W9-BJS-429

1991-1992

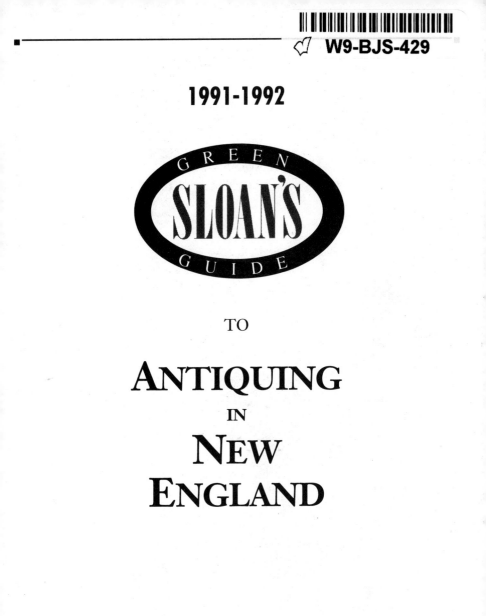

GREEN
SLOAN'S
GUIDE

TO

ANTIQUING
IN
NEW
ENGLAND

Come and Visit My Brand New Store
. . . a Spectacular Post & Beam Setting.

CUPBOARDS & ROSES

- Specializing in 18th & 19th Century ANTIQUE PAINT-DECORATED Furniture from the European Alps.
- Exclusive Import of HAND-CRAFTED REPLICAS and Decorative Accessories.

(One Mile South of the Village Green) Route 7
Sheffield, Massachusetts 01257 • (413) 229-3070

1991-1992

GREEN SLOAN'S GUIDE

TO

ANTIQUING

IN

NEW ENGLAND

Susan P. Sloan
Editor

BOSTON

© 1991 The Antique Press All Rights Reserved.

No part of this book may be reproduced or transmitted in any form or by any means, electronic or mechanical, including photocopying, recording, or by an information storage and retrieval system — except by a reviewer who may quote brief passages in a review to be printed in a magazine or newspaper — without permission in writing from the publisher. This book is sold with the express understanding and agreement that the information and data contained herein will be solely for personal use and will not be used for the creation or updating of mailing lists without express written permission of the publisher. For information, please contact The Antique Press, 105 Charles Street - #140, Boston, MA 02114.

Although the editor has carefully researched all the information contained within the book to ensure its accuracy, no representation is made that it is absolutely accurate and complete. Errors and omissions, whether typographical, clerical or otherwise do sometimes occur and may occur anywhere within the body of this publication. When the reader observes information that needs to be updated, the editor would appreciate being informed. The publisher does not assume and hereby disclaims any liability to any party for any loss or damage by errors or omissions in this publication, whether errors or omissions result from negligence, accident or any other cause.

ISBN 0-929233-02-6
ISSN 1051-6719

Attention: Historical societies, museums, antiques study groups:
This directory is available at quantity discounts on bulk purchases for education, business or sales promotions use. For information, please contact The Antique Press, 105 Charles Street - #140, Boston, MA 02114 (617)723-3001

Printed and bound in the United States of America

TABLE OF CONTENTS

LIST OF MAPS

Acknowledgments

This book was first suggested by Emyl Jenkins, ASA, in the February, 1987 Maine Antiques Digest. It took two and a half years to compile the original database and this second edition reflects the addition or deletion of over 1300 records in the last eighteen months. It also reflects many talents:

Automated Database Publishing, Automated Implementation of Design Specifications, Automated Creation of Fully Page-Numbered Indexes	*Paul Parisi*
Desktop Publishing Consultant & Layout Artist	*Gretchen Wright*
Computer Tech	*Arthur Clarke*
Copy Editor	*Jane Russell* *Anonymous*
Database Software Consultant	*Dennis Cohen/Avden*
Desktop Publishing Software	*Ventura Desktop Publisher*
Linotronic Typsetting	*Microprint/Waltham*
State Maps	*Hartnett House*
Antiquing Maps	*Perugi Designs*
Drawings	*Gail Gardner*
Advertising Sales	*Jane Russell*
Office Staff	*Kara Stepanian*
Chief Strategist	*Arthur Clarke*

The book reflects the support the antiques dealers, and writers and editors in the fields of antiques and decorative arts, who give their wise counsel generously.

SKINNER

Skinner, Inc., Auctioneers and Appraisers of
Antiques and Fine Art

New England's Foremost Auction Gallery

*This rare and important Chippendale Walnut Block-Front Carved Dressing
Table sold recently at a Skinner Americana Auction for $357,500.*

357 Main Street
Bolton, MA 01740
508-779-6241

SKINNER, INC.
*Auctioneers and
Appraisers of Antiques
and Fine Art*

2 Newbury Street
Boston, MA 02116
617-236-1700

Go to one of our auctions and you'll be going once, going twice, going three times...

SKINNER
A real find.

SKINNER, INC.
Auctioneers & Appraisers

Rte. 117, Bolton, MA 01740
(508) 779-6241

2 Newbury Street, Boston, MA 02116
(617) 236-1700

The APPRAISERS' REGISTRY

ALL TYPES OF APPRAISALS OF PERSONAL AND CORPORATE PROPERTY FOR:

Insurance
Estate
Property Division Purposes

*An Association Of Expert Appraisers
Committed To
Privacy, Security And Discretion
In The Handling Of
Fine Arts, Jewelry and Real Estate
Appraisals*

Please Contact
Michael F. Wynne-Willson
President

Box 261 • WESTWOOD, MASSACHUSETTS 02090 • 617/329-4680
FAX: 617/326-6762

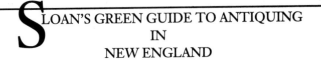

▼

Introduction

INTRODUCTION

SLOAN'S GREEN GUIDE TO ANTIQUING IN NEW ENGLAND is the intelligent guide for antiques buyers, dealers, collectors, knowledgeable travelers, museum curators, interior designers, consultants and ordinary folk planning an antiques tour through New England or a Saturday afternoon "antiquing". It eliminates the guesswork by answering the questions who, where and when with respect to buying, selling and repairing antiques. Whether you have been purchasing antiques in New England for twenty years or you are contemplating the first trip, you will find more useful information between the covers of Sloan's Green Guide than any other single publication.

The New England antiques trade is composed of a large cast of participants in the six states of Connecticut, Maine, Massachusetts, New Hampshire, Rhode Island and Vermont. Included are dealers - retail, private and wholesale; auction houses of all sizes and focus; appraisers; a huge antiquarian book trade; conservators; consultants; repair and restoration specialists and those engaged in the reproduction and replication of antiques. Most of them are here - alphabetized, organized, categorized and indexed - in a fashion enabling you to access them easily.

We have designed this publication to respond to the needs of those being listed and those utilizing the listings. Dealers and other antiques-related businesses are given generous space to describe and list the inventory and/or services they offer. Following the obligatory name, address and telephone number, more detailed facts including business hours, with indications as to seasonal variations, travel directions from easily identified reference points, parking availability and charge cards accepted, if any, are shown to aid you in reaching the appropriate vendor when it is open. The listees are categorized by QuickCodes, i.e. numbers assigned to 87 categories of antiques and antiques-related services. The placement of these QuickCodes at the beginning of each entry enables you to rapidly identify dealers of interest i.e. Americana or Objets d'Art, without reading through the entire listing. Finally, these QuickCodes are the basis for the 87 indices at the end of the book, which list the New England dealers for each of the QuickCode categories i.e., all the New England dealers for (1) Americana, or (56) Nautical/marine items.

As an additional service, we list some services that are not strictly antiques, but of an ancillary nature. Included is the needlework shop on Nantucket which produces beautiful reproductions of hooked rugs, the craftsman in Maine who repairs porch columns that grace many New England period homes and the firm in Massachusetts which sells the only authentic milk paint available in New England. These businesses provide a service to individuals recreating a "period" environment and thus may be of interest to users of the guide.

There are many skilled craftsmen in New England whose services are eagerly sought for the reproduction or replication of fine period antiques - from Goddard and Townsend furniture to fine Chippendale style hardware. The quality of the products and their reputations are excellent and it seems appropriate to list them also.

We have made every attempt to be thorough. This includes thousands of dollars invested in mailings and telephone calls, and hundreds of hours on the phone checking addresses, phone numbers and business hours. Antiques dealers are a ruggedly independent group, and they can close their business spontaneously if they sense that new merchandise might be available down the road. So if a listing is not accurate for the day you visit, it is not for the lack of effort. Readers are encouraged to share information with us, whenever they feel that ours fall short of the mark. Additions, deletions, and amplifications of current listings are welcomed.

How to use this guide

THIS GUIDE IS composed of twelve sections. After the introductory material the first section is devoted to a survey of fine and decorative arts collections and important educational opportunities at selected museums and historic restorations, primarily in New England. These collections are housed in charming museums and mansions, tended by devoted and helpful volunteers. Collections are an invaluable learning tool for the serious antiques buyers wishing to develop an eye for what is right. These institutions warrant your attendance and your financial support, so that the great decorative arts heritage of New England can be maintained, enlarged and adequately secured.

The second section, profiles important periodicals serving the New England antiques community. They provide comprehensive information including calendars, previews, and reviews of auctions, antiques shows and exhibits taking place in New England. "Sandwiched" in amongst this information you may find thought-provoking articles about trends in the trade or almost blow-by-blow descriptions of the latest antiques dispute being adjudicated. It makes for fascinating reading and the periodicals listed are highly recommended.

The 1991 Antiques Show Calendar in the third section provides a monthly listing of antiques shows taking place in New England. The fourth section displays maps and suggested antiquing itineraries in five New England states. In creating these, we have identified the areas in some cases, which are the most heavily populated with antiques shops and in others cases, most heavily populated with group shops, hocking antiques and collectibles. The difference between what you will find on Route 7 in Connecticut and what you will find on Route 4 in New Hampshire is a great as their physical distance. One is primarily formal furniture and one is country antiques and primitives. And when you get into Maine, the York-Wells area displays a handsome collection of both. We suggest where you might go and how you might get there - the rest is up to you.

The next seven sections contain the dealer listings by state preceded by a state map. There are seven sections because although Cape Cod is not a state, for the purposes of this guide it has been treated as such. In order to facilitate Cape Cod antiquing, towns of the three discrete areas of the Cape, and the islands of Nantucket & Martha's Vineyard, are listed in this section. Similarly, all the shops on Martha's Vineyard are treated as if they were in one town, Martha's Vineyard. The designations of Edgartown, West Tisbury, Vineyard Haven and Oak Bluffs are shown on the street address line. Please note in the index that all Cape Cod dealers show a state code of CC, meaning Cape Cod. We assume you know Cape Cod is in Massachusetts.

Antiques dealers constitute the majority of these listings but businesses which provide antiques-related services are also included. Among these are appraisers, auction houses, antiquarian booksellers, restoration and repair services, consultation, conservation, cabinetmaking, replication and reproduction services. The entries are organized alphabetically 1) by state, 2) by city, and 3) by business name. Dictionary-style headers tell you the geographical location of the businesses on a given page.

Dealer entries include the business name, address and phone number, followed by a description, often in the dealer's own words, as to the inventory. Information as to size, hours, days closed, charge cards accepted, services available, year established, associations, travel directions and parking are included. Finally, a maximum of three numbers called "QuickCodes" are shown. "QuickCodes" appear at the beginning of most entries to indicate three categories of antiques or antiques-related services which the business either sells or provides.

Clarification of some terms used in the listings is relevant here. "Assoc" refers to association memberships which the business maintains. Acronyms are shown and these are explained elsewhere in the Guide. "GR12" in the QuickCodes means a group shop with twelve dealers. "MDS20" means a multiple dealer shop with twenty dealers. "FLEA" indicates a flea market.

If you seek antique porcelain dealers in Boston, first refer to the "KEY TO THE USE OF QuickCodes" to determine the QuickCode number for dealers in pottery and porcelain. In this case, it is "63". Run your eye down the right hand margin of the Boston listings for "63" to quickly identify dealers in antique porcelain. For a more comprehensive identification of porcelain dealers in New England refer to the "QuickCode Index" at the back of the book.

There are two (or is it 92?) indexes at the end of the book. The first is an alphabetical listing of all business names, giving the city, state, and page reference. The second index is separated into 87 sections, paralleling the 87 QuickCodes that identify dealers according to the categories of merchandise stocked or services offered. If you are interested in Americana, refer to the Americana index for dealers in all six New England states that specialize in this field. The entire listing of index categories is contained in the "KEY TO THE USE OF QuickCodes". There is an index of multiple dealer and group shops. If you want a large selection, these are the places to frequent and there are over 200 of them in New England. They are the wave of the future, no matter how you feel about it. Finally, there is an index of flea markets.

Sloan's Green Guide is designed to make antiquing easy. We hope it does.

Explanation of a Sample Entry

Woodbury

GERALD MURPHY ANTIQUES LTD.
60 Main St S, 06798
(203) 266-4211   **23 37 39** — *QuickCodes™ showing categories of antiques to be found or services available here: in this case, Clocks/Watches, American Furniture and English Furniture.*

17-19th C English & American furniture, desks, clocks, watercolors, pottery, brass, pewter & glass sold with a guarantee, all in Greek revival house located in the Woodbury historic district. *Pr:* $200/$25000. *Est:* 1984 *Serv:* Purchase estates. *Hours:* Wed-Sun 10-5:30 & by appt. *Size:* Medium. *CC:* MC/V. *Assoc:* WADA. Patricia Murphy-Sadlier. *Park:* On site. *Loc:* I-84 Exit 15: 5MI E on Rte 6.

Price range of inventory
Services available
Associations of which the dealer or business is a member
Charge cards accepted
Parking availability
Year established
Business hours indicating seasonal changes if any
Retail square feet
Travel directions from an easily identified reference point

THOUGHTS ON BUYING ANTIQUES

SLOAN'S GREEN GUIDE is the comprehensive antiques travel guide to New England and a directory of the New England antiques trade. It is written for travelers in New England who seek to identify easily antiques shops and services which meet an individual need. It attempts to present as much factual information as possible about each business, leaving the individual evaluation of the dealer to you, the potential customer. You should not infer from the inclusion of a listing any endorsement on the part of the editor.

The best purchase in any field is an informed purchase. In buying antiques, the knowledge you bring to the selection and purchase of a particular piece will determine the pleasure and satisfaction derived from owning it. It is important to determine the valid criteria for evaluating age and quality. Nothing can surpass knowledge obtained from years of experience and scholarship. This information can be obtained by reading widely articles published in your field of interest in magazines and periodicals covering the antiques trade and collecting, a few of which are mentioned in our section on periodicals. Important information can be obtained in museums and galleries where you can hone your eye on pieces experts consider to be the finer examples. Information can be obtained from the experts, many of whom regularly appear at the lectures, seminars and learning weekends that are held annually in New England institutions on the evaluation, purchase, and care of fine antiques. Antiques shows, in addition to providing a buying opportunity, display thousands of pieces which you may compare and usually handle, carefully, until you can distinguish between the merely acceptable and the truly superb.

Antiques dealers generally love their business and they will respond to an interested, well-informed client. A good dealer cultivates a customer, because although the individual may not purchase today, there is always the possibility that tomorrow he or she may become an avid client, intent on assembling a truly fine collection in a particular field.

ABBREVIATIONS AND TERMS EXPLAINED

Assoc: ASSOCIATIONS A listing of association acronyms indicating the dealer's memberships

By appt only   BY APPOINTMENT ONLY Dealer who does not maintain shop hours. To view the inventory, call ahead for an appointment and an address. One may anticipate this dealer works with the serious collector.

C   CENTURY

CC: CHARGE CARDS accepted

Est: ESTABLISHED Indicates the year in which the dealer entered the antiques trade.

GR20   GROUP SHOP Indicates a collection of antiques and /or collectibles dealers under one roof, in this example: 20 dealers

Int   INTERSECTION

Jct   JUNCTION

L or R   LEFT or RIGHT

Loc: LOCATION Travel directions to the business address from the nearest easily identified reference point

MDS15   MULTIPLE DEALER SHOP Indicates a collection of antiques dealers under one roof, in this example: 15 dealers

MI	MILES
min	MINUTES
N, S, E or W	NORTH, SOUTH, EAST or WEST
Park:	PARKING availability
Pr:	PRICE RANGE Indicates the range of prices in individual pieces in a dealer's inventory
SS	STOP SIGN
Serv:	SERVICES available from this dealer, often at an extra charge. These may include consultation, appraisals, repairs, restorations and shipping, among others.
Shows:	Antiques Show Participation. ELLIS indicates the Ellis Memorial Antiques Show in Boston. WAS indicates the New York City Winter Antiques Show.
Size:	For antiques shops it indicates the square footage of the shop i.e., 500 to 2000 square feet is a medium, 2000 to 10,000 square feet is large and over 10,000 is huge. For antiquarian booksellers it indicates the number of books in inventory. For Flea markets it indicates the number of dealer spaces.
Sum	SUMMER
Win	WINTER

KEY TO THE USE OF
"QuickCodes™"

TO FACILITATE RAPID reference in "Sloan's Green Guide" a coding system is used for identifying 87 selected categories of antiques and antiques-related services. Numbers, referred to as QuickCodes™, have been assigned to these categories. Businesses have been queried as to their inventory and services and then assigned a maximum of three QuickCodes™.

These QuickCodes™ appear on the third line of each entry in bold face type, supplementing the text description. Thus, if one is in Essex, Massachusetts with thirty minutes to spare, one can quickly scan the QuickCodes™ to determine which dealers sell the category of antiques of particular interest. So informed, the reader is able to travel directly to the dealer of choice, bypassing the "pottery and porcelain" dealer when looking for "barometers".

The 87 categories of antiques and antiques-related services and the QuickCodes™ assigned to them appear on the facing page.

1 Americana
2 Andirons/Fenders
3 Antiquities
4 Appraisal
5 Architectural Antiques
6 Arms/Military
7 Art Deco/Art Nouveau
8 Auction
9 Autographs/Manuscripts
10 Barometers
11 Baseball Cards
12 Bookbinding/Restoration
13 Books/Antiquarian
14 Books
15 Bottles
16 Brass/Pewter/Metalware
17 Bronzes
18 Buttons/Badges
19 Cabinet-Makers
20 Cameras/Daguerreotypes
21 Carpets/Rugs
22 Chair Caning
23 Clocks/Watches
24 Coins/Medals
25 Consignment
26 Consultation/Research
27 Country Antiques
28 Crocks/Stoneware
29 Decorative Accessories
30 Decoys
31 Display Stands/Glass
32 Dolls/Toys
33 Ephemera
34 Folk Art
35 French Antiques
36 Furniture
37 Furniture/American
38 Furniture/Continental
39 Furniture/English
40 Furniture/Oak
41 Furniture/Painted
42 Furniture/Pine
43 Furniture/Reproduction
44 Glass

45 Garden Accessories
46 Interior Design
47 Jewelry
48 Lace/Linen
49 Lead Soldiers
50 Lighting
51 Maps
52 Miniatures
53 Mirrors
54 Models
55 Music/Musical Instruments
56 Nautical/Marine Items
57 Needlework/Samplers
58 Objets d'Art
59 Oil Paintings
60 Oriental Art
61 Paperweights
62 Photographs
63 Porcelain/Pottery
64 Post Cards
65 Primitives
66 Prints/Drawings
67 Quilts/Patchwork
68 Repairs
69 Replication
70 Reproduction
71 Restoration/Conservation
72 Scientific/Medical Instruments
73 Sculpture
74 Services to Period Homes
75 Shipping/Packing/Storage
76 Shaker
77 Silver
78 Sporting Art/Equipment
79 Stamps
80 Textiles
81 Tools
82 Tribal Art
83 Victorian Antiques
84 Vintage Cars/Carriages
85 Vintage Clothing/Costumes
86 Wicker
87 Weather Vanes

FLEA = Flea Market
GR10 = Groupshop with 10 dealers
MDS5 = Multiple Dealer Shop 5 dealers

KEY TO ASSOCIATION ACRONYMS

AAA	Appraisers Association of America
AADA	Associated Antique Dealers of America Inc
AADLA	Art & Antique Dealers League of America Inc
ABAA	Antiquarian Booksellers Association of America
ADA	Antique Dealers' Association of America
AIC	American Institute for Conservation of Historic & Artistic Works
ANS	American Numismatic Society
AR	The Appraisers' Registry
ARLIS/NA	Art Libraries Society of North America
ASA	American Society of Appraisers
AWI	American Watchmakers Institute
AWG	Association of Women Gemologists
BADA	British Antique Dealers Association
BCADA	Berkshire County Antiques Dealers Association
BHI	British Horological Institute
CADA	Connecticut Association of Dealers in Antiques Inc
CAI	Certified Auctioneers Institute
CCADA	Cape Cod Antique Dealers Association Inc
ESA	Ephemera Society of America
GIA	Gemological Institute of America
GSAAA	Granite State Antique Dealers & Appraisers Association
IIC	International Institute for Conservation of Historic & Artistic Works
ILAB	International League of Antiquarian Booksellers
ISA	International Society of Appraisers
ISFAA	International Society of Fine Arts Appraisers

JBT	Jewelers Board of Trade
MAA	Maine Auctioneers Association
MABA	Maine Antiquarian Booksellers Association
MADA	Maine Antiques Dealers Association Inc
MJSA	Manufacturing Jewelers & Silversmiths of America
MRIAB	Massachusetts & Rhode Island Antiquarian Booksellers
MSAA	Massachusetts State Auctioneers Association
NAA	National Auctioneers Association
NAADAA	National Antique & Art Dealers Association of America Inc
NADA	National Association of Dealers in Antiques Inc
NAWCC	National Association of Watch & Clock Collectors
NEAA	New England Appraisers Association
NEBA	New England Booksellers Association
NECA	New England Conservation Association
NHABA	New Hampshire Antiquarian Booksellers Association
NHADA	New Hampshire Antiques Dealers Association Inc
NTHP	National Trust for Historic Preservation
ORRA	Oriental Rug Retailers of America
PSMA	Professional Show Managers Association
PVADA	Pioneer Valley Antiques Dealers Association
SSADA	South Shore Antiques Dealers' Association
SADA	Suburban Antique Dealers Association
SNEADA	Southeastern New England Antique Dealers Association Inc
SPNEA	Society for the Preservation of New England Antiquities
VAA	Vermont Auctioneers Association
VABA	Vermont Antiquarian Booksellers Association
VADA	Vermont Antiques Dealers' Association Inc
WADA	Woodbury Antiques Dealer Association

▼

Fine and Decorative Arts Collections

FINE AND DECORATIVE ARTS COLLECTIONS

TOURING EARLY AMERICAN homes and outstanding collections of decorative and fine arts can do much to enhance your knowledge and connoisseurship. With some of the greatest collections located here in New England, or nearby, valuable and worthwhile opportunities abound to do just that. In addition to world-renowned museums in Boston and New Haven, there are dozens of smaller institutions stretching across the landscape from Connecticut to Maine. From the American Impressionist paintings of the Florence Griswold Museum in Old Lyme, Connecticut to the diverse collections of the Currier Gallery in Manchester, New Hampshire, the antiques enthusiast will find superb examples of American and European fine and decorative arts.

Included is folk art at the Shelburne Museum, Shelburne, Vermont; Revere silver, Copley paintings, and American furniture at the Museum of Fine Arts, Boston; Goddard and Townsend furniture at the Museum of Art, RISD, Providence; Chinese Export porcelain at the Peabody Museum of Salem, Massachusetts; the Garvan collection of American painting and decorative arts at Yale in New Haven, Connecticut; and the entire village of Historic Deerfield in Deerfield, Massachusetts. It's a stellar assemblage of antiques and fine art.

In addition, many institutions conduct courses and seminars, lectures and gallery talks on their collections. While some programs are full-time, in-depth courses geared to professionals, others are aimed at collectors and connoisseurs. The following list simply highlights some of the finest opportunities available to those interested in expanding their knowledge of antiques. Because course topics, fees, and dates vary from year to year, it is best to contact the organizations at the address listed for up-to-date information. Fees given here serve as a general guideline. Members often qualify for reduced rates and special programs, and membership fees tend to be quite reasonable.

THE BENNINGTON MUSEUM
West Main Street
Bennington, VT 05201
(802) 447-1571

Hours: March 1 to December 22 Daily 9-5 CLOSED Thanksgiving. In January and February, the Museum is open Saturday and Sunday only.

Admission: Adults $4.50, Senior Citizens $3.50, Family $10.00, Group (10 or more with reservation) $3.50, Children under 12, free. Memberships from $10.

Location: The Bennington Museum is located on West Main Street which is Route 9, one mile west of the intersection of Routes 7 and 9 in downtown Bennington.

THE BENNINGTON MUSEUM, opened in 1928, is a regional museum devoted to exhibitions relating to the art and history of neighboring areas. It houses extensive collections of decorative arts, furniture, paintings, and historical artifacts from Vermont and New England as well as an important collection of American glass and the largest public collection of work by folk artist Grandma Moses.

The museum maintains a collection of 32 paintings by Grandma Moses, a native of nearby Eagle Bridge, New York. She visited Bennington often and painted several views of the town which are on display. There are also works by American painters Joseph Blackburn, Rembrandt Peale, William Jennys, Erastus Salisbury Field, William Morris Hunt, Henry Inman and William Merritt Chase.

Here you will find the Norman A. MacColl pressed glass goblet collection, 19th century free-blown glass, cut and engraved glass, and art glass. There is a collection of over 3,000 pieces of Bennington pottery, 19th century stoneware, and examples of Rockingham, Flint Enamel, Parian and Scroddled ware. Tall, mantel, banjo and shelf clocks made in New England and owned locally are also displayed.

Included in the collection is The Wasp, a 1925 luxury touring car designed and built by Karl Martin in Bennington, which took it's name from the insect it was designed to resemble.

The Genealogy Library, open by appointment, contains more than 3,000 volumes including genealogies, manuscripts, documents and town histories of New England and New York.

Annually in mid-July, the Bennington Museum Antiques Show and Sale is held across the street in the Monument Elementary School.

CAPE ANN HISTORICAL ASSOCIATION
27 Pleasant Street
Gloucester, MA 01930
(508) 283-0455

Hours: Tuesday to Saturday 10-5. CLOSED Holidays and February.

Admission: Adults $3, Senior Citizens and Students $1.50, Children under 12, free. Memberships start at $15.

Location: In the heart of downtown Gloucester, one block N of Main Street and one short block E of City Hall and the Sawyer Free Library. Parking available in the adjacent lot.

IN HIS BOOK "Art Museums of New England," S. Lane Faison says there is no more attractive small museum in New England than the Cape Ann Scientific, Literary & Historical Association. It is truly a special museum, with a beautiful collection housed in an historic residence and lovingly tended by a thoughtful staff. Founded in 1875, it is located in the 1804 home of sea captain Elias Davis.

Here is probably the nation's largest collection of paintings and drawings by Fitz Hugh Lane, a Gloucester native who lived from 1804 to 1865. It includes 32 oil paintings and over 100 drawings. Lane's 19th century scenes of Gloucester and its harbor, the Penobscot Bay area in Maine, and the sailing vessels of the era are precisely composed and rendered in oils in the Luminist style that evokes a tranquil and idyllic period in our history. One can almost feel the mist in the air.

Other painters represented in the collection are Winslow Homer, Maurice Prendergast, Milton Avery, and John Sloan. The Association features displays of American decorative arts including the silver of Paul Revere, China trade objects including a large and beautiful collection of porcelains, carved jades and fans, and more than 260 pieces of fine 19th century furniture. There are collections of jewelry, glassware, basketry, and textiles, including early needlework, linens, and quilts.

The Association is noted for its fisheries and maritime collections relating to Gloucester's 350-year history as a fishing port. The collection includes ship models, scale models, gear, rigging, tools and sailmaking equipment.

The education program includes a series of lectures, symposia, workshops, demonstrations, special events, and tours to outside locations.

STERLING AND FRANCINE CLARK ART INSTITUTE
225 South Street
Williamstown, MA 01267
(413) 458-9545

Hours: Tuesday to Sunday 10-5 and Memorial Day, Labor Day, and Columbus Day. CLOSED Mondays, New Year's, Thanksgiving, and Christmas.

Admission: FREE. Wheelchairs are available. Memberships start at $5.

Location: The Clark Art Institute is located in the northwest corner of Massachusetts in Williamstown at the junction of Rtes. 2 and 7.

SITUATED AMONG THE scenic Berkshire mountains, the Clark Art Institute displays a superb collection of American and European paintings, prints, and silver which reflect a taste for classical art. This collection of Sterling and Francine Clark was formed in France and America between 1912 and 1955, when the Institute was opened. Sterling Clark was a grandson of the partner of sewing machine inventor Isaac Singer.

The permanent collection of art from the Renaissance through the 19th century is noted for an especially fine group of Impressionist paintings, including a large number by Renoir, dating between 1870 and 1880. It also displays works of Monet, Degas, Pissaro, and Sisley; academic masters like Bouguereau, Alma-Tadema, and Gerome; a painting by Gericault and Barbizon artists Millet, Troyon, and Corot. American painters represented include Homer, Sargent, Cassatt, and Remington. The collection of silver is extensive, including examples of American, French, and Dutch craftsmanship. It is particularly strong in 17th and 18th century English silversmiths and Paul de Lamerie is represented by more than 30 pieces. Decorative arts include porcelain from the Meissen, Chantilly, and Sevres factories. Early American glass, and French and American furniture are also displayed.

Exhibits scheduled for the 1991 season include "Irish Decorative Arts" from the National Museum of Ireland, including glass, silver, textiles, and woodwork; "Winslow Homer in the 1890's - Prout's Neck Observed", from the University of Rochester; and 35 paintings by Sir Lawrence Alma-Tadema, member of the Royal Academy and a Victorian Classicist who specialized in genre scenes. Guided tours for groups of adults or school children can be arranged with advance notice, with a nominal charge for adults. Gallery talks are scheduled at 3:00 in the summer. A recorded tour is available for a small fee.

COLONIAL WILLIAMSBURG FOUNDATION
P.O. Box C
Williamsburg, VA 23187
(804) 229-1000

Hours: *Colonial Williamsburg Village is open every day, including Christmas 9-5. DeWitt Wallace Decorative Arts Gallery is open 10-6 daily, Wednesday til 8.*

Admission: *Depending on the level of access you desire: Adult Pass, $19 -$26; Children $12.50 - $17. The cost of the Antiques Forum, $250; Learning Week in Archaeology, $550 for a two-week session, $350 for one-week; all exclusive of room and board.*

Location: *Eastern Virginia on Interstate Route 64, a one-hour drive from Richmond and 2 1/2 hours from Washington. Airports in Richmond, Norfolk, and Newport News. Amtrak has a station in Williamsburg, as does Greyhound Bus.*

COLONIAL WILLIAMSBURG, the one-time capital of Virginia now restored to its 18th century appearance, is a splendid example of a working town in colonial America. Period furnishings fill the houses, both original and reconstructed, and craftsmen in costume demonstrate their trades. The houses illustrate vividly the different social classes and occupational groups of colonial society.

The DeWitt Wallace Decorative Arts Gallery displays antiques from the 17th through the 19th centuries, with more than 8,000 examples of the finest craftsmanship in early American furniture, porcelain and pottery, silver, pewter, brass, and textiles. "Virginia Furniture: 1680-1820" opened in 1990 and is on display indefinitely. Introductory tours of the gallery are offered daily at 1 and 3 p.m. The Abby Aldrich Rockefeller Folk Art Center is closed until the fall of 1991 when a major expansion and renovation will be completed.

Williamsburg will sponsor its widely acclaimed Antiques Forum February 3-8, 1991. The topic of the 1991 Forum is "New Discoveries in the Arts of 18th-Century America." With new emphasis on curatorial and conservation workshops, curators and scholars present their recent findings about antiques in illustrated lectures and informal afternoon sessions. Registration for this popular course is limited to and reservations must be made in the late fall.

The 1991 Learning Weekend will survey "Travel and Transportation in 18th-century Virginia." On selected weekends from January to March "Colonial Weekends" are held. The Department of Archaeological Research sponsors Learning Weeks in Archaeology, during which participants work on excavations at several Historic Area properties. The telephone number for inquiries for 1991 events is (804) 220-7255.

CONCORD MUSEUM
200 Lexington Road
P.O. Box 146
Concord, MA 01742
(508) 369-9609

Hours: *Monday to Saturday 10-4, Sunday 1-4. CLOSED New Years, Easter, Thanksgiving, and Christmas.*
Admission: *Adults $5, Seniors $4, and Children $2. Memberships start at $30.*
Location: *The Concord Museum is located between Lexington Road and the Cambridge Turnpike, about one and one-half miles from Route 2.*

THE COLLECTION OF the Concord Museum is the culmination of the lifetime passion of Cummings E. Davis, who maintained a lunch counter and newsstand in 19th century Concord. Obviously a man of modest means, he collected discarded artifacts from local homes. He also kept records of where they were found and who made them.

Today the Concord Museum, the home of the Concord Antiquarian Society, transports the visitor back through three centuries. Fifteen period rooms, arranged sequentially from 1680-1860, vividly depict the growth and evolution of one of America's most historic communities. From the "keeping room to the Empire Parlor", the decorative arts and domestic artifacts, either owned by Concord area residents or made by Concord area craftsmen, are attractively displayed. The documentation by Cummings Davis helps to forge the connection with the past, chronicling the growth of an early New England town.

Four of these rooms, named in honor of Eleanor Sutton Brown, were recently reinstalled to more accurately reflect room usage in 18th and 19th century Concord. The Green Room is a chamber circa 1721, reflecting the tastes and style of a prominent citizen such as a magistrate or minister. The Queen Anne Room is a bedchamber, reflecting the new emphasis placed on social graces with a tea service set out. The Federal Parlor is a dining room of around 1815, and draws heavily on neo-classical designs popular in post-Revolutionary times.

The Concord Museum displays the lantern that was hung from the steeple of the Old North Church on the night of Paul Revere's ride, relics from the battle at the North Bridge, a large collection of artifacts relating to Thoreau, and the contents of Ralph Waldo Emerson's study. The Museum sponsors lectures intermittently throughout the year.

CURRIER GALLERY OF ART
192 Orange Street
Manchester, NH 03104
(603) 669-6144

Hours: *Tuesday to Saturday 10-4, Thursday til 10, Sunday 2-5. CLOSED Mondays and National Holidays.*

Admission: *FREE. Wheelchair accessible. Memberships range from $20.*

Location: *From N/S/W, I-293 Exit 6 to Elm St, through light to Salmon St, take 7th R on Beech St, continue to 6th light at the museum drive, North Entrance. From N/E/S, I-93 Exit 8 Turn R onto Wellington Rd, which becomes Bridge St, continue through light at Maple St, turn R at Ash St. Take 3rd L at the museum drive, North Entrance.*

THE CURRIER GALLERY of Art, opened in 1929, was financed by former New Hampshire state governor Moody Currier as an art museum for the people of New Hampshire. Moody Currier was a Dartmouth graduate, a classical scholar, linguist, man of letters, and patron of the arts. The Currier's elegant Beaux-Arts building, completed in 1929, is reminiscent of an Italian Renaissance palace.

The antiques enthusiast will find the collections of New England decorative arts to be strong, from the 18th through the late 19th century. New Hampshire furniture makers are well represented, including a number of pieces by the Dunlap family. There are folk art paintings including works by Joseph Davis, Zedekiah Belknap, and portraits by Ammi Phillips. Important American artists represented include Albert Bierstadt, Thomas Eakins, William Merritt Chase, Willard Metcalf, John Singer Sargent, Edward Hopper, and Thomas Hart Benton. The silver collections include pieces by John Coney, Paul Revere I and II, and a growing collection of arts and crafts silver by Arthur Stone, George Gebelein, and Karl Leinonen. The Currier is probably best known for an enormous glass collection which ranges from very early American pieces to pressed glass, cameo glass, and other English, Continental, and American pieces.

In 1991 the Currier will present "Corot to Monet: The Rise of Landscape Painting in France," a traveling exhibition of French Barbizon and Early Impressionist art. The first major scholarly exhibition on this subject mounted in the United States since 1962, it will run from January 27 to April 29, 1991.

The Currier presents lectures, publications and travel programs. Guided tours of the collections and special exhibitions must be arranged in advance through the Education Department.

ESSEX INSTITUTE
132 Essex Street
Salem, MA 01970
(508) 744-3390

Hours: *June to October: Monday to Saturday 9-5; Sundays and Holidays 1-5; November to May: Tuesday to Saturday 9-5, Sundays and Holidays 1-5.*

Admission: *Combination Ticket Adults $5, Senior Citizens $4, Children 6-16 $2.50. Group rates available. Memberships start at $15.*

Location: *The Institute is located in downtown Salem east of the Peabody Museum and W of Washington Square on Essex Street.*

THE ESSEX INSTITUTE, formed in 1848 by the Essex Historical Society and the Essex County Natural History Society, includes a museum, a highly regarded library, and seven period houses.

The Museum contains a picture gallery and a large collection of furniture; decorative arts including ceramics, silver and textiles; toys and games; and historical items of the region. The paintings, portraits of individuals significant in the life of Salem, include works by Greenwood, Blackburn, Copley, Harding, Trumbull, and Stuart.

The Essex Institute maintains seven historic homes on the grounds or nearby, which figure prominently in the architectural history of the region. Included is the John Ward House of 1684, located in the garden of the Institute, and an example of American Colonial architecture. The Crowninshield-Bentley House, built in 1727, is typical of 18th century and pre-Federal architecture.

The Peirce-Nichols House of 1782 is a formal mansion built by the famous architect Samuel McIntire for a prosperous Salem China Trade merchant, Jerathmiel Peirce. Only 24 at the time the house was commissioned, McIntire was inspired by the Georgian style. This classical house also contains carved decorations by McIntire in the Adamesque-style room, which McIntire redecorated.

The Gardner-Pingree House at 128 Essex Street is a McIntire design of 1804, twenty-two years after the Peirce-Nichols house. A handsome brick mansion with a balustraded roof and curving porch with Corinthian columns, it also contains the carvings of McIntire in the decorative motifs on the fireplaces and above the doors. Most of the furniture was made in Salem and contributes to the elegance of the beautifully decorated interior of the house.

The education programs of the Essex Institute include guided tours, lectures, gallery talks, and special school tours.

FLORENCE GRISWOLD MUSEUM
96 Lyme Street
Old Lyme, CT 06371
(203) 434-5542

Hours: June-October: Tuesday to Saturday 10-5, Sunday 1-5; Nov-May: Wednesday to Sunday 1-5.

Admission: Adults $2, Children under 12 and Members no charge. Memberships start at $20.

Location: I-95 Exit 70: second house on the L on the N side of the overpass.

THE FLORENCE GRISWOLD House occupies a unique place in the history of American art, due to the beneficence of its founder. It is here that some of the great American Impressionists of the early 20th century gathered each summer to enjoy Miss Griswold's encouragement, the pastoral nature of the countryside, and the fellowship of their colleagues. In appreciation for the hospitality, impecunious residents often repaired the dilapidated house and left artistic mementos. In 1936 they formed the Florence Griswold Association to care for her, and to maintain her house as a museum of history and art.

The house radiates the spirit of the art colony, for the artists painted landscapes on the door panels and on the walls of the dining room. Across the mantel they painted a caricature of themselves, immortalizing their personalities and camaraderie.

Many of the artists who came to Old Lyme were influenced by the French Barbizon, style which sought to portray an idealized landscape which united man with nature. Rich muted colors dominated sparingly lit Barbizon paintings, conveying a sense of mystery. Lewis Cohen, Henry Ranger, Carleton Wiggins, Will Howe and Allen Talcott were among the artists who painted rural Lyme in this style. When in 1903 Childe Hassam arrived, the artists attracted to the group experimented with the optical effects of color, creating illusions of depth, form, light and atmosphere. Included were Willard Metcalf, William Chadwick, Walter Griffin, Edward Simmons and Edward Rook.

The permanent collection of art includes over 900 paintings, drawings, watercolors and prints by nearly 130 American artists. The archives contain information on the location of the thousands of Old Lyme Art Colony paintings located elsewhere. In addition the world of the Victorian child is explored through an exhibit of the varied Clara Champlain Griswold toy collection. Miniature Victorian houses and kitchens, a tin steamboat, a mechanical carousel and a French doll dressed in Paris finery are displayed.

THE FOGG ART MUSEUM
32 Quincy Street
Cambridge, MA 02138
(617) 495-9400

Hours: Tuesday to Sunday 10-5. CLOSED Mondays, January 1, July 4, Thanksgiving, December 24 and 25.

Admission: General Admission $4; College and university students, senior citizens $2.50; Free to Museum members, Harvard staff and students, children (up to age 18), and on Saturday mornings. Memberships start at $25.

Location: The Fogg Museum is located at the intersection of Broadway and Quincy Streets in Cambridge, one block E of Harvard Square and adjacent to Harvard Yard.

THE FOGG ART Museum, designed by Coolidge, Shepley, Bulfinch & Abbott, was founded in 1891 to house the growing Harvard art collection. The original building was a gift of Elizabeth Perkins Fogg in memory of her husband William Hayes Fogg. In 1927 the Fogg moved to its present home, a neo-Georgian building housing two floors of exhibition galleries overlooking an Italian Renaissance courtyard.

The collections of the Fogg include paintings by Fra Angelico, Rubens, Ingres, Gericault, Van Gogh, Renoir, Monet, Degas, Homer, Pollock and collections of drawings by renowned American and European artists. The Armand Hammer Galleries display Dutch art of the 17th century including paintings by Rembrandt and van Ruisdael, along with examples of Dutch silver and furnishings. They also include paintings of the 18th century of American and French origin and selections from the Hutchinson collection of English silver.

On the second floor and filling two galleries is the Wertheim Collection, one of America's fine collections of Impressionist and post-Impressionist works. Here also is the Fogg's new Decorative Arts Gallery containing 17th, 18th, and early 19th century decorative arts from England and America. The strengths of the Fogg's entire decorative arts collection are in English and American silver, Wedgwood pottery, 17th and 18th century clocks, English and American furniture and 15th and 16th century Italian chests. In addition the Fogg is noted for 19th century French and British paintings, including works from the time of the French Revolution to portraits by Reynolds and Gainsborough.

Exhibits scheduled for 1991 include drawings of Il Guercino, Adolph von Menzel, later Chinese Paintings, and Ceramics of the Song, Jin & Yuan Periods. The regular and special tour schedule can be obtained by calling (617) 495-4544.

GORE PLACE
52 Gore Street off Route 20
Waltham, MA 02154
(617) 894-2798

Hours: *The mansion is open to the public for guided tours from April 15th to November 15th Tuesday-Saturday 10-4, Sunday 2-4. Grounds open year-round during daylight hours.*

Admission: *Adults $4, Seniors $3, Children 12 and under $2. Memberships in Gore Place Society start at $10.*

Location: *From Rte 128/95 Exit 26: 3 Miles E through Waltham center. From MA Turnpike I-90 Exit 17 through Watertown Square to Route 20 W. Midway between Waltham Common and Watertown Square.*

GORE PLACE, DESIGNED in Paris for Christopher Gore, the seventh Governor of Massachusetts, is one of New England's finest examples of Federal period residential architecture. Noted for its oval rooms and recently restored spiral staircase, it is filled with fine early American, European and Oriental furnishings, many of them belonging to the Gore family. The house is situated on a 40-acre estate of gardens, cultivated fields, and woodlands.

The building is thought to be an amalgamation of high-style French intellectual concepts and the Romantic Classicism of Sir John Soane's English Country houses. It is distinguished from contemporary New England buildings by its sophisticated floor plan of ovals and concave and convex wall surfaces, combined with gracious room height. Christopher Gore was considered technologically avant-garde for installing a bathing-tub, a Rumford kitchen and fireplaces, and a ventilator.

The furnishings have been assembled from many of the finest private collections in the Boston area. More than 100 objects originally belonging to Christopher and Rebecca Gore have been returned, including portraits, books from his library, a sideboard, a billiard table, a pair of armchairs, and pieces from three dinner services. The furnishings at Gore Place include masterpieces of American furniture from Baltimore, Philadelphia, Boston, and the New England area. Family portraits include works by Copley, Trumbull, and Stuart. Decorative accessories, spanning the period from c. 1740 to c. 1825, from England, France, and China contribute to the elegance.

The Gore Place Society, founded in 1935, preserves and administers this beautiful mansion, once slated for demolition so that its lands could be divided for a housing development.

HANCOCK SHAKER VILLAGE
Albany Road Route 20, P.O. Box 898
Pittsfield, MA 01202
(413) 443-0188

Hours: *Memorial Day Weekend through October 31 9:30-5. Special events occur year round.*

Admission: *Adults $7.50, Senior Citizens and Students $6.75, Children 6-12 $3.50, Family (2 adults and children in the immediate family) $20. Collectors Forum, $50. Guided tours are offered daily. Memberships start at $25.*

Location: *Hancock Shaker Village is at the junction of Routes 20 and 41, five miles W of downtown Pittsfield, MA. Visitors coming from the N via Rtes 7 and 22 should note that it cannot be reached from Rte 43. Continue on to Rte 20.*

AN OFFSHOOT OF the English Quakers, the Shakers earned their descriptive name from their inspired, spontaneous dancing and trembling during worship services. Hancock was the third of 18 Shaker communities, based on the principles of communal living, equality of sex and race, pacifism, hard work, simplicity and celibacy, to be established in the United States. In 1830 at its height the village numbered 300 inhabitants. The population dwindled slowly for 130 years until, in 1960, the village became a museum.

Hancock Shaker Village is composed of 20 restored buildings on 1,200 scenic acres of meadow and woodland in the Berkshire Hills. Interpreters recreate the daily life and production of the Shaker village, including the faithful reproduction of 19th century Shaker goods including furniture, oval boxes, textiles, tin and iron items, baskets, and brooms. A festival of Shaker crafts and industries takes place the third weekend in August.

Antiques collectors will find the permanent collection of Hancock Shaker Village strong in Shaker artifacts including agricultural tools, baskets, Shaker "Gift" drawings, furniture, folk art, manuscript collections, paintings, textiles, tin and iron.

The annual one-day Collectors' Forum is held in May and covers topics of special interest to Shaker enthusiasts, most recently "Shaker Textiles, Poplarware and Textile Tools." The Forum is staffed by curators from the Village and dealers and collectors of Shaker pieces.

HERITAGE PLANTATION OF SANDWICH
Pine and Grove Streets P. 0. Box 566
Sandwich, MA 02563
(508) 888-3300

Hours: May to October Daily 10-5

Admission: Adults $7, Senior Citizens $6, Children under 12, $3. Memberships start at $30.

Location: From Rte 6A take Route 130 to Pine Street and the Museum. From the Mid Cape Highway take Exit 2 and follow Route 130 N to Grove Street.

LOCATED ON 76 acres of gardens and woodlands one mile from the center of Sandwich Cape Cod's oldest town is the Heritage Plantation of Sandwich. Comprised of a Shaker round barn holding an antique automobile collection, a military museum that contains antique firearms and weapons, military miniatures, native American artifacts and military uniform exhibits. The Art Museum contains a restored and working carousel, folk art, changing art exhibitions, Currier & Ives prints, and antique tools and toys.

The carousel is a 1912 carousel built in Riverside, Rhode Island by Charles I D. Looff, famed for building the first Coney Island carousel in 1876 and features 32 hand-carved flying animals. Other artifacts in the collection span the creative ingenuity of American craftsmen in portraiture, woodcarving, and metalworking. They includes Nantucket Lightship baskets, scrimshaw, weather vanes, toys, trade signs and a vast collection of Anthony Elmer Crowell's bird carvings. It includes cigar store figures by Samuel Anderson Robb and other famous wood carvers; bronzes by Remington, Dallin and Jackson; and early American paintings by Erastus Salisbury Field, William Matthew Prior, and Susan Waters. Heritage Plantation boasts one of the largest collections of Currier & Ives lithographs on public exhibition. Vividly portraying events from America's past, many of the top 50 large and small folio prints produced by the famous New York print firm are on display.

The J. K Lilly III collection of thirty-four antique and vintage cars is housed in the Shaker round barn Village. The star of the collection is the 1930 Dusenberg Model J Tourster custom-made for Gary Cooper. The cars range in age from 1899 to 1937 and include President Taft's 1909 White Steamer the first official U. S. Presidential car. There is also a 1932 Boattail Auburn Speedster, and a Springfield, Massachusetts-made 1922 Rolls Royce.

An extensive program of lectures workshops and gallery talks, are given during the season and the rest of the year. The G. Robert Melber Lectureship Series which is automobile oriented, is held annually in November.

HISTORIC DEERFIELD
The Street Box 321
Deerfield, MA 01342
(413) 774-5581

Hours: Daily 9:30 to 4:30. CLOSED Thanksgiving, Christmas Eve and Christmas.
Admission: Adults $7.50, Children $4. Special group rates for 20 or more with two weeks notice; three- or four-day forums $350-$400. Memberships start at $25.
Location: Historic Deerfield is 40 miles N of Springfield. Take I-91 to Exit 24. Go 6 miles N or Rtes 5 & 10 and turn left onto the village street.

STRETCHED OUT ALONG the main street of Old Deerfield Village in the Connecticut Valley is a remarkable collection of 52 houses, built over a period spanning the early 18th to the 20th centuries. The institution of Historic Deerfield, incorporated in 1951, owns and operates 12 of the houses, which represent the changing styles of Connecticut River domestic architecture. The themes of the guided tour revolve around the collections and the way in which they are exhibited in the houses.

Famous for its exceptional collection of early American furniture, Deerfield exhibits one of the major collections (more than 10,000 objects) of Americana and related decorative arts of the 17th, 18th and early 19th centuries. Holdings include the George Alfred Cluett Collection of American furniture and the Lucius D. Potter Collection of furniture and brass, along with many impressive examples of early American textiles (especially needlework), silver, pewter, glass, brass candlesticks, and paintings.

Historic Deerfield operates an extensive series of educational programs throughout the year. Topics cover just about every interest: historic interiors, design and construction of American furniture, American presentation silver, schoolgirl needlework, identifying base metal artifacts and today's market for Americana.

Three- and four-day forums that focus on a special topic are occasionally offered. College students interested in pursuing a career in the museum or historic preservation field may apply for the nine-week Summer Fellowship Program in Early American History and Material Culture, a well-respected program that is now more than 30 years old.

MUSEUM OF FINE ARTS
465 Huntington Avenue
Boston, MA 02115
(617) 267-9300, weekly events 267-9377, tickets 267-2973

Hours: Museum, including West Wing: Tuesday to Sunday 10-5, Wednesday til 10. West Wing: Thursday and Friday 5-10. Entrances to special exhibition galleries close one-half hour before Museum closing. CLOSED Mondays

Admission: $6 during hours entire Museum is open, $5 when only the West Wing is open. Free to all Saturday 10-12. Members and children free. Memberships start at $35.

Location: Located approximately one mile southwest of Copley Square in the Fenway and on the Arborway branch of the Green Line. Indoor/outdoor parking located adjacent. Wheelchair accessible.

THE HISTORIC CITY of Boston is the home of one of the country's oldest museums, and masterworks from the extensive collections of the Museum of Fine Arts provide valuable records of major historic events as well as examples of the finest works produced in early America.

Holdings include such beautiful American silver objects as Paul Revere's celebrated Sons of Liberty Bowl, a commemorative tankard by Benjamin Burt, and a large and very fine collection of English silver. From the M. and M. Karolik Collection one finds American paintings, American watercolors and drawings, and 18th century American arts. There are exquisitely crafted chests, rockers, settees, and other furniture originally owned by local families who made fortunes on the China or India trades during the clipper ship era; as well as outstanding paintings by renowned artists John Singleton Copley, Fitz Hugh Lane, and Gilbert Stuart. Impressive collections are found in the Asiatic Department, the Textile and Costumes Collections and the European Decorative Arts and Sculpture.

Like many Museums, unable to display their entire collections simultaneously, the MFA organized a 1990 exhibit called "Unlocking the Hidden Museum: Riches from the Storerooms." Visitors explored the issues of condition, conservation, quality, and authenticity, as seen through the eyes of the curators.

Gallery talks and illustrated lectures complement the permanent collections and special exhibitions. With such impressive resources, a fairly extensive program of events is offered from month to month. Listings appear in the calendar sent to members.

MUSEUM OF ART, RHODE ISLAND SCHOOL OF DESIGN
224 Benefit Street
Providence, RI 02903
(401) 331-3511

Hours: Tuesday to Saturday 10:30-5, Thursdays 12-8, Sundays and Holidays 2 - 5. Summer hours June 16 to August 31, Wednesday to Saturday 12-5. CLOSED Mondays, Thanksgiving, Christmas, New Year's, July 4

Admission: Adults $2, Senior Citizens and Children $.50, FREE on Saturday. Wheelchair entrance on North Main Street

Location: From I-95 going E to Cape Cod, take the Wickenden Street exit and follow the signs to Benefit Street. From I-95 W take the South Main Street exit, turn R on College Street and L on Benefit Street.

LOCATED IN THE charming Benefit Street section of Providence, the Museum of Art at the Rhode Island School of Design was founded in 1877 as an art school and a museum. The school serves 2000 students in architecture, ceramics, industrial design and art education. The Museum houses a collection of about 65,000 works of art, portions of which appear in the 45 galleries.

Galleries are arranged around three sides of a courtyard, bounded on the fourth by Pendleton House, the first "American Wing" of any museum in the United States. It houses the bequest of Charles L. Pendleton, one of the first collectors in the field of American decorative arts. The Pendleton collection contains outstanding examples from all the major urban cabinetmaking centers between Portsmouth, New Hampshire and Baltimore. One of the highlights is a Boston bombe chest of drawers; bombe furniture being considered the supreme achievement of Boston cabinetmakers in the 18th century.

Pendleton House also provides a home for two superlative Goddard and Townsend six-shell desks, and an important Philadelphia "slab" table. The two front parlors in Pendleton House replicate the corresponding rooms in Pendleton's own house, which still stands in Providence. Upstairs there is 17th and early 18th-century furniture by both urban and rural turners and joiners, and collections of American decorative arts. .

The Education Department regularly offers a non-credit two-semester introduction to masterpieces of paintings, sculpture, architecture and decorative arts from ancient Egypt to the present. Information on all the Museum's education programs, which are extensive, can be obtained from (401) 331-3511, ext. 349.

MYSTIC SEAPORT INC
50 Greenmanville Ave
Mystic, CT 06355
(203) 572-0711

Hours: *Daily, May 1 to October 31, 9-5, grounds close at 6. November 1 to April 30, 9-4, grounds and some exhibits; 10-4, interpreted exhibits and craft demonstrations. CLOSED Christmas.*

Admission: *Adults, $13.00, Children $6.75. Seaport members, children under four and military in uniform admitted free. Group rates on request. Memberships start at $30.*

Location: *Mystic Seaport is about ten miles E of New London on Route 27, approximately one mile S of Interstate 95, Exit 90. Free parking.*

MYSTIC SEAPORT IS an indoor-outdoor maritime museum including historic ships, boats, buildings, and formal exhibits relating to American maritime history. The primary emphasis is on the maritime commerce of the Atlantic coast during the 19th century and its impact on the economic, social, and cultural life of the United States. The exhibit area covers 17 acres along the Mystic River.

The Museum includes 60 historic buildings, four major vessels, 300 boats, a research library, and substantial collections of maritime artifacts. The ships include America's last surviving wooden whaleship, a full-rigged training ship, and a fishing schooner. The houses, stores, taverns and places of worship, some of them original, others transplanted, are well designed examples of their era.

Several large buildings are devoted to the display of maritime art and artifacts. The Stillman Building houses ship models, paintings, and scrimshaw. The Wendell Building houses an exhibit of British and American figureheads and woodcarvings. The Schaefer Building has changing gallery exhibits of the museum's paintings, prints, and other artifacts.

The White Library, specializing in American Maritime history, contains 350,000 manuscripts and 56,000 ships' plans and charts. Information on maritime folklore, sea chanteys, and the arts and crafts of a seacoast town are available. The education programs of the Seaport are geared to maritime history and other fields of maritime interest.

In mid-July the Museum sponsors Horse and Carriage Weekend, an annual gathering of horses and antique carriages. At the end of the same month there is also an Antique and Classic Boat Rendezvous.

OLD STURBRIDGE VILLAGE
1 Old Sturbridge Village Road
Sturbridge, MA 01566
(508) 347-3362

Hours: May to October, Daily 9-5, November to April, Tuesday-Sunday 9-5. Closed Christmas and New Year's Day.

Admission: Adults $12, Children 6-15 $6, children under 6 free. Individual memberships start at $50.

Location: From Mass Turnpike I-90 Exit 9. From I-84 Exit 2. Follow the signs to Route 20 W. Free parking.

OLD STURBRIDGE VILLAGE is a living history museum, where historically costumed men and women interpret daily life in a rural New England town during the 1830s. The Sturbridge Village Green is surrounded by a Center Meetinghouse, Parsonage, Tavern, Bank, and rural Store. In the context of the museum village, collections of early Americana are more accessible to contemporary visitors.

Small museums house formal displays of traditional crafts. The Glass Exhibit follows the development of the glassmaking process. Included are displays of the glassmaker's tools and moulds, English and American wine and spirit bottles, glass drinking vessels, tumblers and tavern glasses from the late 18th to the early 19th Century. The J. Cheney Wells Clock Gallery contains a superb collection of American clocks including pieces by New England clockmakers Cheney, Benjamin and Simon Willard, Eli Terry, and Seth Thomas. Clock collectors can study examples of wooden works tall clocks, early country clocks, Massachusetts shelf clocks, northern New England clocks, 18th century high style clocks, Willard family shelf, wall, and tall clocks.

The Lighting Exhibit presents lighting devices from early times to the present day, and traces their development, including design, adaptation for different fuels, and evolution of candlestick forms. The Argand lamp, whale oil, and kerosene lamps are included.

Annual events include a three-day antiques conference weekend held in October, during which curators, writers and antiques dealers speak on authenticity, connoisseurship, conservation, and specialized collections. The April Design and Decorations weekend focuses on the architectural features of 18th and 19th century homes, and preserving outbuildings, with lectures and small group discussions. Re-creations of 18th century events occur throughout the year.

PEABODY MUSEUM OF SALEM
East India Square
Liberty and Essex Streets
Salem, MA 01970
(508) 745-9500 (recorded message) (508) 745-1876

Hours: *Year-round Monday to Saturday 10-5, Thursday until 9, Sunday 12-5.*
Closed on national Holidays

Admission: *Adults $4, Senior Citizens and Students $3, Children 6-16 $1.50.*
Families $10. Memberships start at $25.

Location: *Take I-95 N to Rte 128 N to Rte 114 into Salem. Go 2.4 MI on 114,*
then R onto Rte 107 N, Bridge St. Take R opposite Parker Bros, onto St. Peter St,
turn L, then R for municipal parking and Museum.

LOCATED ON EAST India Square in the historic district is the Peabody
Museum of Salem, formed in 1799 by members of the East India Marine
Society to house a collection of "natural and artificial curiosities." Today this
includes 300,000 objects relating to the maritime history of New England, the
natural history of Essex County, and curiosities reflecting everyday life in
India, Japan, China, Africa, and the Pacific Islands during the 1800s.

Recently merged with the China Trade Museum of Milton, the Peabody is the
repository of one of the most beautiful collections of Chinese Export porcelain
in the country. Included in the first floor Export Porcelain galleries of the
newly opened Asian Export Art Wing are general market porcelains, including
those with flower and landscape designs; special order porcelains for the
American market, often adorned with armorial crests or monograms, or
decorated with special motifs; Chinese animal, bird and human figures; and
250 pieces of the finest special order porcelains made for the British and
Continental markets.

Trading in bulk commodities, including tea and textiles, motivated and
supported the trade in luxury goods known as Asian Export Art. Exhibits
include Chinese export gold and silver, decorative arts including paintings,
furniture, and textiles, Japanese export art, depictions of the China coast by
Western artists, goods from Salem's trade with India and depictions of the
Indian people, and architecture and landscapes of the 18th and 19th centuries.
The Museum also has an important collection of ship models, paintings,
and figureheads.

Each year the Museum offers a broad range of educational programs including
guest lectures, symposia, tours for adult and student groups, visitor interactive
demonstrations and special events.

PLIMOTH PLANTATION
Warren Avenue Box 1620
Plymouth, MA 02360
(508) 746-1622

Hours: *April to November Daily 9-5. During July and August Mayflower II is open until 6:30.*

Admission: *Combined admission ticket for all exhibits: Adults $15 Children $10. Pilgrim Village and Wampanoag Settlement only: Adults $12 Children 5-12 $8. Mayflower only: Adult $5.50, Child $3.75.*

Location: *Plimouth Plantation can be reached from Rte 3 Exit 4 at the intersection of Rte 3A and Plimoth Plantation Highway in Plymouth.*

PLIMOTH PLANTATION IS an outdoor living museum of 17th century Plymouth. The museum illuminates the life and times of the English colonists who settled Plymouth Colony and of their Native American neighbors, the Wampanoag Indians. The Museum has three outdoor exhibit areas: the 1627 Pilgrim Village, the Wampanoag Settlement, and Mayflower II.

Through dress, manner, dialect, and world view the costumed interpreters in the Village portray residents of the original English colony. Constructed to appear as it did seven years after the arrival of the Pilgrims, the Village is surrounded by the walls of a palisade, with rough-hewn and clapboarded houses. Speaking in English dialect, the interpreters engage visitors in discussions of politics and religion.

The Wampanoag Settlement depicts the culture of the Native American resident in southeastern New England in the early 17th century. Dome-shaped dwellings made of bent saplings and woven reed mats or bark illustrate the architecture of the Native people. Here the daily routines of this North American Indian tribe come alive for the visitor.

Mayflower II, docked at State Pier in Plymouth Harbor, is a full-scale reproduction of the ship that brought the Pilgrims to the New World in 1620. Built in England, it sailed across the Atlantic in 1957. Aboard the ship staff portray the original Mayflower passengers and crew. Costumed interpreters express their 17th century hopes and concerns for their new life.

The Shelby Cullom Davis Exhibition Galleries enable the visitor to better understand the research and analysis that are necessary to create the Museum's period environment. Each element within the exhibit explores an important source of information on 17th century life. An exhibition of 17th century furniture includes 30 examples of styles common in England in this period.

SANDWICH GLASS MUSEUM
129 Main Street P. O. Box 103
Sandwich, MA 02563
(508) 888-0251

Hours: April to October 9:30-4:40. November, December, February and March Wednesday-Sunday 9:30-4. CLOSED Holidays during November, December and all of January.

Admission: Adults $3, Children 50 Cents, under 6 free. Call for group rates. Memberships start at $10.

Location: From the Sagamore Bridge take Route 6 to Exit 2. Turn L on Route 130 toward Sandwich. Bear L at island. Museum is directly across from Town Hall.

LOCATED IN A charming white clapboard house on Town Hall Square, the Sandwich Glass Museum displays an extensive collection of the famous Sandwich Glass manufactured by the Boston & Sandwich Glass Company (1825-1887) and the Cape Cod Glass Works (1859-1869). Renowned for beautiful colors and fascinating designs, Sandwich Glass is highly prized by collectors today.

The Museum is composed of 13 galleries, arranged chronologically. The exhibits take the viewer through the development and manufacture of several types of glass, starting with early free-blown glass and blown three-mold glass. Shapes and styles on display include candlesticks, tableware, vases, furniture knobs, and tiebacks; colorful mid-period pattern glass in canary, blue, green, and opalescent; and one-of-a-kind presentation pieces made to commemorate special occasions and events.

A display of pressed glass includes the world-famous lacy glass developed at Sandwich. Impressively displayed are Sandwich paperweights and glass decorated by enameling and etching. The cherished dolphin pattern candlesticks of the Cape Cod Glass Company are also on display. In the much celebrated triple dolphin design, the Museum boasts two candleholders, a compote, and the recent acquisition of an opalescent lamp with gilt decoration.

In January and February, the Museum sponsors a Winter lecture series composed of eight sessions on glass design, production, and identification. In August the Museum sponsors the Annual Antique Glass Show and Sale at the Henry Wing School Auditorium. Glass production from around the globe and spanning all periods of manufacture is available for viewing and sale.

The Museum maintains a reference library on the history and production of Sandwich Glass and sells more recent publications in the Museum Shop.

SHELBURNE MUSEUM
Route 7
Shelburne, VT 05482
(802) 985-3346

Hours: *Mid-May through mid-October daily 9-5.*

Admission: *Valid for the "recommended" two consecutive days: Adults $12.50, Children age 6-17, $4.50, $35 Maximum for parents and children under 18.*

Location: *Shelburne is located on Route 7 seven miles south of Burlington and three hundred miles north of New York City.*

THE SHELBURNE MUSEUM, founded in 1947 by Electra Havemeyer Webb, is one of the special treasures of New England. Located on 45 well-tended acres, this assemblage of 35 buildings, predominantly historic, and 200,000 artifacts, includes an outstanding collection of American folk art.

The collections of fine and folk art fascinate the most jaded visitor. Here are superb collections of furnishings and decorative accessories, rugs, quilts, pewter, glass, pottery and porcelain. The Colchester Reef Lighthouse contains galleries of marine art, including paintings, figureheads, and scrimshaw . The Stagecoach Inn houses a collection of American folk sculpture with weather vanes, cigar-store Indians, circus and carousel figures, symbolic eagles, and ship's figures. Dorset House contains a collection of over 1,000 decoys: ducks, geese, swans and shorebirds. The quilt collection, numbering over 800, is noted for quality and superb designs.

The collection of 140 horsedrawn carriages, wagons, sleighs, and coaches contained in the Horseshoe Barn is regarded by many as the outstanding exhibit at the Shelburne. Not to be overlooked is the 892-ton Ticonderoga, a Lake Champlain side-wheeler moved more than two miles overland to this resting place. There is the Kirk Bros. Miniature Toy Circus: more than 5,000 hand carved miniature circus figures.

The Electra Havemeyer Webb Memorial Building, a Greek Revival mansion, contains works of art acquired by Mrs. Webb's parents and moved from their Park Avenue apartment. The Webb Gallery displays 300 years of American painting, including primitive portraits of the colonial period, Luminist painters such as Fitz Hugh Lane, and landscapes from the Hudson River School.

But whatever you find here, and it seems endless, you will find that it is presented with attention to the details of historical accuracy and public education that puts the Shelburne Museum in the front rank of American museums.

SOCIETY FOR THE PRESERVATION
OF NEW ENGLAND ANTIQUITIES
Harrison Gray Otis House
141 Cambridge Street
Boston, MA 02114
(617) 227-3956

Admission: $3 - $5; members free. Membership starts at $25. Modest fees for special events; programs $10 - $200; reduced fees for members.

PRESERVING NEW ENGLAND'S heritage is the aim of the Society for the Preservation of New England Antiquities (SPNEA), which owns 43 historic properties in five states, including 23 house museums and 11 study properties. Founded in 1910 by William Sumner Appleton, the country's first professional preservationist, SPNEA has the largest and best documented collection of New England decorative arts. With 50,000 objects — furniture, wallpapers, ceramics, glass, metal, textiles, and toys — on display, the house museums collectively document daily life in New England over three centuries.

Because SPNEA has extensive documentation for its properties and collections and devotes a great deal of effort to research and interpretation, its house museums are among the best places for collectors to visit to refine their connoisseurship. Many of the houses came to SPNEA with the accumulations of centuries, thus providing remarkable insights into how domestic life has evolved over many generations. Several of the houses, described in more detail below, contain notable collections of decorative arts. A free illustrated House Guide listing all the houses open to the public may be obtained by sending a self-addressed stamped ($.45) envelope to the address above.

Of particular interest to collectors are the following:

CONNECTICUT: Bowen House, Roseland Cottage, Route 169, on the Common, Woodstock (203) 928-4074. Memorial Day weekend to Labor Day weekend: Wed -Sun, 12 - 5; and mid-Sept - mid-Oct: Fri-Sun, 12 - 5, $3. A rare and important surviving example of a Gothic Revival summer estate, notable for its different types of Gothic Revival furniture, Belter furniture and Victorian accessories.

MAINE: Sayward-Wheeler House, 79 Barrell Lane, York Harbor (603) 436-3205. June 1 - Oct 15: Wed - Sun, 12 - 5. $3. Mid-to-late 18th c. furniture, American portraits, 18th c. glass, Chinese Export porcelain, in a house that has remained virtually untouched since the 18th century.

MASSACHUSETTS: Beauport, 75 Eastern Point Blvd, Gloucester, (508) 283-0800. Mid-May - mid-Sept: Mon - Fri, 10 - 4; and mid-Sept - mid-Oct: Mon - Fri, 10 - 4 and Sat, Sun, 1 - 4, $5. Large collections of hooked rugs, glass, silhouettes, Redware, and China trade material, arranged in period settings in a 40-room house overlooking the harbor.

Codman House, Codman Rd, Lincoln, (617) 259-8843. June 1 - Oct 15: Wed-Sun, tours at 12, 1, 2, 3, 4, $3. An 18th c. country house in the English manner, boyhood home of the designer Ogden Codman, Jr. Furnished with French and American antiques and other family furnishings, 1800 - 1930.

Harrison Gray Otis House, 141 Cambridge St, Boston, (617) 227-3956. Open year round: Tue - Fri, 12 - 5 and Sat, 10 - 5. Tours on the hour, last tour at 4, $3. Free-standing brick mansion in the Federal style, furnished with American Federal furniture and decorative arts, with reproduction wallpapers and paint colors based on scientific analysis.

Winslow Crocker House, 250 Route 6A, Yarmouth Port. June 1 - Oct 15: Tue, Thu, Sat, Sun, 12 - 5, $3. Mid to late 18th c. furniture, American portraits, Chinese Export porcelain, 18th c glass, in a Georgian shingle house.

NEW HAMPSHIRE. Barrett House, Main St, New Ipswich. June 1 - Oct 15: Thu -Sun, 12 - 5, $3. Elegant Federal mansion, furnished with late 18th and early 19th c. furnishings, including musical instruments, scenic wallpaper.

Rundlet-May House, 364 Middle St, Portsmouth, (603)436-3205. June 1 - Oct 15: Wed - Sun, 12 - 5, $3. Collection of Federal furniture made in Portsmouth in the early 19th century; English and American prints, glass and ceramics, English and Canton china in a Federal mansion, with gardens and outbuildings.

Today SPNEA is the largest regional preservation organization in the country, with a renowned Conservation Center in Waltham, Massachusetts, which consults on the preservation of historic buildings, conserves fine antique furniture and architectural elements, and develops preservation technology. Its services are available to organizations and individuals around the country. SPNEA offers a variety of educational programs, including lectures, workshops, and courses on architecture and the decorative arts. In its Stewardship Program, SPNEA protects an additional 37 privately owned historic buildings through legal easements. To obtain more information about its programs, services, and publications, write to the address above.

SOTHEBY'S EDUCATIONAL STUDIES
1334 York Avenue
New York, NY 10021
(212) 606-7822

Fees: For the American Arts course is $13,975 (does not cover meals, housing, and supplemental fees); short-term courses, $25-$300.

SOTHEBY'S, THE WORLD-FAMOUS auction house founded in 1744, counts among its staff some of the most knowledgeable experts in the art world. A visit to any Sotheby's auction is a fine way to study antiques and to obtain Sotheby's estimate of their value. Sotheby's year-long educational program, one of the most outstanding, was originally developed at Sotheby's in London as an apprenticeship program for the company's art experts. The Works of Art Program was opened to the general public in 1974, and in 1985 Sotheby's inaugurated the American Arts Course in New York.

The American Arts Course is an accredited full-time, nine-month certificate program of intensive professional study designed primarily for those interested in pursuing careers related to the American art field. The hands-on course emphasizes scholarship, connoisseurship, and practical experience in the workings of the art market.

Lectures, study sessions, field trips, and attendance at art auctions train students to identify period styles from 1650 to the present in the decorative arts (furniture, silver, ceramics, glass, and textiles) and the fine arts (paintings, sculpture, prints, drawings, and photographs).

Enrollment is limited to 24; candidates must demonstrate their qualifications for the program by one of the following: a BA degree in Art History or a related field, substantial experience in the art field, or demonstrated talent in a field such as cabinet-making, interior design, etc. Writing ability and an interview are also required.

Sotheby's Educational Studies also offers short-term courses and symposia from evening lectures to four-day seminars for individuals who want to expand their knowledge of a specific field such as fine arts conservation, antique jewelry or European decorative arts, among others. Specific details on current offerings are available by calling (212) 606-7822.

STRAWBERY BANKE
Marcy Street, P O Box 300
Portsmouth, NH 03801
(603) 433-1100

Hours: May to October daily 10-5. Evenings during the first two weekends in December for the Candlelight Stroll.

Admission: Adults $7, Seniors $6, Children 6-17 $4, Families $18. Special rates for organized groups of 10 or more. Individual memberships start at $30.

Location: One hour north of Boston, I-95 exit 7: take Market Street downtown and follow the directional signs. The museum entrance is located on Marcy Street opposite Prescott Park and the Portsmouth waterfront.

STRAWBERY BANKE MUSEUM is a ten-acre waterfront settlement comprised of 42 historic homes, period gardens, craftshops and exhibitions, depicting more than 350 years of architectural and social change in one of America's oldest neighborhoods, established in 1630.

Salvaged from demolition and urban renewal in the late 1950s, Strawbery Banke offers the visitor seven furnished houses of different time periods, wide ranging exhibits on social history, trades and architecture, historic gardens and landscape, and educational programs for the whole family.

Visitors can stroll through the 1796 Walsh house with its display of interior woodwork and neoclassical furniture, view early craftsmen's tools in the Lowd House, and puzzle over the "split "Drisco House.

Strawbery Banke sponsors a number of symposia during the year. In January they have a two-day symposium of "Collecting New England Decorative Arts," which is held in York Harbor, Maine. In February, the topic at a one day symposium is the urban landscape of early New England. March is reserved for the Women's History Symposium. In October, the annual one-day Architecture Symposium takes place. The Museum sponsors a Brown Bag Lunch Lecture Series at the Portsmouth Public Library which focuses on the history of Portsmouth and specialized Strawbery Banke topics. During the summer, Strawbery Banke offer two-week sessions for children 11-14 years old focusing on historical crafts, games, and aspects of children's s lives during the 18th and 19th centuries.

THE TRUSTEES OF RESERVATIONS
572 Essex Street
Beverly, MA 01915
(508)921-1944

Admission: Varies at each property. Memberships start at $35 and includes admission privileges to properties and the opportunity to attend special events held during the year.

THE TRUSTEES OF RESERVATIONS is the world's first land trust, formed in 1891. In a reversal of the natural order of things, the National Trust in Great Britain used the TTOR'S charter as its model when it started up in 1895. TTOR is one of the largest privately supported land organization in Massachusetts, owning and maintaining 71 properties totalling more than 17,500 acres. These include beaches, wetlands, woodlands, historic houses and formal gardens. Two of the historic houses are notable for their decorative arts collections.

Naumkeag, Prospect Hill Rd, Stockbridge (413)298-3239. Open Late June through Labor Day. From the intersection of Rtes 7 and 102 at the Red Lion Inn in Stockbridge center, take Pine Street north. Bear left on Prospect Hill Road 1/2 MI. Naumkeag, a 26-room gabled mansion designed by Stanford White in 1885, was the summer home of Judge Joseph H. Choate, jurist and ambassador to England at the turn of the century. The house contains notable collections of Chinese export porcelain, antique furniture, elegant rugs and tapestries. Judge Choates daughter, Mabel, had a superior eye for export porcelain and one finds both a handsome 18th century tea and coffee service with a Masonic motif, and an exquisite miniature tea set.

Steven Coolidge Place, 1/2 Mile from Route 125 on Andover street in North Andover, MA. (508)682-3580 Open Sundays 1-5 PM or by appointment mid-April to the end of October. This was the summer home for many years of author and diplomat John Gardner Coolidge and his wife Helen Stevens Coolidge. They filled it with the glorious souvenirs of their travels including pre-18th century ceramics for the Chinese domestic market, Anglo-Irish cut glass, Oriental rugs and fine wall hangings. In addition to the decorative arts, there are beautiful gardens to stroll, which are surrounded by flowering dogwood in season.

Both properties reflect the elegance of gracious country living at the turn of the century.

WADSWORTH ATHENEUM
600 Main Street
Hartford, CT 06103
(203) 278-2670

Hours: Tuesday to Sunday 11-5.

Admission: Adults $3, Students and Senior Citizens $1.50, members and children are free. Free all day Thursday and from 11-1 on Saturday.

Location: On the Main Street side of Atheneum Square, next to the Traveller's Tower.

THE WADSWORTH ATHENEUM'S history began in 1842 with the construction of the Gothic Revival building, containing a library and a fine arts gallery, that was the gift of Daniel Wadsworth. With the additions over the years of the Colt Wing, the Morgan Memorial, the Avery Memorial and the construction of the Goodwin wing it has grown to 36 galleries.

J. Pierpont Morgan figures prominently in the history of the Wadsworth Atheneum for his donation of the Morgan Memorial Building, finished three years before his death, and 1,300 objects ranging from 15th century majolica to 18th century German Silver. His son donated French and German porcelain and decorative arts and the famous Wallace Nutting Collection of Early American furniture.

The Atheneum is renowned for its collections of American art, paintings, sculpture, drawings and decorative arts; French Impressionist paintings; English and American silver; and classical bronzes, among others. In 1989 the Atheneum displayed the sexually explicit photographs of Robert Mapplethorpe, with seemingly minimal disruption to daily life in Hartford, Connecticut.

Gallery talks, running less than an hour, are free with museum admission, as are general tours, offered on Thursday, Saturday and Sunday at 1:00. There are formally organized education programs for adults and lectures. For a weekly recorded listing of museum hours and events call (203)247-9111.

WINTERTHUR
Route 52
Winterthur, DE 19735
(800) 448-3883 or (302) 888-4600

Hours: Tuesday to Saturday 10-4, Sunday 12-4. *CLOSED Mondays, New Year's Day, Easter, July 4, Thanksgiving, and December 24-25.*

Admission: General Admission, Adults $8, Students $6.50. Reserved Tours, Adults $12.50, Members $10, Ages 12-16 $6. Winterthur Guild memberships start at $35. Seminar on American Home, $285; conferences and workshops, $25-$95.

Location: Winterthur is located on Route 52, six miles northwest of Wilmington, Delaware.

NESTLED IN DELAWARE'S Brandywine Valley stands the premier museum of American furniture and decorative arts: Winterthur, the former home of Henry Francis du Pont. This vast collection of American antiques affords an unparalleled opportunity to observe changing styles in American furniture and decorative arts over a 200 year period. Surrounded by spectacular gardens, the grand house contains nearly 200 rooms and displays of outstanding examples of domestic architecture, furniture, textiles, pewter, silver, ceramics, paintings, and prints dating from about 1640 to 1840. Each period room setting is composed with careful attention to every detail.

From mid-June to early August, a series of two-hour subject tours of the museum's collections covering American silver, Federal furniture, American clocks, and Oriental rugs are offered twice daily, at 10:30 and 1:30. Winterthur operates three graduate training programs, a research library, and clinics on identifying and caring for historic and artistic objects. In 1986 the Guild began offering an annual four-day seminar (held in March) on "The American Home." Focusing on a specific period in American design, these seminars explore in lectures & workshops such topics as the Chippendale style period from 1760 to 1790 in lectures and workshops. The annual Winter Institute, a graduate level course in early American decorative arts, will be held January 15 to February 8, 1991.

Reserved tours are available until early April, then resume again in June. "American Interiors" traces the changes in American taste from 1700 to 1840. "A Diverse Nation" examines the ethnic and regional diversity exemplified in the room settings of Shakers, the English, Dutch New Yorkers, and Germans of Pennsylvania, while "American Craftsmanship" focuses on the design history of American decorative arts and the development of furniture construction.

WORCESTER ART MUSEUM
55 Salisbury Street
Worcester, MA 01609
(508) 799-4406

Hours: *Tuesday through Friday 10-4, Saturday 10-5, Sunday 1-5. Free to all Saturday 10-12. CLOSED Mondays, New Year's, Easter, July 4, Thanksgiving, Christmas.*

Admission: *Adults $3.50, Senior citizens and full time college students $2 Members and those 18 and under no charge. Memberships start at $10.*

Location: *From I-90 exit 10 Auburn: Take I-290 E to Worcester, Exit 17. Go L on Rte 9 to Lincoln Sq, proceed through sq. to 3rd set of lights at top of hill, turn R on Harvard St and Museum is on the L at 2nd traffic light.*

THE WORCESTER ART Museum was founded by Stephen Salisbury III in 1896. The Museum is now composed of 42 galleries containing 25,000 objects and is the third largest fine arts museum in New England. It's collections cover the evolution of art and include Classical, Oriental and Medieval sculpture, tapestries, European and American paintings, an American decorative arts gallery; photographs, prints, and drawings.

The Worcester Art Museum is noted for its holdings in American art. Of particular importance are works of New England portraiture including the double portraits of three members of the Freake family, considered two of the finest examples of 17th century American portraiture in existence. Portrait artists from the 18th century represented in the collection in John Singleton Copley, Charles Willson Peale, Joseph Blackburn, Christian Gullagher and Ralph and James Earle.

The collection of American Impressionist paintings includes works by Childe Hassam, Frank Benson, Edmund Tarbell, Mary Cassatt, Maurice Prendergast, John Singer Sargent and James A. Mc N. Whistler. The watercolor art of Winslow Homer, John Singer Sargent, John La Farge and Maurice Prendergast are on display.

In 1991, the Worcester Art Museum will mount exhibits entitled "Pioneers in Bird Illustration" including the work of Catesby, Bewick, Wilson and Audubon; "Toulouse Lautrec Prints;" "Early American Photography: The First Fifty Years" covering the period from 1839 to 1900; "Behind the Seen: Viewing the Masters through Modern Technology" focusing on discoveries made about the museum's collection using radiography; and during the summer, a conservation demonstration on a Flemish work.

YALE UNIVERSITY ART GALLERY
1111 Chapel Street (P O Box 2006 Yale Station)
New Haven, CT 06520
(203) 432-0600

Hours: Tuesday to Saturday 10-5, Thursdays til 8 except Summer, Sunday 2-5. CLOSED New Year's Day, July 4th, Thanksgiving and Christmas.

Admission: FREE, wheelchair accessible. Memberships start at $15.

Location: On the campus of Yale University, at the corner of Chapel and York Streets, opposite the Center for British Art.

THE YALE UNIVERSITY Art Gallery was founded in 1832 by John Trumbull, patriot and artist, who donated more than 100 paintings to Yale College. It has since expanded to become a major art museum with holdings from virtually all national schools and periods in the history of art. It is the oldest university art museum in the Western Hemisphere.

Noteworthy collections at Yale include Italian Renaissance art, early Italian paintings, Greek and Etruscan vases, Italian painting and Medieval art, textiles, African sculpture, Pre-Columbian art, and the Garvan and related collections of American painting and decorative arts, Old Master paintings and a comprehensive collection of master prints, drawings, and photographs.

Included are paintings by Pollaiuolo, Hals, Lorrain, Winslow Homer, Thomas Eakins, John Singleton Copley and John Trumbull; furniture from the Newport workshops of Goddard and Townsend, and Stephen Badlam of Boston; and silver by American silversmiths Edward Winslow and Joseph Richardson.

In early 1991, an exhibit entitled "Master of the Lotus Garden: Bada Shanren and his Art" will feature 80 examples of paintings and calligraphy from North American, European and Asian collections. Other 1991 exhibits scheduled include "Private Delights: The Drawings of Mary Bell", Italian Drawing 1550-1800, Selections from the Permanent collection, and the drawings of 19th century Swiss artist, Felix Vallotton.

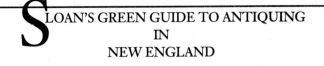

S LOAN'S GREEN GUIDE TO ANTIQUING
IN
NEW ENGLAND

▼

Periodicals

PERIODICALS

DOZENS OF PERIODICALS compete for the attention of the New England antiques enthusiast. Each of these publication brings analysis, information, show schedules and reviews - information that sophisticates so that you may more knowledgeably participate in the pursuit and judge the authenticity of antiques in New England. From the erudite editorials and scholarly articles in The Magazine ANTIQUES through the pages of auction ads in Antiques and The Arts Weekly, to the practical advice in Antiques Exchange, these publications illuminate the antiques trade in New England, and beyond. Hence, a brief overview of a very wide range of periodicals, listed alphabetically.

ANTIQUE EXCHANGE

This little monthly magazine is written, edited, designed and produced by antiques dealer Ed Welch, assisted by his wife Marie, in Winslow, Maine. Ed Welch has been in the business a long time, traveled many miles and happily shares what he knows (and what he thinks) with his readers. He writes on aspects of buying antiques or outlines antiquing tours in Maine. He has a well deserved following, and though you may never go to Maine, you can learn something useful about buying antiques from reading his magazine.

$16 One Year Antique Exchange Magazine, RFD 3, Box 1290, Winslow, Maine 04901

ANTIQUES & THE ARTS WEEKLY

"The Bee," the only weekly antiques newspaper published in New England, is filled with advertising from auctioneers, antiques dealers, show managers and private parties. The paper regularly reviews these events, often devoting a cover to the more noteworthy of them. The Bee has the most complete auction advertising of any New England periodical, in part due to its weekly format. Editor R. Scudder Smith

$35 One Year Antiques & The Arts Weekly 5 Church Hill Rd, Newtown CT 06470 (203)426-8036

ART & ANTIQUES

"Art & Antiques," a monthly magazine, divides it's coverage almost equally between the fine and decorative arts. Among its columnists are well-known names including art critic Hilton Kramer. We like the regular column "Value Judgments", because it educates and informs in a lighthearted style. This is a handsome magazine, and it keeps improving with age. Editor Jeffrey Schaire

$24.00 One Year Art & Antiques, P O Box 840 Farmingdale, New York 10003

ART & AUCTION

Billed as the "magazine of the international art market", it seriously delves into issues of finance and authenticity, and includes thoughtful analyses of sales and trends. Periodically, it tries to answer the question "Where is the market going from here?" other times it outlines an antiques tour or evaluates a new curator or museum. Editor Amy Page.

$42.00 One Year Art & Auction P O Box 11350, Des Moines, IA 50347

MAINE ANTIQUE DIGEST

A monthly paper in six to eight sections covering the marketplace for Americana — country and formal furniture, and fine and folk art. Published in Waldoboro Maine, it keeps its finger on the pulse of the New England antiques trade and attracts 25,000 subscribers in 50 states and foreign countries.

Editor Sam Pennington has many loyal subscribers who appreciate his no-holds barred approach to journalism. He prints the facts as he finds them about shenanigans in the antiques trade, without deference to his advertisers. The tersely worded responses to letters-to-the-editor are often amusing. Sam's bonhomie is apparent in the kindnesses he extends to many worthy organizations. A great read! Editor Samuel C Pennington.

$29 One Year $50 Two Years Maine Antique Digest, Box 645 Waldoboro ME
04572 (207)832-7534 FAX (207)832-7341

The Magazine ANTIQUES

The most scholarly of all the publications, the Magazine ANTIQUES covers the decorative and fine arts, seeking to stimulate appreciation and improve the connoisseurship of its readers. With full-color illustrations, articles cover historic houses, both public and private, ceramics, glass, silver, furniture, textiles, folk art, painting, sculpture, gardens architecture. Regular features include Current and Coming, Queries, Books about antiques, and the thoughtfully composed editorials of Wendell Garrett, now its Editor-at-Large. Since 1922, "the" antiques publication in the United States. Editor Alison Eckhardt Ledes

$38 One Year The Magazine Antiques Old Mill Road POB 1975 Marion OH 43305 1-800/237-2160 FAX(212)941-2897

MASSBAY ANTIQUES

A small monthly paper covering the area within approximately 100 miles of Boston, it is a good source of information about new shop openings. It also prints articles on exhibits, trends in collecting and books reviews. Editor Shannon Aaron

$12 one year, MassBay Antiques, Box 192, Ipswich, MA 01938 (508)356-5141 FAX(508)774-6365

NEW ENGLAND ANTIQUES JOURNAL

A monthly tabloid publication, first published in 1983, containing educational feature articles about antiques, auction reviews and previews, show reviews, a calendar of events, and information about shows at the regional museums. The antiques dealer advertising is organized geographically, which is helpful. Editor Roy Williamson

One Year $19.95 New England Antiques Journal 4 Church St Ware, MA 01082 (413)967-3505 FAX(413)967-6009

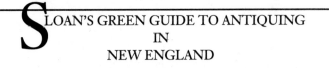

▼

Antiques Show Calendar

ANTIQUES SHOW CALENDAR
1991

Dates	State/City	Show Name & Location	Show Manager
JANUARY			
Jan 1	MA Ashland	Antiques Show Ashland Senior High School	Stephen Allman (802) 334-8894
Jan 1	MA W Springfield	Antique-A-Rama Eastern States Exposition 1305 Memorial Ave	Maven Company (203)758-3880
Jan 1	ME Augusta	New Year's Day Augusta Armory	James Montell (207) 582-2849
Jan 12-13	CT Waterbury	Waterbury Cheshire Antiques Waterbury Cheshire Sheraton 3580 East Main St	Maven Company (203) 758-3880
Jan 13	CT Danbury	Danbury Antiques Market Amber Room Stacey Rd	Sideli & Sideli (518) 392-6711
Jan 13	ME Bath	Bath Antiques Show Bath Junior High Off Congress Ave	P. Thibodeau (207) 443-4407
Jan 12-13	CT Stratford	January Antiques Show CT National Guard Armory Armory Rd	Forbes & Turner (203) 528-0322
Jan 19-20	MA Boston	Copley Plaza Antique Show Copley Plaza Hotel St James & Dartmouth St	Sonia Paine (617) 566-9669
Jan 25-Feb 3	NY New York	Winter Antiques Show 7th Regiment Armory Park Avenue at 67th St	N P Jones (203) 535-1995
Jan 23-27	CT Danbury	Antiques Show Danbury Fair Mall Rte 7 & I-84	Cord Shows Ltd (914) 273-4667

Dates	State/City	Show Name & Location	Show Manager

FEBRUARY . . . .

Feb 8-10	CT Stonington	Stonington Antiques Show Stonington Commnity Center	McElroy-Brodrick (603) 778-8842
Feb 10	ME Bath	Bath Antiques Show Bath Junior High Off Congress Ave	P. Thibodeau (207) 443-4407
Feb 15-17	CT Stamford	Stamford Antiques Show Italian Center Newfield Ave	Wendy Management (914) 698-3442
Feb 16-17	MA Woburn	President's Birthday Antique Northeast Trade Center Exit 35 Off Route 128	Sonia Paine (617) 566-9669
Feb 16-17	CT Stratford	Stratford Armory Antique Stratford Armory Armory Rd & Rte 108	Maven Company (203) 758-3880
Feb 17	CT Danbury	Danbury Antiques Market Amber Room Stacey Rd	Sideli & Sideli (518) 392-6711
Feb 23-24	MA Chestnut Hill	Brimmer & May Ants. Show Brimmer & May School Middlesex Rd	Circa Shows (508) 651-3101
Feb 23-24	MA Holliston	Antiques Show Holliston High School	Stephen Allman (802) 334-8894
Feb 28-Mar 3	MA Boston	Boston Antiques Show Boston Park Plaza Arlington St	Sideli (518) 392-6711

MARCH . . . .

Mar 2-3	MA Cambridge	Buckingham, Browne & Nichols Buckingham, Browne School Gerry's Landing Rd	Sonia Paine (617) 566-9669
Mar 2	ME Portland	March Antiques Market 1945 Congress St	Forbes & Turner (207) 767-3967
Mar 9-10	CT East Windsor	Antiques & Collectibles Show The Ramada Inn Bridge St at I-91	Maven Company (203) 758-3880
Mar 9-10	CT Greenwich	Ephemera Eleven Conference Hyatt Regency 1800 Putnam Ave	Sideli & Sideli (518) 392-6711

Dates	State/City	Show Name & Location	Show Manager
Mar 10	ME Bath	Bath Antiques Show Bath Junior High Off Congress Ave	P.Thibodeau (207) 443-4407
Mar 15-17	MA Newburyport	Newburyport Antiques Show Low Street Armory	McElroy-Brodrick (603) 778-8842
Mar 16	MA Grafton	Capertown Antiques Show Municipal Center	Revival Prom. (508) 839-9735
Mar 16-17	MA Framingham	Antiques Show Keefe Technical High School	Stephen Allman (802) 334-8894
Mar 16-17	CT Old Greenwich	Greenwich Spring Antiques Greenwich Civic Center Harding Rd	Armacost Shows (301) 383-9380
Mar 20-24	NY New York	New York Armory Antique Show 7th Regiment Armory Park Avenue & 67th St	Wendy Management (914) 698-3442
Mar 22-24	CT Hartford	CT Spring Antiques Show State Armory Broad St & Capitol Ave	Forbes & Turner (207) 767-3967
Mar 23-24	MA Westwood	Westwood Antiques Show Westwood High School	Revival Prom. (508) 839-9735

APRIL

Dates	State/City	Show Name & Location	Show Manager
Apr 5-7	RI Providence	Rhode Island Antiques Show Meehan Auditorium Brown University	Sideli & Sideli (518) 392-6711
Apr 6-7	MA W.Springfield	Doll, Toy & Teddy Bear Show New England Building 1305 Memorial Ave	Maven Company (203) 758-3880
Apr 13-14	MA W Springfield	Eastern States Antiques Eastern States Expo 1305 Memorial Ave	Maven Company (203) 758-3880
Apr 13-14	MA Westboro	Heart of New England Hastings School	Revival Prom. (508) 839-9735
Apr 14	MA Northfield	Northfield Antiques Show Pioneer Val Reg'l School Rte 10	Cobblestone (508) 544-7085
Apr 14	CT Danbury	Danbury Antiques Market Amber Room Stacey Rd	Sideli & Sideli (518) 392-6711

Dates	State/City	Show Name & Location	Show Manager
Apr 14	ME Bath	Bath Antiques Show Bath Junior High Off Congress Ave	P. Thibodeau (207) 443-4407
Apr 27-28	CT Stratford	Stratford Doll, Toy Stratford Armory Armory Rd & Rte 108	Maven Company (203) 758-3880

MAY

May 4-5	CT Stafford Spgs	Stafford Srings 700 Stafford Springs Speedway	Revival Prom. (508) 839-9735
May 9-11	MA Brimfield	Brimfield Antiques Mkt Auction Acres Rte 20	J & J Promotions (413) 245-3436
May 18	CT Woodbridge	Woodbridge Antiques Show Center Field	Forbes & Turner (207) 767-3967
May 18-19	NH Ossipee	Ossipee Antiques Festival Flag Gate Farm Rte 28	Water Village (603) 539-5126
May 25-26	NY Rhinebeck	Dutchess County Fairgrounds Rte 9	Bill Walter (914) 758-6186

JUNE

Jun 8-9	CT Farmington	Farmington Antiques Weekend Polo Grounds	Revival Prom. (508) 839-9735

JULY

Jul 6	VT Dorset	Dorset Antiques Show Village Green	Forbes & Turner (207) 767-3967
Jul 6	CT West Hartford	Univ of Hartford Antiques The Sports Center Rte 189	Maven Company 203) 758-3880
Jul 11-13	MA Brimfield	Brimfield Antiques Market Auction Acres Rte 20	J & J Promotions (413) 245-3436
July 20	CT Coventry	Nathan Hale Ant Festival Nathan Hale Homestead South St	Forbes & Turner (207) 767-3967
Jul 26-27	NH Wolfeboro	Wolfeboro Antique Fair & Sale Brewster Academy	Water Village (603) 539-5126

Dates	State/City	Show Name & Location	Show Manager
AUGUST			
Early Aug Wkd	VT Stratton	VADA Antiques Show & Sale Stratton Mtn Base Lodge	Warren Kimble (802) 247-3026
Aug Wkd	VT Manchester	Equinox Antiques Show Equinox Hotel Rte 7	Warren Kimble (802) 247-3026
Aug 6	CT Glastonbury	Glastonbury CT Antiques Hubbard & Main Sts	Forbes & Turner (207) 767-3967
Aug 8-10	NH Manchester	NHADA Antiques Show Center of NH Holiday Inn Rte 44	NHADA (603) 286-4908
Aug 17	CT New London	New London Antiques Show Connecticut College Campus Mohegan Ave	Forbes & Turner (207)767-3967
Aug 18	NH Wolfeboro	Wolfeboro Antiquarian Book Brewster Academy Wolfeboro	Water Village (603) 539-5126
Aug 24	CT Wethersfield	Old Wethersfield Antiques Show Hartford Ave	Forbes & Turner (207) 767-3967
Aug 31-Sep 1	CT Farmington	Farmington Antiques Weekend Farmington Polo Ground	Revival (508) 839-9735
SEPTEMBER			
Sep 12-14	MA Brimfield	Brimfield Antiques Market Auctions Acres Rte 20	J & J Prom. (413) 245-3436
Sep 14-15	ME S Portland	Portland Symphony Orchestra S Portland Armory 680 Broadway	Forbes & Turner (207) 767-3967
Sep 20-22	CT Greenwich	Greenwich Sacred Heart Covent of the Sacred Heart 1177 King St	Wendy Management (914) 698-3442
Sep 25-29	NY New York	New York Armory Antiques Show 7th Regiment Armory Park Ave & 67th St	Wendy Management (914) 698-3442

Dates	State/City	Show Name & Location	Show Manager

OCTOBER

Dates	State/City	Show Name & Location	Show Manager
Oct 4-6	CT Hartford	Connecticut Antiques Show CT State Armory Capitol Ave & Broad St	Forbes/ Turner (207) 767-3967
Oct 5-6	VT Manchester	Equinox Antiques Show Equinox Hotel Rte 7	Warren Kimble (802) 247-3026
Oct 6	NH Ossipee	Ossipee Historical Society Ossipee Town Hall Center Ossipee	Water Village (603) 539-5126
Oct 11-16	NY New York	International Antique Dealers Seventh Regiment Armory Park Ave @ 67th St	Haughton 071-734-5491 (London)
Oct 12-13	NY Rhinebeck	Rhinebeck Antiques Fair Dutchess County Fairgrounds Rte 9	Bill Walter (914) 758-6186
Oct 18-20	CT Wash. Depot	Washington CT Antiques Show Bryan Memorial Town Hall Rte 47	N P Jones (203) 535-1995
Oct 26-27	MA W Springfield	Eastern States Antiques 1305 Memorial Ave	Maven Company (203) 758-3880
Oct 25-27	CT Norwalk	Lockwood-Mathews Mansion Lockwood-Mathews Mansion	Wendy Mgmt (914) 698-3442
Oct 22-27	MA Boston	Ellis Memorial Antiques Show The Cyclorama 539 Tremont St	Fifeld Assoc (703) 765-3469

Dates	State/City	Show Name & Location	Show Manager

NOVEMBER

Nov 2	ME Portland	November Antiques Market 1945 Congress St	Forbes & Turner (207) 767-3967
Nov 2-3	MA W Springfield	Eastern States Ephemera New England Bldg 1305 Memorial Ave	Maven Company (203) 758-3880
Nov 9-10	MA W Springfield	Eastern States Doll, Toy New England Building 1305 Memorial Ave	Maven Company (203) 758-3880
Nov 10	MA Greenfield	Greenfield Antiques Show Greenfield High School Silver St	Cobblestone (508) 544-7085
Nov 22-24	MA Salem	Peabody Museum Antiques Show Hamilton Hall 9 Chestnut St	C. Vining (508) 777-0306
Nov 30-Dec 1	CT Stratford	Stratford Armory Antique Stratford Armory Armory Rd & Rte 108	Maven Company (203) 758-3880

DECEMBER

Dec 6-8	CT Greenwich	Antiquarius Christmas Antiques Greenwich Civic Center Harding Rd	N P Jones (203) 535-1995
Dec 7-8	MA W Springfield	New England Holiday Antiques The Young Building 1305 Memorial Ave	Maven Company (203) 758-3880
Dec 7-8	MA Northampton	Smith Vocational School Rte 9	McElroy-Brodrick (603) 778-8842
Dec 13-15	NY New York	New York Armory Christmas 7th Regiment Armory Park Ave & 67th St	Wendy Management (914) 698-3442

▼

Antiquing Tours

ANTIQUING TOURS

SEVERAL TOURS ARE presented here, varying in length, locale, and the type of antiques to be found. Please keep in mind the following when planning a trip:

1) Dealers are often called away to buy inventory for their shops so the old maxim of "If travelling from a distance, please call ahead" is essential to success.

2) The days on which many dealers regularly close are Sunday, Monday and Tuesday. Read a dealer's hours to be sure the dealer is open on the day you plan to visit.

3) Many shops in Maine, New Hampshire and Vermont are summer shops and are closed for the larger portion of the year. This is especially true the farther north you get. Listings show summer and winter hours when possible.

4) We HIGHLY recommend you carry two AAA Road Maps for New England with you as you are traveling throughout this area.

MAINE

The simplest tour in Maine is to follow Route One north from York to Searsport. There are many fine shops, featuring both country and formal furniture and decorative accessories. In York and Wells, three large multiple dealer shops opened in 1990. Kennebunkport is on this route as well as L.L. Bean in Freeport. Towns of special note include Wiscasset, North Edgecomb, Damariscotta, Camden, Lincolnville and Searsport. The traffic jams on Route 1 in Maine during the summer, especially on weekends can be severe so don't plan a quick tour of Maine shops at these times. Three days minimum would be necessary to cover this route thoroughly.

Up I-95 is Hallowell, an antiques enclave off the beaten path, and you might find it worth your time to take this detour. A short one day trip to Maine from Boston would be to go up I-95 to Exit 3, head east and work your way back to Boston on Route 1. Leave Boston by 8:15 on a weekday to make the first stop by 10:00 am.

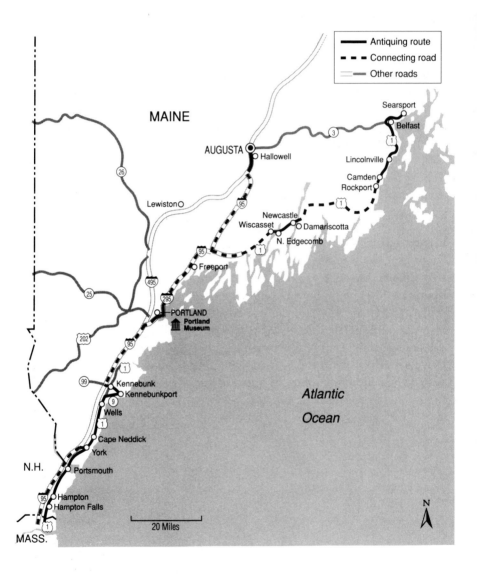

VERMONT AND NEW HAMPSHIRE

Once you move north of Stockbridge, MA, the shops are located further apart, the hours are less predictable and country antiques become more plentiful. Manchester Center, Vermont has a large concentration of antiques shops in and near its center. One could use the attractively restored Equinox Hotel here as a Vermont base and wander north and northeast from this location. If you are interested in Folk Art don't forget the Shelburne Museum in Shelburne, Vermont. Woodstock, Grafton and Newfane are towns with many admirers due to their New England charm and/or the availability of attractive accommodations. A minimum of three days should be allocated to Vermont and the Western portion of New Hampshire west of 93.

In New Hampshire, there are a attractive shops in Peterborough, Hopkinton, Fitzwilliam, Walpole, Sugar Hill and Lyme. There are charming inns in Fitzwilliam, Lyme and Hancock. Route 4 roughly between Rte 202 at the south end and the Epsom traffic circle at the north end is referred to as "Antique Alley." Here you will many shops devoted to primitive and country items, or collectibles, several of them large group shops with dozens of dealers. The regular route of many antiques dealers looking for new inventory, Antique Alley also has many collectibles. Driving south from this area to Hampton and Hampton Falls, you will encounter more group shops and here the merchandise ranges from country to period country to more formal accessories. Route 4 and Hampton Falls can be done in one very long day, if you are determined.

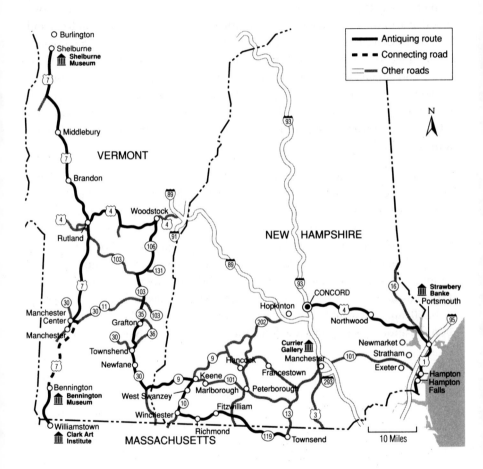

EASTERN MASSACHUSETTS

Numerous day trips can be plotted from Boston. On this map we have shown two trips that are also scenic once you reach antiquing territory. The trip out Rte 2 and Rte 2A through Concord, Acton, Littleton, Groton and West Townsend provides a full range of antiquing opportunities from the wealth of clocks in West Townsend, sophisticated country antiques in Groton and attractive decorative accessories in Concord. Groton is picturebook New England and home of Groton School and Lawrence Academy. The first shot in the Revolutionary War was fired in Concord, a town figuring prominently in the history of this country, and home of the Concord Museum.

Going northeast up the coast you move into an area rich in the history of the China Trade, in the towns of Salem and Gloucester. In Salem you find the Peabody Museum, with an outstanding collection of Chinese Export porcelain, once used for ballast in ships carrying tea and textiles. Gloucester is the home of the Cape Ann Historical Society and the birthplace of Fitz Hugh Lane, who made a visual record of this area in the early 19th century in his beautiful Luminist-style paintings. Marblehead, Salem, Essex and Newburyport are rich in antiques shops. If you only have a day, pick two of these four towns and plan to be at your first stop by 10:00 am. You would have to allot a minimum of two full days to adequately shop the antiques shops in these four towns on the North Shore.

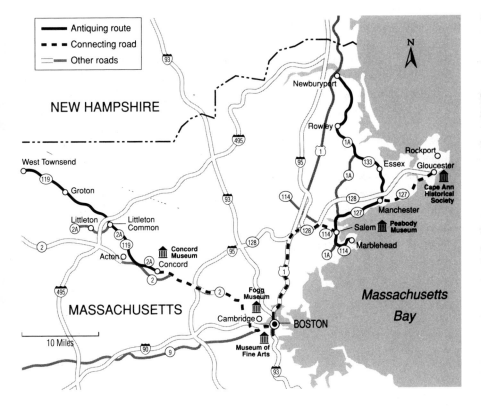

CONNECTICUT AND WESTERN MASSACHUSETTS

The western half of Connecticut and Massachusetts, closest to New York City, is the locale of the largest selection of formal furniture and decorative accessories in New England. The selection available in Greenwich, New Canaan, Woodbury, Connecticut; and Sheffield, Massachusetts is copious. Connecticut also seems to have more shops specializing in antiques of French origin. If you like quality and you are willing to pay for it, the itinerary from Greenwich to Stockbridge, Massachusetts along Route 7, with the essential detour to Woodbury, and perhaps Litchfield, is for you. Towns throughout this area are filled with handsome Gothic Revival and Georgian style homes so the scenery is superb. Bring your checkbook.

Few would have to be reminded that Stockbridge is the home of the Red Lion Inn; adjacent to the famed Tanglewood Music Center and in the heart of the Berkshires. Stockbridge also was the home of Norman Rockwell, if that is your taste. Nearby one finds Chesterwood, summer home of Daniel Chester French of Lincoln Memorial fame, and Naumkeag, a summer home for the Choate family, open to the public and containing a wonderful collection of antique furniture and decorative accessories. Three days minimum should be allocated for covering the area comfortably. Ashley Falls, Great Barrington, South Egremont and Sheffield are replete with antiques shops.

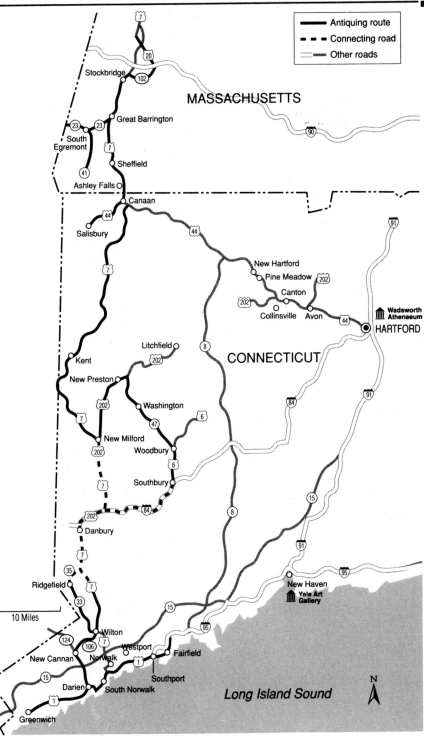

▼

Cape Cod

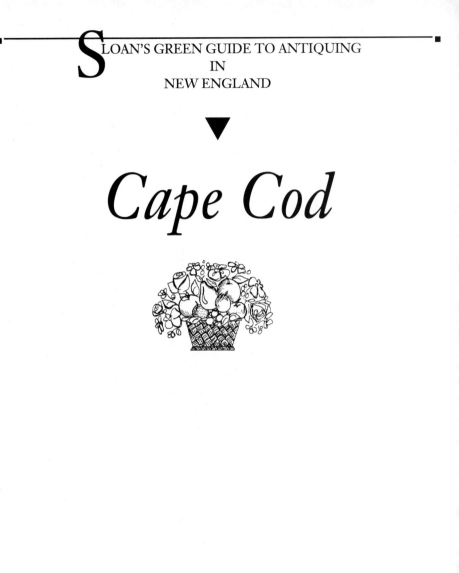

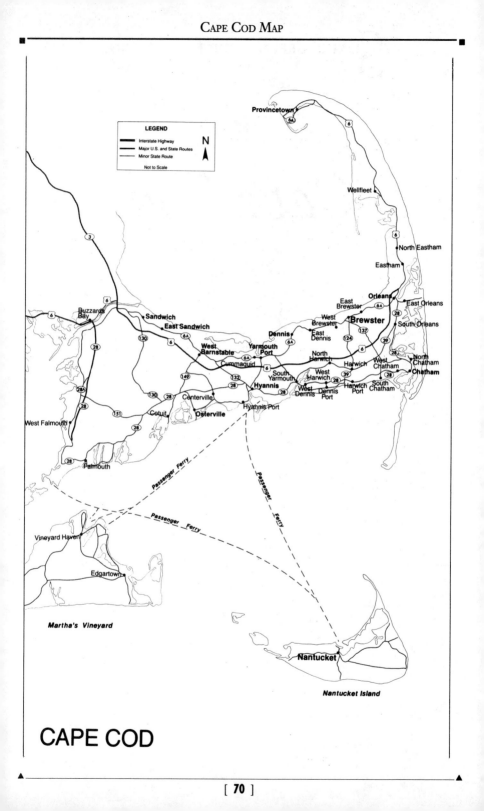

CAPE COD

BARNSTABLE

BARNSTABLE VILLAGE ANTIQUES
3267 Main St Rte 6A, 02630
(508)775-4651 **{GR8}**
Village setting with fine glass, china, vintage jewelry, linens, sterling, ephemera, books, small furniture, Staffordshire, flow blue, prints & choice collectibles. *Est:* 1985. *Serv:* Appraisal, purchase estates. *Hours:* Year round daily 10-5. *Size:* Medium. *Assoc:* CCADA, SADA. Ruth Spetelunas *Park:* In front. *Loc:* Exit 6 Mid-Cape Hwy, R on Rte 6A, Main St.

CAPE COD SHOPPER
3217 Main St Rte 6A, 02630
(508)775-2895 **15 44 64**
Glass & paper antiques & collectibles: 25,000 post cards, sheet music & ephemera, pressed & depression glass, commemorative glass & pottery, bottles & nostalgia collectibles. *Est:* 1983. *Serv:* Appraisal, consultation. mail order. *Hours:* Apr 15-Dec 21 Tue-Sat 10-4, Dec 22-Apr 14 weekends. *Assoc:* CCADA. Jane Sheckells *Park:* In front. *Loc:* From Rte 6 Exit 6: Rte 132 to Rte 6A, turn R, just past Barnstable County Court House in Barnstable Village Ctr.

BREWSTER

WILLIAM M BAXTER ANTIQUES
3439 Main St, 02631
(508)896-3998 **21 37 38**
American, English, Oriental & Continental furniture, rugs, paintings & accessories of the 18th & early 19th C. *Pr:* $100–60000. *Est:* 1960. *Hours:* Jun-Thanksgiving Mon-Sat 10-5, else BY

APPT. *Size:* Medium. *Park:* On site. *Loc:* On Rte 6A in Brewster opposite Nickerson State Park.

BRETON HOUSE
1222 Stoney Brook Rd, 02631
(508)896-3974 **32**
Eclectic selection focusing on children's toys, memorabilia & furniture. *Est:* 1956. *Hours:* Daily 11:30-5. *CC:* MC/V. Jack Saggsser *Park:* On site. *Loc:* At Jct of Stoney Brook Rd & 6A.

WILLIAM BREWSTER ANTIQUES
2912 Main St Rte 6A, 02631
(508)896-4816 **25**
An inventory of functional & eclectic furniture, glass & clocks. *Est:* 1990. *Serv:* Appraisals. *Hours:* Mon-Sat 10-5 by chance or appt. Don & Marge Wilks *Park:* In front.

BREWSTER FARMHOUSE ANTIQUES
716 Main St, 02631
(508)896-9436 **27 44 59**
Country furniture & accessories, glass & oil paintings. *Est:* 1986. *Hours:* Apr 15-Oct 15 daily 10-5, else WEEKENDS ONLY. *Size:* Large. *CC:* MC/V. Patricia W Schultz *Park:* On site. *Loc:* Across the St from Brewster Windmall.

CAPT FREEMAN PERRY HOUSE
1531 Main St, 02631
(508)896-5323 **16 29**
Brass, copper, treen & decorative accessories. *Hours:* Daily 9-5, CLOSED DEC & MAR. *Size:* Medium. *CC:* AX/MC/V. Sarah Cohen *Park:* On site. *Loc:* On Rte 6A.

LAWRENCE FINE PERIOD ANTIQUES
1050 Main St, 02631
(508)896-8381 **29 38**
Beautiful selection of 18th & 19th C fine

paintings, porcelains & furniture. *Est:* 1971. *Serv:* Appraisal, purchase estates. *Hours:* Daily 9-5, CLOSED DEC-MAR. *Size:* Medium. *CC:* AX/MC/V. Mark Lawrence *Park:* In front. *Loc:* Just E of Jolly Whaler Village Motel.

GASKILL CO ANTIQUES
134 Main St Rte 6A, 02631
(508)385-6663   **29 37 59**
Country & formal furniture, silver, paintings & decorative accessories. *Hours:* Wed-Fri, Mon 10-5, Sat-Sun 12-5 CLOSED TUE. *CC:* MC/V. *Loc:* Near Int of Stonybrook Rd & 6A.

BARBARA GRANT-ANTIQUES & BOOKS
1793 Main St Rte 6A, 02631
(508)896-7198   **13 29 65**
Old & out-of-print books, furniture, primitives, old kitchenware, glass, porcelain, prints, linen, decorative accessories, jewelry, collectibles & nostalgia. *Pr:* $1–1000. *Est:* 1980. *Serv:* Purchase estates. *Hours:* Apr-Oct daily 10-5:30, else by chance/appt. *Size:* Medium. *Assoc:* CCADA. *Park:* On site. *Loc:* On Rte 6A between Rte 137 & Rte 124.

THE HOMESTEAD ANTIQUES
2257 Main St Rte 6A, 02631
(508)896-2917   **6 33 56**
Weapons, Victorian canes, nautical items, paintings, prints, scrimshaw, early tobacco advertising tins & signs, garden ornaments, fireplace mantels & accessories, flow blue, carousel animals & decorative wood carvings. *Est:* 1983. *Hours:* Sum: daily 9-5, Oct 15-May 15: Thu-Mon 9-5. *CC:* MC/V. *Park:* On site. *Loc:* 1/2 MI W of Chillingsworth Restaurant.

DONALD B HOWES - ANTIQUES
1424 Main St Rte 6A, 02631
(508)896-3502   **36 59 66**
Folk & fine art, paintings, prints, books, documents & furniture. *Hours:* BY APPT. *Assoc:* CCADA. *Loc:* Almost opposite Fire Museum.

KINGS WAY BOOKS & ANTIQUES
774 Main St Rte 6A, 02631
(508)896-3639   **13 24 48**
Old & out-of-print books & small antiques including crystal, china, glass, silver, rare coins, linens & vintage clothing. *Est:* 1988. *Hours:* Thu-Sun 10-6. *CC:* MC/V. Ella Socky *Park:* On site. *Loc:* Across from the Drummer Boy Museum.

THE PFLOCK'S-ANTIQUES
598 Main St Rte 6A, 02631
(508)896-3457   **2 16 71**
Specializing in copper & brass metalwork including kitchen & nautical items & fireplace equipment. Some furniture. *Serv:* Metal restorations, furniture refinishing. *Hours:* Apr-Nov daily 10-5, Dec-Mar daily 10-4:30. *Size:* Medium. *Assoc:* CCADA. Anne Pflock *Park:* On site. *Loc:* On the S side of Rte 6A in Brewster.

THE PUNKHORN BOOKSHOP
672 Main St, 02631
(508)896-2114   **13 66**
Antiquarian books: American literature, history, limited editions, natural history, prints, publisher's covers & first editions. Exceptional selections in the fields of natural history, classics & Americana. *Serv:* Appraisal, search service. *Hours:* May 15-Sep 15 daily 10-5, else BY APPT. *Assoc:* MARIAB. David L Luebke *Loc:* On the S side of Rte 6A.

EDWARD SNOW HOUSE
ANTIQUES
2042 Main St Rte 6A, 02631
(508)896-2929   **37 59 80**

American formal & country furniture, paintings, textiles in a 1700 Cape Cod house. *Hours:* Call ahead. *Assoc:* CCADA. Elaine Brennan *Park:* On site.

SUNSMITH HOUSE - ANTIQUES
2926 Main St Rte 6A, 02631
(508)896-7024   **32 65 85**

Quilts, linens, toys, dolls, games, primitives, jewelry, country furniture & accessories, vintage clothing, china & glass, used, rare & out-of-print books. *Pr:* $5–1200. *Est:* 1978. *Serv:* Free catalog, purchase estates. *Hours:* Apr-Oct Mon-Sat 10-5 Sun 12-5 by chance/appt. *Size:* Medium. *Assoc:* CCADA. Wendell Smith *Park:* On site. *Loc:* Diagonally across from Ocean Edge Conference Center.

SHIRLEY WALKER ANTIQUES
1792 Main St Rte 6A, 02631
(508)896-8138   **27 34 87**

Distinctive American country antiques & folk art including quilts, weathervanes, painted furniture, toys & appropriate accessories displayed in room settings in the historic Joseph C Lincoln house. *Hours:* Jun-Oct Mon-Sat 10-4 & else by appt. *Assoc:* CCADA. *Park:* In front.

YANKEE TRADER
2071 Main St Rte 6A, 02631
(508)896-7228 FAX
(508)896-7822

Ancient to antique - always the unusual. *Est:* 1958. *Hours:* Daily 10-5, CLOSED Christmas, best to phone ahead. *CC:* AX/MC/V. Stephen/Sheilah Rosen *Park:* On site. *Loc:* Center of Brewster Village.

YORKSHIRE HOUSE
Rte 6A & Crosby Ln, 02631
(508)896-6570   **{GR8}**

Elegant Victorian carriage house featuring period formal & country furniture, marine antiques, Orientalia, kitchenalia, Victoriana, fireplace antiques, Staffordshire & Worcester china & Americana. *Pr:* $10–10000. *Est:* 1985. *Serv:* Appraisal, brochure, interior design. *Hours:* May-Oct Tue-Sun 10-5, Off-season weekends or by appt. *Size:* Large. *CC:* MC/V. *Assoc:* CCADA. Jeffrey Bairstow *Park:* On site. *Loc:* Mid-Cape Hwy Rte 6 Exit 12: W on 6A for 2 MI shop is on R opposite Nickerson State Park Entrance.

BUZZARDS BAY

HERITAGE ANTIQUES & JEWELRY
43 Main St, 02532
(508)759-5886   **47 56 77**

Jewelry, silver, hand-carved whale & ship models by Irving Briggs, nautical items & a wide assortment of decorative antiques & collectibles. *Est:* 1982. *Serv:* Consignments taken. *Hours:* Daily 10-5. *CC:* MC/V. *Assoc:* CCADA. Marjorie M Briggs *Park:* In front & across the street. *Loc:* Across the street from RR station in Buzzards Bay at the Stop lights.

MARKET PLACE
61 Main St, 02532
(508)759-2114   **{GR23}**

Full line of decorative accessories, jewelry, furniture, glass & china. *Est:* 1973. *Hours:* Jun-Oct daily 9:30-5, Nov-May Tue-Sun 9:30-5. *CC:* MC/V. Donna De Felice *Park:* Behind. *Loc:* Across from RR station.

THE OLD HOUSE
291 Head of Bay Rd, 02532
(508)759-4942   **44 63**

Six rooms of early American pressed glass including blown & cut glass, china & porcelain. *Est:* 1935. *Serv:* Annual brochure. *Hours:* Apr-Dec Mon-Sat 9:30-5, Sun BY APPT ONLY. *CC:* MC/V. Pearl B Henshaw *Loc:* 1 MI from Belmont Circle (Grandma's Restaurant).

CENTERVILLE

FOR OLDE TIME'S SAKE
168 Longview Dr, 02632
(508)771-2089   **65 67**

Formal & country furniture, primitives & quilts. *Hours:* BY APPT ONLY. *Assoc:* CCADA. Belle Dienes

CHATHAM

CHAPDELAINE ANTIQUES
585 Main St, 02633
(508)945-1511   **27 44 67**

Specializing in country including furniture, quilts, glass, folk art. Also old mark Hummels & crystal. *Est:* 1986. *Hours:* Mon-Sat 10-5, CLOSED SUN. *CC:* MC/V. *Assoc:* CCADA. Doris Chapdelaine *Park:* Nearby. *Loc:* Next to Chatham T's.

MILDRED GEORGES ANTIQUES
447 Main St, 02633
(508)945-1939   **14 75**

Jewelry, glass, lighting & a nice selection of Americana. *Est:* 1939. *Hours:* Mon-Sat 10-5. *CC:* MC/V. *Park:* Nearby.

HOUSE ON THE HILL
17 Seaview St, 02633
(508)945-2290   **11 33 64**

Post cards, baseball cards, paper Americana, political memorabilia, old advertising items, toys, primitives & glass. *Hours:* Summer daily 10-5 (often til 9), Spring, Fall call for hours. *Assoc:* CCADA. Richard Soffey *Park:* On site. *Loc:* On Seaview St at Main St.

MATTAQUASON ARTS & ANTIQUES
409 Main St, 02633
(508)945-5900   **63 66 67**

Botanical prints, quilts, European & American furniture, silver, Quimper, Majolica, wicker & China Trade porcelain. *Est:* 1987. *Hours:* Jun-Oct daily 10-6 Sun 12-5. *CC:* AX/MC/V. Fleur Hahne Lawrence *Loc:* In Chatham Village.

OLDE VILLAGE COUNTRY BARN
432 Main St, 02633
(508)945-4931   **23 42 56**

Three floors filled with pine furniture, sterling silver, glass, nautical & unusual items. Clocks are a specialty. *Hours:* Year round May-Dec 10-5, Jan-Apr Thu-Sun. *Assoc:* CCADA. Robert M Sequin

SIMPLER PLEASURES
393 Main St, 02633
(508)945-4040   **27**

Country furniture & decorative accessories. *Est:* 1984. *Hours:* Mon-Sat 10-5. *CC:* AX/MC/V. *Park:* On site. *Loc:* On the way to the lighthouse.

THE SPYGLASS
618 Main St, 02633
(508)945-9686   **10 56**

Antique nautical instruments - telescopes, mercurial & aneroid barometers, charts, half-models, lap desks, captains desks, shadow boxes. *Est:* 1981. *Serv:* Telescope repair, reconditioning. *Hours:* Mon-Sat 9-5. *CC:* AX/MC/V. *Assoc:* CCADA. Daniel J Vaughan *Park:* Nearby. *Loc:* Rte 6 Exit 11: Rte 137S to Rte 28, turn L, straight thru rotary on Main St, 1 block on L.

WAYNE'S ANTIQUE CENTER
1300 Main St, 02633
(508)945-4265   **{GR8}**

A very diverse selection of antiques & Deco including an interesting collection of pottery, glass, prints, frames & furniture. *Est:* 1990. *Serv:* Appraisal, purchase estates. *Hours:* Jun-Sep Mon-Sat 12-5; Oct-May Thu-Sat 12-5 & BY APPT. *Size:* Small. Wayne Roberts *Park:* In front. *Loc:* On Main St.

CUMMAQUID

CUMMAQUID FINE ARTS
4275 Main St Rte 6A, 02637
(508)362-2593   **29**

Fine decorative antiques & arts for the table, bar & conservatory, including crystal, porcelain & silver. *Hours:* Jul-Labor Day Tue-Sat 10-5 Spring & Fall Wed-Sun or BY APPT. *CC:* MC/V. Jim Hinkle *Park:* On site. *Loc:* Rte 6 Exit 7: to Yarmouthport, L on Rte 6A for approx 1/2 MI.

ESPRIT DECOR
3941 Rte 6A, 02637
(508)362-2480

18th & 19th C antiques & appropriate accessories, from Folk to Federal. *Hours:* Daily 10-5. *Assoc:* CCADA. Suzanne C Kelly

THE OWL'S NEST ANTIQUES
4083 Main St, 02637
(508)362-4054   **27 32 65**

Country furniture, primitives, dolls & textiles. *Serv:* Furniture refinishing. *Hours:* In season daily 10-5. *Assoc:* CCADA. Nancy Galloni *Park:* In front. *Loc:* On Rte 6A, 4th house E of the post office.

THE PICKET FENCE
4225 Main St Rte 6A, 02637
(508)362-4865   **44 63**

Furniture, depression glass, pottery, porcelain, mirrors & lighting fixtures. *Est:* 1987. *Hours:* Daily 10-5 CLOSED JAN-FEB. *CC:* MC/V. Mary Ann Windsor *Park:* On site. *Loc:* 1 3/4 MI from Barnstable Village lights.

DENNIS

ANTIQUES 608
608 Rte 6A, 02638
(508)385-2755

American, English & Oriental antiques from the 19th & early 20th C. *Hours:* May-Dec daily 11-5 CLOSED WED, Jan-Apr Fri-Mon 11-5. Tom Cardaropoli *Loc:* Rte 6 Exit 8: L on Station Ave, R on 6A, 4 MI down.

ANTIQUES RED LION
601 Main St Rte 6A, 02638
(508)385-4783   **{GR12}**

A multiple dealer co-op with a wonderful variety of antiques & collectibles, including a fine selection of antique American, English & custom mahogany furniture, antique tools, linens, glass, china & more. *Est:* 1985. *Serv:* Appraisal, consultation, Interior design, purchase estates. *Hours:* May-Sep daily 11-5,

Jan-Feb Fri-Mon 11-4 else CLOSED WED. *Size:* Large. *CC:* MC/V. Paul M David, Manager *Park:* On site.

BOSTON BRASS WORKS
Theatre Marketplace Rte 6A, 02638
(508)385-5089   50
Custom & antique lighting & chandeliers. *Est:* 1975. *Hours:* Sum: Mon-Sat 10-4, Sep 15-May 30 Tue-Sat 10-4. *CC:* AX/MC/V. Bill Block *Park:* Nearby. *Loc:* Next to the post office.

CLIPPER SHIPPING & PACKAGING
Betterwood Lane, 02638
(508)385-7007   75
Packaging, crating & shipping smallest to largest items - antiques & fine arts a specialty. *Est:* 1981. *Serv:* Pick-up available, fully insured. *Hours:* Mon-Sat 9-5. *Loc:* Just S of Rte 6A, off Rte 134.

LESLIE CURTIS ANTIQUES
838 Main St Rte 6A, 02638
(508)385-2921   63 86
Distinctive early wicker furniture, Quimper pottery, faux & Brighton bamboo. *Hours:* Seasonal. *Assoc:* CCADA. *Loc:* Rte 6A at Corporation Rd.

DENNIS ANTIQUES
437 Main St Rte 6A, 02638
(508)385-8091   44 63
Quality glassware, Belleek, Waterford, porcelain, pottery, Fiesta, Heisey, Depression glass, early Hall, Lenox. *Hours:* Apr-Nov daily 10-6 & by appt. *Assoc:* CCADA. James J Scott

DOVETAIL ANTIQUES
543 Rte 6A, 02638
(508)385-2478   27 81
Old woodworking & machinists tools & country furniture. *Est:* 1984. *Hours:* Fri-Tue 10-5 CLOSED WED,THU. *Park:* On site. *Loc:* 1/4 MI from Dennis post office.

ELLIPSE ANTIQUES
427 Main St, 02638
(508)385-8626   1 44 50
Specializing in museum quality colored & rare Sandwich glass, Lacy, better kerosene & whale oil lamps, Bennington pottery, historical Staffordshire, & selected 18th & 19th C American accessories. *Pr:* $100–3000. *Est:* 1980. *Serv:* Appraisals. *Hours:* Apr-Oct daily 9:30-dusk, Nov-Mar by chance/appt. *Size:* Medium. *CC:* MC/V. *Assoc:* CCADA, NEAA. *Park:* On site. *Loc:* Rte 6A corner of Black Ball Hill Rd, 1 MI W of Dennis town center, Exit 7 from Rte 6 to Rte 6A, R 4 MI on R.

HYLAND GRANBY ANTIQUES
528 Main St Rte 6A, 02638
(508)771-3070   56
Large inventory of museum-quality 18th & 19th C marine antiques, ship models, scrimshaw, paintings & navigational instruments. *Est:* 1980. *Serv:* Appraisal, consultation. *Hours:* Daily 11-5, CLOSED WED. *Loc:* Call for directions.

HOUSE OF DOLLS
PO Box 208, 02638
(508)385-2325   32
Featuring the finest artist dolls. *Hours:* BY APPT ONLY.

OLDE TOWNE ANTIQUES
593 Main St Rte 6A, 02638
(508)385-5202   {GR10}
A multi-dealer shop with a good selection of fine art, prints, art glass, ephemera, toy soldiers, country, formal & Victorian furniture, Shaker items, accessories & jewelry. *Pr:* $20–2000. *Est:* 1988. *Serv:* Purchase estates. *Hours:* May 15-Sep daily 10-5, Oct-May 14 daily 10:30-5, CLOSED TUE. *Size:* Medium. *Assoc:* CCADA. Walter Jensen *Park:* On site.

RED LION ANTIQUES
601 Main St, 02633
(508)385-4783 **{GR12}**
A multiple-dealer co-op with a fine selection of American, English & custom mahogany furniture, tools, linens, glass, china, etc; decorators & the trade welcome. *Est:* 1985. *Serv:* Appraisal, interior design, purchase estates. *Hours:* May-Sep daily 11-5, Jan-Feb Fri-Mon 11-4. *Size:* Large. *CC:* MC/V. Paul David *Park:* On site.

VILLAGE PEDLAR CLOCK SHOP
623 Main St, 02638
(508)385-7300 **23 59**
A fine selection of antique clocks & oil paintings. *Est:* 1979. *Serv:* Clock repair, appraisal. *Hours:* Mon-Sat 9:30-5:30. *CC:* MC/V. *Assoc:* NAWCC. John Anderson *Loc:* 2 doors down from the Dennis Public Market.

DENNISPORT

THE SIDE DOOR
103 Main St Rte 28, 02639
(508)394-7715 **33 44 64**
Large selection of paper collectibles, post cards, sheet music, photographs, books, china & glass. *Pr:* $1–500. *Est:* 1973. *Serv:* Flow blue matching service. *Hours:* Sum: daily 10-5 Sun 12-4. Win: Fri,Sat 10-5 Sun 12-4. *CC:* AX/MC/V. *Assoc:* CCADA. Frank R Lewy *Park:* In front.

EAST DENNIS

ROBERT C ELDRED CO INC
1483 Main St Rte 6A, 02641
(508)385-3116 **4 8**
Summer auctions weekly, variety of special auctions - Americana, European, Oriental items. July collectors sale. Sep-May general auctions held twice weekly. 10% buyer's premium. *Est:* 1950. *Serv:* Fine arts auction & appraisal, mailing list $6, printed catalogs. *Hours:* Office daily 8:30-5. *Assoc:* AAA. *Park:* On site. *Loc:* Rte 6 Exit 9: L onto Rte 134, to Int of Rte 6A, turn L again, 1/4 MI on L.

EAST ORLEANS

COUNTRYSIDE ANTIQUES
6 Lewis Rd, 02643
(508)240-0525 **39**
Imported English, Irish, Scandinavian & European antique furniture, accessories & collectibles. *Pr:* $25–4500. *Hours:* Jun-Aug Mon-Sat 10-5 Sun 12-4, else CLOSED TUE-WED. *Size:* Large. *CC:* AX/MC/V. *Assoc:* CCADA. Deborah R Rita *Park:* On site. *Loc:* Rte 6 Exit 12 (Orleans): R at light, thru next light, R at 3rd light, approx 1 1/5 MI to Lewis Rd (on R), 1st driveway on R.

EAST ORLEANS ART & ANTIQUES
204 Main St, 02643
(508)255-7799 **1 21 41**
A whimsical mix of 18th & 19th C American country antiques, art & accessories, featuring a huge selection of old & new Kilim rugs & newly painted furniture. *Pr:* $10–3000. *Est:* 1989. *Serv:* Appraisal, consultation, interior design, purchase estates, repairs. *Hours:* Jun-Sep

Wed-Sat 10-5:30, Oct-Dec Fri-Sat 10:15-5:15. *Size:* Medium. *CC:* AX/MC/V. *Park:* On site. *Loc:* On the way to Nauset Beach, across from Fany's farm stand.

EAST SANDWICH

HENRY THOMAS CALLAN FINE ANTIQUE
162 Quaker Meeting House Rd, 02537
(508)888-5372   **8 63**
American samplers & Chinese Export porcelain. *Serv:* Written antiques appraisals for insurance & estate purposes. *Hours:* BY APPT ONLY. *Assoc:* NEAA.

THE GILDED SWAN
685 Rte 6A, 02537
(508)362-2301   **29 47 63**
Fine antique & estate jewelry, export porcelain, Russian icons, enamels, Faberge, African & European decorative accessories. *Serv:* Unconditional guarantee of authenticity. *Hours:* Apr-Dec daily 10:30-5:30. *Assoc:* AAAA CCADA. Ronald A Gray *Park:* In front. *Loc:* On Sandwich/Barnstable line.

HEATHER HOUSE
350 Rte 6A, 02537
(508)888-2034   **42**
Fine antiques, china, jewelry, silver, furniture & quilts. *Est:* 1977. *Hours:* Daily 10-5. *Park:* On site. *Loc:* Off Rte 6, Exit 3 to 6A, turn R.

HORSEFEATHERS ANTIQUES
454 Rte 6A, 02537
(508)888-5298   **29 48 83**
Specializing in linens & lace, Victorian accessories & childhood antiques, interesting smalls. *Est:* 1982. *Hours:* Year round. *CC:* MC/V. *Assoc:* CCADA. Jeanne Gresham *Park:* In front. *Loc:* Next to East Sandwich fire station.

JESSE CALDWELL LEATHERWOOD
39 Discovery Hill Rd, 02537
(508)888-8076   **37 45 56**
American & European furniture & decorative arts, marine items especially ship wool embroideries, exceptional campaign furniture, garden furniture & sculpture. *Pr:* $100–25000. *Hours:* BY APPT. *Size:* Medium. *Assoc:* AADLA. *Park:* On site. *Loc:* Rte 6 Exit 3: N 1 MI to Rte 6A, turn L (W), 1/2 MI to Discovery Hill Rd, turn L, 1/3 MI up dirt Rd to #39.

TITCOMB'S BOOKSHOP
432 Rte 6A, 02537
(508)888-2331   **13**
Two floors of rare & out-of-print books located in charming barn attached to 1790 restored 3/4 Cape Cod home located on historic Old King's Highway including Americana, fishing & hunting, nautical, New Englandiana, Cape Cod. *Serv:* Appraisal, catalog, search service. *Hours:* Daily 10-5 Sun 12-5. *Size:* Medium. *CC:* MC/V. *Assoc:* MARIAB. Ralph & Nancy Titcomb *Park:* On site. *Loc:* 7 MI E of the Sagamore Bridge on Rte 6A, statue of Ben Franklin in front.

FALMOUTH

AURORA BOREALIS ANTIQUES
104 Palmer Ave, 02540
(508)540-3385   **44 63 72**
Pattern glass, historic glass, cut glass, Staffordshire pottery, metalware, paintings, jewelry, porcelain, scientific instruments, ephemera, books, wooden articles, furniture & Orientalia. *Serv:*

Appraisal, consultation, purchase estates. *Hours:* May-Oct daily 11-4 Nov-Dec Sat only, Jan-Apr BY APPT. *Size:* Medium. *Assoc:* CCADA. Maureen E Northern *Park:* On site. *Loc:* 1 1/2 hrs from Boston on way to/from Martha's Vineyard or Nantucket.

CACHE
426 Main St, 02540
(508)548-5222   **27**
Specializing in country antiques & collectibles. *Est:* 1990. *Hours:* Wed-Sun 11-4. Joan Marchand *Park:* In front.

HILARY & PAULETTE NOLAN
376 Palmer Ave, 02540
(508)548-0127   **37**
Genuine early American furniture & accessories. *Hours:* By chance/appt. *Assoc:* NHADA.

HARWICH

THE BARN AT WINDSONG
243 Bank St, 02645
(508)432-8281   **{GR7}**
Formal & country furniture, antique wicker, primitives, early American pattern glass, linens, quilts, flow blue, majolica, prints, & decorative accessories. *Est:* 1988. *Hours:* Sum Mon-Sat 10-5, Sun 12-5; Jan-Mar Fri-Sun 12-4; else, call. *CC:* AX/MC/V. *Assoc:* CCADA. *Park:* On site. *Loc:* Between Harwich & Harwichport.

PATTI SMITH
51 Parallel St, 02645
(508)432-0851   **28**
Specializing in antique decorated blue stoneware. *Pr:* $200–2000. *Serv:* Send SASE for stoneware inventory list. *Hours:* BY APPT ONLY.

SWANSEA ANTIQUES
482 Queen Anne Rd, 02645
(508)432-4651   **27 37 67**
Specializing in quilts, textiles, American Country furniture, primitives, country smalls & accessories. *Serv:* Consultation, interior design. *Hours:* Sum: By chance/appt. *Assoc:* CCADA. Carla R Costanzo *Park:* On site. *Loc:* Rte 6 Exit 10: S on Rte 124 to the 1st L (Queen Anne Rd), 4th house on L.

SYD'S A & J
338 Bank St, 02645
(508)432-3007   **44 47 63**
Heisey & other glass, decorative accessories, china & jewelry. *Hours:* Apr-Oct by chance/appt. Sidney Mercer *Loc:* Just S of Rte 39 on Bank St.

HARWICHPORT

HARWICH BOOKSTORE
390 Main St, 02646
(508)432-0798   **13 14**
A general stock of antiquarian books. *Hours:* Sum: Mon-Sun 10-5, Win: Tue-Sat 10-5. Lee Tighe *Loc:* On Rte 28.

MAGGIE'S ANTIQUES
2 Cross St, 02646
(508)432-4299   **{GR4}**
Specializing in kitchen collectibles, cookbooks, children's books, jewelry, linens & vintage clothing. *Est:* 1989. *Hours:* Year round Tue-Sun 10-5. *Loc:* Just off Rte 28 in the center of Harwichport.

SEVEN SOUTH STREET ANTIQUES
7 South St, 02646
(508)432-4366   **47 63 77**
Silver, jewelry, china & glass. *Est:* 1976. *Hours:* Year round 9:30-5, Appt or call

ahead suggested. Philip Marsh **Park:** Nearby. **Loc:** Around the corner from the post office, just off Rte 28.

HYANNIS

ALBERT ARTS & ANTIQUES
645 Main St, 02601
(508)771-3040   **17 50 63**
American & European antiques including furniture, paintings, porcelains, bronzes & lighting. Jewelry, textiles, & unique decorative accessories. **Serv:** Appraisal, purchase estates. **Hours:** Year round 10-6. **Assoc:** CCADA NEAA. Albert & Iris L Watson

RICHARD A BOURNE CO INC
Corporation St, 02601
(508)775-0797   **4 8**
Auctioning general merchandise, marine items, decoys, antique weapons & glass. Two or three auctions per month year round. Special auctions: Decoy Auction - early July; Marine Sale - August; Americana - Thanksgiving Weekend. 10% buyer's premium. **Serv:** Estate appraisers, catalogs, absentee & phone bidding arranged. **Hours:** Mon-Sat 10-5 by chance or appt. Marie Bagley **Loc:** 1/2 MI W of Airport Rotary Circle on Rte 28.

HYANNIS AUCTION
379 Iyanough Rd, 02601
(508)790-1112   **4 8 25**
A weekly consignment auction house offering expert appraisal service & prompt payment. Handling complete estates & single items. Auction every Saturday night at 6. Accept mail & phone bids. **Serv:** Appraisal, catalog, consultation, pick-up/delivery service available. **Hours:** Mon,Wed,Fri,Sat 10-5 Tue 2-11

Sun 12-5. **Size:** Medium. Donna Johnson **Park:** Nearby lot. **Loc:** Rte 6E Exit 6: R on Rte 132 to rotary, 3rd R onto Rte 28E, 1/4 MI on R across from Grossman's behind Bank of New Eng.

PRECIOUS PAST
315 Iyanough Rd Rte 28, 02601
(508)771-1741   **21 44 48**
Nippon, fiesta, Noritake, Limoges, depression, Pairpoint, cut glass & early American pattern glass. Linens, Oriental rugs, paintings & prints, old dolls & accessories, collectibles, ephemera, toys & furniture. **Hours:** Daily 10-4 CLOSED TUE,SUN. **Park:** On site. **Loc:** Behind Mr. Donut.

STARTING OVER LTD
1336 Phinney's Ln, 02601
(508)775-5088   **71**
Furniture restoration, custom work & fine antiques. **Est:** 1964. **Serv:** Restoration, free pick-up & delivery. **Hours:** Mon-Fri 9-5. **Loc:** At Harborside Landing.

STONE'S ANTIQUE SHOP
659 Main St, 02601
(508)775-3913   **16 36 44**
One of the oldest antiques shops on Cape Cod. **Est:** 1923. **Serv:** Appraisal, interior design. **Hours:** Mon-Sat 9-5 CLOSED SUN. **Size:** Large. E Stone **Park:** On site. **Loc:** W end of Main St.

MARSTONS MILLS

CROCKER FARM
1210 Race Lane, 02648
(508)428-3326   **16 32**
A barn full of interesting old things: iron,

wood & tin. Also featuring antiques for children. **Hours:** By chance/appt. **Assoc:** CCADA. Bunny Warner

MARTHA'S VINEYARD

AUNTIES ATTIC ANTIQUES
224 Edgartown Rd Edgartown, 02539
(508)627-9833   **{GR5}**
A diverse collection of reasonably-priced Americana, furniture, rugs, books, bottles, brass, decoys, glass, linens, porcelain, prints, quilts, jewelry, tools, toys, silver, baskets & lamps. **Pr:** $25–1500. **Est:** 1983. **Serv:** Appraisal. **Hours:** Jun 10-Sep 20 Mon-Sat 10-5, Sep 21-Jun 9 Fri-Sat 10-5. **Size:** Medium. **CC:** MC/V. Judy Brugiere **Park:** In front. **Loc:** In Red General Stores Building on Edgartown Vineyard Haven Rd, Upper Main St Edgartown Triangle Area.

THE BOOK DEN EAST
New York Ave Oak Bluffs, 02557
(508)693-3946   **13**
In a turn of the century carriage barn, a large stock of carefully selected books on Martha's Vineyard, New England, sea & naval history, travel, world history, biography, 1st editions, fine bindings, prints, maps, charts & manuscripts. **Est:** 1977. **Serv:** Purchase estates, search services, catalog (occasional). **Hours:** Jun-Oct Mon-Sat 10-5 Sun 1-5, Nov-May Thu-Sun 11-4, call adv. **Size:** Large. **CC:** MC/V. **Park:** On site. **Loc:** 1/2 MI from Oak Bluffs Ctr on the rd to Vineyard Haven on Martha's Vineyard.

CLOCKTOWER ANTIQUES
Nevins Sq Edgartown, 02539
(508)627-8006   **16 63 77**
Large collection of pottery & porcelain, silver, jewelry, metalwork, glass, prints &

pictures. **Pr:** $25–1800. **Serv:** Purchase estates. **Hours:** May 15-Oct 15 daily 10-5. **Size:** Medium. **CC:** MC/V.

EARLY SPRING FARM ANTIQUES
93 Lagoon Pond Rd Vineyard Haven, 02568
(508)693-9141   **34 36 65**
18th & 19th C country furniture, quilts, hooked rugs, folk art, iron, copper, woodenware & children's items. **Pr:** $5–3000. **Serv:** Brochure, consultation, some restoration. **Hours:** Jun-Oct 15 Mon-Sun 10-4 Sat 2-5 CLOSED WED else Mon-Sun 10-4. Allen Hanson **Park:** On site. **Loc:** Boat to Vineyard Haven, Lagoon Pond Rd at 5 Corners to Hine's Point, on R.

EDGARTOWN ART GALLERY
South Summer St Edgartown, 02539
(508)627-4751   **10 16 39**
Choice English & American furniture, brass, oil paintings, Chinese export porcelain, pottery, barometers in a charming shop in the lobby of the Charlotte Inn. **Est:** 1977. **Hours:** Jun-Sep daily 10-10 weekends 10-5. **Size:** Medium. **CC:** AX/MC/V. Paula Conover **Park:** Nearby lot. **Loc:** 1/2 block S of Main St @ corner of S Summer & Davis Ln.

ISLAND AUCTIONEERS
206 Upper Main St Edgartown, 02539
(508)627-7090   **4 8 25**
Auctioneers of estates, antiques, art collectibles, furniture & household items. **Serv:** Consignments accepted. **Hours:** By appt. Steve Sack

ISLAND TREASURE OF NANTUCKET
258 Edgartown Rd Edgartown, 02539
(508)627-3900   **25 36 59**
Consignment shop accepting quality home furnishings, art, jewelry, quilts, silver, brass, rugs, etc. **Est:** 1990. **Serv:**

Consignment. **Hours:** Year round daily 10-19 Sun 12-5. **Park:** Nearby. **Loc:** At Mariner's Landing.

C W MORGAN MARINE ANTIQUES
Box 2019 Vineyard Haven, 02568
(508)693-3622   **56**

A museum quality marine antiques shop featuring pottery, china & paintings. **Hours:** BY APPT. Frank Rapoza

RED BARN EMPORIUM
Old County Rd West Tisbury, 02575
(508)693-0455   **{GR}**

Also known as the Granary Gallery, a smattering of pine mirrors & interesting pieces in a barn devoted mainly to realistic contemporary art. **Est:** 1954. **Serv:** (800)343-0471. **Hours:** Sum Mon-Sat 10-5. **Loc:** 1/2 MI N of Edgartown-West Tisbury Rd on County Rd.

SHIPWRIGHT GALLERY
15 Dock St Edgartown, 02539
(508)627-7513   **54**

Model ship gallery featuring custom half models, full models, nautical antiques, marine art & carvings. **Pr:** $50–4000. **Est:** 1988. **Serv:** Repairs. **Hours:** Jun-Oct daily 10-5 Nov-Dec weekends CLOSED JAN-MAY. **CC:** AX/MC/V. Joanna Chechile **Park:** Nearby lot. **Loc:** At end of Main St turn L.

EVE STONE & SON ANTIQUES
527 State Rd N Tisbury, 02575
(508)693-0396   **16 37 63**

Featuring 18th & 19th C American furniture & decorative accessories of the period; specialists in metalware, Chinese export porcelain, woodenware, quilts, baskets & lighting. Art consulting services available. **Pr:** $100–15000. **Est:** 1970. **Serv:** Appraisal, conservation, consultation, interior design, purchase est. **Hours:** Memorial Day-Labor Day,

daily 9:30-6. **Size:** Large. **CC:** AX/MC/V. Eve Stone **Park:** On site, in front.

TISBURY ANTIQUES
92 State Rd Vineyard Haven, 02568
(508)693-1196   **21 37 63**

18th & 19th C American furniture, Oriental rugs, pottery & porcelain, glass, Orientalia, Southeast Asian art & lamps. **Serv:** Appraisal, purchase estates. **Hours:** Sum: daily BY APPT. **Assoc:** NEAA.

VINTAGE JEWELRY
Main St Edgartown, 02539
(508)627-5409   **47**

Estate jewelry, antique gold, silver & costume jewelry, collection of glass & china & American Indian items. **Est:** 1983. **Serv:** Repair, restoration. **Hours:** Year round Jul-Aug 10-10. **CC:** MC/V. **Assoc:** NEAA. Susan Freeman **Loc:** At corner of Main & S Summer Sts.

VIVIAN WOLFE ANTIQUE JEWELRY
Main St Edgartown, 02539
(508)627-5822   **47 58 77**

Specializing in a superb assortment of antique jewelry. Also old silver, stones & old American Indian jewelry. **Est:** 1959. **Serv:** Repairs, purchase estates. **Hours:** Jul-Aug 7 days 10-10, Jun & Sep 7 days 10-5. **CC:** AX/MC/V. Vivian Wolfe **Park:** Town lot. **Loc:** In the ctr of town.

NANTUCKET

JANICE ALDRIDGE INC
7 Centre St, 02554
(508)228-6673   **66**

17th-19th C decorative engravings,

botanical, architectural & natural history. English & Continental furnishings & accessories. **Hours:** Late May-Sep.

AVANTI ANTIQUE JEWELRY
4 Federal St, 02554
(508)228-5833   **47**
European & American antique & estate jewelry. **Est:** 1986. **Hours:** Apr-Dec daily 10-5, Win: BY APPT (508/228-4952). **CC:** AX/MC/V. Kathryn Kay **Park:** Nearby. **Loc:** Across from the post office.

FORAGER HOUSE COLLECTION
22 Broad St, 02554
(508)228-5977   **1 34 45**
Folk art, Americana, rugs, quilts, historical, decorative & American master prints, garden accessories for the discriminating collector. **Pr:** $50–10000. **Est:** 1975. **Serv:** Appraisal, conservation, consultation, interior design, repairs. **Hours:** May 15-Dec 15 Mon-Sun 10-6, Dec 16-May 14 BY APPT ONLY. **CC:** AX/MC/V. George Korn **Park:** In front. **Loc:** Located in the ctr of the Historic District.

FOUR WINDS CRAFT GUILD
6 Straight Wharf, 02554
(508)228-9623   **30 54 56**
Nantucket Lightship baskets, scrimshaw, marine items & island memorabilia. **Est:** 1948. **Serv:** Antique baskets bought & appraised. **Hours:** Mon-Sat 9-10 Sun 9-5. **CC:** AX/MC/V. **Park:** Nearby lot.

NINA HELLMAN
48 Centre St, 02554
(508)228-4677   **1 34 56**
Fine selection of nautical antiques, including ship models, navigational instruments, scrimshaw, marine paintings, whaling items, Americana & folk art. **Pr:** $10–10000. **Serv:** Nautical appraisals. **Hours:** May-Dec daily 10-10. **CC:** AX/MC/V.

ISLAND ATTIC INDUSTRIES INC
Miacomet Ave, 02554
(508)228-9405   **1 36 42**
Period American & English furniture, quality used furniture, paintings, prints, books & collectibles. **Pr:** $25–25000. **Est:** 1976. **Serv:** Appraisal, auction, brochure, consultation, purchase estates, repair. **Hours:** May-Dec Mon-Sat 9-5, Jan-Apr Mon-Sat 10-5. **Size:** Large. **CC:** MC/V. Harold B Mathewson **Park:** On site. **Loc:** From Town: Main to Pleasant St to Five Corners, R on Atlantic Ave toward Surfside Rd for 4/5 MI, R onto Miacomet.

VAL MAITINO ANTIQUES
31 N Liberty St, 02554
(508)228-2747   **39 50 56**
English & American furniture, marine items, old hooked rugs, lighting fixtures, weather vanes, Nantucket lightship baskets & decorative accessories. **Est:** 1958. **Serv:** Repairs, restoration. **Hours:** Apr-Dec Mon-Sat 9-5:30, Sun by chance; Jan-Mar CLOSED SUN. **CC:** AX/MC/V. **Loc:** N Liberty St opposite Franklin St.

CLAIRE MURRAY INC
11 S Water St, 02554
(603)543-3924 FAX
(508)228-1913   **21 57**
100% virgin wool hand-hooked rugs in original design. Hooked rug & needlepoint kits available. **Est:** 1986. **Serv:** Catalog ($5-refundable with order), toll-free phone: (800)323-9276. **Hours:** Mon-Sat 9-6 Sun 10-4 during season, else CLOSED SUN,MON. **CC:** AX/MC/V. Claire Murray **Loc:** Between the ferries off Main St.

NANTUCKET HOUSE ANTIQUES
1 S Beach St, 02554
(508)228-4604   **29 34 37**
English & American country furniture,

decorative accessories & folk art. **Serv:** Interior design, furniture repair, appraisal, off island delivery service. **Hours:** Year round.

NANTUCKET LIGHTSHIP
BASKETS
9 Old South Wharf, 02554
(508)228-2326

Lightship baskets in traditional oak construction. **Est:** 1964. **Serv:** Custom orders, repair. **Hours:** May-Oct daily 10-5 & 7-10, else call for appt. **CC:** AX/MC/V. Richard Anderson **Loc:** 1 block over from Main St.

RAFAEL OSONA AUCTIONEER
American Legion Washington St, 02554
(508)228-3942   **8 63 77**

Nine furniture & decorative accessories auctions each year from Memorial Day to Thanksgiving; call for schedule. 18th

Wayne Pratt

AMERICAN ANTIQUES

257 Forest Street
Marlboro, Massachusetts 01752
Telephone (508) 481-2917

6 Candle Street
Nantucket, Massachusetts 02554
Telephone (508) 228-8788
July 4 thru Labor Day

& 19th C furniture, sterling silver, Oriental porcelain, oil paintings, Nantucket baskets & memorabilia, quilts, linens, crystal & more. **Est:** 1980. **Serv:** Shipping, absentee bids, appraisal. **Hours:** Auctions begin at 10; items may be viewed 2 days prior 10-5. **Park:** Nearby lot.

PETTICOAT ROW
19 Centre St, 02554
(508)228-5900   **35 41 48**

English & French country antiques, painted furniture & linens. **Est:** 1986. **Hours:** Year round. Liza Dyche

WAYNE PRATT & CO
6 Candle St, 02554
(508)228-8788   **32 36 37**

Fine American 18th & early 19th C country & formal furniture, specializing in Windsor chairs & featuring a toy showroom. **Serv:** Appraisal. **Hours:** July 4-Labor Day daily 10-5. Marybeth Keene **Loc:** Across from the A & P parking lot.

PROFESSIONAL ART
CONSERVATION
3 Nobadeer Rd, 02554
(508)228-3799   **26 59 71**

Preservation & restoration of fine art. Complete conservation services to dealers, private collectors & museums. **Est:** 1983. **Serv:** Consultation. **Hours:** May 1-Oct 1 BY APPT ONLY. **Assoc:** AIC. Craig Kay **Park:** On Site.

PUFFIN ANTIQUES
28 Washington St, 02554
(508)228-7127   **30 34 56**

Working decoys, folk art, wildlife paintings, shorebirds & nautical items. **Hours:** May-Dec Mon-Thu 10-5, Weekends 10-6. **CC:** AX/MC/V. **Park:** On site. **Loc:** A few blocks over from Main St.

FRANK F SYLVIA ANTIQUES INC
6 Ray's Ct, 02554
(508)228-0960   **56 63 77**

Period furniture, scrimshaw, paintings, silver, porcelain & general line. *Est:* 1927. *Serv:* Appraisal, consultation. *Hours:* Sum: 9-5 CLOSED SUN; or year round BY APPT. *CC:* AX/MC/V. *Park:* Ample. *Loc:* 1 block from Int of Fair & Main Sts, behind Fair Street Museum.

THE TILLER
Easy St, 02554
(508)228-1287   **36 39 63**

One of Nantucket's oldest antiques shops featuring English, American & marine antiques, furniture & decorative accessories. *Est:* 1972. *Hours:* May 25-Oct 10 Mon-Sat 10-4. *Size:* Medium. Howard Chadwick, Mgr *Loc:* Just a few feet from Steamboat Wharf, overlooking Nantucket Harbor.

TONKIN OF NANTUCKET
33 Main St, 02554
(508)228-9697   **56 72**

English furniture with a large selection of silver, Staffordshire, marine & scientific instruments, long case clocks, brass & copper accessories, marine paintings & English prints, ship models, fishing equipment & Nantucket lightship baskets. *Hours:* Year round Mon-Sat 9-5. *Size:* Large. *CC:* AX/DC/MC/V. *Park:* On site.

TRANQUIL CORNERS ANTIQUES
49 Sparks Ave Sanford Boat Bldg, 02554
(508)228-6000   **37 56 67**

Country & formal, American, Canadian & English furniture, accessories, antique, estate jewelry, scrimshaw & quilts. *Hours:* Year round by chance/appt, Win BY APPT ONLY.

VIS-A-VIS LTD
34 Main St, 02554
(508)228-5527   **36 48 67**

Quilts, hooked rugs, furniture, bed & house linens, silver, china, decorative accessories & antique jewelry. *Hours:* Mar-Dec 10-6 by chance/appt; Jan-Feb weekends. *CC:* AX/MC/V.

THE WICKER PORCH
13 N Water St, 02554
(508)228-1052   **77 83 86**

General line of antiques, large selection of restored antique wicker furniture in a seven-room Victorian house. Estate antiques arrive daily. *Pr:* $5–5000. *Serv:* Appraisal, purchase estates, wicker restoration. *Hours:* Late May-Mid Oct 10-5. *CC:* MC/V. Frank McNamee *Park:* Nearby.

LYNDA WILLAUER ANTIQUES
2 India St, 02554
(508)228-3631   **37 63 67**

English & American furniture, paintings, Chinese export porcelain, papier mache, tortoise, majolica, samplers, quilts, faience & brass fireplace fenders & tools. *Est:* 1974. *Hours:* Mid Jun-Mid Oct By chance/appt. *CC:* MC/V. *Loc:* 1 block from Main St.

NORTH CHATHAM

BAYBERRY ANTIQUES
300 Orleans Rd, 02650
(508)945-9060   **27 32 67**

Quality American country furniture, decoys, holiday collectibles, ephemera, Currier & Ives & other prints, postcards & chocolate molds. *Est:* 1987. *Hours:* Sum: daily 10-5, Sun afternoons by chance else BY APPT. *CC:* MC/V. *Assoc:* CCADA. Dick & Carolyn Thompson *Park:* On site. *Loc:* On Rte 28.

PAPYRUS BOOKS & ANTIQUES
302 Orleans Rd Rte 28, 02650
(508)945-2271 **13**
Antiquarian books: general stock featuring American & English literature, biography & detective fiction. *Serv:* Search service. *Hours:* Thu-Mon 12-5. *Assoc:* MARIAB. Katharine Dalton

NORTH EASTHAM

EASTHAM AUCTION HOUSE
Box 1114 Holmes Rd, 02651
(508)255-9003 **8 58**
On Cape Cod, monthly auctions offering antiques & estate furnishings held last Saturday of the month, May-October. *Pr:* $1–4000. *Est:* 1985. *Serv:* Appraisal, accept mail bids, auction, catalog, purchase estates. *Hours:* Office: Tue-Fri 10-3, appt, Previews: 2-7 on sale days. *Assoc:* CAI MSA NAA. Bill Fidalgo *Park:* On site, nearby lot. *Loc:* From Orleans rotary, 4 MI N to lights (Brackett Rd), R, 1/10 MI, R (Holmes Rd).

NORTH HARWICH

MERLYN AUCTIONS
204 Main St, 02645
(508)432-5863 **8 25**
General merchandise auctions most Saturdays February-November at 7, viewing from 1:30-6:30; final auction Thanksgiving weekend. *Serv:* Computerized catalog available. *Hours:* Sun 10-2, Mon-Wed 10-4. *Park:* Nearby.

ONSET

JOSEPH A DERMONT BOOKSELLER
Box 654, 02558
(508)295-4760 **9 13**
Specializing in modern first editions, literary autographs, children's books & proofs. *Pr:* $25–500. *Est:* 1980. *Serv:* Appraisal, free catalog. *Hours:* Daily BY APPT ONLY. *CC:* MC/V. *Assoc:* ABAA MARIAB. *Park:* On site.

ORLEANS

CONTINUUM
#7 Rte 28, 02653
(508)255-8513 **36 50 69**
A small shop specializing in restored electric lighting. Approximately 200 old lamps of all types, original lead crystal shades by Holophane & others are featured; folk art & Americana including old wooden fish decoys. Annual sale on New Year's Day. *Pr:* $100–3000. *Serv:* Appraisal, consultation, repairs, replication, restoration, buy old parts. *Hours:* Jul 5-Sep Mon-Sat 10:30-5 Sun 12-5, else Thu-Mon 10:30-5. *Size:* Medium. *CC:* AX/MC/V. Dan Johnson *Park:* On site. *Loc:* Across from the Christmas Tree Shop.

HAUNTED BOOK SHOP
47 Main St, 02653
(508)255-3780 **13**
Archaeology, natural history, history, art, classical literature, nautical, New Englandiana, poetry. *Serv:* Purchase estates, search service. *Hours:* Sum: Mon-

Thu 9-8 Fri/Sat 10-8; Win: Mon-Thu 9-5 Fri/Sat 10-5. *Assoc:* MARIAB. Drucilla Meany *Park:* Nearby.

FRANK H HOGAN FINE ARTS INC
9 Herringbrook Rd, 02653
(508)255-2676   **4 59**
Fine arts dealer specializing in paintings of the Rockport & Provincetown Schools. *Pr:* $500–15000. *Serv:* Appraisal, consultation, purchase estates. *Hours:* BY APPT ONLY. *Assoc:* ISA. *Park:* On site. *Loc:* Mid-Cape Hwy Exit 12: to ctr of Orleans, then call for directions.

JANE'S COLLECTIQUES
9 Cove Rd, 02653
(508)255-7465   **7 47 85**
20th C, antique & estate gold & silver jewelry, art, objects & small selection of vintage clothing. *Est:* 1989. *Serv:* Accept consignments. *Hours:* May-Dec 15 Daily 10-5, CLOSED WED & SUN. *CC:* MC/V. *Assoc:* CCADA. *Park:* In front. *Loc:* Just off Rte 6A in the ctr of Orleans, 1/2 block N of Main St, opposite town parking lot & behind Land-Ho restaurant.

ORLEANS (SOUTH)

PLEASANT BAY ANTIQUES
540 Chatham Rd Rte 28, 02662
(508)255-0930   **30 34 37**
Large house & barn filled with 18th & 19th C American furniture & accessories, decoys, paintings & marine antiques. *Pr:* $10–25000. *Est:* 1966. *Serv:* Appraisals, consultation, purchase estates. *Hours:* Year round daily 10-5. *Size:* Medium. *CC:* MC/V. *Assoc:* CCADA. Steve Tyng *Park:* In front. *Loc:* 3 1/2 MI S of Int of Rtes 6 & 28.

OSTERVILLE

FERRAN'S INTERIORS
853 Main St, 02655
(508)428-4222   **29 36**
Unusual American, English & European pieces from the 18th-20th C, paintings, prints, quilts, coverlets, linens, china, majolica, Limoges & Roseville. *Est:* 1988. *Serv:* Interior design, consultation. *Hours:* Daily 10-5 CLOSED SUN. *CC:* AX/MC/V. Janet Choate Ferran *Park:* On site. *Loc:* In the farmhouse next to Appleseeds Clothing.

OAK & IVORY
12 Fire Station Rd, 02655
(508)428-9425   **47**
Custom Nantucket lightship baskets & fine ivory jewelry. *Est:* 1985. *Hours:* Mon-Sat 10-5. *CC:* AX/MC/V. *Assoc:* JBT. Robert Marks *Park:* On site. *Loc:* Rte 6 Exit 5: to Osterville, by the fire station.

ELDRED WHEELER
866 Main St, 02655
(508)428-9049   **43**
Handcrafters of fine 18th C furniture reproductions. *Serv:* Catalog ($4). *Hours:* Mon-Sat 10-5 or BY APPT.

A STANLEY WHEELOCK-ANTIQUES
870 Main St, 02655
(508)420-3170   **37 38 39**
General line of American, English & Continental furniture & decorative accessories, china, glass & fine prints. *Hours:* Apr-Dec Mon-Sat 10-5 or BY APPT. *Assoc:* CCADA.

PROVINCETOWN

JULIE HELLER GALLERY
2 Gosnold St, 02657
(508)487-2169   **1 34 59**
Featuring work by early Provincetown
artists, fine estate jewelry, folk art,
Americana & 19th & 20th C decorative
arts. *Hours:* Sum: daily 12-11, Win: daily
12-4. *Assoc:* CCADA. *Park:* Nearby.
Loc: On the beach Town Landing across
from Adams Pharmacy.

THE HOUR GLASS
391 1/2 Commercial St, 02657
(508)487-6524   **16 47 58**
19th & 20th C jewelry & objects of art.
Rare pewter, sterling silver & porcelain
artifacts. *Hours:* Daily from 11 am
CLOSED JAN. *Assoc:* CCADA. Djordje
Soc

INTERIOR ARTS GALLERY
208 Bradford St, 02657
(508)487-2949   **7**
Bakelite jewelry, Chase chrome & Art
Deco advertising, furniture & lighting &
collectibles. *Pr:* $15–2500. *Est:* 1988.
Hours: By chance/appt summer & fall.
Robert F Grabowsky *Park:* In front. *Loc:*
In the E end of Provincetown.

REMEMBRANCES OF THINGS PAST
376 Commercial St, 02657
(508)487-9443   **7 33 55**
An unusual shop of remembrances, both
old & new, from turn-of-the-century to
1950s with emphasis on nostalgia from
the 20s & 30s, including Art Deco,
jewelry, neon, juke boxes & pinball
machines. *Pr:* $25–5000. *Serv:*
Brochure. *Hours:* Apr 15-Oct 15 daily
11-11, Oct 16-Dec 12-4, Jan-Apr 15
wkend. *Size:* Large. *CC:* AX/DC/MC/V.

Helene Lyons *Park:* Nearby lot. *Loc:*
Corner of Pearl & Commercial Sts at the
end of Cape Cod's Rte 6.

SANDWICH

THE BROWN JUG
155 Main St at Jarves, 02563
(508)833-1088   **7 44 50**
Antique glass & Art Nouveau. *Est:* 1935.
Hours: Daily 9:30-5:30. C H Haines *Loc:*
3 doors from Daniel Webster Inn.

FAULCONER HOUSE ANTIQUES
193 Rte 6A, 02563
(508)888-1178   **3 44 50**
Three large rooms of small antiques including Sandwich & other glass, lighting, china, mirrors, maps, prints &
metalwork. *Pr:* $10–500. *Serv:* Purchase
estates. *Hours:* Apr-Oct Mon-Sat 9-5,
Sun 12-5, Nov-Mar BY APPT. *Size:*
Large. *CC:* MC/V. E E Williams *Park:*
On site. *Loc:* On Rte 6A approximately 1
MI E of the Sandwich Glass Museum.

PAUL MADDEN ANTIQUES
146 Old Main St, 02563
(508)888-6434   **34 56 59**
Americana in great variety - paintings,
scrimshaw, Nantucket baskets, folk art,
furniture & decorative accessories - for
the collector & dealer. *Pr:* $25–25000.
Serv: Appraisal. *Hours:* Year round
mornings by appt, afternoons by chance.
Assoc: CCADA. *Loc:* Rte 6 Exit 2: N on
Rte 130 for 1 1/4 MI. Across from Daniel
Webster Inn in Sandwich Village.

MAYPOP LANE
161 Old King's Hwy Rte 6A, 02563
(508)888-1230   **{GR7}**
Tools, kitchen collectibles, furniture,
jewelry, baskets, quilts, rugs, glass, pot-

tery, china & country collectibles.
Hours: Daily 10-4. *CC:* MC/V. *Park:* In
front. *Loc:* On Rte 6A.

SANDWICH ANTIQUE CO-OP
Merchants Square of 6A, 02563
(508)888-0013   **{GR18}**
Specializing in fine antiques & collectibles. *Est:* 1990. *Hours:* Mon-Sat 10-5
Sun 12-5. *Park:* Nearby. *Loc:* In rear of
bldg opposite Angelo's.

SANDWICH AUCTION HOUSE
15 Tupper Rd, 02563
(508)888-1926   **8**
General merchandise auctions every
Saturday night September-May, Wednesday nights June-August. Special auctions include: Americana sale - late
November; Antiques Auction - late September; Antiques & Victoriana sale - late
May. *Serv:* Computerized catalog available. *Hours:* Saturday auctions 7:00 PM
Viewing on Fri-Sat 2-7.

SHAWME POND ANTIQUES
13 Water St Rte 130, 02563
(508)888-2603   **2 44 48**
Andirons & tools, Sandwich glass, fine
linens, accessories & a general line.
Hours: Year round by chance/appt.
Assoc: CCADA. Beverly & James
Turnbull *Park:* In front.

THE STITCHERY IN SANDWICH
179 Old Main St, 02563
(508)888-4647   **27 44 77**
Country accessories, furniture, glass &
silver. *Est:* 1976. *Serv:* B & B suite available all year. *Hours:* Mon-Sat 10-5. *CC:*
MC/V/AX. *Park:* On site. *Loc:* 2 blocks
E of Daniel Webster Inn.

H RICHARD STRAND FINE
ANTIQUES
2 Grove St, 02563
(508)888-3230   **29 36 44**
An authentic collection of antique furniture, lamps, china, paintings - including
an outstanding selection of American
glass - shown in period room settings.
Lighting a specialty. *Serv:* Appraisal.
Hours: All year daily 9-5:30. *Assoc:*
CCADA NEAA. *Park:* On site. *Loc:* Opposite the Sandwich Glass Museum.

TOBEY HOUSE ANTIQUES
44 Water St, 02563
(508)888-1690   **21 50 67**
Braided rugs, baskets, quilts, country
items, early lighting fixtures & accessories. *Est:* 1978. *Hours:* BY APPT
ONLY. Stephanie Palmer *Loc:* Call for
directions.

SANTUIT

ETCETERA ANTIQUES
Rtes 28 & 130, 02635
(508)428-5374   **36**
18th-20th C furniture & accessories. *Est:*
1981. *Hours:* Mon-Sat 10-6, Sun 12-6.
CC: MC/V. Ann Barrett *Park:* Nearby.
Loc: At the end of Rte 130.

SOUTH HARWICH

CAPE COLLECTOR
1012 Main St Rte 28, 02661
(508)432-3701   **13**
Antiquarian books: children's, Cape
Cod, maritime & a general stock. *Hours:*
Daily 1-5. H Jewel Geberth *Loc:* At the
corner of Charles St & Rte 28.

SOUTH YARMOUTH

OLE KENTUCKY QUILTS
10 Indian Memorial Dr, 02664
(508)398-1518   **34 67**
Large inventory of 19th & early 20th C
quilts, American folk art. *Hours:*
Anytime by appt. *Assoc:* CCADA. Jim
Alessio

WELLFLEET

H B WATSON JR & DOROTHY
WATSON
17 School St, 02667
(508)349-9207   **47 50 63**
Antique & estate jewelry, lamps, silver,
small furniture, porcelain & glass. *Serv:*
Estate liquidation, appraisal. *Hours:*
Mon-Sat 10-5 & BY APPT. *Assoc:*
CCADA NEAA. *Loc:* Off Rte 6 at
Schooner's Cove traffic light.

THE FARMHOUSE
Rte 6 & Village Ln, 02667
(508)349-1708   **{GR6}**
Ephemera, oak, pine, glass, china, early
American objects of all kinds & paint-
ings. *Pr:* $1–5000. *Est:* 1988. *Serv:* Pur-

chase estates. *Hours:* Fri-Tue 10-5. *Size:*
Large. *CC:* AX/MC/V. Judy Leckey
Park: On site. *Loc:* 5 MI N of Orleans
Rotary, Rte 6, opposite Wellfleet Drive-In.

FINDERS KEEPERS
3 W Main St, 02667
(508)349-7627   **50 83**
Period, Victorian & second-hand furniture & lighting. *Hours:* Mid Jun-Labor
Day daily 10-5, else Sat-Mon, CLOSED
NOV-MAR. *Loc:* Rte 3 to Rte 6, L at
lights & Wellfleet Center & Harbor
sign, shop is 3/4 MI down St on L.

MORTAR & PESTLE ANTIQUES
Rte 6, 02667
(508)349-2574   **27 42 72**
Country furniture & accessories, pine,
cherry, mortar & pestles, pharmacy
items & microscopes. *Hours:* May-Sep
daily 10-6. *Assoc:* CCADA. Jean Keene
Park: On site. *Loc:* Rte 6, next to Bay
Sails Marine.

WELLFLEET FLEA MARKET
Rte 6, 02667
(508)349-2520   **{FLEA}**
Billed as Cape Cod's biggest flea market,
with antiques, collectibles & other flea
market merchandise. Admission is $1 per
car. *Est:* 1981. *Serv:* Catered,
playground, restrooms, spaces start at
$10 for 18' X 22'. *Hours:* Apr-Oct Sat-

ANDREW'S AXIOMS

The Restoration Principle

A Victorian turned knob handle screwed into an earlier piece of drawer
furniture is irremovable,
but an original brass drop pulls off at the first tug.

Reprinted with permission from *guide to the Antique Shops of Britain 1989.*
copyright The Antique Collectors Club, Great Britain

Sun, Jul-Aug Wed-Thu, Mon Holidays 8-4. *Size:* 200 spaces. *Park:* On site. *Loc:* On the Eastham-Wellfleet line.

WEST BARNSTABLE

BARNSTABLE STOVE SHOP
Rte 149, 02668
(508)362-9913 **74**
Several hundred stoves in stock - genuine Victorian ranges & parlor stoves, ranging from 1850s-1940s. *Serv:* Parts inventory, brochure $1, restoration. *Hours:* Year round.

JEAN KENNEDY ANTIQUES
575 Willow St, 02668
(508)362-3005 **27 65**
Primitives & a general line of country antiques. *Hours:* Mon-Sat 10-4. *Assoc:* CCADA.

LUDWIG'S ANTIQUES
1595 Main St, 02668
(508)362-2791 **27**
18th & 19th C English & American furniture, pottery & Staffordshire. *Hours:* Year round 11-4:30. *Loc:* Rte 6 E, Exit 6 to Rte 132, L onto 6A, shop is opposite Our Lady of Hope Catholic Church.

PACKET LANDING IRON
1022 Rte 6A, 02668
(508)362-2697 **70**
Handmade reproductions of 18th C wrought iron lamps. *Hours:* Tue-Sun 11-5. *Loc:* Between Rtes 132 & 149.

PAXTON'S ANTIQUES
1996 Rte 6A, 02668
(508)362-4913 **16 34 65**
Americana, brass, copper, furniture, glass, china, folk art, primitives & decorative accessories. *Hours:* Daily 10-5. *Assoc:* CCADA. Rita & Don Paxton

SALT & CHESTNUT
WEATHERVANES
651 Rte 6A at Maple St, 02668
(508)362-6085 **5 74 87**
Exclusively devoted to weather vanes - antique & new, miniature replicas. *Pr:* $200–30000. *Est:* 1978. *Serv:* Appraisal, catalog ($2), consultation, repairs, restoration, replication. *Hours:* Wed-Sat 11-5 or by appt. *CC:* MC/V. *Assoc:* CCADA NTHP SPNEA. Marilyn Strauss *Park:* On site. *Loc:* Rte 6A, 1/2 MI past Int of Rtes 6A & 149.

WEST BARNSTABLE ANTIQUES
625 Main St Rte 6A, 02668
(508)362-5120 **36 63**
18th & 19th C furniture & Chinese export porcelain, & stoneware. *Hours:* Daily 10-5. *Assoc:* CCADA. Thomas Slaman

THE WHIPPLETREE
660 Main St Rte 6A, 02668
(508)362-3320 **27 34 81**
A 200 year-old barn with country, folk art, tools & linen. *Hours:* Jun-Dec daily 10-5, Jan-May Wed-Sat 10-5. *Assoc:* CCADA. Merrill Davis

WISTERIA ANTIQUES
521 Main St, 02668
(508)362-8581 **53 63 83**
A fine collection of mirrors, pottery, porcelain, fine china, specialty glass, flow blue, Victoriana, jewelry, small furniture. *Hours:* Open most days 11-5. *CC:* MC/V. *Assoc:* CCADA. Kenneth R DiCarlo *Loc:* On Rte 6A 1 MI E of the Gilded Swan.

WEST BREWSTER

SENTIMENTAL JOURNEY
424 Main St, 02631
(508)385-6388   **44 47 65**
Quality period & turn-of-the-century
furniture, glassware, unusual & unique
collectibles, country items, primitives,
clocks & jewelry. *Hours:* Apr-Nov daily
11-5 & BY APPT. *Assoc:* CCADA.
Linda Cadarette

WEST CHATHAM

1736 HOUSE ANTIQUES
1731 Main St, 02669
(508)945-5690   **41 42 43**
Large inventory of cupboards, chests,
primitives, old paint, old pine cupboards,
trunks & dressers, pine reproductions.
Hours: May-Dec daily 10-5. *Assoc:*
CCADA. John Miller *Loc:* On Rte 28.

FRED'S TRADING POST
1323 Main St Rte 28, 02669
(508)945-9192   **6 63 65**
Country furniture, primitives, flow blue,
ironstone, antique firearms, swords & a
selection of used furniture. *Hours:* Open
Jul & Aug only, call ahead advised. Fred
Greco

WEST DENNIS

RUMFORD ANTIQUES
218 Main St, 02670
(508)394-3683   **44 50**
Depression & pressed pattern glass, oil
lamps & books on antiques. *Serv:* Appraisal, textile conservation. *Hours:*
Summer daily 10-5. *Assoc:* CCADA
SNEADA NEAA. Edna F Anness

WEST FALMOUTH

APROPOS
636 Rte 28A, 02574
(508)457-0045   **37 39**
18th-20th C American & English furniture & accessories attractively displayed
in cottage buildings. *Hours:* Daily; Win:
CLOSED TUE, WED.

VILLAGE BARN ANTIQUE COOP
606 Rte 28A, 02574
(508)540-3215   **{GR8}**
American antiques, country furniture,
china, glass & quilts in a Cape Cod barn.
Hours: Daily 10-5. *Loc:* Next to the Ideal
Spot Motel.

WEST HARWICH

RALPH DIAMOND
ANTIQUES/FINE ARTS
103 Main St Rte 28, 02671
(508)432-0634   **59**
19th & early 20th C American oil &
watercolor paintings specializing in New
England artists including Enneking,
Cahoon, Gifford, Eldred, Chapin,
Batcheller, Leavitt, McKnight. Also
frames, bronze & marble sculpture.
Hours: BY APPT. *Assoc:* CCADA
NEAA.

HOOKED RUG RESTORATION
N Road at Rte 28 Ste 203, 02671
(508)432-0897   **71**
Restoration of hooked rugs done with
expert care; rugs also available for pur-

chase. **Serv:** Conservation, consultation, restoration. **Hours:** Year round BY APPT ONLY. **Size:** Medium. **Assoc:** AIC. Charls J Quigley **Park:** On site. **Loc:** 1 MI E of Dennisport on Rte 28, 2nd 3-story building on L after Bishops Terrace Restaurant.

YARMOUTH PORT

1830 HOUSE ANTIQUES
143 Main St, 02675
(508)362-3820   **44 63**

Beautiful selection of pottery & porcelain, sterling, silver plate, lamps, fine glass attractively displayed in a home in the National Register of Historic Places. **Hours:** Jun-Sep Mon-Sat 10-5. **Assoc:** CCADA. **Park:** In front. **Loc:** On Rte 6A.

BEACH PLUM ANTIQUES
175 Rte 6A, 02675
(508)362-2611   **1 23 50**

A small quality shop offering an eclectic sampling of clocks, lamps, furniture & accessories including Americana from Victorian & early 20th C periods. **Pr:** $10–800. **Est:** 1989. **Serv:** Consultation, purchase estates. **Hours:** Year round Thu-Mon 12-4. W E Russell Jeanne Thompson **Park:** In front. **Loc:** Rte 6 Exit 5: R on to Willow St, R on Rte 6A, shop is 1/2 MI on R.

CC CANCER CONSIGNMENT EXCHANGE
133 Rte 6A, 02675
(508)362-3416   **25 44 63**

American, European & Oriental furniture, accessories & jewelry. **Hours:** Mon-Sat 10-4. **Park:** In front.

DESIGN WORKS
159 Main St, 02675
(508)775-3075   **41 42 63**

Scandinavian country antiques & accessories with a scattering of American & Continental majolica. **Pr:** $5–25000. **Serv:** Appraisal, custom woodwork, interior design, repairs, replication. **Hours:** Daily 10-5 Sun 12-5. **Size:** Large. **CC:** AX/MC/V. Jack Hill **Park:** On site. **Loc:** Rte 6 Exit 7N: to Rte 6A, 3/4 MI on R.

CONSTANCE GOFF ANTIQUES
161 Main St Rte 6A, 02675
(508)362-9540   **21 44 63**

19th C furniture & related accessories, flow blue, ironstone, hooked rugs & glass. **Hours:** Year round daily 10-5 Sun 11-4. **Assoc:** CCADA. **Park:** In front.

BETSY HEWLETT
PO Box 191, 02675
(508)362-6875   **44**

Early American pattern glass. **Serv:** Mail order. **Hours:** BY APPT ONLY. **Assoc:** CCADA. **Loc:** Call for directions.

LIL-BUD ANTIQUES
142 Main St Rte 6A, 02675
(508)362-8984   **44**

Specializing in early American pattern glass - including flint & colored - goblets, wines, tumblers & table sets. **Est:** 1968. **Serv:** Appraisal, catalog ($1), by mail order. **Hours:** Apr-Dec By chance/appt. **Assoc:** CCADA. Walter L Marchant Jr **Park:** In front. **Loc:** Rte 6A, to Ctr of Yarmouth Port.

NICKERSON'S ANTIQUES
162 Rte 6A, 02675
(508)362-6426   **16 27 63**

Country furniture, china, decorative accessories & metalware. **Hours:** Year round 10-5, Sun 12-5. **CC:** MC/V. Reginald & Mary Nickerson **Park:** Nearby. **Loc:** Travel N on Rte 6A.

YARMOUTHPORT ANTIQUES
Formal and Country Furniture, Folk Art,
Glass, China, Linens,
Paintings and Decorative Accessories

Open Daily
10-5

431 Main Street - Route 6A
Yarmouthport, MA 02675
(508) 362-3599

PARNASSUS BOOK SERVICE
Route 6A, 02675
(508)362-6420 **13**
Old books in many specialties including art, maritime affairs, antiques, ornithology, Americana, Slavia, Latin American, Caribbean, Central America, crafts & literary history. *Pr:* $1–5000. *Est:* 1951. *Serv:* Appraisal, catalog, purchase estates, search services. *Hours:* Sum: Mon-Sat 9-8 Sun 12-5, Win: Mon-Sat 9-5 Sun 12-5. *Size:* Medium. Ben Muse *Park:* On site. *Loc:* Rte 6A, across from the Yarmouth Port post office.

TALIN BOOKBINDERY
947 Rte 6A Cranberry Ct, 02675
(508)362-8144 **12 13 71**
Fine bindings, paper conservation & marble papers. *Est:* 1976. *Serv:* Restoration of books, paper conservation. *Hours:* Mon-Fri 9-5. *Park:* Nearby. *Loc:* S side of Rte 6A at the Dennis-Yarmouth town line.

YARMOUTHPORT ANTIQUES
431 Main St, 02675
(508)362-3599 **{GR}**
Formal & country furniture, folk art, glass, china, linens, paintings & decorative accessories. *Hours:* Daily 10-5 BY APPT. *Assoc:* CCADA. Lillian Mc Kinney *Park:* On site. *Loc:* On Rte 6A.

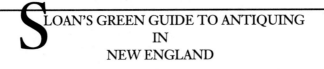
▼

Connecticut

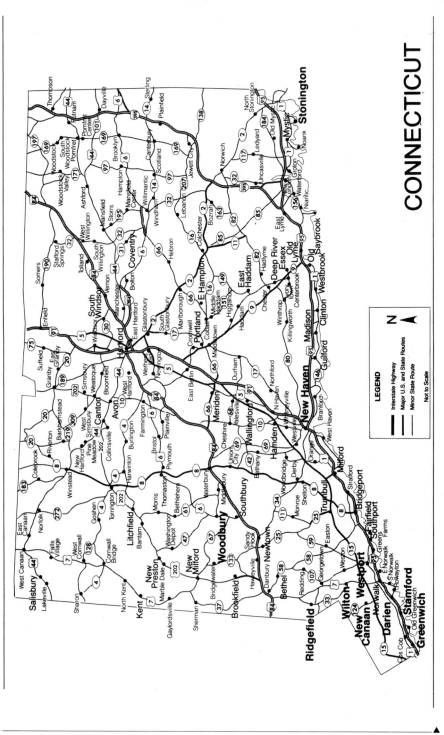

CONNECTICUT

LEGEND

Interstate Highway

Major U.S. and State Routes

Minor State Route

Not to Scale

N

ASHFORD

CLASSICS IN WOOD
PO Box 211, 06278
(203)429-6020   **43**
Reproduction tables, chairs & accessories of the Colonial period. *Serv:* Reproduction, brochure $2.00. *Hours:* Mon-Fri 9-5 BY APPT ONLY. *Loc:* Please call for directions & appt.

JERARD PAUL JORDAN
PO Box 71, 06278
(203)429-7954   **82**
American cowboy and Plains Indian material from the late 19th & early 20th C. *Hours:* BY APPT.

JERARD PAUL JORDAN GALLERY
PO Box 71, 06278
(203)429-7954   **5 74**
An extensive resource of period building & architectural materials through the Federal period including mantels, posts & beams, raised panelled walls, sheathed walls stairways, flooring, fireplace breasts, hearthstones, store counters, cobblestones. *Est:* 1970. *Serv:* Installation, purchase period architectural pieces. *Hours:* BY APPT.

MERRYTHOUGHT
Rte 44, 06278
(203)429-8827   **1 43 65**
18th & 19th C country antiques, furniture & accessories, mostly American, complemented by handcrafted articles from contemporary American artisans - weather vanes, lighting, antique tin items, reproduction Windsor chairs & Colonial tables. *Pr:* $25–5000. *Serv:* Brochure $2, catalog of handcrafted items $2, purchase antiques. *Hours:* Weekends 10-5, weekdays by chance/appt. *Size:* Medium. *CC:* MC/V.

Jeri Dunphy *Park:* On site. *Loc:* Rte 44 approx 1 MI E of Rte 89, next to Scout Camp entrance, look for Sign of the Swan.

AVON

AUTHENTIC REPRODUCTION LIGHTING
Box 218, 06001
(203)677-4600   **50 70**
Authentic reproductions of 18th C tin lighting, realistically priced for use in early homes, electrified or for use with candles - handmade in the Colonial manner. *Serv:* Made-to-order, catalog $2.75. *Hours:* Mon-Fri 9-5.

EAGLE'S NEST
Old Avon Village, 06001
(203)678-0790   **11 24 79**
Baseball cards, coins & stamps sat. *Hours:* Tue-Thu 12-4 Fri 12-5 Sat & Sun 12-6. *Park:* Nearby. *Loc:* 1/2 MI from Avon Old Farms Restaurant.

LAWRENCE C GOODHUE INC
Old Avon Village, 06001
(203)676-1002   **4 37 66**
Specializing in antique decorative prints with an extensive assortment of botanicals, architectural, animals, costumes which complement fine American furniture also in inventory. *Serv:* Appraisal, framing. *Hours:* Tue-Sat 11-5. *Loc:* I-84 Exit 39; N on Rte 10; 1 MI W on Rte 44.

GARLAND AND FRANCES PASS
87 Paper Chase Trail, 06001
(203)673-0787   **13 16 50**
Fine antique metalware including pewter, brass, copper iron & tin.. *Pr:* $100–

7500. *Serv:* Appraisal, illustrated catalog ($2), all items guaranteed & returnable. *Hours:* Mail order only.

RUTH TROIANI FINE ANTIQUES
1 Mulberry Ln, 06001
(203)673-6191   **39 57 59**
17th & 18th C needlework, American & English paintings of animals & children, 17th & 18th C treen, early metalware, early English oak & walnut furniture. *Est:* 1963. *Serv:* Everything guaranteed as represented. *Hours:* BY APPT ONLY. *Assoc:* NHADA. *Shows:* ELLIS. *Loc:* I-84 Farmington Exit.

BANTAM

KENT & YVONNE GILYARD ANTIQUES
Rte 202 W, 06750
(203)567-4204   **27 37 63**
18th & 19th C American country furniture, textiles, china & paintings in a handsome 18th c house. *Est:* 1978. *Serv:* Antique restoration. *Hours:* Daily 10-5 sometimes CLOSED WED, call suggested. *Park:* On site. *Loc:* 4 MI W of Litchfield Ctr.

GOOSEBORO BROOK ANTIQUES
38 Old Turnpike Rd, 06750
(203)567-5245   **28 36 67**
Furniture, baskets, quilts, stoneware & collectibles. *Est:* 1972. *Hours:* All Year. Carolyn Butts *Loc:* 2 MI W of Bantam Ctr, look for signs on Rte 202, 1/8 MI on Old Turnpike Rd.

RICHARD PHELPS ANTIQUES & DESIGN
Rte 202, 06750
(203)567-4388   **27**
Specializing in English & French country furniture, decorative accessories & paintings. *Hours:* Thu-Mon 11-5. Richard Phelps

WESTON THORN ANTIQUES
Rte 202, 06750
(203)567-4661   **39 59 63**
An attractive collection of antique English, Continental & American furniture & old reproductions, paintings, silver, porcelain & rugs, housed in a 2-story building & barn in scenic Litchfield County. *Pr:* $1–10000. *Est:* 1982. *Serv:* Appraisal, purchase estates. *Hours:* Fri,Sun 11-5 Sat 11-5:30, else by chance/appt. *Size:* Large. *Assoc:* AAA. *Park:* On site. *Loc:* Rte 202, 4 MI SW of Litchfield CT.

BARKHAMSTEAD

THE CANE WORKSHOP
Rte 181, 06035
(203)379-7625
Seatweaving including cane, reed & rush. *Serv:* Pickup & delivery in Northwestern CT. *Hours:* Mon-Fri 9-5. Pam Brunell *Loc:* 2 MI N of the Farmington River on Rte 181 in Barhamstead.

BETHANY

THE ANTIQUARIUM
166 Humiston Dr, 06525
(203)393-2723   **13 33**
Antiquarian books & ephemera. *Serv:* Catalogs, appraisal, search service. *Hours:* BY APPT ONLY. *Size:* 20,000 books. *Assoc:* CAB NEAA. Lee & Marian Ash

WHITLOCK FARM BOOKSELLERS
20 Sperry Rd, 06525
(203)393-1240   **13 51 66**

Antiquarian books: Americana, farming, gardening & horticulture, natural history, prints & maps. *Serv:* Appraisal, search service, catalog. *Hours:* Tue-Sun 9-5 CLOSED MON. *Size:* 50,000 books. *Assoc:* ABAA CAB. Gilbert Whitlock

ROBERT B WILLIAMS
57 Lacey Rd, 06525
(203)393-1488   **13 59 66**

Specializing in antiquarian & out-of-print dog books, dog paintings, drawings & etchings, a select group of dog figurines. *Pr:* $15–5000. *Est:* 1980. *Serv:* Appraisal, catalog, purchase estates, search service. *Hours:* BY APPT ONLY. *CC:* MC/V.

BETHEL

J THOMAS MELVIN
20 P T Barnum Sq, 06801
(203)655-5133   **36 59 60**

Furniture, paintings, Oriental porcelains & period brass. *Hours:* BY APPT ONLY.

PICKWICK HOUSE ANTIQUES
153 Greenwood Ave, 06801
(203)743-6170   **21 23 44**

Eight rooms with mahogany formal furniture, china, glass, rugs & tall case clocks. *Est:* 1968. *Serv:* Appraisal, estate sales. *Hours:* Daily 10-6 CLOSED WED,SUN. *CC:* AX/MC/V. *Assoc:* CADA NEAA. Elizabeth Nightingale *Park:* Nearby. *Loc:* Between Wilton & Danbury.

BETHLEHEM

WOODY MOSCH CABINETMAKERS
23 Wood Creek Rd, 06751
(203)266-7619   **19 74 76**

18th C & Shaker antique reproduction furniture, 18th C architectural woodworking & custom cabinetwork. *Est:* 1976. *Hours:* BY APPT. *Park:* On site. *Loc:* Call for directions.

THE NEW ENGLAND SHOP
151 N Main St, 06751
(203)266-7826   **{GR2}**

Five rooms of Victorian reproductions, oak, Oriental, early American primitives, jewelry, country antiques, folk art, dolls, Santa Fe shop, artifacts & classes. *Pr:* $25–2000. *Est:* 1982. *Serv:* Purchase estates. *Hours:* Wed-Sun 12-6. *Size:* Large. *CC:* MC/V. Rena Meyer *Park:* On site. *Loc:* I-84 to Rte 6 to Rte 61. From Woodbury Rte 6 E to Rte 61 N 3/4 MI past Green in Bethlehem. From Litchfield Rte 63S to 132W.

BLOOMFIELD

ARS ANTIQUA BOOKS
50 Silo Way, 06002
(203)242-3466   **13 55**

Antiquarian books specializing in American music & musicology, ethnonomusicology, hymnology, early music, music history & reference, also medieval & Renaissance literature, art & architecture. *Pr:* $5–1000. *Est:* 1983. *Serv:* Catalog (free), search service. *Hours:* By chance/appt. *Size:* 1,000 books. *Assoc:* CAB. Llyn Kaimowitz

BOLTON

AUTUMN POND ANTIQUES
29 Westridge Dr, 06043
(203)643-9709   **1 37 59**
Specializing in 18th & early 19th C
American furniture & accessories. *Serv:*
Purchase estates. *Hours:* By chance/appt
suggested. *CC:* MC/V. *Assoc:* CADA.
Norma Chick *Park:* On site. *Loc:* 84E to
384E Exit 4: toward Bolton.

GRAND VIEW ANTIQUES
22 Hebron Rd, 06043
(203)643-9641   **29 36**
Antique furnishings & accessories.
Hours: Wed-Sat 10-5 Sun 12-5. *Loc:* I-
84E to Rte 384: Exit 5, turn R, 2 MI to
Bolton Ctr, bear R at fork.

HAILSTON HOUSE INC
59 West St Rte 85, 06043
(203)646-2877   **27 36 63**
Two authentic New England barns
brimming traditional furniture, decorative accessories, eclectic lighting, one-of-
a-kind nautical furniture, situated in a
charming country setting accented with
garden ornaments. *Pr:* $10–10000. *Est:*
1976. *Serv:* Consultation. *Hours:* May-
Dec Mon,Fri 11-5 Sat,Sun 10:30-6,Jan-
Apr Sat,Sun 10:30-5. *CC:* MC/V. *Assoc:*
MADA. Frances Hailston *Park:* On site.
Loc: Rte 84 Rte 384 Bolton Exit: Rte 85
S 1 1/2 MI.

BOZRAH

CHARLES GALLERY
431 Fitchville Rd, 06334
(203)889-4901   **59 78**
American 19th & 20th C paintings,

specializing in hunting, fishing &
wildlife. *Hours:* Mon-Fri 10-6, Sat 10-4,
CLOSED SUN. Charles A Connell, Jr
Loc: Rte 2: Exit 23, R at bottom of exit,
L at SS, 1 MI on R.

BRANFORD

YESTERDAY'S THREADS
564 Main St, 06405
(203)481-6452   **47 80 85**
Men's, women's & children's clothing &
accessories from 1840s through 1940s.
Victorian whites, Edwardian wedding
dresses, tuxedoes, day dresses, evening
wear, parasols, vintage textiles & trims &
costume jewelry of all eras. *Est:* 1977.
Serv: Repairs, restoration. *Hours:* Sep-
Jun Mon,Wed,Fri 12:30-5 Sat 10-4, Jul-
Aug by chance/appt. *Park:* In front. *Loc:*
I-95 Exit 55 (Cedar St): toward Bran-
ford, 1.5 MI to end, turn R onto Main St,
approx 3 blocks.

BRIDGEPORT

GRAYNOOK ANTIQUES &
INTERIORS
72 Park Ave S, 06604
(203)334-3621   **29 36 46**
Large 1890 Victorian residence featuring American, European & Oriental antiques. *Est:* 1980. *Serv:* Appraisal,
consultation, interior design. *Hours:*
Daily 9-5 appt suggested. *Size:* Medium.
Henry J Mongelli *Park:* On site. *Loc:*
I-95 Exit 27: to Park Ave, S toward
sound, corner of Linden St & Park Ave.

BRIDGEWATER

THE DOLL ROOM
Rte 133 & Stuart Rd, 06752
(203)354-8442   **32**
Antique & collectibles dolls & doll-related items. *Hours:* By chance/appt.

BRISTOL

RICHARD BLASCHKE
670 Lake Ave, 06010
(203)584-2566   **31 74**
Curved china cabinet glass. *Est:* 1960.
Serv: Cut glass by appt, brochure.
Hours: Mon-Fri 10-4:30 Sat 12-5
CLOSED TUE. *CC:* MC/V. *Park:* On
site. *Loc:* I-84 Exit 31.

DICK'S ANTIQUES
670 Lake Ave, 06010
(203)584-2566   **40 83**
Oak, walnut & Victorian furniture & accessories. *Est:* 1960. *Serv:* Brochure.
Hours: Mon-Fri 10-4:30 Sat-Sun 12-5
CLOSED TUE. *CC:* MC/V. *Park:* On
site. *Loc:* I-84 Exit 31.

FEDERAL HILL ANTIQUES
78 Maple St, 06010
(203)589-3139   **7 66**
Specializing in Art Deco, 30's Deco
prints, old frames. *Est:* 1989. *Hours:* 11-
4:30 CLOSED WED & SUN.

BROOKFIELD

BERT & PHYLLIS BOYSON
23 Cove Rd, 06804
(203)775-0176   **13**
Antiquarian books: children's, illustrated, science, technology & general
nonfiction. *Hours:* BY APPT. *Size:* 3-
4,000 books. *Assoc:* CAB.

EUROPEAN COUNTRY ANTIQUES
833 Federal Rd Rte 7, 06804
(203)775-2872   **27**
18th & 19th C English, Irish & French
country furniture, china & paintings.
Hours: Year round Wed-Sun 11-5. *CC:*
MC/V. *Park:* Nearby. *Loc:* I-84 Exit 7: 3
min.

MC CAFFREY BOOTH ANTIQUES
436 Federal Rd, 06804
(203)775-1629   **36 43**
Antique & reproduction formal furniture. *Serv:* Refinishing, French polishing, restoration. *Hours:* Mon-Sat
11-5:30. *CC:* MC/V. Thomas E Mc Caffrey *Park:* On site. *Loc:* I-84 to Rte 7, L
onto Federal, on Rte 202.

OLD FAVORITES
9 Arrowhead Rd, 06804
(203)775-3744   **32 36 57**
Toys,   household   furnishings,
embroidery, needlework, ceramics,
glassware, Disney, advertising, license
plates, collectibles, paintings, prints &
Oriental rugs. *Hours:* By chance/appt.
Assoc: NEAA.

BROOKLYN

HEIRLOOM ANTIQUES
10 Winding Rd, 06234
(203)774-7017   **36 50 70**

Period furniture & accessories, some formal, some country, some in between. Large inventory of early oil lamps. Reproductions of copper lanterns, iron bridge lamps, tin chandeliers & sconces. *Serv:* Fabric lampshades, lamp parts, lamp repairs, appraisal. *Hours:* Daily 12-5 CLOSED WED. *Assoc:* NEAA. Marcia Laporte *Park:* On site. *Loc:* Rte 169 Brooklyn Ctr S of the traffic light at Int Rte 6, behind Mortlake Fire Company.

BURLINGTON

AMUSEMENT ARTS
P O Box 1158, 06013
(203)675-7653   **73**

Specializing in antique carousel animals. *Serv:* Interested in buying carousel figures. *Hours:* By appt. Bruce Zubee

JOHN CANNINGS ANTIQUES/FURNITURE
Rte 4, 06013
(203)675-7242

American classics perfectly proportioned Windsor chairs, farm tables & stepback cupboards. *Hours:* Thu-Mon 10-5. *Park:* On site. *Loc:* On Rte 4 between the fish hatchery & the Burlington Green.

HADSELL'S ANTIQUES
191 Geo Washington Tnpk, 06013
(203)673-2344   **44**

Two floors of depression glass & quality glass & related items of the era. *Pr:* $25–500. *Est:* 1982. *Serv:* Appraisal, purchase estates, repairs. *Hours:* Fri-Sun 1-5 by chance/appt. *Size:* Medium. Luther A Hadsell *Park:* On site. *Loc:* From Unionville Ctr, S on Rte 177, R at 2nd light after bridge (Burlington Rd), at next SS, R on Geo Washington Tnpk, 1 MI.

CANTERBURY

CACKLEBERRY FARMS ANTIQUES
16 Lisbon Rd, 06331
(203)546-6335   **27**

A small country shop featuring country collectibles. *Pr:* $1–3000. *Serv:* Catering to the trade. *Hours:* By chance/appt. *Size:* Medium. *Park:* On site. *Loc:* Rte 395 Exit 89: Rte 14W to Canterbury, 1st L past firehouse, 600 yds from corner on L.

THOMAS LORD CABINETMAKER
68 N Society Rd, 06331
(203)546-9283   **19 70**

Reproductions of fine cabinet pieces, tables, chairs, lowboys, highboys, desks & chests. *Hours:* BY APPT ONLY. *Loc:* Call for directions & appt.

STONE OF SCONE ANTIQUES
19 Water St, 06331
(203)546-9917   **1 6 13**

Located in the rural setting of Connecticut's quiet corner, featuring a large selection of rare & out-of-print books - New England history a specialty - antique firearms & rare caliber reloading tools, antique jewelry & general line of smalls. *Pr:* $10–3000. *Est:* 1976. *Serv:* Appraisal. *Hours:* Mon-Fri 12-7 Sat 10-7 Sun 10-5. *Size:* 2,400 books. *CC:* MC/V. *Assoc:* CAB. Jan Stratton *Park:* On site.

Loc: I-395N Exit 83A: L on Rte 169, 8 MI, L at Rte 14, 3 MI, L onto Water St, 500 ft on R.

CANTON

1784 HOUSE ANTIQUES
Canton-on-the-Green Rte 44, 06019
(203)693-2622　　　　　**37 44 63**

Quality furniture, paintings, glass, Meissen, Sevres, Limoges & porcelain, specializing in Chinese export. *Hours:* Mon-Sun 10-5. Mrs. Myrtle Colley *Park:* In front. *Loc:* Rte 44: white house with yellow shutters on the village green.

ANTIQUES AT CANTON VILLAGE
Canton Village Rte 44, 06019
(203)693-2715　　　　　**{MDS30}**

Featuring authentic American & European period furniture, clocks, fine paintings, Oriental rugs, porcelains, silver, early lighting, Americana & art glass of the highest quality, many in period room settings. *Pr:* $50–5000. *Est:* 1988. *Hours:* Wed-Mon 10-5 Sun 12-5. *CC:* MC/V. *Assoc:* CADA. *Loc:* From Hartford, I-84W Farmington Exit: follow signs to Farmington Ctr, Rte 10 to Avon, L on Rte 44 to Canton.

BALCONY ANTIQUES
81 Albany Tnpk, 06019
(203)693-2996　　　　　**{GR17}**

Oldest group shop in Connecticut displaying furniture, decorative accessories including paintings, porcelain, china & silver with a wide choice of stock. *Est:* 1972. *Hours:* Mon-Sat 10-4:30. *Park:* On site. *Loc:* On Rte 44.

BOOK STORE
Rte 44, 06019
(203)693-6029　　　　　**13**

General stock of antiquarian books: modern firsts & academic. *Hours:* Wed-Fri 10-6 Sat 10-5 Sun 12-5. *Size:* 10,000 books. *Assoc:* CAB. Stephen Powell

BROKEN SHELL GALLERY
185 Albany Tnpk, 06019
(203)693-2331　　　　　**16 42 66**

Specializing in European polished pine furniture from the 1800's - cottage tables, cupboards, desks, blanket boxes, dressers & footstools, brass, crockery, tins, botanical prints & ironstone platters attractively displayed in Old Church. *Serv:* Interior design, gifts from England. *Hours:* Tue-Sat 10:30-4:30. *CC:* MC/V. Brook Mallory *Park:* In front. *Loc:* Between Rte 10 & Rte 167 across from the Canton Green.

CANTON BARN AUCTIONS
79 Old Canton Rd, 06019
(203)693-0601　　　　　**8**

Auction every Saturday night January-mid December at 7:30, preview 5-7:30. Merchandise from homes, estates. No reserve, no buyers premium, no children allowed. *Serv:* Catered. *Hours:* BY APPT. Richard E Wacht *Park:* On site. *Loc:* Off Rte 44, turn onto Old Canton Rd at Citgo station.

GALWAY STALLARD
136 Dowd Ave, 06019
(203)693-1401　　　　　**48 63 86**

Antique linens, wicker, Staffordshire, furniture, engravings, silver & crystal. *Serv:* Interior design service. *Hours:* Wed-Sat 10-5 Sun 1-5. *Loc:* Going W on Rte 44 past Rte 167 turn S on Dowd Ave.

THE HOUSE OF CLOCKS
148 Albany Tnpk Rte 44, 06019
(203)693-2066   **23 68 71**

Antique clocks & watches bought, sold & restored. Specializing in restoration of wooden cased Federal, Empire & Victorian American clocks. Complete restoration of brass & wooden movements, refinishing, & veneering of wooden cases. Free estimates. *Pr:* $50–7500. *Est:* 1976. *Serv:* Appraisal, consultation, custom woodwork, repairs, restoration. *Hours:* Tue & Thu 10-1, Wed, Fri, Sat 10-4 or by appt. *Assoc:* NAWCC. Robert Galbraith, Jr *Park:* On site. *Loc:* I-84 to Farmington Exit Rte 4: W to Unionville N on Rte 177 to Rte 44,W 1/4 MI. On L next to Margaritaville Restaurant.

CENTERBROOK

BRUSH FACTORY ANTIQUES
33 Deep River Rd Rte 154, 06409
(203)767-0845   **{GR}**

Housed in a newly-renovated historic factory building, furniture & decorative accessories. *Est:* 1988. *Hours:* Tue-Sun 11-5. *CC:* MC/V. *Loc:* I-91 to Rte 9S Exit 4: R off ramp 1/2 MI on L. From I-95 Rte 9N, Exit 4: 3/4 MI on L.

ESSEX EMPORIUM
Middlesex Tnpk Rte 154, 06409
(203)767-1869   **{MD}**

Large selection of quality furniture including armoires, wardrobes, tables & chairs, dressers, chests, mirrors & polished pine, also a group shop featuring art by local artists. *Hours:* Thu-Mon 11-5 Tue, Wed by chance. *CC:* MC/V. *Loc:* Rte 9 Exit 3: follow Rte 154 N approx 1 MI; across from the post office.

THILL'S ANTIQUES
The Factory Bldg 67 Main St, 06409
(203)767-1696   **29 37**

American & European antiques, decorative accessories in a restored factory building. *Est:* 1970. *Serv:* Appraisal. *Hours:* Mon-sat 9-4:30 Sun by chance. *Assoc:* NEAA. Charles W Thill *Park:* In front. *Loc:* I-95 Exit 65 or Rte 9 Exit 4, to Centerbrook.

CHESHIRE

FINE ARTS ASSOCIATES OF CHESHIRE
265 Sorghum Mill Dr, 06410
(203)272-0114   **2 26 59**

Specializing in Gloucester & Rockport artists including Anthony Thieme, F Mulhaupt, Emile Gruppe, MS Pearson, A Cirino, P Cornoyere & Louis Kronberg; photo packet of current works available; authenticity & condition guaranteed. *Pr:* $3000–50000. *Est:* 1980. *Serv:* Appraisal, consultation, purchase estates. *Hours:* Anytime by appt. John & Linda Ladder *Park:* In front. *Loc:* In CT, I-84 to Rte 70 toward center of Cheshire, turn on to Mountain Rd, take 4th L on to Sorghum Mill Dr.

THE MAGNOLIA SHOPPE
908 S Meriden Rd, 06410
(203)272-3303   **36 47 48**

Antiques & collectibles including furniture & smalls, estate jewelry & linens. *Hours:* Tue-Sat 10-5, Sun 1-5. *Assoc:* CADA.

J MUENNICH ASSOCIATES, INC
PO Box 941, 06410
(203)272-5944   **4**

Jewelry appraisal & portable gemological services - diamonds & gemstones/antique & period jewelry. *Hours:* BY APPT ONLY. *Assoc:* AWA GIA ISA. Jill M Muennich, GG

CHESTER

ONE-OF-A-KIND INC
21 Main St, 06412
(203)526-9736   **29 36 47**

A diverse selection of 18th & 19th C furniture, jewelry, silver, rugs, paintings & decorative accessories. *Pr:* $25–5000. *Est:* 1975. *Serv:* Appraisal, brochure, purchase estates. *Hours:* Wed-Sat 10-5 Sun 12-4. *Size:* Medium. *Assoc:* NEAA. Thomas & Cheri-Ann Perry *Park:* In front. *Loc:* I-95 to Rte 9N or I-91 to Rte 9S, Exit 6 to Rte 148E, 1 MI.

PERIOD LIGHTING FIXTURES
1 W Main St, 06412
(203)526-3690   **50 74**

Entirely handmade reproductions of 17th & 18th C chandeliers, lanterns, sconces & lamps in copper, pewter, distressed tin & wood. *Pr:* $275–950. *Serv:* Catalog (refundable)$3. *Hours:* Mon-Fri 8-5 Sat 11-4.

SAGE AUCTION GALLERIES
Rte 154, 06412
(203)526-3036   **4 8**

Auctioning antiques & fine home furnishings from Essex & Clinton homes, including pewter, primitives, silverware, toys, household furnishings, clocks, embroidery, needlework, ceramics, glassware, furniture, rugs, jewelry & watches. *Serv:* Appraisal. *Hours:* Call for appt or schedule. *Assoc:* NEAA. Gloria N Twomey

WILLIAM SCHAFFER PHOTOGRAPHS
4 Water St, 06412
(203)526-3870   **62**

Specializing in 19th & 20th C photographs by American, English, French & Italian photographers. *Hours:* By chance/appt, best to call ahead. *Loc:* I-95 Exit 69: N of Rte 9 to Exit 6.

CLINTON

HEY-DAY ANTIQUES
PO Box 133, 06413
(203)669-8800   **4 21 68**

Specializing in Oriental rugs & carpets. *Est:* 1973. *Serv:* Repair, cleaning, appraisal, purchase estates. *Hours:* BY APPT. *Loc:* Call for directions.

MEURS RENEHAN
101 E Main St, 06413
(203)669-7055   **23 34 65**

European clocks principally early German & Dutch, Japanese clocks, folk art & primitives. *Serv:* Appraisal, restoration, conservation, repair. *Hours:* BY APPT ONLY. *Assoc:* NAWCC. *Loc:* I-95 Exit 63, Rte 81 to Rte 1, then E.

STEPHEN H SMITH, CABINETMAKER
25 Liberty St, 06413
(203)669-9172   **19 37 43**

Specializing in fine handmade beds, from the simple country pencil post style to elegant turned, carved & reeded Federal classics. Fine chests, desks & tables are made to order. *Est:* 1985. *Serv:* Brochure, custom woodwork, reproduction. *Hours:* Appt suggested. Stephen H Smith *Loc:* Convenient to I-95 & US Rte 1 Call for directions.

VAN CARTER HALE FINE ART
36 W Main St Rte 1, 06413
(203)669-4313   **4 26 59**

Fine American paintings, watercolors & prints with an emphasis on Connecticut & New England artists. Art appraisal to the trade with a computer bank of over 13,000 American & Canadian artists with auction records. *Pr:* $300–20000. *Serv:* Specialty is identifying artists from a partial signature. *Hours:* BY APPT. *Assoc:* NEAA. *Park:* On site. *Loc:* I-95 Exit 63: S on 81 for 1/2 MI, R on Boston Post Rd (US1), 6th bldg on L.

ROBERT PAUL WEIMANN III FINE ART
16 W Main St Rte 1, 06413
(203)669-0207   **59**

Specializing in American & European 17th-20th C paintings, including works by Jane Peterson, A., T. Bricher, Bierstadt, Emil Gruppe, Paxton, Metcalf, Robert Weir, H. Hamilton & Joseph Decker. *Est:* 1989. *Serv:* Appraisal. *Hours:* Tue-Sat 10-6 or by appt. Robert P Weimann III *Loc:* I-95 Exit 63: S on Rte 81 and then W on Rte 1. In the Clinton Parkade.

COLCHESTER

LES TROIS PROVINCES
526 Westchester Rd Rte 149, 06415
(203)267-6057   **35 36 63**

One of the country's largest collections of 18th & 19th C country French antique furniture & accessories, tables, armoires & buffets, displayed in period rooms in the historic Champion House. *Est:* 1970. *Hours:* Wed-Sat 10-5 Sun 12-5 or by appt. John Adams *Park:* In front. *Loc:* From Hartford: Rte 2 Exit 16: S to Rte 149, from Middletown: Rte 66E to Rte 16, R onto Rte 149 8 MI N of Goodspeed Opera.

NATHAN LIVERANT & SON
48 S Main St, 06415
(203)537-2409   **37 59**

Fine American antiques & paintings for the discriminating collector displayed in an 1831 meeting house. *Est:* 1920. *Serv:* Will buy a single piece or an entire collection. *Hours:* Mon-Sat 10-5. *Loc:* Located between Hartford & New London.

NADEAU'S AUCTION GALLERY
489 Old Hartford Rd, 06415
(203)537-3888   **8**

Antique & estate auctions. No buyer's premium. *Serv:* Purchase estates, consignments, appraisals, trucking available. *Hours:* Call for appts & schedule. *CC:* MC/V. Edwin Nadeau *Park:* Ample. *Loc:* From Hartford: Rte 84 to Rte 2 toward New London, Exit 17, L at SS, first L then R, first bldg on L.

COLEBROOK

COLEBROOK BOOK BARN
Rte 183, 06021
(203)379-3185   **13**

Antiquarian books: Americana, American & English literature, rare books, salesmen's samples & publisher's leather bindings. *Serv:* Appraisal, catalogs. *Hours:* May-Oct by chance/appt. *Size:* 15,000 books. *Assoc:* ABAA CAB. Robert Seymour

COLLINSVILLE

**COLLINSVILLE ANTIQUES
COMPANY**
One Main St Rte 179, 06022
(203)693-1011   **{GR35}**
A group shop with a large selection of antiques & collectibles located by the Farmington River in the Historic Collins Axe Factory. *Serv:* Delivery. *Hours:* Fri-Mon 9:30-5:30. *Size:* Large. *CC:* MC/V. *Assoc:* NEAA. David Bronkie *Loc:* Rte 84 Exit 39: follow Rte 4 to Rte 179 into Collinsville, between Rtes 4 & 202.

COUNTRY LANE BOOKS
PO Box 47, 06022
(203)489-8852   **13**
Antiquarian books: children's books, Civil War, literature, voyages & Western Americana. *Serv:* Catalog, appraisals. *Hours:* BY APPT ONLY. *Assoc:* ABAA. Edward T Myers

**LAWRENCE GOLDER, RARE
BOOKS**
PO Box 144, 06022
(203)693-8110   **13**
Antiquarian books: rare or scarce Americana, early voyages & travels, the West, Colonial, Indians, wars, Canadiana & the Arctic. *Serv:* Catalog, appraisal. *Hours:* BY APPT ONLY.

CORNWALL BRIDGE

THE BRASS BUGLE
Rte 45, 06754
(203)672-6535   **1 65 80**
In an 18th C barn: furniture, primitives, collectibles, fabrics, quilts, dolls, glass, china, lamps & tools. *Est:* 1962. *Hours:*
May-Nov daily 8-5. *CC:* MC/V. Louise M Graham *Park:* On site. *Loc:* 1 MI off Rte 7 on Rte 45.

HARRY HOLMES ANTIQUES
Rte 7 & Carter Rd, 06754
(203)927-3420   **23 36**
Chairs & dining tables, 18th & 19th C furniture, clocks & accessories. *Est:* 1968. *Serv:* Purchase estates. *Hours:* Daily 9-5 CLOSED WED. *CC:* MC/V. Jeanette Holmes *Park:* On site. *Loc:* 5 MI N of Village of Kent, just below Kent Village State Park.

G K HOLMES ANTIQUES
Rte 7 & 45, 06754
(203)672-6427   **1 37**
Specializing in American 18th & 19th C antique furniture. *Est:* 1959. *Serv:* Restoration. *Hours:* Mon-Sun 8-5. Paula V Holmes

SCANTIQUE
Rte 7, 06754
(203)672-0105   **42**
Specializing in country pine dining tables & chairs. *Serv:* Repairs, custom woodwork. *Hours:* Daily 9-5. Bob Glass *Park:* On site. *Loc:* 3 doors from the Post Office on Cornwall Bridge on Rte 7.

COS COB

THE BOOK BLOCK
8 Loughlin Ave, 06807
(203)629-2990   **9 12 13**
Press books & fine printing, literature, rare books, fine bindings, autograph letters & manuscripts. *Serv:* Appraisals, catalog, restoration, bookbinding. *Hours:* BY APPT ONLY. *Size:* 500 books. *Assoc:* ABAA CAB. David Block

PIERCE-ARCHER ANTIQUES
301 Valley & Palmer Hill Rd, 06807
(203)869-1130   **39**

Fine English antiques, importers of 17th-19th C English furniture & decorative accessories. *Est:* 1967. *Serv:* Master picture framer. *Hours:* Mon-Fri 9:30-5:30 Sat 9:30-4:30. *CC:* AX/MC/V. Eugenia Pierce-Archer *Park:* On site. *Loc:* At the Int.

COVENTRY

ALLINSON GALLERY INC
46 Fieldstone Ln, 06238
(203)742-8990   **4 59 66**

American & European fine prints 1880-1950, paintings & drawings by printmakers, decorative Japanese woodblock prints, small selection of American Impressionist paintings. *Pr:* $100–20000. *Est:* 1977. *Serv:* Appraisal & consultation. *Hours:* BY APPT. *Size:* Medium. *Assoc:* AAA. Jane Allinson PhD *Park:* On site. *Loc:* I-84 Coventry Exit: 8 MI.

COVENTRY ANTIQUE CENTER
Main St Rte 31, 06238
(203)742-1647   **{GR10}**

Furniture, glassware, china, toys & dolls, linens, vintage clothing & collectibles. *Serv:* Doll repair. *Hours:* Wed-Sun 10-5. Mary Woodman

COVENTRY BOOK SHOP
1159 Main St Rte 31, 06238
(203)742-9875   **13**

A general stock of antiquarian books. *Serv:* Appraisal, search service. *Hours:* Tue-Sun 12-5. *Size:* 15,000 books. *Assoc:* CAB. John R Gambino

HANDS OF TIME
209 Woodbridge Rd, 06238
(203)742-9844   **34 65 80**

Antiques, collectibles & folk art featuring fabrics, upholstery, pillows & primitives. *Hours:* Tue-Sat 10-5 by chance/appt. Lynda M Pellegren *Loc:* In the Capt Cyrus Jones House.

MEMORY LANE ANTIQUE CENTER
2224 Boston Tnpk Rte 44, 06238
(203)742-0346   **{GR27}**

Silver, china, glass, furniture, primitives, jewelry, quilts, flow blue, mulberry, tools & toys. *Est:* 1985. *Serv:* Appraisal, consultation, purchase estates. *Hours:* Year round Wed-Sun 10-5. *CC:* MC/V. Gail Dickenson *Park:* On site. *Loc:* I-84 Exit 67: 2 MI S to corner of Rtes 31 & 44.

OLD COUNTRY STORE ANTIQUES
1140 Main St Rte 31, 06238
(203)742-9698   **29 36 70**

Ten rooms of furniture & decorative accessories, including antiques & quality reproduction furniture, porcelain, glass, coin holloware, vintage clothing, & lighting. 18th century through Art Deco. *Est:* 1973. *Serv:* Appraisal, consultation, custom woodwork, purchase estates. *Hours:* Year round Wed-Sun 10-5 & by chance. David Ware Debra Bradshaw *Park:* In front. *Loc:* On Rte 31.

KATHLEEN SULLIVAN-CHILDREN'S BKS
861 Main St, 06238
(203)742-7073   **13**

19th & 20th C children's & illustrated books. *Serv:* Appraisal, search service. *Hours:* BY APPT. *Size:* 1,500 books. *Assoc:* CAB.

VILLAGE ANTIQUES
1340 Main St Rte 31, 06238
(203)742-5701   **{GR12}**

In a reproduction of an 1890s village - a

potpourri of antiques & collectibles, on 2 floors of an old barn. *Pr:* $1–5000. *Est:* 1973. *Serv:* Appraisal, auction, purchase estates, kiln-fired shade matching. *Hours:* Thu-Sun 10-5. *Size:* Large. *CC:* MC/V. *Shows:* RI. *Park:* On site. *Loc:* Corner of Rtes 31 & 275.

WILDFLOWER
1199 Main St Rte 31, 06238
(203)742-7482　　　　　　**27 32 34**
Small, historic shop filled with country antiques, antique toys, unique collectibles, fine contemporary folk art & a large selection of artist teddy bears. *Pr:* $40–3000. *Serv:* Purchase estates. *Hours:* Thu-Sun 12-5. *Size:* Medium. Sylvia R Jucker *Park:* On site. *Loc:* I-84/Rte 31S, directly to Main St in Coventry.

CROMWELL

CUSTOM HOUSE
6 Kirby Rd, 06416
(203)828-6885　　　　　　**29 50**
A specialty shop for custom lamp shades: hand sewn, pierced, botanical, fabric & paper lamination - displayed on antique Chinese porcelain & early oil & kerosene lamps with a selection of antique accessories. *Pr:* $25–1000. *Est:* 1968. *Serv:* Consultation, interior design, custom mounting & wiring. *Hours:* Sep 15-July 15 Tue-Fri 10-4 Sat 9:30-12:30. *Size:* Medium. Eunice Buxton *Park:* On site. *Loc:* I-91 Exit 21: 1st R, 2nd L.

HORTON BRASSES
Nooks Hill Rd, 06416
(203)635-4400　　　　　　**16 70**
Manufacturers of brass hardware for antique furniture. Superior reproductions of Queen Anne, Chippendale, Hep-

plewhite, Sheraton, Victorian & early 1900s drawer pulls, knobs, hinges, finials, escutcheons, iron & architectural hardware. *Est:* 1930. *Hours:* Aug 24-Jul Mon-Fri 9:00-3:45. *CC:* MC/V. *Loc:* I-91 Exit 21: call for directions.

DANBURY

CARNIVAL HOUSE ANTIQUES
17 Padanaram Rd Rte 37, 06811
(203)792-6746　　　　　　**33 44 63**
Three large rooms full of period furniture, carnival & depression-era glass, china, jewelry, pottery, Coca Cola & Pepsi Cola collectibles. *Hours:* Apr-Dec Fri-Sun 12-5 & by appt CLOSED JAN-MAR. *CC:* MC/V. Mary Lou & John Zdanowski *Park:* In front. *Loc:* I-84 (W Exit 6 or E Exit 5): onto Rte 37N, just past McDonald's on R.

DEER PARK BOOKS
27 Deer Park Rd, 06811
(203)743-2246　　　　　　**4 13**
Carefully selected general stock includes prints, photographica & ephemera. *Est:* 1985. *Serv:* Appraisal, catalog, search service, purchase libraries. *Hours:* All year BY APPT. *Size:* 2,000 books. *Assoc:* CAB. Rich & Barbara De Palma *Park:* On site. *Loc:* I-84 Exit 5: 5 min-call for directions.

ORPHEUS BOOKS
4 Abbott Ave, 06810
(203)792-4990　　　　　　**13 55**
Specializing in books about music. *Serv:* Catalog. *Hours:* BY APPT ONLY. *Size:* 3,500 books. *Assoc:* CAB. Irving Goldstein

TIME AFTER TIME
5 Padanaram Rd N Ridge Plaza, 06811
(203)743-2801 **78**
Billiards supplies, custom & antique tables from the mid-1800s, run by a professional billiards player. *Est:* 1958. *Serv:* Billiards room interior design, appraisal, repair, restoration. *Hours:* Mon-Sat, CLOSED WED in JUL/AUG. *Size:* Medium. *CC:* MC/V. Ed O'-Connell *Park:* On site.

DARIEN

1860 HOUSE OF ANTIQUES
682 Post Rd, 06820
(203)655-8896 **{GR4}**
Four rooms & a large barn of country & formal American, English & French furniture, brass, prints, Quimper, mirrors, majolica, copper, lamps, Staffordshire, toys, flow blue, quilts, fireplace furnishings & childhood folk art. *Pr:* $25–2500. *Est:* 1977. *Hours:* Mon-Sat 11-5. *Assoc:* CADA. Lonny Fitz-Gerald *Park:* On site. *Loc:* Between 119 & 12 off I-95.

ANTIQUES UNLIMITED
1090 Post Rd, 06820
(203)655-5133 **34 37 63**
18th & 19th C American furniture with appropriate accessories, formal & country, fine art & folk art, the expected & the unexpected. *Hours:* Mon-Sat 10-5 Sun by chance/appt. *Size:* Large. *CC:* MC/V. *Park:* Nearby lot. *Loc:* I-95 Exit 11: (L from New Haven, R from NYC), 300 ft on R.

GILANN BOOKS
301 West Ave, 06820
(203)655-4532 **11 13 33**
Children's books, first editions, baseball cards & ephemera. *Serv:* Appraisal, catalog, search service, mail order Jul/Aug. *Hours:* BY APPT. *CC:* MC/V. *Assoc:* NEAA. *Park:* On site. *Loc:* Across from Darien Railroad Station.

EMY JANE JONES ANTIQUES
770 Boston Post Rd, 06820
(203)655-7576 **40 42 47**
Seven rooms of furniture in oak, pine, walnut & mahogany, beautiful antique jewelry & accessories. *Serv:* Appraisal, consultation, repair. *Hours:* Mon-Sat 10:30-4:30 Sun 1-5. *CC:* AX/MC/V. *Assoc:* NEAA. *Park:* In front. *Loc:* In the heart of Darien.

LA CALECHE
1089 Post Rd, 06820
(203)655-3993 **35 46**
An elegant shop displaying the finest 17th, 18th & 19th C French antiques with original French paintings, antique mirrors, Quimper, decorative & fine arts personally selected by the French owner. *Pr:* $1500–15000. *Est:* 1987. *Serv:* Consultation, interior design. *Hours:* Mon-Sat 10-5:30 Sun 11-5. *Size:* Medium. *CC:* MC/V. Jany Caroli *Park:* In front. *Loc:* I-95 Exit 11E: on Post Rd 1/5 MI.

H P MC LANE ANTIQUES INC
1076 Post Rd, 06820
(203)655-2280 **16 63 77**
American & English furniture, silver, paintings, brass, boxes, prints, Oriental & European porcelain & lamps. *Hours:* Tue-Sat 10-5, or BY APPT. *Park:* In front. *Loc:* I-95 Exit 11.

PURPLE DOOR ANTIQUES
1975 Post Rd, 06820
(203)655-4742 **{GR4}**
18th & 19th C furniture, quilts, glass, porcelain, redware, stoneware, folk art, toys & more. *Hours:* Daily 10-5 Sun

11-4. *CC:* MC/V. Mary Stasik *Park:* On site. *Loc:* I-95 Exit 10: S on Noroton Ave to Post Rd, L & on L.

CATHERINE SYLVIA REISS
23 Tokeneke, 06820
(203)655-8070 **66**

Antique prints, national historic town views, American, illustrated. *Est:* 1977. *Serv:* Fine matting, framing. *Hours:* Mon-Sat 10:30-5:30. *CC:* MC/V. *Loc:* I-95 Exit 12.

ROSE D'OR
973 & 980 Boston Post Rd, 06820
(203)655-4668 **25 36 44**

Consignment of antiques, furniture, lamps, china, glass, Oriental art, paintings & bronzes. *Hours:* Mon-Sat 10-5 Sun 12-5. *Size:* Large. *Park:* On site. *Loc:* I-95 Exit 11N or 11S: near Darien RR.

WIND-BORNE FRAME & RESTORATION
559 Post Rd, 06820
(203)655-9735 **59 71**

Fine art gallery featuring 19th & early 20th C paintings & prints. Professional fine art conservation services performed by qualified experts. All media & art objects accepted. Antique frame restoration, fine custom framing. *Serv:* Conservation, frame repair, gold leafing, reproduction, restoration,framing. *Hours:* Tue-Sat 10-5. *Size:* Medium. *CC:* MC/V. R Blaikie Hines *Park:* On site. *Loc:* I-95 Exit 13: L off ramp onto Post Rd/Rte 1, 1 MI from Exit on R.

WINDSOR ANTIQUES LTD
1064 Post Rd, 06820
(203)655-2330 **37 63 78**

Large stock 18th & 19th C English & American furniture, Chinese export por-

La Calèche
— *Gallery of Fine French Antiques & Interior Design* —

From Parisian Elegance to Country Charm...
Simply the Finest French Antiques in Fairfield County
— Interior Design by Jani Caroli —

1089 Post Road
Darien, CT
(East of Exit 11, I-95)

203-655-3993

Mon– Sat 10 a.m.–5:30 p.m.
Sunday by appointment

celains, samplers, folk art, sporting art, paintings & fireplace equipment. *Est:* 1975. *Hours:* Mon-Sat 10:30-5, CLOSED AUG. David Kemp *Park:* On site. *Loc:* I-95 Exit 13 or 11.

DEBORAH WITHERSPOON
155 Old Kings Highway, 06820
(203)656-0127
Carrying furniture, paintings & decorative accessories. *Hours:* Tue-Sat 10-5 by chance/appt.

DEEP RIVER

JAS E ELLIOTT ANTIQUES
453 Winthrop Rd, 06417
(203)526-9455   **4 39 63**
Specializing in British pottery & porcelain of 18th & 19th C, Federal, Empire & Regency furniture, early ABC plates & mugs & other fine quality decorative accessories. *Pr:* $50–10000. *Est:* 1959. *Serv:* Appraisal, consultation, purchase estates. *Hours:* May-Dec Fri-Sat 12-5, else BY APPT. *Size:* Medium. *Assoc:* AADLA CINOA NEAA. *Shows:* ELLIS, PA, DC. *Park:* On site. *Loc:* I-95 Exit 64: Rte 80, Jct of 145.

W B GOTTLEIB - BOOKS
385 Winthrop Rd, 06417
(203)526-9462   **13**
Antiquarian books: modern first editions, poetry, travel, juveniles & theatre. *Hours:* Daily 12:30-5:30. *Size:* 3,000 books. *Assoc:* CAB. William B Gottleib *Loc:* On Rte 80.

RIVERWIND ANTIQUE SHOP
68 Main St Rte 154, 06417
(203)526-3047   **{GR20}**
Furniture, Oriental rugs, quilts, sterling, jewelry, primitives, linens, books & glass

in a restored 1860 house. *Pr:* $5–5000. *Est:* 1985. *Hours:* Wed-Sat 10:30-5 Sun 12-5 Mon-Tue by chance. *Size:* medium. *CC:* MC/V. Peggy Maraschiello *Park:* On site. *Loc:* I-95 Exit 69: to Rte 9, Exit 5 E to Rte 154 (Main St) to corner Spring St.

SARA SAMPSON ANTIQUES
15 Hemlock Terr Extension, 06417
(203)526-9168   **44 23 50**
Flow blue china & clocks & Sandwich glass overlay lamps. *Hours:* BY APPT. *Assoc:* CADA.

SECOND CHANCE ANTIQUES
87 Warsaw St, 06417
(203)526-4251   **36 44 63**
A large selection of quality furniture, country cupboards & accessories, antiques, glass, china, jewelry & collectibles. *Est:* 1989. *Hours:* Daily 10-5 or by appt. *CC:* MC/V. *Loc:* On Rte 80.

DON SLATER & SONS ANTIQUES
Rte 154 & Union St, 06417
(203)526-9757   **42**
An enormous selection of Irish country pine antiques & furnishings. *Hours:* Weekends 10-5 or by appt.

THE YELLOW VICTORIAN
116 N Main St, 06417
(203)526-2944   **85{GR3}**
A full line of vintage clothing, furniture, glass, jewelry & assorted collectibles. *Hours:* Mon-Tue 11-5, Wed-Sat 11-7, Sun 12-7. *Loc:* Rte 9 Exit 5: on Rte 154 (Main St).

DERBY

BOOKS BY THE FALLS
253 Roosevelt Dr Rte 34, 06418
(203)734-6112   **13 14**
Four rooms of antique & out-of-print books in an old red brick building by the waterfall including poetry, philosophy, classics, art, occult, horror & fantasy. *Est:* 1983. *Serv:* Appraisal, search service. *Hours:* Year round daily 10-5. *Size:* 25,000 books. *Assoc:* CAB. Ronald A Knox *Park:* In front. *Loc:* Rte 8 Exit 15: L thru town, 1 MI to old red brick factory by waterfall.

DURHAM

HODGE PODGE LODGE
265 Main St, 06422
(203)349-8015   **29 36**
Furniture & decorative accessories. *Hours:* By chance/appt. *Assoc:* CADA. George Gorton

EAST HADDAM

CONNECTICUT RIVER BOOKSHOP
Goodspeed Plaza, 06423
(203)873-8881   **4 13**
General out-of-print & rare books, specializing in nautical, hunting & fishing, New England, art & architecture, children's & Americana subjects. *Pr:* $10–500. *Est:* 1987. *Serv:* Nautical catalog, appraisal, search service. *Hours:* Thu-Sat 10:30-5 Sun 1-5 or by appt. *Size:* 25,000 books. *Assoc:* CAB. Frank Crohn *Park:* On site. *Loc:* I-95 Exit 69: Rte 9N to Exit 7 (E Haddam), located right in town.

HOWARD & DICKINSON
48-50 Main St, 06423
(203)873-9990   **59**
English & American antiques, accessories & paintings. *Hours:* Daily by chance/appt. *Loc:* I-95 Exit 7: to East Haddam.

MAGIC HORN LTD
95 Ray Hill Rd, 06423
(203)873-1346   **13 33**
Children's & illustrated, big little books, limited ephemera & general stock of antiquarian books. *Serv:* Limited search service. *Hours:* Sat-Sun 11-6 by chance/appt. Fred Miller

JIM MILLER ANTIQUES
Rte 82, 06423
(203)873-8286   **82 85**
Tribal jewelry & pottery from the Amazon jungle, deco furniture, lamps, American Indian artifacts, vintage clothing & antique jewelry. *Est:* 1948. *Hours:* Daily 11-6 Tue-Thu by chance. *Loc:* 2 MI from Goodspeed Opera House on the way to Gillette Castle.

OLD BANK HOUSE GALLERY
90 Main St, 06423
(203)873-8224   **60 66 78**
In a handsome 1820 bank overlooking the CT river, an extensive selection of antique & original prints, beautiful French matting & marbleized papers. Interesting collection of books & antiques provide pleasant browsing. *Pr:* $25–8000. *Est:* 1979. *Serv:* Custom framing, conservation, interior design. *Hours:* Everyday BY APPT. Winifred Rapp *Park:* On site. *Loc:* Rte 9 Exit 7: toward Goodspeed Opera House, located 1 MI N of Goodspeed on Rte 149.

EAST HAMPTON

BIBLIOLATREE
190 E High St Rte 66, 06424
(203)267-8222 **13**

Antiquarian books. *Hours:* Every after-noon after 1, including weekends. *Size:* 50,000 books. *Assoc:* CAB. Paul O Clark

CONNECTICUT YANKEE BOOKSHOP
95 Main St, 06424
(203)267-8865 **13**

General stock of antiquarian books. *Serv:* Search service. *Hours:* Wed-Sat 10-6, Sun 12-4. *Size:* 7,000 books. *Assoc:* CAB. Robert J Brooks

OLD BANK ANTIQUES
66 Main St, 06424
(203)267-0790 **{GR30}**

Furniture from every period attractively arranged & accented with glassware, Orientals, clocks, mirrors & a large selection of jewelry. *Pr:* $5–2500. *Est:* 1984. *Hours:* Wed-Sun 10-5 Thu 10-9. *Size:* Large. *CC:* AX/DC/MC/V. *Park:* Nearby lot. *Loc:* I-84 Exit 55: Rte 2, Exit 13, R onto Rte 66, L at 2nd light.

OPERA HOUSE ANTIQUES
95 Main St, 06424
(203)267-0014 **36 59 83**

Country & formal furniture, Victoriana, glassware, accessories, paintings, prints & collectibles. *Est:* 1986. *Serv:* Appraisal, auction, purchase estates. *Hours:* Wed-Sun 10-5. *Size:* Medium. *Park:* On site. *Loc:* From Hartford: Rte 2 Exit 13: R onto Rte 66, L at 3rd light.

PAST AND PRESENT
89 Main St, 06424
(203)267-0495 **47**

Antiques, jewelry, collectibles & quality used furniture. *Hours:* Wed-Sun 11-5 or BY APPT. Doreen Pierce *Park:* On site. *Loc:* 20 MI S of Hartford.

MARTIN ROENIGK
26 Barton Hill, 06424
(203)267-8682 **55**

Specializing in antique mechanical music, disc & cylinder music boxes, band organs, organettes, some phonographs, coin pianos, mechanical birds - always something interesting. *Pr:* $5–20000. *Serv:* Appraisal, repairs, buying & selling. *Hours:* BY APPT ONLY. *Size:* Medium. *Park:* On site. *Loc:* Call for directions.

EAST LYME

STEPHEN & CAROL HUBER INC
82 Plants Dam Rd, 06333
(203)739-0772 **34 41 57**

Needlework specialists covering English & American 17th-19th C. Samplers, silk embroideries, tent stitch pictures, bedcovers, domestic handwoven fabrics always in stock. American painted furniture 17th-19th C & appropriate accessories. *Pr:* $25–200000. *Serv:* Appraisal, conservation, consultation, interior design. *Hours:* Appt suggested. *Size:* Large. *Loc:* Please call for directions & appt.

EAST NORWALK

THE CLOCKERY
14 Van Zant St, 06855
(203)838-1789 **23 68 71**
Antique clock specialists with 100 clocks on display in the showroom. *Pr:* $100–8000. *Est:* 1973. *Serv:* Repair, restoration. *Hours:* Tue-Sat 10-4:30. *CC:* MC/V. *Assoc:* AWI BHI NAWCC. Floyd Taylor *Park:* On site. *Loc:* I-95 Exit 16: to Rte 136, 1/2 MI S.

EASTON

RED SLEIGH
1093 Black Rock Tnpk, 06612
(203)268-2783 **34 42 65**
Affordable country pine, primitives, folk art & interesting smalls. *Pr:* $10–1500. *Serv:* Consultation, purchase estates, repairs, restoration. *Hours:* By chance/appt. *Size:* Large. *Assoc:* CADA. William Pirozzoli *Park:* On site. *Loc:* Merritt Parkway.

ELLINGTON

PINNEY STREET ANTIQUES
50 Pinney St, 06029
(203)871-1406 **{GR}**
A multi-dealer shop in a restored 1830 homestead with oak, pine & mahogany furniture, wicker furniture, Amish quilts, jewelry, books & glassware. *Est:* 1990. *Hours:* Daily 10-5 Sun 12-5 Thu til 8 CLOSED TUE-WED. *Loc:* Close to Rtes 190 & 20.

ENFIELD

ENCORE CONSIGNMENT
150 Enfield St, 06082
(203)741-6685 **25 29 36**
One of area's largest consignment stores featuring furnishings, antiques & collectibles. Antique dealer booths also on premises. Thousands of items. *Pr:* $25–2500. *Est:* 1989. *Serv:* Consignment, purchase estates. *Hours:* Tue 12-4 Wed-Sat 10-5. *Size:* Large. Robert Milner *Park:* On site. *Loc:* I-91 Exit 49: 200 yards S.

ESSEX

ARNE E AHLBERG
Rte 153, 06426
(203)767-2799 **37**
18th & early 19th C antique American country & formal furniture & decorative accessories. *Hours:* Wed-Sat 11-5. *Park:* In front.

A MATHEWS ANDERSON ANTIQUES
2 Captains Walk, 06426
(203)767-1214 **21 27 44**
An antique barn with 3 floors of country furniture, Oriental rugs, flint glass & collectibles. Herb garden, herbs & dried arrangements. *Est:* 1986. *Serv:* Brochure. *Hours:* Apr-Dec Wed-Sun, Jan-Mar BY APPT. *Size:* Medium. *Park:* On site. *Loc:* I-95S Exit 68 (Essex/Hartford): Rte 9, Exit 3, R 1/2 MI on Rte 154, on corner of Rte 154 & Captains Walk.

PATRICIA & KEITH BARGER
59A Main St, 06426
(203)372-2536   **21 37 39**

18th & 19th C American & English furniture & antique tall case clocks. *Hours:* Wed-Sun 11-5 or by appt.

FRANCIS BEALEY AMERICAN ARTS
3 S Main St, 06426
(203)767-0220   **1 37 59**

Fine period American furniture of the 18th & early 19th C, American Impressionist paintings - fireplace furnishings a specialty. *Pr:* $1000–100000. *Serv:* Consultation. *Hours:* Sep 15-Jun 30 Mon-Sat 11-4, else Mon-Fri 11-4. *Size:* Medium. *Park:* Nearby lot. *Loc:* 4 MI N of I-95, from the W: Exit 65 (Rte 153), from the E: Exit 69 (Rte 9 to Exit 3).

BONSAL-DOUGLAS ANTIQUES
2 Essex Sq, 06426
(203)345-3914 FAX
(203)767-3240   **38 56 59**

Marine paintings, early European furniture, period accessories in historic town of Essex. Sherry often served in the late afternoon. *Serv:* Conservation, interior design, consultation, select estate purchases. *Hours:* Tue-Sat 11-5. Isabelle D Seggerman *Park:* On site. *Loc:* I-95 Exit 69: Rte 9, Exit 3 (Essex) which is Rte 154, follow signs & rd directly into Main St Essex.

ESSEX ANTIQUES CENTER
8 Main St, 06426
(203)767-1291   **{GR22}**

In an historic 1800 Colonial in the village center, 18th & 19th C American & English furniture, 19th & 20th C paintings & prints, white Ironstone & Staffordshire, 19th C lighting including Oriental porcelain, Sandwich Glass, Art Glass, silver, porcelain. *Hours:* Daily 11- 5 Sun 12-5. *CC:* MC/V. *Park:* Private parking. *Loc:* In the ctr of Main St in a white colonial.

ESSEX AUCTION & APPRAISAL
PO Box 27, 06426
(203)767-1204   **4 8 25**

Liquidators of estate & household contents, commercial & residential, single pieces or entire contents, direct purchases or consignment. *Serv:* Appraisal, accept mail/phone bids, mailing list. *Hours:* BY APPT. *Assoc:* ASA ISA. *Loc:* Call for directions.

ESSEX COLONY ANTIQUES
Rte 153 & Ingham Hill Rd, 06426
(203)767-1156   **{GR10}**

A twelve room restored 1792 red colonial with country & formal furniture & accessories, a fine arts gallery & antique Oriental rugs. *Est:* 1986. *Serv:* Purchase estates. *Hours:* Daily 10:30-5:00. *CC:* AX/MC/V. Frank Coulom *Park:* On site. *Loc:* I-95 Exit 65N: 3 MI.

THE ESSEX FORGE
Old Dennison Rd, 06426
(203)767-1808   **2 50 70**

Reproduction chandeliers, indoor lighting, sconces, fireplace equipment, lanterns & standing lamps. *Est:* 1969. *Hours:* Mon-Sat 10-5. *CC:* MC/V. Wallace Lawder *Park:* On site. *Loc:* 1st door on L on North Main St.

HASTINGS HOUSE
Box 606, 06426
(203)767-8217   **45 60 80**

Textiles, objets d'art, European & Oriental antiques, Japanese scrolls & screens, unusual 19th C garden furniture & statuary. *Est:* 1968. *Serv:* Purchase estates. *Hours:* BY APPT ONLY. *Assoc:* AADLA. *Shows:* WAS. Philip H McNemer *Loc:* Call for Appt.

VALLEY FARM ANTIQUES
134 Saybrook Rd, 06426
(203)767-8555   **6 16 63**

Furniture, guns, pewter, jewelry, china & glass. *Est:* 1960. *Serv:* Appraisal, consultation, purchase estates. *Hours:* Tue-Sat 10-4. Ellsworth E Stevison *Park:* Nearby. *Loc:* 2 min off I-95.

WHITE FARMS ANTIQUES
2 Essex Sq, 06426
(203)767-1876   **37**

Specializing in 18th & 19th C American country furniture & accessories. *Est:* 1985. *Hours:* Tue-Sat 10-5. Dan Stix *Park:* Nearby. *Loc:* In the center of town.

FAIRFIELD

JAMES BOK ANTIQUES
1954 Post Rd, 06430
(203)255-6500   **16 29 36**

Period furniture, early brass & accessories. *Hours:* By chance/appt. *Assoc:* NHADA. *Loc:* On US Rte 1.

CONNECTICUT BOOK AUCTION GALLERY
251 Carroll Rd, 06430
(203)259-1997   **8 13 51**

Three scheduled book auctions annually of used & rare books, maps, photographs & ephemera from estates & collections. No buyers' premium, no reserves & no bidding by consignors. *Est:* 1976. *Serv:* Appraisal, accept mail/phone bids, catalog, purchase estates. *Hours:* BY APPT ONLY. Y J Skutel *Park:* On site. *Loc:* Easy access from the RR station & I-95 in the center of Fairfield.

ENSINGER ANTIQUES LTD
3921 Park Ave, 06432
(203)374-1586   **36 63**

Specializing in Chinese export porcelain & period furniture. *Hours:* Sum BY APPT ONLY. Gail Ensinger

PATTY GAGARIN ANTIQUES
975 Banks North Rd, 06430
(203)259-7332   **21 29 41**

Fine American painted furniture, weather vanes, rugs & accessories. *Hours:* BY APPT ONLY. *Loc:* 10 min from Merrit Pkwy or I-95.

JOSKO & SONS AUCTIONS
407 Meadowbrook Rd, 06430
(203)255-1441   **8**

Periodic auctions of antiques & collectibles from area homes. *Serv:* Auctioneer. *Assoc:* NEAA. William J Josko

A LUCAS BOOKS
89 Round Hill Rd, 06430
(203)259-2572   **13**

19th & 20th C first editions. *Serv:* Appraisal, search service. *Hours:* Please phone first. *Size:* 13,000 books. *Assoc:* CAB. Alexander Lucas

MUSEUM GALLERY BOOK SHOP
360 Mine Hill Rd, 06430
(203)259-7114   **13 14**

Specializing in books on the fine arts. *Hours:* BY APPT. *Size:* 17,000 books. *Assoc:* CAB. Henry B Caldwell

LLOYD RALSTON GALLERY
173 Post Rd, 06430
(203)255-1233   **1 8 32**

One of New England's largest toy & train galleries, including mechanical & still banks, cast iron, comic tin, tin cars, Schoenhut circus, games, dolls, Disneyana, trains & accessories, Americana, fire collectibles, lamps, arcade machines & more. *Serv:* Appraisal, auction, catalog($18). *Hours:* Mon-Sat 10-4, Sun BY APPT. *Size:* Medium. *Park:* On site. *Loc:* I-95 Exit 23, 1/2 MI to Post Rd.

WINSOR ANTIQUES
43 Ruane St, 06430
(203)255-0056 **35 39**
Specializing in English & French country furniture & English Windsor chairs, furnishings from the 17th to late 19th C & a large selection of decorative accessories. *Pr:* $25–20000. *Est:* 1983. *Hours:* Year round Tue-Sat 10-5. *Size:* Large. *CC:* MC/V. *Assoc:* CADA. Paul Winsor *Park:* On site. *Loc:* I-95 Exit 21 (Mill Plain Rd): S to Jct Rte 1, L on Post Rd to 1st light, R on Ruane St, 1st bldg on L.

FALLS VILLAGE

R & D EMERSON, BOOKSELLERS
103 Main St, 06031
(203)824-0442 **13**
In an old church: antiquarian & rare books. *Hours:* Thu-Mon 12-5 CLOSED Tue-Wed. *Size:* Large. *CC:* MC/V. *Assoc:* ABAA CAB. Robert C Emerson *Park:* In front.

FARMINGTON

LILLIAN BLANKLEY COGAN ANTIQUARY
22 High St, 06032
(203)677-9259 **37**
Specialist in 17th & 18th C original New England furniture & the appropriate accessories - nothing post-revolutionary. *Est:* 1928. *Hours:* BY APPT ONLY. *Assoc:* AADLA. *Shows:* WAS. *Loc:* Situated at "Hearts & Crowns".

FARMINGTON ANTIQUES WEEKEND
Farmington Polo Grounds, 06032
(603)363-4515
600 exhibitors many under tents in a polo field in the middle of CT held in June & September. Admission is $3 for adults, early admission at 7am on Saturday is $10. *Est:* 1980. *Serv:* Free parking. *Hours:* Jun 8-9 & Aug 31-Sep 1, 1991 Sat 10-6 Sun 9-4. Don Mackay *Park:* Free. *Loc:* I-84 Exit 39: 9 MI W of Hartford.

GOLDEN SALES & AUCTIONS
PO Box 1321, 06034
(203)676-9178 **8**
Auctions consisting of a variety of antiques & collectibles, services include estate & consignment auctions. *Serv:* Appraisal, accept mail & phone bids, consultation, purchase estates. *Hours:* BY APPT ONLY. *Size:* Medium. *CC:* MC/V. *Assoc:* NAA. Robert Jacques *Park:* On site. *Loc:* I-84 Exit 34: Crooked St Exit to Woodford Ave.

GAYLORDSVILLE

BITTERSWEET SHOP
Rtes 7 & 55, 06755
(203)354-1727 **{GR14}**
Formal & country furniture, 18th C English furniture, Quilts, paintings, baskets, tools. *Est:* 1978. *Hours:* Apr-Dec daily 10-5, Sun 12-5 CLOSED WED. *CC:* MC/V. Mark Estabrooks *Park:* On site. *Loc:* 40 min N of Danbury on Rte 7.

MICHAEL HALL ANTIQUES
Kent Rd Rte 7, 06755
(203)355-4750 **50 60 80**
American & European furniture, pottery, porcelain, glassware, textiles, linens,

lighting fixtures, chandeliers & Oriental works-of-art. *Hours:* By chance/appt. *Park:* On site. *Loc:* From Gaylordsville Iron Bridge, on Rte 7 less than 1/4 MI on Housatonic River side, travelling N.

GLASTONBURY

MAURER & SHEPHERD, JOYNERS
122 Naubuc Ave, 06033
(203)633-2383   **70 74**

Reproduction of authentic 17th & 18th C Colonial joinery - windows, door frames & columns. *Est:* 1976. *Serv:* Consultation, reproduction. *Hours:* Mon-Fri 8:30-5:30. Hap Shepherd *Loc:* 5 min outside of Hartford, off Rte 2.

MARY S SWIFT ANTIQUES
1401 Main St, 06033
(203)633-2112   **30 34 36**

A small friendly shop next to an 18th C house, with country furniture, hooked rugs, quilts, decoys & unusual accessories. *Pr:* $25–2000. *Est:* 1972. *Serv:* Appraisal. *Hours:* Daily by chance/appt. *Size:* Medium. *Park:* On site. *Loc:* Main St is Rte 17 in Glastonbury.

ROY & BETSY THOMPSON ANTIQUES
1224 Main St, 06033
(203)659-3695   **1 36**

Specializing in 17th & 18th C New England furniture & decorative accessories & 19th C American paintings. *Est:* 1968. *Serv:* Appraisal, consultation. *Hours:* BY APPT. *Assoc:* ADA. *Park:* On site. *Loc:* From Hartford: Rte 2E Exit 7: follow S Glastonbury signs approx 3 MI on L.

GRANBY

FIN N' FEATHER GALLERY
36 Lakeside Dr, 06035
(203)653-6557   **13**

Antiquarian books specializing in hunting & fishing with some related natural history. *Serv:* Catalogs, search service. *Hours:* BY APPT ONLY. Barry Small

GRANBY ANTIQUES EMPORIUM
381 Salmon Brook, 06035
(203)653-2355   **{GR20}**

Multi-dealer shop offering antiques & collectibles in an 1840 colonial including a wide selection of tools, toys, linens, glass, prints, primitives, pine, mahogany, oak & country furniture. *Pr:* $10–3000. *Est:* 1980. *Hours:* Year round daily 12-5, Sat-Sun 10-5. *Size:* Medium. *CC:* MC/V. Vern Thompson *Park:* On site. *Loc:* On Rte 10-202, 1 MI N of Granby Ctr.

WILLIAM & LOIS M PINKNEY
240 N Granby Rd, 06035
(203)653-7710   **13 66**

Antiquarian books: Western Americana, New England, New York, limited editions club, first editions, children's books, cookbooks, natural history, hunting & fishing, sheet music, prints, literary biography & criticism. *Serv:* Appraisal, search service. *Hours:* Mon-Fri 9-5, call ahead on weekends. *Size:* 12,000 books. *Assoc:* ABAA CAB.

GREENWICH

AMERICAN TRADITION GALLERY
335 Greenwich Ave 2nd fl, 06830
(203)869-8897 **59**
Specializing in American painters 1830-1930, especially Connecticut artists.
Serv: Appraisal. *Hours:* Sum: Tue-Fri 11-4 or BY APPT.

ANTAN ANTIQUES LTD
12 W Putnam Ave, 06830
(203)661-4769 **29 35 59**
French & English 18th & 19th C decorative accessories & furniture. *Est:* 1978. *Hours:* Mon-Sat 10:30-5. *CC:* AX/MC/V. Monique Olmer *Park:* On street. *Loc:* Corner of Greenwich Ave.

ANTIQUES & INTERIORS AT THE MILL
334 Pemberwick Rd, 06831
(203)531-8118 **29 36**
A beautiful collection of 18th & 19th C antique furniture & accessories in the railroad building of a restored mill. *Pr:* $20-6000. *Est:* 1985. *Serv:* Appraisal, consultation, interior design. *Hours:* Jan 2-Dec 25 Tue-Sat 10:30-5 & BY APPT. *Size:* Medium. *CC:* MC/V. Doris W Ross *Park:* On site. *Loc:* Merritt Pkwy King St Exit: (from S:R, from N:L) on King, at 2nd light, L on Glenville, 1st R after Fire Station.

BETTERIDGE JEWELERS INC
117 Greenwich Ave, 06830
(203)869-0124 **4 47**
From pre-Columbian to Tiffany: Carefully chosen antique & estate jewelry for the serious collector. *Serv:* Appraisal. *Hours:* Tue-Sat 9-5. *Assoc:* AAA. Albert E Betteridge III *Loc:* Off Post Rd, 2 blocks down on the L.

CHELSEA ANTIQUES OF GREENWICH
14 W Putnam Ave, 06830
(203)629-2224 **4 24 63**
Four showrooms of English & American furniture, Persian rugs, sterling silver, English & Continental porcelain, crystal, bronze, Oriental porcelain, art & print section 18th & 19th C works, jewelry, gold & silver coins. *Pr:* $15-15000. *Est:* 1949. *Serv:* Appraisal. *Hours:* Year round Mon-Sat 10:30-5. *Size:* Medium. *Assoc:* NEAA. *Park:* Nearby lot. *Loc:* On Boston Post Road in central Greenwich opposite "Greenwich Chateau" the highest building in town.

CONSIGNMENTS ETC
283 Greenwich Ave, 06830
(203)661-7370 **25**
Formal & period furniture & decorative accessories including English, French, tables, sideboards, wing chairs, desks, breakfronts, Oriental porcelains, silver, china, chandeliers, lamps, mirrors & linens. *Hours:* Mon-Sat 10:30-5:30. *Loc:* I-95 S Exit 3 (Arch St): L off exit, Greenwich St is approx 2 blocks down on Arch.

ESTATE TREASURES OF GREENWICH
1162 E Putnam Ave, 06878
(203)637-4200 **25 39 47**
A large, quality consignment shop of antiques, furniture, china, sterling, glassware & estate jewelry, specializing in beautiful 19th C English furniture in mahogany or country pine. *Est:* 1978. *Hours:* Mon-Sat 10-5:30 Sun 12-5. *CC:* MC/V. *Assoc:* CADA. Lillian London *Park:* In front. *Loc:* I-95 Exit 5: L 1/2 block.

GREENWICH GALL OF AMERICAN ART
6 W Putnam Ave, 06830
(203)622-4494   **59**
Fine quality investment paintings of the 19th to 20th C, both American & European. *Pr:* $1000–20000. *Serv:* Appraisal, conservation, consultation, repairs, restoration. *Hours:* Tue-Sat 10-5. Abby M Taylor *Park:* In front, nearby lot. *Loc:* I-95 Exit 3: follow signs to bus district, 1st bldg at the head of Greenwich Ave.

RENE GROSJEAN ANTIQUES
51 Greenwich Ave, 06830
(203)869-7114   **23 47**
Antique & estate jewelry & watches. *Est:* 1943. *Serv:* Restoration, repair. *Hours:* Tue-Sat 9:30-5. *Park:* In front. *Loc:* 1 block from Post Rd.

GUILD ANTIQUES
384 Greenwich Ave, 06830
(203)869-0828   **29 37 39**
English & American furniture, Chinese export porcelain & decorative accessories. *Hours:* Mon-Sat 10-5. *CC:* MC/V. George Rich *Park:* In front. *Loc:* 2 MI from Exit 3, NY Thruway.

HALLOWELL & CO
340 W Putnam Ave, 06830
(203)869-2190   **6 72 78**
Fine vintage sporting & collector firearms. *Pr:* $500–50000. *Serv:* Appraisal, catalog, purchase estates. *Hours:* Mon-Sat 10-6. *Size:* Medium. *CC:* AX/MC/V. Morris L Hallowell *Park:* In front. *Loc:* West Putnam Ave is US Rte 1.

HENRI-BURTON FRENCH ANTIQUES
382 Greenwich Ave, 06830
(203)661-8529   **35**
Quality 18th & 19th C French furniture & accessories from country to formal; armoires, commodes, tables, chairs, Quimper, faience, lamps & decorative objects. *Est:* 1987. *Hours:* Mon-Sat 10-5. *Size:* Large. *CC:* MC/V. *Park:* On street. *Loc:* I-95 Exit 3: (from NYC: L, from New Haven: R), follow to Greenwich Ave turn R, located at the foot of Greenwich Ave.

LIBERTY WAY ANTIQUES
One Liberty Wy, 06830
(203)661-6417   **29 36 44**
Furniture, art, decorative accessories & early American pattern glass. *Est:* 1987. *Serv:* Appraisal. *Hours:* Mon-Sat 10-5:30. *CC:* AX/MC/V. Joy Shannon *Park:* On site. *Loc:* I-95 Exit 3: follow Arch St N, cross Greenwich Ave, L to Mason St, L on Elm St, 2nd parking lot drive.

PROVINCES DE FRANCE
22 W Putnam Ave, 06830
(203)629-9798   **35 59**
Fine French 18th & 19th C antiques - a large selection of provincial & country furniture, faience & accessories, fine paintings, watercolors & prints. *Hours:* Mon-Sat 10-5:30, CLOSED SUN. *Size:* Medium. *CC:* AX/MC/V. Jenny Kechejian *Park:* In front. *Loc:* I-95 Exit 3: 1/2 block from Greenwich Ave, on Rte 1.

DONALD RICH ANTIQUES
360 West Putnam Ave, 06830
(203)661-6470   **29 37 39**
18th & 19th C formal English & American furniture & decorative accessories. *Est:* 1990. *Serv:* Retail & Trade. *Hours:* Tue-Sat 10-5 by chance or appt. *Park:* Ample parking. *Loc:* At Lamp Post common.

SCHUTZ & COMPANY
Dewart Rd, 06830
(203)629-3387 **4**
Appraisal of 19th & 20th C American & European painting & sculpture. **Hours:** BY APPT ONLY. **Assoc:** AAA. Herbert Schutz

SOPHIA'S GREAT DAMES
One Liberty Wy, 06830
(203)869-5990 **47 80 85**
Quality antique clothing & period accessories from the 1880s-1950s, nostalgia & collectibles, specializing in costume jewelry, Victorian wedding gowns; quality costume rental. **Est:** 1981. **Hours:** Mon-Sat 10-5:30. **Size:** Medium. **CC:** AX/MC/V. Sophia Scarpelli **Park:** On site. **Loc:** 1 MI off I-95.

VINTAGE LADIES
71 Church St, 06830
(203)661-6546 **3 36 80**
Collectibles from pillows to posts, preferably old, painted & whimsical. **Pr:** $25–5000. **Est:** 1976. **Serv:** Consultation, custom woodwork, purchase estates, repairs, restoration. **Hours:** Sep-May Mon-Fri 11-5, Jun-Aug Mon-Fri 10-5, Sat 10-1. **CC:** MC/V. **Park:** In front. **Loc:** Exit 95 at Greenwich, R on Railroad Ave, L on Mason St to E Putnam Ave, cross Putnam & you are on Church St.

GUILFORD

A SUMMER PLACE
37 Boston St, 06437
(203)453-5153 **29 67 86**
A large selection of fine antique wicker, quilts & small antiques with a from the sea motif. **Serv:** Interior design. **Hours:** By chance/appt. **CC:** No. Mary Jean Mc-

Laughlin. **Park:** On site. **Loc:** E of New Haven take Exit 58 from Rt 95, then go S a few blocks to the GuilfordGreen.

ARNE E AHLBERG
1090 Boston Post Rd, 06437
(203)453-9022 **1 37**
18th & early 19th C antique American country & Formal furniture & decorative accessories. **Serv:** Appraisal. **Hours:** Sat 10-5, Weekdays by chance/appt.

CORNUCOPIA ANTIQUE CONSIGNMENTS
1058 Boston Post Rd, 06437
(203)453-8677 **25 47 80**
Two floors of furniture, china, glass, silver, paintings, jewelry & textiles. **Est:** 1985. **Serv:** Interior design. **Hours:** Jun-Dec Tue-Sat 10-5 Sun 11-3, Jan-May CLOSED SUN. **Size:** Medium. **CC:** MC/V. **Park:** On site. **Loc:** I-95 Exit 58: Rte 77, turn toward Guilford, at traffic light turn R, 3rd bldg on L, red carriage.

LAMB HOUSE FINE BOOKS
21 Boston St, 06437
(203)453-8803 **13**
Select out-of-print titles of 20th C literature, New England history, Americana, decorative arts, architecture, antiques, travel & exploration, gardening & children's literature for the collector. **Hours:** Tue-Sat 10-5 Sum: also Sun 12-5. **Assoc:** CAB. Lory McCaskey **Loc:** On-the-Green.

HADLYME

BUSINESS IN THE BARN
32 Town St Rte 82, 06439
(203)526-3770 **27 38 40**
Large showrooms of American painted country, English country oak & formal

Continental furniture. Custom lamps & tray tables a specialty. *Hours:* Fri-Sat 11-5, Sun 12-5.

FULTON'S FOLLY
Ferry Rd, 06439
(203)526-9025

18th & 19th C furniture & accessories. *Hours:* BY APPT. *Assoc:* CADA.

HAMDEN

AMERICAN WORLDS BOOKS
PO Box 6305 Whitneyville Station, 06517
(203)776-3558   **13**

Antiquarian books: American literature, scholarly studies of American authors, American cultural history & business history. *Serv:* Catalogs, appraisal, search service. *Hours:* BY APPT ONLY. *Size:* 9,000 books. *Assoc:* CAB. Nolan E Smith

ANTIQUE BOOKS
3651 Whitney Ave Rte 10, 06518
(203)281-6606   **13**

Antiquarian books in 3 buildings emphasizing early Americana in all fields except poetry & fiction with specialties in history, Civil War, early schoolbooks, science. *Pr:* $10–300. *Serv:* Catalog, appraisal. *Hours:* By chance/appt suggested. *Size:* 30,000 books. *Assoc:* CAB. Willis O Underwood *Park:* On site. *Loc:* I-91 Exit 10: Rte 10 (Whitney Ave), R after the 4th light.

BOOKCELL BOOKS
90 Robinwood Rd, 06517
(203)248-0010   **13**

Antiquarian books: the sciences, technology, China & Japan. *Serv:* Catalogs,

appraisal, search service. *Hours:* BY APPT ONLY. *Size:* 8,000 books. *Assoc:* CAB. Dorothy Kuslan

GALLERY 4
Mt Carmel Center 2985 Whitney, 06518
(203)281-6043   **44 48 77**

Antiques, silver, cut glass, Limoges, linens, books, trade cards, china, pattern glass, quilts, fine art, Eskimo, American Indian, Oriental art. *Est:* 1976. *Hours:* Mon-Sat 10-6. *CC:* MC/V. *Loc:* I-95 Exit 10: 200 yds N on R.

MC BLAIN BOOKS
2348 Whitney Ave, 06518
(203)281-0400   **13**

A general line of antiquarian books including those on Africa, Asia, the Pacific, Black America, Latin America, the Middle East, Russia & Eastern Europe. *Serv:* Catalogs. *Hours:* BY APPT ONLY. *Size:* 10,000 books. *Assoc:* ABAA CAB. Philip & Sharon Mc Blain *Park:* On site. *Loc:* 2 blocks off Wilbur Cross Parkway.

HARTFORD

BACON ANTIQUES
95 Maple Ave, 06114
(203)524-0040   **36 44 63**

Furniture, decorative accessories, glass & china. *Est:* 1947. *Serv:* Appraisal, purchase estates. *Hours:* Mon-Sat 9-5. *CC:* MC/V. *Park:* On street. *Loc:* 100 yds from Main St.

THE JUMPING FROG
161 S Whitney St, 06105
(203)523-1622   **13**

Antiquarian books: modern first editions, military history, biography, literary criticism, autographed books, illustrated, science fiction, mysteries, drama, music, sports, Norman Rockwell covers & advertisements. *Est:* 1983. *Serv:* Appraisal, catalog ($1), purchase estates. *Hours:* Wed-Sat 12-6 Thu til 9 Sun 1-6, else by chance/appt. *Size:* 17,000 books. *Assoc:* CAB. Bill McBride *Park:* In front. *Loc:* I-84 Exit 46: R at 2nd Light, 1/2 block on L.

HARWINTON

JOHN M DAVIS INC
PO Box 262, 06791
(203)485-9182 **37 39 60**
English & American furniture, accessories & Chinese export porcelain. *Est:* 1973. *Serv:* Appraisal, conservation, purchase estates, interior design. *Hours:* BY APPT ONLY. *Loc:* 10 min E of Litchfield.

RYAN'S ANTIQUES
8 Burlington Rd Rte 4, 06791
(203)485-9600 **27 81**
Tools, kitchen items, large variety of antiques & collectibles & country furniture. *Hours:* Sum: daily by chance/appt. *Loc:* Rte 8 Exit 42: E 3 MI on Rte 4.

HEBRON

DAVID & DALE BLAND ANTIQUES
124 Slocum Rd, 06248
(203)228-3514 **36**
Specializing in 18th C furniture. *Hours:* Fri-Sat by chance or appt.

HEBRON VILLAGE ANTIQUES
105 Main St Rte 66, 06248
(203)228-1876 **27 29 36**
Featuring country & formal furniture & decorative accessories. *Est:* 1989. *Hours:*

Thu-Sun 10-5. *Assoc:* NEAA. Raymond Laskey Paul Pomprowicz *Loc:* Rte 2 Exit 13: to Hebron Ctr, on the L.

HIGGANUM

NEVER SAY GOODBYE
658 Killingworth Rd, 06441
(203)345-4854 **85**
Collectibles, curiosities, vintage clothing & accessories. *Hours:* Wed-Fri 11-4, Sat-Sun 11-6. Faith Zila *Loc:* Rte 9 Exit 9: R at end of exit, approx 1 MI on L.

IVORYTON

COMSTOCK HSE ANTIQUE RESTORATION
28 Comstock Ave, 06442
(203)767-2211 **68 69 71**
Conservation of fine antique furniture. *Serv:* Conservation, repairs, restoration. *Hours:* BY APPT ONLY. *Assoc:* NEAA. Timothy D Robin *Park:* On site.

JEWETT CITY

COLLEGE MART
Wedgewood Dr, 06351
(203)642-6248 **{FLEA}**
Indoor/outdoor flea market with antiques & collectibles & other flea market merchandise. *Hours:* Every Sun 9-4. *Size:* 150 spaces.

JEWETT CITY EMPORIUM
124 N Main St Rte 12, 06351
(203)376-9808 **{GR20}**
Antiques, collectibles, estate jewelry,

diamonds, coins, furniture, linens & old lace. *Est:* 1983. *Serv:* Appraisal. *Hours:* Wed-Sun 10-5. *Size:* Large. *CC:* MC/V. Deanna Denis *Loc:* I-395 Exit 84: 1 1/2 MI on Rte 12.

PACHAUG FLEA MARKET
Rte 138, 06351
(203)376-3102   {FLEA}

Indoor/outdoor flea market with antiques & collectibles. *Serv:* Space rental is $15. *Hours:* May-Oct Sun 9-4. *Size:* 50 Dealers. Deanna & John Denis *Loc:* I-395 Exit 85 Pachaug Grange On Route 138.

WALTON ANTIQUES INC
Box 307, 06351
(203)376-0862   1 37

Specializing in American antiques of the 17th-early 19th century. *Serv:* Written guarantee, buy back policy, purchasing. *Hours:* Mon-Sat BY APPT ONLY.

KENT

AN AMERICAN GALLERY
31 S Main St, 06757
(203)927-3243   1 34 59

Specializing in American paintings, furniture & folk art. *Est:* 1990. *Hours:* Fri-Sat 11-5:30 Sun 12-5 or by appt. Frederic I Thaler *Loc:* Across from the Kent Greenhouse.

THE COMPANY STORE
Rte 7 N, 06757
(203)927-3430   34 39 65

A selection ranging from primitive to formal furniture, original painted grain pieces, folk art, paintings, clocks, decoys, radios silver tools accessories. *Est:* 1989.

Serv: Restoration. *Hours:* Tue-Sat 10-5 by chance/appt. *Loc:* Opposite Sloane-Stanley Museum.

THE FORRERS
92 N Main St Rte 7, 06757
(203)927-3612   27 32 81

Early American country & formal furniture, accessories, early glass, toys, banks, tools, folk art & Staffordshire china. *Est:* 1959. *Serv:* Purchase estates. *Hours:* Daily 9-5 by chance/appt. *Size:* Medium. *CC:* AX/MC/V. Vivian G Forrer *Park:* On site. *Loc:* Rte 7, 35 MI N of Danbury.

GOLDEN THISTLE ANTIQUES
Rte 7, 06757
(203)927-3790   37 38 63

American & European furniture, porcelain & glass. *Est:* 1967. *Hours:* Fri-Mon 11-5, else BY APPT. *Park:* Nearby. *Loc:* Ctr of town.

KENT ANTIQUES CENTER
Kent Station Sq Main St, 06757
(203)927-3313   {GR8}

Quality country antiques, accessories & collectibles from the 18th-20th C located in a restored 150 year-old farmhouse. Featuring English silver, men's wrist watches, early tools, paintings/prints, toys, quilts & early glass. *Hours:* Daily 11-5 CLOSED THU. *CC:* MC/V. *Loc:* On Rte 7 behind the RR station, N of the monument.

ELIZABETH S MANKIN ANTIQUES
Rte 341 E, 06757
(203)927-3288   37 59 63

American formal & country period furniture, paintings, accessories & English ceramics. *Est:* 1953. *Hours:* Mon-Sat 10:30-5. *Assoc:* NHADA. Elizabeth S Mankin *Park:* On site. *Loc:* Approx 2 MI from traffic light in Kent.

MAVIS
Rte 7 N, 06757
(203)927-4334　　　　　　**29 44 48**

Spacious shop with general line of antiques & collectibles including glass, china, linens, jewelry & kitchenware, stencilled furniture with complementary decorative accessories; also a B & B. *Est:* 1973. *Hours:* Mon-Sat 11-6 Sun 12:30-6:30. *CC:* MC/V. Mavis L Scholl *Park:* On site. *Loc:* 3 MI N of town or 3 MI S of Kent Falls.

OLDE STATION ANTIQUES
Main St Rte 7, 06757
(203)927-4493　　　　　　**29 36**

American, French & English fine antiques & reproductions. *Serv:* Interior design, restoration. *Hours:* Daily 10-5 CLOSED MON. *CC:* MC/V. Gene Stillwagon *Park:* On site. *Loc:* N of the ctr of town.

PAULINE'S PLACE
Main St Rte 7, 06757
(203)927-4475　　　　　　**47**

A collection of Victorian, Georgian, Art Deco & Contemporary jewelry in 14K, 18K & 21K gold. Precious stones, enamel & gold. *Est:* 1978. *Serv:* Antique jewelry & watch repair. *Hours:* May-Dec 12-5 CLOSED WED Jan-Apr Fri-Mon 12-5 CLOSED TUE-THU. *CC:* AX/MC/V. *Park:* In front. *Loc:* Approx 1/4 MI N of Main St monument.

TERSTON & CO
Kent Green, 06757
(203)927-4774　　　　　　**42**

Specializing in English pine antiques & decorator fabrics. *Hours:* Tue-Sat 10-5 by chance or appt.

KILLINGWORTH

THE BERGERON'S ANTIQUES
294 Rte 81, 06417
(203)663-2122　　　　　　**38 40 42**

Furniture: including English oak pub tables, Continental armoires & American. *Pr:* $25–5000. *Est:* 1972. *Serv:* Purchase estates, repairs, restoration. *Hours:* By Chance/Appt. *Size:* Large. *CC:* MC/V. *Assoc:* CADA. Rebecca Bergeron *Park:* On Site.

LEWIS W SCRANTON ANTIQUES
224 Roast Meat Hill, 06417
(203)663-1060　　　　　　**16 28 41**

Specializing in early American painted furniture in as-found condition, New England slipware, redware, stoneware & other related early accessories. *Est:* 1968. *Serv:* Purchase estates. *Hours:* By chance/appt suggested. *Assoc:* ADA. *Shows:* RI. *Park:* On site. *Loc:* I-95 Exit 63: Rte 81N, 5 MI, R at circle onto Rte 80, approx 1 MI, R at 1st crossroad, 3rd house on R.

LAKEVILLE

BAD CORNER ANTIQUES & DECORATION
Rtes 41 & 44, 06039
(203)435-9369　　　　　　**33 36 65**

A restored Victorian carriage house featuring two floors of primitives, American advertising & furniture. *Est:* 1965. *Hours:* May-Oct daily 11-5. Gail A Vaill *Park:* On site. *Loc:* Adjacent to Iron Masters Motel.

LEBANON

THE ETCETERA SHOPPE
760 Trumbull Hwy, 06249
(203)642-6847 **48 85**
Antique baby dresses, vintage clothing, linen & lace. *Est:* 1981. *Serv:* Repair & restoration of antique gowns, period & floral designs. *Hours:* Mid Aug-Dec Wed-Sat 10:30-5, else by chance/appt. Nancylee S Gaucher *Park:* On site. *Loc:* I-395, Rte 32N out of Norwich, to Rte 87.

LEONE'S APPRAISERS & AUCTIONEERS
Barker Rd, 06249
(203)642-6248 **8**
Estate sales, antiques & collectibles auctions. *Hours:* BY APPT. *Assoc:* NAA NEAA. Robert A Leone

LISBON

MR & MRS JEROME BLUM
45 Ross Hill Rd, 06351
(203)376-0300 **16 37 50**
American 18th & early 19th C furniture, decorative arts & brass. Early lighting & fireplace equipment. *Hours:* BY APPT ONLY. *Assoc:* NHADA. *Shows:* ELLIS. *Loc:* I-395 Exit 84: (Jewett City).

LITCHFIELD

ANTIQUES 'N THINGS
Harris Plains Rd Rte 202, 06759
(203)567-9664 **32 40**
Specializing in oak furniture, collectibles, toys & trains. *Hours:* Daily 11-5. *Loc:* Just W of town.

D W LINSLEY INC
Rte 202 W, 06759
(203)567-4245 **39 40 42**
Exceptional English country pine & period oak furniture displayed on 3 floors. *Est:* 1973. *Hours:* Thu-Sun 11-5. *Size:* Medium. *CC:* AX. *Park:* On site. *Loc:* 2 MI from Litchfield adjacent to the White Memorial.

LITCHFIELD ANTIQUES CENTER
85 West St, 06759
(203)567-8826 **{GR10}**
A handsome collection of formal & country furniture & decorative accessories in a pink Victorian house just beyond the Litchfield Village Green. *Est:* 1989. *Serv:* Appraisal, purchase estates. *Hours:* Daily 10-4 Sun 12-4 CLOSED TUE. *Park:* In front. *Loc:* Just W of the Green on 202.

LITCHFIELD AUCTION GALLERY
Harris Plains Rd Rte 202, 06759
(203)567-3126 **4 8**
Sunday auctions held twice monthly featuring Americana, fine art & folk art. 10% buyers premium. *Serv:* Appraisal, accept mail/phone bids, brochure, catalog, consultation. *Hours:* Tue-Fri 9:30-5, CLOSED non-auction weekends. *Size:* Large. *CC:* MC/V. *Park:* On site. *Loc:* From N: Rte 7 to Rte 63 to 202W, From NYC: Rte 684 to 84 in Danbury, Brookfield Exit (Rtes 7 & 202) follow Rte 202.

THOMAS MC BRIDE ANTIQUES
West St, 06759
(203)567-5476 **44 59 77**

Furniture, decorations, silver, American & European paintings, Victorian, early American & French glass. *Est:* 1966. *Hours:* Mon-Fri 9:30-5 weekends BY APPT, CLOSED Dec 15-Apr. *Park:* On site. *Loc:* Red barn next to Town Hall.

JOHN STEELE BOOK SHOP
South St near the Green, 06759
(203)567-0748 **13 64**

Antiquarian & second-hand books, Connecticut history, post cards. *Hours:* Tue-Sat 11-5:30 Sun 1-5 & BY APPT. *Size:* 20,000 books. *Assoc:* CAB. William Keifer *Loc:* Next to the Litchfield Historical Society.

HARRY W STROUSE
322 Maple St, 06759
(203)567-0656 **58 77**

Two rooms of 18th & 19th C antiques & decorations in a 1749 house. Specializing in silver & objets d'art, furniture, glass, china, rugs, tools, paintings, prints, fabric, pewter, crocks, andirons, books, brass, copper & wrought iron. *Pr:* $25–5000. *Est:* 1971. *Serv:* Appraisal, auction, consultation, interior design, purchase estates. *Hours:* By chance/appt. *Size:* Medium. *Park:* On site. *Loc:* 1 1/2 MI N from Rte 202, just past Our Lady of Grace Church.

PETER H TILLOU - FINE ARTS
185 Prospect St, 06759
(203)567-5706 **34 59 73**

European & American paintings of 17th-19th C, 18th C American furniture, sculpture & American folk art. *Est:* 1955. *Serv:* Estates & collections purchased. *Hours:* By chance/appt. *Shows:* WAS. *Loc:* Call for appt.

THOMAS D & CONSTANCE R WILLIAMS
Brush Hill Rd, 06759
(203)567-3334 **16 37 63**

Specializing in American furniture, 18th-19th C pewter & Chinese Export porcelain. *Hours:* By chance. *Loc:* Off Rte 202 W of downtown.

WOOD*WORKS
The Cove Rte 202, 06759
(203)567-9767 **68 71**

American & European antiques restoration, fine woodworking, French polishing, faux finishes, marbleizing & grain painting. *Est:* 1975. *Hours:* BY APPT. Barry Strom *Park:* On site. *Loc:* On Rte 202 headed toward Bantam.

MADISON

ANTIQUES AT MADISON
837 Boston Post Rd, 06443
(203)245-7856 **35 37 39**

American, English & French furniture & antique decorative objects. *Pr:* $100–3000. *Est:* 1986. *Hours:* Apr-Jan 15 Wed-Sat 11-5 Sun 1-5, Jan 16-Mar Sat 11-5 Sun 1-5. *Size:* Medium. *CC:* AX/MC/V. Joan Fernandez *Park:* On site. *Loc:* I-95 Exit 61: to downtown Madison.

KIRT & ELIZABETH CRUMP
387 Boston Post Rd Rte 1, 06443
(203)245-7573 **23 37**

18th & 19th C clocks including tall case clocks, pillar & scroll & other shelf clocks & mantle clocks, period timepieces & American furniture. *Est:* 1976. *Serv:* Appraisal, consultation, repair & restoration of clocks only.

Hours: By chance/appt. **Assoc:** ADA BHI NAWCC. **Park:** On site. **Loc:** I-95 Exit 61: approx 1 MI.

P HASTINGS FALK SOUND VIEW PRESS
170 Boston Post Rd, 06443
(203)245-2246   **26 59 66**
Specialist in 19th & early 20th C American art, paintings by women & vintage photographs. Publisher of 25,000 entry biographical dictionary "Who Was Who in American Art", dictionary of signatures & monograms of American artists. **Serv:** Brochure, catalog, consultation, purchase estates. **Hours:** BY APPT ONLY. **CC:** MC/V. Peter H Falk **Loc:** Call for Appt & directions.

NOSEY GOOSE
33 Wall St, 06443
(203)245-3132   **27 41 86**
Painted & country furniture, related accessories, antique wicker & quilts. **Est:** 1980. **Hours:** Mon-Sat 10-5. **CC:** MC/V. Betty-Lou Morawski **Park:** On site. **Loc:** I-95 Exit 61S: Rte 1, L at light, 1st L off Rte 1.

ON CONSIGNMENT OF MADISON
77 Wall St, 06443
(203)245-7012   **25 36 77**
Consignment furniture, china, porcelain, Oriental rugs & silver. **Est:** 1985. **Serv:** Consignment shop. **Hours:** Tue-Sat 10-5. **Park:** On site. **Loc:** From Boston Post Rd: US Rte 1, L onto Wall St, between library & post office on Wall St.

ORDNANCE CHEST
PO Box 905, 06443
(203)245-2387   **6 24 78**
Antique firearms, books, medals, edged weapons - mostly pre-WW II, pre-1898 weapons & military collectibles. **Pr:** $10–1500. **Est:** 1976. **Serv:** Appraisal,

catalog (3 issues/$10), purchase estates, search service. **Hours:** BY APPT ONLY. **CC:** MC/V. **Loc:** Call for directions.

RIVER CROFT
220 River Rd, 06443
(203)245-4708   **16 68 71**
Repair, restoration, polishing of brass, copper, iron, perform fabrication, welding, brazing, soldering of metals & electrified lamps. **Serv:** Repairs, restoration. **Hours:** Mon-Fri 9-5 Sat 9-12. Bob Cole **Park:** On site. **Loc:** I-95 Exit 62S: L onto Rte 1, 1st L onto Mill Rd, 3/4 MI, sign hangs from tree at end of driveway on R.

SCHAFER AUCTION GALLERY
82 Bradley St, 06443
(203)245-4173   **4 8**
Auctions approximately twice monthly, always on Sunday evening at 7 with a 2-hour preview before-hand. Quality home furnishings & antiques. Left bids. **Est:** 1969. **Serv:** Appraisal, consignment. **Hours:** By chance. **Assoc:** CAA NAA. **Park:** On site. **Loc:** I-95 Exit 61: S on Rte 79, 1st L, 3rd bldg on R.

MANCHESTER

BOOKS & BIRDS
519 E Middle Tnpk, 06040
(203)649-3449   **13**
Antiquarian books: general stock used & rare, including birds, nature, Connecticut, antiques, arts, collectibles, hunting & fishing, military & history, gardening, cooking & children's books. **Serv:** Appraisal, search service. **Hours:** Tue-Sat 11-4:30 Thu til 8, call for Sun & Mon hours. **Size:** 35,000 books. **CC:** MC/V. **Assoc:** CAB. Gil Salk **Park:** On site. **Loc:** 1 MI E of Main St on Rtes 6 & 44.

CONNECTICUT CANE & REED CO
134 Pine St Box 762, 06040
(203)646-6586 **22**
Complete stock of all chair seating & wicker repair supplies. Largest selection on the East Coast. *Serv:* Antique restoration & basketry supplies, same day shipments. *Hours:* Mon-Fri 9-5 Sat 10-4. *Size:* Large. *CC:* AX/MC/V. Joanne Parkinson *Park:* On site. *Loc:* Off Rtes 44 & 6.

MANSFIELD CENTER

SHEILA B AMDUR - BOOKS
PO Box 151, 06250
(203)423-3176 **13**
Antiquarian books relating to medicine, psychiatry & New England. *Hours:* BY APPT. *Size:* 3,000 books. *Assoc:* CAB.

JACK COLLINS WOODWORKING
RR1 Box 243, 06250
(203)455-0086 **70 71**
Restoration lumber - authentic new materials for restoration. Seasoned wide Eastern white pine, red oak, white oak, Pennsylvania cherry, hard maple, genuine mahogany, slow growth Northern hard pine & clear pine. *Serv:* Custom milling, brochure $1.00 restoration lumber. *Hours:* BY APPT.

MARBLE DALE

LIMEROCK FARMS ANTIQUES
Rte 202, 06777
(203)355-1208 **27**
Country American furniture, tables & cupboards in cherry & pine. *Est:* 1977. *Hours:* Sat-Sun 11-5 or BY APPT.

Leilah J Diekman *Park:* On site. *Loc:* 4 MI from New Milford toward Litchfield.

EARL J SLACK ANTIQUES
Rte 202 & Wheaton Rd, 06777
(203)868-7092 **37 39 59**
English & American furniture, paintings, English & Oriental porcelains thoughtfully displayed in a 19th C house. *Est:* 1968. *Hours:* Sat,Sun 11-5. *Loc:* Between New Milford & Litchfield by a red brick church.

MARLBOROUGH

THE CONNECTICUT GALLERY
4 Austin Dr, 06447
(203)295-9543 **17 59 66**
Fine American art of all periods, specializing in Connecticut Impressionism & contemporary art. Major to minor masterpieces, paintings, sculpture, drawings & prints. Ten-room Victorian house with sculpture garden in rural setting 15 min from Hartford. *Est:* 1985. *Serv:* Brochure, catalog, appraisal, consultation. *Hours:* Tue-Sat 10-5 or BY APPT. *Size:* Large. *Park:* On site. *Loc:* From Hartford Rte 84 to Rte 2E to Exit 12, straight off exit, first house on L, a yellow & white Victorian.

MERIDEN

DUNN'S MYSTERIES OF CHOICE
251 Baldwin Ave, 06450
(203)235-0480 **13**
Antiquarian books: detective fiction, true crime, Ayn Rand, H.L. Mencken, libertarianism, atheism & anarchism. *Serv:*

Catalog. **Hours:** BY APPT ONLY. **Size:** 10,000 books. **Assoc:** CAB. William Dunn

FAIR WEATHER ANTIQUES
763 Hanover Rd, 06450
(203)237-4636   **33 36 64**
Decorative antiques, furniture, post cards, ephemera & collectibles. **Hours:** Mon,Thu-Sat 11-4, Oct-Apr Sun 1-4. **Assoc:** CADA.

ORUM SILVER CO
51 S Vine St, 06450
(203)237-3037   **68 71**
Expert repair work of old silver & antiques, soldering, dents removed, fabrication of lost parts, buffing, cleaning & polishing of all types of metals. Dresser sets restored, knife blades replaced, sterling pieces repaired & refinished. **Serv:** Brochure, repairs, restoration. **Hours:** Mon-Fri 8-4. Joe Pistilli **Park:** In front. **Loc:** I-691 in Meriden: travelling W Exit 6, travelling E Exit 5.

MIDDLE HADDAM

MIDDLE HADDAM ANTIQUES
Rte 151, 06456
(203)267-9221   **27 83**
Antiques & collectibles specializing in country & Victorian smalls. **Hours:** Daily 10-5 & evenings BY APPT. Janet Freidenberg **Park:** On site. **Loc:** 1 block from Cobalt Center.

MIDDLEBURY

MICHAEL C DOOLING
72 North St, 06762
(203)758-8130   **13**
Antiquarian books: Americana, architecture, art, bindings & travel. **Serv:** Appraisal, catalog. **Hours:** Evenings & weekends BY APPT. **Size:** 1,000 books. **Assoc:** CAB. Michael Dooling

MIDDLETOWN

COUNTRY ANTIQUES AT MIDDLETOWN
808 Washington St, 06457
(203)344-8536   **36 40 83**
Five-room historic house & barn filled with Victorian, formal, country & primitive furnishings, china & collectibles, specializing in Victorian oak, walnut & quality mahogany furniture. **Pr:** $10–2000. **Serv:** Appraisal, auction, consultation, interior design, purchase estates, repair. **Hours:** May 15-Aug Fri-Sun 11-5 or by appt. **Size:** Medium. **CC:** MC/V. **Park:** On site. **Loc:** From Hartford: I-91S, Rte 66 Washington St Exit: 2 MI on R. From New Haven: I-91N, Rte 66 Middletown Exit: 5 MI on L.

IBIS BOOKS & GALLERY
49 Rapallo Ave, 06457
(203)347-4957   **13**
Antiquarian books: poetry, books on books, illustrated Arabian Nights, Connecticut. **Serv:** Search service. **Hours:** Tue-Sat 11:30-5:30 Sun 10-2. **Size:** 3,000 books. **Assoc:** CAB. Susan Allison

MILFORD

ANTIQUES OF TOMORROW
93-95 Gulf St, 06460
(203)878-4561   **40 59 60**
Antiques, furniture, dolls, toys, paintings
& Orientalia. *Pr:* $25–1000. *Est:* 1974.
Serv: Appraisal, consultation, custom
woodwork, purchase estates, repairs.
Hours: Daily 10-3:30. *Size:* Medium.
CC: MC/V. Mary Paternoster *Park:* On
site. *Loc:* 4 min from either Merritt or
Wilbur Pkwys.

JENNY LEES ANTIQUES
4 Daniel St, 06460
(203)878-5068   **32 36**
18th C furniture, dolls & accessories.
Serv: Auction. *Hours:* Mon-Sat 10-4 or
by chance. Ginny Kabe *Loc:* Rte 1 Milford Post Rd Exit, in Milford center.

MILFORD EMPORIUM
16 Daniel St, 06460
(203)878-3677   **40 43**
Refinished turn-of-the-century oak &
walnut furniture & reproductions. *Est:*
1976. *Hours:* Mon-Fri 3-6 Sat 10-4 Sun
9-3. Peter Goodfellow *Park:* On site.
Loc: 1 block from post office.

MILFORD GREEN ANTIQUES GALLERY
19-21 River St, 06460
(203)874-4303   **33 66**
Mostly Victorian to Art Deco, antiques,
collectibles & decorative accessories, including furniture, glass, china, radios,
prints (Norman Rockwell, Maxwell Parrish & the printed art of the Golden
Age), ephemera & magazines. *Pr:* $25–
2500. *Est:* 1987. *Serv:* Conservation,
purchase estates, matting & framing.
Hours: Tue-Sat 11-5, Monday by
chance/appt. *Size:* Medium. *CC:* MC/V.

Assoc: CADA. Dave Williams *Park:* In
front, nearby lot. *Loc:* Rte 15S, R off Exit
56, straight for 5 MI; Rte 15N, Exit 54,
R at end of connector, R at 2nd light, 1/2
MI to downtown.

STOCK TRANSFER
119 Broad St, 06460
(203)874-1333   **25 36 47**
Large consignment shop specializing in
fine home furnishings, collectibles,
jewelry & paintings. *Est:* 1982. *Hours:*
Tue-Sat 10-4. *Size:* Large. *Park:* On
site.

TREASURES & TRIFLES
580 Naugatuck Ave, 06460
(203)878-7045   **36 47**
Furniture, advertisements & jewelry.
Hours: Daily 12-5. Billy Byrnes

MONROE

MONROE ANTIQUE CENTER
418 Main St Rte 25, 06468
(203)268-9805   **{GR8}**
Variety of antiques & collectibles,
specializing in country furniture, costume jewelry & children's books, sheet
music, Deco, fiesta, blue willow, Max-
field Parrish & Wallace Nutting prints.
Est: 1980. *Hours:* Tue-Fri 11:30-4:30
Sat,Sun 11:30-5. *Size:* Medium. Barbara
A Gilmore *Park:* On site. *Loc:* Located
in red house corner of Pepper St & Rte
25.

MOODUS

PEDDLERS VILLAGE
34 Plains Rd, 06469
(203)873-2387   **{MDS}**
Antiques & collectibles in the 1852 Nelson Clark Richmond house including furniture, jewelry, baskets, ephemera, glassware & collectibles. *Serv:* Consignments taken. *Hours:* Year round Tue-Sun 10-5:30. *Loc:* Rte 2 Exit 16 or Rte 9 Exit 7: at Jct of Rtes 149 & 151.

MORRIS

MARTINGALE FARM ANTIQUES
Rte 61 South St, 06763
(203)567-5178   **27**
Two-story barn with country furniture & accessories. *Est:* 1984. *Hours:* Thu-Mon 10-5. *Assoc:* CADA. *Park:* On site. *Loc:* 10 MI N of Woodbury, next to the Morris Historical Society.

T'OTHER HOUSE ANTIQUES
66 Litchfield Rd, 06763
(203)567-9283   **44 63**
China, pattern glass & general line. *Est:* 1948. *Hours:* By chance/appt. *Park:* On site. *Loc:* Near White Flower Farms.

MYSTIC

5 CHURCH STREET ANTIQUES
5 Church St, 06355
(203)536-0610   **25 29**
Antiques consignment shop. *Serv:* Appraisals, estate sale management. *Hours:* May-Dec Fri-Tue 10:30-5, Jan-Apr Sat,Sun 10:30-5. *Size:* Medium. *CC:*
MC/V. *Park:* In front. *Loc:* Rte 27 at Mystic Seaport, S towards downtown, R on Holmes St, L onto Church St, 1st L into large parking lot.

MYSTIC FINE ARTS
Factory Square Courtyard, 06355
(203)572-8141
Fine arts auction house specializing in American & European paintings, watercolors, prints & sculpture in six sales a year. *Serv:* Appraisal, consignments accepted, restoration. *Hours:* By appt. Albert E Goring

MYSTIC RIVER ANTIQUES MARKET
14 Holmes St, 06355
(203)572-9775   **{GR35}**
Fine antiques, collectibles, memorabilia, paintings, books, furniture & pottery in an attractive riverside setting. *Est:* 1985. *Hours:* Year round daily 10-5. *CC:* MC/V. Linda R Schuster *Park:* On site. *Loc:* I-95 Exit 90: S on Rte 27 to Holmes St.

ORIENTAL RUGS LTD
4 E Main St, 06355
(203)572-9233   **21**
Large selection of antique Oriental carpets & selection of new carpets. *Est:* 1980. *Serv:* Appraisal, consultation. *Hours:* Mon-Sat 10-5 or BY APPT. *CC:* MC/V. *Assoc:* NHADA. Karen DiSaia *Park:* In rear. *Loc:* I-95 Exit 89: S to Rte 1, turn L.

LYNN M ROTH
14 Holmes St, 06355
(203)536-8955   **13**
Antiquarian books on art, decorative arts, antiques, architecture, photography, quaint, literature. *Hours:* BY APPT. *Assoc:* CAB.

TRADE WINDS GALLERY
20 W Main St, 06355
(203)536-0119   **51 66**
Specializing in antique maps & prints from around the world & a general line of art. *Pr:* $25–1500. *Est:* 1974. *Hours:* Jun-Sep Mon-Sat 10-6 Sun 11-5, else CLOSED SUN. *Size:* Medium. *CC:* AX/MC/V. Thomas K Aalund *Park:* In front. *Loc:* Just W of the drawbridge in downtown Mystic.

NAUGATUCK

ALBERT JOSEPH & CO
538 Andrew Mountain Rd, 06770
(203)723-1821   **40 83 27**
Oak, Victorian & country furniture & accessories of the period. *Hours:* BY APPT. *Assoc:* CADA.

PEDDLER'S MARKET
Rte 63 New Haven Rd, 06770
(203)729-5398   **{FLEA}**
Flea market with antiques, collectibles & other flea market merchandise. Admission is free. *Est:* 1980. *Serv:* Catered, Space rental starts at $25. *Hours:* May-Oct Sun dawn to dusk. *Size:* 72 spaces. *Park:* Free parking. *Loc:* Between New Haven & Waterbury on Rte 63.

TOUCHMARK ANTIQUES
140 Partridgetown Rd, 06770
(203)723-8667   **36**
18th & 19th C furniture & accessories. *Hours:* BY APPT. *Assoc:* CADA.

NEW CANAAN

ACAMPORA ART GALLERY
134 Elm St, 06840
(203)966-6090   **59**
Specializing in 19th-early 20th C American paintings with focus on Hudson River School & American Impressionists. *Pr:* $2400–75000. *Est:* 1970. *Hours:* Tue-Sat 10-4. *Park:* In front. *Loc:* From Merritt Pkwy going N Exit 37: L to middle of town to SS, L turn 1/2 block on L - Elm St.

BUTLER FINE ART
One East Avenue, 06840
(203)966-2274   **59**
Specializing in 19th & early 20th C American paintings focusing on New England artists. *Est:* 1989. *Serv:* Appraisal, professional restoration. *Hours:* Mon-Sat 10-4. Jane Butler Sara Tarr

ENGLISH HERITAGE ANTIQUES, INC
13 South Ave, 06840
(203)966-2979   **39 59 63**
Fine English 18th & 19th C formal furniture, paintings, porcelain & accessories displayed on three spacious gallery levels. Everything guaranteed to be as represented. Located in the heart of the beautiful village of New Canaan. *Est:* 1978. *Serv:* Brochure, purchase estates. *Hours:* Mon-Sat 10-5. *Size:* Large. *CC:* AX/MC/V. *Assoc:* AADLA CINOA NEAA. Cecily C Megrue *Park:* Nearby lot. *Loc:* Merritt Pkwy Exit 37: N 2 MI, opposite Mobil, 1 hr from NYC.

HASTINGS ART, LTD
110 Main St, 06840
(203)966-9863   **59**
Fine 19th & 20th C American paintings, specializing in Hudson River School &

American Impressionism. *Serv:* Appraisal, conservation, restoration. *Hours:* Wed-Sat 10:30-4:30. *CC:* MC/V. *Park:* In front. *Loc:* From NYC: Exit 37, L at bottom of ramp, to New Canaan, 1st shop on Main St.

MARTHA JACKSON QUILTS
Main Street Cellar 120 Main St, 06840
(203)966-8348   **63 67**
Specializing in 19th & early 20th century quilts: appliques, patchworks, geometrics & Amish. Some flow blue china. *Hours:* Mon-Sat 10-5 By appt 203-637-2152 & at fine shows. *CC:* MC/V. Martha Jackson *Park:* In front & nearby lot. *Loc:* Merritt Pkwy Exit 37 (Rte 124): to New Canaan. R on Cherry St, L onto Main St. Shop at Int of Elm & Main.

LISSARD HOUSE
282 Brushy Ridge Rd, 06840
(203)972-3473   **42 66 78**
Irish pine furniture, antiques & reproductions, sporting painting & prints. *Est:* 1987. *Serv:* Irish tea room on premises. *Hours:* Tue-Sat 9:30-5. *CC:* AX/MC/V.

MAIN STREET CELLAR ANTIQUES
120 Main St, 06840
(203)966-8348   **{MDS8}**
A handsome collection of painted furniture, garden furniture, quilts, pine, folk art, ceramics & early prints. *Est:* 1984. *Hours:* Mon-Sat 10-5. *CC:* MC/V. Jane Apuzzo *Park:* On street. *Loc:* I-95 Exit 15, Rte 7 to Rte 123N to Rte 106S, L on Main St; From Merritt Pkwy: Exit 38, Rtes 123N & 106S as above.

MANOR ANTIQUES
90 Main St, 06840
(203)966-2658   **35 39**
Direct importer of personally selected fine quality English & French period furniture & objets d'art. *Pr:* $50–20000. *Est:* 1983. *Serv:* Appraisal, interior design. *Hours:* Mon-Sat 10-5 Sun 12-4 & BY APPT. *Size:* Medium. *CC:* AX/DC/MC/V. *Assoc:* NEAA. Florence M Byrne *Park:* Nearby lot, in front. *Loc:* Merritt Pkwy Exit 38N (Rte 123) to Rte 106, L on Rte 105 to Main St (Rte 124), R on Main St.

THE MORRIS HOUSE
Box 1524, 06840
(203)966-9778   **37**
Fine American furniture & decorative accessories from the early American scene pre-1840. *Pr:* $50–50000. *Est:* 1944. *Serv:* Consultation. *Hours:* BY APPT ONLY. Joan Morris *Park:* On site.

NEW CANAAN ANTIQUES
120 Main St, 06840
(203)972-1938   **{MDS5}**
Fine quality period American, English & French furniture, 19th C paintings, 18th & 19th C porcelains & other fine accessories beautifully displayed in 7 rooms in one of New Canaan's earliest buildings. *Est:* 1984. *Serv:* Brochure. *Hours:* Mon-Sat 10-5. *Size:* Large. *Park:* Nearby lot. *Loc:* Merritt Pkwy Exit 37 or 38: to Ctr of New Canaan, corner of Main & Elm Sts.

ROSEMARY
26 Forest St, 06840
(203)966-5167   **45**
Antiques, furniture & decorations for home & garden. *Hours:* Mon-Sat 10-5. *Loc:* Near Gates Restaurant.

SALLEA ANTIQUES INC
66 Elm St, 06840
(203)972-1050   **2 29 39**
Specializing in fine boxes of all sizes, shapes & styles. Furniture, Chinese export porcelain, Japanese Imari, brass,

fireplace equipment, paintings, lamps & more. *Hours:* Mon-Sat 10-5, sometimes Sun. *CC:* MC/V. *Shows:* ELLIS. Sally B Kaltman *Park:* Nearby. *Loc:* On the corner of Elm St & South Ave.

JOYCE SCARBOROUGH ANTIQUES
3 South Ave, 06840
(203)972-3644   **39 42**

English country furniture - especially pine - plus accessories & kitchenware. *Pr:* $5–4000. *Est:* 1974. *Hours:* Mon-Sat 10-5 Sun BY APPT. *CC:* AX/MC/V. *Park:* Nearby lot. *Loc:* Ctr of town across from municipal parking lot.

SEVERED TIES, INC
111 Cherry St, 06840
(203)972-0788   **29 36**

Furniture, decorative accessories, art, silver & estate jewelry. *Serv:* Consignments. *Hours:* Mon-Sat 10-5 Sun 1-5. *Assoc:* CADA NEAA. William E Dale *Park:* Adjacent. *Loc:* Off Merritt Pkwy.

THE SILK PURSE
118 Main St, 06840
(203)972-0898   **25 29 36**

A large consignment shop for fine home furnishings. *Hours:* Mon-Sat 10-5 Sun 12-5. *CC:* MC/V. *Park:* Nearby.

THE STUDIO
86 Main St, 06840
(203)966-1332   **50**

Custom lamps & lampshades & miscellaneous English antiques. *Serv:* Interior design, bridal registry. *Hours:* Mon-Sat 10-5:30. *CC:* MC/V. *Park:* Nearby. *Loc:* Across the street from the town hall on Main St.

NEW FAIRFIELD

APPLE TREE HILL ANTIQUES
402 Rte 37, 06812
(203)746-7250   **27 29 83**

A country barn full of furniture & accessories. *Pr:* $2–2000. *Est:* 1989. *Serv:* Consultation, custom woodwork, interior design, repairs, restoration. *Hours:* May-Oct Fri-Sun 11-5 or by chance/appt; Sep-Apr BY APPT ONLY. *Size:* Large. Terry Froehlich *Park:* On site. *Loc:* 4 1/2 MI from center of New Fairfield (N on Rte 37); 3 MI E of Rte 22 (NY) via Havilland Hollow Rd.

ANDREW'S AXIOMS

When you have a brilliant idea for collecting something hitherto rare, undiscovered and full of potential, you will suddenly notice that the shops are full of them.

Reprinted with permission from *guide to the Antique Shops of Britain 1989*. copyright The Antique Collectors Club, Great Britain

NEW HARTFORD

GALLERY FORTY FOUR
Rte 44, 06057
(203)379-2083 **59**
Specializing in 19th & early 20th C American paintings. *Est:* 1966. *Serv:* Framing, restoration, appraisal. *Hours:* Tue-Sat 10-5. *Park:* On site. *Loc:* 7 min from Rte 8 & Rte 44 in Winsted CT opposite the post office.

VILLA'S AUCTION GALLERY
Rte 7 N, 06057
(203)379-7151 **8**
Specializing in estate & antiques auctions. 10% buyers premium. *Hours:* Call for appt or schedule. Richard Villa *Park:* On site. *Loc:* From Hartford: Follow Rte 44 W to Canaan Ctr, take Rte 7N.

NEW HAVEN

ARK ANTIQUES
Box 3133, 06515
(203)387-3754 **16 77**
Fine American craftsman silver, jewelry & metalwork of the early 20th C, with special focus on the Arts & Crafts Movement. *Pr:* $50–35000. *Serv:* Catalog $10, 3 consecutive catalogs $25. *Hours:* Sep 15-Jun BY APPT & shows. Rosalie Berberian *Loc:* Call for appt & directions.

EDWIN C AHLBERG
441 Middletown Ave, 06513
(203)624-9076 **37 71**
Formal & semi-formal antiques & New England furniture. *Serv:* Repairs, refinishing, appraisals. *Hours:* Mon-Fri 8-5 Sat 8-12. *Shows:* ELLIS. *Loc:* I-91 Exit 8: On Rte 17.

ANN MARIE'S VINTAGE BOUTIQUE
1569 Chapel St, 06511
(203)787-1734 **47 85**
Vintage clothing, beaded & mesh antique bags, embroidered shawls & deco jewelry.

ANTIQUE CORNER
859 Whalley Ave, 06515
(203)387-7200 **{GR5}**
Three floors of antiques including American & European furniture, oil paintings, antique & estate jewelry, art glass, quilts, silver, fine prints, maps, books, autographs, crystal & china. *Est:* 1981. *Serv:* Appraisal, consultation, purchase estates. *Hours:* Mon-Sat 10:30-5 Sun 12-4. *Size:* Medium. *CC:* MC/V. Rhona Harris *Park:* On site. *Loc:* Merritt Pkwy Exit 59.

THE ANTIQUES MARKET
881 Whalley Ave, 06515
(203)389-5440 **39 63 72**
Extensive stock of old Wedgwood, Irish Belleek & period English furniture, paintings, scientifics & other treasures. *Est:* 1968. *Serv:* Mail orders. *Hours:* Daily 10:30-5. *CC:* AX/MC/V. *Assoc:* CADA. Miriam Levine *Park:* On site. *Loc:* Merritt Pkwy Exit 59.

ARETHUSA BOOK SHOP
87 Audubon St, 06511
(203)624-1848 **13**
Antiquarian books on ancient & world history, fiction, art & architecture, travel, science, children's & cooking. *Hours:* Mon-Sat 10:30-6 Sun 1-5. *Size:* 7,500 books. *Assoc:* CAB. John Gearty

BRYN MAWR BOOK SHOP
56 1/2 Whitney Ave, 06510
(203)562-4217 **13**
Antiquarian books: art, biography, psychology, psychiatry, travel, fine litera-

ture. *Hours:* Win: Wed-Fri 12-3 Sat 10-1, Sum: Wed-Thu 12-3.. *Size:* 20,000 books. *Assoc:* CAB. Meigs, Carter & Darling

CITY POINT ANTIQUES
19 Howard Ave, 06509
(203)776-2202 **66 80**
Early textiles, prints, decorative accessories, Yale memorabilia & Dutch tiles. *Est:* 1980. *Hours:* Sat-Sun 10-5 or BY APPT. *Loc:* Opposite Chart House.

THOMAS COLVILLE INC
58 Trumbull St, 06511
(203)787-2816 **59 66**
Specializing in antiques from the 19th & early 20th C, French & Dutch paintings, watercolors & drawings. Also a broad range of 19th C American Art with emphasis on landscapes & George Inness. *Est:* 1972. *Serv:* Appraisal, consultation, purchase estates, repair. *Hours:* BY APPT. *Park:* Nearby. *Loc:* I-91 Exit 3.

FROM HERE TO ANTIQUITY
900 Whalley Ave, 06515
(203)389-6722 **37 59 63**
Specializing in 19th & 20th C American art & art pottery. A great variety of quality Americana, folk art, furniture & glass. *Pr:* $50–25000. *Est:* 1983. *Serv:* Appraisal, consultation, interior design, purchase estates, repairs. *Hours:* Daily by chance/appt. *Size:* Medium. *CC:* MC/V. D B Smernoff *Park:* On site. *Loc:* Merritt Pkwy Exit 59.

GIAMPIETRO ANTIQUES
153 1/2 Bradley St, 06511
(203)787-3851 **34 59**
American folk art & decorative art for the serious collector. *Est:* 1977. *Hours:* BY APPT ONLY. *Assoc:* ADA. Kathryn Giampietro *Loc:* Call for directions.

SALLY GOODMAN ANTIQUES
901 Whalley Ave, 06515
(203)387-5072 **44 47 77**
One of New Haven's largest dealers in antique & estate jewelry. Large selection of sterling silver. Dealer trade welcome. *Est:* 1976. *Serv:* Appraisal, consultation, purchase estates, repairs. *Hours:* Oct-Dec daily 10-5, Jan-Sep 10-5 CLOSED SUN. *Size:* Medium. *CC:* MC/V. *Assoc:* GIA. Steven Goodman, GIA *Park:* On site. *Loc:* Merritt Pkwy Exit 59: 1 1/2 MI down road on L.

ANDREW'S AXIOMS

Angles Rules on Corner Cupboards

1. A corner cupboard will remain permanently affixed to the wall only until filled with china or porcelain; then it will fall.

2. When it falls, it will hit a perfect satinwood surface on the way down.

3. The effort to catch it while it is falling will cause more damage than if you just let it fall.

Reprinted with permission from *guide to the Antique Shops of Britain 1989*.
copyright The Antique Collectors Club, Great Britain

HAROLD'S LTD INC
871-873 Whalley Ave, 06515
(203)389-2988   **37 47 63**

Fine European & American antiques - Irish pine to American four poster beds, china, jewelry, silver, Oriental rugs, lighting fixtures & Orientalia. *Est:* 1968. *Serv:* Appraisal, purchase estates, restoration. *Hours:* Mon-Sat 10-5 Sun 12-4. *CC:* AX/MC/V. *Assoc:* NEAA. *Park:* On site. *Loc:* Merritt Pkwy Exit 59: R onto Whalley Rd, 1 1/2 MI.

HER MAJESTY'S ANTIQUES
317 Bassett St, 06511
(203)787-0096   **63 83**

Located in Gowie-Normand house - New Haven's only Victorian museum. All substyles of Victorian furniture. Diverse & colorful selection of advertising tins & many patterns of Roseville pottery. *Serv:* Consultation, interior design. *Hours:* BY APPT. *Size:* Medium. *CC:* MC/V. Seth C Hawkins *Park:* On site. *Loc:* Rte 15 Exit 60 (Dixwell Ave): S 1 1/2 MI to Bassett St, R for 1 block.

PETER G HILL & ASSOCIATES
100 Orange St, 06508
(203)624-5101   **5**

Architectural antiques. *Hours:* Mon-Sat 9:30-5:30. *Loc:* Downtown New Haven exit off interstate, Exit 1, go R at the light, R again at 3rd light onto Chapel St, next R onto Orange.

JASMINE
One Elm St, 06510
(203)785-1430   **29 36**

Fine 18th & 19th C American, English & Chinese furnishings & accessories. A source for reproduction fabrics, tapestries & bed linens. *Est:* 1983. *Serv:* Interior design. *Hours:* Mon-Sat 10-6, Sep-Dec 24 extended evening hrs. *Size:* Medium. *CC:* AX/DC/MC/V. *Assoc:* NTHP. David Gillman *Park:* On site.

Loc: Rte 91 Trumbull St Exit: L onto Orange St, L onto Elm St, 1 block on the L across from WTNH 8.

MILTON H KASOWITZ
895 Whalley Ave, 06515
(203)389-2514   **16 47 77**

General line of furniture & decorative accessories including brass, copper, jewelry, glass, lamps, gold & silver. *Est:* 1953. *Serv:* Appraisal, purchase estates. *Hours:* Mon-Sat 10-4:30. *CC:* DC/MC/V. *Park:* In back. *Loc:* Down the street from Harold's Ltd.

WILLIAM REESE COMPANY
409 Temple St, 06511
(203)789-8081   **13**

Antiquarian books: Western & general Americana, English literature, some early printed & color plate books. *Serv:* Catalog, appraisal. *Hours:* Mon-Fri 9-5 BY APPT ONLY. *Size:* 10,000 books. *Assoc:* ABAA CAB. William Reese

R W SMITH-BOOKSELLER
51 Trumbull St, 06510
(203)776-5564   **13**

Art reference - especially American Colonial to the present, photography, architecture & 20th C design & American decorative arts. *Pr:* $10–3500. *Est:* 1975. *Serv:* Catalog($3.50), purchase estates, search service a specialty. *Hours:* By chance/appt. *Size:* 20,000 books. *Assoc:* ABAA ARLIS/NA CAB ILAB NEBA. Raymond W Smith *Park:* In front. *Loc:* I-91 Exit 3: thru light at end of Exit, 1 block on R in John Slade Ely House.

C A STONEHILL INC
282 York St, 06511
(203)865-5141   **9 13**

English literature & history, incunabula & manuscripts. *Serv:* Appraisal. Robert J Barry Jr

VILLAGE FRANCAIS
555 Long Wharf Dr, 06511
(203)562-4883 **35**

Country French antiques & fabrics from Provence. **Hours:** Mon-Fri 10-4 & by appt. **Loc:** I-95 Exit 46: In the Long Wharf Maritime Center.

WEST GATE ANTIQUES
896 Whalley Ave, 06515
(203)387-2078 **23 36 58**

Fine selection of antiques, objets d'art & furniture. **Est:** 1972. **Serv:** Appraisal, consultation. **Hours:** Mon-Sat 11-5. **CC:** MC/V. Christopher S Velush **Park:** On site. **Loc:** Merritt Pkwy Exit 59: R off ramp 2 MI.

WHITLOCK'S INC
17 Broadway, 06511
(203)562-9841 **13**

Attractive antiquarian & rare books in all fields, specializing in Connecticut, local history & British out-of-print imports. **Est:** 1900. **Serv:** Appraisal, purchase estates, search services. **Hours:** Mon-Sat 9:30-5:30. **Size:** Large. **CC:** MC/V. **Assoc:** CAB. Reverdy Whitlock **Park:** Nearby lot. **Loc:** Located in downtown New Haven.

NEW MILFORD

BRUCE W ANDERSON ANTIQUES
264 Kent Rd N, 06776
(203)355-3042 **23 40 59**

Antique & custom furniture including Victorian, Empire, oak, clocks & paintings. **Est:** 1980. **Hours:** Tue-Sat 10-5 by chance or appt. **Assoc:** NAA NEAA. **Park:** On site. **Loc:** From Rte 84 to Rte 7N which is Kent Rd.

AUCTION BARN
Rte 109, 06776
(203)355-3866 **8**

Antique & estate auctions from local homes. No buyer's premium. **Serv:** Purchase estates, accept consignments. **Hours:** Auction every Fri at 7. Ted Gall, Auctioneer **Loc:** Midway between New Milford & Washington on Rte 109.

BIT OF COUNTRY
24 Park Lane Rd Rte 202, 06776
(203)354-6142 **27 40**

Antique oak furniture, solid brass beds & white iron beds. **Est:** 1981. **Hours:** Daily 10-5:30 Sun 11-4. **CC:** MC/V. **Park:** On site. **Loc:** I-84 Exit at Rte 7.

THE BROWSER'S BOX
148 Candlewood Mt Rd, 06776
(203)354-4932 **60 44 50**

Orientals, glass, one-of-a-kind items & miniature lamps. **Hours:** BY APPT. **Assoc:** CADA. Doris & Ray Poirot

CRICKET HILL CONSIGNMENT
49 Bank St, 06776
(203)354-8872 **25 43 63**

Formal & country antiques, reproduction furniture, porcelain, glass & accessories. **Est:** 1982. **Hours:** Daily 11-5 CLOSED TUE. **CC:** MC/V. **Park:** On site. **Loc:** 1 block off the Village Green.

ELEPHANT'S TRUNK FLEA MARKET
Rte 7, 06776
(203)355-1448 **{FLEA}**

Flea market with antiques & collectibles & other flea market merchandise. **Serv:** Catered, rental spaces (20' x 25') available w/o reservations. **Hours:** Apr-Mid Nov Sun 7:30-4:30. **Size:** 165 dealers. **Park:** Ample parking for 1000 cars. **Loc:** I-84 Exit 7: 7 MI N of Danbury.

LIME ROCK FARM ANTIQUES
184 Chestnutland Rd, 06776
(203)355-1208 **36**

Antique furniture, art & accessories.
Hours: Sat-Sun 11-5 or BY APPT. *Assoc:*
CADA. Leilah J Diekman

PHOENIX ANTIQUE
RESTORATION
5 Old Town Park Rd #20, 06776
(203)354-6646 **19 71**

18th C cabinet work, fine French polishing, painted finishes, veneer & carving.
Serv: Antique furniture, repair, restoration, refinishing, faux marbling. *Hours:*
Mon-Fri 7:30-4, Sat-Sun BY APPT.
Paul Gannon *Park:* On site. *Loc:* R off
Rte 7S onto Sullivan Rd, R onto Town
Park Rd.

RIVER HOUSE INC
Rte 202, 06776
(203)350-3577 **39 63 66**

English formal & country furniture,
Chinese export porcelain, framed
engravings & prints. *Hours:* Fri-Sun
10:30-5.

TIMELESS BOOKS
8 Caldwell Dr, 06776
(203)355-4839 **13**
A general stock of antiquarian books:
juvenile series & children's illustrated.
Hours: BY APPT. *Size:* 2,000 books.
Assoc: CAB. Tony A Saia

TRI-COUNTY LIQUIDATORS
Rte 109, 06776
(203)355-3866 **8**

Auction every Friday night at 7, viewing
begins at 6. *Hours:* Shop open Sat 11-4.
Ted Gall *Loc:* Located at New Milford
Auction barn.

THE TRUNK SHOP ETC
52 Railroad St, 06776
(202)350-4427

Specializing in rare & unusual trunks,
also a wide range of accessories. *Hours:*
By chance/appt. *Assoc:* NHADA.
Nicholas Wood

LEON VANDERBILT ANTIQUES
7 Main St on the Green, 06776
(203)350-6080 FAX
(203)350-6080 **37 38 71**

Displaying fine European & American
furniture from the 18th & 19th centuries. *Est:* 1973. *Serv:* Restoration services, structural, French polishing,
veneer & inlay. *Hours:* Mon-Sat 10-5
Sun 12-5 & by appt. Gary & Hilary Leon
Loc: Near the top of the Green.

LEON ✿ VANDERBILT
Antiques

Displaying exquisite European and American furniture
from the 18th and 19th centuries.
Also specializing in restoration and conservation.

Daily 10-5, Sun 12-5 & by appointment. Closed Tuesdays.
Showroom: 7 Main St New Milford, CT 06776 Tel & Fax 203/ 350-6080
Restoration: 22A Bennitt St New Milford, CT Tel 203/ 354-5662

NEW PRESTON

BLACK SWAN ANTIQUES
Rte 45 Main St, 06777
(203)868-2788   39
17th & 18th C English country furniture, unique examples of Elizabethan, William & Mary & Queen Anne pieces, framed engravings, paintings, prints, American & Continental furniture & decorations. *Est:* 1985. *Serv:* Purchase antiques. *Hours:* Thu-Mon 10-5 Sun 12-5, CLOSED TUE & WED. Hubert van Asch van Wyck *Loc:* Rte 202 on Rte 45.

BRITANNIA BOOKSHOP
Church St, 06777
(203)868-0368   13 58 66
Antiquarian bookshop specializing in old British & Irish books, old prints, paintings & curios. Situated in an historic 18th C village in a restored cider mill overlooking a dramatic waterfall & mill pond. *Hours:* Fri-Sun 11-6 or by chance or appt. *Size:* 10,000 books. *CC:* AX/MC/V. *Assoc:* CAB. Barbara C Tippin *Park:* On site. *Loc:* I-84 E Exit 7: to Rte 7, N to New Milford, 202 E to Rte 45 New Preston Ctr.

THE R COGSWELL COLLECTION
Five Main St, 06777
(203)868-9108   37 67
American 18th & 19th C furniture & accessories of the period. Large collection of fine quilts, wooden rocking horses & pull toy horses. *Pr:* $25–20,000. *Est:* 1986. *Serv:* Purchase estates. *Hours:* Apr-Sep Thu-Mon 11-5, Oct-Mar Fri-Sun 11-5 for appt 868-7819. *Size:* Medium. *CC:* MC/V. Raymond Ahlers

BLACK SWAN ANTIQUES

Main Street · New Preston, CT
203·868·2788

Our specialty is early English furniture and accessories, including framed engravings, paintings and prints. We also feature American and Continental furniture and decorations.

Thursday–Saturday & Monday 10 a.m. to 5 p.m.
Sunday Noon to 5 p.m.

Park: On site. **Loc:** I-84 New Milford Exit: Rte 202 into New Preston to Main St.

TIMOTHY MAWSON BOOKS & PRINTS
Main St, 06777
(203)868-0732   **13 66**

Gardening & horticulture, cookery & gastronomy, decorative arts & botanical prints. **Serv:** Catalog, appraisal, search service. **Hours:** Thu-Sun 11-5:30 or BY APPT. **Size:** 5,000 books. **Assoc:** ABAA CAB. **Park:** Nearby.

NEW PRESTON ANTIQUES CENTER
Church St, 06777
(203)868-9651   **{GR8}**

A fine selection of furniture, decorative accessories, tramp art & unique examples from the 17th to the 20th C from eight quality dealers. **Est:** 1990. **Hours:** Thu-Mon 10-5. **Park:** Nearby.

JONATHAN PETERS
5 Main St, 06777
(203)868-9017   **29 48**

Unique collection of fine & imported linens & home accessories including furniture, wicker, baskets, handmade bandboxes, frames, English botanicals, flower holders & Limoges boxes. **Hours:** Mon-Sat 11-5 Sun 12-5. **CC:** AX/MC/V. Betsey Nestler **Park:** Nearby. **Loc:** In the center of New Preston.

TREBIZOND RARE BOOKS
Main St, 06777
(203)868-2621   **13**

Antiquarian books: English, Continental & American literature, voyages & travels, Americana & 18th C British books. **Serv:** Appraisal, catalog. **Hours:** By chance/appt. **Size:** 2,000 books. **Assoc:** CAB. Williston Benedict

TRUMPETER
Five Main St, 06777
(203)868-9090   **9 66 83**

19th & 20th C prints - historical & architectural - Victorian smalls & framed autographs. **Est:** 1978. **Serv:** Framing. **Hours:** Thu-Mon 11-5. **CC:** AX/MC/V. **Park:** On site. **Loc:** Just past Jct of Rtes 202 & 45.

VILLAGE BARN & GALLERY
Main St, 06777
(203)868-0502   **25**

Consignments, country furnishings, accessories & art. **Serv:** Lamp repair. **Hours:** Thu-Mon 12-5:30 Sat 10-5:30. **CC:** MC/V. **Park:** In front.

NEWINGTON

CONNECTICUT ANTIQUE WICKER
1052 Main St Rear, 06111
(203)666-3729   **86**

A large selection of antique wicker from Victorian to Bar Harbor. **Est:** 1980. **Serv:** Restoration, purchase estates, consultation, appraisal. **Hours:** BY APPT, please call for hours. Henry Spieske **Park:** On site. **Loc:** Call for directions.

DOLL FACTORY
2551 Berlin Tnpk Rte 5-15, 06111
(203)666-6162   **85**

Vintage clothing from the 1920s to present. **Serv:** Rental. **Hours:** Tue-Sat 1:30-6:30. **Size:** Medium. **CC:** MC/V. Louise S Chinelli **Park:** On site. **Loc:** From Hartford, Rte 91S, Rte 15-5 which is Berlin Tnpk to Newington CT.

NEWTOWN

BANCROFT BOOK MEWS
86 Sugar Ln, 06470
(203)426-6338 **13 33**
Antiquarian books: music, theatre & dance, scores, librettos, ephemera. *Serv:* Catalog, search service. *Hours:* BY APPT. *Size:* 3,000 books. *Assoc:* CAB. Eleanor Bancroft

JANE COTTINGHAM ANTIQUES
187 S Main St, 06470
(203)426-4000 **66**
English & American furniture, old photographs, botanical prints & early advertising, vintage children's furniture, toys, cupboards, folk art & paintings. *Hours:* Tue-Sat 10-5 Sun 12-5. *Loc:* Corner Pecks Lane & Rte 25.

THE PAGES OF YESTERYEAR
Old Hawleyville Rd, 06470
(203)426-0864 **13**
Nonfiction antiquarian books. *Serv:* Appraisal. *Hours:* BY APPT. *Size:* 2,000 books. *Assoc:* CAB. John Renjilian

POVERTY HOLLOW ANTIQUES
Poverty Hollow Rd, 06470
(203)426-2388 **44 50 63**
Furniture, lamps, china & glass. *Hours:* Thu-Sun or by chance. Marge Bennett *Loc:* Short distance from I-84.

NIANTIC

BOOK BARN
41 West Main St, 06357
(203)739-5715 **13**
A general stock of antiquarian books.

Serv: Search service. *Hours:* Seven days 11-6. *Size:* 18,000 books. *Assoc:* CAB. Randi White Chuck Howard

NOANK

STONE LEDGE ART GALLERIES
59 High St, 06340
(203)536-7813 **59**
Specializing in fine 19th C oils, acrylics & photographic fine art. *Serv:* Framing, restoration, art appraisal. *Hours:* Tue-Sat 9-5. *CC:* MC/V. *Park:* In front. *Loc:* 3 Sts from Universal supermarket.

NORFOLK

NOBODY EATS PARSLEY
114 Litchfield Rd Rte 272 S, 06058
(203)542-5479 **33 27**
Small items, ephemera & furniture, especially country. *Est:* 1982. *Serv:* Appraisal. *Hours:* Wed-Sun 10-4. *Park:* On site. *Loc:* Rte 44 to Norfolk, Rte 272S, 10 houses up on the R.

NORTH HAVEN

FARM RIVER ANTIQUES
26 Broadway, 06473
(203)239-2434 **83**
Museum quality American furniture of the Victorian period (1830-1890) in original & authentically preserved condition shown in a restored firehouse. *Pr:* $1000–100000. *Est:* 1972. *Serv:* Purchase estates. *Hours:* Sep-Jul Tue-Sat Appt suggested, Aug Tue-Sat APPT ONLY. *Size:* Large. *Park:* On site. *Loc:*

From New Haven: I-91N Exit 11, 1st 3 R turns to Broadway; From Hartford: I-91S Exit 12, L on Washington, R on Broadway.

NORWALK

BARTER SHOP
140 Main St Rtes 7 & 123, 06851
(203)846-1242   **15 33 55**
Three buildings of antiques, collectibles, old books, magazines, old records, post cards, bottles, ephemera, Victorian, oak, Art Deco furniture, tools, pictures, prints, paintings & frames, musical instruments, photographica & militaria. *Pr:* $1–15000. *Hours:* Year round Mon-Sun 11-6, Before 11 & eves til 8:30 by chance. *Size:* Huge. *CC:* MC/V. Richard A Bucciarelli *Park:* On site. *Loc:* CT Thruway Exit 15 (Rte 7): 1/4 MI S on Rte 123 (7) OR Merritt Pkwy, Exit 39 (Main Ave), 1 MI S on L.

BRASWELL GALLERIES
125 West Ave, 06854
(203)838-3319   **8**
Auctions once monthly featuring furniture, lamps, Oriental rugs, clocks, paintings, prints & etchings. *Serv:* Consignments, auction, appraisal. *Hours:* Mon-Fri 10-4 or BY APPT. Gary Braswell *Loc:* Near Maritime Center in Norwalk.

EAGLES LAIR ANTIQUES
565 Westport Ave, 06851
(203)846-1159   **37 59**
Specializing in American & Continental furniture, fine art, paintings & decorative accessories. *Est:* 1970. *Serv:* Consultation, repair. *Hours:* Daily 10-6, Sat-Sun by chance. *CC:* AX/MC/V.

Alexis Mihura *Park:* On site. *Loc:* Merritt Pkwy Exit 41: S 1 MI to Westport, Rte 1, L 1 MI.

GALLERY II LTD
14 Orchard St, 06850
(203)853-9225   **36 50**
A distinctive collection of furniture, camphor wood boxes, cabinets, chairs, accessories, 19th C hanging lanterns etched shades. *Est:* 1990. *Hours:* By appt only. *Loc:* Behind Loehman's Plaza.

NORWICH

1840 HOUSE ANTIQUES
47 8th St, 06360
(203)887-2808   **27**
Country furniture & accessories. *Est:* 1964. *Hours:* By chance/appt. *Assoc:* CADA. Olive J Buddington

NORWICHTOWN ANTIQUE CENTER
221 West Thames St, 06360
(203)887-1870   **{GR25}**
Pine, oak collectibles, glassware & estate jewelry. *Hours:* Tue-Sat 11-5, Sun 12-4:30. *Loc:* Rte 32S, 1 MI from Norwich Inn.

OLD GREENWICH

NEW ENGLAND SHOP
250 Sound Beach Ave, 06870
(203)637-0326   **21 44 63**
China, glassware, rugs & furniture. *Hours:* Mon-Sat 9-5. Barbara Reagan *Park:* Accessible.

OLD LYME

THE COOLEY GALLERY
25 Lyme St, 06371
(203)434-8807   **59 71**
Specializing in fine American paintings - Hudson River School, Connecticut Impressionists & Contemporary Realists. *Est:* 1984. *Serv:* Appraisal, period framing, restoration. *Hours:* Mon-Sat 10-5, else BY APPT. Jeffrey W Cooley *Park:* In front. *Loc:* I-95 Exit 70.

THE ELEPHANT TRUNK
24 Lyme St, 06371
(203)434-9630   **25 29 39**
Quality consignments, French, American & English furniture, rugs, chandeliers, paintings, porcelains & Oriental artifacts. *Hours:* Tue-Sat 10-4 or BY APPT. *Park:* In front. *Loc:* I-95 Exit 70: S on Rte 156.

MICHAEL BLACK DESIGNS
23 Lyme St, 06371
(203)434-8909   **38 60**
Antique Continental & Oriental furniture & decorative accessories for the discriminating collector. *Est:* 1987. *Hours:* Tue-Sat 10-5 or BY APPT. R Michael Black *Park:* In front. *Loc:* I-95 Exit 70.

GARY R PARTELOW REPRODUCTIONS
34 Lyme St, 06371
(203)434-2065   **43 70**
Reproduction of classic American designs - some 17th & all 18th C - Windsor, Queen Anne, Chippendale & ladderback chairs, candlestick tables, mahogany lowboys & highboys. *Est:* 1983. *Serv:* All furniture is custom. *Hours:* Mon-Sat 8:30-5. *Park:* In front. *Loc:* I-95 Exit 70.

WHITLEY GALLERY
60 Lyme St, 06371
(203)434-9628   **59 60 63**
18th & 19 C American & European furniture, specializing in Impressionists of the Old Lyme Colony, Oriental art, pottery, porcelain, crystal & decorative accessories. *Hours:* Wed-Sat 10:30-5 & by appt. Joseph Whitley *Park:* In front. *Loc:* I-95 Exit 70.

OLD MYSTIC

PAUL BROWN-BOOKS
Hendel Building Rte 27 & I-95, 06372
(203)536-9689   **13**
Antiquarian books: nautical, military, Americana & general stock. *Hours:* Tue-Sun 12-5. *Size:* 6,000 books. *Assoc:* CAB.

OLD MYSTIC ANTIQUE FLEA MARKET
Rte 27 at I-95, 06372
(203)536-2223   **{FLEA}**
Indoor & outdoor, between 20 & 60 dealers carrying large variety of good collectibles & antiques. *Est:* 1974. *Serv:* Catered. Space rental starts at $20. *Hours:* Year round Sun 10-5. *Size:* 45 spaces. Sonny Hendel *Park:* Free parking. *Loc:* I-95 Exit 90: from N - directly across st; from S - L of 27, 200 yards.

OLD SAYBROOK

ANTIQUES DEPOT OF SAYBROOK JCT.
455 Boston Post Road, 06475
(203)395-0595   **{GR}**
A group shop with furniture, china, glass & decorative accessories. *Est:* 1990.

Serv: Delivery service. **Hours:** Wed-Sun 10-5 Thu til 7:30 CLOSED MON-TUE. **CC:** MC/V. Gary Woods **Park:** On site. **Loc:** I-95 N Exit 67: S on 154, 1/2 MI on R; 1-95 S Exit 68: L at 1st light, 1/5 MI on R; From Rte 9, S on 154, 3/4 MI.

JAMES DEMOREST ORIENTAL RUGS
1 Great Hammock Rd, 06475
(203)388-9547   **21**
Specializing in the purchase & sale of antique Oriental rugs. **Serv:** Appraisal. **Hours:** By chance/appt. **Loc:** On the corner of Old Boston Post Rd & Great Hammocks.

ESSEX-SAYBROOK ANTIQUES VILLAGE
985 Middlesex Tnpk, 06475
(203)388-0689   **{GR85}**
Furniture, primitives, glass, china, brass clocks, linens, jewelry, paintings, silver, pottery, decoys & toys. **Est:** 1983. **Serv:** Truck & UPS shipping. **Hours:** Year round daily 11-5. **CC:** AX/MC/V. Judith Ganswindt **Park:** On site. **Loc:** I-95 Exit 69: Rte 9, Exit 2, L at end of ramp, 1/2 MI to Village.

HARBOR BOOKS
168 Main St, 06475
(203)388-6850   **13**
General stock of used hardcover & paperback books. **Pr:** $1–100. **Est:** 1988. **Serv:** Search services. **Hours:** Tue-Fri 9:30-5:30 Sat 10-5, CLOSED SUN. **CC:** MC/V. Judy Gallicchio **Park:** In front, nearby lot.

THE HOUSE OF PRETTY THINGS
49 Sherwood Terr, 06475
(203)388-3727   **44 32 63**
Glass: art, Victorian, early Americana, cameo, cut, pressed & modern. Also porcelain, dolls, figurines & some furniture.

Est: 1975. **Serv:** Purchase estates. **Hours:** Mon-Sat 11-5. **CC:** MC/V. **Assoc:** CADA NEAA. Frank Burton **Park:** On site. **Loc:** Rte 154 S (Main St), R at lights at Fire House, 1st R is Sherwood Terr.

LITTLE HOUSE OF GLASS
1560 Boston Post Rd, 06475
(203)399-5127   **44 63**
Furniture, china & glass. **Est:** 1956. **Hours:** Daily 10-5, call ahead advised. **Park:** In front. **Loc:** I-95 Exit 66: approx 2 MI.

NEW CREATION ANTIQUES
816 Middlesex Tnpk, 06475
(203)388-4344   **26 68 71**
Conservation of fine antique furniture by an experienced craftsman who served a 5-year guild-style apprenticeship to acquire his trade. Period-sensitive repair, restoration of original finishes, period fabrics for reupholstery. 18th & 19th C furnishings. **Pr:** $25–25000. **Est:** 1980. **Serv:** Appraisal, conservation, consultation, interior design, custom woodwork. **Hours:** Apr-Dec Tue-Sat 10-5 Appt suggested; Jan-Mar Fri-Sat 10-5. **Assoc:** NEAA. Michael L Poletti **Loc:** I-95 E Exit 67: L toward Essex, on R side of Rte 154 N, 1/2 MI before Essex town line.

PRESENCE OF THE PAST
488 Main St, 06475
(203)388-9021   **63**
Haviland & Noritake china. **Est:** 1977. **Serv:** China matching. **Hours:** BY APPT ONLY. Jan Fenger **Loc:** Call for directions.

SWEET PEA ANTIQUES
851 Middlesex Tnpk Rte 154, 06475
(203)388-0289   **44 47 63**
China, glass, estate jewelry, furniture & decorative accessories. **Est:** 1983. **Hours:**

Wed-Sun 11-5. **CC:** MC/V. **Park:** On site. **Loc:** 5 min from I-95, to Rte 154N, on the L.

TOUCH OF CLASS
1800 Boston Post Rd, 06475
(203)399-6694 **86**
Antique & reproduction wicker. **Est:** 1977. **Serv:** Repair, restoration. **Hours:** Spring-Fall daily 10-6. **CC:** MC/V. **Park:** On site. **Loc:** I-95 Exit 66: on Rte 1.

VAN'S ELEGANT ANTIQUES
998 Middlesex Tnpk Rte 154, 06475
(203)388-1934 **32 48 85**
Antique dolls & related items, glassware, furniture, vintage clothing, linens & jewelry. **Hours:** Daily 11-5 or by appt. **CC:** MC/V.

ORANGE

SHANNON FINE ARTS INC
517 Boston Post Rd, 06477
(203)393-2033 **59**
American painting from 1840-1940 featuring Connecticut artists, American Impressionism & select European works. **Est:** 1976. **Hours:** Tue-Sat 11-5:30 & by appt. **CC:** MC/V. Gene Shannon **Loc:** Call for directions.

PAWCATUCK

CHRISTOPHER & KATHLEEN COLE
120 S Broad St, 06379
(203)599-2188 **16 27 65**
Specializing in American country antiques, cast wrought iron for the hearth, treenware, architectural elements, accessories & furniture. **Pr:** $20–1000. **Est:**

1979. **Hours:** All year by chance/appt. **Size:** Medium. **CC:** MC/V. **Park:** On site. **Loc:** I-95 Exit 91: S off ramp to N Main St, 1/3 MI, L on N Main St to Rte 1E, 3 MI.

DOUGLAS HOWARD
74 Liberty St Rte 2, 06379
(203)599-1797 **60**
Dealer in small decorative objects, curios, Orientalia, Deco, Disney, oddments. **Hours:** Tue-Wed & by chance 10-5. **Park:** Nearby. **Loc:** I-95 Exit 92: S on Rte 2.

WOODS ANTIQUES
38 W Broad St Rte 1, 06378
(203)535-4851 **40 83 86**
Oak & Victorian furniture, wicker, fine china, glass & estate jewelry. **Hours:** Mon-Fri 10-4 Sat, Sun 10-2.

PINE MEADOW

1847 HOUSE ANTIQUES
Church St off Rte 44, 06061
(203)379-0575 **27 63**
Country antiques & accessories in a rustic shop: coverlets, cupboards, baskets, pottery & country furniture. **Est:** 1978. **Serv:** Purchase estates. **Hours:** Thu-Tue 12:30-5 CLOSED WED. Barbara C Krohner **Park:** On site. **Loc:** Across from the Tackle Shop.

PINE MEADOW ANTIQUES
Rte 44, 06061
(203)379-9333 **36**
Vast assortment of 19th & 20th C furniture & collectibles, American & English country & Victorian antiques. **Est:** 1973. **Serv:** Auctioneers, estate appraisal, lamp shade specialists. **Hours:** Daily 10-5. **CC:**

MC/V. *Assoc:* NAA. Rae Cameron *Park:* On site. *Loc:* Between Canton & Winsted.

PLAINVILLE

ATLAS AMUSEMENT
86 Whiting St, 06062
(203)793-9611   **78**
Specializing in antique pool tables with over two dozen on display. *Serv:* By chance/appt. *Hours:* Appt suggested.

ROBERT T BARANOWSKY
337 New Britain Ave, 06062
(203)747-3833
A general line of quality antiques. *Hours:* Daily afternoons or by chance/appt. *Loc:* I-84 Exit 34: 1 min off exit.

THE BOOK EXCHANGE
327 New Britain Ave, 06062
(203)747-0770   **13**
A general stock of antiquarian books: literature, science fiction, philosophy, religion, comics, mysteries, bestsellers, occult, counterculture & used records. *Hours:* Mon,Wed,Sat-Sun 10-6 Thu,Fri 10-8. *Size:* 60,000 books. *Assoc:* CAB. Paula Rose *Loc:* On Rte 372.

JEFF JACOBS FLEA MARKET INC
161 Woodford Ave, 06062
(203)242-1849   **{FLEA}**
A weekly, Sunday show with a variety of merchandise including glass, furniture, political, paper, Oriental, antique jewelry, lace & linens, etc. Admission 50 cents. *Pr:* $25–3000. *Est:* 1984. *Serv:* Cafeteria, restrooms. *Hours:* Every Sun 9-4. *Size:* 55-100 dealers. Jeff Jacobs *Park:* Free parking on site. *Loc:* I-84 W Exit 34 (Crooked St): turn L, R at traffic lights, 1/2 MI on R.

WINTER ASSOCIATES INC
21 Cooke St Box 823, 06062
(203)793-0288   **1 8 66**
Appraisals for estate & insurance of antiques & household furnishings, purchase or take on consignment single items or entire estates, antiques & fine furnishings auctions. *Serv:* Catalogs ($3/$5), consultation. *Hours:* Mon-Fri 9-5. *CC:* MC/V. *Assoc:* NEAA. Linda Stamm *Park:* On site. *Loc:* NYC train to Berlin,CT; Robertson Airport in Plainville OR I-84 Exit 34: Rte 372W, R after 3rd light, 2 hrs from NYC/Boston.

PLANTSVILLE

CARRIAGE FORGINGS ANTIQUES
24 West St, 06479
(203)276-8225   **44 50 77**
Furniture, lamps, glass & silver. *Hours:* Wed-Sat 10-5. *Park:* On site. *Loc:* I-84 Exit 30.

VILLAGE ANTIQUES STORE
69 West Main St, 06479
(203)628-2498   **{GR}**
Dolls, toys, & unusual items. *Hours:* Wed-Sat 10-3. *Loc:* I-84 Exit 30.

POMFRET

EBENEZER GROSVENOR REV. INN
Rte 44 Box 242, 06258
(203)928-4994
Antiques & collectibles in a charming country setting. *Hours:* Tue-Sat 10-5 by chance/appt. Nancy & Charles Thorpe *Loc:* On Rte 44 near Int of 169.

OLD STUFF ANTIQUES & COLLECTIBLE
Rte 44, 06258
(203)928-6961   **36 40 44**
Hoosiers, jelly cupboards, period furniture, mahogany, oak, glassware, jewelry, doll clothes, dolls & toys. *Hours:* Fri-Sun 11-5 or by appt. *Loc:* Halfway between Jct of 97 & 169.

POMFRET ANTIQUE WORLD
Rte 101, 06258
(203)928-5006   **{GR90}**
Furniture, pottery, porcelain & country paintings. *Est:* 1984. *Hours:* Daily 10-5 CLOSED WED. *CC:* MC/V. *Park:* On site. *Loc:* I-395 Exit 93: To Pomfret, W from Int of Rtes 169 & 101.

J THOMPSON ANTIQUES
Rte 169, 06258
(203)928-3713   **27 63 80**
Specializing in country furniture, Redware & textiles. *Hours:* Sum: Wed-Sat 11-5. Joyce Aicher *Park:* On site. *Loc:* On Rte 169 between Rtes 44 & 171.

POMFRET CENTER

POMFRET BOOK SHOP
Rtes 44 & 169, 06259
(203)928-2862   **13 51 64**
New England books & town maps, atlases, prints & post cards. *Serv:* Catalog, appraisal, search service. *Hours:* BY APPT. *Size:* 8,000 books. *Assoc:* CAB. Roger Black

PRISCILLA HUTCHINSON ZIESMER
Box 174, 06459
(203)774-4429   **29 37 59**
American furniture pre-1845, paintings, textiles, folk art, baskets & other accessories. *Hours:* BY APPT ONLY. *Assoc:* ADA. *Shows:* RI. Priscilla H Ziesmer

PUTNAM

GRAMS & PENNYWEIGHTS
75 & 83 Main St, 06260
(203)928-6624   **{FLEA}**
Indoor antiques & collectibles market under one roof. *Serv:* Catered. *Hours:* Sun 9-4. Paul Kenyon *Park:* Ample parking. *Loc:* On Rte 44.

GRAMS & PENNYWEIGHTS ANTIQUES
39 Front St Rte 44, 06260
(203)928-3422   **{GR100}**
A multi-dealer shop featuring 18th & 19th C country & formal furniture silver, art glass, Oriental rugs, lamps, jewelry, quilts, paintings, pottery, dolls & toys, memorabilia, bronzes, primitives, collectibles & objets d'art. *Pr:* $25-20000. *Est:* 1987. *Serv:* Appraisal, custom woodwork, doll hospital, purchase estates, repairs. *Hours:* Thu-Tue 10-5 Sun 9-4 CLOSED WED. *Size:* Huge. Paul Kenyon *Park:* On site. *Loc:* I-395 Exit 97: Rte 44W to Front St downtown Putnam.

REDDING

MELLIN'S ANTIQUES
PO Box 115, 06875
(203)938-9538   **37 63 66**
Specializing in Canton Chinese export porcelain maintaining a large selection of forms supplemented with high quality 17th & 18th C brass, unusual decoratives boxes, 19th C bird & flower prints in

custom frames all in a pleasing room setting. *Pr:* $25–10000. *Est:* 1977. *Serv:* Appraisal, brochure, consultation, interior design. *Hours:* By chance/appt. *Size:* Medium. *Assoc:* ADA. Rich Mellin *Park:* On site. *Loc:* Off Rte 7 Fairfield County, call for directions.

SERGEANT
Great Pasture Rd, 06875
(203)938-9366   **5 37**
18th & 19th C American furniture, architectural elements, French & English furniture. *Serv:* House restoration service. *Hours:* BY APPT ONLY. *Assoc:* AAA. *Shows:* RI. Gary Sergeant *Park:* In front. *Loc:* 1 MI S of Redding ctr.

TURKEY HILL BOOKS
4 Packer Brook Rd, 06896
(203)938-8833   **13**
Antiquarian books: firsts, fiction, children's signed, limited editions & fine bindings. *Serv:* Appraisal, catalog, search service. *Hours:* BY APPT. *Size:* 5,000 books. *Assoc:* CAB. Jack Grogins

RIDGEFIELD

ANTIQUE POSTER COLLECTION GALL.
17 Danbury Rd, 06877
(203)438-1836   **66**
A gallery devoted to authentic lithography posters from 1840-1930. *Est:* 1969. *Hours:* Tue-Sat 10-4. *Loc:* Rte 35 Girolmetti Court.

ATTIC TREASURES
58 Ethan Allen Hwy Rte 7, 06877
(203)544-8159   **29 44 46**
Small shop chock full of furniture, decorative accessories & more. *Pr:* $1–

1000. *Est:* 1980. *Hours:* Daily 11-5. *Park:* On site. *Loc:* 10 MI S of I-84 on Rte 7.

COUNTRY VILLAGE ANTIQUES CENTER
346 Ethan Allan Hwy Rte 7, 06877
(203)438-1100   **{GR10}**
Ten shops featuring country furniture, antique fishing tackle, tools, primitives, linens, glass, china & quilts housed in an 18th C home. *Hours:* Mon-Sat 10:30-5:30 Sun 12-5. Bonnie Olbrich *Park:* On site. *Loc:* Between Rtes 102 & 35.

GERALD GRUNSELL & ASSOCIATES
450 Main St, 06877
(203)438-4332   **4 23 71**
Dealers in fine European 18th & 19th C clocks. *Est:* 1953. *Serv:* Restorations undertaken, appraisals, nationwide delivery & set-up. *Hours:* Tue-Sat 9-5. *Assoc:* FBHI NAWCC. *Park:* Nearby. *Loc:* 20 min N of I-95.

HUNTER'S CONSIGNMENTS INC
426 Main St, 06877
(203)438-9065   **25 44 63**
Quality antiques & furnishings, antique jewelry, china, crystal & silver. *Est:* 1986. *Hours:* Mon-Sat 10-5 Sun 12-5. *CC:* MC/V. *Park:* On site.

IRISH GLEN ANTIQUES
346 Ethan Allan Hwy, 06877
(203)431-3979   **42**
Featuring architectural Irish pine furniture, French fruitwood, English Pine & decorative accessories. *Hours:* Tue-Sat 10-5 by chance/appt. Valerie Flowers

ISLAND HOUSE ANTIQUES
20 Prospect St, 06877
(203)431-6326   **3 42**
The Irish Shoppe: Antique pine from the Irish countryside & 18th C antiques.

Hours: Mon-Sat 10-5:30 Sun 12-5. **Size:** Medium. **CC:** AX/MC/V. **Park:** In front. **Loc:** On Rte 7.

THE RED PETTICOAT
113 West Ln Rte 35, 06877
(203)431-9451   1 43

Located in the 1740 Benjamin Rockwell house, seven rooms of 18th & 19th C antiques, fine reproductions, lamps, collectibles, accessories, folk art, old wicker & ephemera all in a beautiful country setting. **Pr:** $5–10000. **Serv:** Purchase estates. **Hours:** Tue-Sun 11-6. **Size:** Large. **CC:** MC/V. **Park:** On site. **Loc:** Rte 35S, West Ln Ridgefield, 4 MI S of fountain.

RIDGEFIELD ANTIQUES CENTER
Copps Hill Common Rte 35, 06877
(203)438-2777   {GR24}

18th, 19th & 20th C furniture, paintings, porcelain, glass, textiles, country pieces & decorative accessories. **Est:** 1989. **Hours:** Mon-Sat 10-5 Sun 12-5. Louise Dobson **Loc:** In back lower level.

RIDGEFIELD ANTIQUE SHOPS
197 Ethan Allen Hwy, 06877
(203)431-3702   {GR5}

Furniture, dolls, toys & smalls. **Hours:** Daily 11-5. Lois Dickson **Park:** Ample. **Loc:** On Rte 7.

THE SILK PURSE
470 Main St, 06877
(203)431-0132   36 63 77

Two large shops full of furniture, silver, china, glassware & pictures from the finest homes in Fairfield county. **Pr:** $25–2500. **Hours:** Mon-Sat 10-5 Sun 12-5. **Size:** Medium. **CC:** MC/V. **Park:** In front.

UNDER THE DOGWOOD TREE
39 Silver Hill Rd, 06877
(203)438-9860   47

Victorian, contemporary & estate jewelry. **Est:** 1986. **Serv:** Appraisal, consultation, repairs, restoration. **Hours:** Wed-Sat 10:30-5. **CC:** MC/V. Marty Brayer **Loc:** Across from the post office.

RIVERTON

ANTIQUES AND HERBS OF RIVERTON
Rte 20, 06065
(203)379-3673   48 77

Victorian silver plate, new linens & baskets. **Hours:** Tue-Sat 11-4:30 Sun 12-4. **Loc:** Off Rte 44.

UNCOVERING THE PAST
1 Taylor Rd, 06065
(203)379-7916   36 53 71

Repairs, restorations, stripping, refinishing, mirror resilvering & metal cleaning performed on premises by trained professionals, serving both the homeowner & the dealer, work guaranteed. **Est:** 1989. **Serv:** Pickup & delivery available, appraisal, repairs, replication. **Hours:** Sep-May Mon-Thu 10-4, Sat 10-3, Jun-Aug Mon-Thu 10-4 Sat 9-1. Wendy Larsen-Beneke **Park:** On site. **Loc:** From Hartford: Rte 84W - Rte 8N, R at end of Hwy, L at light to continue on 8N, 1 3/4 MI, R on to Rte 20, 3/4 MI L on Taylor.

ROWAYTON

SALISBURY

KEVIN B MC CLELLAN
APPRAISER/AUC
147 Rowayton Ave, 06853
(203)866-2122   **1 4 8**
Estate specialists. Appraisals for insurance, estate tax, liquidation or equi-
table distribution. Auctions & estate
sales. New York gallery placement.
Terms to consignor - 10-25%. No
buyers premium. *Serv:* Appraisal, accept
mail bids, consultation. *Hours:* Mon-Sat
10-4 Appt suggested. *CC:* MC/V. *Assoc:*
ASA. Kevin B Mc Clellan, ASA *Park:* In
front, nearby lot. *Loc:* I-95 E, Exit 12, R
on to Rte 136, approx 2 MI on R.

WILLIAMS PORT ANTIQUES
143 Rowayton Ave, 06853
(203)866-7748   **25 29 36**
Period furniture & gentlemen's antiques,
plus selective antique consignments.
Serv: Appraisal. *Hours:* Mon-Sat 10-5,
Sun by chance/appt. *CC:* MC/V. *Assoc:*
CADA NEAA VADA. Andy Williams
Park: In front. *Loc:* I-95 Exit 11 or 12: to
Rte 136, 1 1/2 MI to Rowayton Ctr.

ROXBURY

THOMAS CHIPMAN ANTIQUES
Roxbury Sta Rte 67, 06783
(203)354-8911   **5**
American antiques & antique building
materials. *Hours:* BY APPT. *Loc:* Directly on Rte 67.

AVERY & COX LTD
Academy St, 06068
(203)435-0062   **39**
17th, 18th & 19th C English & Continental furniture & accessories. *Hours:*
Wed-Sat 10-5, Sun 11-3, or by appt; Call
ahead in winter. Sylvia Cox *Park:* On
site. *Loc:* On Rte 44.

BUCKLEY & BUCKLEY ANTIQUES
Main St Rte 44, 06068
(203)435-9919   **37 50 57**
Specialize in William & Mary, country
Queen Anne & other high forms of
American country furniture (1680-1860)
& period accessories. *Est:* 1976. *Serv:*
Appraisal, consultation, interior design,
purchase estates. *Hours:* Wed-Mon 11-5
Sun 1-5 appt suggested. *Size:* Medium.
Assoc: BCADA. Don & Gloria Buckley
Park: On site. *Loc:* Rte 44, 1/4 MI W of
Town Hall.

RUSSELL CARRELL
Rte 44, 06068
(203)435-9301   **41 63**
18th & early 19th C painted furniture &
pottery. *Est:* 1946. *Hours:* BY APPT
ONLY. *Loc:* Call for directions.

LION'S HEAD BOOKS
Academy St, 06068
(203)435-9328   **13**
Antiquarian & new books on gardening,
landscape, design, architecture. *Serv:*
Appraisal, catalog, search service. *Hours:*
Mon-Sat 10-5 & mail order. *Size:* 10,000
books. *Assoc:* CAB. Mike McCabe

SALISBURY ANTIQUES CENTER
Library St off Rte 44, 06068
(203)435-0424   {GR10}
Formal English & American, country & primitive furniture, paintings, Jewelry & smalls. *Est:* 1981. *Hours:* Daily 11-5. *CC:* MC/V. Nick Collin *Park:* In front. *Loc:* Off Rte 44 in downtown Salisbury behind the Library.

THREE RAVENS ANTIQUES
Main St Rte 44, 06068
(203)435-9602   1 30 67
Unusual American antiques & accessories, American paintings & graphics, woodcarvings, early furniture, unusual pottery, weather vanes, stoneware, decoys & architectural elements. *Hours:* Open daily by chance/appt. *Assoc:* BCADA. Florie & Harold Corbin *Loc:* At Int of Rtes 41 & 44 in Salisbury near the White Hart Inn.

AMERICAN ANTIQUES
FOLK ART
COUNTRY FURNITURE
ARCHITECTURAL
ELEMENTS
EARLY DECORATIVE
ACCESSORIES

THE HAROLD CORBINS

P.O. Box 677, Main Street
Salisbury, CT 06068
Tel. (203) 435-9602

SHERMAN

PAST TIME BOOKS
Rte 39 N, 06784
(203)354-2515   13
A general stock of antiquarian books: illustrated, children's classics, New England authors, self-help & how-to books, medieval studies, archaeology & ancient history. *Serv:* Appraisal, search service. *Hours:* By chance/appt. *Size:* 4,000 books. *Assoc:* CAB. Steve Lorusso

THE PICKET FENCE
Rte 37, 06784
(203)355-4911   67
A collection of American antique quilts & antique collectibles. *Hours:* Sum: Sat-Sun 11-5, else by chance/appt, call ahead suggested.

SCARLET LETTER BOOKS & PRINTS
Box 117, 06784
(203)354-4181   13 66
Antiquarian books: children's, illustrated, 19th C wood engravings & original illustrator art. *Hours:* BY APPT ONLY. *Assoc:* ABAA. Kathleen A Lazare

SIMSBURY

C RUSSELL NOYES
9 Hopmeadow St, 06089
(203)658-5319   16 27 37
Country & formal furniture of the 18th & 19th C, woodenware, tin, copper, brass & decorative accessories. *Est:* 1955.

Hours: Daily 9-5 CLOSED JAN-MAR 15. **Park:** On site. **Loc:** On Rte 10 between Avon & Simsbury.

ation, consignments. **Hours:** BY APPT. Brian Riba **Park:** On site. **Loc:** S of Hartford.

SOMERS

SOUTH NORWALK

ANTIQUE & FOLK ART SHOPPE
62 South Rd Rte 83, 06071
(203)749-6197   **34 48 53**
Tables, chests, lampshades, linens, redware, stoneware, folk art, paintings, rugs, mirrors & signs. **Serv:** Custom lampshades. **Hours:** Tue-Sat 10-4. Falkowski **Loc:** Off Rte 190, Rte 83 S.

ANTIQUES & ART ASSOCIATES
54 Springfield Rd Rte 83 N, 06071
(203)749-4061
Selling antiques from an 1820 house & barn. **Serv:** Delivery, shipping. **Hours:** Wed-Mon 10-5, Thu til 7, CLOSED TUE. Tom Corcoran

BC BOOKS
64 Field Rd, 06071
(203)763-1315   **13**
Antiquarian books: a general stock. **Serv:** Search service. **Hours:** Tue-Sat 10-5. **Size:** 8,000 books. **Assoc:** CAB. Charlie Belsen

SOUTH GLASTONBURY

RIBA AUCTIONS
Main St, 06073
(203)633-3076   **4 8**
Three auctions of autographs, photographs, prints, posters & historical ephemera. 10% buyer's premium. **Est:** 1984. **Serv:** Appraisal, catalog, consult-

BEAUFURN INC
35 S Main St, 06854
(203)838-3221   **43**
Imported French & English antique reproduction furniture. **Pr:** $300–8000. **Serv:** Catalog $10, interior design, reproduction. **Hours:** Mon-Fri 9-5, Sat 10-5. **Size:** Large. **CC:** MC/V. **Park:** Free in nearby lot. **Loc:** From NYC: I-95 N, Exit 14, R on Fairfield Ave, to 3rd light at railroad bridge, R on S Main St; Park beyond storefront on R.

FAIENCE
120 Washington St, 06854
(203)853-4444   **36 46**
French tableware & antique & reproduction furniture. **Serv:** Interior design services. **Hours:** Tue-Sat 10-5:30 Sun 1-5. **CC:** AX/MC/V. Sue Westphal **Park:** On site. **Loc:** In Historic District of South Norwalk.

MECHANICAL MUSIC CENTER INC
89B N Main St, 06854
(203)852-1780   **55**
Various automatic music instruments, victrolas, music boxes, player pianos & self-playing organs. **Est:** 1975. **Serv:** Reproducing pianos & piano rolls, restoration, repair. **Hours:** Tue-Sat 9:30-4:30. **CC:** MC/V. Fran Mayer **Park:** On site. **Loc:** Adjacent to Maritime Ctr.

OLD WELL ANTIQUES
135 Washington St, 06854
(203)838-1842   **27 32 41**
American country painted furniture,

period furniture & accessories, vintage toys & holiday goods. **Pr:** $1–5000. **Est:** 1985. **Hours:** Tue-Sat 11-5. Patrick J Padula **Park:** Nearby lot. **Loc:** I-95 Exit 15.

WASHINGTON STREET BOOK STORE
119 Washington St, 06854
(203)866-9204   **13**
General stock of antiquarian books in all subjects. **Hours:** Daily 10-6, extended hrs during summer & before Christmas. Christopher Grahame-Smith

SOUTH WILLINGTON

SOUTH WILLINGTON ANTIQUES
Rte 32, 06279
(203)429-5595   **5 29 36**
Fourteen rooms & barn with furniture & decorative accessories - everything from the early country furniture to pieces of the 50s & period costumes. Resource for decorators, dealers & theatre groups. **Pr:** $1–5000. **Est:** 1958. **Serv:** Appraisal, restoration, delivery. **Hours:** Wed-Sun 10-4 or BY APPT. **Size:** Large. **CC:** MC/V. Donna Burns **Park:** On site. **Loc:** I-84 Exit 70: S approx 4 MI on the L.

SOUTH WINDSOR

COUNTRY BARN
1135 Sullivan Ave, 06074
(203)644-2826   **27 34 65**
Large 150-year-old barn featuring antique country furniture, primitives, kitchen collectibles & folk art. **Pr:** $50–25000. **Est:** 1982. **Serv:** Purchase estates. **Hours:** Year round daily 10-5. **Size:**

Large. Jo Patelli **Park:** On site. **Loc:** I-84N S Windsor Exit: L on Buckland to Sullivan Ave.

TIME PAST ANTIQUES
673 Main St, 06074
(203)289-2119   **23**
American, English & Continental clocks & fine antiques. **Est:** 1981. **Serv:** Appraisal, consultation, restoration & repairs (guaranteed). **Hours:** Mon-Fri 9-5, weekends BY APPT. **CC:** MC/V. **Assoc:** NAWCC. **Park:** On site. **Loc:** Just across the Bissell Bridge on Rte 91; 6 MI from downtown Hartford.

JOHN A WOODS, APPRAISERS
347 S Main St, 06074
(203)289-3927   **4 14 26**
A medical book dealer offering appraisals of books, documents & manuscripts. **Est:** 1976. **Serv:** Catalog, consultation, purchase estates, library development. **Hours:** By appt only. **Assoc:** AAA ASA.

SOUTHBURY

BEAUX ARTS
348 Main St S, 06488
(203)264-9911   **66 59 71**
Featuring 17-19th C etchings & engravings with occasional stock of 19th & early 20th C watercolors, oils & charcoals. Specializing in French matteing & period framing. **Serv:** Restoration, archival/restoration framing. **Hours:** Mon-Fri 10-5:30 Sat 10-4:30. **CC:** AX/MC/V. **Assoc:** PPFA. Peter Miller CPF **Park:** In front/rear. **Loc:** I-84 Exit 15: R at light, next L, shop is 3/4 MI on R, bordering city of Woodbury.

CHISWICK BOOK SHOP INC
Professional Bldg Village St, 06488
(203)264-7599   **13**
Illustrated, press, rare & press books, book arts & Officina Bodoni. *Hours:* BY APPT ONLY. Herman & Aveve Cohen

COUNTRY FARE
45 Quaker Farms Rd, 06488
(203)264-7517   **50**
Antique lamps & unusual lighting fixtures. *Serv:* Custom mounting, repairs, parts, antique lamp restoration. *Hours:* Tue-Fri 10-5 Sat 10-3. *Loc:* Rte 67 to Rte 188 S.

THE HONEY POT
88 Main St S, 06488
(203)264-9966   **4 47**
Antique jewelry including: rings, bracelets, brooches, pins, pendants, necklaces, earrings, chains, watch chains, fobs, diamonds & stickpins. *Serv:* Repair, bead & pearl restringing. *Hours:* Tue-Fri 10-5 Sat 10-4. *CC:* MC/V. *Loc:* I-84 Exit 15: rear of bldg.

LE MANOIR COUNTRY FRENCH ANTIQUE
Box 63, 06488
(203)264-4650   **35 38 63**
Fine quality 18th & 19th C French provincial furniture & accessories & old Quimper faience. *Pr:* $35–15000. *Hours:* By appt only. *Park:* On premises. *Loc:* I-84 to Southbury Exit 15.

NEW TO YOU LTD
29 Bullet Hill Rd, 06488
(203)264-2577   **25**
Consignment home furnishings including antiques, quality used furniture & accessories. *Serv:* Broom clean service for moving & estate settlements. *Hours:* Tue-Sat 10-5 or by chance/appt. *CC:* MC/V.

SOUTHPORT

CHELSEA ANTIQUES
293 Pequot Ave, 06490
(203)255-8935   **47 77 83**
A Victorian style shop with furniture, decorative accessories, fine estate & antique jewelry, depression glass, silver plate & sterling. *Serv:* Consignments. *Hours:* Tue-Sat 10:30-5. *CC:* AX/MC/V. Pat Everson *Loc:* I-95 Exit 19.

GWS GALLERIES
2600 Post Rd, 06490
(203)255-4613   **59**
American & English formal furniture & decorative accessories & oil paintings. *Hours:* Mon-Sat 9:30-5:30. Graham Stiles

PAT GUTHMAN ANTIQUES
281 Pequot Rd, 06490
(203)259-5743   **16**
Antiques & accessories for the kitchen & keeping room from America, England & the Continent. *Serv:* Demonstrations, lectures, guest exhibitors. *Hours:* Tue-Sat 10-5 & BY APPT. *Shows:* ELLIS. *Loc:* I-95 Exit 19.

HANSEN & CO
244 Old Post Rd, 06490
(203)259-5424   **4 6**
Appraisals of antique firearms & military accoutrements. *Serv:* Consultation, purchase estates. *Hours:* Mon-Fri 9-6 Sat 9-4. *CC:* MC/V. *Assoc:* AAA. Kenneth M Levin

POMEROY ANDERSON
PO Box 787, 06490
(203)255-3095   **4 26**
Independent fine arts appraiser, specializing in paintings & sculpture.

Art consultant, lecturer, author & researcher. **Serv:** Appraisal, auction, consultation, purchase estates. **Hours:** BY APPT. **Assoc:** ASA. Margaret P Anderson ASA

J B RICHARDSON GALLERY
362 Pequot Ave, 06490
(203)259-1903   **21 34 37**
American country & formal furniture, folk art & Oriental rugs. **Hours:** Thu-Sat 11-5 or BY APPT. **Assoc:** ADA.

THE STATION
96 Station St, 06490
(203)254-3739   **29 36 45**
Antiques, art & decorations for home & garden. **Est:** 1990. **Hours:** Wed-Sat 11-5. **Loc:** I-95 Exit 19.

THE STOCK MARKET
3519 Post Rd, 06490
(203)259-1189   **37 38 39**
English, Continental & American formal & country furniture, silver, paintings & decorative accessories. **Hours:** Mon-Sat 10:30-5.

TEN EYCK-EMERICH ANTIQUES
351 Pequot Ave, 06490
(203)259-2559   **37 63**
18th & 19th C English & American furniture & porcelain. **Hours:** Tue-Sat 11-5.

STAFFORD SPRINGS

STAFFORD SPRINGS 700
Rte 140 West St, 06076
(508)839-9735
May 4 & 5, 1991 antiques weekend at Stafford Motor Speedway with over 700 dealers. Admission $3. **Est:** 1990. **Serv:** Delivery service available. **Hours:** Sat 9-

5 Sun 9-5 Early Admission Saturday 7:00am $20. **Size:** Huge. **CC:** MC/V on $100up. Revival Promotions **Park:** Acres of free park on gravel. **Loc:** I-90 Exit 8: S on Rte 32. I-84 E to Exit 70 or I-91 to Rte 140 E. From Brimfield Rte 19 S.

STAMFORD

FENDELMAN & SCHWARTZ
555 Old Long Ridge Rd, 06903
(203)322-7854   **4**
Fine arts, antiques & household contents appraisal firm for probate, fine arts insurance, gift & IRS evaluations. Sale of art or antiques collections can be handled privately, at public sale or auction. **Serv:** Appraisal. **Hours:** BY APPT. **Assoc:** AAA ASA ISA. Jeri Schwartz

STEVE NEWMAN FINE ARTS
201 Summer St, 06905
(203)323-7799   **73**
19th & 20th C American & European sculpture, paintings, watercolors, prints, art glass, sterling silver. **Serv:** Purchase estates. **Hours:** Fri by chance/appt.

RAPHAEL'S ANTIQUE RESTORATION
655 Atlantic St, 06902
(203)348-3079   **71**
Antique furniture restoration, veneer replacement, carving & French polishing. **Est:** 1947. **Serv:** References available. **Hours:** Mon-Fri 8-5 Sat 8-2:30. **Park:** On site. **Loc:** I-95S Exit 7 (Atlantic St): 2 blocks turn L, under thruway & railroad bridges, 1 block on R.

UNITED HOUSE WRECKING INC
535 Hope St, 06906
(203)348-5371   **5 29 45**
The antique, the unique & the unusual

in Connecticut, featuring architectural pieces, antiques, furniture & memorabilia with large selection of outdoor garden furniture, concrete fountains, statuary urns & much more. *Serv:* Shipping & delivery. *Hours:* Mon-Sat 9:30-5:30 Sun 12-5. *Size:* Huge. *CC:* AX/MC/V. Ross Lodato *Park:* On site. *Loc:* I-95 Exit 9S, R on to Courtland Ave (Rte 106), L on Glenbrook Rd, R on Hope St, beyond Glenbrook Shopping Center.

STONINGTON

NEIL B EUSTACE
156 Water St, 06378
(203)535-2249   **29 37**

American formal furniture, decorative arts & accessories of the 18th & early 19th C. *Hours:* By chance/appt. *Park:* Nearby. *Loc:* Near the corner of Water & Pearl Sts in the village.

HUDNUT ANTIQUES
123 Water St, 06378
(203)535-3886   **29 37 63**

American furniture, porcelain, china, decorative accessories in a little shop down the stairs. *Est:* 1989. *Serv:* Buy antiques. *Hours:* Mon-Sat 10-5. *CC:* AX. Mary L Oakes *Park:* Nearby.

KING CANE
19 Pearl St, 06378
(203)535-3470   **22 68 77**

Specializing in gold, silver, coins & antiques, also cane webbing, hand cane, Hong Kong grass, miscellaneous weaves, outdoor furniture, rattan repair, reed, rush natural & fiber, shaker, splint, wicker spray-painting. *Est:* 1970. *Serv:* Chair seat weaves, chair repair, basket & wicker

repair. *Hours:* Mon-Sat 9-5. Clarence H June *Park:* Nearby. *Loc:* In the village a few feet off Water St.

MARY MAHLER ANTIQUES
117 Water St, 06378
(203)535-2741   **29 36**

Specializing in 18th & 19th C furniture & accessories. *Hours:* Mon-Sat 11-5 or by appt. *Park:* Nearby. *Loc:* In the village.

RONALD NOE ANTIQUES
135 Water St, 06378
(203)535-2624   **29 36**

Specializing in mahogany dining furniture & formal accessories. *Hours:* Mon-Sat 10-5 Sun 12-4. *Size:* Medium. *CC:* MC/V. *Park:* Nearby. *Loc:* In the village.

OPUS I
120 Water St, 06378
(203)535-2655   **21 36 63**

18th & 19th C furniture, Rose Medallion, Canton, brass, paintings, Windsor chairs & Oriental rugs. *Hours:* Sum: Mon-Fri 11-4, Win: By chance/appt. Carolyn Gunn *Loc:* In the village.

ORKNEY & YOST ANTIQUES
148 Water St, 06378
(203)535-4402   **21 29 37**

18th & 19th C American furniture, Oriental rugs, paintings & appropriate accessories of antique & international appeal. *Pr:* $20–25000. *Est:* 1972. *Serv:* Auction, purchase estates. *Hours:* Mon-Sat 10-5 most Suns. *Size:* Large. *CC:* AX/MC/V. *Shows:* Hartford, RI. Carolyn & Neil Orkney *Park:* On site. *Loc:* I-95 Exit 91: follow signs to Stonington Borough, 3 min off I-95, on Water St in the village.

PEACEABLE KINGDOM
145 Water St, 06378
(203)535-3434   **25 44 77**

Consignment shop with a varied line of furniture, pottery & porcelain, silver. *Est:* 1977. *Hours:* Tue-Sat 10-5 Sun-Mon by appt. *Size:* Medium. *CC:* V/MC. Bertrand F Bell *Park:* Nearby. *Loc:* In the village.

QUESTER GALLERY
77 Main St On The Green Box 446, 06378
(203)535-3533 FAX
(203)535-3860   **54 56 78**

Extensive collection of 19th & 20th C paintings, sculptures & prints, specializing in maritime, sporting, wildlife & American Impressionist subjects. Sea-focused collection includes fine ship & yacht models, furniture & other special things. *Pr:* $500-1000000. *Est:* 1860. *Serv:* Appraisal, restoration, framing, consultation, catalog ($12). *Hours:* Mon-Sat 10-5 Sun 12-5. *Size:* Large. *Assoc:* ISA NEAA. James P Marenakos *Park:* In front. *Loc:* From N: I-95 Exit 91: L for 1/3 MI, L on N Main thru light, L @ SS, R @ next SS, over RR overpass, L on High, 1 block.

QUIMPER FAIENCE
141 Water St, 06378
(203)535-1712   **63**

The U S retail store for Quimper, a French pottery made since 1690. This shop stocks antique Quimper as well as pieces made currently in the original factory located in Quimper, France. *Est:* 1690. *Serv:* Catalog ($2). *Hours:* Mon-Sat 10-5. *CC:* MC/V. Sarah Janssens *Park:* Nearby. *Loc:* In the village.

MARGUERITE RIORDAN INC
8 Pearl St, 06378
(203)535-2511   **1 57 59**

American furniture, fine paintings & works of art for the serious collector. *Hours:* BY APPT. *Shows:* WAS. *Loc:* In the village.

VICTORIA STATION
109 Water St, 06378
(203)535-3258   **36 59 63**

A charming selection of 19th C furniture, paintings, glass & china. *Hours:* Weekends 10-5 or BY APPT. Virginia A Anderson *Park:* Nearby. *Loc:* In Stonington Village.

WATER STREET ANTIQUES
114 Water St, 06378
(203)535-1124   **38 39 59**

English & Continental furniture, paintings & accessories. *Est:* 1987. *Hours:* Daily 10-5 & by appt. *CC:* MC/V. Anne Murphy *Park:* Nearby. *Loc:* In the village.

STONY CREEK

STONY CREEK VILLAGE STORE
118 Thimble Island Rd, 06405
(203)488-3060   **44 63**

Antiques, furniture, pottery, porcelain & glass. *Est:* 1960. *Serv:* Purchase estates, manage estate sales, auctioneer. *Hours:* Mon-Sun 9-5. Alice Green *Park:* In front. *Loc:* I-95 Exit 56 S: 1 1/2 MI.

STORRS

RAINBOW BOOKS
146 Moulton Rd, 06268
(203)429-5343   **13**

Children's antiquarian books & some general stock. *Serv:* Search service. *Hours:* BY APPT. Caroline C Lucal

STRATFORD

AMERICA'S PAST
82 Boston Ave, 06497
(203)378-7037   **59**
19th & 20th C American paintings.
Hours: Wed-Fri 11-4. Ivan Seresin *Loc:*
I-95 Exit 32: 4 min away.

LORDSHIP ANTIQUE AUTO INC
5 Prospect Drive, 06497
(203)377-3454   **4 71 84**
Appraisal & restoration of classic, exotic
& antique automobiles; also high-tech
paint work. *Est:* 1969. *Serv:* Shipper,
broker & consultant for banks, insurance
co's & Fed agencies. *Hours:* Mon-Fri 7-
4, Sat BY APPT, Sun CLOSED. *Assoc:*
NADA. Kevin Biebel

RON'S READING ROOM
235 Wilbar Drive, 06497
(203)378-9018   **13**
Antiquarian books specializing in
military science, children's books,
Americana, leather sets, mysteries, nautical, aviation, hunting & fishing. *Serv:*
Appraisals, search service. *Hours:* By
appt 9-12 & 5-9. *Size:* 8,000 books.
Assoc: CAB. Ron Weston

SUFFIELD

NIKKI & TOM DEUPREE
480 N Main St, 06078
(203)668-7262   **7 34 41**
Small, top quality inventory constantly
changing, with emphasis on design &
condition. *Pr:* $100–30000. *Serv:* Ap-
praisal. *Hours:* Appt suggested. *Assoc:*
ADA. *Loc:* 5 MI N of Bradley International Airport.

THOMPSON

RUSSIAN BEAR ANTIQUES
Box 33 RR 2, 06277
(203)928-4276   **29 37**
Fine American 18th & 19th C furniture
& accessories. *Serv:* Appraisal, purchase
estates. *Hours:* Sat,Sun 1-5 or by
chance/appt. Camille Strong *Loc:* 15 MI
S of Worcester, MA, 1 1/2 MI from Int
of 395 & 44.

TOLLAND

THE HOMESTEAD
46 Tolland Green, 06084
(203)872-0559   **27 34 63**
Antiques & collectibles including
country crafts, tole, folk art, baskets, pottery, pewter. *Hours:* Daily 10:30-5. *CC:*
MC/V. *Park:* Nearby. *Loc:* I-84 Exit 68.

TORRINGTON

COUNTRY AUCTION SERVICE
PO Box 1532, 06790
(203)542-5212   **8 25**
Purchase & sale of antique furniture, furnishings & collectibles - single items &
complete estates - consignment arrangements available. Inquiries handled with
discretion. No buyer's premium. *Serv:*
Estate appraisal & liquidation, consultation, purchase estates. *Hours:* BY
APPT. *Assoc:* NAA. I Joseph Stannard
Loc: Call for directions.

NUTMEG BOOKS
354 New Litchfield St Rte 202, 06790
(203)482-9696   **13 33**

Used, rare & out-of-print books, paper
& ephemera. *Serv:* Catalog, appraisal,
search service. *Hours:* Daily 12-5, or by
chance/appt; call advised on weekdays.
Size: 20,000 books. *CC:* MC/V. *Assoc:*
CAB. Deborah Goring *Park:* On site.
Loc: 1/2 MI from downtown W toward
Litchfield.

PIT'S ANTIQUES & FURNITURE
35 Water St, 06790
(203)482-5317   **40 83**

Specializing in Victorian, oak,
Mahogany, early American & collec-
tibles. *Est:* 1990. *Hours:* Sat-Wed 10-6
Thu-Fri 10-9.

PURE SILVER & GOLD
8 Water St, 06790
(203)489-0019   **47**

Specializing in antique & estate jewelry.
Hours: Tue-Sat 10-5, Thu til 9. Bret Van
Scteras *Loc:* Rte 8 Torrington Exit: shop
located in center of downtown area.

WRIGHT'S BARN & FLEA MARKET
Rte 4, 06790
(203)482-0095   **{FLEA}**

Indoor/outdoor market with antiques &
collectibles. *Hours:* Year round Sat-Sun
10-4:30. John Wright *Loc:* On Rte 4 between Torrington & Goshen.

TRUMBULL

APPRAISAL ASSOCIATES
93 Canterbury Ln, 06611
(203)268-6403   **4 84**

Appraisal of classic & vintage cars. *Est:*

1973. *Serv:* Appraisal, consultation.
Hours: Mon-Sat BY APPT. *Assoc:* ASA.
Ralph G Okrepkie

GWENDOLYN DONAHUE
Old Barn Rd, 06611
(203)268-3988   **27**

Country antiques. *Hours:* BY APPT.
Loc: Call for appt & directions.

ZIMMERS HEIRLOOM CLOCKS
124 Strobel Rd, 06611
(203)261-2278   **23 71**

Wide variety of clocks including banjo,
long case, mantel & others. *Serv:* Clock
restoration, buy & sell. *Hours:* By
chance/appt.

WALLINGFORD

ANTIQUE CENTER OF WALLINGFORD
28 South Orchard St, 06492
(203)269-7130   **{GR3}**

A renovated barn filled with oak & other
furniture, country items, pottery, pressed
glass, tinware, post cards, book &
collector's items. A browser's paradise.
Pr: $1–1000. *Est:* 1966. *Hours:* Daily
1-5. *Size:* Medium. *Park:* On site. *Loc:* 1
block E of Rte 5, across from the
cemetery.

FROM THE BARN
28 S Orchard St, 06492
(203)269-3017   **36**

Furniture & related items. *Hours:* 1-5
daily or BY APPT. *Assoc:* CADA. Lorry
& George Mellor

THE HAVERLY'S ANTIQUES
28 S Orchard St, 06492
(203)269-8135
General & varied line of antiques.
Hours: Daily 1-5. *Assoc:* CADA.

IMAGES, HEIRLOOM LINENS/LACE
32 N Colony Rte 5, 06492
(203)265-7065   **46 48 80**
A unique antiques shop specializing in
American & European estate linens/lace
& other early textiles - linen sheet sets,
shams, banquet cloths, especially hard-
to-find large tablecloths, rounds,
squares, runners, doilies, pillowcases,
quilts & coverlets. *Pr:* $2–1200. *Est:*
1988. *Serv:* Appraisal. *Hours:* Mon-Fri
10-4 Sat 11-4 or by chance/appt. *CC:*
MC/V. Debra S Bonito *Park:* On site.
Loc: I-91 Exit 13, 4 MI; Merritt Pkwy
Exit 64, 2 min.

MAISON AUCTION COMPANY INC
128 East St, 06492
(203)269-8007   **4 8**
Antique & estate auctions. No buyer's
premium. *Serv:* Appraisal, auctioneer.
Hours: Call for appt & schedule. Bill
Ulbrich *Loc:* I-91 Exit 12: R onto Rte 5N
to 2nd signal light. L over RR bridge
onto John St. R at end onto East St.

LEE MOHN ANTIQUES & ART
30 N Colony Rd, 06492
(203)269-3313   **58 63 64**
A general line of antiques specializing in
American Arts & Crafts pottery & Indian
arts. *Est:* 1988. *Hours:* Mon-Sat 12-4 or
by chance/appt. *Size:* Medium. *Park:*
On site. *Loc:* I-91 Exit 13: 2 MI N on Rte
5 OR Wilbur Cross Pkwy Exit 66, 2 MI
S.

WALLINGFORD ANTIQUES
COLLECTIVE
36 N Main St 2nd Fl, 06492
(203)265-9037   **{GR15}**
Quality group shop with clocks, furniture, silver, quilts, glass, china, inkwells,
lighting fixtures, post cards, vertu,
decorative accessories, books, microscopes & ephemera. *Pr:* $5–5000.
Hours: Thu-Sun 10-4. *Assoc:* NAWCC.
Park: In front. *Loc:* I-91 Exit 14 OR
Merritt Pkwy Exit 64: in Simpson Court
at corner of Center St.

WASHINGTON DEPOT

S CALCAGNI FINE ARTS &
ANTIQUES
Titus Rd, 06794
(203)868-7667   **37 39 60**
Fine art & antiques specializing in dining
tables, chairs, sideboards, mirrors, china
& Chinese export porcelain. *Est:* 1978.
Serv: Appraisal, purchase estates,
repairs, conservation. *Hours:* Mon-Sat
12-5. *Park:* On site. *Loc:* I-84 Exit 15:
Rte 6 to Rte 47 to Washington.

DES JARDINS ORIENTAL RUGS
4 Green Hill Rd Rte 47, 06794
(203)868-9495   **4 21 71**
Offering one of the largest collections of
fine antique & decorative rugs in New
England. *Serv:* Professional restorations
& cleaning, appraisal, consultation,
repairs. *Hours:* Wed-Sun 10-5, appt suggested. *Size:* Medium. *CC:* AX/MC/V.
Gale Des Jardins

HICKORY STICK BOOKSHOP
Rte 47, 06794
(203)868-0525   **13**
Antiquarian books: Connecticut, New
England, Alexander Calder, Gladys

Taber & Eric Sloane. *Serv:* Search service. *Hours:* Mon-Sat 9-6 Sun 11-5. *Size:* 2,500 used. *Assoc:* CAB. Thomas P Whitney

MICHAEL S MAC LEAN ANTIQUES
18 Titus Rd, 06794
(203)868-9425   **27 38 39**

Specializing in country French, painted Venetian, English & Irish furniture & unusual accessories. *Est:* 1990. *Serv:* Appraisal, interior design. *Hours:* Daily 10-5:30 CLOSED TUE. *CC:* AX. *Assoc:* ISFAA. *Park:* In front. *Loc:* From S: I-84 Rte 6N: L Rte 47 to Washington Depot; From N: Rte 202 to Rte 47.

K MAISONROUGE ANTIQUES LTD
11 Green Hill Rd, 06794
(203)868-9427   **13 35 38**

One large floor of fine European Continental furniture & objets d'art from the 17th C to the present. *Pr:* $25–15000. *Est:* 1990. *Hours:* Tue-Sun 9-6. *Size:* Small. *Park:* In front. *Loc:* Rte 47 to Litchfield, in Washington Depot.

THE TULIP TREE COLLECTION
Washington Mews Rte 47, 06794
(203)868-2802   **21 41 42**

A carefully selected collection of antique & reproduction painted, pine furniture & reproduction upholstered furniture, complemented by rag & kilim rugs, lamps & accessories. *Pr:* $10–3000. *Serv:* Appraisal, interior design, reproduction, architectural design. *Hours:* Year round Tue-Sun. *Size:* Large. *CC:* AX/MC/V. Robert B Winston *Park:* Nearby lot. *Loc:* From S: I-84 Rte 6 N: L Rte 47 to Washington Depot From N: Rte 202 to Rte 47 to Washington Depot.

WATERTOWN

CRAIG FARROW CABINETMAKER
70 Seminole Rd, 06795
(203)263-0495   **68 70 71**
Specializing in early New England 17th & 18th C furniture copies. *Est:* 1979. *Serv:* Repairs, restoration, reproduction. *Hours:* Tue-Sat 9-5. *CC:* MC/V. *Park:* On site.

WEST CORNWALL

DEBORAH BENSON BOOKSELLER
River Rd, 06796
(203)672-6614   **13**
Antiquarian books: early medical, diabetes, modern firsts, fore-edge, books about books, Alice In Wonderland & inscribed books. *Serv:* Catalog, appraisal, search service. *Hours:* By appt. *Size:* 10,000 books. *Assoc:* CAB. Deborah Covington

BARBARA FARNSWORTH
Rte 128, 06796
(203)672-6571   **13**
Antiquarian books: horticulture, art, literature, prints & decorated trade bindings. *Serv:* Appraisal, catalogs. *Hours:* Sat usually 9-5 else by chance/appt. *Size:* 50,000 books. *Assoc:* ABAA CAB.

WEST HARTFORD

SAMUEL S T CHEN
104 Shepard Rd, 06110
(203)561-0765   **4**
Appraisal of Oriental art - including painting & calligraphy, jade &

hardstones, pottery & porcelain, bronze & cloisonne & snuff bottles. *Est:* 1977. *Serv:* Appraisal. *Hours:* BY APPT ONLY. *Assoc:* AAA.

ROBIN FERN GALLERY
165 Robin Rd, 06119
(203)233-2781   **59**
Specializing in 19th & 20th C American & European art. *Pr:* $200–7000. *Hours:* BY APPT ONLY. Elizabeth B Beksha *Park:* In front. *Loc:* I-84 Exit 43.

FINITNEY & COMPANY
976 Farmington, 06107
(401)596-6210   **48 58**
English & American antiques furniture & smalls, American fine arts, French linens. *Hours:* Mon-Sat 10-5. Barbara B Eyre *Loc:* I-84: In W Hartford Cen.

DAVID E FOLEY BOOKSELLER
76 Bonnyview Rd, 06107
(203)561-0783   **13**
Antiquarian books: fishing, hunting, natural history & related fields. *Serv:* Catalogs, appraisals search service. *Hours:* By appt. *Size:* 2,000 books. *Assoc:* CAB.

ALICE KUGELMAN
19 Sunset Terr, 06107
(203)521-6482   **4**
Independent appraiser specializing in 18th & 19th C furniture & silver, estate liquidation & museum consultant. *Est:* 1970. *Hours:* BY APPT. *Assoc:* ASA.

WEST HARTFORD BOOK SHOP
322 Park Rd, 06119
(203)232-2028   **13**
General stock of used, antiquarian, out-of-print & rare books. *Serv:* Appraisal, search service. *Hours:* Mon-Sat 11-5 Thu 11-9. *Size:* 10,000. *Assoc:* CAB. Michael Polasko

WEST HAVEN

THE ADVANCED COLLECTOR
423 Saw Mill Rd, 06516
(203)932-1728   **59**
Specializing in 19th-20th C American art. *Hours:* Tue-Sat 10-5 by chance/appt. *Assoc:* NEAA. Michael G Bodyk

ARTISTIC VENTURES GALLERY
608 Second Ave, 06516
(203)934-0191   **59**
"Art between the wars", American paintings - 1920s-1940s, dealer to dealer. *Pr:* $1000–10000. *Serv:* Purchase estates. *Hours:* BY APPT ONLY. Lydia Bornick *Park:* Nearby lot. *Loc:* Call for directions.

JOSEPH LOUIS NACCA
52 Fern St, 06516
(203)933-4668   **36 37 83**
18th & 19th C furniture, specializing in the Empire period. *Pr:* $100–5000. *Serv:* Repairs, restoration, refinishing. *Hours:* Mon-Fri 8-4:30 Sat 8-12 CLOSED SUN, appt suggested. *Park:* In front. *Loc:* I-95 Exit 43: make a R U-turn, go up Highland St, 2nd L is Fern, 2nd house on R.

WEST REDDING

LINCOLN & JEAN SANDER INC
235 Redding Rd Rte 107, 06896
(203)938-9873   **37**
18th C New England furniture & related accessories. *Serv:* Appraisal, consultation. *Hours:* BY APPT. *Assoc:* ADA. *Park:* In front. *Loc:* 12 MI from Rte 84, 2 MI from Rte 7, 10 MI from Merritt Pkwy.

WEST WILLINGTON

RONALD & PENNY DIONNE
7 Glass Factory Schoolhouse Rd, 06279
(203)487-0741   **29 37**
American furniture & decorative accessories with emphasis on the 18th C.
Hours: BY APPT. *Assoc:* NHADA. *Loc:*
I-84 Exit 69: 1 MI E.

WESTBROOK

THE CAPTAIN STANNARD HOUSE
138 S Main St, 06498
(203)399-7565   **{GR3}**
Federal, Victorian & country furniture.
Est: 1987. *Hours:* Daily 11-5. *Size:*
Medium. *CC:* AX/MC/V. Elaine
Grandmaison *Park:* On site. *Loc:* I-95
Exit 65: R 1/4 MI into town cen, L at 2nd
light, at end of st.

TROLLEY SQUARE ANTIQUES
1921 Boston Post Rd, 06498
(203)399-9249   **44 47 63**
A lovely shop full of antiques & collectibles, including jewelry, glass, china,
tools, furniture, toys & miscellaneous
items. *Pr:* $5-2500. *Serv:* Conservation,
purchase estates. *Hours:* Daily 10-6.
Size: Medium. *CC:* MC/V. *Park:* On
site. *Loc:* I-95 Exit 66: to Boston Post Rd
R to Old Kelsey Pt Rd, I-95 from New
Haven Exit 65: to Boston Post Rd, turn
L to Trolley Sq.

WILD GOOSE CHASE
356 East Pond Meadow Rd, 06498
(203)345-3459   **36**
Antiques & furniture. *Hours:* Thu-Sun
10-5. John Iverson

WESTON

MILLICENT RUDD BEST
190 Goodhill Rd, 06883
(203)227-3966   **4**
Furniture & decorative arts, porcelain,
ceramics & silver. *Serv:* Appraisal, estate
sale service. *Hours:* BY APPT ONLY.
Assoc: AAA.

SANDI OLIVER FINE ART
11 Tubbs Springs Dr, 06883
(203)226-4469   **4 59 72**
Dealers in 19th & 20th C fine art, oil
paintings, sculpture, scientific, & medical instruments, American & European
clocks, Americana, Federal & Empire
furniture, early 16th, 17th & 18th C
European furniture, nautical & marine
items & garden statuary. *Est:* 1979. *Serv:*
Appraisal, purchase estates. *Hours:* BY
APPT. *Park:* On site. *Loc:* Off Rte 53.

WESTPORT

AMERICAN CLASSICS
80 Post Rd E, 06880
(203)221-1282   **1 34**
Americana including folk, American Indian, Western & carousel art. *Hours:*
Wed-Sat 11-5. *Loc:* I-95 Exit 17: in
downtown Westport.

CASA DI ORO
979 Post Rd E, 06880
(203)221-1555   **68 71 77**
Antique silver restoration including silver plating, re-polishing, flatware
refinishing, removal of engraving, re-engraving. Antique repairs including
enamel restoration & porcelain repairs.

Antique jewelry repairs & refinishing. **Hours:** Tue-Sat 11-6. Boris **Park:** In front/rear. **Loc:** 1-95 Exit 18: 2 min.

CONNECTICUT FINE ARTS, INC
2 Gorham Ave, 06880
(203)227-8016   **4 59 66**

Art appraisals of 19th & 20th C American & European drawings, paintings, prints & sculpture. Buying & selling 19th & 20th C works of art. **Est:** 1968. **Serv:** Appraisal, consultation. **Hours:** BY APPT ONLY. **Assoc:** AAA. Burt Chernow

CONSIGNMART
877 Post Rd E, 06880
(203)226-0841   **25 36 77**

Consignments of antiques, jewelry, paintings, furniture, silver & Oriental rugs. **Hours:** Mon-Sat 10-5:30. **Park:** Ample. **Loc:** I-95 Exit 18.

COUNTRY SWEDISH ANTIQUES
35 Post Rd W, 06880
(203)222-8212   **27**

Direct import of Swedish antiques & reproductions. **Pr:** $100–5000. **Est:** 1985. **Hours:** Mon-Sat 10-5. **Size:** Medium. **CC:** MC/V. Dick De Jounge **Park:** On site. **Loc:** I-95 Exit 17: to Int of Rte 1, or Merritt Pkwy, Exit 41 to Int of Rte 1.

THE FAMILY ALBUM
283 Post Rd E, 06880
(203)227-4888   **34 47 67**

Antique jewelry, quilts, vintage prints & folk art. **Hours:** Mon-Sat 9:30-5:30. **CC:** MC/V. Wendy Heyman **Park:** Playhouse Square. **Loc:** Next to Westport County Playhouse, Exit 40 or 41 off Merritt Pkwy.

FRIEDMAN GALLERY
139 W Post Rd E, 06880
(203)226-5533   **7 47 50**

Specialize in 20th C decorative arts with an emphasis on Art Deco, furniture, jewelry, lighting, radios & juke boxes. **Pr:** $50–10000. **Est:** 1980. **Hours:** Tue-Sun 10:30-5:30. **Size:** Medium. **CC:** AX/MC/V. Michael Friedman **Park:** Nearby lot. **Loc:** Downtown Westport across from the post office.

GUTHMAN AMERICANA
Box 392, 06881
(203)259-9763   **13**

Antiquarian books on American Revolution, French & Indian War & Colonial warfare. **Hours:** BY APPT ONLY. **Assoc:** ABAA. **Shows:** WAS. William H Guthman **Loc:** Call for directions.

JORDAN DELHAISE GALLERY LTD
1 Riverside Ave, 06880
(203)454-1830   **38 58 59**

Eclectic 18th & 19th C European furniture & accessories, 19th & 20th C works of art, photography & the unusual in Westport's antiques corner. **Pr:** $100–20000. **Est:** 1982. **Serv:** Appraisal, consultations **Hours:** Mon-Sat 10:30-5:30, Sun by appt. **Size:** Medium. George Jordan Michel Delhaise **Park:** In front, nearby lot. **Loc:** Merritt Pkwy Exit 41: Rte 33 S, corner of Jct 33 & Rte 1 OR I-95, Exit 17, Rte 33 N, at traffic light of Jct 33 & Rte 1.

DORVAN MANUS RESTORATION/GILDING
179 Compo Rd S, 06880
(203)227-8602   **37 39**

Restoring precious objects - gilt frames, mirrors, lacquer trays, painted furniture. Also, select small antique furniture &

accessories at wholesale & retail. *Serv:* Restoration of gilt mirrors. *Hours:* May-Nov BY APPT.

OLD LIBRARY ANTIQUES & ART CTR
7 Post Road E, 06880
(203)454-0134 {GR26}
Antiques, estate jewelry, pottery, crafts, art. *Hours:* Mon-Sat 10-6, Thu til 8 Sun 12-6. Harriet Lebish *Loc:* I-95 Exit 17 or Merritt Pkwy Exit 42.

PARC MONCEAU
18 Riverside Ave Rte 33, 06880
(203)227-8887 27 35
18th & 19th C country French furniture & accessories including armoires, buffets, tables, chairs, bureaus & many interesting accessories. *Est:* 1985. *Serv:* Restoration. *Hours:* Tue-Sat 10-5. *Size:* Large. Joanna Farber *Park:* Nearby lot. *Loc:* I-95 Exit 17: N on Rte 33 to 18 Riverside Ave OR Merritt Pkwy, Exit 41, S on Rte 33 to 18 Riverside Ave.

PRINCE OF WALES
1032 Post Rd E, 06880
(203)454-2335 39 42
Specialists in fine quality 18th & 19th C English pine furniture with an excellent selection of armoires, linen presses, Welsh dressers, desks, tables. *Hours:* Tue-Sat 10-5 Sun 1-5 BY APPT. *Size:* Large. *CC:* MC/V. *Park:* Accessible.

PROFESSIONAL ART CONSERVATION
4 Bauer Place, 06880
(203)254-3233 26 59 71
Preservation & restoration of fine art. Complete conservation services to dealers, private collectors & museums. *Serv:* Consultation. *Hours:* Sep 1-Jun 1 BY APPT ONLY. *Assoc:* AIC. Craig Kay *Park:* In front.

SAM SLOAT COINS, INC
136 Main St, 06881
(203)226-4279 24 79
Buy & sell coins, stamps & precious metals. *Est:* 1961. *Serv:* Appraise estates of coins. *Hours:* Mon-Fri 9-5 Sat 9-12. *Park:* On site. *Loc:* I-95 Exit 17 OR Merritt Pkwy Exit 42.

THINGS
142 Main St, 06880
(203)254-3714 36 77 78
Interesting mix of furniture, silver, wood carvings, Orientalia, hunt prints & country Japanese. *Pr:* $5–9000. *Serv:* Interior design. *Hours:* Mon-Sat 10:00-5:30 Sun by chance, Nov 24-Dec 24 Sun 12-5. *Size:* Medium. *CC:* AX. Barbara Kelley *Park:* Nearby lot. *Loc:* I-95 Exit 17: N to Post Rd, R 2 blocks, L onto Main St, 2nd block on R OR Merritt Pkwy Exit 41.

TODBURN
243 Post Rd W, 06880
(203)226-3859 27 32 86
Fine quality antique wicker, accessories, country furniture & folk art. *Serv:* Restoration of wicker furniture. *Hours:* Tue-Sat 10-5 or call ahead. Don Jobe GG Anderson *Park:* On site. *Loc:* I-95 Exit 17.

WESTPORT ANTIQUES & COLLECTIBLES
5 Post Rd W, 06880
(203)454-0523
Furniture, pottery & glassware. *Est:* 1989. *Hours:* Mon-Sat 10-5 Sun 12-4.

WETHERSFIELD

CLEARING HOUSE AUCTION GALLERIES
207 Church St, 06109
(203)529-3344   **4 8**
Family-owned & operated full-time auction gallery, 2 sales per week. One major catalog auction per month, usually on Friday. Auctions every Wednesday at 7 pm, with a one hour preview. *Est:* 1947. *Serv:* Appraisal, auction. *Hours:* Office: daily 8-5, gallery: BY APPT. *CC:* MC/V. Thomas G Le Clair *Park:* On site for 300 cars. *Loc:* I-91 Exit 26 (Marsh St): S of Hartford.

WILLIMANTIC

EASTERN CONNECTICUT FLEA MARKET
Rtes 31 & 32, 06226
(203)456-2578   **{FLEA}**
Indoor/outdoor market with antiques, collectibles. *Est:* 1978. *Serv:* Catered, restrooms, space rental begins at $15. *Hours:* Every Sun 8-3. *Size:* 100 spaces. *Park:* Free parking. *Loc:* At the Mansfield Drive In.

ERNEST S ELDRIDGE AUCTIONEER
201 Church St, 06226
(203)423-0525   **8**
Complete auction service with bi-weekly

auctions. *Serv:* Appraisal, accept phone bids, consultation, no buyer premium. *Hours:* Call for appt & schedule. *Assoc:* CAA. *Park:* In front. *Loc:* 30 MI E of Hartford.

WILTON

ARCHIVES HISTORICAL AUTOGRAPHS
119 Chestnut Hill Rd, 06897
(203)226-3920   **9 13**
Autograph letters, documents, manuscripts & signed books. *Hours:* By appt only. *Assoc:* ABAA. Warren P Weitman

AMABEL BARROWS ANTIQUES
372 Ridgefield Rd, 06897
(203)762-9054   **4**
Management of estate sales, specializing in antiques. Complete household furnishings (minimum value $15,000) sold in situ. *Pr:* $1-30000. *Est:* 1965. *Serv:* Appraisal. *Hours:* ESTATE SALES ONLY. *Assoc:* CADA NEAA.

WARREN FETT
52 Millstone Rd, 06897
(203)762-3998   **35 39 59**
Specializing in English & French country antiques, paintings & accessories. *Hours:* By appt. Warren Fett

GREEN WILLOW ANTIQUES
Cannon Crossing, 06897
(203)762-0244   **36 44 63**
An old fashioned antique shop in a country setting with furniture, early glass, china, jewelry, art glass, American pottery & silver. *Serv:* Appraisal, consultation, purchase estates. *Hours:* Tue-Sun 11-5. *CC:* MC/V. *Assoc:* NEAA CCADA. Lynn Brinker *Park:* On site.

Loc: From Merritt Pkwy: Rte 7N to Cannon Rd, 1 block to Cannon Crossing, From I-84: Rte 7S to Cannon Rd, etc.

GRYPHON'S CREST ANTIQUES
426 Danbury Rd, 06897
(203)762-7577   **37**

18th & 19th C furnishings from Great Britain. *Hours:* Tue-Sat 10-5 or by chance/appt. *Loc:* Located in Talbot House.

THE PINE CHEST, INC.
30 Deepwood Rd, 06897
(203)762-0521   **27 37 74**

American country furniture & accessories - specializing in mid 18th-late 19th C items. *Est:* 1985. *Serv:* Custom woodwork, repairs. *Hours:* BY APPT. *Assoc:* CADA. Michael West *Park:* On site. *Loc:* Call for directions.

THOMAS SCHWENKE, INC
300 Danbury Rd Rte 7, 06897
(203)834-2929   **37**

A large showroom stocked with fine period American Federal furniture, American Federal Classics replica furniture collection & period accessories. Toll free (800)FED-FURN. *Serv:* Appraisals, restoration, upholstery, custom manufacture, interior des. *Hours:* Tue-Sat 10-5 Sun 1-5. *Size:* Large. *CC:* MC/V. *Assoc:* ADA, NAADAA. *Park:* On site. *Loc:* In the Elijah Betts House.

GEORGE SUBKOFF ANTIQUES INC
643 Danbury Rd Rte 7, 06897
(203)834-0703   **37 39 59**

A large shop stocked with fine period American, English & Continental furniture of the 18th & early 19th C, good paintings & decorations. *Hours:* Tue-Sat 10-5:30 Sun 12-5. *Size:* Large. *Assoc:* AADLA. *Park:* On site. *Loc:* On Rte 7.

VALLIN GALLERIES
516 Danbury Rd, 06897
(203)762-7441   **45 60**

Chinese & Asian art & antiques, fine porcelains, pottery, paintings, textiles & Oriental garden ornaments from neolithic through 19th C. *Est:* 1940. *Serv:* Purchase estates or single items. *Hours:* Wed-Sat 10:30-5 Sun 1-5, else BY APPT. *Assoc:* AADLA ASA CINOA. Peter Rosenberg *Park:* In front. *Loc:* On Rte 7.

MARIA & PETER WARREN ANTIQUES
1030 Ridgefield Rd, 06897
(203)762-7353   **35 37 39**

Period American, English & French furniture, antiques & decorative arts. *Hours:* BY APPT ONLY.

WAYSIDE EXCHANGE
300 Danbury Rd, 06897
(203)762-3183   **21 29 36**

Furniture, rugs & decorative accessories. *Est:* 1961. *Hours:* Mon-Sat 10:30-5 Sun 12-5. *Park:* On site. *Loc:* Rte 7.

WINDHAM

THE TIN LANTERN
273 Back Rd, 06280
(203)423-5676   **50 70**

Reproductions of traditionally handmade early American chandeliers, sconces, lanterns & reflector ovens. *Serv:* Tin tools bought & sold. Cane, reed & shaker tape chair seat weaving. *Hours:* Mon-Fri 9-5 Wed 1-5 Sat 9-2. A J Styger *Loc:* 5 MI E of Willimantic at Windham Center.

The Guide to the Antique Shops of Britain, 1991

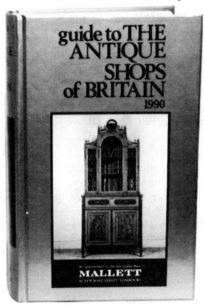

is the indispensable reference guide for antique hunters planning a trip to England. This brand new edition contains 20 percent more information than the previous edition. With the busy traveler in mind, information is listed alphabetically both by town and by specialty. Stock details and a listing of business hours will save you countless hours of wasted effort.

1,000 pages, 470 illustrations, 70 in full color, $29.95.

"the incomparable, ultimate antique dealers' guidebook."

-Emyl Jenkins

Order from your favorite bookstore or from:

Antique Collectors' Club
Market Street Industrial Park
Wappingers Falls, NY 12590

To find out more about our art and antique reference books or to order a free catalog call our toll free number (800) 252-5231.

WINDSOR

**CEDRIC L
ROBINSON-BOOKSELLER**
597 Palisado Ave, 06095
(203)688-2582　　　　**13 51 66**
Antiquarian books: Americana, architecture Civil War & Confederacy, American literature, voyages, travels & exploration, maps & prints. *Serv:* Catalog, appraisal. *Hours:* Mon-Sat 9-5 BY APPT. *Size:* 15,000 books. *Assoc:* ABAA CAB.

WINSTED

LAUREL CITY
462 Main St, 06098
(203)379-0325　　　　**24 47**
Specializing in coins, estate jewelry & antiques. *Serv:* Buying gold & silver coin, single pieces or collections. *Hours:* Mon-Fri 10-5 or by chance/appt.

VERDE ANTIQUES & BOOKS
64 Main St, 06098
(203)379-3135　　　　**13 33**
Antiquarian books: first editions, children's illustrated & ephemera. *Serv:* Appraisal. *Hours:* Wed-Sat 12-5. *Size:* 750 books. *Assoc:* CAB CADA. Ginny Dethy

WOODBRIDGE

MIRIAM LILLIAN
26 Overhill Rd, 06525
(203)387-3196　　　　**47 77**
Jewelry, silver, Satsuma & other quality mix. *Hours:* By chance/appt. *Assoc:* CADA.

HH PERKINS CO
10 S Bradley Rd, 06525
(203)389-9501　　　　**14 22 36**
Supplies quality seat weaving materials including caning, Shaker tape, natural/fibre rush & basketry supplies, including reeds, handles & instructions. *Est:* 1914. *Serv:* Catalog & instruction materials, consultation, repairs. *Hours:* Year round Mon-Sat 9-5, Sat 9-12, Sun CLOSED. *CC:* MC/V. Raymond DeFrancesco *Loc:* I-91 S Exit 59: L at bottom of ramp (15 S), thru 3 sets of lights, R on Bradley Rd.

RED BARN OF WOODBRIDGE
378 Amity Rd, 06525
(203)389-4536　　　　**{GR15}**
An antique co-op displaying an array of unusual antiques. *Est:* 1990. *Hours:* Wed-Sat 10-4 Sun 12-4. *Loc:* On Rte 63.

WOODBRIDGE BOOK STORE
Meeting House Ln The Center, 06525
(203)387-3815　　　　**13**
A general stock of antiquarian books. *Hours:* TUE ONLY 10-4. *Assoc:* CAB. Dianne Goodrich

WOODBURY

JOEL EINHORN AMERICAN FURNITURE
819 Main St N, 06798
(203)266-9090 **23 34 36**
Fine quality American 18th & 19th C furniture, folk art, clocks & ship paintings for the beginning & advanced collector. Special emphasis on Federal furniture & American tall clocks. Frequently one or two woodie station wagons available. *Pr:* $500-100000. *Serv:* Appraisal, consultation, purchase estates. *Hours:* Mar-Nov Thu-Sun 11-5 appt suggested, Dec-Feb Sat-Sun 11-5. *Size:* Medium. *Park:* On site. *Loc:* I-84 Exit 15 7 1/2 MI N on US 6.

ANTIQUE FURNITURE RESTORATION
187 Washington Rd, 06798
(203)266-4295 **71**
French polishing, restoration of old finishes, veneers & inlays, complete & proper structural restoration. *Serv:* Will purchase antique furniture in any condition. *Hours:* Mon-Sat 9-5. Mark Bieluczyk *Loc:* From Canfield Corner 1 MI on L on Rte 47.

THE BAY TREE ANTIQUES
745 Main St N, 06798
(203)263-5611 **29 39 66**
Ten showrooms of fine imported 18th & 19th C English formal & country furniture as well as accessories in a pre-Revolutionary home & barn. *Pr:* $25–10000. *Est:* 1985. *Hours:* Mar-Dec Wed-Sat 10-5 Sun 11-5 & BY APPT. *Size:* Large. *CC:* MC/V. James R Buc-

Hamrah's

Serving New England with Quality Oriental Rugs Since 1895

Our many years of experience
are reflected in the quality of our carpets.

Woodbury, CT 06798
Wed–Sun 10–5

115 Main Street North (Route 6)
203•266•4343
Appointments Suggested

zynski *Park:* On site. *Loc:* Rte 84 Exit 15
(Rte 6): N thru Southbury & Woodbury,
2 MI N of Woodbury town ctr.

BOOKS ABOUT ANTIQUES
139 Main St N, 06798
(203)263-0241   **14**
Specializing in books relating to antiques, decorative arts, folk art, fine arts,
interior design, architecture & crafts. *Pr:*
$4–350. *Est:* 1988. *Serv:* Special orders,
search service. *Hours:* Mon-Sat 10-5:30
Sun 12-4. *Size:* Medium. *CC:*
AX/MC/V. *Assoc:* ABA. Greg Johnson
Park: In front. *Loc:* I-84 Exit 15: E on
Rte 6, approx 5 1/2 MI on L.

BRASS RING ANTIQUES, INC.
97 Main St N, 06798
(203)266-4615   **43 47 63**
General line specializing in Victorian antiques & accessories, also Roseville,

jewelry, furniture reproductions & more.
Hours: 11-5 Tue-Sun. *CC:* MC/V. Joan
Ruggiero *Park:* On site. *Loc:* Rte 6 off
I-84.

BRITISH COUNTRY ANTIQUES
50 Main St N, 06798
(203)263-5100   **35 39 42**
Eleven spacious house & barn
showrooms featuring exceptional quality
authentic 18th & 19th C English &
French country furniture in pine, fruitwoods, elm & oak, paint-decorated armoires, many unusual accessories,
known for beautifully-finished antiques.
Est: 1977. *Serv:* Brochure, custom
woodwork, interior design. *Hours:* Year
round Tue-Sun 10-5. *Size:* Large. *CC:*
MC/V. Ed Adolph *Park:* On site. *Loc:*
I-84 Exit 15: Rte 6 E for 5 MI, on R, 1 hr
45 min from NYC.

COUNTRY ANTIQUES

Eleven showrooms featuring exceptional quality 18th & 19th C. English and French Country Furniture in Pine, Fruitwoods, Elm and Oak, Paint-Decorated Armoires and many unusual Accessories.

DIRECT IMPORTERS

- Beautifully finished authentic antiques in <u>excellent</u> condition
- Friendly personal service
- Design assistance
- Cabinet work for customized interiors
- Deliveries easily arranged
* * * * * * * * * * * *
Open 10-5 Tues. thru Sun.
(203) 263-5100

50 Main Street North (Route 6), Woodbury, CT 06798
*** 1¾ hr. Country Drive from NYC ***

CARRIAGE HOUSE ANTIQUES
403 Main St S, 06798
(203)266-4021   **1 37 59**
A choice selection of American furniture from 1760-1840, as well as 19th C American & English paintings. *Pr:* $500–10000. *Serv:* Brochure, consultation. *Hours:* BY APPT ONLY. *Size:* Medium. *CC:* MC/V. *Assoc:* WADA. Nancy Huebner *Park:* On site. *Loc:* Across from the cannon & Civil War monument on Main St.

HAROLD E COLE ANTIQUES
661 Washington Rd, 06798
(203)263-3332   **1 37 71**
17th, 18th & 19th C New England furniture & accessories for advanced dealers & collectors. *Est:* 1960. *Serv:* Appraisal, consultation, purchase estates, restoration. *Hours:* By chance/appt. *Park:* On site. *Loc:* 3 MI from Int of Rtes 47 & 6.

COUNTRY LOFT ANTIQUES
88 Main St N, 06798
(203)266-4501   **35**
A beautifully refurbished rustic 125 year-old barn specializing in country French antiques & accessories. *Est:* 1985. *Hours:* Wed-Sat 10-5 Sun 12-5. Carole Winer *Park:* On site. *Loc:* 1/5 MI N of Jct 47 on Rte 6.

CROSSWAYS ANTIQUES
4 Main St S, 06798
(203)263-4100   **16 39 53**
English Georgian furniture & accessories of the period including porcelains, trays, mirrors, brass & prints. *Est:* 1964. *Hours:* Mon-Sat 10:30-5 Sun 1-5. *Size:* Medium. James E Boudreau *Park:* In front. *Loc:* At the corner of Rtes 6 & 47.

DARIA OF WOODBURY
82 Main St N, 06798
(203)263-2431   **34 37 65**
18th & 19th Century American country & formal furniture, folk art, early textiles & accessories. *Est:* 1968. *Serv:* Appraisal, consultation, purchase estates. *Hours:* Daily 10-5. Daria & Wayne Mattox *Park:* On site.

DAVID DUNTON/ANTIQUES
Rte 132 off Rte 47, 06798
(203)263-5355   **1 37 59**
Antiques of the highest quality from the American Federal period with appropriate accessories. *Est:* 1974. *Serv:* Conservation. *Hours:* Thu, Sun 1-5, Fri-Sat 10:30-5, by chance/appt, call ahead. *Size:* Large. *Park:* In front. *Loc:* I-84 Exit 15: Rte 6 to Rte 47, L on 47 to Rte 132 R onto 132, 2nd house on L. 10 min from I-84.

GILDAY'S ANTIQUES
1917 Main St N, 06798
(203)274-1555   **37 50**
Fine 19th C American furniture, lamps, paintings & Oriental rugs. *Est:* 1985. *Serv:* Purchase estates, interior design service. *Hours:* Wed-Sun 10-5:30 or BY APPT. *CC:* MC/V. Ed Gilday Healy *Park:* On site. *Loc:* Near the Watertown Line, Exit 15 on I-84, E on Rte 6, 10 MI.

GRASS ROOTS ANTIQUES
12 Main St N, 06798
(203)263-3983   **29 44 77**
18th & 19th C country & formal antiques on 2 floors in a renovated silk mill - including glass, china, pictures, silver, jewelry & decorative accessories. *Est:* 1972. *Serv:* Purchase estates. *Hours:* Tue-Sat 11-5 Sun 1-4. *CC:* MC/V. Ethel Greenblatt *Park:* In front. *Loc:* I-84 Exit 15.

KENNETH HAMMITT ANTIQUES
346 Main St S, 06798
(203)263-5676   **2 37 53**
Authentic 18th & 19th C American furniture & accessories - mostly formal -

including highboys, lowboys, chests, tables, chairs, candlestands, mirrors, silver, paintings, rugs, samplers & fireplace tools. **Est:** 1954. **Serv:** Fully guaranteed. **Hours:** Mon-Sat 10-5:30. **Size:** Large. **Park:** On site. **Loc:** I-84 Exit 15: approx 6 MI.

HAMRAH'S ORIENTAL RUGS
115 Main St N, 06798
(203)266-4343   **21 80**
A wonderful collection of carefully selected & unusual antique rugs, including antique, Persian, Caucasian, Aubusson rugs & needlepoints - a haven for the collector, the decorator & novice alike. **Est:** 1895. **Serv:** Washing & restoration available. **Hours:** Wed-Sun 11-5 or by appt. **CC:** AX/MC/V. **Park:** On site.

FRANK C JENSEN ANTIQUES
142 Middle Rd Tnpk, 06798
(203)263-0908   **37**
17th, 18th & 19th C American furniture & accessories. **Est:** 1953. **Serv:** Reproductions, restorations. **Hours:** By chance/appt, please call ahead. **Park:** On site. **Loc:** I-84 Exit 15: R at 3rd light, off Rte 6, 1/2 MI on R.

MILL HOUSE ANTIQUES
Rte 6, 06798
(203)266-4326 FAX
(203)263-3446   **29 35 39**
One of America's largest collections of English & French antique furniture, chandeliers, accessories & works of art thoughtfully displayed in 17 showrooms. **Est:** 1964. **Hours:** Mon-Fri 9-5, Sat-Sun 9:30-5, CLOSED TUE. **Size:** Large. **Park:** On site. **Loc:** I-84 Exit 15: 9 MI N. 4 MI N of Woodbury.

A walk in the country

Come meander through our 17 showrooms filled with superb English and French antique furniture, accessories, chandeliers and works of art. We call it Mill House of Woodbury. You'll call it a revelation.

Mill House Antiques

1964   TWENTY-SEVEN YEARS OF CHOICE   1991

Rt. 6, 4 mi. north of Woodbury, CT (203) 263-3446
We're open 9-5 every day of the week but Tuesday

GERALD MURPHY ANTIQUES LTD
60 Main St S, 06798
(203)266-4211   **23 37 39**
17-19th C English & American furniture, desks, clocks, watercolors, pottery, brass, pewter & glass sold with a guarantee, all in a Greek revival house located in the Woodbury historic district. *Pr:* $200–25000. *Est:* 1984. *Serv:* Purchase estates. *Hours:* Wed-Sun 10-5:30 & by appt. *Size:* Medium. *CC:* MC/V. Patricia Murphy-Sadlier *Park:* On site. *Loc:* I-84 Exit 15: 5 MI E on Rte 6.

NININGER & COMPANY LTD
4 Main St S, 06798
(203)266-4661   **19 70 71**
Occasional tables of distinction with a fine selection for sale in the gallery; designers & crafters of special order furniture, restorers & conservators of fine antiques. *Pr:* $600–6000. *Est:* 1979. *Serv:* Brochure, conservation, custom woodwork, repairs, replication, reproduction. *Hours:* Wed-Mon 10:30-5 Sun 1-5. *Size:* Medium. *CC:* MC/V. *Park:* In front. *Loc:* At the Int of Rtes 6 & 47.

ART & PEGGY PAPPAS ANTIQUES
PO Box 335, 06798
(203)266-0374   **1 5 43**
17th, 18th & 19th C American antiques & reproductions, 18th, 19th & 20th C architectural elements for restoration & decoration, including hardware, flooring, beams, mantles, windows, doors & cutstones. *Serv:* Consultation, custom woodwork, purchase estates, replication, reproduction. *Hours:* BY APPT ONLY.

THE POLISHED SNEAKER
137 Main St S, 06798
(203)266-4847   **25 36**
Consignment antiques & used furniture. *Est:* 1986. *Hours:* Tue-Fri 11-4, Sat-Sun

12-5. *CC:* MC/V. *Park:* In front. *Loc:* Next door to the blacksmith shop, in the same building as the florist.

RAMASE
266 Washington Rd Rte 47, 06798
(203)263-3332   **5 74**
General old building materials including hewn beams, wide flooring, paneled room ends, wall boards, doors, moldings, mantels, old window glass, old brick, early American hardware, cupboards & weathered barn siding. *Est:* 1960. *Hours:* Fri-Sat 8-4 BY APPT. Harold Cole *Park:* On site. *Loc:* 1 1/2 MI from Int of Rtes 46 & 7.

JEAN REEVE ANTIQUES
813 Main St S, 06798
(203)263-5028   **29 47 83**
A large collection of vintage jewelry, unique & unusual collectibles, art, pottery, glass & china. *Pr:* $25–500. *Est:* 1986. *Hours:* Wed-Mon 11-4, Sat 11-5, CLOSED TUE, SUN. *Park:* On site. *Loc:* Rte 6 to Woodbury, shop next door to the 'Tique Mart.

MONIQUE SHAY ANTIQUES & DESIGN
920 Main St S, 06798
(203)263-3186   **36 41**
Three large barns of 19th C Canadian antiques including painted armoires, cupboards, tables & chairs. *Pr:* $100–10000. *Hours:* Daily 10-5. *Size:* Huge. *Park:* On site. *Loc:* I-84 Exit 15: to Rte 6N, 3 MI on L.

'TIQUE MART
Rte 6, 06798
(203)758-1571   **{FLEA}**
Flea market with antiques, crafts, collectibles & other flea market merchandise. Free admission. *Est:* 1967. *Serv:* Catered, rentals start at $15. *Hours:* Late Apr-Nov Sat 9-5. *Size:* 150 dealers.

Park: Free parking. *Loc:* I-84 Exit 15: 5 MI N on Rte 6 to Woodbury to the corner of Rte 6 & Middle Quarter Rd.

VIGUES ART STUDIO
434 Main St S, 06798
(203)263-4088   71

Paintings cleaned, relined, new varnish, complete restoration of gold leaf frames. *Hours:* Daily 10-5, Mon & Thu til 8. *CC:* MC/V. *Loc:* 10 min from I-84.

ROBERT S WALIN AMERICAN ANTIQUES
547 Flanders Rd, 06798
(203)263-4416   1 29 37

18th & 19th C American furniture, accessories & folk art. *Est:* 1966. *Serv:* Purchase estates. *Hours:* By chance/appt suggested. *Assoc:* ADA. *Park:* On site. *Loc:* I-84 to Rte 6, 3 MI N of the town of Woodbury.

MADELINE WEST ANTIQUES
Main St S (At War Memorial), 06798
(203)263-4604   29 60

Decorative accessories for the intermediate & advanced collector, Oriental paintings, prints, fine porcelain & Staffordshire plates. *Est:* 1960. *Hours:* Daily 10-5.

WEST COUNTRY ANTIQUES
334 Washington Rd Rte 47, 06798
(203)263-5741   29 35 39

Specializing in 18th & 19th C English & French country furniture & decorative accessories in a large 19th C barn. *Est:* 1982. *Hours:* Wed-Mon 10-5. *Size:* Large. *CC:* MC/V. Judy & Ralph Mueller *Park:* On site. *Loc:* I-84 Exit 15: 1 1/2 MI N of Main St on Rte 47.

WOODBURY BLACKSMITH & FORGE CO
161 Main St S, 06798
(203)263-5737   2 16 70

Early American wrought iron hardware, custom fireplace tools, accessories, brackets, hangers & hooks, latches, hinges, door knockers & foot scrapers, also reproduction of American 18th C firebacks. *Est:* 1976. *Serv:* Catalog ($3), repairs, replication, reproduction. *Hours:* Mon-Fri 9-5, Sat 9-2. *CC:* MC/V. Charles W Euston *Park:* On site. *Loc:* On Rte 6 off I-84.

WOODBURY HOUSE
494 Main St S, 06798
(203)263-3407   1 4 23

Fine books in all categories, bindings, Americana & clocks. *Est:* 1968. *Serv:* Appraisal, search service. *Hours:* Thu-

West Country Antiques

ENGLISH & FRENCH ANTIQUES

OPEN 10-5, CLOSED TUESDAYS • ROUTE 47, WOODBURY, CT • 203-263-5741
Exit 15 From I-84 - 1.6 Miles • North on Route 47 From Main Street Woodbury

Sun 12-5. *Size:* 3000 books. *CC:* MC/V. *Assoc:* CAB CADA ISA NEAA. Bernie McManus *Park:* On site.

WOODBURY PEWTERERS
Rte 6, 06798
(203)263-2668   **16 70**
Reproduction of early American pewter - including pieces from the Henry Ford Museum, the Mystic Seaport collection & a personal collection. Some factory seconds at a discount. *Serv:* Repairs of their own pieces. *Hours:* Mon-Sat 9-5, Christmas-Apr Mon-Fri. Ray Titcomb *Park:* On site. *Loc:* I-84 Exit 15, 3 MI N on Rte 6.

LES CLASSIQUES
693 Main St S 2nd level, 06798
(203)266-0210   **35 70**
Specializing in authentic French antiques & iron furnishings. *Est:* 1989. *Serv:* Fine French fabrics, reproductions. *Hours:* Thu-Sun 11-6 or BY APPT. *CC:* MC/V.

WOODSTOCK

BO & CO
RR 2 Roseland Park Road WM #11, 06281
(203)928-3939   **13**
Antiquarian books: technology & social history (English & American 1837-1900). *Serv:* Catalogs. *Hours:* By appt only. *Size:* 2,000 books. *Assoc:* CAB. Elizabeth B Wood

CHERYL R WAKELY ANTIQUES
Child Hill Rd, 06281
(203)928-6148
19th C furniture, textiles & accessories. *Est:* 9. *Hours:* Daily 12-4 or by appt. Cheryl Wakely *Loc:* Off rte 169 on Child Hill Rd.

WOODSTOCK (SOUTH)

SCRANTON'S SHOPS
Rtes 169-171, 06281
(203)928-3738   **{GR90}**
Seven rooms of antiques & handcrafted items in an early New England blacksmith's shop. *Est:* 1982. *Hours:* Mon-Fri 11-5 Sat,Sun 10-6. *Size:* Large. *CC:* DC/MC/V. *Park:* On site. *Loc:* I-395 Exit 97: toward Putnam, R on 171 for 5 MI, on the L across from fairgrounds.

WOODSTOCK ANTIQUE CENTER
Jct Rtes 171 & 169, 06267
(203)928-3190   **{GR30}**
Featuring a diverse line of antiques & collectibles including country furniture, primitives, advertising ephemera, china & glass. *Est:* 1989. *Serv:* Buy, wholesale & retail. *Hours:* Mon, Tue 10-5, Thu-Sun 10-6 CLOSED WED. *CC:* MC/V. David & Judy Rondeau *Park:* On site. *Loc:* From Sturbridge: Rte 169S off Rte 20; From Hartford: Rte 44 to Rte 169.

WOODSTOCK VALLEY

NORMAN C HECKLER & CO
Bradford Corner Rd, 06282
(203)974-1634   **8**
Full-service auction company specializing in auction sales of bottles, flasks, fruit jars & glass objects. *Est:* 1988. *Serv:* Accept mail bids, phone bids, appraisals, picture catalogs. *Hours:* Auctions five times a year - office hours from 9-5. *Park:* On site. *Loc:* Auctions held at St. Philip Ctr on Rte 44 in Warrenville, CT.

YALESVILLE

VICTOR A DENETTE
BOOKS/EPHEMERA
31 Chapel St, 06492
(203)269-9818   **13**
A general stock of antiquarian books.
Serv: Appraisal, search service. *Hours:*
Tue-Fri 9-5. *Size:* 10,000 books. *Assoc:*
CAB.

UNIQUE ANTIQUES &
COLLECTIBLES
409 Main St, 06492
(203)265-7255   **23 55 83**
Interesting shop in turn of century post
office with a diverse line of antiques &
collectibles & a bargain barn. *Pr:* $1–
2500. *Est:* 1984. *Serv:* Appraisal, purchase estates, repair, restoration. *Hours:*
Tue-Fri 10-5 Sat 11-5 Sun by
chance/appt. *Size:* Medium. Rick Ter-
mini *Park:* On site. *Loc:* I-91 Exit 15: Rte
68W to Main St.

Maine

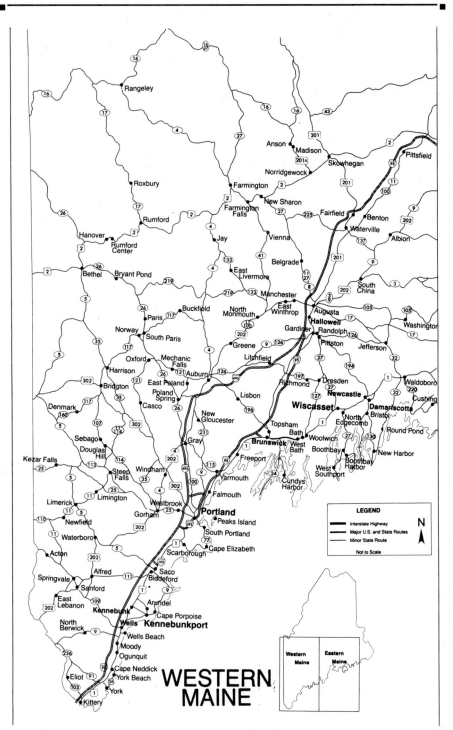

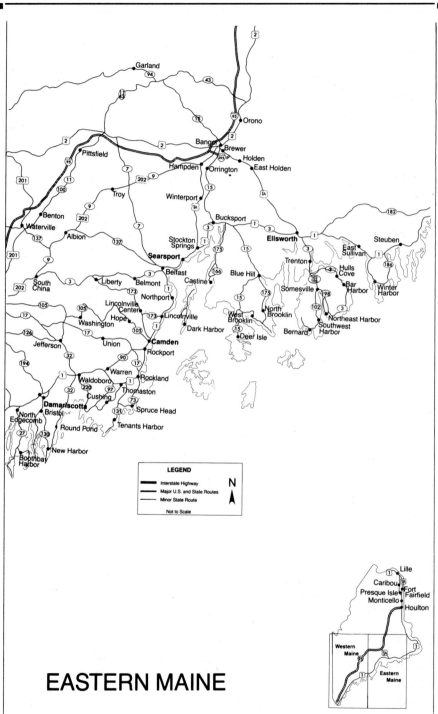

EASTERN MAINE

ACTON

GOOSE POND FARM
Rte 109 & Goose Pond Rd, 04001
(207)636-2664   **65 23 44**

Primitives; household furnishings; clocks; ceramics, glassware; American & English furniture; modern American painting; prints; Turkish, Persian, Caucasian & Chinese rugs & antique jewelry. *Serv:* Appraisal. *Hours:* By chance/appt. *Assoc:* NEAA. Jeanne Fulton

ALFRED

ALFRED TRADING COMPANY
Village Sq, 04002
(207)324-8355   **27 40 42**

Country antiques, tools, oak & pine furniture, quilts, linens & tins. *Hours:* Open all year daily 10-5. *CC:* MC/V. Fred Price *Loc:* On the square in center village.

PATRICIAN DESIGNS
1 Court St, 04002
(207)324-3555   **27 40**

Refinished oak furniture, country & Victorian accessories. *Est:* 1978. *Hours:* Sum: daily 12-5, Win: by chance/appt. *CC:* MC/V. Patricia Marley *Loc:* Rtes 202, 4 & 111.

SHIRETOWN ANTIQUE CENTER
Rte 202, 04002
(207)324-3755   **{GR50}**

Country furniture, primitives, oak & collectibles. *Est:* 1983. *Hours:* Jun-Sep Mon-Sat 10-5 Sun 1-5 Oct-May

CLOSED TUE. *Size:* Medium. *CC:* MC/V. Joan Sylvester *Park:* In front. *Loc:* 1 MI N of Alfred Village Sq.

ANSON

PHILL A MC INTYRE & DAUGHTERS
PO Box 231, 04911
(207)696-5809   **8**

Antique & estate auctions usually held at the Morrill auction facility in Gray, Maine. 10% buyer's premium. *Serv:* Auctioneer.

ARUNDEL

ARUNDEL ANTIQUES
US Rte 1,
(207)985-7965   **{GR200}**

A large group shop featuring a wide selection of antiques. *Hours:* Daily 10-5 CLOSED TUE,WED. Joanne S Desjardins *Loc:* Between Biddeford & Kennebunk.

AUBURN

MORIN'S ANTIQUES
195 Turner St, 04210
(207)782-7511   **40**

Specializing in refinished oak for home & office, always at least 300 pieces in stock. *Serv:* Refinishing & delivery service. *Hours:* Mon-Fri 9-5. Diane Landry, Mgr

ORPHAN ANNIE'S
96 Court St, 04210
(207)782-0638 **7 77 85**

Art glass by Tiffany, Durand, Steuben, Galle, Daum, Leverre Francais, decorative lighting from Art Nouveau & Art Deco periods, perfumes, jewelry, vintage clothing, pottery, silver, Orientalia & collectibles. *Pr:* $5–5000. *Est:* 1977. *Serv:* Purchase estates. *Hours:* Mon-Sat 10-5 Sun 12-5. *CC:* AX/MC/V. Daniel Poulin *Park:* On site. *Loc:* ME Tnpk Exit 12: 4 MI to Auburn, R at 3rd light, 4 blocks, on R, across from County Court House.

AUGUSTA

PINE TREE STABLES ANTIQUES
1095 Riverside Dr, 04330
(207)622-4857 **23 44 50**

Art glass, baskets, primitives, watches, clocks, cut glass, flow blue, majolica, lamps, lanterns, prints, brides baskets, rose bowls, Roseville, Nippon, other fine glass & china. *Hours:* Tue-Sun 9-5, anytime by appt CLOSED MON & JAN-FEB. *Assoc:* MADA. Harold Bulger *Loc:* On Rte 201.

READING TREASURES BOOKSHOP
W River Rd, 04330
(207)622-2047 **13**

A general collection of antiquarian books with an emphasis on early children's literature, Maine books & New England writers. *Serv:* Search service. *Hours:* Year round Tue-Fri afternoons Sat mornings or BY APPT. *Assoc:* MABA. Gertrude Harrington

WHITE BARN ANTIQUES
Riverside Dr, 04330
(207)622-6096 **32 44 63**

Victorian antiques, china, toys furniture. *Serv:* Appraisals, consultation. *Hours:* Apr 15-Dec 15 Mon-Sat 10:30-3 Sun by chance/appt. *Assoc:* MADA. Eleanor N Merrill *Loc:* Rte 201N, 6 MI N of Memorial Bridge.

BANGOR

T J BURKE ORIENTAL RUGS
48 Columbia St, 04401
(207)942-8872 **21**

Antique/semi-antique Oriental rugs, carpets, kilims, tapestries & tribal trappings. *Pr:* $100–35000. *Est:* 1978. *Serv:* Appraisal, cleaning, purchase estates, repairs, restoration. *Hours:* Mon-Fri 10-5:30 Sat 10-2 Sun BY APPT, call ahead. *Size:* Medium. *Park:* In front. *Loc:* I-95 Hammond St Exit: Columbia St is 1 block up from Main St; from Main St 2nd L (Cross St) to Int with Columbia St.

GAMAGE ANTIQUES
60 Main St, 04401
(207)945-6226 **36 50 59**

Formal & country furniture, lamps, paintings, rugs, china, glass & jewelry. *Hours:* All year Mon-Sat. *Assoc:* MADA. Hedda Gamage

LIPPINCOTT BOOKS
624 Hammond St, 04401
(207)942-4398 **13 33**

Four centuries of old & rare books, wide variety of subjects - especially Maine, ephemera, periodicals & some uncommon books. *Pr:* $1–1000. *Est:* 1975. *Serv:* Appraisal, purchase estates. *Hours:*

Mon-Fri 10-5:30, Sat 10-5. *Assoc:* MABA. Bill Lippincott *Park:* In front. *Loc:* I-95 Exit 46: bear R, 1/2 MI on R.

1983. *Serv:* Catalog. *Hours:* BY APPT. *CC:* MC/V. *Assoc:* MABA. *Park:* On site.

BAR HARBOR

ALBERT MEADOW ANTIQUES
10 Albert Meadow, 04609
(207)288-9456   **44 47 77**

A small summer shop filled with fine decorative arts including Art Nouveau, Arts & Crafts, lamps, sterling silver & estate jewelry. Always a nice selection of Tiffany, Galle, Loetz, Steuben, Rookwood, Gorham & Navajo weavings. *Est:* 1987. *Hours:* Jun 15-Oct 15 Daily 10-7. *CC:* MC/V. *Park:* On site. *Loc:* 75 Ft from the big, black clock on Main St at the Village Green.

GRANDMA'S ATTIC
112 Cottage St, 04609
(207)667-4024   **32 77 81**

A large selction of toys, dolls, tools, silver, glass, pottery, door stops, furniture, etc. *Hours:* Daily 10-6. *Park:* On street. *Loc:* Between Rte 3 and downtown.

ROSE W OLSTEAD
200 Main St, 04609
(207)288-5494   **1 37**

A select grouping of American period furniture & decorative accessories displayed in room like settings - including nautical items, lighting devices & metal ware. *Est:* 1946. *Hours:* Mon-Sat 10-5:30.

STEVE POWELL
The Hideaway, 04609
(207)288-4665   **13**

Large stock of antiquarian mystery books & related items. *Pr:* $5–1500. *Est:*

BASS HARBOR

ONCE UPON A TIME
Rte 102, 04563
(207)244-3745   **27 47 67**

Extensive collection of silver, gold & costume jewelry, country antiques & collectibles, quilts, linens, china & country furniture displayed in a small barn. *Pr:* $5–500. *Est:* 1971. *Hours:* May 15 - Sep 15 seven days 9-6 by chance/appt. *Size:* Medium. *CC:* MC/V. Doris Simon *Park:* In front. *Loc:* 3 MI S of Southwest Harbor on Rte 102.

BATH

JAMES E ARSENAULT BOOKSELLER
3 North St, 04530
(207)443-1510   **13 33 66**

A carefully selected cross-section of better books; including art, architecture, antiques, literature, Americana, natural history, travel & old, unusual or significant dictionaries. Serious prints (not from books) often on hand. Photos autographs, paper. *Pr:* $15–2000. *Est:* 1987. *Hours:* BY APPT ONLY. *Assoc:* MABA. James E Arsenault *Park:* In front. *Loc:* 1/2 MI up-river from Bath Ironworks just off Washington St on corner of North & Front Sts.

FRONT STREET ANTIQUES
190 Front St, 04530
(207)443-8098 **27 40 63**
Specializing in pine, oak, country, textiles, Staffordshire & ironstone. *Hours:* Daily 10-5 Sun by chance.

RECENT PAST
17 Western Ave, 04530
(207)443-4407 **48 83**
Victorian & country specializing in textiles & linens. *Hours:* By chance/appt. Pauline J Thibodeau

TRIFLES
21 Elm St, 04530
(207)442-8474 **29**
Decorative accessories - antique smalls of the 19th C, emphasis on classically oriented pieces. *Est:* 1986. *Serv:* English tea room serving lunch & afternoon tea. *Hours:* Mon-Fri 11-4 rainy Sats. Helen Robinson *Park:* In front. *Loc:* 2 blocks from Rte 1 in downtown Bath.

BELFAST

ANDREWS & ANDREWS
Rte 1, 04915
(207)338-1386 **4 8**
Auctioneers offering antiques from area estates. *Serv:* Appraisal, absentee bids accepted upon approval. *Hours:* Call for appt or schedule. Daniel W Andrews

APEX ANTIQUES
98 High St, 04915
(207)338-1194 **5 36 38**
A Victorian carriage house featuring American & European formal & country furniture, architectural details & accessories. *Est:* 1978. *Serv:* Consultation, interior design, repairs, some reproduction, restoration. *Hours:* May-

Nov: daily 9-6, Win: by chance/appt. *Size:* Medium. *Assoc:* MADA. Giacomo P D'Avanzo *Park:* On site.

BOOKLOVER'S ATTIC
Rte 1, 04915
(207)338-2450 **13**
Antiquarian books: American first editions, music, maritime, aviation, Americana, science fiction, hunting, fishing, exploration, recordings (lp's): jazz, Broadway shows, sound tracks, classical & vocal. *Hours:* May-Oct 11-6 daily CLOSED TUE. *Assoc:* MABA. Peter Plumb *Park:* Nearby. *Loc:* Rte 1 N just over bridge.

AVIS HOWELLS ANTIQUES
21 Pearl St, 04915
(207)338-3302 **37 60 76**
In a white Victorian home, specializing in things Shaker & Canton. American furniture pre-1850. *Hours:* By appt. *Assoc:* MADA. Avis Howells *Loc:* At corner Court & Pearl Sts.

IRONWOOD ART & ANTIQUES
77 High St, 04915
(207)338-5367 **7 16 29**
Decoratives from all eras including Art Nouveau, Art Deco, craftsman & Moderne; tribal & folk art as well as country primitives & paintings, in an eclectic gallery setting. *Pr:* $25–2500. *Est:* 1989. *Serv:* Interior design. *Hours:* May-Dec Tue-Sat 10-4, Jan-Apr Sat 10-4 or by appt. *Size:* Medium. *Assoc:* MADA. Jude Nickerson *Park:* In front, nearby lot. *Loc:* S 1 block from town ctr traffic light.

BELGRADE

BORSSEN ANTIQUES
Rte 135, 04917
(207)495-2013 **40**
A large selection of oak furniture - wholesale & retail. *Est:* 1967. *Serv:* Restoration, refinishing, delivery, shipping. *Hours:* All year daily. *Loc:* 1 1/2 MI S of Town Hall.

BERNARD

1895 SHOP
1 Steamboat Wharf Rd, 04612
(207)244-7039 **23 44 64**
Glass, china, collectibles, post cards, lamps & clocks. *Hours:* Seasonal Jun-Sep open most days in the summer-call advised. *CC:* MC/V. Louise Kelley *Park:* Off street. *Loc:* Off Rte 102.

ANTIQUE WICKER
Just Off Rte 102, 04612
(207)244-3983 **86**
Two hundred pieces of antique wicker in stock at all times. *Est:* 1976. *Serv:* Will ship anywhere. *Hours:* Sum: daily 10-5, Win: anytime by chance/appt. Edward Higgins *Park:* On site. *Loc:* 4 MI beyond Southwest Harbor.

NANCY NEALE TYPECRAFT
Steamboat Wharf Rd, 04612
(207)244-5192 **12 16**
Specialists in antique wood type & other items relating to printing: type trays, type sticks & complete fonts. Unique museum-like shop displaying type made from 1880s to 1940s. Cuts used for illustrations & newspapers, Hebrew type & German type. *Serv:* Catalog, mail order, collages representing family history made to order. *Hours:* Jun-Aug by chance/appt.

THE OLD RED STORE
2 Steamboat Wharf Rd, 04612
(207)244-3349 **44 63**
Mainly china, glass & small furniture. *Est:* 1974. *Hours:* Jun 15-Sep 15 Mon-Fri 10-1 2-5, else by chance/appt. Paul Hinton *Park:* Nearby.

BIDDEFORD

BIDDEFORD ANTIQUE CENTER
Rte 1, 04005
(207)284-6433 **{GR40+}**
Furniture, paintings, primitives, linens, fine glass, china & collectibles. *Est:* 1987. *Hours:* Daily 9:30-4:30 Nov-Mar CLOSED TUE,WED. *CC:* MC/V. Dolly Curran *Park:* On site. *Loc:* I-95 Exit 4: N on Rte 111 to Rte 1, S about 1 1/2 MI.

ELI THE COBBLER ANTIQUES
30 Morin St, 04005
(207)282-1028 **44 47**
Oriental & art glass & jewelry. *Est:* 1972. *Hours:* Year round Mon-Fri 9-3. *Loc:* Just around the corner from the Biddeford Antique Center.

BLUE HILL

EMERSON ANTIQUES
Main St, 04614
(207)374-5140 **29**
Antiques & decorative accessories - mostly New England & pre-1845. *Est:*

1963. *Hours:* Mon-Fri 10-5 Sat 11-3, call ahead suggested in winter. *CC:* MC/V. Brad Emerson *Park:* On street.

LIROS GALLERY
Main St, 04614
(207)374-5370 **51 59 66**
Fine paintings, old prints, maps & Russian icons. *Est:* 1966. *Serv:* Restoration. *Hours:* Year round Mon-Fri 9-5 Sat BY APPT. *CC:* AX/MC/V. *Park:* On street. *Loc:* Next to Jonathan's Restaurant in Blue Hill.

BOOTHBAY

BLUE UNICORN
Rte 27, 04537
(207)633-6499 **44**
Furniture, flint, Heisey, toy glass & china. *Hours:* Seasonally daily 10-5 Sun 12-5. *Assoc:* MADA. John Stengele *Loc:* Next to Texaco station.

SWEET WOODRUFF FARM
Rte 27, 04537
(207)633-6977 **27 41**
Wonderful country shop & herb farm located in the barn of an early sheep farm. Painted country antiques are the specialty. *Est:* 1988. *Serv:* Bed & Breakfast in the 1767 house. *Hours:* Open most days, call ahead advised. *Size:* On site. *CC:* MC/V. *Loc:* 4 1/2 MI on Rte 27 (Boothbay from Rte 1).

BOOTHBAY HARBOR

BAY STREET ANTIQUES
2 Bay St, 04538
(207)633-3186 **3 44 63**
Art glass (Tiffany, Nash, Daum, Galle,

Schneider), early 20th C American art pottery (Newcomb, Ohr, Rookwood, Grueby), paintings, American Indian baskets & pottery, Art Nouveau, Arts & Crafts, Art Deco, Chinese items, Japanese prints, folk art, ephemera. *Pr:* $5–20000. *Est:* 1980. *Hours:* Jun 15-Sep 30 Mon-Sat 10-5. *Assoc:* MADA. Tom R Cavanaugh *Loc:* Follow Atlantic Ave to Bay Street, turn L (E side of Boothbay Harbor).

COLLECTOR SHOP
Lakeside Dr & Middle Rd, 04538
(207)633-2215 **23 36 44**
Furniture, glass, china, clocks, lamps, tin & post cards. *Est:* 1982. *Hours:* Most days 10-5. Ed Swett *Park:* On site. *Loc:* 5th business on L after Boothbay post office.

GLEASON FINE ART
27 McKown St, 04538
(207)633-2336 **59 66**
19th & 20th C American paintings, with emphasis on artists who have ties to the Boothbay Harbor region, including Monhegan Island. *Pr:* $5–10000. *Est:* 1987. *Serv:* Appraisal, consultation, purchase estates. *Hours:* May-mid Oct Tue-Sat 10-5, else by chance/appt. *CC:* AX/MC. Dennis Gleason *Loc:* Rte 27 to Boothbay Harbor, in farmhouse 3 doors up from gourmet shop on R.

JOSEPHINE HURD ANTIQUES
92 Commercial St, 04538
(207)633-4732 **44**
Early glass & large selection of Portland glass patterns. *Hours:* Jul-Oct daily 10-4. *Assoc:* MADA. *Loc:* White house with goblets in the window.

BREMEN

CONNELL FINE ARTS
Broad Cove Rte 32,
(207)529-5426   **59**

Specializing in 19th and early 20th C paintings, bronzes & Oriental rugs. *Est:* 1986. *Serv:* Appraisal, consultation, purchase estates, estate sale service. *Hours:* Appt suggested. *Assoc:* MADA NHADA VADA. Neal J Connell *Park:* On Site. *Loc:* From Waldoboro Rte 1: 6 MI S on Rte 32.

BREWER

FRAN & DEAN'S ANTIQUES
21 Silk St, 04112
(207)989-5740   **65 81**

Tools & primitives. *Hours:* BY APPT ONLY. Frances Pennypacker

MCLEOD MILITARY COLLECTIBLES
RFD 1 Box 1598, 04412
(207)843-6205   **6 20**

Maine's only shop devoted to military antiques, all wars & all nations - Nazi, Japanese, GI, Viet Cong, Union or Confederate. *Pr:* $1–1000. *Serv:* Appraisal, catalog, consultation, purchase estates. *Hours:* Daily 12-5. *CC:* MC/V. Ralph McLeod *Park:* In front. *Loc:* Rte 1A Holden on R side of Rd 3 MI from I-395 Rte 1A interchange.

SCOTT'S BOOKS
121 Parker St, 04412
(207)989-2459   **13**

Antiquarian books: hard covers, nonfiction & many subjects. *Hours:* Year round by chance/appt. *Size:* 12,000 books. *Assoc:* MABA. Scott Servisky

BRIDGTON

RICKER HOUSE ANTIQUES
22 N High St, 04009
(207)647-5069

Fine antiques & accessories. *Serv:* Colonial lamp shades. *Hours:* Tue-Sat 10-5 by chance/appt.

WALES & HAMBLEN ANTIQUE CENTER
134 Main St, 04009
(207)647-8344   **{GR30}**

Victorian, oak & country furniture & decorative accessories. *Serv:* Restoration, refinishing. *Hours:* Daily 10-5.

BRISTOL MILLS

BACKWARD GOOSE
Rte 130, 04539
(207)677-2017   **36 44 65**

Specializing in glass, china, furniture, & primitives. *Hours:* Daily 10-5 by chance or appt. Elizabeth Huff *Park:* Nearby.

JOSEPH P RICE ANTIQUES
Rte 130, 04539
(207)563-8848   **36 44**

General line with an emphasis on furniture, ironstone, Staffordshire early ceramics. *Hours:* Sum: daily 10-5, weekends only in Sep, Win: CLOSED. *Assoc:* MADA.

BROOKLIN

CREATIVE ANTIQUES
Rte 173, 04616
(207)359-8525   **29 41 66**
Decorative objects, painted furniture, hooked rugs, prints & unusual things. *Hours:* Aug-Sep by chance/appt. *Assoc:* MADA. *Loc:* 1 MI S of village.

BROOKS

FINE ART RESTORATION
RFD#2 Box 1440, 04921
(207)722-3464   **71**
Specializing in the conservation & restoration of oil paintings. Will supply free wood box for shipping of paintings. *Est:* 1960. *Serv:* Written estimates upon receipt of Polaroid. *Hours:* BY APPT. John Squadra

BRUNSWICK

BRUNSWICK ART AND ANTIQUES
PO Box 631, 04011
(207)725-2642   **5 56 59**
Fine 19th & 20th C oil paintings, paper items, military collectibles, nautical items, jewelry & Oriental carpets. *Serv:* Appraisal, restoration & framing. *Hours:* Sum 10-5 or BY APPT. *Assoc:* MADA. Guenter E Adam

CROSS HILL BOOKS
9 Noble St, 04011
(207)729-8531   **13**
Specializing in nautical books. Catalogs issued concerning sea, ships, sailing, maritime & naval history & yachting. *Pr:*

$5–500. *Est:* 1977. *Serv:* Appraisal, free catalog, search services. *Hours:* BY APPT. *Assoc:* MABA. William W Hill *Park:* In front. *Loc:* US Rte 1, Pleasant St to Main St, R onto Main St S for 1/2 MI, R on Noble 2nd house on L.

ROBERT E DYSINGER - BOOKS
5 Stanwood St, 04011
(207)729-1229   **13**
19th C Americana & American literary first editions. *Serv:* Search service. *Hours:* By chance/appt. *Assoc:* MABA.

GORDON'S BOOKSHOP
14 Center St, 04011
(207)725-2500   **13**
Antiquarian books: travel, natural science, art, WW I, WW II, maritime & marine. *Hours:* Mon-Sat 10-5. *Assoc:* MABA. Marilyn A Gordon

MARILYN NULMAN, BOOK REPAIR
9 Noble St, 04011
(207)729-6449   **12 68**
Book repair & book binding, acid-free slipcases. *Hours:* BY APPT ONLY. *Assoc:* MABA.

OLD BOOKS
136 Maine St, 04011
(207)725-4524   **13**
Large selection with emphasis on literature. *Hours:* Mon-Sat 10-5 CLOSED THU,SUN. *Assoc:* MABA. Clare C Howell *Loc:* Over It's Academic.

CHARLES VINCENT - BOOKS
1 Maple St, 04011
(207)729-7854   **13**
Rare antiquarian books & collectibles in all subjects. *Hours:* By chance/appt. *Assoc:* MABA.

WALFIELD THISTLE
381 Bath Rd, 04011
(207)443-3986 **13**
Antiquarian books - used, out-of-print & scarce books. *Hours:* Mon-Sat 10-5. *Size:* 8,000 books. *Assoc:* MABA. Jean Thistle

BRYANT POND

MOLL OCKETT
Rte 26, 04219
(207)665-2397 **13 33 44**
Specialize in out-of-print books, Maine writers, nature, history & travel plus ephemera. *Pr:* $1–300. *Est:* 1968. *Serv:* Appraisal, purchase estates. *Hours:* Apr-Oct Thu-Mon 10-5. *Size:* Large. *Assoc:* MABA. Basil Sequin *Park:* On site. *Loc:* On Rte 26, between Bethel & Norway.

CAMDEN

ABCDEF BOOKSTORE
23 Bay View St, 04843
(207)236-3903 **13**
Antiquarian books: Americana, European history, literature, music & art - a thoroughly diverse selection. *Est:* 1967. *Hours:* May-Oct 10:30-5 CLOSED JAN-MAR. *Size:* 100,000 books. *Assoc:* ABAA MABA. Lilian Berliawsky *Park:* Nearby. *Loc:* Near the harbor.

AMERICAN COUNTRY
COLLECTION
27 Mountain St Rte 52, 04843
(207)236-2326 **27 34 80**
Tools, folk art, woodenware, tinware, kitchenware, iron, textiles, glass & china. Specializing in country accessories.

Hours: All year by chance/appt. James/Marjorie Tenety *Park:* In back. *Loc:* Across from the library.

CANDLELIGHT & COBBLESTONES
Melvin Heights Road, 04843
(207)236-8222 **36 44**
Small furniture, glass, kitchenware, tin, general line & collectibles. *Hours:* Year round daily 9-5 Win: by chance/appt. Isabella Davies *Loc:* 1 1/4 MI from ctr of town straight up John St.

DOORYARD BOOKS
82 Mechanic St, 04843
(207)236-2544 **13**
Antiquarian books including Maine books, children's fiction, history, fine arts, nautical, cooking, Judaica, biography, natural history, first editions, bridge, science fiction & mysteries. *Hours:* May-Nov 12-5 other times by appt. *Assoc:* MABA. Steve Stevens

LEVETT'S ANTIQUES
24B Bayview St, 04843
(207)236-8356 **29 36**
18th & 19th C furniture & accessories. *Est:* 1976. *Hours:* Mon-Sat 10-5. Georgia G Levett *Park:* On site. *Loc:* 1/2 block off Rte 1 in ctr of town.

RED LANTERN
28 Limerock St, 04843
(207)236-3813 **28 77**
Kitchen things, crocks & jugs, silver, general line. *Hours:* Jun-Sep 11-4 or by chance/appt. Patricia A Linden *Loc:* 2 blocks from the library.

THE RICHARDS ANTIQUES
93 Elm St Rte 1, 04843
(207)236-2152 **36 50**
Furniture & accessories for the discriminating collector, lamps a specialty. Large inventory of Woodstock & other fine lamp shades. *Pr:* $1–5000. *Est:* 1948.

Serv: Purchase estates, lamp repair.
Hours: By chance/appt CLOSED
WED,SUN. Chad Richards **Park:** In
front. **Loc:** Rte 1, on L entering Camden
from S.

SCHUELER ANTIQUES
10 High St Rte 1, 04843
(207)236-2770   1 36 59
Located in a renovated carriage house,
where a range of American furniture,
decorative accessories, complimentary
art, decoys & paintings are attractively
displayed. **Est:** 1947. **Hours:** Jun 15-Oct
15 Tue-Sun 10-5. **Size:** Medium. **Assoc:**
MADA. Gay Schueler **Park:** On site.
Loc: Thru Camden heading N, R at top
of town (where Rte 1 heads toward Belfast), 4th house on L.

STARBIRD
17 Main St, 04843
(207)236-8292   27
Unusual portable country antiques &
furniture. **Hours:** Daily 10-5 CLOSED
FEB-MAR. **CC:** MC/V/AX. **Park:**
Nearby. **Loc:** Two doors from the library.

STONE SOUP BOOKS
35 Main St, 04843
                             13 14 33
Out-of-print books - specializing in
Maine, maritime & poetry. **Est:** 1982.
Hours: May 1-Oct 31 daily 10:30-5 Nov-
Apr Wed-Sun 10:30-5. **Size:** 10,000
books. **Assoc:** MABA. Paul Joy **Park:** In
front. **Loc:** Ctr of downtown Camden, on
waterfront side of Main St.

CAPE ELIZABETH

HANSON'S CARRIAGE HOUSE
3 Two Lights Rd, 04107
(207)767-3608   27 76 80
Country furnishings, textiles, primitives,
Shaker & Indian items. **Hours:** BY
APPT. **Assoc:** MADA. Jean Hanson **Loc:**
En route to lighthouses, off Rte 77.

LOMBARD ANTIQUARIAN MAP &
PRINTS
Box 281, 04107
(207)799-1889   13 51 66
Rare 16th-19th C maps, charts of all
world regions, specializing in Maine &
New England, Winslow Homer wood
engravings, early botanical, natural history & architectural engravings. **Serv:**
Catalog, sale by phone & mail, search
service. **Hours:** BY APPT ONLY. **Assoc:**
ABAA MABA MADA. Reginald T Lom-
bard Jr

CAPE NEDDICK

THE BARN AT CAPE NEDDICK
US Rte 1, 03902
(207)363-7315   {GR24}
Smalls, glass, oak & pine furniture, pot-
tery & general line of antiques attractive-
ly displayed in pristine barn. **Est:** 1986.
Hours: Daily 10-5. **CC:** MC/V. Stephen
Le Blanc **Park:** On site. **Loc:** I-95 York
Exit: Rte 1, 3 MI N.

COLUMBARY ANTIQUES
Rte 1, 03902
(207)363-5496   {GR}
A collection of furniture, framed prints,

collectibles, glass & china. *Hours:* Tue-Sat 10-5 by chance/appt. Lynn & Fred Leisentritt *Park:* In front.

CRANBERRY HILL
ANTIQUES/LIGHTING
1284 Rte 1 Box 84, 03902
(207)363-5178 **1 29 50**
General line of antiques in as found condition, largest lampshade/lamp parts selection north of Boston. *Est:* 1971. *Serv:* Appraisal, repairs, reproduction, restoration, purchase estates. *Hours:* Daily 9:30-5, CLOSED TUE. *Size:* Large. *CC:* MC/V. Tony & Dorothy Anni *Park:* On site. *Loc:* I-95N York Exit: E to Rte 1N, L on to Rte 1N, 3 1/5 MI on L diagonal from Cape Neddick Inn.

CAPE PORPOISE

PADDY'S COVE ANTIQUES
Ward Rd, 04014
(207)967-4842 **27 65**
Country furniture, cupboards & primitives. *Est:* 1976. *Hours:* May-Nov daily (except Tue) 10-5, Win: By chance/appt. *Assoc:* MADA. Priscilla Flannery *Park:* On site. *Loc:* 2 MI from Kennebunkport off Rte 9.

CARIBOU

AUNTIE BEA'S ANTIQUES
Madawaska Rd, 04736
(207)498-8721 **44**
Depression, carnival, pattern, cut glass, tin primitives, baskets, small furniture, dolls & doll furniture,. *Hours:* Sum: by appt only. Roger Thompson *Loc:* Off I-89 on the Madawaska Rd.

THE BARN DOOR
724 N Main St, 04736
(207)492-0432 **23 67 81**
Cupboards, primitives, clocks, oil lamps, quilts, tools, tin, woodenware, furniture, advertising items, brass bells & wooden sculptures. *Est:* 1968. *Hours:* Sum: Tue-Sat 9-5, Win: Fri-Sat 9-5. Valeska Lombard *Park:* Nearby. *Loc:* Just N of the airport.

CHARLOTTE'S DOLLS
Madawaska Rd Box 6980, 04736
(207)498-8937 **32**
Approximately 1400 dolls, antique & new, large & small, some ready for display & others in need. Doll accessories, stands, shoes, socks & doll dusters. *Hours:* Year round daily 9-9 by chance/appt. Charlotte St Peter *Park:* On site. *Loc:* From Caribou: Off Rte 1 to Rte 89 on access hwy to Madawaska Rd, 5th house on R.

CASTINE

BARBARA FALK - BOOKSELLER
Rte 166A, 04421
(207)326-4036 **13 33**
Antiquarian books: literature, children's, women writers & ephemeral material. *Hours:* Year round by chance/appt call ahead. *Size:* 15,000 books. *Assoc:* MABA.

CORNISH

CORNISH TRADING COMPANY
Main St, 04020
(207)625-8387 **{GR}**
Antiques & collectibles. *Hours:* May-Oct daily 10-5 CLOSED TUE,

CLOSED APR. Greg Wilfert *Loc:* In the Masonic Hall next the park in the ctr of town.

CUNDYS HARBOR

BOOK PEDLARS
Holbrook St, 04011
(207)729-0087   **13**
Out-of-print Maine books, children's illustrated books & Americana. *Hours:* By chance/appt. *Assoc:* MABA. Wally O'-Brien

CUSHING

NEVILLE ANTIQUES
Pleasant Point Rd, 04563
(207)354-8055   **10 29 63**
Barometers, nautical antiques, English & Chinese porcelains, & decorative accessories. *Pr:* $50–3000. *Serv:* Barometers restored & repaired, appraisal, conservation, consultation. *Hours:* By chance/appt. *CC:* MC/V. *Assoc:* MADA. C Neville Lewis *Loc:* 9 MI from Thomaston off Rte 1.

DAMARISCOTTA

R & B BENNETT
Bristol Rd, 04543
(207)563-5013   **44 50 81**
Quality early American pattern glass (1830-1890), including Portland & Sandwich, lamps & some early tools. *Hours:* Jun to mid Oct, by chance/appt. *Assoc:* MADA. Roger & Bee Bennett *Loc:* Call for directions.

COOPER'S RED BARN
Bus Rte 1, 04543
(207)563-3714   **13 44 81**
Two story barn filled with books, furniture, glass, antique tools & old picture frames. *Est:* 1945. *Hours:* Daily 9-5. *Size:* Large. *Park:* On site. *Loc:* 3/4 MI heading E out of Damariscotta.

DRUM & DRUM
Main & Elm Streets, 04543
(207)563-1772   **32 37 67**
Specializing in early American furniture & accessories, theorems, quilts, gameboards & signs. *Hours:* Tue-Sat 10-5.

LOON'S LANDING ANTIQUES
Courtyard Shops off Main St, 04543
(207)563-8931   **27**
Specializing in country furniture & lots of smalls. *Hours:* Mon-Sat 10-5 by appt.

THE MAPLES
Bristol Rd, 04543
(207)563-8565   **27 30 83**
Country & Victorian antiques, crafts, folk art & decoys. *Est:* 1985. *Hours:* May-Oct daily 10-5, else BY APPT. *Park:* On site. *Loc:* 2 MI from downtown on Rte 130 heading S.

THE OLD PRINT SHOP
Elm St in Northey Sq, 04543
(207)563-5632   **66**
Specializing in decorative antique prints. *Hours:* Mon-Sat 10-5 by chance/appt. *Park:* Nearby.

PINE CHESTS & THINGS
Bristol Rd, 04543
(207)563-3267   **27 30 65**
Primitives, country furniture, looms, spinning wheels & duck decoys. *Est:* 1962. *Hours:* By chance/appt. *Assoc:* MADA. Richard Else

PATRICIA ANNE REED ANTIQUES
Bristol Rd HC 61, 04543
(207)563-5633   **5 34 59**
Gallery full of Americana, early furniture, paintings, porcelain, toys, fabrics, folk art, architectural pieces & decorative objects. *Serv:* Appraisal, consultation, interior design, purchase estates. *Hours:* May 15-Oct Mon-Sat 9-6 Sun by chance/appt. *Size:* Medium. *Park:* On site. *Loc:* A short distance from Baptist Church, toward Pemaquid Point.

PETER/JEAN RICHARDS FINE ANTIQUE
Bristol Rd Route 130, 04543
(207)563-1964   **37 39 77**
Fine 18th & early 19th C American & English furniture, silver & accessories. *Serv:* Appraisal, consultation, purchase estates. *Hours:* May 15-Oct weekdays, else BY APPT. *CC:* AX/MC/V. *Assoc:* MADA NHADA. Jean & Peter Richards *Park:* On site. *Loc:* Rte 1, Business Rte 1 into Damariscotta, S on Rtes 129-130, toward Pemaquid & Bristol, 1/2 MI to shop in red barn on L.

SCHOONER GALLERIES
Biscay Rd, 04543
(207)563-5647   **27 66**
Specializing in antiques & country collectibles, paintings & prints. *Hours:* Mon-Sat 10-5 by chance/appt.

THRU THE LOOKING GLASS
Bus Rte 1, 04543
(207)563-1929   **36 44 53**
Specializing in furniture, glass, mirrors, collectibles. *Hours:* Tue-Sat 10-5 by chance or appt.

DEER ISLE

BELCHER'S ANTIQUES
Reach Rd RR1 Box 359, 04627
(207)348-9938   **27 34 56**
Three large rooms & two floors in attached barn of a 19th C farmhouse featuring country antiques, folk art, nautical & advertising items. *Pr:* $50–1500. *Est:* 1984. *Hours:* Jun-Dec daily 10-5, Jan-May by chance/appt. *Size:* Large. *CC:* MC/V. Linda Friedmann *Park:* In front. *Loc:* Rte 15 S on Deer Isle; 1/10 MI from the Reach Rd monument.

DENMARK

BRUCE D COLLINS FINE ART
RR1 Box 113, 04022
(207)452-2197   **8**
Periodic auctions of American & European paintings & graphics. 10% buyer's premium. Absentee & telephone bidding can be arranged. *Serv:* Auctions, consignments accepted, catalogs. *Hours:* Call for appts & schedule. *Loc:* Auctions held at Seaboard Auction Gallery, Rte 236 Eliot ME. Rte 95 N Exit 3B.

C E GUARINO
Berry Rd, 04022
(207)452-2123   **8 51 66**
Absentee auction house holding six auctions a year in historical American ephemera, antique prints, maps, photographs, posters & Indian artifacts. *Est:* 1973. *Serv:* Auction, mailing list, appraisal. *CC:* MC/V. *Park:* On site. *Loc:* Rte 117 1 MI from the Village of Denmark.

DOUGLAS HILL

THE GALLERY SHOP
Jones Museum of Glass & Ceramics, 04024
(207)787-3370   **44**
18th - 20th C, American, English, Continental & Far Eastern glass & ceramics; related books & slides. *Serv:* Identification services, dealer discounts. *Hours:* May 15-Nov 10 Mon-Sat 9:30-5, Sun 1-5. *CC:* MC/V. *Assoc:* MADA. Dorothy-Lee Jones *Park:* Ample parking. *Loc:* ME Tnpk Exit 8: Rte 25 to Gorham, R at lights on to 114, go 19 MI to E Sebago; follow signs to museum.

DRESDEN

MATHOM BOOKSHOP & BINDERY
Blinn Hill Rd, 04342
(207)737-8806   **9 12 13**
Antiquarian books: A general stock with an emphasis on Maine, New England, British & American literature, signed modern & first editions, antiquarian, women's studies, historical, scholarly, remainders. *Hours:* By chance/appt best to call ahead. *Assoc:* MABA. Lewis Turco

EAST HOLDEN

COUNTRY STORE ANTIQUES
Bar Harbor Rd Rte 1A, 04429
(207)843-7449   **27 40 59**
In an 100 year old general store, two floors of oak, country pine, cottage pine, mahogany, walnut, wicker, rugs, lamps, china & paintings attractively displayed in room settings. *Est:* 1960. *Serv:* Shipping within US, interior design, repair, restoration. *Hours:* Sum:Jun-Oct 14 Mon-Sat 10-5; Xmas:Nov 15-Dec 23 Wed-Sat 11-5. Francine Grant *Park:* In front. *Loc:* 10 min from Bangor, 20 min form Ellsworth Jct 1A & 46.

EAST LEBANON

MICKLESTREET RARE BOOKS/MOD 1STS
RFD 1, 04027
(207)457-1042   **13**
Antiquarian books: Medicine, architecture, Americana, literature, theatre & fine printing. *Serv:* Catalogs issued. *Hours:* BY APPT ONLY. *Size:* 10,000 books. *Assoc:* MABA. Viola Morris *Loc:* Off Rte 202 corner of New Road and Jim Grant Rd.

EAST LIVERMORE

ALDEN PRATT, BOOKS
Rte 106, 04228
(207)897-6979   **13**
Used & out-of-print books, including Maine town & country histories, books of local interest & Civil War. *Hours:* BY APPT. *Assoc:* MABA. *Loc:* Rte 133 to Rte 106N, 1 MI.

EAST WINTHROP

BERRY PATCH ANTIQUES
Rte 202 Marshview Crossing, 04343
(207)395-4270   **27 65**
Specializing in country, primitives, furniture, glass & Maine artists. *Hours:* Thu-Sun 10-5.

LAKESIDE ANTIQUES
Rte 202, 04364
(207)377-2616   **{GR48}**
Two floors of pine, oak, walnut, Victorian furniture, cupboards, chests, tables, tools, toys & Victorian accessories. *Hours:* Daily 7-5, Win: CLOSED MON,TUE. Ormond Piper *Loc:* 4 MI W of ME Tnpk exit 15 on Rte 202.

ELIOT

BOOKS & AUTOGRAPHS
287 Goodwin Rd, 03903
(207)439-4739   **9 13 62**
Signed & limited editions of 20th C writers, autographs, letters, manuscripts, signed photographs with emphasis on the performing arts, including the opera, movies & theatre. *Hours:* Year round BY APPT ONLY. *Assoc:* ABAA MABA. Sherman R Emery

SEABOARD AUCTION GALLERY
Rte 236, 03903
(207)439-5585 FAX
(207)439-4515   **8**
Antique & estate auctions. *Serv:* Estate appraisal. *Assoc:* MAA NHAA NAA. Martin Willis *Loc:* I-95 Exit 3B Southbound Exit 2 in Kittery Rte 236 N Approx 3 MI on L, 5 MI from Portsmouth.

ELLSWORTH

BIG CHICKEN BARN-BOOKS & ANTIQUE
Rte 1, 04605
(207)667-7308   **13**
Antiquarian books, magazines & paperbacks including Maine, nautical, religion, Americana, mysteries, children's, cookbooks & medical. *Hours:* Mar-Dec Daily 9-5 Jan-Feb weekends only. *Size:* 110,000 books. *Assoc:* MABA. Annegret Cukierski *Loc:* Halfway between Bucksport & Ellsworth.

CALISTA STERLING ANTIQUES
Bayside Rd Rte 230, 04605
(207)667-8991   **29 36**
Formal & country period furniture & accessories in 2 shops. *Est:* 1951. *Hours:* May-Oct 9-5 CLOSED SUN Nov-Apr by chance/appt. *CC:* MC/V. *Assoc:* MADA. *Park:* In front. *Loc:* 4 MI from ctr of Ellsworth, look for signs.

CINDY'S ANTIQUES
Bucksport Rd, 04605
(207)667-4476   **40 77 86**
Country, Victorian, oak furniture, wicker, smalls, decoys, flint glass & silver. *Hours:* Daily. *Assoc:* MADA. Lawrence Clough *Loc:* 3 MI N of Ellsworth on Rte 1.

DOWNEAST ANTIQUE CENTER
40 Water St, 04605
(207)667-9351   **{GR13}**
Furniture, decorative accessories, jewelry, post cards & toys. *Est:* 1988. *Serv:* Chair caning. *Hours:* Year round Mon-Sat 9-5 Sun 12-5, CLOSED Dec 26-Jan 1. *CC:* MC/V. A L Jenkins *Park:* On site. *Loc:* 1 block from Union River Bridge on Water St.

EASTERN ANTIQUES
52 Dean Street, 04605
(207)667-4033　　　　**33 55 85**
A good selection of furniture, silver, cut glass, Edison phonographs, paintings, vintage clothing & advertising. *Hours:* Daily 9-5.

EUSTIS

MAC DONALD'S MILITARY
Coburn Gore, 04936
(207)297-2751　　　　**13 62**
Civil War books, papers & photographs, other military & wars & Maine fish & game. *Serv:* Catalogs issued every six weeks - send two stamps. *Hours:* BY APPT ONLY. *Assoc:* MABA. Thomas L MacDonald

FAIRFIELD

JULIA & POULIN ANTIQUES
Skowhegan Rd, 04937
(207)453-2114　　　　**40**
Warehouse full of antique oak, walnut, & mahogany furniture. *Est:* 1967. *Serv:* Antiques, estates, fine furnishings bought & sold. *Hours:* Mon-Sat 9-5. *CC:* MC/V. Arthur Julia *Park:* In front. *Loc:* I-95 Exit 36: 1 MI.

JOHN D JULIA ANTIQUES
Rtes 23 & 201, 04937
(207)453-9460　　　　**40 42 86**
Oak, pine, mahogany, wicker & walnut furniture & smalls. *Est:* 1972. *Serv:* Hand carved decoys & wooden animals. *Hours:* TO THE TRADE, call suggested. *Size:* Huge. *Loc:* I-95 Exit 36.

JAMES D JULIA AUCTIONEERS
Skowhegan Rd Rte 201, 04937
(207)453-7904　　　　**8 30 59**
Dealing in fine quality furniture, jewelry, paintings. Special catalog auctions include decoys. Also a showroom with items for sale. *Pr:* $10–100000. *Serv:* Appraisal, brochure, catalog (free), purchase estates. *Hours:* Mon-Fri 9-5. *Size:* Medium. *Assoc:* MAA MADA NAA. *Park:* In front. *Loc:* I-95 Exit 36: on Rte 201, 1 MI N of Fairfield Village.

THISTLE'S
16 Main St, 04937
(207)453-9817　　　　**13 36 66**
Antiquarian books - Maine, New England, Americana, hunting, fishing, mystery ephemera & prints. *Pr:* $10–500. *Serv:* Purchase estates. *Hours:* Mon-Sat 10-5. *Size:* Medium. *Assoc:* MABA. David G Thistle *Park:* On site. *Loc:* I-95 Exit 35 (Fairfield): 1 MI S on Main St.

FALMOUTH

HARD CIDER FARM ORIENTAL RUGS
45 Middle Rd Rte 9, 04105
(207)775-1600　　　　**21**
Fine Oriental rugs - antique to modern, large collection of Persian & tribal rugs. *Est:* 1975. *Serv:* Appraisal, conservation, consultation, repairs, restoration. *Hours:* Tue-Sat 10-5 appt appreciated. *Size:* Medium. *CC:* AX/MC/V. R W Tirrell *Park:* On site. *Loc:* I-295 Exit 10 (Falmouth): Rte 9W, L onto Middle Rd, 1 4/5 MI.

FARMINGTON

ANTIQUES FROM POWDER HOUSE HILL
North St RR1 Box 1000, 04938
(207)778-2946   **81**
Specializing in quality tools, functional & collectible. *Hours:* By chance/appt. *Assoc:* MADA. Wendell A Sweatt *Loc:* At Court House take Anson St for 3/4 MI, R on North St, 1st house.

MAPLE AVENUE ANTIQUES
23 Maple Ave, 04938
(207)778-4850   **27 65**
Country furniture, primitives & accessories. *Hours:* By chance/appt. *Assoc:* MADA. Frank P Dingley *Loc:* Street between Annadales garage and Irving gasoline station on Rte 2.

TOM VEILLEUX GALLERY
Rtes 4 & 149, 04938
(207)778-3719   **59 66**
American Impressionists & American women artists for the discriminating collector. Provincetown prints. *Est:* 1972. *Serv:* Purchase American paintings, appraisals, consultation, restoration. *Hours:* BY APPT ONLY. *Loc:* Call for appt & directions.

FARMINGTON FALLS

FALLS BOOK BARN
Main St, 04940
(207)778-3429   **13 33**
Antiquarian books: biography, classics, cooking, criminology, history, juvenile, Maine, nature, poetry, religion, fiction & ephemera. *Hours:* Mar-Nov by chance/appt, call ahead advised. *Assoc:* MABA. Ethel Emerson *Loc:* 3/10 MI off Rte 2.

FORT FAIRFIELD

JANDRA'S WOODSHED
24 High St, 04742
(207)473-7331   **36 44 50**
Furniture, china, glass, oil lamps & stoneware. *Serv:* Restoration, cabinetwork. *Hours:* Mon-Sat 9-5, call ahead suggested. *Assoc:* ISA. John C Anderson *Loc:* Across from the hospital, right in the village.

FREEPORT

BOOK CELLAR
36 Main St, 04032
(207)865-3157   **13**
Nostalgic fiction, juveniles & biography. *Serv:* Search service. *Hours:* Year round mornings, mostly mail order. *Assoc:* MABA. Dean Chamberlin

FREEPORT ANTIQUE MALL
Rte 1, 04032
(207)865-0607   **{GR55}**
Primitives, jewelry, glass, china, pottery, stoneware, furniture & toys on two & a half floors. *Hours:* Daily year round 10-5. Howard Washburn *Loc:* I-95N Exit 17: 5 min S of downtown Freeport.

OLD THYME SHOP
207 Main St, 04032
(207)865-3852   **27**
Country pieces & accessories. *Hours:* Mon-Fri 10-4. Barbara Perry

PORT 'N STARBOARD
Box 165, 04032
(207)865-6648   **54 56 66**

Ship & shore merchants with marine antiques, paintings, folk art, prints, ephemera, photography, maps, charts, books, instruments, scrimshaw, ship models, 1/2 hulls, folk art & decoys. *Pr:* $3–3000. *Est:* 1984. *Serv:* Appraisal, consultation, interior design. *Hours:* BY APPT ONLY. *CC:* AX/MC/V. Michael Leslie

GARDINER

BUNKHOUSE BOOKS
Rte 5A, 04345
(207)582-2808   **13**

Maine town & county histories, non-fiction & fiction on Maine, sporting books, novels & general books. *Hours:* May-Oct weekday afternoons. *Size:* 12,000 books. *Assoc:* MABA. Isaac Davis

MCKAY'S ANTIQUES
75 Brunswick Ave, 04345
(207)582-1228   **16 63 65**

Metals, pottery, early china, iron, brasses, tin, firkins & primitives. *Est:* 1980. *Hours:* Sum: daily 10-5 CLOSED MON, Win: by chance/appt. *CC:* MC/V. Irene McKay *Park:* Nearby. *Loc:* On Rte 201 beside 7-11.

MORRELL'S ANTIQUES
106 Highland Ave, 04345
(207)582-4797   **44 63 83**

Quality glass (art, cut & pattern), fine china & choice Victorian collectibles. *Hours:* By chance/appt. *Assoc:* MADA. Hazel I Morrell

PORT OF GARDINER ANTIQUES
269 Water St, 04345
(207)582-2441   **{GR}**

Antique estate jewelry, furniture, glass, china & collectibles. *Hours:* Tue-Sat 9-5. Loretta Brinzow *Park:* In rear.

FRED ROBBINS
210 Brunswick Ave Rte 201, 04345
(207)582-5005   **6 20 49**

Military, political & campaign material, daguerreotypes & lead soldiers. *Est:* 1968. *Serv:* Appraisal. *Hours:* Mon-Sat 10-5. *Assoc:* NPIC PTAD. *Park:* Nearby. *Loc:* 2 MI from I-95.

GARLAND

FREDERICA DEBEURS - BOOKS
Upper Garland Rd, 04939
(207)924-7474   **13**

Antiquarian book shop: Specializing in fine & decorative arts, Maine authors, mathematics, science & technology. *Pr:* $1–850. *Est:* 1981. *Serv:* Appraisal, free catalog, search service. *Hours:* By chance/appt. *Assoc:* MABA. *Park:* On site. *Loc:* From Dexter, 5 MI E on Rte 94, take dirt road on L (sign), bookstore is just beyond bend to R.

GORHAM

COUNTRY SQUIRE ANTIQUES
105 Mighty St, 04038
(207)839-4855   **21 44 59**

Bohemian, cranberry & satin glass, porcelain, Limoges lamps, paintings, rugs & furniture. Also Early American refinished country furniture. *Est:* 1972. *Hours:* Appt preferred. *Assoc:* MADA.

Ed Carr *Park:* On site. *Loc:* 11 MI from Exit 8 on ME Tnpk, 4 MI from ctr of Gorham, 1 MI off Rte 114N.

LONGVIEW ANTIQUES
20 Longview Dr, 04038
(207)839-3020   **21 65 67**
Primitives, quilts, paintings, hooked rugs & country furnishings in a three-room shop with a country setting. *Hours:* All year Mon 10-5 or by chance/appt. *Assoc:* MADA. Helen A Woodbrey

GRAY

THE BARN ON 26 ANTIQUE CENTER
Rte 26 Poland Spring Rd, 04039
(207)657-3470   **{GR20}**
Oak, pine, primitives, country items, furniture & glass. *Est:* 1977. *Hours:* May-Oct Wed-Fri 10-4, Sat-Sun 9-5 else by chance/appt. *CC:* MC/V. Fran Demers *Park:* Ample. *Loc:* I-95 Exit 11: 3 1/2 MI.

HALLOWELL

ACME ANTIQUES
163 Water St, 04347
(207)622-2322   **{GR}**
Vintage clothing, jewelry, toys & collectibles. *Hours:* Year round Thu-Sun, else by chance/appt. *Loc:* I-95N Exit 30A.

BERDAN'S ANTIQUES
151 Water St, 04347
(207)622-0151   **27 34 65**
Furniture, coverlets, folk art, primitives, stoneware, quilts, advertising items & country items. *Est:* 1963. *Hours:* Appt

suggested CLOSED SUN & HOLIDAYS. *Assoc:* MADA NHADA. Betty M Berdan *Loc:* Downtown.

BRASS AND FRIENDS ANTIQUES
121 Water St, 04347
(207)626-3287   **50**
Restored antique lighting including chandeliers, sconces, floor & table lamps, restored & ready for installation. *Est:* 1987. *Serv:* Lamp repairs, restoration, rewiring & polishing. *Hours:* Year round Mon-Sat 10-5. *CC:* MC/V. *Park:* On street. *Loc:* On the corner of Central & Water St.

D & R ANTIQUES
202 Water St, 04347
(207)623-3020   **23 44 50**
Clocks, china, glass & lamps. *Hours:* Daily 9-5. Rowland Hastings

GINNY'S ANTIQUES
165 Water St, 04347
(207)622-2322   **{GR}**
A group shop with old bottles, post cards, glassware & collectibles. *Hours:* Year round, daily. *Loc:* Rte 95N Exit 30A: follow signs.

GRANITE CITY ANTIQUES
113 Water St, 04347
(207)626-3334
Hummel, Lladro, toys, paintings & prints bought & sold. *Hours:* All year by chance/appt.

HATTIE'S ANTIQUES
148 Water St, 04347
(207)622-0110   **47**
Fine antique jewelry bought & sold; also buying scrap gold & silver. Antique lamps, clocks, art glass & furniture bought & sold. *Serv:* Appraisals. *Hours:* Mon-Sat 10-4:30. Elery L Beale

JOHNSON-MARSANO ANTIQUES
121 Water St, 04347
(207)623-1230   **47 77**
Antique jewelry, sewing collectibles &
unusual sterling objects. *Est:* 1980.
Hours: Mon-Sat 10-5. *Park:* Nearby.
Loc: On the corner of Water & Central
Sts.

**JAMES LE FURGY ANTIQUES &
BOOKS**
168 Water St, 04347
(207)623-1771   **1 37 59**
American painted furniture & accessories pre-1860 in original condition,
19th & 20th C American paintings,
American Indian art, new & out-of-print
reference books on the fine & decorative
arts. *Pr:* $20–2000. *Serv:* Appraisal, pur-
chase estates. *Hours:* Mon,Wed,Fri,Sat
10-5 appt suggested. *Size:* Medium.
Park: In front. *Loc:* ME Tnpk Augusta
Exit: Rte 202, toward Augusta at rotary
turn R on State St S to Hallowell (State
St becomes Water St).

MAINELY ANTIQUES
200 Water St, 04347
(207)622-7922   **44 63**
In a shop overlooking the Kennebunk
River: Specializing in American pottery,
Fiesta, Heisey, Lalique, Steuben,
majolica & Roseville. *Hours:* Daily 10-4
CLOSED SUN.

DAN MC LAUGHLIN ANTIQUES
108 Water St, 04347
(207)623-8888   **36**
High quality furniture of the Victorian &
turn-of-the-century eras; general line of
antiques. *Hours:* Year round by
chance/appt.

MEMORIES
190 Water St, 04347
(207)623-2274   **{GR7}**
Victorian & country furniture, jewelry,

quilts, paintings, glass, china, collec-
tibles. *Est:* 1989. *Serv:* Purchase estates.
Hours: Jul-Sep 10-5, Oct-Jun 10-5, Sun
by chance/appt. *Size:* Medium. *CC:*
MC/V. *Park:* In front, nearby lot. *Loc:*
Rtes 27 & 201 between Gardiner &
Augusta; on the beautiful Kennebec
river.

MOTHER GOOSE ANTIQUES
168 Water St, 04347
(207)623-1752   **47 77 83**
Fine antique & estate jewelry specializing in Victorian, Arts & Crafts, & Tiffany jewelry. *Est:* 1982. *Hours:* Open
year round 9:30-5:00. *CC:* AX/MC/V.
Loc: In the downtown.

NO 5 KENNEBEC ROW ANTIQUES
124 Water St, 04347
(207)622-1888   **36 44 47**
Furniture, glassware, jewelry, sterling &
Oriental rugs. *Est:* 1987. *Serv:* Appraisal.
Hours: Mon-Sat 10-5 or by appt. *CC:*
MC/V. Dan Pomerleau *Loc:* I-95 N Exit
30A.

SILVER THREADS
Water St, 04347
(207)685-4961   **80 85**
European textiles & linens, vintage
clothing from 1870-1970, lamps, furniture, radios, curios & fine & costume
jewelry. *Hours:* Year round til early evening.

JOSIAH SMITH ANTIQUES
181 Water St 2nd fl, 04347
(207)622-4188   **44 60 63**
Emphasizing early glass & ceramics,
Oriental items with Japanese pottery a
specialty, art pottery, art from all periods
small, decorative furniture & accessories.
Pr: $25–2500. *Est:* 1980. *Hours:* All year
most days 10-5. *Assoc:* MADA. Bruce

Weber & Jeff Wainoris *Park:* Nearby lot. *Loc:* On Rte 201 (Water St), entrance to 2nd fl shop is on Academy St.

LEON TEBBETTS BOOK SHOP
164 Water St, 04347
(207)623-4670   13
Antiquarian books: a general collection in all categories of fiction & nonfiction. *Hours:* Jun-Oct daily 10-5, Nov-May Sat 10-5 & by appt. *Size:* 30,000 books. *Assoc:* MABA.

HANOVER

LYONS' DEN ANTIQUES
Rte 2, 04237
(207)364-8634   23 30 36
Glass, china, tools, clocks, 18th & 19th C furniture, primitives & decoys on two floors in the barn. *Hours:* Daily 9-5. *Size:* Large. Nancy Lyons *Park:* On site. *Loc:* 10 MI W of Rumford.

HARRISON

BACKWARD GLANCE ANTIQUE MALL
Main St, 04040
(207)583-6306   {GR}
Antiques, collectibles & reference books. *Hours:* Thu-Mon 9-4.

JEFF KOOPUS
Maple Ridge Rd, 04040
(207)583-4860   70
Specializing in authentic handcrafted country & formal furniture. All work done on a custom basis by commission. *Serv:* Reproduction furniture.

HOPE

THE BLUEBERRY PATCH
Box 975, 04847
(207)763-4055   1 44
Early Americana & collectibles. Fine collection of carriage/wagon wheels, wagons & sleighs. *Est:* 1986. *Serv:* Brochure, purchase estates. *Hours:* BY APPT: Jun 15-Oct 5 Mon-Sat 10-6 Sun 1-6, call ahead. *Size:* Large. Merle V Zimmer *Park:* On site. *Loc:* From downtown Camden, Rte 105W, approx 7 1/2 MI.

HULLS COVE

HULLS COVE TOOL BARN
Breakneck Rd, 04644
(207)288-5126   59 81
Featuring a large selection of old tools, also furniture, books & prints. *Hours:* Jun-Oct 15 daily else Thu-Sun 9-5 or by appt. Skip Brack *Loc:* Rte 3 towards Bar Harbor, turn onto Breakneck Rd at the Hulls Cove General Store.

JAY

RIVER OAKS BOOKS
RFD 2 Box 5505, 04239
(207)897-3734   13
Antiquarian books: a general collection with emphasis on illustrated books, mystery, Americana, juvenile, nature, Maine books. *Serv:* Mail order. *Hours:* Year round by chance/appt. *Assoc:* MABA. Nick Bogdon *Loc:* Just off Rte 140.

JEFFERSON

BUNKER HILL ANTIQUES
Rte 213, 04348
(207)563-3167   **27 65 67**
Primitives, country furniture & accessories, quilts, hooked rugs, coverlets, decorative items & paintings. *Hours:* By chance/appt. *Assoc:* MADA. Joanne Johnston

KENNEBUNK

THOMAS & CELESTE DYNAN
Rte 1 N, 04043
(207)985-7763   **36 59**
Small but select collection of antique paintings & American & English formal furniture & accessories. *Pr:* $500–10000. *Hours:* May 15-Oct 11-4 by chance/appt; Nov-May 14 BY APPT ONLY. *Size:* Medium. *CC:* MC/V. *Park:* On site. *Loc:* 1 MI N of traffic light in center of Kennebunk.

PERRY HOPF
13 Mechanic St, 04043
(207)985-4654   **70**
18th C period reproduction framing in five styles of hand planed molding with acid free backing & matting & period finishes suitable for prints, documents & needlework. *Hours:* By chance/appt.

JJ KEATING INC
Rte 1 N, 04043
(207)985-2097   **8 70**
Full array of antiques as well as antique reproductions. *Est:* 1957. *Serv:* Appraisal, auction, purchase estates, reproduction. *Hours:* May-Oct Tue-Sun, Nov-Apr Thu-Sat. James J Keating *Loc:* I-95 Exit 3: N on US Rte 1.

JUDITH A KEATING, GG
Rte 1 N, 04043
(207)985-4181   **4**
Appraisals of antique & estate jewelry, watches, silver & antique ladies' accessories including fans, pocketbooks, sewing. *Serv:* Appraisal by appt. *Hours:* Wed-Sat 11-5 & by appt. *Assoc:* MADA. *Loc:* I-95 Exit 3: Rte 1 N.

RICHARD W OLIVER AUCTIONEERS
Rte 1 Plaza 1, 04043
(207)985-3600   **8**
Auctioneers of antiques, decoys, Oriental art, glass, china, golf & fishing items, guns. 10% buyer premium, 20% deposit on mail/phone bids. *Serv:* Appraisal, purchase estates, mailing list. *Hours:* Mon-Fri 9-5 Sat 10-4. *Assoc:* NAA NEAA. Betsy Brown *Park:* On site. *Loc:* I-95 Exit 3: E to US Rte 1, then L.

RIVERGATE ANTIQUES MALL
Old Post Rd Rte 1 N, 04043
(207)985-6280   **{GR100}**
Full line of antiques & collectibles, china, glass, furniture, jewelry & pottery. *Est:* 1987. *Hours:* Year round daily 10-5. *CC:* MC/V. *Park:* On site. *Loc:* 1/2 MI N of Kennebunk on Rte 1.

VICTORIAN LIGHT/WATERTOWER PINES
29 York St Rte 1 S, 04043
(207)985-6868   **50 71**
Victorian & turn-of-the-century chandeliers, wall sconces, floor & table lamps in a 120 year-old carriage barn. Kerosene, gas & early electric lighting in original condition or completely restored. *Pr:* $5–30000. *Serv:* Brochure, consultation, repairs, restoration. *Hours:*

Mon-Sat 9:30-5 Sun 12:30-5 appt suggested. *Size:* Medium. *CC:* AX/MC/V. Judy Oppert *Park:* In front. *Loc:* I-95 Exit 3: to Kennebunk, Rte 1S, look for Watertower which is at back of property.

KENNEBUNKPORT

ANTIQUES ON NINE
61 Western Ave, 04046
(207)967-0626   **35 37 38**

Featuring formal & country furnishings both American & Continental, architectural elements, books, art, textiles, accessories. Fresh merchandise daily. Summer lodging available in housekeeping cottages near the beach. *Pr:* $10–10000. *Est:* 1980. *Serv:* Appraisal, auction, interior design, purchase estates. *Hours:* Year round daily 9-5. *Size:* Large. *CC:* MC/V. Jim Biondi *Park:* On site. *Loc:* On the Kennebunk-Kennebunkport town line, Rte 9, 3 1/2 MI E of Rte 1, between Wells & Kennebunk Exits 2 & 3 off ME Tnpk.

CATTAILS ANTIQUES
Rte 35 Lower Village, 04046
(207)967-3824   **27 59 66**

Country furniture, baskets, quilts, paintings, prints, wicker furniture, linens, silver, country accessories, some Shaker smalls, folk art & nautical items. *Pr:* $5–2500. *Est:* 1977. *Serv:* Appraisal, consultation, interior design, framing, B & B available. *Hours:* May-Oct 15 Mon-Fri 10-5 Sat 9-5 Sun 11-5, else by chance. *CC:* AX/MC/V. *Assoc:* MADA. Cathleen Ellenberger *Park:* On site. *Loc:* I-95 Exit 3 (in ME): S on Rte 35, 4-5 MI, on L; B & B available in home.

GIBRAN ANTIQUE GALLERY
Ocean Ave, 04046
(207)967-5556   **47 77 83**

Estate jewelry, old Hummels, Victorian furnishings & silver. *Est:* 1985. *Hours:* Sum: daily 10-9, Oct-Christmas Fri,Sun. *CC:* MC/V. *Park:* Nearby. *Loc:* Across from the old Fire Station.

THE GOOSE HANGS HIGH
Pearl St, 04046
(207)967-5717   **65**

A barn full of antiques including American primitives, small things, wood, tin & glass. *Est:* 1968. *Hours:* Apr-Nov by chance/appt CLOSED SUN. *Assoc:* MADA. Jean Pineo *Loc:* Look for the goose over the barn entrance across from the Captain Jefferd's Inn.

MARITIME MUSEUM SHOP
Ocean Ave, 04046
(207)967-2918 FAX
(207)967-4195   **17 56**

Nautical & general antiques, bronzes, paintings, campaign & camphorwood furniture, scrimshaw & navigational instruments. *Hours:* May 15-Nov 15 daily 10-5, including Sun. *Park:* On site. *Loc:* At Booth Tarkington's former Boathouse.

NAUTICAL ANTIQUES
Box 765, 04046
(207)967-3218   **56 59**

Specialist in marine antiques, scrimshaw, marine paintings, carvings, folk art, campaign furniture & prisoner of war work. *Est:* 1972. *Serv:* Appraisal, catalog $3. *Hours:* BY APPT ONLY. *Size:* Medium. John F Rinaldi *Park:* On site. *Loc:* 1 1/2 hours from Boston, 1/2 hour from Portland.

OLD FORT INN & ANTIQUES
Old Fort Ave, 04046
(207)967-5353   **30 44 65**
Selection of period antiques including
English & European country pine,
decoys, primitives, china, cut glass &
early advertising items. *Pr:* $25–900.
Hours: Apr 15-Dec 15 daily 9-5, Dec
16-Apr 14 BY APPT ONLY. *CC:*
AX/DC/MC/V. Sheila Aldrich *Park:* In
front. *Loc:* I-95 Exit 3: L on Rte 35,
follow signs to Kennebunkport, over
drawbridge, R to Ocean Ave, L at
Colony Hotel, R, 1/4 MI.

**MARIE PLUMMER & JOHN
PHILBRICK**
Rte 9 Spring St at Dock Square, 04046
(207)967-5282   **29 36 50**
Early American furniture & accessories
from the 17th & 18th C located in an
18th C house; specialties include lighting, stoneware & redware, Delft &
country mirrors. *Pr:* $500–10000. *Est:*
1975. *Serv:* Appraisal, interior design.
Hours: Mon-Fri 10-5 Call ahead. *Size:*
Small. *Assoc:* MADA. Marie Plummer
Park: On site. *Loc:* I-95 Exit 2: Rte 1N
to Rte 9 into Kennebunkport Village;
From N: I-95 Exit 3, Rte 35 into Kennebunkport, L on Rte 9.

PORT ANTIQUES
Ocean Ave, 04046
(207)967-5119   **47 77**
Antique & estate jewelry, collectibles, sil-
ver, furniture & paintings. *Est:* 1985.
Serv: Appraisal, purchase estates. *Hours:*
Tue-Sun 9-5. *CC:* AX/MC/V. Chris
Coughlin *Park:* Nearby. *Loc:* Corner of
Arundel Wharf.

**RANDS ANTIQUES ON RAND
GREEN**
Western Ave Rte 9, 04046
(207)967-4887   **29 42**
Refinished English pine furniture &

decorative accessories. *Est:* 1944. *Hours:*
Mar-Dec daily 10-5. *CC:* MC/V. *Park:*
Nearby. *Loc:* I-95 Exit 3: to Rte 9.

SAML'S STAIRS ANTIQUES
27 Western Ave Rte 9, 04046
(207)967-2850   **36 59 77**
18th & 19th C furniture, paintings, silver, china & accessories. *Est:* 1986. *Serv:*
Appraisal, consultation, repair. *Hours:*
Mon-Sat 10-4 BY APPT ONLY
CLOSED WED. Bruce L Johnson *Loc:*
Just off Rte 1.

WINDFALL ANTIQUES
Ocean Ave PO Box 2600, 04046
(207)967-2089   **60 63 77**
Porcelain, American & European silver,
19th C art, Orientalia, bronze & glass.
Hours: Apr-May weekends Jun-Oct
daily 10-5 CLOSED TUE. *Assoc:*
MADA NEAA. Anne Kornetsky *Park:*
Nearby. *Loc:* Near Colony Hotel.

WINTER HILL FARM
Wildes District Rd, 04046
(207)967-5879   **27 70 71**
English, Continental & American furniture accented with fine accessories displayed in a restored barn. Custom built
reproduction tables & other furniture
available. Specializing in the restoration
of fine antique furniture. *Pr:* $10–3000.
Est: 1985. *Serv:* Repairs, restoration,
replication, reproduction. *Hours:* Apr-
Nov 9:30-5, Dec-Mar Mon, Wed-Sat
10-5. *Size:* Medium. Carol Dickinson
Park: On site. *Loc:* From Kennebunkport, Rte 9E, to Maine St, bear L
at fork, 1/2 MI on Wildes District Rd, on
L atop hill.

KINGFIELD

PATRICIA BUCK EMPORIUM
Main Street, 04947
(207)265-2101 **40 83**
Specializing in Victorian & oak furniture. *Hours:* Daily 10-6. *CC:* AX/MC/V. Patricia Buck

KITTERY

WILLIAM CORE DUFFY
Box 445, 03904
(207)439-6414 **77**
Early American silver for the knowledgeable collector. Exceptional silver from all periods. *Est:* 1976. *Serv:* Appraisal, purchase estates. *Hours:* BY APPT ONLY. *Loc:* Call for directions.

THE WINDSOR CHAIR
36 Rogers Rd, 03904
(207)439-2164 **43**
Handcrafted 18th C reproduction Windsors & fine period furniture. *Est:* 1983. *Hours:* BY APPT. *CC:* MC/V. Madeleine Godnig *Park:* On site. *Loc:* I-95 Exit 2 (Kittery): to Rte 236S, at traffic circle continue 3/4 MI, bear R at fork at cemetery, on L.

LIMERICK

RYAN M COOPER
PO Box 149, 04048
(207)793-8863 **56 62**
19th & 20th C maritime photography, including sailing vessels, naval vessels, steamers, whaling vessels, yachting & harbor views. Some maritime objects including paintings & artifacts. *Hours:* BY APPT. *Assoc:* PHSNE. *Loc:* Call for directions.

TOM JOSEPH & DAVID RAMSAY
Rte 5, 04048
(207)793-2539 **1 5 45**
Early American furniture in original paint, paintings, folk art, garden statuary, architectural items & student lamps. *Est:* 1976. *Hours:* BY APPT. *Assoc:* ADA NHADA PTADA. *Loc:* On Rte 5, 50 yds from Jct of Rte 160.

LIMINGTON

EDWARD & ELAINE CASAZZA
Rte 25, 04049
(207)637-2599 **21 59 65**
Furniture, primitives, paintings, rugs & country. *Hours:* Year round Mon-Sat 8-4:30.

ROBERT O STUART
Jo Joy Rd, 04049
(207)793-2305 FAX
(207)793-4522 **1 29 37**
Specializing in fine 18th & 19th C American furniture & decorative accessories. *Est:* 1976. *Serv:* Appraisal, restoration, consultation. *Hours:* Mon-Sat 9-5 Sun 1-5. *Park:* On site. *Loc:* Off Rte 117, 28 MI W of Portland.

LINCOLNVILLE

ANTIQUES AT CLARKS CORNER
Slab City Rd & Rte 52, 04849
(207)763-3702 **27 32 33**
Furniture, country, oak, ephemera, advertising signs, Coca Cola ads & other Coca Cola memorabilia, children's furni-

American Furniture
and
Decorative Accessories

Robert O. Stuart

*Queen Anne flat-top
highboy, walnut
and burl walnut
veneer, Massachusetts,
circa 1730-1750,
containing a secret
document drawer
in the cornice moulding;
retains a mellow
bronze patina.
Dimensions: 69"H., 38"W.
(bottom case), 20¾"D.*

Come visit us in Limington, just 28 miles west of Portland.
Jo Joy Road (off Route 117) P.O. Box 104, Limington, Maine 04049 (207) 793-4522
Fax: (207) 793-2305

ture, old wooden wheelbarrows, old cash registers, soda fountain accoutrements. *Est:* 1987. *Serv:* Refinishing of country oak, out-of-state delivery. *Hours:* Jun-Labor Day 10:30-5 Weekends Spring & Fall. Rich Roberts *Park:* In front. *Loc:* Rte 1 to Rte 173 at Isleboro Ferry Slip. Take 1st R after shop sign (Slab City Rd) and go to end. Approx 5 MI from Rte 1.

COUNTRY PATCH ANTIQUES
Rte 235, 04849
(207)763-4069   **27 65 67**
Country antiques, primitives, quilts, linens, vintage clothing, advertising, kitchenwares, blue willow, children's items, country furniture & accessories; Dealers welcome. *Est:* 1980. *Hours:* May-Sep Daily 9-5, Sun by chance WIN: Thu-Fri by chance/appt. *Size:* Medium. Pat Aho *Park:* On site. *Loc:* 7 MI N of Camden, From Camden: Rte 52 to Lincolnville Center, Rte 235 for 4/5 MI.

DUCK TRAP ANTIQUES
Rte 1, 04849
(207)789-5575   **44 63**
Large selection of flow blue for the beginner or advanced collector, china, glass, pewter & furniture. *Hours:* May-Nov call for appt. *Assoc:* MADA. Natalie Mac Innis *Loc:* 7 MI N of Camden.

ENTELECHY ANTIQUES
PO Box 62 Rte 17, 04849
(207)789-5177   **27 37 66**
A general line of antiques with emphasis on 18th C furniture & embellishments, country pieces, prints & paintings, together with selected items that go with antiques but do not themselves have age. *Hours:* Wed-Sat 9-6, Sun when flag is out & always by appt. *CC:* MC/V. Lincoln/Shirley Reid *Park:* On site. *Loc:* Rte 173, first house on L up from blinking light on Rte 1 at Lincolnville Beach.

FIELDWOOD ANTIQUES
Rte 52, 04849
(207)763-3926   **27**
Antique country furniture, decorations & accessories. *Hours:* May-Oct 9-5. Arlene W Lepow *Loc:* 5 MI from Camden, follow Rte 52.

LINCOLNVILLE BEACH

BETTY'S TRADING POST
Rte 1, 04849
(207)789-5300   **24 32 36**
Furniture, glass, jewelry, dolls & old coins. *Hours:* Year round daily 10-6. Betty Smith *Loc:* Across from the ferry landing next to the post office.

GOOSE RIVER EXCHANGE
Rte 1, 04849
(207)789-5241   **13 20 33**
Books, post cards, photographica, posters, advertising & ephemera. A unique paper-Americana specialist. *Pr:* $2–2000. *Est:* 1977. *Hours:* Jul-Sep 4 daily 10-6, else by chance/appt. *Size:* Medium. Kenneth N Shure *Park:* In front. *Loc:* Rte 1 in Lincolnville Beach, opposite Lobster Pound Rest.

MAINE ANTIQUE MERCHANTS LTD
Rte 1 (Northport), 04849
(207)338-1444   **{GR12}**
Antiques of the early American community. *Hours:* May 15-Oct 15 Tue-Sat, Win: by chance/appt. Ellen Katona Bob Lutz *Loc:* 2 1/2 MI N of Lincolnville Beach.

NORTH HOUSE FINE ANTIQUES
Rte 1 Waterside, 04849
(207)789-5252   **29 36 63**
Quality 18th & 19th C decorative arts &

furniture with emphasis on English ceramics. *Pr:* $50–5000. *Hours:* Jun-Sep by chance/appt. *Size:* Medium. *CC:* MC/V. *Assoc:* MADA. Judith Noel *Park:* In front. *Loc:* Rte 1, 6 MI N of Camden or 10 MI S of Belfast.

THE RED BARN
587 Rte 1, 04849
(207)236-2749   **36 44 45**

A big barn full of grand old things including china, glass, jewelry, furniture, tools, dolls, miniatures & garden sculpture. *Hours:* Open most months 10-4. Nancy Ann Baer

SIGN OF THE OWL
RR2 Box 85, 04849
(207)338-4669   **40 60 63**

General selection including some pine & oak furniture, china, glass, specialize in Orientalia - old & reproduction - porcelain & art. *Pr:* $20–1200. *Est:* 1986. *Serv:* Appraisal, interior design, bed & breakfast. *Hours:* May-Oct daily 10-6, Nov-Apr Wed-Sun 11-5. *Size:* Medium. *CC:* AX/MC/V. John E Trowbridge *Park:* On site. *Loc:* US Rte 1, 9 MI N of Camden.

LISBON

OLD LISBON SCHOOLHOUSE
ANTIQUES
Rte 196, 04252
(207)353-6075   **{GR3}**

Large Victorian schoolhouse filled with a general line from 1800 to 1950s. *Pr:* $10–500. *Est:* 1973. *Serv:* Appraisal, consultation, purchase estates. *Hours:* Apr 15-Nov 15 Thu, Sat 10-4 or by chance/appt call ahead. *Size:* Large.

Burtt Warren *Park:* On site. *Loc:* I-95 at Topsham take Rte 196N, or at Auburn, Rte 196S, to Lisbon.

LOVELL VILLAGE

KNOLLWOOD ANTIQUES
Historic Village Block Rte 5, 04051
(207)925-3059

Furniture, decorations, lighting, carpets, mirrors, paintings & 18th-19th C engravings. *Est:* 1990. *Hours:* Mon-Fri 10-5 by chance or appt. *CC:* MC/V/AE. Richard La Vigne *Loc:* 45 min W on Rte 302 Top Rte 5 N.

MADISON

BOOKS BOUGHT AND SOLD
125 Main St, 04950
(207)696-8361   **13**

Antiquarian books: Better used, out-of-print esoteric books, literature, history & records. *Serv:* Paperbacks traded. *Hours:* Year round daily 8:30-5. *Assoc:* MABA. C Seams

---

MANCHESTER

BLUE WILLOW FARM ANTIQUES
Worthing Rd, 04351
(207)623-4893   **63**

Blue willow, collectibles & country crafts. *Est:* 1984. *Hours:* Jun-Oct Mon-Fri 1-5, else by chance/appt. Vicki Oliver *Park:* On site. *Loc:* 1 1/2 MI off Rte 17.

CHARLES ROBINSON RARE BOOKS
Pond Rd, 04351
(207)622-1885   **13 51 66**
Rare & fine books in many fields. Illustrated books, maps & fine prints of the 19th & 20th C a specialty. Science, medicine & travel. Prints, lithographs & books containing original art. *Pr:* $25–2000. *Est:* 1974. *Serv:* Appraisal, auction. *Hours:* BY APPT ONLY. *Assoc:* MABA. *Loc:* Rte 202, 2 1/2 MI, on L.

MECHANIC FALLS

MCMORROW AUCTION COMPANY
Box 825 RFD #1, 04256
(207)345-9477   **8**
Antiques, commercial, farm & estates. *Serv:* Auction, appraisal. *Assoc:* CAI. Jody McMorrow

MOODY

THE GRAY'S ANTIQUES
Rte 1 & Tatnic Rd, 04054
(207)646-8938   **{GR7}**
A quality group shop with 2 floors in the shop & 2 floors in an attached barn featuring Victorian, oak & country furniture, art & prints, glass, china, sterling, linens & decorative accessories. *Est:* 1987. *Hours:* Jun-Oct daily 10-5, Nov-May CLOSED TUE. *CC:* MC/V. Jean Gray *Park:* On site. *Loc:* Just over the Ogunquit line.

KENNETH & IDA MANKO
Seabreeze Dr, 04054
(207)646-2595   **27 34 87**
Offering a choice stock of country furniture, paintings & folk art for the advanced collector, dealer & decorator.

One of the finest 19th C antique weathervane selections in New England. *Est:* 1973. *Serv:* Appraisal, consultation. *Hours:* Summer & Fall: daily 9-5 or by chance. *Assoc:* NEAA. *Park:* On site. *Loc:* I-95 Exit 2; Rte 109 E to Rte 1, Rte 1 S 2 1/2 MI to Eldridge Rd, E to Seabreeze.

NEW GLOUCESTER

LOUISE NOVAK - BOOKS
Rte 231, 04260
(207)926-3302   **13**
Antiquarian books: emphasis on Maine authors, non-fiction & nature. *Hours:* Year round Apr-Dec 10-5 Win: by appt. Best to call ahead. *Assoc:* MABA.

NEW HARBOR

RICHARDSON BOOKS LTD
Box 169, 04554
(207)677-2429   **13**
Antiquarian books: Jane Austen, Virginia Woolf, the Bloomsbury Group, Winston Churchill. *Serv:* Catalogs issued. *Hours:* BY APPT ONLY. *Assoc:* MABA. Peggy Richardson

NEWBURGH

GARY W WOOLSON, BOOKSELLER
Rte 9,
(207)234-4931   **13 51 66**
General line of used & antiquarian books, maps, prints & a few paintings. Specializing in Maine, natural history, literature, art/architectural history. *Pr:*

$1–500. *Est:* 1967. *Serv:* Appraisal, lists. *Hours:* BY APPT ONLY. *Assoc:* MABA. *Park:* On site. *Loc:* I-95 Exit 43: toward Winterport on Rte 69, Rte 9, 2 MI, sign in front.

NEWCASTLE

BARN STAGES BOOKSHOP
Pump St, 04553
(207)563-8335   **13**
A general, eclectic, balanced collection of used & out-of-print books both hardback & paperback-gathered for readers & browsers, categorically arranged. An annex 2 miles from the main shop houses 6,000 children's books. *Pr:* $1–50. *Est:* 1985. *Hours:* May 15-Oct 15 Mon-Fri 1-5 ANNEX Sun 1-5 only else by chance. *Size:* 20,000 books. *Assoc:* MABA. Barbara W Yedlin *Park:* On site. *Loc:* Pump St; 1/10 MI from Main St (Bus Rte 1).

DIFFERENT DRUMMER ANTIQUES
Glidden St Off Bus Rte 1, 04553
(207)563-1836   **50**
Lighting devices & a variety of furniture, textiles, toys, tin & accessories. *Est:* 1983. *Serv:* Consultation, purchase estates, estate tag sales. *Hours:* Apr-Oct daily 10-5, Nov-Mar by chance/appt. *Size:* Medium. *Assoc:* MADA. J M Waner *Park:* On site. *Loc:* 100 ft off Bus Rte 1, signs posted.

FOSTER'S AUCTION GALLERY
Rte 1, 04553
(207)563-8150   **8**
Fine antiques, 15-20 estate sales per year, Aug 1-2 annual summer auction - Americana, fine arts. Accept mail/phone bids, 10% buyers premium. *Est:* 1953. *Serv:* Appraisal, estate liquidation, mail-ing list. *Hours:* Daily 9-4. *Assoc:* MAA NAA. Robert L Foster Jr *Park:* On site. *Loc:* From Wiscasset, 3 MI N, on L, on Rte 1.

FOSTERS FLEA MARKET/ANTIQUE MALL
US Rte 1, 04553
(207)568-8150   **{FLEA}**
Flea market with antiques, collectibles & other flea market merchandise. Free admission. *Est:* 1978. *Serv:* Catered, rentals begin at $5. *Hours:* May-Sep Sun 7-4:30; late Apr-Oct Sat 7-4:30. *Size:* 50 spaces. *Park:* Free parking. *Loc:* On Rte 1 in Newcastle.

MARY HODES
Mills Rd Rte 215, 04553
(207)563-5151   **16 36 81**
Furniture, Mettlach, pewter, tin, china, tools & sewing items. *Est:* 1970. *Hours:* Apr-Oct daily 11-5. *Loc:* 1 MI from Rte 1.

CONSTANCE H HURST ANTIQUES
Bus Rte 1 at Newcastle Sq, 04553
(207)882-7354   **29 39**
Imported 17th, 18th, 19th C English period furniture & accessories. *Serv:* Purchase estates. *Hours:* Mon-Sat 10-5, Win: Mon-Sat 10-4. *Park:* Nearby. *Loc:* From Rte 1N, take Bus Rte 1.

KAJA VEILLEUX ART & ANTIQUES
Newcastle Sq Bus Rte 1, 04553
(207)563-1002   **23 47 59**
Furniture, paintings, sconces, rugs, clocks, jewelry & decorative items. *Serv:* Appraisal, estate auctions. *Hours:* Daily 9-5, Win: CLOSED SUN. *Assoc:* MADA NEAA.

MILLING AROUND
Academy Hill, 04553
(207)563-1241   **27 80**
Antiques, textiles, bobbins & country

furnishings. *Est:* 1979. *Hours:* Sum: afternoons & weekends, else BY APPT. *Assoc:* MAA. Dirk Poole *Park:* Nearby. *Loc:* US Rte 1 Newcastle/Damariscotta Exit: 1st L.

NEWCASTLE ANTIQUES
Rte 1, 04553
(207)563-5714 **3 56 59**
Oil paintings, antiquities, early American furniture & accessories & marine antiques. *Est:* 1978. *Hours:* Daily. Ellen Perez *Loc:* 4 MI N of Wiscasset Bridge.

SAIL LOFT
Main St, 04553
(207)563-5671 **13**
Antiquarian books: illustrated, children's & natural history. *Pr:* $2–450. *Est:* 1933. *Serv:* Appraisal, search service. *Hours:* Summer: by chance/appt. *Assoc:* MABA. CT & Sherry Hughes *Park:* In front. *Loc:* At the bridge on Main St.

NEWFIELD

JOHN BAUER/SONIA SEFTON ANTIQUES
Elm St, 04056
(207)793-8950 **1 27 82**
American Indian art & American period furniture & accessories. *Pr:* $150–15000. *Serv:* Appraisal, purchase estates. *Hours:* BY APPT ONLY.

NORTH BERWICK

YOUNG FINE ARTS GALLERY, INC.
PO Box 313, 03906
(207)676-3104 **59 66**
Paintings, watercolors, drawings, prints.

Serv: Auctions 5 times a year. illustrated listing $15. *Hours:* BY APPT. George Young *Loc:* Auctions at Seaboard Gallery in Elliot, ME.

NORTH EDGECOMB

THE DITTY BOX
Rte 1, 04543
(207)882-6618 **1 57 63**
In an 1840 meeting house featuring a large collection of American furniture & decorations, with emphasis on country items. Staffordshire portrait figures, samplers, pewter & Currier & Ives prints. *Pr:* $10–3000. *Est:* 1963. *Serv:* Appraisal, brochure. *Hours:* Jun 23-Oct 15 Mon-Fri 10:30-5, else by chance/appt. *Size:* Medium. *Assoc:* MADA. Muriel & George Lewis *Park:* On site. *Loc:* W side of Rte 1, on North Edgecomb/Newcastle line, 2 MI N of Wiscasset Bridge - 2 MI S of Foster's Auction Gallery.

EDGECOMB BOOK BARN
Cross Point Rd, 04556
(207)882-7278 **13**
Antiquarian books: including rare, specializing in illustrated, children's, marine, Americana & Maine books. *Hours:* Sum: daily 11-6, Win: BY APPT. *Size:* 30,000 books. *Assoc:* MABA. Frank McQuaid

MAH ANTIQUES
Eddy Rd, 04556
(207)882-6960 **66**
Prints: botanicals, historical & natural history. *Hours:* Mar-Nov BY APPT ONLY. Sally S Walt *Park:* On site. *Loc:* 1 MI from Rte 1 across the river from Wiscasset.

JACK PARTRIDGE
Rte 1, 04556
(207)882-7745   **1 39 58**

18th C English & American furniture, paintings & objets d'art. *Est:* 1927. *Hours:* May-Oct 15 daily 9:30-6. *Loc:* 3 MI N of Wiscasset facing Pioneer Motel on R going N on Rte 1.

NORTH MONMOUTH

JOYCE B KEELER - BOOKS
Wilson Pond Rd, 04265
(207)933-9088   **13**

Antiquarian books: diverse general collection, including science fiction & fantasy, children's books 1870-1970, nostalgic fiction, regional Americana & Maine books. *Serv:* Mail order. *Hours:* BY APPT ONLY. *Assoc:* MABA.

NORTHEAST HARBOR

PINE BOUGH
Main St, 04662
(207)276-5079   **1 13 50**

Dealing in select 18th, 19th & 20th C American antiques, accessories in treen, iron, glass, American lighting a specialty. Also antiquarian books & ephemera. *Pr:* $1–10000. *Serv:* Appraisal, consultation, purchase estates. *Hours:* Jun-Aug Mon-Sat 10-5, else by chance/appt. *CC:* AX/MC/V. JoAnne Fuerst *Park:* In front. *Loc:* Within 5 MI of Acadia Nat'l Park, at head of Sea St, on Main St in heart of Village.

NORTHPORT

LORD SEAGRAVE'S
Coastal Rte 1, 04915
(207)338-1424   **9 13 33**

Autographs, manuscripts, antiquarian books, decoys, ephemera, oak furniture, maps, nautical & marine items, post cards, prints, glass, Civil War items & primitives. *Pr:* $10–5000. *Serv:* Appraisal, auction, catalog ($1), purchase estates. *Hours:* Daily 10-5. *Size:* Medium. *CC:* MC/V. *Assoc:* MABA. Ron Seagrave *Park:* On site. *Loc:* Rte 1, 10 MI N of Camden.

NORWAY

DIXON'S ANTIQUES
16 Deering St, 04268
(207)743-6881   **16 37 66**

Early New England furniture, pressed glass, Wedgwood, prints & paintings, primitives, copper & ironware. *Hours:* BY APPT. *Loc:* Rte 26 from ME Tnpk in Grey, ME, 20 MI.

OGUNQUIT

BEAUPORT INN ANTIQUES
96 Shore Rd, 03907
(207)646-8680   **44 63**

Small furniture, china, glass & decorative accessories. *Hours:* Daily in season, else Thu-Mon. Dan Pender *Park:* On site. *Loc:* Off US Rte 1 on the road to Perkins Cove.

POTPOURRI ANTIQUES
Rte 1, 03907
(207)646-3529　　　　　**23 47 77**
Specializing in fine antique jewelry. *Pr:* $5–5000. *Est:* 1961. *Serv:* Auction, consultation, purchase estates. *Hours:* May-Oct 15 by chance/appt. *Assoc:* MADA. Thomas N Zankowich *Park:* On site. *Loc:* 1 1/4 MI N of Ogunquit Ctr.

ORLAND

BROOKSIDE ANTIQUES
The Castine Rd Rte 175, 04472
(207)326-8220　　　　　**27 59**
Country furniture, paintings, Canton, hooked rugs, baskets, iron & more. *Hours:* All year by chance/appt. *Size:* Small. *Assoc:* MADA. Sam Braden *Park:* On site. *Loc:* Between Orland & Castine, 6 MI off Rte 1.

ORONO

THE GREEN DOOR ANTIQUE SHOP
92 Main St, 04473
(207)866-3116　　　　　**44 63 77**
European & American antiques, period Irish silver a specialty, china & glass. *Serv:* Appraisal & estate sales. *Hours:* By chance/appt, call ahead. *Assoc:* MADA. Eileen O'Callaghan

ORRINGTON

MERRIMAC'S ANTIQUES
Rte 15 River Rd, 04474
(207)989-2667　　　　　**40 44 83**
One floor of glass, china, baskets. One room of furniture - Victorian, oak & some pine, dealing mainly in art glass. *Pr:* $25–5000. *Serv:* Appraisal. *Hours:* May-Oct 20 by chance/appt. *Assoc:* MADA. Mary MacDonald

OXFORD

MEETING HOUSE ANTIQUES
Rte 26 at Jct Rte 121, 04270
(207)539-8480　　　　　**{GR}**
A group shop with country, oak, walnut, mahogany & pine furniture, glass & paintings. *Hours:* Daily 9-5. Stephen Sears

TILLSON'S ANTIQUE CENTER
Rte 26, 04270
(207)539-2339
Antiques, primitives & some collectibles. *Hours:* Year round Daily 10-5, sometimes open earlier. *Park:* On site. *Loc:* Approx 15 MI N of Gray Exit off ME Tnpk.

UNDERCOVER ANTIQUE & FLEA MARKET
Rte 26, 04270
(207)539-4149　　　　　**{GR50}**
Fifty dealers under one roof with good selection of collectibles. *Hours:* Daily 10-5.

WAGON WHEEL ANTIQUE MALL
Rte 26, 04270
(207)539-4393   **{GR}**
A collection of books, post cards, furniture & collectibles. *Hours:* Daily 10-5.

PALERMO

A REAL MAINE COUNTRY STORE
Old Rte 3, Palermo Village, 04354
(207)993-2772   **5 29 83**
Located in a 1920's country store & featuring decorative antiques from Victorian to 1950's & many architectural antiques. *Est:* 1990. *Serv:* Appraisal, purchase estates. *Hours:* Mid Jun-Dec Thu 8-4, Fri-Sat 10-4, else BY APPT. June Nerber *Park:* In front. *Loc:* From Augusta: 18 MI on Rte 3; From Belfast: 15 MI on Rte 3, R to Palermo Village.

PARIS

HAUNTED BOOKSHOP
Paris Hill, 04271
(207)743-6216   **13**
Antiquarian books: general collection of used, out-of-print & rare books. *Serv:* Search service. *Hours:* Year round by chance/appt, extended summer hours. *Assoc:* MABA. Wini Mott

PEAKS ISLAND

ROBERT T FOLEY ANTIQUES
PO Box 82, 04108
(207)766-2261   **34 65**
Folk art & primitives. *Hours:* BY APPT ONLY. Robert T Foley

PITTSFIELD

KENNISTON'S ANTIQUES
Rte 2, 04967
(207)487-5032   **36 63 77**
Primitives, glass, china, furniture, paintings, jewelry, baskets, silver & books. *Hours:* Apr-Nov or BY APPT. Barbara Kenniston

PITTSTON

PHIPPS OF PITTSTON
Rte 27, 04345
(207)582-3555   **28 42 63**
Pine & other natural wood furniture, ironstone, yellow ware, glass & china & other decorator items. *Hours:* Spring-Fall daily 10-5 CLOSED SUN else year round BY APPT. *Assoc:* MADA. Maggi Phipps *Loc:* 3 MI from Gardines Bridge South, & 5 MI from Wiscasset North.

KENNETH E TUTTLE ANTIQUES
Rtes 194 & 27, 04345
(207)582-4496   **21 37 84**
18th & early 19th C American country & formal furniture. *Est:* 1967. *Serv:* Everything guaranteed as represented. *Hours:* Year round Mon-Fri 9-5 Sat-Sun By chance/appt. *Assoc:* MADA.

POLAND SPRING

CIDERPRESS BOOKSTORE
Cleve Tripp Rd RFD 1, 04274
(207)998-4338   **13**
Antiquarian books: a general collection with emphasis on literature, science, history, philosophy, natural history & books

by & about women. *Hours:* Mar 15-Dec 15 by chance/appt. *Assoc:* MABA. Virginia Chute *Loc:* From Rte 26 take Range Hill Rd.

PORTLAND

F O BAILEY ANTIQUARIANS
141 Middle St, 04101
(207)774-1479   **4 8**
One of Maine's oldest auction houses dealing in fine furniture, paintings, rugs, glassware, porcelain, gold & silver items. 10% buyer's premium. *Est:* 1819. *Serv:* Appraisal, auctioneers, restoration & refinishing. *Hours:* Mon-Fri 9-5 Sat 10-4. *Assoc:* MADA. Joy Piscopo *Loc:* I-295 Exit Franklin St: at 5th set of lights turn R onto Middle St, gallery on R at next Int.

BARRIDOFF GALLERIES
26 Free St, 04101
(207)772-5011   **59**
Specializing in 19th & 20th C American paintings. *Est:* 1975. *Serv:* Appraisal, consultation, auction. *Hours:* Mon-Fri 10-5 Sat 12-4. Annette Elowitch *Park:* Nearby. *Loc:* 2 blocks from the Portland Museum.

CARLSON AND TURNER BOOKS
241 Congress St, 04101
(207)773-4200   **9 13 66**
Antiquarian books: good selection of reference books, fine art & decorative prints. *Est:* 1974. *Serv:* Appraisal. *Hours:* Tue-Sat 10-5 most Sun 12-5 Irregular hours in April. *Size:* 40,000 books. *CC:* MC/V. *Assoc:* MABA. Norma C Carlson *Loc:* I-295 Franklin St Exit: R at 2nd light, 150 yds on L across from Eastern Cemetery.

GEORGE L COLLORD III
295 Forest Ave Suite 262, 04101
(207)773-6803   **23 72**
Rare watches, clocks, mechanical antiques - specializing in the purchase & sale of unusual & complicated American & European wrist & pocket watches; scientific & mechanical items also a specialty, including telescopes, microscopes, typing & sewing mach. *Est:* 1976. *Serv:* Patek Philippe, Rolex & other high grade pocket & wristwatches wanted. *Hours:* BY APPT ONLY 9-6 daily. *Assoc:* NAWCC.

CREIGHTON'S COUNTRY STORE
96 Commercial St, 04101
(207)774-7611   **27**
Specializing in country antiques. *Hours:* 7-7 Daily. *Loc:* Near the Int of Commercial & Franklin.

CUNNINGHAM BOOKS
762A Congress St, 04104
(207)775-2246   **13**
Antiquarian books: an organized general collection of used & out-of-print books. *Hours:* Year round Mon-Sat 10:30-5:30PM. *Assoc:* MABA. Joan Pickard

FLYNN BOOKS
466 Ocean Ave, 04103
(207)772-2685   **13**
Antiquarian books: a general collection, including rare & fine press books, Americana, the West & selected Maine & New England books. *Hours:* BY APPT ONLY. *Assoc:* MABA. Anita Flynn *Park:* On site. *Loc:* I-295 Exit 8 (Washington Ave): L at 3rd light onto Ocean Ave, corner of Victor Rd, red house.

MILK STREET ANTIQUES
8 Milk St, 04101
(207)773-8288   **28 34 67**

Fine 18th & 19th C American country & formal furniture, pottery, china, stoneware, toys, paintings, quilts, textiles, Oriental rugs, folk art & decoys. *Est:* 1976. *Serv:* Wholesale to the trade. *Hours:* Mon-Sat 10-6. *CC:* MC/V. Kimberly Washam *Park:* Nearby. *Loc:* Next to the Regency.

THOMAS MOSER
CABINETMAKERS
415U Cumberland Ave, 04101
(207)774-3791   **19**

Solid cherry furniture. *Serv:* Catalog ($9). *Hours:* Mon-Sat 9-5. *CC:* MC/V. *Loc:* I-95N Exit 6A: onto 295 N, take Exit 6A again (Forest Ave), showroom located on corner of Forest & Cumberland Aves.

NELSON RARITIES, INC
One City Center 8th Fl, 04112
(207)775-3150   **7 23 47**

Extensive collection of estate jewelry, specializing in Art Deco, Art Nouveau & period jewelry, also stones, watches & silver. *Serv:* Purchase estates, catalog, 1-800-882-3150. *Hours:* Daily 9:30-5. *Assoc:* MADA. Andrew Nelson

F M O'BRIEN ANTIQUARIAN
BOOKS
38 High St, 04101
(207)774-0931   **9 13 66**

Specializing in Americana & general literature, with an emphasis on Maine books, autographs, paintings & prints. *Est:* 1934. *Serv:* Appraisal, build collections for libraries. *Hours:* BY APPT ONLY. *Assoc:* ABAA MABA. *Park:* On site. *Loc:* I-95 Exit 7 at S Portland: follow Gull signs to waterfront Commercial St to High St up to 5th house on L with long drive.

OCTAVIA'S ANTIQUES
247 Congress St, 04101
(207)772-2668   **50 83**

Victorian era furniture, accessories & lighting. *Est:* 1983. *Hours:* Year round Tue-Sat 10-5:30. *Loc:* 2 min off I-95.

OUT-OF-PRINT SHOP
112 High St, 04101
(207)775-3233   **13**

Antiquarian books: a general collection of nonfiction. *Hours:* Wed-Fri 11-6 Sat 12-5:30. *Assoc:* MABA. Pat Murphy

PAST TENSE ANTIQUES
247 Congress St, 04101
(207)772-3355

Eclectic selection of antiques from all periods specializing in 1950s memorabilia. *Est:* 1988. *Hours:* Year round Tue-Sat 11-6. Calvin S Muse *Park:* On street.

PORTLAND EXPO FLEA MARKET
239 Park Ave, 04102
(207)874-8200   **{FLEA}**

Heated indoor flea market including antiques, fine art, a variety of collectibles & other flea market merchandise; substantial block book discounts available for dealers. *Est:* 1981. *Serv:* Catered. *Hours:* Late Oct-Late Mar Sun 9-4. *Size:* 150 spaces. *Park:* Free parking on site. *Loc:* From ME Tnpk: Exit 6A or 7, follow I-295 to Exit 5A (Congress St), L on St John St, R on to Park Ave; Park 200 yds on L.

MARY ALICE REILLEY
83 India St, 04101
(207)773-8815   **42 44 65**

A large selection of pine, also primitives, glass, china & country accessories. *Hours:* Tue-Sat 11-5 by chance/appt. *Assoc:* MADA.

REMEMBER WHEN
15 Pleasant St, 04101
(207)761-7946　　　　　**48 59 80**

A small shop with collectibles, decorative accessories, clothing & beautifully presented vintage textiles, especially linens. Some furniture & art work. *Pr:* $25–500. *Est:* 1987. *Hours:* Apr 20-Oct 20 Tue-Sat 10-6, Oct 21-Apr 19 Tue-Sat 11-5. Emily Materson *Park:* In front. *Loc:* I-295 Exit 7: S to Fore St, turn R, up Pleasant St at Int with Fore (at blinking light).

ALLEN SCOTT/BOOKS
89 Exchange St, 04101
(207)774-2190　　　　　**13**

Antiquarian books: carefully selected collection of quality books for collectors & libraries including first editions, art, architecture, psychology, travel, Americana, maritime, literature, books on books & history. *Hours:* Year round Mon-Sat 11-6 & BY APPT. *Size:* 10,000 books. *Assoc:* MABA. *Loc:* In the Old Port Exchange.

VENTURE ANTIQUES
101 Exchange St, 04101
(207)773-6064　　　　　**44 63 67**

19th C furniture, china, glassware, quilts, lamps & decorative accessories. *Hours:* Mon-Sat 10-5. *Assoc:* MADA. Isabel Thacher

WEST PORT ANTIQUES
17 Pleasant St, 04104
(207)774-6747　　　　　**36 67 80**

Small shop located in historic Old Port section of Portland featuring a full range of antiques including furniture, carefully selected smalls & textiles. *Pr:* $5–5000. *Est:* 1988. *Serv:* Interior design. *Hours:* Tue-Sat 11-5 or by chance/appt; off-season BY APPT ONLY. *CC:*

AX/MC/V. Mary Ingalls *Park:* In front, local garage. *Loc:* 1 block S of Civic Center.

WILMA'S ANTIQUES & ACCESSORIES
255 Congress St, 04101
(207)772-9852　　　　　**27 44 63**

Country & formal furniture, fine glass & china, braided & hooked rugs, paintings & accessories. *Est:* 1979. *Serv:* Purchase estates. *Hours:* Mon-Sat 10-5. *Size:* Medium. *CC:* MC/V. *Assoc:* MADA. Wilma D Taliento *Park:* On site. *Loc:* I-95 Franklin St Exit, thru 4 sets of lights, turn L, thru 1 set of lights, diagonally across from Levinsky's.

GERALDINE WOLF
26 Milk St, 04104
(207)774-8994　　　　　**47**

Antique & estate jewelry. *Hours:* BY APPT ONLY. *Assoc:* MADA.

PORTLAND (SOUTH)

J. GLATTER BOOKS
146 Ocean St, 04106
(207)799-7283　　　　　**13**

Antiquarian books: Hardcover & paperback books for the teacher, student, collector & reader. *Hours:* Year round Tue-Fri 11-5 Sat 12-4. *Size:* 12,000 books. *Assoc:* MABA. Jack Glatter

PRESQUE ISLE

THE COUNTRY STORE
667 Main St, 04769
(207)764-6192　　　　　**32 36 44**

General line of antiques & collectibles. *Serv:* Purchase estates. *Hours:* Mar-Dec

Mon-Sat 10-5, Jan-Feb Mon-Sat 12-4.
Size: Large. *CC:* MC/V. Angie Graves
Park: On site. *Loc:* Diagonally across
from McDonald's.

RANGELEY

BLUEBERRY HILL FARM
Saddleback Rd, 04970
(207)864-5647   **44 67**
Antiques, quilts, glass, advertising,
country furnishings & collectible fishing
items. *Hours:* Jul-Aug daily 10-4.
Stephanie/Don Palmer

RICHMOND

THE LOFT ANTIQUES
9 Gardiner St, 04357
(207)737-2056   **29 48 85**
Early clothing, accessories, fine laces,
linens & decorative items. *Hours:* By
chance/appt. Kay Pierce *Loc:* I-95 Exit
26.

ROCKPORT

EARLY TIMES ANTIQUES CENTER
Rte 90, 04856
(207)236-3001   **{GR}**
A select group of dealers with diverse
offerings including furniture of all
periods, decorative accessories, jewelry,
post cards & collectibles. *Hours:* Mar-
Dec Mon-Sat 9-4:30 Most Sun 12-4:30.
George & Martha Martens

**JOAN HARTMAN ELLIS ANTIQUE
PRINT**
19 High St, 04856
(207)236-4524   **66**
18th & 19th C engravings, lithographs &
woodcuts, including botanicals, natural
history, American & European views &
caricatures. *Pr:* $25–500. *Est:* 1962.
Hours: Appt suggested. *Park:* In front.
Loc: In Rockport Village on Amesbury
Hill.

KATRIN PHOCAS LTD
19 Main St, 04856
(207)236-8654   **37 39 59**
Two floors of English & American furniture of 17th, 18th & 19th C, accessories
& fine art at harborside. *Pr:* $25–10000.
Est: 1987. *Hours:* Jun-Sep Tue-Sat 10-5,
JUL, AUG BY APPT. *CC:* AX/MC/V.
Assoc: MADA. *Park:* In front.

WINDY TOP ANTIQUES
59 Pascal Ave, 04856
(207)236-4514   **16 18**
Small, tidy shop specializing in buttons
& lace, copper & brass, china, glass &
some soft goods. *Est:* 1970. *Serv:* Button
appraisal. *Hours:* May-Oct 15 Mon-Fri
10-5 by chance/appt. Marion H Magee
Park: On site. *Loc:* Rte 1N to Rte 90 at
Waldoboro, to dead end, shop on R, next
to general store.

ROUND POND

CARRIAGE HOUSE
Rte 32, 04564
(207)529-5555   **13 66**
Antiquarian books: emphasis on nonfic-
tion, large & varied selection of
Americana, marine & illustrated books,
prints, furniture & primitives. *Est:* 1961.
Hours: Sum: daily 10-5 Win: by

chance/appt. *Assoc:* MABA. Roy Gillespie *Loc:* 1 MI S of Round Pond Village.

THE HOLMES
Rte 32, 04564
(207)529-5788   **27 29 59**

Country furniture, primitives, paintings & decorative accessories. *Hours:* Jul-Aug Mon-Fri 10-5 or BY APPT. *Park:* On site.

ROUND POND VILLAGE ANTIQUES
Rte 32, 04564
(207)529-5592   **27**

Specializing in furniture & accessories for the country home. *Hours:* Thu-Sun 10-4.

TIME AND AGAIN ANTIQUES
Rte 32 S, 04564
(207)677-2715   **36 44 63**

Carrying fine pattern glass, including Portland & Sandwich; china, including flow blue, Mulberry & white ironstone; 19th & 19th C furniture; selection of whale oil lamps. *Pr:* $50–3000. *Est:* 1982. *Serv:* Purchase estates. *Hours:* May-Oct daily 9-4, Nov-Apr by chance/appt. *Size:* Medium. *Assoc:* MADA. June Staples *Park:* On site. *Loc:* From Damariscotta, Rte 130 to New Harbor for about 13 MI, L on Rte 32, shop is approximately 2 1/2 MI.

ROXBURY

YANKEE GEM CORP
Rte 17, 04275
(207)364-4458   **6 24 32**

Large barn offering glass, china, pewter, primitives, guns, coins, toys, furniture & paintings. *Hours:* May-Nov Daily, Sat &

Winters by chance. *CC:* MC/V. *Assoc:* MADA. Ann A Mc Crillis *Loc:* 9 MI N off Rte 2.

RUMFORD

CONNIE'S ANTIQUES
190 Lincoln Ave, 04276
(207)364-8886   **48 64 85**

Clothing, linens, post cards, dolls, jewelry, toys, furniture, primitives, glass & china. *Hours:* By chance/appt, call advised. *Assoc:* MADA. Constance P Goudreau *Loc:* 1/3 MI off Rte 2, big blue house on top of hill.

RUMFORD CENTER

GROVE FARM ANTIQUES
Star Rte, 04278
(207)369-0259   **29 66 85**

Glass, paintings, prints, decorative arts & vintage clothing. *Hours:* May-Oct by chance/appt. Burton S de Frees *Loc:* From Rte 2 at Rumford Ctr go N 6 MI, then 1 1/2 MI on E Andover Rd.

SACO

F P WOODS, BOOKS
48 Ferry Rd, 04072
(207)282-2278   **13 76**

Specializing in Americana, literature, Shaker, utopian & communal material. *Pr:* $20–4000. *Est:* 1978. *Serv:* Appraisal, catalog, purchase estates, search service. *Hours:* Year round: by chance/appt. *Assoc:* MABA. Frank P

Woods *Park:* On site. *Loc:* Rte 1, N of
Saco take R off Main onto Beach out to
Ferry Rd.

SANFORD

BOOK ADDICT
Pine Tree Dr, 04073
(207)324-2243   **13**
Antiquarian books: a general collection
including biography, history, adventure,
nature, sports & fiction arranged by
author. *Hours:* May-Oct BY APPT.
Assoc: MABA. David H Foshey

J LEEKE PRESERVATION
CONSULTANT
2947 Country Club Rd #2, 04073
(207)324-9597   **5 26 74**
Helping homeowners, tradesmen, con-
tractors, architects & museums understand their historic buildings - involving
problem solving, project management,
planning, maintenance, programming &
training.   Practical restoration reports.
Serv: Conservation, consultation, repair,
restoration, replication, reproduction.
Hours: By appt only - call or write for
details.

SCARBOROUGH

CLIFF'S ANTIQUE MARKET
Rte 1, 04074
(207)883-5671   **{GR65}**
Furniture: pine, oak, walnut, mahogany
& country; glass, china art, jewelry,
books, rugs, silver & post cards. A broad
selection. Work with dealers. *Est:* 1984.
Serv: Custom woodwork, purchase estates, restoration. *Hours:* Apr-Nov daily
10-5; Dec-Mar CLOSED TUE-WED.

Size: Huge. *CC:* MC/V. Cliff & Joan
Caton *Park:* On site. *Loc:* ME Tnpk Exit
5: 6 1/2 MI N on Rte 1, just S of
Portland, across from Scarborough
Downs.

TOP KNOTCH ANTIQUES
14 Willowdale Rd, 04074
(207)883-5303   **40**
Antiques, collectibles & oak furniture,
signs, toys & tools. *Serv:* Consignments
accepted. *Hours:* Daily & some evenings. *Park:* On site. *Loc:* From Rte 1
follow signs.

SEARSPORT

ANTIQUES AT THE HILLMANS
Rte 1, 04974
(207)548-6658   **28 50 67**
Fine china, lamps, dolls, linens,
stoneware, quilts, Victorian walnut, oak
& country furniture. *Hours:* Apr-Oct
daily, else chance/appt. *Assoc:* MADA.
Les Hillman *Loc:* 2 3/4 MI N of town.

THE CAPTAIN'S HOUSE ANTIQUES
E Main St, 04974
(207)548-6344   **21 37 60**
Formal American furniture of the 18th &
19th C. Specializing in Chinese export
porcelain with a large selection of Can-
ton & Rose Medallion. Mandarin-
Oriental carpets. *Hours:* Jun-Aug
Mon-Sat 10-5 Sun 1-5. *Size:* Medium.
Assoc: MADA. Elizabeth Hoeschle
Park: On site. *Loc:* 2 1/2 MI N of
Searsport on US 1, between Camden &
Bar Harbor.

GOLD COAST ANTIQUES
Rte 1, 04974
(207)548-2939   **32 50 52**
Antique dolls, doll accessories, doll

dressmaking, old ivory, china, signed cut glass, Limoges, paintings, early oil lamps, miniatures & furniture. *Hours:* By chance/appt. Vasco Baldacci

HART-SMITH ANTIQUES
US Rte 1, 04974
(207)548-2412   **36 59**
American country & period furniture & paintings. *Hours:* Year round by chance/appt.

PRIMROSE FARM ANTIQUES
Rte 1, 04974
(207)548-6019   **28 76 80**
Country antiques, furniture, textiles, Shaker items, stoneware, baskets, tools, fine glass, china & ironstone. *Est:* 1973. *Hours:* Apr-Oct daily 9-5 CLOSED SUN, Win BY APPT. *Assoc:* MADA. Liz Dominic *Loc:* 3 MI N of Village.

PUMPKIN PATCH ANTIQUE CENTER
Rte 1, 04974
(207)548-6047   **{GR25}**
Eclectic array of Americana & Maine antiques in a two-story shop. *Hours:* Daily 9-5, Win BY APPT. *Assoc:* MADA. Bob Sommer

RED KETTLE ANTIQUES
Rte 1, 04974
(207)548-2978   **27 32 40**
Victorian walnut & oak furniture, country furniture & accessories, dolls, toys, linen & stoneware. *Hours:* All year by chance/appt. *Assoc:* MADA. Ginny Middleswart *Loc:* 3 MI N of Village on Rte 1.

SKOWHEGAN

MAIN(E)LY BOOKS
178 Madison Ave, 04976
(207)474-3185   **13**
Antiquarian books: hunting, fishing, music, entertainment & military history. *Hours:* Year round BY APPT ONLY. *Assoc:* MABA. Robert Chandler

SOUTH CASCO

VARNEY'S VOLUMES
Quaker Ridge Rd, 04077
(207)655-4605   **13**
General collection of out-of-print & rare books with specialty in children's & Maine. *Pr:* $5–250. *Est:* 1978. *Serv:* Mail orders anytime. *Hours:* Jul-Aug daily 10-5 CLOSED WED & SUN, else by chance/appt. *Assoc:* MABA. A. Lois Varney *Park:* On site. *Loc:* 25 MI NW of Portland just off Rte 302 between Portland & White Mts, turn R at Thomas Inn & Playhouse.

SOUTH CHINA

COUNTRY ANTIQUES
Rte 32 Off Rte 3, 04358
(207)445-2315   **1 15 27**
Country furniture, specializing in pine - refinished & original paint - country smalls & primitives, kitchen utensils, iron, spongeware, yellow ware, redware, stoneware, & old tools. *Hours:* Daily by chance/appt. Karl Rau *Park:* In front. *Loc:* Rte 3E from Augusta, turn S onto Rte 32, 100 yds to shop.

GRAY MATTER SERVICE
Rte 3, 04358
(207)445-2245　　　　　　　　**13**

Books: rare, used, out-of-print, collectibles, folk art & antiques. *Hours:* May-Nov Mon-Thu 10-5 Fri-Sun 1-5, Mar-Apr Sat-Sun 10-5. *Assoc:* MABA. Mabel Charles

SOUTHWEST HARBOR

MARIANNE CLARK FINE ANTIQUES
Main St Rte 102, 04679
(207)244-9247　　　　**27 29 37**

Authentic 18th & 19th C country & formal furniture & accessories, also paintings & folk art. *Pr:* $25–25000. *Hours:* Mon-Sat 10-5. *Size:* Large. *Assoc:* AADA MADA. *Park:* On site. *Loc:* Rte 1 thru Ellsworth, to Int of Rte 102, to SW Harbor, on Mt Desert Island, Acadia National Park.

SPRINGVALE

HARLAND EASTMAN - BOOKS
66 Main St Rte 109, 04083
(207)324-2797　　　　　**13 14**

Old & rare books, a general collection with emphasis on Maine local history, Maine nonfiction, Maine authors, 19th & 20th C boys' & children's books. *Pr:* $5–500. *Serv:* Appraisal. *Hours:* By chance/appt Best to call if coming a distance. *Size:* Medium. *Assoc:* MABA. *Park:* In front. *Loc:* 1 1/2 MI N of Int of Rtes 109 & 202, no sign.

GEORGE E MILKEY BOOKS
7 Frost St #2, 04083
(207)324-5510　　　　　　　**13**

Antiquarian books: out-of-print & rare books including Americana, literature, ships & the sea, natural history & scholarly books. *Hours:* Year round daily 9-9. *Assoc:* MABA. George Milkey

SPRUCE HEAD

ELFAST'S ANTIQUES
Patten Point Rd, 04859
(207)594-9377　　　　**63 67 80**

Specialize in a large selection of British china & pottery, including stick sponge, gaudy Welsh, blue & white, soft paste, yellowware & ironstone, as well as quilts, rugs, textiles, country furniture & related accessories. *Est:* 1972. *Hours:* Jun-Oct daily 10-5, Sep-Jun by chance/appt. *Assoc:* MADA. Bruce Elfast *Loc:* Follow signs from Rte 1 between Thomaston & Rockland.

STEEP FALLS

WARD'S BOOK BARN
Box 6, 04085
(207)675-3348　　　　　　　**13**

Antiquarian books: old fiction - much before 1900 - biography, military & rare books. *Hours:* Year round daily 9-8. *Assoc:* MABA. Ellery Ward

STOCKTON SPRINGS

BRICK HOUSE ANTIQUES
Rte 1 at Sandy Point, 04981
(207)567-3173   **17 37 81**
18th & 19th C American & French furniture, primitives, art glass, china, tools, metals, bronzes, lamps & paintings. *Hours:* Jun-Sep or by chance. *Assoc:* MADA. Violet K Paddock

VICTORIAN HOUSE/BOOK BARN
E Main St, 04981
(207)567-3351   **13**
Antiquarian books: large selection of old, out-of-print & scarce books. *Serv:* Mail & phone orders, search service. *Hours:* Apr-Dec daily 8-8 Jan-Mar by chance/appt. *Assoc:* MABA. Andrew B MacEwen

THOMASTON

ANCHOR FARM ANTIQUES
184 Main St, 04861
(207)354-8859   **47 63 77**
Two large rooms featuring sterling silver, jewelry, china, lamps, tools & furniture. *Est:* 1975. *Serv:* Appraisal, purchase estates. *Hours:* May-Oct, Win by chance/appt. *Size:* Large. *Assoc:* MADA. Muriel D Knutson *Park:* In front. *Loc:* Rte 1 next to ME State Prison.

WEE BARN ANTIQUES
4 1/2 Georges St, 04861
(207)354-6163   **32 36 47**
Offering fine, fun smalls including, furniture, accessories, silver, jewelry, art glass, toys & fine china. *Est:* 1972.

Hours: Apr-Oct daily 9-4:30, Nov-Mar by chance/appt. *Assoc:* MADA. Gwen B Robinson *Loc:* Just off Rte 1.

TOPSHAM

ANTIQUES AT TOPSHAM FAIR MALL
100 Old Lewiston Rd 2-10, 04086
(207)729-7913   **{GR75}**
A large group shop with furniture, jewelry, glass & china, Victoriana, country, Oriental art, paintings & baseball cards. *Est:* 1987. *Hours:* Seven day 9:30-5:30 Sun 12-5. *Size:* MEDIUM. *CC:* AX/MC/V. Shirley Short, *Mgr Park:* In front. *Loc:* I-95 Exit 24: Turn R at Mc Donald's and you are in Topsham Fair Mall.

MERRYMEETING ANTIQUES
Pleasant Point Rd, 04086
(207)729-9251   **44 59 63**
Specializing in fine art & cut glass, china, pewter & paintings. *Hours:* All year by chance/appt. *Assoc:* MADA. Ellie V Carver

TOWN HILL

WEST EDEN ANTIQUES
Rte 102,
(207)288-3062   **27 28 77**
Country furniture, tin, quilts, iron woodenware, stoneware, paintings, art work, silver, white ironstone & rugs. *Hours:* Daily 9-5. Bob Hylander

TRENTON

MAYO AUCTIONEERS & APPRAISERS
Rte 3 Bar Harbor Rd, 04605
(207)667-2586   **4 8 25**
Downeast Maine's only full-time auction & appraisal service, located on the doorstep to Bar Harbor & Acadia National Park. *Est:* 1974. *Serv:* Appraisal, auction. *Hours:* Year round by chance/appt. *Size:* Large. *CC:* MC/V. *Assoc:* CAI NAA NEAA. Wayne A Mayo *Park:* On site. *Loc:* 7 MI from Ellsworth on Rte 3.

TRENTON ANTIQUE CENTER
Rte 3 Bar Harbor Rd, 04605
(207)667-7323   **65 86**
Quality furnishings, antique wicker, country, folk art & primitives. *Est:* 1953. *Hours:* May-Oct Mon-Sat 11-4. *Loc:* 7 MI from Ellsworth on the way to Bar Harbor.

TROY

GREEN'S CORNER ANTIQUES
Rte 202, 04987
(207)948-2355   **27 40 83**
A large barn full of oak, mahogany & pine furniture, thousands of small items, doorstops, kitchenware, toys, signs, tools & stoneware. Also stock farm-related items - cupboards, frames & lighting. *Pr:* $1–1000. *Est:* 1975. *Serv:* Appraisal, consultation, purchase estates, repairs. *Hours:* Year round daily, appt suggested. *Size:* Large. Ron Reed *Park:* On site. *Loc:* From Waterville, Rte 139, Rte 202 in Unity, 4 MI on L N of Unity.

WALDOBORO

CENTRAL ASIAN ARTIFACTS
Main & Jefferson Sts, 04572
(207)273-2490   **21 47**
Oriental carpets, Rosewood, lapis jewelry. *Hours:* Sum: Wed,Thu 1-4, Fri 10-8, Sat 10-5.

WILLIAM EVANS FINE CABINETMAKER
W Main St, 04572
(207)832-4175   **70 71**
Period reproductions & restoration of quality period furniture. Trained by Dutch master cabinetmaker. *Est:* 1973. *Serv:* Conservation, custom woodwork, reproduction, restoration, consultation. *Hours:* By chance/appt. *Park:* On site. *Loc:* Old Rte 1 (Main St) in the village, by the bridge.

TRUEMAN AUCTION CO
Feyler's Corner, 04572
(207)832-6062   **8**
Friendly auction company with low commission rates & prompt settlement of accounts. Entire estates or single items handled. Terms to consignor vary & buyer's premium is 10%. *Serv:* Appraisal, accept mail bids, brochure, catalog, consultation. *Hours:* Daily 7-7. *Assoc:* NAA. Lawrence B Trueman *Loc:* On Rte 220, approximately 2 1/2 MI W of Moody's Diner in Waldoboro, office only.

WARREN

ABLE TO CANE
67 Main St, 04864
(207)273-3747 **22**
Caning, basketry, wicker material, Nantucket Lightship desks & basket molds. *Serv:* Repairs on all types of antique seats. *Hours:* By chance/appt. *Loc:* Off Rte 1.

WARREN VILLAGE

VILLAGE ANTIQUE GROUP SHOP
Union & Main Sts, 04864
(207)273-2860 **{GR14}**
Country, linens, silver, jewelry, glass, china & collectibles. *Hours:* May-Oct daily 10-4. *Loc:* 1 block off of Rte 90.

WASHINGTON

THE LILAC SHED ANTIQUES
Rte 17, 04574
(207)845-2263 **16 28 63**
Pottery & porcelain, glass, paintings, prints, ironware, tools, brass & lighting, specializing in kitchen range grates & range parts. *Hours:* Year round daily. Kenneth L Spahr *Loc:* 1/3 MI W of Rte 220.

WATERBORO

WATERBORO EMPORIUM
Rte 202, 04067
(207)247-4128 **11 42 80**
Pine & oak furniture, baseball cards, jewelry, ephemera, linens, rugs, textiles, depression & pattern glass. *Hours:* Sep-May Fri-Sun 10-4 Jun-Aug 9-5. Sherry Porter *Loc:* On the Square.

WELLS

1774 HOUSE ANTIQUES
Rte 1, 04090
(207)646-3520 **27 65 67**
Cupboards, country, primitives, quilts, decorative accessories & small furniture - always interesting & unique items. *Hours:* Daily. Stan Tufts *Park:* In front. *Loc:* Across from Bo-Mar Hall, Rte 1 N.

THE ARRINGTONS
Rte 1, 04090
(207)646-4124 **13**
Rare, new used books, prints, post cards, ephemera, with emphasis on military, non-fiction & literary criticism. *Hours:* Jun-Oct 9-6, else 10-5. *Assoc:* MABA, MADA. Eleanor Arrington

BO-MAR HALL ANTIQUES
Rte 1, 04090
(207)646-4116 **{GR114}**
Furniture, glass, china, jewelry, paintings, brass items, clocks pottery & textiles. *Hours:* Daily 10-5. *Park:* In front. *Loc:* I-95 Exit 2: Rte 109 E, N on Rte 1, on the L.

THE BOOK BARN
US Rte 1, 04090
(207)646-4926 **9 11 13**
Large general book stock, autographs, baseball cards & comics stock; wholesale section for quantity buyers. *Serv:* Appraisal, catalog (no charge), purchase estates. *Hours:* Apr-Nov daily 10-5, Dec-Mar Sat,Sun 10-5. *Size:* Medium. *CC:* MC/V. *Assoc:* MABA. Ann Polizzi *Park:* Nearby lot. *Loc:* I-95 Exit 2: L at ramp onto Rte 109E, R to Rte 1S, 100 yds on L, next to shopping ctr.

COUNTRY HOUSE ANTIQUES
US Rte 1, 04090
(207)646-5507 **33 40 42**
Refinished oak & pine furniture, ephemera, tinware, china, glass & primitives, country accessories, wooden ware & advertising items all displayed in an old carriage barn & house. *Hours:* Apr-Oct Tue-Sun 10-5, Jan-Mar weekends 10-5. *Assoc:* MADA. Edward T Goebel *Park:* On site. *Loc:* I-95 Exit 2: Rte 109 E to Rte 1, N on Rte 1, on the L.

COREY DANIELS
Shady Ln Drakes Island, 04090
(207)646-5301 **34 37 45**
Large selection of visually appealing European antiques for house & garden, choice American folk art & furniture. *Est:* 1971. *Serv:* Purchase estates. *Hours:* Daily by chance/appt. *Loc:* I-95 Exit 2: N on Rte 1, R on Drakes Island Rd, R on Shady Ln.

EAST COAST BOOKS
Depot St Rte 109, 04090
(207)646-3584 **9 13 66**
Collection of used & out-of-print books & remainders, specializing in fine art prints, drawings, watercolors, historical paper & autographs of the 17th thru 20th C. *Pr:* $10–5000. *Est:* 1976. *Serv:* Appraisal, auction (accept mail bids),

catalog, purchase estates. *Hours:* Apr-Oct daily 10-6 Nov-Dec 10-5 Jan-Mar by chance/appt. *CC:* AX/MC/V. *Assoc:* MABA. Merv Slotnik *Park:* On site. *Loc:* I-95 Exit 2: 1/2 MI E of Exit.

THE FARM
Mildram Rd, 04090
(207)985-2656 **16 39 53**
Specializing in English antiques with a large stock of English formal & country furniture, mirrors, lighting, silver, pottery & porcelain, metalware & Chinese export porcelain for the discriminating collector. *Pr:* $25–20000. *Hours:* Sum: daily 10-4 CLOSED WED. Win: weekends. *Size:* Large. Thomas Hackett *Park:* On site. *Loc:* I-95 Exit 2: Rte 109 E to Rte 1, Rte 1 N to Coles Hill Rd, L to Mildram Rd, Farm on R.

HARDING'S BOOK SHOP
US Rte 1, 04090
(207)646-8785 **13 51 66**
A very large stock of quality old & rare books, maps & prints, Maine & New England town histories meticulously arranged. *Hours:* Apr-Dec daily 9-5, Jan-Mar Fri-Sun 9-5. *Size:* Large. *Assoc:* ABAA MABA MADA. Douglas N Harding *Park:* On site. *Loc:* I-95 Exit 2: E to Rte 1, N on Rte 1, beyond Drake Island Rd on the L.

HEYDAY ANTIQUES & FINE ART
Wells Union Antique Center, 04090
(207)646-3766 **37 38 59**
Specializing in 18th - early 20th C paintings by listed American & European artists; American furnishings & unusual accessories largely out of local estates. *Pr:* $100–15,000. *Est:* 1978. *Serv:* Appraisal, expert shipping guaranteed. *Hours:* Year round by chance/appt. *CC:* AX/MC/V. *Assoc:* MADA GSAAA. Tony

K Pescosolido *Park:* In front. *Loc:* I-95 Exit 2: L onto Rte 109 to Rte 1. At light take L, 1/4 MI on the R..

R JORGENSEN ANTIQUES
Rte 1, 04090
(207)646-9444   1 29 42

An extensive, elegant antiques shop presenting a choice selection of fine period furniture & accessories, including American, English & Continental, formal & country pieces, featuring 17th, 18th & 19th C antiques for the enthusiast/collector/decorator. *Est:* 1971. *Hours:* Jan-Nov Daily 10-5 CLOSED WED, Dec BY APPT ONLY. *Size:* Huge. *Assoc:* ADA MADA NHADA. *Park:* On site. *Loc:* Maine Turnpike Exit 2 (to Wells & Sanford); L to Rte 1, R going S, 2 1/2 MI; Large sign on the R.

MACDOUGALL-GIONET ANTIQUES/ASSOC
US Rte 1, 04090
(207)646-3531   {GR60}

Wells' oldest antiques shop in an 18th C restored barn. Two floors with a wide range of American, English & Continental antique furniture & smalls in room settings. No golden oak or depression glass. *Pr:* $10–25000. *Est:* 1965. *Serv:* Estate & insurance appraisals. *Hours:* Year round 9-5. *Size:* Large. *CC:* MC/V. RG Mac Dougall & AJ Gionet *Park:* On site. *Loc:* ME Tnpk Exit 2: L to Rte 1, then L for 1 MI. Big red sign, house & barn on L.

OLD GLORY
Rte 1, 04090
(207)646-4392   {GR}

A multi-period group shop in integrated room settings with American furniture, mirrors, lighting, glass, china, textiles, prints & paintings & decorative accessories. *Hours:* Daily 10-5. *CC:*

AX/MC/V. Bonnie Salmon Sue Horn *Park:* In front. *Loc:* I-95 Exit 2: 150 yards N of Jct of US Rtes 1 & 9 in Wells.

A DAVID PAULHUS BOOKS
Burnt Mill Rd, 04090
(207)646-7022   13 59 66

Antiquarian books - emphasis on Americana & fine bindings, paintings & prints. *Hours:* Year round by chance/appt. *Assoc:* MABA.

RIVERBANK ANTIQUES
Rte 1 - Wells Union Antique Ctr, 04090
(207)646-6314   5 38 45

Two floors of 18th & 19th C American, English & Continental furniture & decorations, featuring garden ornaments & architectural elements. *Pr:* $5–10000. *Est:* 1976. *Serv:* Purchase estates. *Hours:* May-Nov Mon-Sat 10-5 Sun 12-5, Mar-Apr CLOSED TUE-THU. *Size:* Large. Lynn E Chase *Park:* On site. *Loc:* I-95 Exit 2: Rte 1, 1/4 MI N, bldg #9 at Wells Antique Ctr.

WELLS ANTIQUE MART
Rte 1, 04090
(207)646-8153   {GR85}

Furniture, decorative accessories, glass, china, quilts, metalwork, jewelry, lace & linens, quilts. *Hours:* Year round: daily 9-5 CLOSED TUE. *Park:* In front. *Loc:* I-95 Exit 2.

WELLS UNION ANTIQUE CENTER
US Rte 1, 04090
(207)646-6612   {GR15}

Nine individually owned shops with 15 dealers carrying a wide range of country, formal, American, English & Continental furniture, paintings & accessories, garden statuary, architectural, glass, china, jewelry & collectibles. *Pr:* $1–10000. *Est:* 1982. *Hours:* May-Nov daily, Dec-Apr call ahead CLOSED TUE, WED. *Size:* Huge. *CC:* MC/V.

Park: On site. **Loc:** I-95 Exit 2: L off Exit on Rte 109, to Rte 1, at light take L, 1/4 MI on R.

WEST BATH

F BARRIE FREEMAN ANTIQUES
Quaker Point Farm RFD 1 Box 688, 04530
(207)442-8452   **13 29**
New England decorative arts in fine condition & original surface & rare books specializing in western Americana, travel, exploration & mapping. **Pr:** $10–50000. **Serv:** Appraisal, consultation, interior design. **Hours:** Daily 8-3 BY APPT. **Size:** Large. **Assoc:** MABA. F Barrie Freeman **Park:** On site. **Loc:** 3 MI from Rte 1 in Bath; Congress & Western Ave exit; Please call for you will never find us without better directions.

WEST BROOKLIN

LOUISA GOODYEAR ANTIQUES
Old Friends Barn, 04616
(207)359-8949   **27 33 65**
Maine furniture, country implements, primitives, oddities & collectibles. **Pr:** $1–500. **Est:** 1970. **Serv:** Purchase estates. **Hours:** May 15-Oct 15 Mon-Sat 11-5, Oct 16-May 14 by chance/appt. **Park:** On site. **Loc:** 5 MI from Dear Isle Bridge, or Sedgewick, L toward Brooklin, 1 MI.

WEST ROCKPORT

HERITAGE ANTIQUES
Rte 17, 04865
(207)236-3800   **66**
General line including fine & collectible art & prints. **Hours:** Jun-Oct daily until 8 or by chance. Jaye S Umberger **Loc:** 1/4 MI W Jct Rtes 17 & 90.

NICE STUFF
1 Park St, 04865
(207)236-3495
General line of antiques & collectibles. **Hours:** Mar-Dec 10-5 CLOSED SUN. Dorothy Callaway **Loc:** Located at the corner of Rtes 17 & 90.

WEST SOUTHPORT

CATHERINE HILL ANTIQUES
Cozy Harbor, 04576
(207)633-3683   **32 36 65**
Furniture, primitives, toys, decorative items in the shed. **Hours:** By chance/appt. **Loc:** 1 block off Rte 27 between Boothbay Harbor & Newagen.

WESTBROOK

PEG GERAGHTY-BOOKS
41 The Hamlet, 04092
(207)854-2520   **13 33**
Antiquarian books: emphasis on children's books, Americana & paper ephemera. **Hours:** Year round BY APPT ONLY. **Assoc:** MABA.

WINDHAM

CIDER MILL ANTIQUE MALL
Rte 302, 04062
(207)892-5900   **{GR}**
Furniture, glass, jewelry, china, oak,
mahogany, period clothing & primitives.
Hours: Daily 10-5 Thu til 7. *Loc:* ME
Tnpk Exit 8: Go R, turn L at 2nd light;
On Rte 302 about 8 MI on R.

WINTER HARBOR

POND HOUSE ANTIQUES
Main St E, 04693
(207)963-2992   **16 28 66**
Large shop featuring primitives, country,
pewter, copper, brass, stoneware, decoys,
quilts, paintings, prints. *Pr:* $25–1000.
Est: 1985. *Serv:* Purchase estates. *Hours:*
May 15-Oct 15 daily 9-5 by chance/appt.
Size: Large. Elsie R Fanning *Park:* In
front. *Loc:* Rte 1N out of Ellsworth, Rte
186 on the way to spectacular Schoodic
Point.

WISCASSET

HOPE R ANGIER
Sheepscot Stenciling, 04578
(207)586-5692   **70**
Reproduction theorem paintings on an-
tiqued velvet. *Serv:* Color brochure,
price list. *Hours:* BY APPT.

COACH HOUSE ANTIQUES
Pleasant St, 04578
(207)882-7833   **36 59 65**
Country & formal furniture, primitives,
paintings & unusual accessories. *Est:*
1966. *Hours:* All Year, Win: by
chance/appt. *Assoc:* MADA. William
Glennon

ELLIOTT HEALY
Middle Street, 04578
(207)882-5446   **13 51 62**
Photography books & images, fine arts,
books on antiques, illustrated &
children's books, prints & maps. *Est:*
1972. *Hours:* BY APPT ONLY. *CC:*
V/MC. *Assoc:* MABA. *Park:* On street.
Loc: Just a short distance off Rte 1 in
center Wiscasset.

LILAC COTTAGE
Main St On The Green Rte 1, 04578
(207)882-7059   **16 37 39**
19th C American & English furniture,
porcelain & brass & pretty things. *Est:*
1964. *Hours:* Jun-Oct daily 10-5
CLOSED SUN. *Assoc:* MADA. Shirley
Andrews *Park:* In front.

MARINE ANTIQUES
US Rte 1, 04578
(207)882-7208   **54 56 72**
Selected marine antiques including ship
paintings, scrimshaw, models, instruments & carvings, also campaign furniture. *Pr:* $500–50000. *Serv:* Appraisal,
consultation. *Hours:* By chance/appt.
Size: Large. John T Newton *Park:* In
front.

**MARSTON HOUSE AMERICAN
ANTIQUES**
Main St at Middle St, 04578
(207)882-6010   **1 32 41**
18th & 19th C American country furniture & accessories in original paint,
primitives, folk art, birdhouses, baskets,
toys, quilts, rugs & linens. *Pr:* $100–
10000. *Est:* 1987. *Hours:* Apr-Oct daily
10-5, else by chance/appt. *Size:*
Medium. *CC:* AX/MC/V. Paul

Mrozinski *Park:* On site. *Loc:* Rte 1 to
Wiscasset, in ctr of town at corner of
Main St (Rte 1) & Middle St.

MUSICAL WONDER HOUSE
18 High St, 04578
(207)882-7163   **55**
Antique music boxes, wind-up
phonographs, records & player pianos.
Pr: $950–150000. *Est:* 1963. *Serv:* Ap-
praisal, conservation, consultation, purchase estates, repairs, rest. *Hours:* May
2-Oct daily, else BY APPT ONLY. *CC:*
AX/MC/V. Danilo Konvalinka *Park:* In
front. *Loc:* Rte 1 to Wiscasset, 50 MI N
of Portland, 150 MI N of Boston.

NONESUCH HOUSE
1 Middle St, 04578
(207)882-6768   **{GR9}**
18th & early 19th C formal & country
furniture, accessories, paintings, prints,
quality smalls, nautical & folk art. *Est:*
1982. *Hours:* Apr-Nov daily 10-5. *CC:*
MC/V. Dan Anspach Terry Lewis *Park:*
Nearby. *Loc:* 80 ft from Rte 1.

MARGARET BROCKWAY
OFSLAGER
Rte 1, 04578
(207)882-6082   **21 34 59**
In one of Maine's most beautiful villages,
carefully selected antiques & decorative
items from Maine are exhibited in a late
18th C house, featuring folk art, hooked
rugs, paintings & country furniture.
Hours: Mid Jun-Oct daily, appt suggested, CLOSED SUN. *Loc:* At Main &
Summer St.

AARON & HANNAH PARKER
ANTIQUES
US Rte 1, 04578
(207)882-6511   **32 48 67**
Decorative accessories, quilts, linens,
toys, formal furniture, ironstone &
ephemera. *Est:* 1983. *Hours:* Year round

daily 9-5, Jan-Feb By chance/appt. *Size:*
Large. *CC:* MC/V. *Assoc:* MADA. *Park:*
On site. *Loc:* 2 1/2 MI S of Wiscasset.

PORRINGER & BRUCE MARCUS
ANTIQUE
Water St, 04578
(207)882-7951   **37**
Specializing in 17th, 18th & 19th C furniture. *Est:* 1976. *Serv:* Appraisal, consultation. *Hours:* Year round Mon-Sat
10-4:30. Barbara Darling *Park:* Nearby.
Loc: On the waterfront by the Old Ships.

PORTSIDE ANTIQUES
Main St, 04578
(207)882-6506   **27 37 77**
18th & 19th American country & formal
furniture, paintings, Oriental rugs, sterling silver & clocks. *Hours:* Year round
call ahead in winter. Edward J O'Rourke
III

QUALITY GLASS & ANTIQUES
MALL
Rte 1, 04578
(207)882-7595   **{GR13}**
Group shop dealing in primitives, fine
furniture, dolls, glass & china, ephemera,
jewelry, tools, prints, paintings, marine
antiques, wicker & books. *Est:* 1989.
Hours: May-Dec daily 10-5; Jan-Apr
Wed-Sun 10-5. *Size:* Medium. *CC:*
D/MC/V. Ned Robbins *Park:* Nearby
lot. *Loc:* Rte 1 just before railroad tracks
& bridge in Wiscasset; shop is on R if
travelling N from Portland.

SHEILA & EDWIN RIDEOUT
12 Summer St, 04578
(207)882-6420   **27 57 63**
American, English 18th & 19th C pottery, samplers, needlework pictures,
country & furniture. *Hours:* Sum: Tue-
Fri 10:30-6 else by chance/appt Jul by
appt.

SPRIG OF THYME ANTIQUES
US Rte 1, 04578
(207)882-6150   **34 41 65**
Early Cape Cod house filled with country painted furniture & proper accessories, folk art & other country needs. *Serv:* Interior design. *Hours:* Apr-Oct daily 10-5, else by chance/appt. Linda P Heard *Park:* On site. *Loc:* Just S of the village.

PATRICIA STAUBLE ANTIQUES
Rte 1 & Pleasant St, 04578
(207)882-6341   **{GR4}**
American country & period furniture & accessories, art, folk art, pottery, textiles, hooked rugs, paintings, quilts, decoys, nautical items, Victorian jewelry,. *Pr:* $50–12000. *Est:* 1965. *Serv:* Appraisal, interior design, purchase estates. *Hours:* All year, Nov-May appt suggested. *Size:* Large. *CC:* V. *Assoc:* MADA. Patricia Stauble *Park:* On site. *Loc:* Rte 1 - in town.

TWO AT WISCASSET
Main St, 04578
(207)882-5286   **1 34 50**
Three & a half rooms of decorative arts, country furniture with original paints or finish, folk art, toys, early lighting & hooked & braided rugs. *Pr:* $25–2500. *Est:* 1972. *Hours:* Apr 15-Nov 15 Mon-Sat 11-5, Sun by chance/appt, else BY APPT. *Assoc:* MADA. Doris Stauble *Park:* On site. *Loc:* On Rte 1.

WISCASSET BAY GALLERY
Water St, 04578
(207)882-7682   **59 66 71**
Specializing in fine 19th & early 20th C American & European paintings with a focus on New England artists. *Pr:* $250–10000. *Est:* 1985. *Serv:* Appraisal, brochure, conservation, purchase estates, restoration. *Hours:* May-Oct Tue-Sat 10-5, Nov-Dec 21 Fri 10-4. *Size:*

Medium. *CC:* MC/V. *Assoc:* NEAA. Keith S Oehmig *Park:* On site. *Loc:* N on Rte 1, last road on L before bridge, S on Rte 1, 1st road on R after bridge.

YARMOUTH

GERALD W BELL AUCTIONEER
139 Main St, 04096
(207)989-3357   **8**
Auctioning antiques & estate jewelry. 10% buyer's premium. *Serv:* Accept phone bids.

THE RED SHED
12 Pleasant St, 04096
(207)865-4228   **36 48 77**
Four rooms of antique furniture & accessories including sterling & Victorian silver, fine china, jewelry, glass, linens & post cards. *Hours:* Mar-Dec 23 daily 10-4 CLOSED SUN. *Assoc:* MADA.

A E RUNGE ORIENTAL RUGS
106 Main St, 04096
(207)846-9000   **21**
Specializing in older rugs & carpets & better quality new rugs in traditional designs & colors. *Serv:* Handwashing, insurance appraisals. *Hours:* Mon-Sat 10-5:30. *Loc:* On Main St near the overpass.

W M SCHWIND, JR ANTIQUES
17 E Main St Rte 88, 04096
(207)846-9458   **36 59 66**
Shop in 1810 house featuring country & formal furniture, paintings, prints, ceramics, glass, rugs & related accessories. *Est:* 1967. *Hours:* Year round, Sum: Mon-Sat 10-5. *Assoc:* MADA.

YORK

BELL FARM ANTIQUES
244 Rte 1 S, 03909
(207)363-8181   **{GR22}**
Two floors of antiques, art & prints, silver, china, toys, furniture, exceptional linens, primitives, quilts & Victoriana. *Est:* 1989. *Hours:* Year round Daily 10-5 Sun 12-5. *Size:* Large. *CC:* MC/V. Judy & Rex Lambert *Park:* On site. *Loc:* I-95 York Exit: 1 MI S on Rte 1.

FORLANO & FORLANO
Chases Pond Rd, 03909
(207)363-7009   **21**
Specializing in antiques & old decorative Oriental carpets, textiles & accessories. *Est:* 1960. *Serv:* Cleaning & repair. *Hours:* Daily 10-5, call ahead advisable. Larry Forlano *Park:* On site. *Loc:* I-95 York Exit: W to Chase's Pond Rd, then 1/2 MI N.

GORGEANA ANTIQUES
80 Southside Rd, 03909
(207)363-3842   **44 63**
Specializing in fine quality glass, china & collectibles including early American pattern glass, Sandwich Glass & Heisey. *Hours:* All year 10-4, by chance/appt. *Assoc:* MADA. Julia Upham *Loc:* 1/2 MI E of Rte 1S of York River.

MARITIME AUCTIONS
935 Rte 1 PO Box 322, 03909
(207)363-4247   **8**
Nautical auctions, firehouse, railroad, scientific instrument auctions, absentee bids, 10% buyers premium, maritime art. Auctions held at Seaboard Auction Gallery. *Serv:* Catalog ($15), mailing lists, consignments. *Hours:* Jun-Sep daily 9-5, else BY APPT ONLY. Chuck DeLuca *Park:* On site.

OLDE STUFF SHOPPE
#2 Rte 1, 03909
(207)363-4517   **27 33 63**
Antiques & collectibles including early country furniture, oak, pine, mahogany, advertising items, pottery & glassware. *Hours:* Tue-Sat 10-5 by chance /appt. Dean Rutherford Jane Bean *Loc:* Just S of the York exit on Rte 1.

POST ROAD ANTIQUES & BOOKS
Chases Pond Rd, 03909
(207)363-7922   **1 13 29**
General line of American period, formal & country antiques, paintings & prints & old & rare books in a small shop. *Hours:* Tue-Sat 10-5 or BY APPT. Richard Holland

WITHINGTON/WELLS
Cider Hill Rd Rte 91, 04909
(207)363-7439   **27 34 29**
Country furniture, folk art & decorative objects. *Hours:* Call ahead advised. *Assoc:* NHADA. Bob & Nancy Withington

YORK ANTIQUES GALLERY
Rte 1, 03909
(207)363-5002   **{MDS}**
Quality multiple dealer shop offering a diversified selection of antiques with an emphasis on American country furniture & accessories displayed in a large restored three story barn. *Est:* 1989. *Hours:* Year round daily 10-5. *Size:* Large. *Assoc:* NHADA. Gail & Don Piatt *Park:* On site. *Loc:* I-95 Yorks Ogunquit Exit: 9/10 MI N on Rte 1 (last on before toll); 10 min from Portsmouth.

YORK BEACH

SAMUEL WEISER BOOKS
PO Box 612, 03910
(207)363-7253   **13**
Antiquarian books specializing in Oriental philosophy, metaphysics, religion, folklore & archeology; quality general stock. *Pr:* $3–5000. *Est:* 1936. *Hours:* BY APPT ONLY. *Assoc:* ABAA MABA. Glen Houghton

YORK HARBOR

SERENA COLBY GALLERY
Rte 1A, 03911
(207)363-5662   **44 63 83**
An eclectic collection of quality antiques with an emphasis on fine glass & china featuring Portland & Staffordshire. A fine selection of paintings by American artists in one of southern Maine's oldest shops. *Est:* 1975. *Serv:* Appraisal, brochure, conservation, repairs, restoration. *Hours:* Apr-Oct Mon-Sat 10-3 or BY APPT. *CC:* AX/CB/MC/V. Thelma/Laurence Ladd *Loc:* E of Rte 1 on Rte 1A.

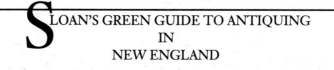

▼

Massachusetts

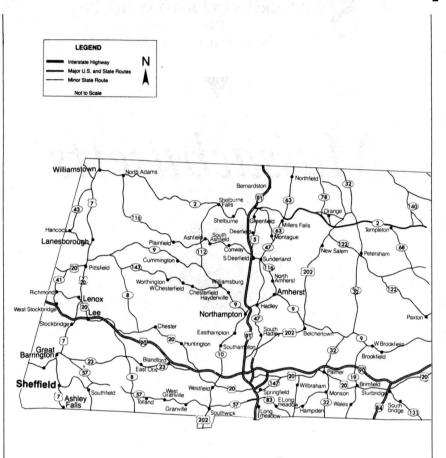

Western
Massachusetts

Eastern
Massachusetts

WESTERN
MASSACHUSETTS

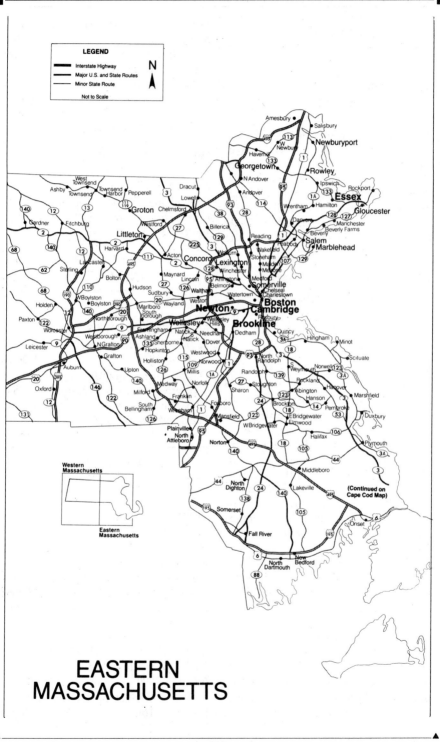

EASTERN
MASSACHUSETTS

ABINGTON

ABINGTON AUCTION GALLERY
728 Brockton Ave, 02351
(617)857-2001 **8**
An antiques & quality household merchandise auction gallery specializing in Americana & Victorian items. All auctions conducted Sat at 6:30 with a 3-hour preview. *Est:* 1985. *Serv:* Appraisal, auction, estates purchased. *Hours:* Office Mon-Fri 10-5. Charles D Glynn *Park:* On site. *Loc:* 15 min from Rte 24 on Rte 123, 20 min from Rte 3.

ACTON

ENCORES
174 Great Rd Rte 2A, 01720
(508)263-1515 **29 36 38**
Over 400 pieces of hand-selected European country antique furnishings - furniture, oil paintings, crocks, stoneware & copper; also featuring an outstanding collection of armoires, cupboards, sideboards, tables, chairs, dressers, desks, beds & washstands. *Pr:* $25–3500. *Est:* 1980. *Serv:* Consultation, interior design, repairs, replication, reproduction. *Hours:* Mon-Sat 10-5 Sun 12:30-5. *Size:* Large. *CC:* MC/V. Nancy Lenicheck *Park:* In front. *Loc:* I-95, Rte 2 W for 9 MI; at rotary take 2nd Exit, Rte 2A/119, 1 1/2 MI on L.

SEAGULL ANTIQUES
60 Great Rd, 01720
(508)263-0338 **7 36 77**
An ever changing array of quality antiques from period to deco - furniture, sterling & accessories. *Pr:* $25–5000.

Serv: Appraisal, purchase estates. *Hours:* Sep-Jun Mon-Sat 10-4:30 Sun 12:30-4:30, Sum: Mon-Sat 10-4:30. *Size:* Medium. *CC:* MC/V. Carole Siegal *Park:* In front. *Loc:* I-495 Exit 31: to Littleton Common, Rte 2A E, 10 min to Great Rd, OR Rte 128, to Rte 2W, to Rte 2A W, 15 min to Great Rd.

WINDSOR HOLLOW ANTIQUES
128 Great Rd Rte 2A, 01720
(508)263-3955
Specializing in fine antiques & collectibles. *Hours:* Mon-Sat 10-5 Sun 12-5. Jim & Sheila

AMESBURY

FELTNER ANTIQUES
72 Haverhill Rd Rte 110 W, 01913
(508)388-1935 **29 36 86**
Oak, walnut, mahogany, wicker & decorative accessories. *Hours:* Thu-Sat 10-5 Sun 12-5 or by appt. *CC:* MC/V. *Loc:* I-495 Exit 53 or Exit 54: 3 min.

AMHERST

ALBION USED BOOKS
30 Main St, 01002
(413)256-1221 **13 14**
Antiquarian books: general stock including used books & academic presses. *Serv:* Appraisal, search service. *Hours:* By chance, call ahead advised. *Assoc:* MARIAB. James Murphy

AMHERST ANTIQUARIAN MAPS
Mc Clellan St, 01002
(413)256-8900 **51 66**
Old, rare, original maps, charts & prints from the 16th-19th C. *Pr:* $10–3000.

Serv: Occasional catalog ($2), search service. *Hours:* Year round by chance appt. *CC:* MC/V. *Assoc:* MARIAB. Jon Kimmel Rosenthal *Park:* In front. *Loc:* In Amherst Cen, less than 1/4 MI from the Post Office.

BOOK MARKS
1 E Pleasant St, 01002
(413)549-6136   **13**
Antiquarian books: photography, art, architecture, illustrated, literary criticism, literature & music. *Hours:* Mon-Sat 10-5. *Assoc:* MARIAB. Fred Marks *Loc:* Located in the Carriage Shops.

R & R FRENCH ANTIQUES
657 S Pleasant St, 01002
(413)253-2269   **2 36**
18th & 19th C furniture, lighting, fireplace tools, ceramics, pewter & textiles. *Hours:* Tue-Sat by chance/appt. *Assoc:* PVADA. Rachael C French *Loc:* Corner of S Pleasant & E Hadley Rd on Rte 116.

GRIST MILL ANTIQUES
Rte 116S & Mill Ln, 01002
(413)253-5296   **33 36 44**
An eclectic collection of furniture, glass, ephemera, advertising, post cards, political memorabilia, posters, kitchenware & fountain pens housed in a 240-year old grist mill. *Est:* 1984. *Serv:* Consultation, interior design, purchase estates. *Hours:* Feb-Dec Thu-Tue 10-5 Sun 12-5 CLOSED WED. *Size:* Medium. *Assoc:* PVADA. Hill & Ronya Boss *Park:* On site. *Loc:* Rte 116, 1 MI S of Amherst Commons.

LEIF LAUDAMUS, RARE BOOKS
62 Orchard St, 01002
(413)253-5188   **13**
Antiquarian books: bibliography, early printing, history of science, incunabula, medicine, Bibles, illustrated, foreign language & rare books. *Serv:* Appraisal, catalog, purchase estates & collections. *Hours:* BY APPT. *Assoc:* MARIAB.

ROSENTHAL PAPER RESTORATION
Mc Clellan St, 01002
(413)256-0844   **71**
Conservation & restoration of flat printed paper. *Hours:* BY APPT ONLY. *Assoc:* AIC NECA. Bernice Masse Rosenthal

VALLEY BOOKS
199 Pleasant St, 01002
(413)256-1508   **13 14**
Two floors of used, discounted new & old books on all subjects, first editions & out-of-print books, specializing in literature, the arts, history & sports. *Est:* 1975. *Serv:* Appraisal, catalog. *Hours:* Year round Mon-Fri 10:30-5:30 Sat 10-5 Sun 12-5. *Size:* Medium. *CC:* MC/V. *Assoc:* MARIAB NEBA. Lawrence & Charmagne Pruner *Park:* In rear. *Loc:* I-91 Amherst Exit (Rte 9E): 6 MI to lights at Amherst College, turn L, go thru 2 lights, store on R.

WOOD SHED ANTIQUES
156 Montague Rd, 01002
(413)549-1720   **16 65**
Specializing in New England primitives, games, tole, iron & treenware textiles. *Pr:* $25–250. *Serv:* Brochure. *Hours:* Daily by chance/appt. *Assoc:* PVADA. Bea & Harlan Wood *Park:* On site. *Loc:* On Rte 63.

ANDOVER

ALPHABET BOOKS & ANTIQUES
68 Park St, 01810
(508)475-0269   **13**
General stock antiquarian books, Irish literature & some antiques. *Serv:* Appraisal, search service. *Hours:* Tue-Sat 10-5, call ahead. *Assoc:* MARIAB. Brendan Roche

ANDOVER BOOKS & PRINTS
68 Park St, 01810
(508)475-1645   **13 51 66**
General stock of unusual, scholarly & fine books, prints, calligraphy, paper ephemeral & other book-related item. *Pr:* $1–500. *Est:* 1977. *Serv:* Appraisal, catalog, search service, repairs, restoration. *Hours:* Tue-Sat 10-5. *Size:* Medium. *CC:* MC/V. *Assoc:* ABAA MARIAB. V David Roger *Park:* On site. *Loc:* Located across from Park St Village, 2 blocks E of Main St & Old Town Hall.

BARBARA FINE ASSOCIATES
271 Highland Rd, 01810
(508)475-5812   **51 66 78**
In a converted barn, one of the largest collections of 16th-20th C decorative prints in New England: natural history, botanicals, nautical, sporting, maps, views, Oriental, architecture, golf, legal, medical & handpainted French mats & period frames. *Est:* 1977. *Serv:* Appraisal, conservation, consultation, interior design, purchase estates. *Hours:* Mon-Fri appt suggested CLOSED WED. *Size:* Medium. *CC:* MC. *Park:* In front, nearby lot. *Loc:* 128 N to 93 N to 125 Andover, R on Hillside Rd (turns into Highland Rd).

NEW ENGLAND GALLERY INC
350 N Main St, 01810
(508)475-2116   **37**
18th C American furniture & accessories. *Est:* 1969. *Serv:* Appraisal, purchase estates. *Hours:* Tue-Sat 9-4 appt suggested. Robert A Blekicki *Park:* Nearby. *Loc:* I-495 Exit 41A.

ARLINGTON

IRREVERENT RELICS
106 Massachusetts Ave, 02174
(617)646-0370   **1 28 42**
Specializing in a country look for folks with city sophistication & city spaces. Full of the weird & wonderful from hooked rugs to pastoral paintings. *Pr:* $5–2500. *Serv:* Conservation, consultation, interior design, purchase estates, repairs. *Hours:* Tue,Wed 12-6 Thu 12-8 Fri 12-5 Sat 10-6, call ahead advised. *Size:* Medium. Kristin Duval *Park:* On site. *Loc:* 2 blocks N of Int of Rte 16 & Massachusetts Ave, approx 1 1/2 MI N of Porter Sq, 3 MI N of Harvard Sq.

PAUL KLAVER
5 Viking Ct #43, 02174
(617)643-7167   **3 4 33**
Specializing in firefighting antiques & related items exclusively. *Pr:* $25–2500. *Est:* 1987. *Serv:* Appraisal, auction, consultation, purchase estates. *Hours:* BY APPT ONLY. *Assoc:* SPNEA. Paul Klaver

SCIENTIA BOOKS
432A Massachusetts Ave, 02174
(617)643-5725   **13**
Specializing in antiquarian books on medicine, science & evolution, scholarly books on history of medicine & history of science. *Est:* 1985. *Serv:* Appraisal,

catalog, search service. *Hours:* BY APPT ONLY. *Assoc:* ABAA MARIAB. Malcolm J Kottler *Loc:* From Rte 128, take Rte 60 (Pleasant St), 1 MI then R at Int of Pleasant & Massachusetts Aves.

SECOND TYME AROUND
1193A Massachusetts Ave, 02174
(617)646-5789   **47 48 77**
Antique & costume jewelry, linens, sterling & furniture. *Hours:* Mon, Tue, Fri, Sat 10-5; Thu 10-8. *CC:* MC/V. *Park:* In front.

THE WAY WE WERE
1267A Massachusetts Ave, 02174
(617)648-7016   **47 67**
Specializing in antique & costume jewelry; also, furniture, china, glass, quilts & collectibles. *Hours:* Tue-Fri 11-4 Sat 11-2. Gloria

ASHBY

COUNTRY BED SHOP
Richardson Rd, 01431
(508)386-7550   **19 43 70**
Country & high style reproduction beds, chairs & tables. Each piece made to order. *Pr:* $1000–8000. *Est:* 1972. *Serv:* Catalog ($4), replication, reproduction, custom work. *Hours:* Mon-Sat 8-5 appt suggested. Alan W Pease *Park:* On site. *Loc:* Call for directions.

ASHLEY FALLS

DON ABARBANEL
E Main St, 01222
(413)229-3330   **16 57 63**
Needlework, brass, metalwork, English pottery, Delft, Chinese export porcelain, fine furniture of the 17th, 18th & 19th C, & formal accessories. *Hours:* Daily 10-5, call ahead in winter. *Assoc:* BCADA. *Park:* In front. *Loc:* Just off Rte 7A at Lewis & Wilson.

ASHLEY FALLS ANTIQUES
PO Box 35 Rte 7A, 01222
(413)229-8759   **36 47 1**
Extensive collection of authentic early American furniture & furnishings & carefully-selected antique jewelry & buttons located in a picturesque brick building facing Village Park in the historic district. *Pr:* $2–20000. *Est:* 1957. *Serv:* Consultation, purchase estates, all items guaranteed. *Hours:* Year round daily 9:30-5:30. *Size:* Medium. Jeanne Cherneff *Park:* In front. *Loc:* 4 MI S of Sheffield, MA on Rte 7A, 1 MI N of CT border.

CIRCA
Rte 7A, 01222
(413)229-2990   **38 63**
Important collections of majolica & Canton, sophisticated oddments, 18th & 19th C furniture & accessories. *Hours:* Fri-Mon 10-5. *Assoc:* BCADA. *Park:* On site.

LEWIS & WILSON
E Main St, 01222
(413)229-3330   **39 59 60**
English, French & Oriental furniture, paintings, china, ginger jars & lighting fixtures. *Hours:* Daily 10-5. *Assoc:* BCADA. Don Lewis *Park:* On site. *Loc:* Renovated train station, green with yellow trim, just off Rte 7A.

RUSSELL LYONS
Rte 7A, 01222
(413)229-2453   **29 38**
Continental furniture & decorative accessories. *Hours:* Daily by chance/appt. *Park:* In front.

ROBERT THAYER AMERICAN
ANTIQUES
E Main St, 01222
(413)229-2965 **1 37**
Specializing in Americana. *Serv:* All
items unreservedly guaranteed as represented. *Hours:* By chance/appt. Robert
Thayer *Park:* On site. *Loc:* Just off Rte
7A.

THE VOLLMERS
Rte 7A, 01222
(413)229-3463 **6 27 59**
18th & 19th C country & formal furni-
ture, accessories & antique firearms.
Hours: Daily 10-5, TUE by chance.
Assoc: BCADA. Diana B Vollmer *Park:*
On site.

ATHOL

ANTIQUES TOOLS & CATALOGS
Box 177, 01331
(508)249-5990 **81**
Fine American antique tools & related
catalogs. Author of "Patented Transi-
tional & Metallic Planes in America
1827-1927"(just reprinted with updates,
available from author for $55, post paid).
Serv: Appraisal, catalog $5 (Publications
list free), purchase estates. *Hours:* Year
round BY APPT. Roger K Smith *Loc:*
Call for directions.

AUBURN

AUBURN ANTIQUE & FLEA
MARKET INC
773 Southbridge St Rte 12, 01501
(508)832-2763 **{FLEA}**
Flea market with antiques, collectibles,
crafts & other flea market merchandise.

Serv: Catered, spaces start at $10, indoor
spaces Sun, outdoors Sat only. *Hours:*
Year round Sat (weather permitting) -
Sun 9-4. *Size:* 150 spaces. *Loc:* I-90 Exit
10, OR I-290 Exit 8, OR I-395 Exit 7:
follow Rte 12S 1/2 MI.

BELMONT

CROSS & GRIFFIN
468 Trapelo Rd, 02178
(617)484-2837
General line of furniture & decorative
accessories. *Est:* 1961. *Hours:* Tue-Sat
10-4. *CC:* MC/V. *Park:* On street. *Loc:*
Rte 128, Trapelo Rd Exit: toward Belmont, 4 MI at Waverly Square.

THE IN PLACE
5 Bartlett Ave, 02178
(617)489-4161 **44**
Specializing in glass. *Est:* 1965. *Hours:*
Tue-Sat 11-4, Sum: By chance. Irene
Northway

PAYSON HALL BOOKSHOP
80 Trapelo Rd, 02178
(617)484-2020 **13**
Antiquarian bookseller with a general
stock & books on Ireland & the Irish.
Serv: Appraisal, catalog, search service.
Hours: Tue-Fri 12-5 Sat 10-4. *Assoc:*
MARIAB. Clare M Murphy *Park:* Nearby.

BERNARDSTON

BERNARDSTON BOOKS
503 South St Rte 5, 01337
(413)648-9864 **13 14**
Out-of-print books: history, biography,
anthropology, military, natural history,

Black history, fiction classics, theology & religion, philosophy of history, linguistics, sociology, art & music, poetry & literary criticism. *Pr:* $5–500. *Est:* 1986. *Serv:* Conversation, purchase estates. *Hours:* By chance/appt. *Size:* Large. *Assoc:* MARIAB. A L Fullerton *Park:* On site. *Loc:* I-91 Exit 28: Rte 10S OR I-91 Exit 27: Rte 5N.

BEVERLY

JEAN S MC KENNA BOOK SHOP
10 Longview Terr, 01915
(508)922-3182　　　　　　　**13**
Antiquarian books: biography, children's, illustrated, literature, local history & fiction. *Serv:* Appraisal, search service. *Hours:* BY APPT. *Assoc:* MARIAB.

PRICE HOUSE ANTIQUES
137 Cabot St, 01915
(508)927-5595　　　　**36 86 71**
A huge shop filled with an ever-changing inventory featuring quality antique oak, mahogany & wicker furniture & accessories; plus, loads of smalls, carousel figures occasionally. *Pr:* $15–5000. *Est:* 1976. *Serv:* Consultation, purchase estates, repairs, restoration, refinishing. *Hours:* Mon-Sat 10-5, Sun by chance. *CC:* MC/V. Kathy Pignato *Park:* Nearby lot. *Loc:* Rte 128 to Rte 62E, 2 MI take R onto Cabot St, 1/2 MI on L.

BLANDFORD

ROBERT F LUCAS
Main St, 01008
(413)848-2061　　　　　　**9 13**
Antiquarian books: 19th C Americana,

Thoreau, transcendentalism, 19th C Hawaiiana, Poe, manuscript Americana & whaling. *Serv:* Appraisal, catalog. *Hours:* BY APPT. *Assoc:* ABAA. *Loc:* On Rte 23.

BOLTON

SKINNER INC
Rte 117, 01740
(508)779-6241　　　　　　**4 8**
One of New England's largest auction galleries with 60 auctions annually, including Americana, Victoriana, dolls & toys, Arts & Crafts, Oriental rugs, prints & paintings, bottles & glass, jewelry, American Indian art & 20th C esign. *Serv:* Fine art & antiques appraisal, nine catalog subscriptions available. *Hours:* Mon-Fri 10-5, auctions most frequently held on Sat. *Size:* Large. Nancy Skinner *Park:* On site. *Loc:* I-495 Exit 27: E on Rte 117 towards Boston, Skinner is on the L.

BOSTON

ALBERTS-LANGDON INC
126 Charles St, 02114
(617)523-5954　　　　　　**60 63**
Fine Far Eastern art, ceramics, paintings & furniture. *Serv:* Appraisal. *Hours:* Sep-Jul Mon-Fri 10-4. Russell Alberts *Park:* Nearby. *Loc:* At the corner of Charles & Revere Sts.

ANTIQUE IRELAND INC
103B Charles St, 02114
(617)248-0789　　　　　　**42**
Specializing in Irish antique pine furniture, including dressers, tables, wardrobes & chests. *Est:* 1990. *Hours:*

Mon-Sat 11-5:30, Sun 12-4. Mary O'-Sullivan *Park:* On street. *Loc:* Two blocks from Boston Common, between Pinckney & Revere Sts.

ANTIQUE PORCELAINS LTD
33 Fayette St, 02116
(617)426-5779 **35 60 63**
A fine collection of Chinese export, Staffordshire, Imari, faience & other choice pieces in a restored Federal townhouse in downtown Boston. *Serv:* Consultation, interior design. *Hours:* BY APPT. *Size:* Medium. Anne F Kilguss *Park:* Nearby lot. *Loc:* From Arlington St go S to Piedmont St, turn L 1 block, R on Church St, 3 blocks to Fayette St, 4th house on L.

ARABY RUG
667 Boylston St, 02116
(617)267-0012 **21**
Antique & semi-antique rugs from the Middle East. *Serv:* Expert cleaning & washing, rugs demothed & stored. *Hours:* Mon-Sat 9-6. *Assoc:* NEAA. Arthur Mahfuz *Loc:* Across from the Boston Public Library.

ARS LIBRI
560 Harrison Ave, 02118
(617)338-5763 FAX
(617)357-5212 **13 66**
Dealers in rare & scholarly books on the fine arts, illustrated books from 15th-20th C; Stock of art reference material includes monographs, catalogues, Raisonne periodicals & documents relevant to all periods & fields of art

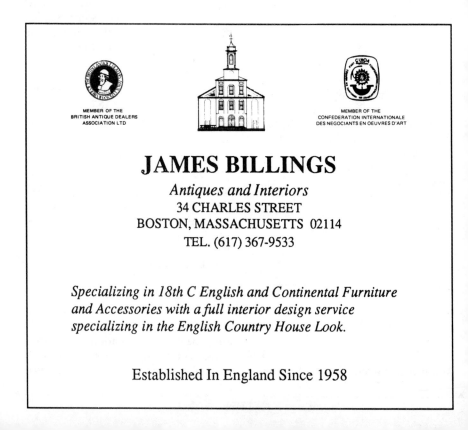

MEMBER OF THE
BRITISH ANTIQUE DEALERS
ASSOCIATION LTD

MEMBER OF THE
CONFEDERATION INTERNATIONALE
DES NEGOCIANTS EN OEUVRES D'ART

JAMES BILLINGS

Antiques and Interiors
34 CHARLES STREET
BOSTON, MASSACHUSETTS 02114
TEL. (617) 367-9533

Specializing in 18th C English and Continental Furniture and Accessories with a full interior design service specializing in the English Country House Look.

Established In England Since 1958

history. *Serv:* Purchase libraries & books on fine arts. *Hours:* Mon-Fri 9-6 Sat 11-5. *Assoc:* ABAA. Elmer Siebel

ARVEST GALLERIES INC
77 Newbury St, 02116
(617)247-1418   **59 73**
19th & early 20th C American art. *Est:* 1973. *Serv:* Appraisal, conservation, restoration. *Hours:* Daily 9-5. *Size:* Medium.

AUTREFOIS ANTIQUES
125 Newbury St, 02116
(617)424-8823   **35 50 53**
Antique French, English & Italian country furniture & accessories with chandeliers, lighting & Oriental porcelain. *Pr:* $50–10000. *Serv:* Custom lamp mountings. *Hours:* Mon-Sat 10-5:30. *Size:* Medium. *CC:* AX/MC/V. Maria Rowe *Park:* In front. *Loc:* One block from Copley Square.

BEDELLE INC
50 School St, 02108
(617)227-8925   **17 47**
Antique jewelry, bronzes, glass & paintings. *Hours:* Mon-Fri 10-2 & by appt. *Size:* Medium. Charles Richman *Park:* Nearby garage. *Loc:* Down from the Parker House.

BELGRAVIA ANTIQUES INC
222 Newbury St, 02116
(617)267-1915   **29 36 60**
A unique collection of 18th & 19th C English & French furniture interspersed with Deco pieces, decorative lamps, mirrors & Oriental porcelain. *Pr:* $25–15000. *Hours:* Mon-Sat 10-5:30. *Size:* Medium. *CC:* AX/MC/V. Carolyn Woods *Park:* Nearby. *Loc:* Between Exeter & Fairfield Streets.

JAMES BILLINGS ANTIQUES
34 Charles St, 02114
(617)367-9533   **29 38 39**
18th & early 19th C English & Continental furniture, paintings, prints & accessories. *Pr:* $250–25000. *Serv:* Complete interior design service. *Hours:* Mon-Sat 10-6. *Size:* Medium. *CC:* AX/MC/V. *Assoc:* BADA CINOA. James Billings *Park:* In front. *Loc:* On the corner of Charles & Chestnut Sts, 1 block from the Boston Public Garden.

THOMAS G BOSS-FINE BOOKS
355 Boylston St, 02116
(617)421-1880   **9 13**
Rare & collectible books, fine bindings & bookplates. Specializing in 1890, Art Nouveau, Arts & Crafts: illustrated, press books, imprints, posters, Art Deco, books about books. *Pr:* $25–50000. *Serv:* Appraisal, catalog. *Hours:* Tue-Fri 9-5 Sat 10-4 Mon by chance/appt, CLOSED SUN. *Size:* Medium. *CC:* AX/MC/V. *Assoc:* ABAA MARIAB. Thomas G Boss *Park:* Nearby. *Loc:* Near the corner of Arlington & Boylston, next to the Arlington St Church.

BOSTON ANTIQUE COOPERATIVE I&II
119 Charles St, 02114
(617)227-9811   **{GR14}**
In the heart of Beacon Hill two levels with a diverse selection from 17th C to Art Deco. *Est:* 1981. *Hours:* Daily 10-6 Sun 12-6. *CC:* MC/V. *Park:* Nearby.

BOSTON BOOK ANNEX
906 Beacon St, 02215
(617)522-2100   **9 13**
Antiquarian books: American & English literature, first editions, autographs & manuscripts, East Asian studies. *Est:* 1979. *Serv:* Appraisal, catalog, search service, purchase estates, restoration.

Hours: Mon-Sat 10-10 Sun 12-10. **CC:** MC/V. **Assoc:** ABAA MARIAB. Helen Kelly **Park:** In front, nearby lot. **Loc:** W of Fenway Park.

THE BOSTON HAMMERSMITH
46 Westland Ave Ste 42, 02115
(617)542-1949 **68**

Expert repairs of silver, pewter & Sheffield. **Est:** 1973. **Serv:** Repairs, restoration. **Hours:** Mon-Fri 8-4. Kristina Karnalovich

BRATTLE BOOK SHOP
9 West St, 02111
(617)542-0210 **4 9 13**

One of Boston's oldest & largest antiquarian bookstores, 3 floors of used & rare books. **Pr:** $1–25000. **Serv:** Appraisal, purchase estates, 1-800-447-0210. **Hours:** Mon-Sat 9-5:30. **Size:** Large. **CC:** AX/MC/V. **Assoc:** ABAA MARIAB. Kenneth Gloss **Park:** Nearby lot. **Loc:** Between Washington & Tremont in downtown Boston, 1 block from Jordan Marsh, off the Boston Common.

BRODNEY INC
811 Boylston St, 02116
(617)536-0500 **29 47 77**

A full line shop with an extensive inventory of fine quality paintings, antique & estate jewelry, pottery & porcelain, silver & holloware, antique clocks & objets d'art. **Serv:** Always looking to purchase single items & estates. **Hours:** Mon-Sat 9:30-5 Jul,Aug CLOSED WEEKENDS. **Assoc:** AADLA. Richard G Brodney **Park:** Nearby. **Loc:** Opposite Prudential Center & Hynes Convention Center.

BROMER BOOKSELLERS INC
607 Boylston St 2nd fl, 02116
(617)247-2818 **4 13**

Antiquarian books: Specializing in rare books of all periods, featuring literary first editions, private press & illustrated books, fine bindings, children's & miniature books. **Est:** 1975. **Serv:** Appraisal, catalog, purchase estates. **Hours:** Mon-Fri 9:30-5:30, often Sat 10-4. **CC:** AX/MC/V. **Assoc:** ABAA ILAB MARIAB. Anne & David Bromer **Park:** Nearby. **Loc:** Corner of Dartmouth & Boylston Sts in ctr of Copley Sq. 2nd floor of only office bldg at that Int. On the Green Line.

MAURY A BROMSEN ASSOCIATES INC
770 Boylston St, 02199
(617)266-7060 **4 9 13**

Antiquarian books: autographs, bibliography, Americana & Latin Americana. **Serv:** Appraisal. **Hours:** BY APPT. **Assoc:** ABAA. **Park:** Nearby.

ANDREW'S AXIOMS

Traveller's Observation

No antique shop opens before 10 a.m.
The one you get to at 10:30 a.m. won't open that day.

Reprinted with permission from *guide to the Antique Shops of Britain 1989.*
copyright The Antique Collectors Club, Great Britain

BUDDENBROOKS
753 Boylston St, 02116
(617)536-4433   **13 14 66**
Antiquarian books: literature, fine illustrated books, explorations & voyages, fine bindings, fishing & hunting, sets & children's books. *Est:* 1975. *Serv:* Appraisal, catalogs, search service. *Hours:* Mon-Fri 8-11, Sat-Sun 9-11. *Size:* Large. *CC:* AX/MC/V. *Assoc:* ABA ABAA MARIAB NEBA. Martin Weinkle *Park:* Nearby lot. *Loc:* I-91 Prudential Ctr Exit: Copley Sq to Boylston St, between Exeter & Fairfield.

CAMDEN PASSAGE LTD
120 Brookline Ave, 02215
(617)421-9899   **3 29 66**
American & European antiquities, custom furnishings, antique prints & accessories. *Est:* 1989. *Serv:* Design service by appt. *Hours:* Mon-Sat 10-5, July-Aug CLOSED SAT. *Park:* On street. *Loc:* 2 blocks west of Kenmore Square.

**NEW ENGLAND CENTER/
ANTIQUE CONSERVATION**
PO Box 370, 02130
(617)524-2899   **68 71 74**
Restoration of antique furniture, wooden artifacts, paintings. Decorative carving, wood & brass inlay, painted surfaces, structural stabilization, gilding & decorative veneer, upholstery, rushwork & caning & French polish. *Est:* 1974. *Serv:* Appraisals, pickup & delivery, consultation. *Hours:* Mon-Fri 8-5. *Assoc:* AIC NEAC. Robert A Lamboy

HOWARD CHADWICK ANTIQUES
40 River St, 02108
(617)227-9261   **2 29 36**
A small shop on Beacon Hill filled with American & English furniture, brasses, pictures, porcelains & lamps. *Est:* 1979. *Serv:* Appraisal, consultation. *Hours:* Oct 15-May 15 Mon-Sat 11-4, else Tue-

Thu 11-4. *Loc:* 2 short blocks N of Beacon St on River St, 1/2 block W of Charles St.

CHILDS GALLERY
169 Newbury St, 02116
(617)266-1108   **59 66 73**
Fine American & European paintings, prints, drawings, watercolors & sculptures. *Est:* 1937. *Serv:* Appraisal, consultation, restoration of frames. *Hours:* Tue-Fri 9-6 Sat,Mon 10-5. *Assoc:* ABAA. *Shows:* ELLIS. D. Roger Howlett III *Park:* Nearby.

CHOREOGRAPHICA
82 Charles St, 02114
(617)227-4780   **13**
Antiquarian books: antiques, cookery, dance, embroidery, needlework, music, theatre, opera & art. *Hours:* Mon-Sat 9:30-5 Sun 9-4. *Assoc:* MARIAB. Ernest Morrell *Park:* Nearby.

THE COLLECTOR
63 Harvard Ave, 02134
(617)787-5952   **55 62 82**
Five rooms full of cameras, antique & vintage furniture, African & ethnic art, paintings, rugs, coins, photographs, mission, oak, musicals, wicker & pottery. *Pr:* $5–5000. *Serv:* Appraisal, conservation, consultation, purchase estates, repair, restoration. *Hours:* Mon-Sat 11-5 Sun BY APPT. *Size:* Large. *CC:* AX/MC/V. Steven Berkovitz *Park:* In front. *Loc:* Corner of Rte 9, Brookline Hills stop on Green Line.

WOMEN'S EDUCATIONAL UNION
Collector's Shop, 356 Boylston St, 02116
(617)536-5651   **25 47 48**
Consignment antiques: A distinctive selection of American furniture, lighting fixtures, silver, oil paintings, Orientalia, pottery & porcelain, crystal, glassware, Native American art, metalwork, fine

linens & decorative accessories. *Hours:* Mon-Sat 10-6. Delores V Cleland *Park:* Nearby. *Loc:* 1/2 block W of the Public Garden on Boylston St right down the street from Shreve, Crump & Lowe.

ISABELLE COLLINS OF LONDON
115 Newbury St, 02116
(617)266-8699   **39 42**

Specialist in antique English country & pine furniture. *Hours:* Tue-Sat 10-5. *Park:* Nearby. *Loc:* Between Clarendon & Dartmouth Sts.

COMENOS FINE ARTS
81 Arlington St, 02116
(617)423-9365   **59 66 73**

American Impressionist paintings concentrating on the Boston School - featuring paintings, watercolors & drawings. *Est:* 1976. *Serv:* Consultation, purchase estates, appraisal. *Hours:* Mon-Sat 9:30-

5:30 Sun 12-5. *Size:* Medium. *CC:* MC/V. *Assoc:* NEAA. Rose Ann O'-Connor *Park:* On site (valet). *Loc:* Opposite Park Plaza Hotel, up the street from Ritz-Carlton & Public Garden.

CRANE COLLECTION
121 Newbury St, 02116
(617)262-4080   **59**

Gallery of American paintings featuring 19th & early 20th C art including Boston School, Hudson River School, American Impressionism & Tonalist works. Changing quarterly exhibitions. Artists include: Bruce Crane, George Inness & William Metcalf. *Pr:* $1000–100000. *Serv:* Appraisal, conservation, consultation, repairs. *Hours:* Tue-Sat 10-5. *Size:* Medium. *CC:* AX. Gael Crasco *Park:* Nearby lot. *Loc:* On Newbury St between Clarendon & Dartmouth Sts.

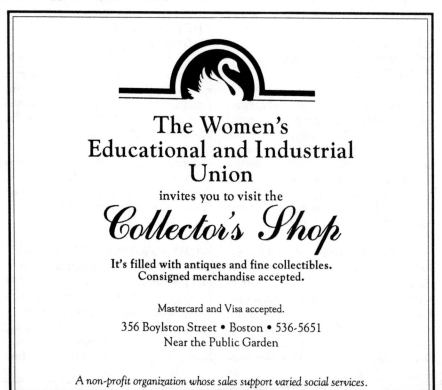

The Women's Educational and Industrial Union

invites you to visit the

Collector's Shop

It's filled with antiques and fine collectibles.
Consigned merchandise accepted.

Mastercard and Visa accepted.

356 Boylston Street • Boston • 536-5651
Near the Public Garden

A non-profit organization whose sales support varied social services.

DIVINE DECADENCE
535 Columbus Ave, 02118
(617)266-1477   **7 29 36**

An innovative shop featuring a unique blend of 20th C interior furnishings, specializing in Art Deco, moderne & mid-century - including designer furniture, sculpture, lighting, vintage rattan, neon clocks, jukeboxes & advertising. *Serv:* Custom neon. *Hours:* Tue-Sat 12-6 Sun 12-5 or BY APPT. *CC:* AX/MC/V. *Loc:* From Copley Pl, Dartmouth St E, L onto Columbus Ave, 8 blocks on L.

JEAN-JACQUES DUBOIS
64 W Cedar St #6, 02114
(617)695-9259

Restoration of antique fine furniture, specializing in period materials & methods, contemporary conservation techniques, French polishing, preservation of antique finishes & structurally-sound repairs. *Serv:* Restoration, repairs. *Hours:* BY APPT ONLY. *Loc:* Call for directions & appointment.

EUGENE GALLERIES
76 Charles St, 02114
(617)227-3062   **51 59 66**

Fine prints - botanicals, historical & city views, maps, paintings & books. *Est:* 1954. *Serv:* Framing. *Hours:* Mon-Sat 10:30-5:30. *CC:* MC/V. Barbara Fischer *Park:* Nearby garage. *Loc:* Between Mt Vernon & Pinckney Sts.

ROY K EYGES INC
38 Newbury St 2nd Fl, 02116
(617)247-8400   **4 47 77**

Estate & period jewelry, silver, china, glass, diamonds, colored stones, silver flatware & art objects in a 19 C period showroom. *Est:* 1941. *Serv:* Appraisal, estates purchased. *Hours:* Mon-Sat 9:30-4:30. *Assoc:* AAA. *Loc:* Between Arlington & Berkeley Sts.

FINDERS KEEPERS
93 Charles St, 02114
(617)742-1416   **{GR3}**

A small, charming shop on Beacon Hill with a nice selection of furniture, small Oriental rugs, paintings, prints, porcelain & silver; a great spot for unusual decorative accessories. *Pr:* $25–1000. *Est:* 1990. *Hours:* Sep-May daily 11-6, CLOSED MON; Jun-August Tue-Sat 11-6. Constance Mc Carrens *Park:* In front. *Loc:* At the corner of Charles & Pinckney Sts.

FINE TIME VINTAGE TIMEPIECES
279 Newbury St, 02116
(617)262-0444 FAX
(617)536-5858   **23 47 68**

Specializing in timepieces - wristwatches, clocks, jewelry & pocketwatches including Patek Philippe, Cartier, Breguet, Rolex, Le Coultre, Movado & Audemars. Repeaters, chronographs, moonphases. *Est:* 1983. *Serv:* Appraisal, repair, restoration, search services. *Hours:* Sum: Tue-Sat 11-6, Win: Tue-Sun 11-6. *Assoc:* NAWCC. William Zeitler *Park:* Nearby garage. *Loc:* Corner of Gloucester & Newbury Sts.

THE FINEST HOUR
274 Newbury St, 02116
(617)266-1920   **23 68 71**

In an elegant Boston townhouse - wide selection of vintage wristwatches & exotic watchbands in dozens of skins & colors. *Pr:* $150–5000. *Serv:* Repair, restoration, purchase old/unusual watches. *Hours:* Mon-Sat 11-7 Sun 1-5. Thomas Thompson *Loc:* Near the Arlington or Copley MBTA stops in Boston.

FIRESTONE AND PARSON
Ritz Carlton Hotel, 02108
(617)266-1858   **47 77**

Period jewelry from the Victorian era to

the present, English & early American silver. **Pr:** $500–100000. **Serv:** Appraisal, brochure, purchase estates. **Hours:** Oct-May Mon-Sat 9:30-5, Jun-Sep Mon-Fri 9:30-5. **Assoc:** NAADAA. Edwin Firestone **Park:** Nearby. **Loc:** Across from the Public Garden.

THE FORTRESS CORPORATION
99 Boston St, 02127
(617)288-3636　　　　　　**26 71 75**
The highest quality packing, crating, moving & storage services available at an affordable price—plus appraisals, video documentation, insurance & liquidation assistance. High security, modern, climate controlled to museum quality standards.. **Est:** 1988. **Hours:** Mon-Fri 8-6, Sat 9-3. **CC:** MC/V. Jim Levis, President **Park:** On site. **Loc:** Exit 16 off the Southeast Expressway - Rte 93 S.

FUSCO & FOUR ASSOCIATES
1 Murdock Terr, 02135
(617)787-2637　　　　　　**4 7 66**
Specialists in Art Deco & Art Moderne, as well as fine prints & works of art on paper from 1900-1950 with an emphasis on American & European modernist artists. **Est:** 1979. **Serv:** Appraisal, consultation, personal curatorial services, catalog ($10). **Hours:** BY APPT ONLY. Tony Fusco & Robert Four **Loc:** Call for directions.

GOODSPEED'S BOOK SHOP INC
7 Beacon St, 02108
(617)523-5970　　　　　　**13 51 66**
Rare books, prints, autographs, genealogies & Americana. **Hours:** Mon-Fri 9-5 Sat 10-3, Jun 15-Labor Day CLOSED SAT. **Assoc:** ABAA. George T Goodspeed **Park:** Nearby lot. **Loc:** 1 block E of the State House.

We have Museum Quality® Storage all locked up in Boston.

Beneath the inflated lock and chain we display on our building for special occasions, Boston's most sophisticated storage facility is always ready to safeguard your valuable art and antiques against damage and theft.

　　Only the Fortress combines the security and convenience of Safe Deposit Room℠ storage with a full range of moving and storage services that include expert packing, crating and video inventory.

　　For a limited time, lease a storage unit for six months and The Fortress will rebate you the first month! Call us at (617) 288-3636 for details.

99 BOSTON STREET
BOSTON, MA 02125
(617) 288-3636
FAX (617) 436-2491
MUSEUM QUALITY MOVING & STORAGE℠

GRAND TROUSSEAU
88 Charles St, 02114
(617)367-3163   **47 85**
A small, romantic shop on Beacon Hill filled with antique clothes & jewelry. Carrying wearable clothing from 1890-1940 in all sizes, Victorian & Edwardian gowns & wedding dresses, beaded flapper dresses, embroidered shawls & all manner of accessories. *Pr:* $25–1000. *Est:* 1985. *Serv:* Consultation on re-creating a total period look. *Hours:* Mon-Sat 11-7 Sun 12-5. *CC:* AX/MC/V. Candace Elgood *Park:* Local garage.

GEORGE I GRAVERT ANTIQUES
122 Charles St, 02108
(617)227-1593   **29 38**
Specializing in decorative European furniture & accessories. *Est:* 1958. *Hours:* Mon-Fri 10-5 or by appt. *Park:* Nearby. *Loc:* At the corner of Charles & Revere Sts.

GROGAN & COMPANY
890 Commonwealth Ave, 02215
(617)566-4100   **4 8**
Boston's only full service auction & appraisal company. *Est:* 1987. *Serv:* Appraisal, accept mail/phone bids, catalog, consultation, purchase estates. *Hours:* Mon-Fri 9-5:30 Sat,Sun BY APPT. Michael B Grogan *Park:* On site.

H GROSSMAN ANTIQUES
51 Charles St, 02114
(617)523-1879   **1 37 63**
American furniture, china & glass. *Est:* 1923. *Hours:* Mon-Sat 9-5. Hyman Grossman *Park:* Nearby. *Loc:* On Beacon Hill.

GUIDO
118 Newbury St, 02116
(617)267-0569   **59 71**
19th & 20th C American & Boston School paintings & gold leaf frames. *Est:*

1967. *Serv:* Restoration, gold leaf frames, appraisal. *Hours:* Tue-Sat 9:30-5:30. *Loc:* Clarendon & Dartmouth Sts.

HALEY & STEELE INC
91 Newbury St, 02116
(617)536-6339   **1 56 66**
Print dealers & custom picture framers, specializing in 18th, 19th & 20th C published prints, English sporting art, American topographical & historical views, botanicals, natural history & marine. *Pr:* $25–3500. *Est:* 1899. *Serv:* Appraisal, catalog, conservation, consultation, interior design, repairs. *Hours:* Sep-Jun Tue-Fri 10-6 Sat 10-5 Jul/Aug Tue-Fri 9-5 Sat 10-5. *Size:* Medium. *CC:* AX/MC/V. Terri Adams *Park:* Nearby lot. *Loc:* Between Berkeley & Clarendon Sts in the Back Bay.

HARPER & FAYE INC
60 Federal St, 02110
(617)423-9190   **4 47**
Fine antique & estate jewelry in gold & platinum. *Pr:* $450–25000. *Est:* 1985. *Serv:* Appraisal, consultation. *Hours:* Please call for hours. *CC:* AX/MC/V. *Assoc:* GIA. *Park:* Local garage. *Loc:* MBTA Red Line to Downtown Crossing. R 1 block down Washington St, R down Franklin St, L opposite the Shawmut Bank.

HERITAGE ART
105 Charles St #230, 02114
(617)523-2793   **1 26 59**
Oil, watercolor & pastel artwork of rediscovered 19th & early 20th C painters in the Boston area; period Tonalist, Luminist, & Impressionist paintings of Boston & greater metropolitan subjects. *Pr:* $500–5000. *Est:* 1986. *Serv:* Appraisal, consultation, purchase estates. *Hours:* BY APPT &

SHOWS. Fred Gorman & Jane Russell *Park:* Local garage. *Loc:* In Boston on Beacon Hill.

HOMER'S JEWELRY & ANTIQUES
44 Winter St, 02108
(617)482-1973   **47 77**

Antique & estate jewelry, silver. *Est:* 1882. *Hours:* Mon-Sat 9:30-5, win til 6. Dan Cohen *Park:* Local garage.

PRISCILLA JUVELIS INC
150 Huntington Ave Suite SDL, 02115
(617)424-7687 FAX
(617)424-1895   **9 13 66**

Antiquarian books: artist books, art bindings, fine bindings & printing, first editions, illustrated books, literature, manuscripts & drawings. *Pr:* $500–500,000. *Est:* 1980. *Serv:* Appraisal, occasional catalog. *Hours:* BY APPT ONLY. *Assoc:* ABAA MARIAB. *Park:* Local garage. *Loc:* Near Copley Square next to the Colonnade Hotel.

KAY BEE FURNITURE COMPANY
1122 Boylston St, 02215
(617)266-4487   **17 21 23**

Used furniture, Oriental rugs, clocks, bronzes, paintings, china, glass & prints. *Hours:* Mon-Fri 9-5:30 Sat 9-5. Leonard Kadish *Loc:* Between the Fenway & Massachusetts Ave.

KNOLLWOOD ANTIQUES
517 Columbus Ave, 02118
(617)536-8866   **29 36 50**

Located in the historic South End at Greenwich Park, a two-level shop containing furniture, decorations, lighting, carpets, mirrors, paintings & 18th-19th C engravings. *Est:* 1988. *Serv:* Consultation, interior design. *Hours:* Jan-late Nov Mon-Sat 9-6 Wed til 9, else Mon-Sun 9-9. *Size:* Medium. *CC:* MC/V. Richard A Lavigne *Park:* On Site. *Loc:* From Prudential Ctr take W Newton St to corner of Columbus, take R, go 2 blocks to corner of Greenwich Park & Columbus Ave.

LESLIE'S & MAYFAIR ANTIQUES
49 Charles St 2nd fl, 02114
(617)248-1933   **{GR3}**

Collection of small furniture, folk art, samplers, rugs, tools, lamps, mirrors, prints, jewelry, glass, porcelain, brass, decorative accessories & Art Deco. *Pr:* $10–1500. *Est:* 1987. *Serv:* Purchase estates. *Hours:* Wed-Sat 11:30-6 Sun 12-5. *Assoc:* SADA. *Park:* Local garage. *Loc:* On Charles St 2 blocks from the Public Garden.

LONDON LACE
167 Newbury St 2nd fl, 02116
(617)267-3506   **48 80**

Specializing in fine linens, lace window-

Jane Russell
Fred Gorman

By appointment
(617)523-2793

HERITAGE ART

Nineteenth and early twentieth century paintings
by New England artists

105 Charles St. #230   Boston, MA 02114

coverings, bedspreads & pillowcases. *Pr:* $25–200. *Serv:* Brochure. *Hours:* Mon-Sat 10-5:30. *Size:* Medium. *CC:* MC/V. *Park:* Copley Place parking lot. *Loc:* Between Dartmouth & Exeter Sts.

SAMUEL L LOWE JR ANTIQUES INC
80 Charles St, 02114
(617)742-0845   **1 56 59**
Fine Americana with a large selection of museum-quality American marine paintings & prints, ship models, scrimshaw, china, instruments, marine books, steamship memorabilia, China trade items, furniture & folk art. *Est:* 1964. *Serv:* Consultation, marine interior design. *Hours:* Sep-Jun Mon-Fri 10:30-5 Sat 10:30-4, Summer by chance/appt. *Size:* Medium. *Park:* In front. *Loc:* On Charles St between Mt Vernon & Pinckney Sts.

MARCOZ ANTIQUES INC
1 Design Center Pl Ste 328, 02211
(617)357-0211   **35 38**
Importers of fine 18th & 19th C English & French antiques, displayed in a large showroom. *Pr:* $500–50000. *Serv:* Purchase estates, reproduction. *Hours:* Mon-Fri 9-5 daily, Sep-Jun 1st Wed each month 9-8. *Size:* Large. *Park:* On site. *Loc:* South Station exit from expressway.

MARCOZ ANTIQUES & JEWELRY
177 Newbury St, 02116
(617)262-0780   **29 39 53**
Fine selection of English formal furniture & accessories. *Serv:* Antiques & estates purchased. *Hours:* Mon-Sat 10-6. *CC:* AX/MC/V. Marc S Glasberg *Park:* Nearby.

MARIKA'S ANTIQUE SHOP INC
130 Charles St, 02114
(617)523-4520   **29 47 77**
A widely varied shop selling a broad selection of jewelry, silver, porcelains & paintings including European, Oriental & American antiques with an emphasis on wholesale trade. *Est:* 1945. *Serv:* Always interested in purchasing estates. *Hours:* Tue-Sat 10-5 & BY APPT. *Size:* Medium. *CC:* MC/V. *Park:* Local garage. *Loc:* Corner of Charles St & Revere Sts 1 block from Charles subway stop.

NELSON-MONROE ANTIQUES
PO Box 8863, 02114
(617)492-1368   **63 77**
18th & early 19th C English & Continental pottery & porcelain, China trade porcelain & silver, old Sheffield plate. *Pr:* $200–10000. *Serv:* Appraisal. *Hours:* BY APPT. *Assoc:* AADLA. *Shows:* ELLIS. James M Labaugh

THE NEWBURY GALLERIES ANTIQUES
29 Newbury St, 02116
(617)437-0822   **29 38 53**
A carefully-chosen selection of Continental furniture, mirrors & decorative accessories. *Serv:* Interior design. *Hours:* 11-6 daily & BY APPT CLOSED SUN, MON. *Size:* Medium. Carolyn Tribe *Park:* Nearby. *Loc:* 1 1/2 blocks W of the Public Garden.

NEWBURY STREET JEWELRY & ANTIQUE
255 Newbury St, 02116
(617)236-0038   **46 63 77**
Silverware, ceramics, china, porcelain, modern American painting, sculpture, 19th C American art, Latin American & Oriental art, Persian rugs, antique jewelry, precious metals & watches. *Est:* 1986. *Serv:* Appraisal. *Hours:* Daily 10-5. *CC:* MC/V. *Assoc:* NEAA. Doris Nichols *Park:* Nearby lot. *Loc:* Between Fairfield & Gloucester Sts.

THE NOSTALGIA FACTORY
324 Newbury St, 02115
(617)236-8754 **1 13 33**
Original old advertising: posters, signs, tins & trade cards & an extensive selection of ephemera including catalogs, programs, post cards, rare books, royalty collectibles & movie memorabilia. *Pr:* $15–1200. *Serv:* Appraisal, interior design. *Hours:* Daily 11-7. *Size:* Medium. *CC:* AX/DC/MC/V. Rudy Franchi *Park:* Local garage. *Loc:* In the 1st block E of Massachusetts Ave.

O'NEAL ANTIQUARIAN BOOKSELLERS
234 Clarendon St, 02116
(617)266-5790 **13**
Specializing in fine & rare books, bindings, English & American first editions. *Pr:* $25–& up. *Est:* 1969. *Serv:* Appraisals, brochure, catalog, purchase estates. *Hours:* Mon-Sat 9-5. *CC:* AX/MC/V. *Assoc:* ABAA MARIAB. David L O'Neal *Park:* Nearby. *Loc:* Near the corner of Newbury & Clarendon, 2 blocks from Copley Square.

PEPPER & STERN RARE BOOKS INC
355 Boylston St 2nd Fl, 02116
(617)536-7072 FAX
(617)421-1880 **9 13**
Antiquarian books: English & American literature, detective fiction, rare cinema material, autographs & manuscripts. *Serv:* Appraisal, catalog. *Hours:* Mon-Sat 9-5, Sat 10-4. *Assoc:* ABAA MARIAB. Peter L Stern *Park:* Nearby. *Loc:* Near the Int of Boylston St & the Public Garden.

PERIOD FURNITURE HARDWARE CO
123 Charles St, 02114
(617)227-0758 **50 70**
Located in historic Beacon Hill, a storehouse of brass hardware & accessories for the discriminating dealer or homeowner. Highest quality reproduction furniture & door hardware, light fixtures, bath accessories, fireplace equipment & weather vanes. *Pr:* $5–2500. *Serv:* Catalog ($4.50), reproduction. *Hours:* Mon-Fri 8:30-5 Sat 10-2, Jul-Aug CLOSED SAT. *CC:* MC/V. *Park:* Local garage. *Loc:* At the N end of Charles St on famed Beacon Hill.

EDWARD T POLLACK BOOKS
236 Beacon St, 02116
(617)437-1095 **13**
Antiquarian books: art, artists, photography, architecture & design, illustrated, children's & fine prints. *Serv:* Catalog. *Hours:* BY APPT ONLY. *Assoc:* MARIAB.

RERUNS ANTIQUES
125B Charles St, 02114
36 50 53
Reasonably-priced antiques & furniture from Beacon Hill & greater Boston. *Pr:* $1–500. *Serv:* Purchase estates. *Hours:* Mon-Sat 1:30-5:30. *CC:* MC/V. Sarah Gorman *Park:* Local garage. *Loc:* MBTA Red Line to Charles St stop.

ROLLY-MICHAUX LTD
290 Dartmouth St, 02116
(617)536-9898 **35 59 63**
Fine 18th C French furniture & decorations. *Hours:* Tue-Sat 11-5:30 or by appt. *Loc:* At the Vendome, corner of Commonwealth & Dartmouth.

C A RUPPERT
121 Charles St, 02114
(617)523-5033 **29 39 63**
18th, 19th & early 20th C English, Continental & American furniture & decorative accessories. *Est:* 1988. *Hours:* Mon-Sat 10-5. *Park:* Nearby lot.

SHALLCROSS & LORRAINE
60 Pinckney St, 02114
(617)720-2133 **21 71**

Oriental rug restorers - invisible restorations including texture matched wool, custom spinning & custom dyeing to restore all types of damage. *Est:* 1975. *Hours:* By appt only. Holly L Smith

SHER-MORR ANTIQUES
82 Charles St, 02114
(617)227-4780 **13 60 66**

General line with emphasis on Orientalia, featuring decorative prints & used & antiquarian books. *Pr:* $4–2000. *Hours:* Mon-Sat 9-5 Sun 9-4. *Size:* Medium. *CC:* MC/V. Jack Sherman *Loc:* Boston's Antique Shop Row just off Storrow Dr.

SHOP ON THE HILL
84 Chestnut St, 02114
(617)523-0440 **29 41 45**

Trompe l'oeil furniture, antiques & decorative accessories in a charming shop on a side street of Beacon Hill. *Hours:* Wed-Sun 12-6:30 call ahead. Paul F MacDonald *Park:* Nearby garage. *Loc:* 1 block W of Charles St & 1 block N of Beacon St.

SHREVE, CRUMP & LOW
Antiques Dept 330 Boylston St, 02116
(617)267-9100 **39 63 66**

Large selection of fine English, American & Chinese export, 18th & early 19th C furniture, ceramics, glass, prints & paintings. *Pr:* $50–30000. *Est:* 1865. *Serv:* Purchase estates, 1-800-225-7088. *Hours:* Sep-Jun Mon-Sat 9:30-5:30, Jul-Aug CLOSED SAT. *Size:* Medium. *CC:* AX/MC/V. *Shows:* ELLIS. James D Shaffer *Park:* Local garage. *Loc:* I-90 Copley Sq Exit: across from the Public Garden at Boylston & Arlington Sts.

SKINNER INC
2 Newbury St, 02116
(617)236-1700 **8 47 55**

Boston office of New England's largest auction gallery. This location specializes in regular auctions of jewelry & musical instruments. *Serv:* Auction & appraisal. *Hours:* Mon-Fri 10-5. Nancy Skinner *Park:* Nearby. *Loc:* At the corner of Arlington & Newbury Sts above Burberry's. Auctions often held at Ritz Carlton across the st.

SOTHEBY'S
101 Newbury St, 02116
(617)247-2851 **8**

Boston office of the famous auction house. *Est:* 1744. *Serv:* Auctioneer. *Hours:* Please call ahead. Patricia E Ward

VOSE GALLERIES OF BOSTON INC
238 Newbury St, 02116
(617)536-6176 **59**

19th C American & 20th C American Impressionist paintings up to 1925. *Est:* 1841. *Serv:* Referrals for restoration services. *Hours:* Mon-Fri 8-5:30 Sat 9-4. *Shows:* ELLIS. Abbot W Vose *Park:* Nearby.

ALFRED J WALKER FINE ART
158 Newbury St, 02116
(617)247-1319 **59**

19th & 20th C American paintings specializing in the Boston School. *Est:* 1978. *Serv:* Appraisal, consultation, restoration. *Hours:* Tue-Sat 10-5. *Park:* Nearby. *Loc:* Dartmouth & Exeter Sts above the Copley Society.

WENHAM CROSS ANTIQUES
232 Newbury St, 02116
(617)236-0409 **27 29 63**

18th & 19th C country furniture & decorative objects including Quimper, Majolica, quilts, hooked rugs, paintings

& folk art. *Pr:* $25–10000. *Est:* 1979.
Serv: Purchase estates. *Hours:* Mon-Sat
10-5. *CC:* AX/MC/V. *Assoc:* NHADA
NSAA. Emily Lampert *Park:* Nearby
lot. *Loc:* Between Exeter & Fairfield Sts.

CHARLES B WOOD III INC
116 Commonwealth Ave, 02116
(617)247-7844   **13**
Antiquarian books: science & technology, architecture, photography, decorative arts, landscape gardening & book
arts. *Serv:* Catalog. *Hours:* BY APPT
ONLY. *Assoc:* ABAA MARIAB. *Park:*
Nearby.

BRIDGEWATER

DAM' YANKEE SHOP
36 Central Sq, 02324
(508)697-2934   **40**
Refinished antique oak furniture including press back chairs, round & square
tables, beds, chests, hoosiers, roll top
desks, medicine cabinets, wardrobes &
bookcases. *Est:* 1972. *Hours:* Mon-Sat
9-5 Sun 11-4. *Assoc:* NEAA. Jim
Manchester *Loc:* 3 MI off Rte 24.

BRIGHTON

DERBY DESK COMPANY
140 Tremont St, 02135
(617)787-2707   **36 68 71**
American & European desks circa 1850-
1890. *Pr:* $2500–25000. *Est:* 1981. *Serv:*
Consultation, interior design, repairs,
restoration, customizing. *Hours:* Open
all year Mon-Sat 10:30-5. *Size:* Medium.
Kal Unger *Park:* In front. *Loc:* I-90 Exit
17: 10 min from downtown Boston. Follow signs to Brighton.

BRIMFIELD

BRIMFIELD
Rte 20 Auction Acres, 01010
(413)245-3436
Outdoor antiques shows featuring over
700 exhibitors from the US & Canada.
Est: 1959. *Serv:* Catered, showers,
spaces start at $100, motel info 508-597-
8155. *Hours:* 1991 DATES: May
9,10,11, July 11,12,13 Sep 12,13,14.
Size: Huge. Jill Lukesh Judith Mathieu
Park: Acres of on site parking. *Loc:* I-90
Exit for Rte 84.

BRIMFIELD ANTIQUES
Haynes Hill Rd, 01010
(413)245-3350   **2 16 59**
Offering one of the finest selections of
antique fireplace equipment, specializing
in fine Federal furniture, paintings &
accessories. *Serv:* Conservation, appraisal. *Hours:* BY APPT. *Assoc:* AAA
ADAA. *Shows:* ELLIS. Richard N
Raymond *Loc:* 8 MI W of Old
Sturbridge Village.

BROCKTON

BEN GERBER & SON INC
386 Pleasant St, 02401
(508)586-2547   **4**
China, glass, silver & jewelry. *Est:* 1946.
Serv: Appraisal for estates. *Hours:* Mon-
Sat 9-3:30. *Assoc:* AAA.

BROOKLINE

ANTIQUERS III
171A Harvard St, 02146
(617)738-5555   **7**
Specializing in Art Deco & 20th C
decorative arts. *Pr:* $100–25000. *Est:*
1972. *Serv:* Appraisal, consultation, interior design, purchase estates, bidding.
Hours: Mon-Fri 10-5, Sat 11-5. *Size:*
Medium. *CC:* AX/MC/V. Mark Feldman
Park: In front. *Loc:* Next to Stop & Shop
parking lot.

APPLETON ANTIQUES
195 Harvard St, 02146
(617)566-5322   **7 50 83**
Victorian & Art Deco, furniture, lighting
& decorative accessories. *Est:* 1978.
Serv: Appraisal, consultation, purchase
estates, repairs, restoration of lamps.
Hours: Mon-Sat 10-6 Sun By Appt. *Size:*
Medium. *CC:* MC/V. *Park:* On street.
Loc: 1 block from Coolidge Corner.

AUTREFOIS II
130 Harvard St, 02146
(617)566-0113   **35 38 50**
Large selection of country French &
Continental furniture, Oriental porcelains, decorative accessories & lighting; a support & storage store for the
Newbury St store, to open late 1990 or
1991. *Serv:* Custom mounted lamps.
Size: Medium. *CC:* AX/DC/MC/V.
Park: Nearby.

CYPRESS TRADING POST
144 Cypress St, 02146
(617)566-5412   **17 60 63**
Two medium sized floors of unusual
items, including porcelain, bronze
Oriental & European art & some furniture. *Pr:* $15–9000. *Est:* 1970. *Hours:*
Year round by chance/appt, call ahead

suggested. *Size:* Medium. Dick Maccini
Park: On site. *Loc:* Corner of Rte 9 &
Cypress St in a blue house.

THE FRAME GALLERY
300 Harvard St Rear, 02146
(617)232-2070   **68 70 71**
Hand-shaped, hand-carved & gilded picture frames custom designed. Creative
French & English matting. *Serv:*
Authentic restoration, custom woodwork, repairs, replication. *Hours:* Tue-Sat 10-6 appt suggested. *Size:* Medium.
CC: MC/V. Michael Allen *Park:* On site.
Loc: Coolidge Corner, facing the Centre
St parking lot.

JERRY FREEMAN LTD
1429 Beacon St, 02146
(617)731-6720   **29 37 53**
18th, 19th & 20th C furniture, decorative accessories, paintings & mirrors.
Est: 1978. *Serv:* Interior design, purchase estates. *Hours:* Mon-Sat 11-5.
Size: Medium. *CC:* MC/V. *Park:* In
front. *Loc:* 3 blocks from Coolidge
Corner on the Green Line (C Route).

TIM GALLAGHER ANTIQUES
Arcade Bldg 318 Harvard Ave #7, 02146
(617)566-2555   **29 36 59**
19th C American & European antiques,
including furniture, art work, framed
engravings, decorative accessories & collectibles. *Serv:* Purchase estates, restoration. *Hours:* Tue-Sat 10-5 Mon BY
APPT. *CC:* MC/V. *Park:* Nearby lot.

GENOVESE STAINED GLASS STUDIO
15 Littell Rd, 02146
(617)738-6367   **68 70**
Repair & restoration of stained & leaded
glass:windows, lamps, mirrors & period
pieces. Reframing & sizing of old
panels. Brass, zinc, wood, glass etching
& protective shields (lexan) installed.

Est: 1982. *Serv:* Free estimates, pick up & delivery available. *Hours:* By chance/appt. Emanuel Genovese *Park:* In front. *Loc:* In the heart of Brookline at Coolidge Corner, 3 blocks S on Harvard St, L on Alton Pl, 1 block, L on Littel Rd.

ROSINE GREEN ASSOCIATES INC
45 Bartlett Crescent, 02146
(617)277-8368   **68 69 71**

Experts in restoration of art objects, Oriental lacquer, paintings, frames, porcelains, metals, furniture & designing display stands. *Est:* 1955. *Serv:* Appraisal, conservation, custom woodwork, repairs, replication. *Hours:* Mon-Fri 9-5, Sat 10-12, Appt suggested. *Assoc:* AAA AIC. Ehiel Rits *Park:* On site. *Loc:* Off Washington St between Beacon St & Commonwealth Ave.

RENOVATORS SUPPLY
1624 Beacon St, 02146
(617)739-6088   **50 70 74**

Period hardware, plumbing & lighting supplies. *Serv:* Reproduction. *Hours:* Mon-Sat 10-6, Tue & Thu 9:30-5:30. *Size:* Medium. *CC:* MC/V. *Park:* In front. *Loc:* Between Coolidge Corner & Cleveland Circle.

NANCY A SMITH APPRAISAL ASSOC
7 Kent St, 02146
(617)566-1339   **4 26**

An association of personal property appraisers specializing in furniture, clocks, silver, metals, rugs, textiles, ceramics & glass, fine arts & architectural interior elements. Reports prepared for insurance/estate planning, estate taxation, gift values. *Serv:* Appraisal, consultation. *Hours:* Daily 9-5. *Assoc:* AAA ASA CPPC SPNEA. *Loc:* Brookline Village.

THE STRAWBERRY PATCH
12 Cypress St, 02146
(617)566-0077   **40**

Quality refinished oak furniture & brass accessories. *Pr:* $200–800. *Est:* 1981. *Hours:* Thu-Sat 8:30-5:30 Sun 12-3. *Size:* Medium. *CC:* AX/MC/V. Myrna Aschenbrand *Park:* In front. *Loc:* 3 blocks from Rte 9.

BROOKLINE VILLAGE

A ROOM WITH A VIEUX
220 Washington St, 02146
(617)277-2700   **35 50 53**

Specializing in French furniture, armoires, French stoves, mirrors & decorative accessories. *Est:* 1988. *Hours:* Mon-Sat 10-6. Jeffrey Diamond *Park:* In front. *Loc:* 1 block from Rte 9.

THE ANTIQUE COMPANY
311 Washington St, 02146
(617)738-9476   **29 47 77**

Antique jewelry & silver, 19th & 20th C fine & decorative arts. *Pr:* $5–15000. *Est:* 1978. *Serv:* Purchase estates. *Hours:* Mon-Sat 10-5. *Size:* Medium. *CC:* AX/MC/V. Toby Langderman *Park:* Nearby lot. *Loc:* 1 block from Rte 9.

NEAL BECKERMAN ANTIQUES
31 Harvard St, 02146
(617)232-6414   **7 38 73**

Continental furniture, fine paintings, sculpture, deco, tapestries, folk art & garden statuary. *Pr:* $100–25000. *Est:* 1973. *Serv:* Purchase estates, appraisal. *Hours:* Mon-Fri 9:30-5:30 Sat, Sun 12-5:30. *Size:* Medium. Ellen Carlino *Park:* In front. *Loc:* 3 blocks from stop on MBTA Green Line.

BROOKLINE VILLAGE BOOKSHOP
23 Harvard St, 02146
(617)734-3519   **13 14**
Americana, biography, children's, local history & nautical. *Pr:* $5–1000. *Serv:* Appraisal, catalog. *Hours:* Mon-Sat 10-6 Thu til 9. *Size:* 30,000 books. *CC:* AX/MC/V. *Assoc:* ABAA MARIAB. James Lawton *Loc:* I-95 to Rte 9E: to Washington St in Brookline Village, L on Washington by taking R around Fire Station, R at 1st fork.

BROOKLINE VILLAGE ANTIQUES
18 Harvard St, 02146
(617)734-6071   **38 39 53**
18th & 19th C English, Continental & American furniture, paintings & restored lighting. *Hours:* Mon-Sat 10-6 Sun 11-7. Herb Hough *Loc:* 2 blocks from Rte 9.

TOWNE ANTIQUES
256 Washington St, 02146
(617)731-3326   **37 38 39**
Large selection of mahogany, cherry, & walnut furniture & mirrors on two floors in the center of Brookline Village. *Pr:* $500–5000. *Est:* 1970. *Serv:* Purchase estates, appraisal, auctioneers. *Hours:* Mon-Sat 9-6. *Size:* Huge. *CC:* DC/MC/V. Francis J O'Boy *Park:* Nearby. *Loc:* Brookline Village on the MBTA Green line, 1 block off Rte 9.

CAMBRIDGE

JAMES R BAKKER ANTIQUES INC
370 Broadway, 02139
(617)864-7067   **8 59 66**
Cambridge's only fine arts auction & appraisal service featuring regular sales of paintings, prints & sculpture. *Serv:* Appraisal, auction, catalog, purchase estates. *Hours:* Mon-Fri 10-5 Sat BY APPT. *Size:* Medium. *Assoc:* ADA MSAA. *Loc:* Walking distance from Central & Harvard Sqs in Cambridge.

BERNHEIMER'S ANTIQUE ARTS
52C Brattle St, 02138
(617)547-1177   **3 47 60**
Like a museum - featuring rare & unusual art objects from around the world, including ancient, European, Asian, Islamic, Pre-Columbian & Native American art & antique jewelry - a family tradition since 1864. *Est:* 1963. *Serv:* Appraisal. *Hours:* Mon-Sat 10-5. *Size:* Medium. *CC:* AX/DC/MC/V. *Assoc:* AAA. G. Max Bernheimer *Park:* Nearby lot. *Loc:* On Brattle St, 1 block from the center of Harvard Sq & the Harvard MBTA stop.

ROBIN BLEDSOE BOOKSELLER
1640 Massachusetts Ave Rear, 02138
(617)576-3634   **13**
Antiquarian books: Horses, sporting art, art history, architecture, archaeology, graphic design, photography, female artists & gardens. *Serv:* Appraisal, catalog, search service. *Hours:* Tue-Fri 10-5 Sat 10-6 & BY APPT. *CC:* MC/V. *Assoc:* ABAA MARIAB. *Park:* In front. *Loc:* Between Harvard & Porter Squares, opposite Quality Inn.

SHARON BOCCELLI & CO ANTIQUES
358 Broadway, 02139
(617)354-7919   **29 63 83**
General line of antiques - wholesale. *Est:* 1978. *Serv:* Appraisal, auction. *Hours:* Sat 10-6. *Size:* Medium. *Park:* In front.

CHRISTIE, MANSON & WOOD
PO Box 2723, 02238
(617)576-0400   **4 8 25**
Specialists in the disposal of fine arts &

antiques from collections & estates. *Serv:* Auction, appraisal. *Hours:* By appt only. Elizabeth Chapin

CITY LIGHTS
2226 Massachusetts Ave, 02140
(617)547-1490   **50 83**

Large selection of fully restored antique lighting 1850-1930, ceiling fixtures, wall sconces, table & floor lamps. *Pr:* $250–5000. *Est:* 1976. *Serv:* Catalog ($5). *Hours:* Tue-Sat 10-6 Thu til 7:30. *Size:* Medium. *CC:* MC/V. Chris Osbourne *Park:* In front. *Loc:* Int Rte 2 & Alewife Brook Pkwy OR Red Line to Davis Sq.

EASY CHAIRS
375 Huron Ave, 02138
(617)491-2131   **27 40 50**

Vintage oak, wicker & rattan, brass lamps & country store items. *Pr:* $2–4000. *Est:* 1980. *Serv:* Purchase estates. *Hours:* Mon-Sat 10-5:30. *Size:* Medium. Lee Joseph *Park:* In front. *Loc:* 1 MI N of Harvard Sq.

FLEUR DE LIS GALLERY
52C Brattle St, 02138
(617)864-7738   **44 47 63**

Antique jewelry, colored glass, European hand-painted china, classic furniture, Quimper, Victorian frames, Oriental art & old Victorian plate. *Est:* 1981. *Hours:* Tue-Sat 11:30-4:30 call ahead. *Size:* Medium. Silvia Burger *Park:* Nearby lot. *Loc:* At the ground floor next to Bernheimer's.

HAMPSHIRE BOOKS
157 Hampshire St, 02139
(617)354-3536   **13**

General stock of old & rare books. *Hours:* Sun-Mon 12-5, Wed-Sat 12-6. *Assoc:* MARIAB. Frank Crowley

HOWARD ANTIQUES
1654 Massachusetts Ave, 02138
(617)354-5544   **29 44 63**

A good selection of metalware, pottery & porcelain, glass, country furniture. *Hours:* Tue-Fri 12-5:30 Sat 10-4. *Park:* On street. *Loc:* Between Harvard & Porter Square at the corner of Shepherd St.

F B HUBLEY & CO
364 Broadway, 02139
(617)876-2030   **4 8 25**

Auctioneers & estate appraisers since 1935; specializing in estate liquidation & consignments of antiques, fine arts, & custom furniture or furnishings. Buyer's premium. *Serv:* Appraisal, auction, purchase estates. *Hours:* Mon-Fri 8:30-5. *Assoc:* AAA. *Loc:* Midway between Harvard University & Kendall Sq.

HURST GALLERY
53 Mt Auburn St, 02138
(617)491-6888   **3 4 82**

In a sun-lit gallery 3 blocks from Harvard's Fogg Museum, antiquities & ethnographic art: African, American Indian, Oceanic, Pre-Columbian, Asian & Classical. Special exhibitions & catalog sales. *Pr:* $50–50000. *Est:* 1977. *Serv:* Appraisal, conservation & mounting, restoration, catalog, free newsletter. *Hours:* Tue-Sat 12-6 Thu til 8. *Size:* Medium. *CC:* AX/DC/MC/V. *Assoc:* ASA ISA. Norman Hurst *Park:* Nearby lot. *Loc:* 4 blocks off JFK St Harvard Sq.

KEEZER'S HARVARD COMMUNITY EXCHANGE
140 River St, 02139
(617)547-2455   **85**

Reasonably priced classic clothing, traditional styles, tuxedos & overcoats. *Est:* 1895. *Hours:* Daily 10-6. *Size:* Large. *Park:* On site. *Loc:* I-90 Cambridge Exit: 1/4 MI from Memorial Dr.

LAMP GLASS
2230 Massachusetts Ave, 02140
(617)497-0770 **50 70**
Large selection of glass shades & antique reproductions including student shades, torchier, gas, GWTW globes, cased glass, etched sconce & chandelier glass & prisms. *Est:* 1984. *Serv:* Reproduction. *Hours:* Wed,Fri,Sat 10-6 Thu 10-7:30. *Size:* Medium. *CC:* MC/V. Tania Maxwell *Park:* In front.

MATZ & PRIBELL
366 1/2 Broadway, 02139
(617)661-6200 **1 8 35**
Specializing in important catalogued estate auctions, as well as stocking in the gallery for sale, a fine selection of period American, Continental & English furniture, paintings & decorative accessories from New England homes. *Pr:* $50–20000. *Est:* 1976. *Serv:* Appraisal, interior design, purchase estates, auction, catalog. *Hours:* Tue-Sat 10-5 CLOSED SUN, MON. *Size:* Medium. *CC:* AX/MC/V. *Park:* In front. *Loc:* Approximately 1 MI from Harvard College's Fogg Art Museum, located in the heart of the Cambridge antiques district.

H MENDELSOHN FINE EUROPEAN BOOKS
1640 Massachusetts Ave Rear, 02138
(617)576-3634 **13**
Antiquarian books: architecture, decorative arts, gardening & printing history thoughtfully selected & displayed with attention to quality & condition. *Serv:* Catalog. *Hours:* Tue-Sat 10-5. *Assoc:* MARIAB. Harvey L Mendelsohn *Park:* Nearby.

THE MUSIC EMPORIUM
2018 Massachusetts Ave, 02140
(617)661-2099 **55 71**
Vintage guitars, banjos, mandolins, concertina, wooden flutes, stringed instruments & dulcimers. *Pr:* $10–15000. *Est:* 1977. *Serv:* Appraisal, conservation, repair, restoration. *Hours:* Mon-Sat 11-5:30 Th 11-8. *Size:* Medium. *CC:* MC/V. *Park:* Nearby lot. *Loc:* Red Line to Porter Sq, 3 block walk.

CARL R NORDBLOM AUCTIONEER
PO Box 167 Harvard Square, 02138
(617)491-1196 **8**
Auctioneer with approximately six auctions annually of primarily 18th & early 19th C American furniture, paintings, Oriental rugs & decorative accessories. Terms to consignor 10% over $500. 10% buyers' premium. *Est:* 1973. *Serv:* Appraisal of American antiques, purchase estates. *Hours:* Call for appt & auction schedule.

OLD PRINT SHOP
1700 Massachusetts Ave, 02138
(617)354-5700 **66**
A charming collection of old prints including architectural, botanical, animals, bird, historical, equinine, maps. *Est:* 1989. *Hours:* Mon 1-6, Tue-Sat 11-6, Thur 11-7. *Park:* On street. *Loc:* On the way to Porter Square at the corner of Martin St.

KARIN J PHILLIPS ANTIQUES
348 Broadway, 02139
(617)547-9433 **36 60**
Eclectic selection of furniture & accessories ranging from early 19th C to fabulous 50s. *Pr:* $20–8000. *Est:* 1978. *Serv:* Appraisal, purchase estates. *Hours:* Mon, Tue, Wed, Sat 10:30-4, else by chance. *Park:* In front. *Loc:* From Harvard, take Massachusetts Ave under the underpass and bear R on Broadway.

POSTAR ANTIQUES
356 Broadway, 02139
(617)576-0463
Buying & selling quality antiques for over 60 years. *Est:* 1917. *Serv:* Appraisal, consultation, purchase estates. *Hours:* By chance. *Size:* Medium. Henry Postar *Park:* In front. *Loc:* Between Central & Inman Sqs, 10 min from downtown Boston.

SADYE & COMPANY
182 Massachusetts Ave, 02139
(617)547-4424   **{GR7}**
Vintage clothing, jewelry & accessories. *Est:* 1988. *Hours:* Mon-Sat 11-6 Sun 12-4. Alma Libby

SEARLES RARE WATCHES
124 Mt Auburn St Suite 200, 02138
(617)576-5810   **23**
Specializing in rare watches. *Hours:* By appt only. David B Searles II

THE STARR BOOK SHOP
29 Plympton St, 02138
(617)547-6864   **13**
Antiquarian books: literary criticism & biography, literature, philosophy, sets & scholarly remainders. *Serv:* Catalog, wholesale available. *Hours:* Mon-Sat 10-6 Sun 12-6. *Assoc:* MARIAB.

A TOUCH OF CLASS
1309 Cambridge St, 02139
(617)491-7000   **36 83**
Specializing in Victorian antiques. *Serv:* Appraisal, auction, purchase estates, restoration. *Hours:* Daily 9:30-6. *Size:* Large. *CC:* MC/V. *Assoc:* AAA NEAA. *Park:* In front. *Loc:* 1/2 MI from Harvard Sq.

WEINER'S ANTIQUE SHOP
356 Broadway, 02138
(617)864-5312   **29 36 63**
A large selection with variety & quality.

Continuous family ownership for 94 years. *Pr:* $25–10000. *Est:* 1896. *Serv:* Appraisal, purchase estates. *Hours:* Mon-Fri By chance/appt please call first. *Size:* Medium. *CC:* MC/V. *Assoc:* AAA NAWCC. Paul Weiner *Park:* On Street.

CANTON

GABRIEL'S AUCTION CO INC
611 Neponset St, 02021
(617)821-2992   **4 8**
Estate, antique & consignment auctions of art, collectibles, rugs, furniture, militaria & firearms. *Est:* 1974. *Serv:* Appraisal, auction, consignment, conduct on site & fund raising auctions. *Hours:* Mon-Fri 10-5 by chance or appt. *Assoc:* AAA CAI MSAA NAA. Evan N Gavrilles *Loc:* I-95 Exit 11-A.

CHARLESTOWN

BUNKER HILL RELICS
207 Main St, 02129
(617)241-9534   **17 60 63**
Orientalia, Oriental rugs, porcelain, art glass, bronzes, marble busts, silver, furniture & miscellaneous collectibles. *Serv:* Purchase estates. *Hours:* Tue-Fri 11-5:30 Sat 9:30-5:30 & BY APPT.

CHELMSFORD

CHERYL NEEDLE BOOKS
212 North Rd, 01824
(508)256-0455   **13**
Antiquarian books: general stock includ-

ing Americana, ephemera, the arts, science, travel & social sciences. **Serv:** Appraisal. **Hours:** BY APPT ONLY. **Assoc:** MARIAB. Cheryl/Matthew Needle

CHESTERFIELD

CHESTERFIELD ANTIQUES
Rte 143, 01012
(413)296-4252   1 37
Specializing in American 18th & 19th C furniture & accessories, especially high country & formal American furniture circa 1780-1840. **Hours:** Daily (a call ahead advised). **Assoc:** BCADA NHADA VADA. Jack Geishen **Park:** On site. **Loc:** I-91 Exit 9W: between Pittsfield & Northampton, 20 min W of Northampton.

CHESTNUT HILL

BOOK & TACKLE SHOP
29 Old Colony Rd, 02167
(617)965-0459   13 64
Antiquarian Books: geology, ichthyology, fishing & hunting, medicine, music, postcards & nautical; Summer location in Watch Hill, RI (401)596-0700. **Serv:** Appraisal, catalog, search service. **Hours:** By appt. **Assoc:** MARIAB. B L Gordon

SONIA PAINE
616A Hammond St, 02167
(617)566-9669   47 60 77
French & Oriental estate jewelry, silver, porcelain, Russian & French enamel. **Est:** 1968. **Serv:** Purchase estates, appraisal, promoter of major antiques

shows. **Hours:** Tue-Sat 12-4 & BY APPT. **Assoc:** AAA SADA. **Park:** Nearby. **Loc:** Corner of Rte 9 & Hammond St.

DALE POLLOCK APPRAISAL
SERVICES
Box 193, 02167
(617)277-4962   4
Appraisals of jewelry & silver for insurance, probate, property division, donations & sale. **Est:** 1979. **Serv:** Appraisal, consultation. **Hours:** BY APPT ONLY. **Assoc:** ASA GIA AR.

MAGDA TISZA RARE BOOKS
130 Woodchester Dr, 02167
(617)527-5312   13
Antiquarian books: foreign languages (mainly French & German), literature, philosophy & illustrated books. **Pr:** $25–2500. **Est:** 1975. **Serv:** Appraisal, catalog. **Hours:** BY APPT. **Assoc:** ABAA MARIAB.

CONCORD

THE BARROW BOOKSTORE
79 Main St, 01742
(508)369-6084   13
Antiquarian books: transcendentalism, Concord & its writers, Thoreau, the Alcotts, literature, children's books, local history & nature. **Serv:** Search service. **Hours:** Mon-Sat 9:30-5 Sun 12-5. **Assoc:** MARIAB. Pamela Fenn **Park:** On street, nearby lot.

BOOKS WITH A PAST
17 Walden St 2nd Fl, 01742
(508)371-0180   13
Antiquarian books: Concord authors, Thoreau, Alcotts, Hawthorne, Concord history, transcendentalism, natural history & music. **Serv:** Search service.

Hours: Mon-Sat 10-5. *Assoc:* MARIAB. Bonnie Bracker *Park:* On street. *Loc:* Just off Main Ave.

CONCORD ANTIQUES
32 Main St Basement Level, 01742
(508)369-8218   {GR10}
A carefully chosen & thoughtfully displayed selection of beautiful quilts, paintings, samplers, English & Oriental porcelain, sterling, linens, crystal, fine American furniture & country accessories & jewelry. *Pr:* $25–1000. *Hours:* Mon-Sat 10-5 Sun 1-5. *CC:* MC/V. *Assoc:* SADA. Mary Ann Boynton *Park:* In front. *Loc:* In the center of town.

CONCORD PATRIOT ANTIQUES
1595 Main St Rte 62, 01742
(508)263-0105   36 44 77
Large selection of early antiques, including Chippendale, East Lake, Victorian, Gothic country & oak. Glassware includes Chelsea, Staffordshire, Bohemian, Limoges, Nippon/Noritake & Bisque. Also carrying jade, ivory, silver & cloisonne. *Hours:* Weekdays BY APPT, weekends & holidays 9-4. Tom & Lorrie Graham

JOSLIN HALL RARE BOOKS
Box 516, 01742
(508)371-3101   13 14
Specialists in scarce & out-of-print books on the decorative arts & American fine arts, especially references on American decorative arts of the 18th & 19th C. *Pr:* $25–2500. *Est:* 1981. *Serv:* Brochure, catalog (free), purchase libraries, search service. *Hours:* BY APPT ONLY. *Assoc:* MARIAB.

BERNICE JACKSON FINE ARTS
Box 1188, 01742
(508)369-1718 FAX
(508)369-9088   66
Vintage European & American posters & poster-related graphics 1895-1950. *Est:* 1976. *Serv:* Appraisal, fine arts consultant. *Hours:* BY APPT. *CC:* MC/V. *Loc:* Call for directions.

CONWAY

CONWAY HOUSE
Rte 116 Ashfield Rd, 01341
(413)369-4660   16 50 65
All 18th & 19th C samplers, primitives, paintings, lighting devices, copper, brass, iron, Staffordshire, textiles & furniture. *Est:* 1963. *Serv:* Appraisal. *Hours:* Appt advised. *Assoc:* ADA NHADA VADA. Jack & Ray Van Gelder *Park:* On site. *Loc:* I-91N Exit 24: I-91S Exit 25: take Rte 116 to Conway, 6 1/2 MI.

ROBERT L MERRIAM
Newhall Rd, 01341
(413)369-4052   13
Out-of-print books on a wide variety of subjects, specializing in bibliography, decorative arts & Americana. This bed & breakfast in an attractive country setting permits evening browsing. *Serv:* Appraisal, catalog. *Hours:* Sun 1-5 or by chance/appt. *Size:* 10,000 books. *Assoc:* MARIAB. *Park:* In front. *Loc:* From S: Rte 91 Exit 24: Rtes 5 & 10 to Rte 116 to Conway. In Conway Shelburne Falls Rd to Newhall Rd.

SOUTHPAW BOOKS
Elmer Rd, 01341
(413)369-4406   13 66
Antiquarian books: first editions, women, labor & radical studies, photography & small quantity of socially related graphics. *Serv:* Catalog, search service, appraisal. *Hours:* By appt. *Size:* 15,000. *Assoc:* MARIAB. Eugene Povirk *Loc:* 2

MI from the int of Rte 116 & Shelburne Falls Rd in the ctr of Conway or call for specific directions.

CUMMINGTON

B SHAW ANTIQUES
Rte 9, 01026
(413)634-2289   **36**

Large stock of furniture - oak, walnut, Victorian, wicker, early pine, primitives, desks, round tables, sets of chairs, rockers & brass beds - primarily to the trade. *Pr:* $25–500. *Hours:* By chance/appt.

DANVERS

CROSSMAN-VINING ANTIQUES
98 High St, 01923
(508)777-0306   **29 36 59**

Gallery of fine period antique furniture, paintings, porcelains & accessories in room settings with a special emphasis on the China trade. *Pr:* $100–35000. *Est:* 1989. *Serv:* Conservation, purchase estates, restoration. *Hours:* Mon-Sat 9-5. *CC:* MC/V. Carl Crossman & Christine Vining *Park:* On site. *Loc:* Rte 128 Exit 23N: on Rte 35 at the Framemakers Bldg in Danvers.

SPRAGUE HOUSE ANTIQUES
59 Endicott St, 01923
(508)774-3944   **37**

Period & fine custom furniture of investment quality in original or professionally restored condition. *Hours:* By chance/appt. Ron Hodgdon *Loc:* Rte 128 Exit 24.

DEDHAM

CENTURY SHOP
626 High St, 02026
(617)326-1717   **4 8**

A general line of antiques. *Serv:* Purchase estates, appraisal, auctions. *Hours:* Daily 11-4:30 CLOSED FRI,SUN. *Assoc:* SADA. Eleanor Woodward *Loc:* Near Court House.

DEDHAM ANTIQUE SHOP
622 High St, 02026
(617)329-1114   **1 37**

Large stock of authentic American furniture & accessories - fourth generation in American antiques. *Serv:* Private & trade enquiries invited. *Hours:* By chance/appt. *Assoc:* SADA. Simon Nager

HENRY HORNBLOWER III
176 Court St, 02026
(617)329-3226   **36 59 66**

Paintings, prints & furniture. *Est:* 1965. *Serv:* Purchase estates, appraisal. *Hours:* BY APPT ONLY, privately & primarily to the trade. *Loc:* Call for directions.

DEERFIELD

ANTIQUE CENTER OF OLD DEERFIELD
Rte 5, 01341
(413)773-3620   **{GR20}**

A multiple dealer shop featuring formal & country furnishings, accessories, glassware, china, collectibles, linens & reference books. *Est:* 1979. *Hours:* Daily 10-5 CLOSED MON. *CC:* MC/V. Arthur Breuer & James Reddy *Loc:* I-91 Exit 24: Rte 5 for 7 MI.

ELLIE'S ANTIQUE CENTER
Rtes 5 & 10, 01342
(413)774-5692 {GR35}
Antiques & collectibles. *Pr:* $5–1000. *Est:* 1987. *Serv:* Brochure. *Hours:* Tue-Sun 10-5. *Size:* Large. *CC:* MC/V. *Assoc:* PVADA. *Park:* On site. *Loc:* 1 1/4 MI S of Historic Deerfield.

DEERFIELD (SOUTH)

DOUGLAS AUCTIONEERS
Rte 5, 01373
(413)665-2877 4 8
Western New England's largest auction gallery, two auctions a week year round. 10% buyer's premium. *Est:* 1968. *Serv:* Appraisal, brochure, consultation, purchase estates. *Hours:* Mon-Fri 8-4:30 Sat 9-12. *Assoc:* CAI NAA. Douglas P Bilodeau *Park:* On site. *Loc:* I-91 Exit 24: 2 MI N.

INTERNATIONAL AUCTION SCHOOL
Rte 5, 01373
(413)665-2877 8
New England's only auction school. Licensed by the Commonwealth of Massachusetts, Department of Education. *Est:* 1978. *Serv:* Auction, brochure. *Hours:* Mon-Fri 8-4:30 Sat 9-12. *Size:* Huge. Douglas P Bilodeau *Park:* On site. *Loc:* I-91 Exit 24: 2 MI N.

DRACUT

THE ANTIQUARIAN SCIENTIST
Box 367, 01826
(508)957-5267 13
Antiquarian books & instruments, history of science, medicine, natural history, science, technology & antique scientific instruments. *Serv:* Appraisal, catalog. *Hours:* BY APPT. *Assoc:* MARIAB. Raymond Giordano

DUXBURY

DUXBURY GALLERIES ANTIQUES & ART
590 Washington St, 02331
(617)534-5529 28 37 63
Furniture, primitives, china, stoneware, in a charming shop on the road into town. *Hours:* By chance/appt. *Size:* Small. *CC:* MC/V. Jack Corn *Park:* Nearby.

FOLK ART ANTIQUES
449 Washington St, 02331
(617)934-7132 44 63 77
A very pretty little shop with china, silver, furniture, paintings, decorative accessories, Export porcelain & painted furniture. *Est:* 1980. *Hours:* Mon-Sat 11-5. *CC:* MC/V. Lee Adams *Park:* Nearby. *Loc:* From Rte 3A take Rte 14 E toward water; at flag pole turn R, 1 MI on L.

SNUG HARBOR ANTIQUES
449 Washington St, 02331
(617)934-9049 {GR9}
Located in Duxbury's historic waterfront district & featuring early iron, toys, jewelry & silver, oak & pine furniture, books & paper, paintings & prints, & intriguing collectibles & primitives. *Pr:* $5–3000. *Est:* 89. *Serv:* Appraisal. *Hours:* Year round Tue-Sat 11-5, Sun 12-5. *Size:* large. *CC:* MC/V. *Assoc:* SSADA. Bob Dente *Park:* In front. *Loc:* From Int of Rtes 3A & 14, go E on St George St to R on Washington St.

WICKHAM BOOKS
Box 203 Snug Harbor, 02331
(617)934-6955   **13**
Antiquarian books: Children's, nautical, Massachusetts history & general stock. *Serv:* Search service. *Hours:* Tue-Sat 10-5. *Assoc:* MARIAB. Miriam & Al Wickham

EAST ARLINGTON

HENRY DEEKS
PO Box 1500, 02174
(617)488-1862   **13 52**
Civil War, vintage photographs, postcards, Americana & objects of the period. *Hours:* BY APPT ONLY. *Assoc:* MARIAB.

EAST BRIDGEWATER

ANTIQUES AT FORGE POND
35 N Bedford St Rte 18, 02333
(508)378-3057   **{GR5}**
Multi-dealer shop featuring glass, china, dolls, furniture & post cards. *Est:* 1974. *Serv:* Brochure, purchase estates. *Hours:* Daily 11-5. *Size:* Medium. *Assoc:* HAAD SSADA. Marie A Davis *Park:* In front. *Loc:* On Rte 18.

EAST LONGMEADOW

THE LAYNE GALLERIES
51 Prospect St, 01028
(413)525-1200   **47 66**
Jewelry, prints, paintings, bronzes, general antiques & collectibles. *Hours:* Tue-Fri 10:30-5 else by chance/appt.

CC: MC/V. *Assoc:* PVADA. Evangeline/Mark Layne *Park:* On street. *Loc:* From ctr of town, just a few hundred feet on Prospect St.

EASTHAMPTON

GLASKOWSKY & COMPANY
180 Main St, 01027
(413)527-2410   **1 16 83**
Carrying American 18th & 19th C furniture, andirons, fenders, paintings, prints, maps, clocks, toys, mechanical banks, bronzes, lamps, art pottery, china, glass, silver, pewter, copper, brass, wrought iron, quilts, coverlets, Baccarat paperweights. *Est:* 1947. *Serv:* Appraisal. *Hours:* By chance/appt. *Park:* In front. *Loc:* On Rte 10 4 MI S of Northampton.

SCHOEN & SON BOOKSELLERS
1 Cottage St, 01027
(413)527-4780   **13**
Specializing in used & antiquarian scholarly books, Judaica, psychoanalysis, American imprints, German books & social sciences; buy & sell significant collections & libraries. *Est:* 1983. *Serv:* Appraisal, catalog, purchase estates, search services. *Hours:* By chance/appt. *Assoc:* MARIAB. Kenneth Schoen *Park:* In front. *Loc:* 1/2 hour N of Springfield, 10 min from Northampton & five colleges.

ELMWOOD

DOING ANTIQUES AT ELMWOOD
734 Bedford St, 02337
(508)378-2063   **{GR7}**
Large selection of Royal Doulton including figurines, character jugs, series

ware, flambe. Also Royal Bayreuth, Orientalia, jewelry, paintings, prints, pottery & porcelain, displayed in a 19th C general store with the oldest working post office in NE. *Pr:* $25–700. *Est:* 1985. *Serv:* Appraisal, brochure, purchase estates. *Hours:* Tue-Fri 10:30-4 Sat,Sun 10-5. *Size:* Large. Paul Dewing *Park:* On site. *Loc:* Rte 24N or S to Rte 106E, Int of Rtes 18 & 106 to East Bridgewater.

ESSEX

AMERICANA ANTIQUES
48 Main St, 01929
(508)768-6006   **40 42 50**

Country pine & walnut with Victorian oak furniture & brass lighting a specialty. *Pr:* $25–2500. *Est:* 1969. *Hours:* Daily 10-5. *CC:* AX/MC/V. *Assoc:* NSADA. Kenneth Monroe *Park:* On site. *Loc:* Rte 128N Exit 15: to Essex.

ANNEX ANTIQUES
69 Main St, 01929
(508)768-7704   **{GR3}**

A diversified line of antiques featuring country furniture complemented by first & second period antiques & accessories. *Est:* 1958. *Serv:* Purchase estates. *Hours:* Mon-Sat 10-5 Sun 11-5. *Size:* Large. *CC:* MC/V. Barbara Dyer-Reymond *Park:* On site. *Loc:* On Causeway overlooking Essex River.

AS TIME GOES BY ANTIQUES
63 Main St, 01929
(508)768-7479   **36**

Furniture: particularly dining room tables. *Hours:* Daily 11-5 CLOSED WED. *CC:* MC/V. *Park:* On street. *Loc:* Downtown Essex.

BLACKWOOD MARCH
3 Southern Ave, 01929
(508)768-6943   **8**

Auctions of fine arts & antiques. 10% buyer's premium. *Serv:* Auction & appraisal. *Hours:* Call for appt or schedule. Michael March *Loc:* At Burnham's Corner in South Essex.

BRICK HOUSE ANTIQUES
166 Main St Rte 133, 01929
(508)768-6617   **36 59 63**

Antique furniture, textiles paintings, jewelry, china & collectibles displayed in a 200-year-old brick house. *Hours:* Wed-Sun 10:30-4:30. Cathie Beattie *Park:* In front. *Loc:* At Burnham's Corner in South Essex.

P A BURKE ANTIQUES INC
140 Main St, 01929
(508)745-9478   **38 39 53**

One of two large shops carrying 18th & 19th C English & Continental furniture, Chinese export porcelain & accessories. *Pr:* $500–25,000. *Hours:* Year round by chance/appt. Paul A Burke Jr *Park:* On site.

CHEBACCO ANTIQUES
38 Main St Rte 133, 01929
(508)768-7371   **{GR10}**

Featuring American pine & country furniture & related accessories, including quilts, textiles, pottery, porcelain & stoneware. *Pr:* $25–500. *Est:* 1981. *Hours:* Daily 10:30-4:30. *Size:* Medium. *CC:* AX/MC/V. *Assoc:* SADA. Jane Adams *Park:* In front. *Loc:* Rte 128N Exit 15 (School St): turn L toward Essex, At Int Rte 133, go L, 1 MI on R.

CHRISTIAN MOLLY ANTIQUES
Rte 133, 01929
(508)768-6079   **44 47 77**

American & European antiques, furniture, porcelain, glass, silver & jewelry.

Hours: Mon-Sat 10-5 Sun 12-5. **Assoc:** NSADA. **Park:** In front. **Loc:** Rte 128 Exit 15: about 1 1/2 MI.

COMENOS FINE ARTS & ANTIQUES
140 Main St Lower Level, 01929
(508)768-3325   **38 73 77**

Specializing in fine art, with period furniture & decorative accessories including paintings, sculpture, silver, porcelain & more. **Est:** 1990. **Hours:** Mon-Sat 11-5, Sun 3-6. **CC:** MCV. Lori Watston **Park:** In front. **Loc:** Just N of Burnham's corner on Rte 133.

COUNTRY CORNER ANTIQUES
57R John Wise Ave, 01929
(508)768-7702   **27**

Country & cottage furniture, accessories & collectibles. **Hours:** Tue-Sat 10-5. Paul Schroeter **Park:** On site. **Loc:** In the lower level of the Friendship Antiques barn on Rte 133.

R C COVIELLO ANTIQUES
155 Main St, 01929
(508)768-7365

Featuring 18th, 19th & 20th C furniture & decorative accessories. **Est:** 1987. **Hours:** Daily 10-5. **CC:** AX/MC/V. Robert C Coviello **Park:** On street. **Loc:** Rte 128 N from Boston, Exit 15 toward Essex, located on Rte 133 just N of Burnham's Corner.

JOHN CUSHING ANTIQUE RESTORATION
113 Martin St, 01929
(508)768-7356   **68 71**

Antique furniture restoration: repairs, hand stripping, veneer work, hand-rubbed oil finishes, varnishes & shellac finishes. **Serv:** Consultation, custom woodwork, repairs, restoration. **Hours:** APPT ESSENTIAL. **Assoc:** NSADA.

Park: In front. **Loc:** Rte 22 from ctr of Essex: 1/2 MI from Jct of Rtes 22W & 133 on R side of road, sign in front.

EMMONS & MARTIN ANTIQUES
165 Eastern Ave Rte 133, 01929
(508)768-3292   **{GR2}**

Furniture, mirrors, paintings, porcelain, decorative accessories, rugs. **Est:** 1990. **Hours:** Daily 11-5. **Size:** Medium. Cheryl B Emmons **Park:** On site. **Loc:** Rte 128 N Exit 14: 2 1/2 MI on L Across from So Essex Antiques.

FRIENDSHIP ANTIQUES
John Wise Ave Rte 133, 01929
(508)768-7334   **21 36**

A discriminatingly chosen collection of period decorative furniture, including paintings, rugs, silver, china, glass & a 3000-volume library. **Pr:** $50–50,000. **Est:** 1968. **Serv:** Appraisal: estate & insurance; auction. **Hours:** Tue-Sat afternoons (appt suggested). **CC:** MC/V. William S Friend **Park:** On site. **Loc:** 1 MI N of Int of Rtes 133 & 22.

HOWARD'S FLYING DRAGON ANTIQUES
136 Main St Rte 133, 01929
(508)768-7282   **44 45**

A general line of antiques, handcrafts & statuary. **Est:** 1972. **Hours:** Daily 10:30-6. **CC:** AX/MC/V. Laura Howard **Park:** Nearby. **Loc:** Rte 128N Exit 15: 4 MI in the ctr of town.

L A LANDRY ANTIQUES
164 Main St, 01929
(508)768-6233   **4 8 58**

Buying, selling, appraising & auctioning fine antiques on the North Shore of Boston for over fifty years. **Pr:** $25–150000. **Est:** 1938. **Serv:** Appraisal, auction, conservation, consultation, interior design, repairs. **Hours:** By chance/appt suggested. **Assoc:** AAA AR. Robert E Landry

Park: Nearby lot. *Loc:* Rte 128N to Rte 133W, on Rte 133 on Burnham's Corner in South Essex.

MAIN STREET ANTIQUES
44 Main St, 01929
(508)768-7039   {GR5}

Four floors of fine quality 18th, 19th & 20th C antiques & collectibles attractively displayed in a restored, Victorianized 18th C New England home. *Pr:* $1–3000. *Est:* 1983. *Serv:* Appraisal, consultation, interior design, purchase estates, repairs. *Hours:* Daily 10-5. *Size:* Large. *CC:* AX/MC/V. Robert C Coviello *Park:* On site. *Loc:* Rte 128N Exit 15: toward Essex, 3 MI, turn L onto Main St, 1/4 MI up on R.

ELLEN NEILY ANTIQUES
157 Main St, 01929
(508)631-8224   {GR2}

American formal & country painted furniture, folk art, silver, export porcelain & art. *Est:* 1985. *Hours:* Mon-Sat 10-5 Sun 12-5. *CC:* V/MC. *Assoc:* NHADA NEAA. *Park:* In front. *Loc:* Near Burnham's Corner in S Essex.

NORTH HILL ANTIQUES
155 Main St, 01929
(508)768-7365   37 46 59

Located on the 1st floor of a restored 19th C house, featuring a collection of quality 18th & 19th C European & American furniture & accessories. *Pr:* $100–5000. *Est:* 1988. *Serv:* Appraisal, consultation, interior design, purchase estates, repairs. *Hours:* Daily 10-5. *Size:* Medium. *CC:* MC/V. Sylvia G Kaplan *Park:* In front. *Loc:* Rte 128N Exit 15: toward Essex, 3 MI, turn L onto Main St, 200 yds up on L.

RIDER & CLARKE ANTIQUES
144 Main St Rte 133, 01929
(508)768-7441   21 39 59

Fine period, formal & decorative furniture, paintings, Oriental rugs & works of art from the 18th & 19th C. *Pr:* $500–50000. *Serv:* Appraisal, conservation, consultation, purchase estates, restoration. *Hours:* Tue-Sat 11-5 Sun 12-6 open Mon Hol. *Size:* Large. Jon Rider *Park:* On site. *Loc:* Rte 128N Exit 14: Rte 133 approx 3 1/2 MI to Essex. 1/4 MI on R after turning onto Main St.

RO-DAN ANTIQUES
67 Main St, 01929
(508)768-3322   37 38 63

Oriental porcelain, 18th & 19th C American & European furniture. *Hours:* Mon 9-5 Fri-Sat 10-5 Sun 12-5 CLOSED TUE-THU. *Loc:* Rte 128 N Exit 15 (toward Essex): 3 MI, turn L on Main St 1/4 MI up on R.

STEPHEN SCORE ANTIQUES
159 Main St, 01929
(508)768-6252   34 41 65

American primitive paintings, painted furniture, folk art & decorative accessories. *Hours:* Weekends 12-5 & BY APPT. *Park:* Nearby. *Loc:* At Burnham's Corner in Essex.

THE SCRAPBOOK
34 Main St Rte 133, 01929
(508)768-7404   51 66

Antique prints, maps & botanicals - from the 15th through 19th C including architectural, natural history & sporting. *Est:* 1970. *Serv:* Custom framing, French mats. *Hours:* Year round 10-5. *Assoc:* NSADA. Vincent Caravella *Park:* On street. *Loc:* Behind the White Elephant Shop.

SOUTH ESSEX ANTIQUES
166 Eastern Ave, 01929
(508)768-6373   **{GR6}**
A variety of decorative & unusual items
from all periods & cultures, jewelry, eth-
nography, furniture & decorative objects
& paintings. *Pr:* $25–7000. *Est:* 1982.
Serv: Appraisal, purchase estates. *Hours:*
Mon-Sun 10-5. *Size:* Medium. William
Taylor *Park:* On site. *Loc:* Rte 128N Exit
14: L 2 1/2 MI to Essex, on R, low white
building surrounded by parking lot.

SUSAN STELLA ANTIQUES
166 Main St, 01929
(508)768-6617   **{GR4}**
18th & 19th C furniture, paintings,
quilts, antique garden furniture, porcelains including Export, brass, period
accessories & marine antiques. *Pr:* $25–
5000. *Est:* 1978. *Serv:* Appraisal. *Hours:*
Daily 10:30-5. *Size:* Medium. *CC:*
MC/V. *Assoc:* NEAA. Susan Stella *Park:*
On site. *Loc:* Rte 128N Exit 15: toward
Essex, 3 MI, across from SS entering
Essex, white brick building.

TRADEWINDS ANTIQUES
63 Main St, 01929
(508)768-3327   **36 56 59**
Specialists in walking sticks, also a fine
selection of Federal furniture, nauticals,
paintings & porcelains located in a 19th
C building overlooking the Essex river.
Pr: $25–3000. *Est:* 1980. *Hours:* Jun 15-
Oct 15 Tue-Sun 11-5; mid Oct-mid Jun
Wed-Sun 11-4. *CC:* MC/V. N Taron
Park: In front, nearby lot. *Loc:* Rte 128
N Manchester School St Exit.

A P H WALLER & SONS ANTIQUES
140 Main St Rte 133, 01929
(508)768-6269   **17 38 60**
A superior collection of period Oriental
pieces, bronzes, paintings, ceramics &
Continental furniture in a new
showroom. *Est:* 1975. *Hours:* Wed Fri-

Sat 10:30-5 Sun by chance. *Size:*
Medium. Allen P Waller *Park:* In front.
Loc: Just N of Burnham's corner on the
R.

THE WHITE ELEPHANT SHOP
32 Main St, 01929
(508)768-6901   **25 27 63**
One of New England's oldest consignment shops featuring collectibles, china,
books & furniture. *Pr:* $1–1500. *Est:*
1953. *Serv:* Appraisal, auction, brochure,
conservation, custom woodworking,
repairs. *Hours:* Mon-Sat 10-5, Sun 12-5.
Size: Large. Thomas Ellis *Park:* On
street. *Loc:* Rte 128 Exit 14: to Essex;
From NH: Rte 95 to Rte 133 to Essex.

EVERETT

THE TINNING COMPANY
69 Norman Street, 02149
(617)389-3400   **15 58 71**
Retinning of copper cookware. Cost is
diameter of pan + depth X $3.50. *Hours:*
Mon-Fri 9-5. *Loc:* I-93N Exit 30: Rte
16E thru Wellington Cir, thru 2 overpas-
ses, 2 1/2 blocks from Afco Research at
Rotary.

FAIRHAVEN

FANTASY HOUSE ANTIQUES
32 Cedar St, 02719
(508)993-8558   **50 63**
Specializing in Mt Washington, Pairpoint & Gundersen; also carrying
Limoges, silver plate & lamps. *Serv:* Appraisal, purchase estates. *Hours:* BY
APPT ONLY. *Assoc:* SNEADA. Kenneth L Tobergta Sr

EDWARD J LEFKOWICZ INC
43 Fort St, 02719
(508)997-6839 **13 51 56**
Specialize exclusively in rare & antiquarian books, manuscripts, charts & prints relating to ships & the sea, voyages, naval history & science, navigation & shipbuilding, whaling & marine art. *Pr:* $25–10000. *Est:* 1974. *Serv:* Appraisal, catalog. *Hours:* BY APPT ONLY. *CC:* MC/V. *Assoc:* ABAA MARIAB. *Park:* On site. *Loc:* E on Rte 6 from New Bedford, 2nd R after bridge onto Main St, Follow Main St to End, L, 1st R is Fort St.

GENEVIEVE C PELTZ
723 Washington St, 02719
(508)996-0921 **44 36**
Glass, china & furniture. *Hours:* By chance/appt. *Assoc:* SNEADA.

FALL RIVER

COLLECTORS JUNCTION
791 Plymouth Ave, 02721
(508)674-9586 **{GR}**
Four large rooms featuring furniture, clocks, glass, paintings, lamps, old toys & dolls, country store advertising & old jewelry. *Est:* 1986. *Serv:* Appraisal, brochure, purchase estates. *Hours:* Apr-Oct Mon-Sat 10-4. *Size:* Large. *Assoc:* SNEADA. Faith Wong *Park:* On site. *Loc:* I-195 Exit 7: halfway between Providence RI & Cape Cod MA.

DORCAS BOOKS
133 Keeley St, 02723
(508)675-1904 **13**
Antiquarian books: American & English first editions, detective fiction, children's, explorations & voyages, biography & illustrated. *Serv:* Appraisal,

catalog, search service. *Hours:* By chance/appt. *Assoc:* MARIAB. Stanley Kay

LIGHTHOUSE ANTIQUES & PROMOTIONS
PO Box 5065, 02723
(508)679-3572 **44**
Speicalizing in art glass. Estates bought & sold. *Hours:* After 3. *Assoc:* SNEADA. John Domingos

YANKEE EXCHANGE
203 Plymouth Ave Bldg 7, 02722
(508)672-9890 **36**
Specializing in fine used furniture, antiques, & collectibles. *Hours:* Daily 10-9 Sun 12-6. *Loc:* Located at Durfee Union Mill Place.

FITCHBURG

JOHN CLEMENT FINE ART
52 Buttrick Ave, 01420
(508)345-5863 **59 60 66**
Small but carefully chosen selection of decorative & historical prints, drawings & maps of all periods. Occasional offerings of master prints, drawings & paintings from a lifetime collection. *Est:* 1985. *Serv:* Purchase estates & collections. *Hours:* BY APPT TO THE TRADE ONLY. *Loc:* Call for appt & directions.

FLORENCE

LA CHAISE DE FRANCE
30 N Maple St, 01060
(413)584-9645
Furniture restoration, specializing in 18th & 19th C French & Americanupholstery, horsehair

upholstering & fabric walls & ceilings.
Hours: Mon-Fri 9-5, Weekends BY
APPT.

FOXBORO

POND HOUSE WOODWORKING
39 Main St, 02035
(508)543-8633   19 68 71
Conservation of furniture, gilt frames &
wooden artifacts, specializing in French
& American veneered furniture, mar-
quetry & parquetry, gilding & gilding
conservation. Located in a carriage
house attached to an old Victorian house.
Est: 1975. *Serv:* Conservation, custom
woodwork, repairs, restoration, gilding.
Hours: Mon-Fri 9-6, Sat-Sun BY APPT.
Size: Medium. *Assoc:* AIC NTHP
SPNEA. John Philibert *Park:* On site.
Loc: I-95 approx 20 MI N of Providence
RI, take Rte 140 to Foxboro, 7 houses
beyond Foxboro Ctr on R (Rte 140 is
Main St).

FRAMINGHAM

AVERY'S ANTIQUES
74 Franklin St, 01701
(508)875-4576   37 65
Early American furniture & accessories,
beds, primitives & Victorian upholstered
furniture. *Hours:* Mon-Fri 8-5 Sat 8-12.
Assoc: SADA. *Loc:* Next door to the
former Registry of Motor Vehicles.

FRANKLIN STREET ANTIQUES
10 Franklin St, 01701
(508)875-8948   {GR}
Two floors of furniture, primitives,
linens, china, glass, pottery, books, prints
& jewelry. *Serv:* Purchase estates,

moving sale services. *Hours:* Mon-Sat
10-5 or BY APPT. *Size:* Large. *Assoc:*
SADA. Dorothy M Fitch

THE HARDYS' HALL
52 Union Ave, 01701
(508)620-9029   16 63 66
Wallace nutting, Fiestaware & kitchen
iron. *Hours:* Tue-Sat 10-5:30 Sun &
Mon by chance/appt. Peggy Hardy

LEW HORTON'S
450 Waverly St, 01701
(617)237-2735   6 30 78
Specializing in firearms, fishing gear,
decoys, sporting art, books & advertising
materials, military & sporting related
items. *Est:* 1947. *Serv:* Appraisals.
Hours: Mon-Tue 10-5, Wed-Fri 10-8,
Sat 9-5, Sun 12-5. *Loc:* Across from the
old Train Station & Ebenezer's Restaurant.

VINTAGE BOOKS
117 Concord St, 01701
(508)875-7517   13
Used, rare & out of print books in all
categories; 35,000 books in stock. *Serv:*
Search service, special orders, catalog
(Quaker Books). *Hours:* Tue-Sat 10-6
Fri 10-9. *Size:* 35,000 books. *Assoc:*
MARIAB. Nancy & David Haines

FRANKLIN

JOHNSTON ANTIQUES
789 W Central St, 02038
(508)528-0942   24 51 79
Formal furniture & accessories, china,
brass, copper, pottery, jewelry, Orientalia, paintings, prints, maps, early paper,
Shaker, coins, stamps & primitives. *Serv:*
Appraisal. *Hours:* Daily 10-5 & BY

APPT. *Assoc:* SADA. Claire & James Johnston *Loc:* Rte 495W Exit 17: to Rte 140.

GARDNER

IRENE'S BOOK SHOP
49 W Broadway, 01440
(508)632-5574   **13 64**
Collectable & rare books in all categories including Americana, children's books literature, magazines, New Englandiana, poetry, postcards. *Est:* 1967. *Serv:* Appraisal, catalog, search service. *Hours:* Mon-Sun 1-5 & BY APPT. *Assoc:* MARIAB. Irene M Walet *Park:* In front. *Loc:* On Rte 2A, 5 houses down from ctr of S Gardner.

GEORGETOWN

THOMAS A EDISON COLLECTION
51 W Main St, 01834
(508)352-9830   **55**
Wind-up phonographs, disc & cylinder records, piano rolls & music boxes. *Pr:* $100–3800. *Est:* 1978. *Serv:* Repairs, appraisal. *Hours:* Daily 10-5, CLOSED MON,THU. *Size:* Medium. *CC:* MC/V. *Assoc:* AAA. Ralph Woodside *Park:* In front. *Loc:* I-95 to Rte 133, 1 1/2 MI W; in Sedler's Antique Village.

JANE FIELD BOOKS
14 North St, 01833
(508)352-6641   **13**
Antiquarian books: biography, military & general. *Serv:* Search service. *Hours:* BY APPT. *Assoc:* MARIAB. Marcia Jane

PHEASANT HILL ANTIQUES
Nelson St, 01833
(508)352-2287   **36 66 67**
Offering country & formal American furniture, textiles & graphics, particularly those related to the American South. Extensive stock of Harvardiana. *Pr:* $100–10000. *Est:* 1986. *Serv:* Purchase estates. *Hours:* BY APPT ONLY.

SCALA'S ANTIQUES
28 W Main St, 01833
(508)352-8614   **{GR8}**
Three floors of antiques & collectibles including jewelry, country formal, vintage clothing, depression glass & dolls. *Serv:* Insurance & estate appraisal. *Hours:* Tue-Sun 11-5. *Size:* Large.

SEDLER'S ANTIQUE VILLAGE
51 W Main St Rte 97, 01833
(508)352-8282   **{GR30}**
Furniture, quilts, glass, pottery, porcelain & folk art. *Est:* 1977. *Hours:* Daily 10-5 Fri til 9. *CC:* MC/V/DC. *Park:* On site. *Loc:* I-95 Rte 133 Exit: through town 1 1/2 MI in Georgetown.

GLOUCESTER

BANANAS
78 Main St, 01930
(508)283-8806   **47 85**
A large selection of vintage clothing, accessories & costume jewelry ranging from the turn of the century to the 60s. *Pr:* $5–250. *Est:* 1975. *Hours:* Mon-Sat 10-5 Sun 1-5. *Size:* Medium. *CC:* MC/V. Richard A Leonard *Park:* In front. *Loc:* Rte 128N to end, Exit to downtown Gloucester.

BEAUPORT ANTIQUES
45 Main St, 01930
(508)281-4460   **29 36 63**

Furniture, china & decorative accessories. *Hours:* Mon-Sat 10:30-3:30. Lois Derrick *Park:* Nearby. *Loc:* Downtown.

BURKE'S BAZAAR-POET'S ANTIQUES
Rte 133, 01930
(508)283-4538   **59**

Fine paintings. *Hours:* Tue-Sat 10-5. *Size:* Medium. Edward Leaman *Park:* On site. *Loc:* On the border between Gloucester & Essex.

CAPE ANN ANTIQUES/ ORIENTAL RUGS
1083 Washington St Lanes Village, 01930
(508)281-3444   **21 36 59**

Oriental rugs, paintings, jewelry, stained glass & furnishings. *Pr:* $5–5000. *Serv:* Appraisal, purchase estates. *Hours:* By chance/appt. *Size:* Large. *CC:* AX/MC/V. Mark Longval *Park:* On site. *Loc:* Rte 128 to Rte 127N 4 MI N of first rotary.

GLOUCESTER FINE ARTS
PO Box 133, 01930
(508)281-3638   **4**

Fine arts & American antiquities appraiser, artist reps, exhibitors, show producers & publishers, speaker services. *Est:* 1970. *Serv:* Appraisal, auctions, conservation & research services, estate liquidation. *Hours:* BY APPT ONLY. *Assoc:* ISA NAA SPNEA. John MacFarlane

WILLIAM N GREENBAUM
179 Concord St, 01930
(508)283-0112   **51 66**

Art prints - old masters, early English mezzotints, 20th C American, British, European & Japanese woodblocks, fine drawings & watercolors. *Pr:* $50–2000. *Hours:* BY APPT ONLY.

JER-RHO ANTIQUES
352 Main St, 01930
(508)283-5066   **4 44 47**

China, glass, estate jewelry, extensive art glass, furniture, prints & paintings. *Serv:* Buy & sell estates, appraisal. *Hours:* Tue-Sun 10-6. *Size:* Medium. *CC:* AX/MC/V. *Assoc:* NEAA NSADA. Jerry & Rhoda Grushka

MAIN STREET ARTS & ANTIQUES
124 Main St, 01930
(508)281-1531   **{GR10}**

Paintings, jewelry, ephemera, post cards, wicker, textiles, second-hand furniture, china, glass & books. *Est:* 1988. *Serv:* Appraisal, auction, consultation, purchase estates. *Hours:* Mon-Sat 10:30-5 Sun 12:30-5. *Size:* Medium. *Assoc:* ISA NADA. David B Cox *Park:* On street. *Loc:* In the center of business district.

TEN POUND ISLAND BOOK CO
3 Center St, 01930
(508)283-5299   **4 13**

Old & rare books of all kinds, with specialties in maritime, local history & fine & decorative arts. *Pr:* $5–5000. *Est:* 1976. *Serv:* Appraisal, catalog, consultation, purchase estates. *Hours:* Year round Mon-Fri 12-5 Sat 10-5. *Size:* Medium. *CC:* MC/V. *Assoc:* ABAA MARIAB NEAA. Gregory Gibson *Loc:* Corner of Center & Main St in ctr Gloucester.

GRAFTON

GREAT BARRINGTON

GRAFTON FLEA MARKET INC
Rte 140 Grafton-Upton Town Line, 01519
(508)839-2217   **{FLEA}**
Indoor/outdoor flea market with antiques, collectibles, baseball cards, stamps & coins & much more. Adults 50 cents, children free. *Est:* 1970. *Serv:* Catered, space rental $20. *Hours:* Mar-Dec Sun-Mon & Holidays 9-5. *Size:* 200 spaces. *Park:* Free parking. *Loc:* I-90 to 495 S, then Exit 21B to Rte 140.

PEGGY PLACE ANTIQUES
119 George Hill Rd, 01519
(508)839-2703   **27 65**
Country pieces, primitives, cubbies & cupboards, toys & lighting. *Hours:* Thu-Sun 11-5 Mon-Wed By Chance. *Assoc:* SADA. Peggy Marshall *Loc:* Off Rte 140 1 MI from Common.

REVIVAL PROMOTIONS INC
PO Box 388, 01509
(508)839-9735
May antiques weekend at Stafford Motor Speedway with over 700 dealers.Admission $3. *Est:* 1990. *Serv:* Delivery service available. *Hours:* Sat-Sun 9-5, early admission Sat 7 a.m., $20. *CC:* MC/V ($100+). Bob & Abby McInnis *Park:* Acres of free park on gravel. *Loc:* I-90 Exit 8: S on Rte 32. I-84 E to Exit 70 or I-91 to Rte 140 E. From Brimfield Rte 19 S.

MADISON
177 Main St, 01230
(413)528-3017   **5 55**
Architectural elements & fragments, signs, musical instruments, ceramic door knobs, brass plates & fittings. *Est:* 1989. *Hours:* Thu-Mon 10:30-5:30. Reginald Madison. *Loc:* Across the street from The Country Dining Room.

BY SHAKER HANDS
14 Lake Ave, 01230
(413)528-1450   **27 37 76**
Specializing in Shaker & American furniture & accessories. *Est:* 1987. *Serv:* Appraisal, consultation. *Hours:* BY APPT. Jim Johnson *Park:* On site. *Loc:* 5 blocks W of Int of Rte 7 & Taconic Ave in Great Barrington.

BYGONE DAYS
969 Main St Rte 7S, 01230
(413)528-1870   **42**
A large collection of used, antique & reproduction country pine furniture & round oak. *Pr:* $5–1000. *Est:* 1981. *Serv:* Repairs. *Hours:* Mon-Sun 10:30-5. *CC:* MC/V. Ted Portnoff *Park:* On site. *Loc:* S of the fairgrounds.

CORASHIRE ANTIQUES
Rtes 7 & 23 at Belcher Sq, 01230
(413)528-0014   **27 29 37**
American country furniture & accessories in the red barn. *Hours:* Daily 9-5. *Assoc:* BCADA. Nancy Dinan *Park:* Nearby.

ANDREW'S AXIOMS

Ugly antiques acquire beauty as soon as their value rises.

Reprinted with permission from *guide to the Antique Shops of Britain 1989.*
copyright The Antique Collectors Club, Great Britain

COUNTRY DINING ROOM
ANTIQUES
178 Main St, 01230
(413)528-5050   **44 63 77**

Specializing in antiques for the dining room: silver, linens, china, pottery, crystal, furniture, rugs & paintings for a completely coordinated dining room. *Est:* 1989. *Hours:* Sum 10-6 daily, Win Thu-Mon 11-5:30 or by chance. *CC:* MC/V. *Assoc:* BCADA. Sheila Chefetz *Park:* On street. *Loc:* At the N end of town.

THE EMPORIUM ANTIQUE
CENTER
319 Main St, 01230
(413)528-2731   **{GR20}**

Glassware, rare books, prints, silver, primitives, country furniture, Art Deco, advertising & jewelry. *Hours:* Daily 10-5 Sun 12-4 CLOSED TUE. Terry Whitcomb *Park:* Nearby. *Loc:* In the ctr of town.

JONESES ANTIQUES
740 S Main St, 01230
(413)528-0156   **36 45 81**

Huge collection of everything from garden statuary to china. *Hours:* Daily 8:30-5. *Park:* On site. *Loc:* Across from Barrington Fair.

KAHN'S ANTIQUE & ESTATE
JEWELRY
38 Railroad St, 01230
(413)528-9550   **47 58 77**

Antique & estate jewelry of all periods & silver smalls. *Pr:* $25–10000. *Est:* 1974. *Serv:* Appraisal, purchase estates, repairs, custom work. *Hours:* Mon-Sat 10-5, Sun by chance/appt. *CC:* AX/DC/MC/V. *Assoc:* BCADA. Steven Kahn *Park:* Nearby. *Loc:* 1 block W of Rte 7.

PAUL & SUSAN KLEINWALD INC
578 S Main St, 01230
(413)528-4252   **29 37 53**

18th & 19th C American, English & Continental furniture & decorative accessories of excellent quality. *Serv:* Insurance & estate appraisals. *Hours:* Anytime by chance/appt. *Assoc:* BCADA. *Park:* In front. *Loc:* On Rte 7.

J & J LUBRANO
39 Hollenbeck Ave, 01230
(413)528-4164 FAX
(413)528-5799   **9 13 66**

Musical autographs & manuscripts, early printed music & rare books on music & dance. *Pr:* $100–10000. *Est:* 1977. *Serv:* Appraisal, catalog, purchase library estates. *Hours:* BY APPT ONLY. *Assoc:* ABAA MARIAB. John Lubrano *Loc:* Call for directions.

MEMORIES
306 Main St, 01230
(413)528-6380   **65**

Large, eclectic selection of antiques, primitives, collectibles, unusual accessories, Art Deco, books, maps, prints, lighting fixtures, phonographs, radios, old copper, old toys, sleds & bicycles, stoves & scales & much more. *Pr:* $25–15000. *Est:* 1990. *Serv:* Purchase estates. *Hours:* Daily 10-5:30, CLOSED TUE. *Size:* Large. *CC:* AX/MC/V. Mario & Karen Tsakis *Park:* In front, nearby lot. *Loc:* Center of Great Barrington on Main St (Rte 7) at railroad station 4 MI N of Sheffield & 5 MI S of Stockbridge.

GEORGE R MINKOFF INC
RFD 3 Box 147, 01230
(413)528-4575   **9 13 66**

Antiquarian books: 19th & 20th C English & American literature, signed & presentation copies, illustrated books, manuscripts, letters & original drawings. *Est:* 1967. *Serv:* Appraisal, catalog $5, purchase estates. *Hours:* Year round Mon-Fri 9-5 weekends BY APPT. *Size:* Large. *CC:* MC/V. *Assoc:* ABAA. *Park:* On site.

MULLIN-JONES ANTIQUITIES
525 S Main St Rte 7, 01230
(413)528-4871   **27 35 63**
Importers of 18th & 19th C French country, formal & garden antiques; Provence is the specialty; furniture, colorful pottery, iron urns, gilded mirrors & sconces, chandeliers & tiles. *Pr:* $40–12000. *Est:* 1986. *Serv:* French decorator fabrics & window lace; ship anywhere. *Hours:* Daily 10-5 Tue BY APPT. *Size:* Medium. *Assoc:* BCADA. Patrice Mullin *Park:* On site. *Loc:* Rte 7 (S Main St) between fairgrounds & Int of Rtes 7, 41 & 23, 1/2 MI S of downtown business district.

RED HORSE ANTIQUES
Rtes 7 & 23, 01230
(413)528-2637   **27 36**
Two floors of furniture & accessories of all periods. *Est:* 1966. *Hours:* Daily 10-5 CLOSED TUE. April Ehrenman *Park:* On site.

SNYDER'S STORE
945 S Main St, 01230
(413)528-1441   **27 65 67**
Country, oak & rustic furniture, tramp art, primitives, quilts, linen, jewelry, architectural details, mantels & garden pieces. *Hours:* Apr-Dec 20 daily 12-5, Jan-Mar weekends & BY APPT. *Assoc:* BCADA. Shirley Snyder *Park:* Nearby. *Loc:* On Rte 7.

GREENFIELD

THE SELECTIVE READER
658 Bernardston Rd, 01301
(413)774-5594   **13**
Antiquarian books: automobilia, aeronautica & cookery. *Serv:* Catalog, search service. *Hours:* Call ahead advised. *Assoc:* MARIAB. Earl/Gwendolyn Kelton

GROTON

BOSTON ROAD ANTIQUES
498 Boston Rd Rte 119, 01450
(508)448-9433   **{GR4}**
American country furniture & decorative accessories, featuring primitives, folk art & Shaker. *Hours:* Daily 9-5. Richard Walker *Loc:* 495 Exit 31: approx 4 1/2 MI W.

PAM BOYNTON
82 Pleasant St Rtes 111 & 225, 01450
(508)448-5031   **29 36**
Specializing in 18th & 19th C furniture & accessories. *Est:* 1948. *Hours:* Daily by chance/appt. *Assoc:* NHADA. *Park:* On site. *Loc:* 2 blocks off Main St.

GROTON ANTIQUES
134 Main St Rte 119, 01450
(508)448-3330   **{MDS40}**
Specializing in fine Americana & country including 17th & 18th C furniture, metalwork, cabinet pieces, rugs, needlework, paintings, pine & porcelain. *Est:* 1977. *Serv:* Restoration shop on the premises. *Hours:* Daily 10-5. *Park:* On site. *Loc:* On Rte 119, behind Jos Kilbridge Antiques.

IMAGINE
Main St, 01450
(508)448-5044   **36 83**
Country & formal American furniture, jewelry, paintings, prints, porcelain, Arts & Crafts. *Est:* 1981. *Serv:* Framing. *Hours:* Mon-Sat 10-5. Marilyn Mc Grath *Park:* In front. *Loc:* On Rte 119 in Groton center.

JOSEPH KILBRIDGE ANTIQUES
134 Main St Rte 119, 01450
(508)448-3330   **1 39 60**
18th & 19th C formal & country furniture & fine arts at one of the largest dealers in Massachusetts. *Pr:* $100–20000. *Est:* 1970. *Serv:* Purchase estates, restoration. *Hours:* Open 7 Days 10-5. *Size:* Large. *Assoc:* NADA. Joseph Kilbridge *Park:* On site. *Loc:* From 495 take Rte 119 W 6 MI to (Groton Center) next to the Groton Inn.

MATTOZZI & BURKE ANTIQUES
228 Main St Rte 119, 01450
(508)448-3038   **29 36**
In a renovated colonial, 18th & 19th C period furniture & accessories. *Hours:* By chance/appt, call ahead is advised. *Assoc:* NHADA SADA. James Mattozzi *Park:* In front. *Loc:* On Rte 119 in center of town.

THE MEADOW GALLERY
134 Main St Rte 119, 01450
(508)448-3330   **27 29 37**
Formal & country furniture and decorative accessories attractively displayed. *Est:* 1986. *Hours:* Daily 10-5. *Size:* Medium. *Park:* On site. *Loc:* Behind Jos Kilbridge & Groton Antiques.

OLD FASHIONED MILK PAINT COMPANY
436 Main St, 01450
(508)448-6336   **46 70 74**
The only authentic early paint available.

Manufacturer & distributor of genuine milk paint in powder form. For restoration or reproduction of furniture, walls & woodwork. Eight authentic colors. Wholesale & retail. *Est:* 1974. *Serv:* Brochure (3 stamps), restoration. *Hours:* Year round Mon-Sat 9-5. Charles E Thibeau *Park:* On site. *Loc:* Rte 495 Exit 31W: 8 MI on Rte 119, 1 MI W of Groton on Rte 119 take driveway on R just before railroad bridge.

HADLEY

HADLEY ANTIQUES CENTER
Rte 9, 01035
(413)586-4093   **{GR70}**
70 dealers offering an ever-changing stock of antiques & collectibles. *Est:* 1982. *Hours:* Daily 10-5 CLOSED WED. *Size:* Large. *CC:* MC/V. Sue Allen *Park:* On site. *Loc:* I-91 N Exit 19 or I-91 S Exit 20: follow Rte 9 3 MI E, big, gray bldg on R.

HOME FARM ANTIQUES
Rte 9, 01035
(413)584-8810   **50 71**
Specializing in antique furniture restoration; antique furniture & accessories. *Pr:* $10–1000. *Est:* 1976. *Serv:* Custom woodwork, repairs, proper & careful restoration. *Hours:* By chance/appt CLOSED SUN MON. *Assoc:* PVADA. Bob Berra *Park:* On site. *Loc:* On Rte 9, 3 MI E of Jct with I-95 (Exit 19).

KEN LOPEZ BOOKSELLER
51 Huntington Rd, 01035
(413)584-4827   **13**
Antiquarian books: detective fiction, first editions, modern literature, poetry, science fiction & fantasy & Vietnam War literature, American Indian literature.

Serv: Appraisal, catalog, search service.
Hours: BY APPT ONLY. **Assoc:** ABAA
MARIAB.

MOUNTAIN CREST ANTIQUES
45 Lawrence Plain Rd Rte 47S, 01035
(413)586-0352   **27 34 87**
18th & 19th C country furniture & accessories in paint, also folk art & a good
selection of old weathervanes. **Pr:** $75–
5000. **Est:** 1980. **Hours:** By chance/appt.
Size: Medium. Marion & Ray Szala
Park: In front. **Loc:** MA Tnpk Exit 4, Jct
91N to Exit 19 (Hadley), 1 MI on Rte 9,
then 2 MI on Rte 47 S.

OLDE HADLEY FLEA MARKET
Lawrence Plain Rd Rte 47 S, 01035
(413)586-0352   **{FLEA}**
Flea market with antiques, collectibles &
other flea market merchandise. Free admission. **Est:** 1980. **Serv:** Catered, rental
space is $15 reservations not required.
Hours: Sun 8-5, dealer shopping at 6:00
am. **Size:** 100 spaces. **Park:** Free parking.
Loc: I-91N Exit 19: 2 MI from Hadley
Ctr on Rte 47 S.

HALIFAX

WILLEM & INGER LEMMENS
ANTIQUES
394 Plymouth St Rte 106, 02338
(617)293-2292   **1 4 37**
Period American furniture & appropriate accessories from the 17th, 18th
& early 19th C. All items guaranteed as
represented. **Pr:** $25–20000. **Est:** 1970.
Serv: Appraisal, auction, purchase estates. **Hours:** By chance/appt, call if coming from a distance. **Size:** Medium.
Assoc: ADA NEAA SADA. **Park:** On
site. **Loc:** 1/2 MI W of the Int of Rtes 106
& 58 on Rte 106 in Halifax.

HAMILTON

ELMCRESS BOOKS
161 Bay Rd Rte 1A, 01982
(508)468-3261   **13 33 64**
Antiquarian books: books about books,
ephemera, natural history, nautical,
prints, royalty & Third World. **Serv:** Appraisal, catalog, search service. **Hours:**
Tue-Sat 12-5. **Assoc:** MARIAB NEAA.
Britta Cressy

HANOVER

JOAN F CADDIGAN
778 Washington St, 02339
(617)826-8648   **8**
Antiques & collectibles auctions, estate
liquidations. No buyer's premium. **Serv:**
Auction, appraisal mailing list. **Hours:**
By chance/appt. **CC:** MC/V. **Assoc:**
MSAA NAA CAI.

HANOVER ANTIQUES CENTRE
1130 Washington St Rte 53, 02339
(617)826-0059   **32 65 67**
Specializing in jewelry, furniture, dolls &
toys, china & porcelain, primitives, sterling silver & wicker. **Est:** 1990. **Serv:**
Appraisal, brochure, consultation, purchase estates. **Hours:** Mon-Sat 10:30-
4:30 Sun 12-4. **Size:** Medium. **CC:**
MC/V. Pat Farrington **Park:** On site.
Loc: 1 MI S of Hanover Mall on Rte 53.

HOLLY LANE GALLERIES
778 Washington St, 02339
(617)826-8648
A collection of furniture, accessories,
collectibles & bric a brac. **Serv:** Auction,

appraisal, estate liquidation. *Hours:* Tue-Sat 10-5 or by chance. *CC:* MC/V. *Assoc:* SSADA. Joan Caddigan *Park:* In front.

LLOYD ANTIQUES
140 Broadway at Four Corners, 02339
(617)826-9232   **5 27 59**
Country furniture, architectural pieces, trunks, metalwork & paintings. *Est:* 1980. *Serv:* Estate liquidation. *Hours:* By chance/appt. *Assoc:* SSADA. Paul Lloyd *Park:* In front. *Loc:* At the int of Broadway & Washington Sts.

RESTORATION RESOURCES
200 Webster St, 02339
(617)878-3794   **5 46 71**
Authentic & reproduction items for the home including architectural pieces, hardware, unusual mantels, moldings, doors, stained glass, classic pedestal sinks, claw foot tubs, bath fixtures & accessories, woodwork & ornamental plaster. *Pr:* $10–12000. *Est:* 1987. *Serv:* Appraisal, repairs, restoration. *Hours:* Daily 10-6, Sat 10-5, CLOSED SUN. *Size:* Large. *CC:* MC/V. *Park:* In front. *Loc:* Rte 3S, Exit 13, L off exit, L at lights, L under overpass into parking lot.

TIMES PAST
195 Washington St, 02339
(617)826-3736   **{GR30}**
Located in the historic Hanover Academy building. Antiques, collectibles, china, glass, pottery, small furniture, jewelry, antiquarian books, primitives, country furniture, pewter, linen, quilts, tools, oak furniture & depression glass. *Hours:* Daily 11-5. *Park:* Nearby. *Loc:* At Hanover Four Corners just off Rtes 53 & 139.

HARVARD

CORNUCOPIA INC
325 Ayer Rd, 01451
(508)772-0023   **43**
Handcrafted Windsors & dining furniture in pine, cherry & curly maple. *Est:* 1972. *Serv:* 24-page catalog ($2), reproductions to order, replication. *Hours:* Appt suggested. *CC:* MC/V. Bill Cory *Park:* On site. *Loc:* Call for directions.

THE HARVARD ANTIQUE SHOP
Harvard Common, 01451
(508)456-9011   **21 27 76**
Country, Shaker, a large selection of Oriental rugs & original paint. *Hours:* Wed 10-4 else by chance/appt. *Assoc:* AAA. Pat Hatch *Park:* On site. *Loc:* Rte 2 or I-495 to Rte 110, 2 MI to ctr of town.

PAULA T MC COLGAN INC
170 Old Littleton Rd, 01451
(508)456-3786   **41**
Specializing in quality country furniture, artifacts & decorative accessories & garden accents. *Serv:* Consultant for period interiors. *Hours:* Weds 10-4 or by appt. *Assoc:* NHADA VADA. *Loc:* 1 1/2 MI from Rte 495.

HAVERHILL

CONSTANCE MORELLE BOOKS
1282 Broadway, 01832
(508)374-7256   **13 33**
Antiquarian books: American literature, biography, children's books, ephemera, Massachusetts history, natural history, cookery, embroidery, needlework, litera-

ture & sheet music. *Serv:* Catalog, search service. *Hours:* Call ahead. *Assoc:* MARIAB.

HAYDENVILLE

BRASSWORKS ANTIQUES CENTER
132 Main St, 01039
(413)268-7985   {GR}
A varied collection of glassware, primitives & Victorian furniture. *Hours:* Mon-Sat 10-5 Sun 12-5. Susan Kostek *Park:* On site. *Loc:* On Rte 9, 6 MI from downtown Northampton.

HINGHAM

A T GARRITY GALLERY FINE ART
30 Harbor View Dr, 02043
(617)749-0643   59
Specializing in late 19th & early 20th C American & European paintings. *Serv:* Semi annual auction of paintings, consignments. *Hours:* By appt only.

PIERCE GALLERIES INC
721 Main St Rte 228, 02043
(617)749-6023   4 59
One of New England's largest 19th - 20th C American art galleries, specializing in American Impressionism, art from 1840 - 1940 & Super Realism. *Est:* 1968. *Serv:* Appraisal, catalog ($3-50), conservation, consultation, purchase est. *Hours:* BY APPT ONLY. *Size:* Large. *Assoc:* AAA. Patricia Jobe Pierce *Park:* On site. *Loc:* Rte 3 Exit 14: L off exit 3 1/2 MI, 3-story Victorian house set back from street with circular driveway.

HOLDEN

DAVIDIAN AMERICANA
4 Boyden Rd, 01520
(508)829-9222   1 27 28
Specializing in country furniture & accessories, pantry boxes, stoneware, baskets & early toys. *Est:* 1970. *Serv:* Appraisal. *Hours:* Mon-Tue BY APPT, Wed-Fri 10-4, Sat-Sun by chance. *Size:* Medium. *Assoc:* SADA. *Park:* On site. *Loc:* S of the Int of Rte 122A and 31 just off 122A.

VILLAGE ANTIQUES
1 Zottoli Rd Rte 122A, 01520
(508)829-6708   44 48 50
Furniture, glass, baskets, oil lamps, frames & linens. *Est:* 1984. *Hours:* Tue-Fri 10-5:30 Sat 10-2, Sum: CLOSED SAT. Hal Corey *Park:* In front. *Loc:* Behind Luddy Chevrolet.

HOLLISTON

WILDER SHOP
400 Washington St, 01746
(508)429-4836   50 87
Antiques, refinished furniture & accessories, handcrafted lighting & weather vanes. *Hours:* Mon-Sat 10-5 Sun 1-5. *Assoc:* SADA. The Brighams *Loc:* Jct of Rtes 16 & 126.

THE YANKEE PICKER
86 Church St, 01746
(508)429-6155   50
Large eclectic selection of antiques including glass & collectibles. *Hours:* Thu-Sat 10-5 Sun 12-5. Sylvia Stickney *Loc:* Located at the corner of Church & Grove Sts.

HOPKINTON

HERITAGE ANTIQUES
216 Wood St, 01748
(508)435-4031   **21 36 58**
Quality antiques, furniture & accessories, rugs & objets d'art. *Hours:* Tue-Fri 9-5 weekend evenings by chance/appt. *Assoc:* SADA. Clifton L Gilson *Loc:* Rte 135.

HUDSON

THE NEW ENGLAND ANTIQUE TOY MALL
65 Main St, 01749
(508)568-0856   **32 33 54**
Wind-ups, battery ops, lead & cast playsets, character items, space toys, Disneyana, premiums, advertising, games, trains, TV-related ephemera, vehicles, models, Beatles & puzzles. *Serv:* Always buying. *Hours:* Daily 12-5:30. *CC:* AX. *Park:* Free. *Loc:* Jct Rtes 62 & 85, 1 MI from Rtes 495 & 290.

JAMAICA PLAIN

BOSTON BOOK ANNEX
705 Centre St, 02130
(617)522-2100   **9 13**
Antiquarian books: American & English literature, first editions, autographs & manuscripts & East Asian studies. *Serv:* Appraisal, catalog, purchase estates, repairs, search service. *Hours:* Mon-Sat 10-10, Sun 12-10. *CC:* MC/V. *Assoc:* ABAA, MARIAB. Helen Kelly *Park:* nearby.

J R BURROWS & COMPANY
818 Centre St, 02130
(617)524-1795   **21 71 74**
Historical design merchants specializing in imported carpets, wallpapers & textiles used for the restoration of historic buildings & interiors. *Est:* 1985. *Serv:* Design consultation for period revival interiors. Catalog $5. *Hours:* BY APPT. John R Burrows

LAME DUCK BOOKS
90 Moraine St, 02130
(617)522-6657   **13**
American & European literary & philosophical first editions, autographs & manuscripts. *Serv:* Appraisal, catalog, search service. *Hours:* BY APPT ONLY. *Assoc:* MARIAB. John Wronoski

KINGSTON

LANGENBACH FINE ARTS & ANTIQUES
164 Elm St Rte 80, 02364
(617)585-6529   **36 59 60**
Specializing in American country & period furniture, paintings, Oriental rugs & decorative accessories. *Est:* 1990. *Hours:* By chance/appt. Gary Langenbach *Loc:* Rte 3 Exit 9: 1 1/2 MI from exit. 40 min S of Boston.

LANESBOROUGH

AMBER SPRING ANTIQUES
29 S Main St Rte 7, 01237
(413)442-1237   **27 81**
American furnishings large & small, tools, pottery, advertising, country store & unusual trivia. *Est:* 1957. *Hours:* Mon-Sat 10-5, Sun 12-5. *Size:* Medium. *Assoc:*

BCADA. Gae & Larry Elfenbein **Park:** On site. **Loc:** 5 MI N of Pittsfield on Rte 7.

SAVOY BOOKS
Bailey Rd, 01237
(413)499-9968   13

Antiquarian books: horticulture, agriculture, domestic arts, Americana, American & English literature before 1900. **Serv:** Appraisal, catalog. **Hours:** BY APPT. **Assoc:** ABAA MARIAB. Robert Fraker

SECOND LIFE BOOKS INC
55 Quarry Rd, 01237
(413)447-8010   13

Antiquarian books: agriculture, first editions, literature, women, signed & fine press books. **Serv:** Appraisal, catalog. **Hours:** BY APPT. **Assoc:** ABAA MARIAB. Russell Freedman

WALDEN'S ANTIQUES ART & BOOKS
1 Main St Rte 7, 01237
(413)442-5346   13

General line of antiques & 1000's of books. **Est:** 1955. **Serv:** Estate liquidation. **Hours:** Apr-Nov daily by chance/appt. William C Walden **Loc:** Across from the Federated Church.

LEE

AARDENBURG ANTIQUES
144 W Park St, 01238
(413)243-0001   29 37

Early 19th C American furniture & accessories. **Hours:** Weekends by chance, else BY APPT. David Hubregsen **Park:** Nearby.

CAROPRESO GALLERY
136 High St, 01238
(413)243-3424   4 8

Specializing in estate liquidation & 18th & 19th C Americana auctions with auctions one Saturday a month. **Est:** 1962. **Serv:** Auction, appraisal, brochure. **Hours:** Mon-Fri 9-5. Louis E Caropreso **Loc:** Parallel to Rte 20.

FERRELL'S ANTIQUES & WOODWORKING
67A Center St, 01238
(413)243-0041   41 71 76

Fine line of country furniture & accessories in original condition. Shaker furniture, painted country pieces. **Serv:** Repair, restoration, custom woodwork, replication, reproduction. **Hours:** Mon-Fri 10-5, Sat 12-5. **Size:** Medium. **CC:** MC/V. Glenn Ferrell **Park:** On site. **Loc:** I-90 Exit 2: R on Rte 20 to Town Green, R on Main to end, R & immediate L into parking lot, shop at rear.

HENRY B HOLT INC
PO Box 699 - Golden Hill, 01238
(201)316-9735 FAX
(413)243-3184   4 59 71

Dealer in 19th & early 20th C American paintings will advise on the disposal of individual paintings or estates. **Serv:** Appraisal, restoration, purchase estates, conservation. **Hours:** BY APPT ONLY. **Assoc:** AAA BCADA. **Loc:** Rte 20N from Lee to Golden Hill Rd, opposite Black Swan Motel follow Golden Hill Rd to 1st T Int, L.

THE KINGSLEIGH 1840
32 Park St Rte 20, 01238
(413)243-3317   47 53 83

Jewelry, small furniture, mirrors & collectibles - all part of a unique 1840 Victorian house & bed & breakfast. **Pr:** $5–500. **Est:** 1985. **Serv:** Purchase estates, repairs, restoration. **Hours:** Jun-

Sep daily 10-6, Oct-May Fri,Sat 10-5 Sun 11-4. *Size:* Medium. *CC:* AX/MC/V. Linda Segal *Park:* On site. *Loc:* I-90 Exit 2: Rte 2W for 3/4 MI.

PEMBROKE ANTIQUES
28 Housatonic St Rte 20, 01238
(413)243-1357   **34 37 76**
Shaker furniture & accessories, 18th & 19th C folk art, paintings & furniture. *Hours:* Sat-Sun 10-5 weekdays BY APPT. Morton B Dobson Jr *Park:* Nearby.

LENOX

CHARLES L FLINT ANTIQUES INC
64 Housatonic, 01240
(413)637-1634   **1 34 76**
American & European furniture, oil paintings, folk art, accessories & Shaker. *Serv:* Appraisal & consultations on Shaker. *Hours:* Mon-Sat 10-5 Sun by chance/appt. *Park:* In front. *Loc:* One block from the boutiques on Church St.

OCTOBER MOUNTAIN ANTIQUES
136 East St, 01240
(413)637-0439   **27 34 76**
Country & Shaker furniture & 18th & 19th C folk art. *Hours:* May-Dec 10 by chance/appt. Betty Fleishman *Park:* Nearby. *Loc:* Off Rte 720, take Walker St to East St & follow signs.

STONE'S THROW ANTIQUES
57 Church St, 01240
(413)637-2733   **36 63 77**
19th C American, English & French furniture, china, glass, inkstands, frames, prints, perfumes, silver & Orientalia attractively displayed in a well stocked shop. *Hours:* May-Oct daily 10-5, Nov-

Apr Thu-Mon. *Size:* Medium. *CC:* AX/MC/V. *Assoc:* BCADA. Sydelle S Shapiro *Park:* On site.

MARY STUART COLLECTIONS
81 Church St, 01240
(413)637-0340   **77**
Silver, silver smalls, linen & occasional pieces of furniture. *Est:* 1980. *Hours:* Mon-Sat 10:30-5 Sun 11-4. *CC:* AX/MC/V. *Park:* Ample. *Loc:* 2 blocks N of Walker St.

LENOXDALE

ANTIQUE RESTORATION AT GRANARY
14 Golden Hill Rd, 01242
(413)637-0867   **36 71**
Antique furniture. *Est:* 1954. *Serv:* Restoration. *Hours:* Daily 9-6. Jerry J Vuolo *Loc:* From Rte 7 in Lenox take Walker St toward Lenoxdale, R at Church St which becomes Golden Hill Road.

LEXINGTON

EVA AROND
52 Turning Mill Rd, 02173
(617)862-6379   **13**
Antiquarian books specializing in juveniles (including foreign languages), fine literature, fine & performing arts, cookbooks & general out-of-print. *Est:* 1978. *Serv:* Appraisal, catalogs, purchase estates. *Hours:* BY APPT ONLY. *Assoc:* MARIAB. *Loc:* Rte 128/I-95 Exit 31B: 1 1/2 MI from exit, call for directions.

FANCY FLEA ANTIQUES
1841 Massachusetts Ave, 02173
(508)862-9650 **{GR}**

An extensive collection of pottery, porcelain, glass, sterling silver, antique jewelry & decorative accessories. **Pr:** $25–2000. **Hours:** Tue-Sat 10-5:30. **CC:** MC/V. **Park:** In front. **Loc:** Opposite the Boston Federal Savings Bank.

GALLERY ON THE GREEN LTD
1837 Massachusetts Ave, 02173
(617)861-6044 **59**

American & European oils & works on papers. **Est:** 1980. **Serv:** Referrals on framing & restoration. **Hours:** Tue-Sat 10-5. **Park:** On street. **Loc:** Just short of the Minuteman statue.

LINCOLN

BROWN-CORBIN FINE ART
Sandy Pond Rd, 01773
(617)259-1210 **26 40 59**

Specializing in fine 19th & early 20th C American paintings, watercolors & drawings, with emphasis on Luminists, American Pre-Raphaelites & Impressionists selected with a view toward quality & importance. **Pr:** $2000–250000. **Serv:** Appraisal, consultation. **Hours:** BY APPT. Jeffrey Brown Kathryn Corbin

WILKERSON BOOKS
31 Old Winter St, 01773
(617)259-1110 **13**

Antiquarian books: gardening, landscape design & decorated trade bindings. **Serv:** Appraisal, catalog, search service. **Hours:** Call ahead. **Assoc:** ABAA MARIAB. Robin Wilkerson

LITTLETON

ANTIQUES AT SIGN OF THE BLUEBIRD
287 Great Rd, 01460
(508)486-3067

General line of quality antiques. **Pr:** $10–10000. **Est:** 1971. **Serv:** Appraisal. **Hours:** Tue,Wed 12-5 Thu-Sat 10-5. **CC:** MC/V. **Assoc:** SADA. James Baird **Park:** On site. **Loc:** I-495 Exit 31: to Rte 2A/119, E to Littleton Cen, continue thru lights for 1/4 MI, on L.

BLUE CAPE ANTIQUES
620 Great Rd Rte 119, 01460
(508)486-4709 **6**

Eclectic assortment of antiques including furniture, paintings, militaria. **Est:** 1963. **Hours:** Wed-Sat 11-5. Norman Caron **Park:** On site. **Loc:** 495 Exit 31: 1 MI W.

HAMLET ANTIQUES
161 Great Rd, 01460
(508)952-2445 **41**

Scandinavian furniture, painted & unpainted, clocks, paintings & rugs. **Serv:** Wholesale to the trade. **Hours:** Mon-Sat 10-5 Sun 12-5. Stephen de Mont **Park:** On site.

UPTON HOUSE ANTIQUES
275 King St Rte 2A-110, 01460
(508)486-3367 **27 46**

Antiques in the country manner, featuring furniture & smalls in original condition - some with paint. **Est:** 1984. **Serv:** Early interiors decorating service with room consultation & written proposal. **Hours:** Tue,Thu,Fri 10-3 Sat 10-4 Sun by chance. **CC:** MC/V. Eileen Poland **Loc:** Rte 495 Exit 30: R, 1000 ft.

LONGMEADOW

LE PERIGORD
805 Williams St, 01106
(413)567-0262   **35**
French & American country & city furniture, lighting, pottery, clocks, iron, garden - 18th C thru Nouveau & Deco. *Hours:* Tue-Sat 10-5 or BY APPT. *Size:* Medium. J D Roberts *Park:* Nearby. *Loc:* I-91 Exit 49: next to post office; 3 MI S of Springfield.

MALDEN

EXCALIBUR HOBBIES LTD
63 Exchange St, 02148
(617)322-2959   **6 49**
Lead soldiers & toys, military items & strategic games. *Pr:* $5–500. *Serv:* Appraisal, catalog (free listing), purchase estates, repairs, restor. *Hours:* Year round Mon-Sat 10-6, Fri 10-8, Sun (Dec only) 12-5. *Size:* Large. *CC:* MC/V. *Park:* Free in local garage. *Loc:* I-93 Exit 32: Rte 60E for approx 2 MI, L on Commercial St, R on Exchange St; 1 1/2 blocks from Rte 1; 2 MI W on Rte 60.

MANSFIELD

THE FAINTING COUCH
25 Tremont St, 02048
(508)339-7733   **85 47**
Vintage apparel & any wearable items, such as jewelry, gloves, hats & shoes. *Hours:* BY APPT. *Assoc:* SNEADA. Margarita Prestwich

FROG HOLLOW ANTIQUES
82 Stearns Ave, 02048
(508)339-8066
A country shop of antiques, vintage collectibles, curiosities & newer good things from area homes & estates. *Serv:* Appraisal, consultation. *Hours:* Thu-Sat 11-5 BY APPT. *Size:* Medium. *Assoc:* SADA. Cal Vizedom *Park:* On site. *Loc:* I-95 Exit 7A (Mansfield): Rte 140 to Rte 106, L on 106 to Stearns Ave, L on Stearns Ave to #82 on L.

MARBLEHEAD

THE ANTIQUE SHOP
92 Washington St, 01945
(617)639-0413   **44 60 63**
Orientalia, cut glass & hand painted china, furniture & silver. *Hours:* Daily 12-5. *CC:* AX/MC/V. Edith Harris Eleanor Meyers *Park:* Nearby. *Loc:* Across from The Town House.

ANTIQUEWEAR
82 Front St, 01945
(617)631-4659   **18**
Antique buttons of the 1800s fashioned to jewelry. *Pr:* $25–300. *Est:* 1970. *Serv:* Appraisal, consultation, purchase estates, repairs. *Hours:* May-Dec Thu-Sun, else BY APPT. *CC:* AX/DC. Jerry Fine *Loc:* Across from the Landing Restaurant, 1 block from Marblehead Antique Exchange on the harbor front.

THE BLACK GOOSE
28 Atlantic Ave, 01945
(617)639-0465   **36 44**
Antiques, used furniture, glass, dolls & gifts. *Pr:* $10–600. *Hours:* Year round daily 1:30-5:30. *Size:* Large. *CC:* MC/V. Jean A Lee *Park:* Nearby. *Loc:* Across from Marblehead Savings.

BRASS & BOUNTY
68 Front St, 01945
(617)631-3864   **50 56**

Nautical antiques, restored gas & electric chandeliers. *Serv:* Restoration. *Hours:* Daily 9-5:30. *Size:* Medium. *CC:* MC/V. Maryanne Dermody *Park:* Nearby. *Loc:* Just across from The Landing on the harbor.

E R BUTLER & SONS
25 Mugford St, 01945
(617)631-4031   **75**

Packing & crating of antique & other items, shipping arranged for, phone estimates subject to inspection of item. *Est:* 1948. *Serv:* From Eastern Mass 1-800-287-4031. *Hours:* Mon-Sat 10-4. *CC:* MC/V. Wayne Butler *Park:* On site. *Loc:* Go to end of Pleasant St (Rte 114), L, L again at Old Town House (yellow bldg in middle of st) across from church.

CALICO COUNTRY ANTIQUES
79 Washington St, 01945
(617)631-3607   **27 67**

Specializing in antique quilts, country furniture & accessories. *Hours:* Mon-Sat 10-5, Sun 12-5.

CROWN & EAGLE ANTIQUES
235 Washington St, 01945
(617)631-0198

Antiques & unusual collectibles. *Hours:* Daily 10-5. *CC:* MC/V. Egea Branscombe

EVIE'S CORNER
96 Washington St, 01945
(617)639-0007   **5 17 74**

Architectural bronzes & marble, featuring antique leaded glass & period furniture. *Est:* 1978. *Hours:* Weekends 12-5 or BY APPT. *Park:* Nearby street.

FIVE HONEST LADIES
120 Pleasant St, 01945
(617)631-7555

Furniture & decorative accessories. *Hours:* Mon-Sat 10-5, Sun 1-5. *CC:* MC/V. *Park:* Nearby.

HEELTAPPERS ANTIQUES
134 Washington St, 01945
(617)631-7722   **36 63 77**

18th & 19th C country & formal furniture, silver, glass, porcelains & accessories. *Serv:* Consultation. *Hours:* Tue-Sat 11-5. *Size:* Medium. *CC:* MC/V. *Assoc:* NSADA. *Park:* Nearby. *Loc:* In the Historic District.

HISTORICAL TECHNOLOGY INC
6 Mugford St, 01945
(617)631-2275   **72**

Antique scientific instruments & early associated books. *Serv:* Subscription to 2 issues of illustrated catalog - $12. *Hours:* BY APPT ONLY. Saul Moskowitz

MARBLEHEAD ANTIQUES
118 Pleasant St, 01945
(617)631-9791   **29 36 63**

Formal & country furniture, American & Continental decorative accessories. *Est:* 1968. *Serv:* Appraisal, consultations, interior design. *Hours:* Mon-Sun 12-5 CLOSED THU. *Size:* Medium. *CC:* MC/V. *Assoc:* NSADA. Harriet Norman *Park:* In front. *Loc:* Across from the movie theatre.

MUCH ADO
7 Pleasant St, 01945
(617)639-0400   **13**

Two floors of old, out-of-print & rare books including children's books, women's literature, nautical & first editions. *Serv:* Appraisal, catalog, search service. *Hours:* Mon-Fri 9:30-6 Sat,Sun 10:30-6 & BY APPT. *Assoc:* MARIAB. Nash Robbins

OLD TOWN ANTIQUE CO-OP
108 Washington St, 01945
(617)631-9728 **{GR5}**
Delightful assortment of American antiques & accessories, concentrating on wicker, quilts, oak & pine furniture, prints & jewelry. *Est:* 1979. *Serv:* Appraisal, catalog, interior design, purchase estates, restoration. *Hours:* Daily 10-5 Sep-Jun CLOSED WED. *Size:* Medium. Marla B Segal *Park:* Nearby. *Loc:* In the center of the village.

S & S GALLERIES
231 Washington St, 01945
(617)631-7595 **2 27 36**
Estate furniture, country & formal, antiques, jewelry & fireplace equipment. *Hours:* Tue-Sat 10:30-4. *Size:* Medium. *CC:* MC/V. *Park:* Nearby.

SACKS ANTIQUES
38 State St at Front St, 01945
(617)631-0770 **39 63 77**
Marblehead's oldest antique shop, fine English furniture & china, large collection of silver objects of art. *Pr:* $25–5000. *Est:* 1912. *Serv:* Appraisal, purchase estates. *Hours:* Daily CLOSED SUN. *CC:* AX/DC/MC/V. Stanley S Sacks *Park:* Nearby lot (side). *Loc:* 17 MI N of Boston, located opposite the Town Landing, look for famous gold eagle.

MARION

THE HOBBY HORSE
339 Front St, 02738
(508)748-0763 **36 29**
Buying daily from Plymouth County homes, a varied & changing stock of furniture & decorative accessories. *Est:* 1959. *Hours:* By chance/appt. *Assoc:* SNEADA. Robert E Mower *Loc:* I-195 Exit 20 S.

THE WICKER PORCH
335 Wareham Rd Rte 6, 02738
(508)748-3606 **77 83 86**
General line of antiques, large selection of restored antique wicker furniture. Estate antiques arrive daily. *Pr:* $5–5000. *Serv:* Appraisal, purchase estates, wicker restoration. *Hours:* Jun-Sep Thu-Tue 10-5, Oct-May Fri-Mon 10-5. *Size:* Large. *CC:* MC/V. *Assoc:* SPNEA NEAA. *Loc:* I-95 Rte 105 Exit: 1st lights, L onto Rte 6, E 1/2 MI on L.

Wayne Pratt

AMERICAN ANTIQUES

257 Forest Street
Marlboro, Massachusetts 01752
Telephone (508) 481-2917

6 Candle Street
Nantucket, Massachusetts 02554
Telephone (508) 228-8788
July 4 thru Labor Day

MARLBORO

MARSHFIELD

PAGE & PARCHMENT
20 Fay Ct, 01752
(508)481-2282   13

Antiquarian books: literature, technical books, design & general stock. *Hours:* BY APPT ONLY. *Assoc:* MARIAB. Val Paul Auger

WAYNE PRATT & CO
257 Forest St, 01752
(508)485-5491 FAX
(508)481-2917   32 36 37

A large selection of fine American 18th & early 19th C furniture, both country & formal - specializing in Windsor chairs & featuring a toy showroom for the collector. *Serv:* Appraisal. *Hours:* BY APPT ONLY. *Size:* Large. *Assoc:* ADA NHADA. Wayne Pratt *Park:* In front. *Loc:* From Boston, I-90W to 495N Exit Rte 20W, from Hartford, Rte 84 to I-90 to 495N Exit Rte 20W.

THE SHELLEY GALLERIES
34 Main St, 01752
(508)481-5694   40 50 63

Miller lamps, oak furniture, primitives, Victorian items, mahogany, smalls, collectibles & a selection of Limoges, Staffordshire & Minton. *Serv:* Accept consignments. *Hours:* Tue-Sat 10-6.

WAYSIDE ANTIQUES
1015 Boston Post Rd, 01752
(508)481-9621   40 42 86

Quality Victorian, walnut, mahogany, oak, wicker, pine, early furniture & accessories in an historic setting. *Serv:* Appraisal. *Hours:* Mon-Sat 10-5. *Assoc:* SADA. Buck Colaianni *Loc:* Next to Wayside Country Store.

ANTIQUES AT EAGLE'S NEST
40 Main St, 02050
(617)837-7244   {GR5}

Furniture, jewelry, vintage clothing, trunks, linens, china, glass, prints, collectibles. *Est:* 1989. *Serv:* Theatrical rental & some consignment. *Hours:* Mon-Sat 11-5 Sun 12-5. *Size:* Medium. *CC:* MC/V. *Assoc:* SSADA. *Park:* On site. *Loc:* Rte 3A just off Jct of Rte 139 near fairgrounds.

WILLIS HENRY AUCTIONS
22 Main St, 02050
(617)834-7774   4 8 76

Nation's only auction gallery featuring annual sales of Shaker furniture & accessories, specializing in American Indian & African art, Americana & estate sales. 10% buyers premium. *Serv:* Appraisal, accept mail/phone bids, catalog, consultation, purchase estates. *Hours:* Mon-Fri 9-5 appt suggested. *Loc:* Call for directions to specific auctions.

LORD RANDALL BOOKSHOP
22 Main St, 02050
(617)837-1400   13

A selected general stock of antiquarian books with an emphasis on New England & literature, art & children's books, housed in a 100-year-old heated barn. *Pr:* $1–1000. *Est:* 1972. *Serv:* Appraisal, purchase estates, search service. *Hours:* Tue-Sat 11-5. *Size:* 20,000 books. *Assoc:* MARIAB. Gail Wills *Park:* On site. *Loc:* Rte 3S from Boston, Marshfield Exit: R onto Rte 139, 2 1/2 MI to 1st light, L on Rte 3A, 1st bldg on R.

MELROSE

ROBINSON MURRAY III
BOOKSELLER
150 Lynde St, 02176
(617)665-3094   **13**
Rare & unusual books: 18th & 19th C
Americana, early American imprints,
pamphlets, broadsides, American literature, Black history. *Serv:* Appraisal,
catalogs. *Hours:* BY APPT. *Assoc:*
MARIAB.

STARR BOOK CO INC
44 W Wyoming Ave, 02176
(617)662-2580   **13**
Antiquarian books: American literature,
Americana, English literature, first edi-
tions, literary criticism & biography, fic-
tion, translations & nonfiction. *Serv:*
Appraisal, search service. *Hours:* Mon-
Fri 9:30-5 Sat 9:30-4. *CC:* MC/V. *Assoc:*
MARIAB. Norman Starr *Park:* On site.
Loc: 10 Min N of Boston.

MIDDLEBORO

CHARLES & BARBARA ADAMS
15 Prospect St, 02346
(508)947-7277   **37**
Early American furniture, iron, brass,
Bennington pottery & appropriate accessories. *Hours:* BY APPT ONLY.
Assoc: ADA. *Loc:* Call for directions.

MILFORD

DUNBAR'S GALLERY
76 Haven St, 01757
(508)634-8697   **1 32 34**
Offering a wide variety of quality toys &
advertising in fine condition: early
American, German & Japanese tin toys,
mechanical & still banks, comic character & Disney toys, horse drawn &
automotive cast iron toys, posters, signs,
automobilia & folk art. *Serv:* Appraisal,
consultation, purchase estates, repairs &
restoration. *Hours:* Mon-Fri 8-5, Appt
suggested. *Size:* Medium. *CC:* MC/V.
Assoc: AAA SADA. Howard Dunbar
Park: On site. *Loc:* Rte 495, Exit 21B (W
Main St & Upton), 1st L on to South St,
2 1/2 MI, L on to Haven St, 1 MI down
on L side.

MONTAGUE

THE BOOK MILL
Greenfield Rd, 01351
(413)367-9959   **13 14**
Antiquarian books: general stock featuring academic presses. *Serv:* Appraisal,
search service. *Hours:* By chance, call
ahead advised. *Assoc:* MARIAB. James
Murphy

PETER L MASI BOOKS
17 Central St, 01351
(413)367-2628   **13**
Antiquarian books: American technical
books, pamphlets ranging from architecture & decorative arts to engineering,
business, agriculture, medicine, cooking
& textiles; trade catalogs; lively arts,
American social, religious & educational
history. *Pr:* $10–500. *Est:* 1978. *Serv:*

Catalog. *Hours:* By chance/appt. *Assoc:* ABAA MARIAB. *Loc:* Next door to the Town Hall in Montague Center.

KARL SCHICK
15 Depot St, 01351
(413)367-9740   **13**

Antiquarian books: science & medicine, philosophy, psychiatry, psychology & rare books. *Hours:* BY APPT ONLY. *Assoc:* ABAA.

MONTEREY

TEA ROOM ANTIQUES
Rte 23, 01245
(413)528-4415   **27**

A village shop featuring country furniture, smalls & collectibles. *Hours:* Mid-May-Mid Oct 10:30-4:30 CLOSED WED. *Assoc:* BCADA. Judy Durlach *Loc:* Rte 23 W from Great Barrington.

NATICK

VANDERWEG ANTIQUES
77 Worcester Rd Rte 9, 01760
(508)651-3634   **29 36 83**

19th C furniture, lamps, mirrors, clocks, paintings, porcelains emphasizing European items. *Pr:* $25-2000. *Est:* 1988. *Serv:* Consultation. *Hours:* Mon-Sat 10-5. *Size:* Medium. *CC:* MC/V. *Assoc:* SADA. *Park:* On site. *Loc:* Rte 9 W, just over Wellesley line in between Honeybaked Ham & Renjeau Galleries.

NEEDHAM

GEORGE A DOWNER FINE ARTS
Box 905, 02192
(617)449-0971   **59**

Investment-quality oil paintings, primarily American Impressionists & watercolors. *Est:* 1978. *Serv:* Appraisal, buying/selling. *Hours:* BY APPT. *Loc:* Call for directions.

KLOSS VIOLINS
1200 Great Plain Ave, 02192
(617)444-4383   **4 55**

Stringed, bowed instrument appraisal & restoration, trade & sale of early & contemporary instruments. *Serv:* Expertise in museum conservation, restoration, baroque conversion. *Hours:* Tue-Fri 1-6 BY APPT. Horst Kloss

ON CONSIGNMENT GALLERIES
1090 Great Plain Avenue, 02192
(617)444-4783   **25**

Furniture, glass, china, sterling, jewelry, lamps, mirrors, chandeliers, glass, objets d'art, pottery, bronzes, copper & brass. *Serv:* Accept consignments. *Hours:* Mon-Sat 10-5:30 Fri til 8 Sun 1-5. *CC:* MC/V.

STEWARTS OF NEEDHAM
190 Nehoiden St, 02192
(617)444-0124

Antiques for amateur & expert in a simple country setting - general line of furniture, china, glass, ironware & quilts. *Est:* 1927. *Hours:* BY APPT please. *Assoc:* SADA. Mrs Sidney Stewart *Loc:* Off Rte 135.

TREFLER ANTIQUE RESTORING STUDIO
99 Cabot St, 02194
(617)965-3388　　　　**68 71**
Master restorers - crystal, porcelain, jade, ivory, wood, paintings, objets d'art & metal. *Est:* 1948. *Serv:* Appraisal, conservation, custom woodwork, repairs, replication & more. *Hours:* Mon-Fri 9-5 Sat 10-2 or BY APPT. *Assoc:* AIC IIC. Leon Trefler *Park:* On site. *Loc:* Rte 128 Exit 19A (Newton Highlands): 3/4 MI, R after Federal Express gray bldg, 100 yds up on L.

ESTHER TUVESON-BOOKS & EPHEMERA
30 Brookside Rd, 02192
(617)444-5533　　　　**13**
Antiquarian books: Americana, children's, fine arts, first editions, illustrated & nonfiction special interests. *Serv:* Search service. *Hours:* Call ahead. *Assoc:* MARIAB.

THE WICKER LADY INC
925 Webster St, 02192
(617)449-1172　　　　**68 71 86**
Specializing in antique & new classic wicker furniture, custom upholstery for wicker & will search to order unusual wicker pieces. *Est:* 1980. *Serv:* Refinishing, repair, restoration. *Hours:* Mon-Fri 10-5:30. Charlie Wagner *Park:* In front. *Loc:* Rte 128 Exit 17 (Rte 135): toward Needham Ctr, approx 1 MI from Rte 128, L on Webster, driveway between Texaco & 1st house.

NEW BEDFORD

BROOKSIDE ANTIQUES
44 N Water St, 02741
(508)993-4944　　　　**44**
New England's finest collection of 19th C art glass & a large collection of New Bedford glass. *Serv:* Appraisal, consultation, purchase estates, mail order list. *Hours:* Jun-Dec Mon-Sat 10-5, Jan-May Tue-Sat 10:30-4:30. *Size:* Medium. *CC:* MC/V. *Assoc:* SNEADA. Louis O St Aubin Jr *Park:* In front. *Loc:* Directly E of the Whaling Museum.

LANDMARK ANTIQUES
36 N Water St, 02740
(508)990-8818　　　　**29**
Antiques, decorative accessories & unique items. *Hours:* Mon-Sat 10-5. *Assoc:* SNEADA. Nancy Morris Douglas *Loc:* Behind the Whaling Museum.

NEW BEDFORD ANTIQUES COMPANY
85 Coggeshall St, 02746
(508)993-7600　　　　**{GR200}**
One of New England's largest group shops with a wide selection of jewelry, silver, glass, American, Victorian, oak & custom mahogany furniture, clocks & toys, Art Deco, china, pottery, ephemera, bronzes, Orientalia, ivories & paintings. *Pr:* $50–2000. *Est:* 1986. *Serv:* Purchase estates. *Hours:* Year round Mon-Sat 10-5 Sun 12-5. *Size:* Huge. *CC:* DC/MC/V. *Assoc:* SNEADA. Susan Carr *Park:* On site. *Loc:* I-95 Exit 16E or 17W: 20 min from the Bourne Bridge.

NEW MARLBOROUGH

MARLBORO COTTAGE ART & INTERIORS
144 S Sandisfield Rd Rte 183, 01230
(413)229-2170   **46 53 71**

Decorative accessories & fabrics, paintings, prints, mirror & pedestals, historic interiors & reverse painting on glass. *Est:* 1985. *Serv:* Interior design service, gold leaf restoration, fancy paint finishes. *Hours:* Anytime by appt or 8-8 by phone. *Assoc:* BCADA. Barry Webber *Loc:* Rte 57 thru New Marlborough Ctr R at fork up South Sandisfield Rd   2 MI on L.

NEW SALEM

THE COMMON READER BOOKSHOP
Old Main St, 01355
(508)544-3002   **13 33**

Antiquarian books: American literature, literary criticism, biography, women, theatre, ephemera, history & Americana. *Serv:* Appraisal, search service. *Hours:* May-Oct Wed-Sun 10-5. *Assoc:* MARIAB. Dorothy Johnson & Doris Abramson *Loc:* Just off Rte 202.

NEWBURYPORT

MICHAEL J BAUMANN
2 Federal St, 01950
(508)465-2439   **1 37**

Specializing in American antiques. *Hours:* Daily 10-5.

JOHN J COLLINS JR
74A Water St, 01950
(508)462-7276   **21**

Specializing in old & antique Oriental rugs for the collector & decorator. *Hours:* Mon-Sat 10-5, Sun 1-5. *Assoc:* ADA NHADA.

PAUL & LINDA DE COSTE
288 Merrimack St, 01950
(508)462-2138   **16 56 72**

18th & 19th C furniture & accessories, folk & nautical items with specialties in scientific instruments & metal of the 17th, 18th & 19th C. *Hours:* BY APPT. *Assoc:* NHADA. *Loc:* Call for directions.

PETER EATON
39 State St, 01950
(508)465-2754   **37**

Fine New England 18th C furniture selected for knowledgeable collectors. *Est:* 1970. *Serv:* Appraisal, consultation, photography. *Hours:* Mon-Sat 10-5 Sun by appt. *Assoc:* ADA NHADA. *Shows:* Hartford, NHADA, ADA. *Park:* Nearby. *Loc:* In the heart of downtown Newburyport.

ELIZABETH'S 20TH CENTURY
41 State St, 01950
(508)465-2983   **7 47 85**

A large assortment of Art Deco & designer 50s furniture & furnishings - Russell Wright, Frankart, Saarinen & Bertoia. Large assortment of costume jewelry & some precious metals & stones. *Pr:* $25–8000. *Est:* 1979. *Hours:* Mon-Sat 10-6 Sun 2-6; Jun-Dec Thu-Fri til 9. M Elizabeth Baratelli *Loc:* I-95N Exit 57 (Newburyport): R on High St 3 MI. State St is main business st; Corner of State & Essex.

FEDERAL STREET LIGHTHOUSE
37 Market Sq, 01950
(508)462-6333   **50**
Period reproduction lighting &
hardware. *Hours:* Mon-Sat 11-5 Sun 2-
5. Cheryl B Smith

JOPPA BAY ANTIQUES
37 State St, 01950
(508)465-3099
Estate furniture 1840-1940 & accessories. *Hours:* Daily 10-5, Thu-Fri til 9,
Sun til 6, else by chance. Duncan Mac
Burns

LEPORE FINE ARTS
Horton's Yard 58 Merrimac St, 01950
(508)462-1663   **59**
American & European paintings from
the 19th & 20th C with a focus on the
years 1870-1930. Works by such artists
as: Laura Hills, C H Davis, Theresa
Bernstein, Theodore Wendel &
Gertrude Fiske in a gallery overlooking
Newburyport's historic waterfront. *Serv:*
Appraisal, conservation, interior design,
purchase estates. *Hours:* May-Oct Tue-
Fri 11-5 Sat 10-5, Nov-Apr Thu,Fri 11-
5 Sat 10-5. *Park:* Nearby.

PLUM BUSH ANTIQUES
97 Water St, 01950
(508)462-0407   **36 44 85**
A general line of antiques including
vintage clothes, furniture, glass, jewelry
& dolls. *Est:* 1989. *Hours:* Mon-Sat 9-5
Sun 12-5.

**CHRISTOPHER L SNOW
ASSOCIATES**
Two Inn St, 01950
(508)465-8872   **4 8**
Twenty-eight years experience with antiques, fine arts, Americana & paintings
offering accurate, confidential & professional appraisal service for insurance
companies, private collectors, executors,
individuals, corporate trustees & banks.
Est: 1960. *Serv:* Appraisal, auction, purchase estates. *Hours:* Mon-Fri 10-4, appt
suggested. *Assoc:* AAA. *Park:* Nearby
lot. *Loc:* Located in the heart of
Newburyport's historic Market Sq on
Inn St.

SOMEWHERE IN TIME
27 State St, 01950
(508)462-4545   **40 44 75**
Offering a fine selection of Victorian furniture as well as elegant glassware & interesting accessories. *Pr:* $25–4000. *Est:*
1988. *Serv:* Purchase estates, restoration, refinishing, delivery & shipping.
Hours: Daily 10-5 Sun 12-5, later during
summer & on holidays. *Size:* Medium.
CC: AX/MC/V. Stuart F Frye *Park:* In
front. *Loc:* I-95 Exit 57: E on Rte 113 to
Newburyport, follow signs to
downtown. 3 min from I-95, 20 min
from Portsmouth.

NEWTON

THE BOOK COLLECTOR
375 Elliot St, 02164
(617)964-3599   **13 14**
Antiquarian books: American literature,
general history, Massachusetts history,
science & theatre. *Pr:* $1–500. *Serv:* Ap-
praisal, search service. *Hours:* Mon-Sat
10-5. *Size:* Medium. *Assoc:* MARIAB.
Theodore & Neil Berman *Park:* Nearby
lot. *Loc:* Rte 9E 1/4 MI, W New-
ton/Waban Exit: R at SS on Ellis St, R at
SS up hill to Chestnut St, R at light to
Elliot, 50 ft to lot.

BRASS BUFF ANTIQUES
977 Chestnut St, 02164
(617)964-9388   **16 71 72**
Specializing in scientific & medical in-

struments, nautical items, lighting, sconces, candlesticks, cannons, fireplace equipment, tools, kitchenware, copper, selected furniture, armor, hardware & doorknobs. **Pr:** $3–10000. **Est:** 1973. **Serv:** Polish brass & copper, iron & metals restored, conservation, repairs. **Hours:** Tue-Sun 1-5, call first. **Size:** Medium. **Assoc:** SADA. Mel Rosenburg **Park:** In front. **Loc:** Rte 9W Chestnut St Exit: L under Rte 9, 1st shop on R at top of hill.

PETER D COWEN
PO Box 181, 02168
(617)899-1955 **59 66**

Fine 19th C bird & flower prints, specializing in Audubon, Catesby & Redoute in the finest condition & American 19th C paintings. **Pr:** $1000–100000. **Est:** 1977. **Serv:** Consultation, purchase estates. **Hours:** BY APPT ONLY. **Loc:** Call for directions.

GIVE & TAKE CONSIGNMENT SHOP
799 Washington St, 02160
(617)964-4454 **25**

Consignment furniture, jewelry, china & glass. **Est:** 1981. **Serv:** Accept consignments. **Hours:** Mon-Sat 10:30-5. **CC:** MC/V. **Park:** On street. **Loc:** Just below Walnut St.

HARD-TO-FIND NEEDLEWORK BOOKS
96 Roundwood Rd, 02164
(617)969-0942 **13 57**

Embroidery & needlework, lace, quilting, knitting, crocheting & textiles. **Serv:** Appraisal, catalog, search service. **Hours:** Call ahead. **Assoc:** ABAA MARIAB. Bette S Feinstein

PAST TENSE
284 California St, 02158
(617)244-5725 **33**

A general line of antiques featuring furniture, Americana, collectibles & ephemera, magazines. **Serv:** Consignment shop. **Hours:** Tue 10-Sat 10-5 other times by chance. Martha Ryan David Harr **Loc:** 1/2 MI from Watertown Square; California St is parallel to Rte 16.

SUNDERLAND BOOKS
457 Centre St, 02258
(617)332-9880 **13**

Modern first editions, mysteries, espionage fiction & a general stock. **Serv:** Catalog. **Hours:** BY APPT ONLY. **Assoc:** MARIAB. Sheila Brownstein

NEWTON CENTRE

EDWARD MORRILL & SON
27 Country Club Rd, 02159
(617)527-7448 **13**

Antiquarian books: science, sports & nature, reference, travel & Americana. **Hours:** BY APPT ONLY. **Assoc:** ABAA. Samuel R Morrill

SUZANNE SCHLOSSBERG BOOKS
529 Ward St, 02159
(617)964-0213 **13**

Antiquarian books: children's, first editions & illustrated. **Serv:** Appraisal, catalog, search service. **Hours:** BY APPT ONLY. **Assoc:** ABAA MARIAB.

NEWTON HIGHLANDS

MARCIA & BEA ANTIQUES
One Lincoln St, 02161
(617)332-2408   **27 40 67**
19th C American country furniture, pine, oak, mirrors, quilts, baskets, rugs & accessories. *Hours:* Mon-Sat 10-5 Thu til 8 Sun 1-5. *Assoc:* SADA.

NEWTON LOWER FALLS

ARTHUR T GREGORIAN INC
2284 Washington St, 02162
(617)244-2553   **21**
6000 new & antique Oriental rugs. *Hours:* Mon,Tue,Thu,Fri 9-6 Wed 9-9 Sat 9-5. *Park:* In front.

NEWTON UPPER FALLS

ECHO BRIDGE MALL
381 Eliot St, 02164
(617)332-3328   **{GR13}**
American furniture including oak, Arts & Crafts, Art Nouveau, Art Deco, porcelain & pottery, jewelry, sterling silver flatware, prints & glass. *Est:* 1975. *Serv:* Purchase estates, repair silver. *Hours:* Tue-Sat 11-4, CLOSED SUN. *CC:* MC/V. Steve Nelson *Park:* In front. *Loc:* Near Rtes 9 & 128: Eliot Street at the corner of Chestnut.

NORTH WIND FURNISHINGS INC
1005 Chestnut St, 02164
(617)527-7724   **40 71 83**
One of the area's best selections of restored, turn-of-the-century furniture (oak, walnut, mahogany & wicker); no reproductions. Accessories include lighting, quilts, brass & iron beds. Custom restoration & repairs a specialty. *Est:* 1978. *Serv:* Appraisal, brochure, purchase estates, repairs, restoration. *Hours:* Tue-Sat 10-5. *CC:* MC/V. Neil & Joyce Friedman *Park:* In front. *Loc:* Rte 128 to Rte 9 E, Chestnut St exit.

NEWTONVILLE

AROUND THE CORNER ANTIQUES
10 Austin St, 02160
(617)964-1149   **36 44 47**
Furniture, textiles, jewelry & glassware. *Hours:* Mon-Sat 10-4. *Loc:* Across from Star Market.

NORFOLK

ROBERT F GRABOWSKY
87 Cleveland St, 02056
(508)528-5140   **7**
Interior arts: Art Deco, Art Moderne & fine antiques from the 18th-20th C & collectibles including radios, lunch boxes, board games, toys. *Serv:* Appraisal, consultation. *Hours:* By appt only.

NORFOLK ANTIQUES
16 Carson Circle, 02056
(508)528-0056   **40**
A large, constantly changing selection of quality furniture & furnishings in a country setting. Specializing in popular styles of oak, mahogany, cherry & period pieces. Also, fine collectibles, paintings, toys, rugs & the unusual. Expert restoration. *Pr:* $50–1500. *Serv:* Restoration, appraisal, brochure, consultation, purchase estates, repairs. *Hours:* Mon, Wed-

Sat 10-6, Sun 12-5, CLOSED TUE. *Size:* Large. *CC:* MC/V. Peter J Kane *Park:* On site. *Loc:* Less than 20 MI from Boston; Rte 115 location next to Norfolk commuter train depot, behind Post Office, in Norfolk Ctr.

NORTH ADAMS

STATIONHOUSE ANTIQUES CENTER
Rte 8 Heritage State Pk, 01247
(413)662-2961   **{GR40}**

A full line of antiques & collectibles displayed in a restored freightyard building. *Est:* 1987. *Hours:* Apr-Dec daily 10-5:30 Jan-Mar Thu-Mon 10-5. *Size:* Large. *CC:* MC/V. Donella Markham *Park:* Ample. *Loc:* Rte 8, just S of Main St & Rte 2, follow signs to Heritage Park.

NORTH AMHERST

PIONEER AUCTION OF AMHERST
Jct Rtes 116 N & 63, 01059
(413)253-9914   **8**

Antique & estate auctions, including an annual Labor Day auction. 10% buyers premium. *Hours:* Call for appt or schedule. Bruce Smebakken *Loc:* Jct of Rtes 116N & 63.

NORTH ANDOVER

ROLAND B HAMMOND INC
169 Andover St, 01845
(508)682-9672   **37 59 77**

American silver, furniture & paintings.

Est: 1951. *Serv:* Estate appraisals. *Hours:* Appt suggested. *Shows:* ELLIS. *Loc:* Call for directions.

NORTH ATTLEBORO

RYAN'S ANTIQUES & AUCTIONS
PO Box 3225, 02761
(508)695-6464   **4 8 26**

Antiques, collectibles & specialty auctions held the 2nd & 4th Wednesdays of every month at the K of C Hall Rte 123, So. Attleboro MA at 6:30 PM. *Est:* 1985. *Serv:* Appraisal, auction, brochure, consultation, purchase estates. *Hours:* Wed 4-11 or by appt. *Size:* Medium. *Assoc:* MAA NAA NEAA SNEADA. *Park:* On site. *Loc:* From S: I-95 N to Exit 2B L at 1st Light W on Rte 123. From N, E or W: Rte 495 or Rte 128 to I-95 S to Exit 3. W on Rte 123.

NORTH BROOKFIELD

J & S ENTERPRISES
27 Grove St, 01535
(508)867-2478   **{GR8}**

A quality group shop featuring period furniture, building materials & accessories. *Est:* 1989. *Serv:* Auctions, purchase estates. *Hours:* Mon & Thu 10-12 & 1-4 Wed 4-8 Sat-Sun 10-5 by chance/appt. Joe Craig & Sara Hunt *Park:* On site. *Loc:* Rte 67N to Central St, last building on L.

NORTH CHELMSFORD

RARE FINDS AT THE MILL
73 Princeton St, 01863
(508)251-8170   **{GR20}**
A collection of distinctive furniture &
decorative accessories including jewelry,
Victorian & primitive furniture, art pottery, Mission, prints, glass, Art Nouveau
& Art Deco. *Est:* 1988. *Hours:* Mon Sat
12-5 Sun 12-5. *Park:* On site. *Loc:* Rte 3
Exit 32: Rte 3A/4 N, to the Mill Complex 1 1/2 MI on L.

NORTH DARTMOUTH

S HANKIN TEXTILE CONSERVATION
1365 Tucker Rd, 02747
(508)993-4176   **4 26 71**
Protection for valuable antiques fabrics
with preservation storage systems, conservation consultations & professional
services. *Est:* 1985. *Serv:* Appraisal, conservation, consultation. *Hours:* BY
APPT ONLY. Susan Hankin

NORTH READING

MAC SONNY'S FLEA MARKET
Main St Rte 28, 01864
(617)532-0606   **{FLEA}**
Indoor/outdoor flea market with antiques, collectibles & other flea market
merchandise. Admission is 50 cents. *Est:*
1973. *Serv:* Rental space start at $25 for
an 11' X 12' space. *Hours:* Every Sun
8-5. *Size:* 300 spaces. *Park:* Free Parke-
ing. *Loc:* Rte 128 to Rte 28 N; from Rtc
93 take Rte 62 E.

NORTH WEYMOUTH

BRIDGE ANTIQUES
398 Bridge St Rte 3A, 02191
(617)335-9264
A general line of antiques. *Hours:* By
chance/appt. Fran Tucci

NORTHAMPTON

ALEXANDER'S JEWELRY
207 Main St, 01060
(413)586-9552   **23 68**
Specializing in antiques jewelry &
vintage wristwatches. *Serv:* Appraisal,
watch repair, purchase estates. *Hours:*
TO THE TRADE. *CC:* AX/MV/V.
Assoc: NAWCC. *Park:* Nearby. *Loc:*
Across the street from City Hall.

AMERICAN DECORATIVE ARTS
9 3/4 Market St, 01060
(413)584-6804   **7 40**
Modern design from 1890 - 1960 including mission oak, art deco & fifties
modern, furniture & accessories. *Pr:*
$25–5000. *Est:* 1977. *Serv:* Appraisal,
consultation, purchase estates. *Hours:*
Thu-Tue 10-6 Sun 12-5. *Size:* Medium.
CC: MC/V. *Assoc:* PVADA. *Park:* In
Front. *Loc:* I-91 Exit 18: to light in ctr of
town, R, then 1st L. In the Antique Center of Northampton.

ANTIQUE CENTER OF NORTHAMPTON
9 1/2 Market St, 01060
(413)584-3600   **{GR40}**
Three floors in a restored historic building featuring mission furniture & accessories, Art Deco & Art Nouveau, country
& formal furniture, lighting, books, 50s

modern jewelry, American Indian items, toys, pottery & wrist watches. **Pr:** $10-10000. **Est:** 1987. **Serv:** Purchase estates. **Hours:** Mon-Sat 10-6 Sun 12-5 CLOSED WED. **Size:** Large. **CC:** MC/V. **Assoc:** PVADA. C Kennedy **Park:** In front. **Loc:** From S: I-91 Exit 18: N on Rte 5 to 1st light, R, L at next light(Market St), from N: I-91 Exit 20: S on Rte 5, L on Market.

BARBARA L FERET BOOKSELLER
136 Crescent St, 01060
(413)586-0384   **13**

Antiquarian books on cookery, wine & gastronomy. **Serv:** Appraisal, catalog, search service. **Hours:** BY APPT. **Assoc:** MARIAB.

GEORGE FINE KILIMS
12 Main St, 01060
(413)527-8527   **21**

Oriental flatweaves featuring rugs, wall hangings & cushions. **Hours:** Daily by chance/appt. **Loc:** Upstairs at 12 Main St.

GLOBE BOOKSHOP
38 Pleasant St, 01060
(413)584-0374   **13**

Antiquarian books: fine arts, literature, local history, philosophy, poetry, classical literature, fine printing, first editions, limited editions & children's. **Serv:** Appraisal, search service. **Hours:** Mon-Sat 9-9 Sun 10-5. **Assoc:** MARIAB. Mark Brumberg

L & M FURNITURE
1 Market St, 01060
(413)584-8939   **28 32 40**

Oak furniture, toys, Roseville pottery, crocks, wicker, glassware & graniteware. **Hours:** Mon-Sat 11-5. **Assoc:** PVADA. Marge Farrick

SETH NEMEROFF BOOKSELLER
46 Green St, 01060
(413)586-2220   **13**

Select, diverse stock of unusual & scholarly books in most fields, emphasizing fine & folk art, art history, symbolism, psychology, religion, ancient studies, travel, some old picture frames & artworks. **Serv:** Appraisal, catalog, search service, purchase estates. **Hours:** By chance most days 10-3, or by appt. **Assoc:** MARIAB. **Park:** In front. **Loc:** I-91 to Northampton, W on Main St, L at West St (see signs for Rte 66 W & North Star Rest), bear R on to Green St.

NORTH KING ANTIQUE CENTER
881 North King St, 01060
(413)585-0707   **{GR20}**

Two floors of antiques & collectibles in a newly renovated, air conditioned building with glassware, furniture, books & ephemera. **Pr:** $5-3000. **Est:** 1990. **Hours:** Year round Mon-Sat 10-5, Sun 12-5. **Size:** Large. **Assoc:** PVADA. **Park:** On site. **Loc:** I-91 Exit 21: N on Rtes 5 & 10, 1/4 MI on R; From N on 5 & 10, 3 1/2 MI N of Northampton center, before Danco Designs Center.

PAULSON'S EPHEMERA ETCETERA
52 Green St, 01060
(413)584-0722   **14 33 64**

An interesting shop with antiquarian paper, old prints, Victorian greeting cards, trade cards & scraps, collectibles, old post cards & used books. **Pr:** $1-1000. **Est:** 1981. **Serv:** Appraisal, purchase estates, repairs, restoration. **Hours:** Year round Tue-Sat 10-5,. **Size:** Small. **CC:** MC/V. **Assoc:** ESA MARIAB. Barbara C Paulson **Park:** Nearby. **Loc:** Main St becomes Green Street in Northampton.

LILIAN C STONE ANTIQUES
42A Green St, 01060
(413)586-4090   **16 52 77**

Specializing in sterling, crystal, porcelain, brass, furniture & miniatures. *Est:* 1969. *Hours:* By chance/appt. *Loc:* Across from the Smith College campus & parking lot.

VALLEY ANTIQUES
15 Bridge St, 01060
(413)584-1956   **40 43 83**

Antiques & reproduction oak furniture including a line of Victorian walnut items. *Hours:* Mon-Sat 10-5, Sun 1-5. *CC:* MC/V. *Park:* In rear. *Loc:* On Rte 9.

NORTHFIELD

KEN MILLER'S FLEA MARKET
Warwick Ave, 01360
(413)498-2749   **{FLEA}**

Outdoor flea market with antiques, collectibles. Free admission. *Est:* 1965. *Serv:* Catered, space rental starts at $6. *Hours:* May-Sep Sun 7-3. *Size:* 50 spaces. *Park:* Free parking. *Loc:* I-91, Exit 28 N.

NORTON

NORTON FLEA MARKET
Rte 140, 02766
(508)339-8554   **{FLEA}**

Flea market with over 500 dealer spaces. Admission is $1.00 children free. *Est:* 1971. *Serv:* Catered, rental space is $20 for 20' X 20'. *Hours:* Apr 15-Oct Sun-Mon Holidays, 5:30am til ?. *Size:* 500 spaces. *Park:* Free parking. *Loc:* I-495 Exit 11.

NORWELL

SOUTH SHORE ANTIQUE CENTER INC
295 Washington St, 02061
(617)659-7722   **{GR75}**

In a 250 year old colonial barn, a varied selection including antique quilts, furniture, china, stoneware, decoys, glass, linens, country collectibles. *Est:* 1989. *Hours:* Mon-Sat 10-5, Sun 12-5. *Size:* Large. *CC:* AX/MC/V. *Park:* On site. *Loc:* Rte 3 Exit 14: N on Rte 228, R at traffic light onto Rte 53, 1 1/3 MI on L.

STONEHOUSE ANTIQUES
Rte 53, 02061
(508)878-0172   **36 53 81**

Furniture, tools, mirrors, glass shades, Oriental rugs, lamps & fireplace equipment. *Est:* 1940. *Hours:* Daily 11-5 CLOSED WED, SUN. Marie Anderson *Park:* On site. *Loc:* 1 MI E of 228 on Rte 53 on R.

NORWOOD

COUNTRY TURTLE
1101 Washington St, 02062
(617)769-3848   **{GR3}**

Furniture, accessories, linens, tools, glass, textiles & primitives. *Est:* 1986. *Serv:* Appraisal, custom woodwork, purchase estates. *Hours:* Tue-Sat 11-4. *CC:* DC/MC/V. *Assoc:* SADA. Barbara Cohen *Park:* Nearby lot. *Loc:* I-95 to Rte 1 to Norwood: Dean St, L onto Washington, 1 1/2 blocks.

ORANGE

ARMCHAIR BOOKS
107 Main St, 01364
(508)575-0424   **13**
Antiquarian books: New England town histories, genealogy, cookery, first editions. *Hours:* Tue-Sat 9-6 Sun-Mon 10-6, call ahead advised. *Assoc:* MARIAB. Ed Rumrill *Loc:* Shop in Building 38 Antique Ctr on S Main St.

BLDG 38 ANTIQUE CENTER
57 S Main St, 01364
(508)544-3800   **{GR30}**
Two floors of dealers in a renovated brick building on the river with a wide variety of quality antiques & collectibles. *Est:* 1987. *Hours:* Mon-Sat 9-6 Sun 10-6. *Size:* Large. *CC:* AX/MC/V. *Park:* Nearby lot. *Loc:* Rte 2 Rte 122 Orange Exit: on Main St in downtown Orange.

ORANGE TRADING COMPANY
57 S Main St, 01364
(508)544-6683   **33 55**
A unique shop specializing in jukeboxes, slot machines, arcade games, coke machines & advertising. *Est:* 1980. *Serv:* Appraisal, restoration. *Hours:* Daily 9-6 Fri,Sat til 8. *Size:* Large. *CC:* MC/V. *Assoc:* AAA. Gary H Moise *Park:* In front. *Loc:* Rte 2 to Rte 122 Orange Exit: in the ctr of Orange.

STOCKWELL DECORATING & ANTIQUES
80 New Athol Rd Rte 2A, 01364
(508)575-0340   **50**
Small antiques, custom lamps, silk shades & lamp conversions. *Serv:* Decorating service, custom draperies. *Hours:* Daily CLOSED WED,SUN. *Assoc:* PVADA. Jerome Willard

PALMER

QUABOAG VALLEY ANTIQUE CENTER
10 Knox St, 01069
(413)283-3091   **{GR50}**
Two floors of fine glass, pottery, toys, clocks, jewelry, books & furniture, including over 500 pieces of oak, mahogany, walnut & country. *Pr:* $1–5000. *Est:* 1983. *Serv:* Appraisal, brochure, consultation, custom woodwork, purchase estates. *Hours:* Tue-Sat 9-5 Sun 12-5. *Size:* Huge. David Braskie *Park:* On site. *Loc:* I-90 Exit 8: 1 MI, take Rte 32 thru 2 sets of lights on to Main St, 1/4 MI up to Knox St.

PEABODY

AMERICANA ANTIQUES
South Ln Rte 1, 01960
(508)535-1042   **36 83**
Furniture only - period, Federal, Empire & Victorian. *Pr:* $25–25000. *Est:* 1968. *Hours:* Fri, Sat 9-5. M Meehan *Park:* On site.

HERITAGE CANING COMPANY
28 Foster St, 01960
(508)531-5094   **22 68 71**
Press & hand cane, fiber rush, porch weave, herringbone, Shaker tape, seat weaving of all kinds, stripping & refinishing. Materials available for sale. *Est:* 1969. *Serv:* Appraisal, consultation, conservation, chair repairs a specialty. *Hours:* Year round Mon-Fri 8:30-4. John Newman *Park:* On site. *Loc:* In Peabody Sq 1 1/2 blocks from Monument, across from Bank of New England branch.

PEMBROKE

ENDLESS ANTIQUES
95 Church St, 02359
(617)826-7177   **{GR6}**

Pine & oak furniture, jewelry, linens, fine glass & china; specializing in dolls & doll supplies. *Pr:* $2–2000. *Est:* 1987. *Serv:* Doll hospital, purchase estates. *Hours:* Daily 11-5 Wed til 8. *Size:* Medium. *CC:* MC/V. *Assoc:* SSADA. Marie A Davis *Park:* In front. *Loc:* Rte 3S Exit 12: R on Rte 139S, 1/4 MI on L.

FOUR CORNERS ANTIQUES
236 Water St at Rte 139, 02359
(617)826-2838   **{GR}**

A varied selection of furniture, vintage pocket & wrist watches, primitives, wicker, pine, toys & garden ornaments. *Hours:* Mon-Sat 11-5. *Assoc:* SSADA. Dave Hutton *Park:* On site. *Loc:* At the Int of Water St and Rte 139.

PETERSHAM

GROUND FLOOR ATTIC ANTIQUES
West St, 01366
(508)724-3297   **28 81 83**

Country & Victorian furniture, tools, china, prints, lamps, kitchenware, stoneware & glass located in an 1860s building. *Hours:* Wed-Sun 10:30-5:30. *Assoc:* PVADA. Hank Sherwood *Loc:* Off the Common.

PITTSFIELD

BERKSHIRE ANTIQUES
1716 W Housatonic St Rte 20, 01201
(413)447-9044   **5 37 59**

In a converted greenhouse, a general line of American & European furniture; always a large inventory. *Est:* 1985. *Serv:* Appraisal, consultation, purchase estates. *Hours:* Apr 16-Dec 20 Thu-Sun 10-5. *Size:* Large. Paul Fenwick *Park:* On site. *Loc:* Rte 20: 1/4 MI E of the Hancock Shaker Museum.

BERKSHIRE HILLS COINS & ANTIQUES
111 South St Rte 7, 01201
(413)499-1400   **24 27 47**

Small shop specializing in estate gold & costume jewelry, sterling items, old tools, baseball cards, restored oak furniture, decorative accessories & large selection of collectible coins. *Est:* 1987. *Serv:* Appraisal, consultation. *Hours:* Mon-Sat 10-5:30 or by chance/appt. *Size:* Small. *CC:* MC/V. Peter & Pauline Karpenski *Park:* In front. *Loc:* 1/2 block N on Rte 7 past Rte 20, Pittsfield.

GREYSTONE GARDENS
436 North St, 01201
(413)442-9291   **47 48 85**

A full line of ladies' & men's vintage & antique clothing & jewelry set in an environment of country ease & Victorian elegance. *Pr:* $1–500. *Est:* 1980. *Serv:* Brochure $1. *Hours:* All year Mon-Sat 11-6 Thu 11-9. *Size:* Medium. *CC:* MC/V. *Park:* In front. *Loc:* N of the town green on North St (Rte 7).

OCTOBER MOUNTAIN LEADED GLASS

109 South St, 01201
(413)442-3022   **46 70 71**

Custom designed window & cabinet panels. Beveled & etched glass, lamps & mirrors. Antique windows bought & sold. **Pr:** $15–1000. **Serv:** Appraisal, conservation, consultation, interior design, repairs. **Hours:** Tue-Sat 10-5, Mon by chance. Dwight O'Neil **Park:** On site. **Loc:** From Lenox to Pittsfield take Rte 7-20 which becomes South St; shop is on the R 1/2 block past Housatonic St.

PLAINFIELD

DICK HALE ANTIQUES

Main St Rte 116, 01070
(413)634-5317   **36 42**

Barn full of as-found & refinished antiques & accessories - specializing in pine & cherry. **Pr:** $25–3000. **Serv:** Purchase estates. **Hours:** Daily 11-4:30 or by chance/appt. **Size:** Medium. **Assoc:** BCADA PVADA. **Park:** On site. **Loc:** I-91 to Rte 116W to Plainfield OR Rte 9 to Rte 116N to Plainfield, OR Rte 2 to Rte 112S to Rte 116, then W.

"If the truth be told, I prefer Biedermeier."

Drawing by P. Steiner; © 1990
The New Yorker Magazine, Inc.

PLAINVILLE

BRIAR PATCH ANTIQUES
62 Spring St, 02762
(508)695-1950 **1 28 65**
Shop located in 19th C barn, featuring country furniture & smalls, stoneware, quilts, baskets, toys, dolls, tinware, woodenware & collectibles. *Pr:* $5–600. *Serv:* Appraisal, purchase estates. *Hours:* By chance/appt. *Assoc:* SADA. Marie Oldread *Park:* On site. *Loc:* I-495 Exit 15: Rte 1A to Plainville, 2 1/5 MI, L on Broad St, R on Spring St.

PLYMOUTH

ANTIQUES UNLIMITED INC
96 Long Pond Rd, 02360
(508)746-4100 **37 38 39**
A 3000 square foot showroom exhibiting American & European antiques. Search service is a specialty. *Pr:* $250–12000. *Serv:* Consultation, purchase estates, domestic & international search service. *Hours:* Mon-Sat 10-5 Sun 12-4 or BY APPT. *Size:* Large. Lawrence B Bill *Park:* On site. *Loc:* Rte 3, Exit 5: 1/4 MI W on Long Pond Rd.

VILLAGE BRAIDER
117 Sandwich, 02360
(508)746-9625
General line of antiques & collectibles. *Hours:* Tue-Sat 11-5. *Loc:* Across from the fire station on Rte 3A S.

THE YANKEE BOOK & ART GALLERY
10 North St, 02360
(508)747-2691 **13**
A quaint rare & out-of-print bookshop with an attached art gallery specializing in local history, fine bindings, children's books & antique & contemporary art, originals & prints. *Est:* 1981. *Serv:* Appraisal, catalog, purchase estates, search service. *Hours:* Mon-Sat 10-5. *Size:* Medium. *CC:* AX/DC/MC/V. *Assoc:* MARIAB. Charles F Purro *Park:* Nearby lot. *Loc:* SE Expressway to Rte 3S Exit 6(Rte 44): R on Rte 44 to traffic light, R at light, L on North St.

RANDOLPH

B & B AUTOGRAPHS
PO Box 465, 02368
(617)986-5695 **9**
Specializing in presidential signers, letters & documents authenticity guaranteed. *Pr:* $250–50000. *Est:* 1976. *Serv:* Appraisal, purchase estates. *Hours:* BY APPT ONLY. Barry Bernstien

RAYNHAM

COUNTRY PLACE FLEA MARKET
Rtes 24 & 44, 02767
(617)823-8923 **{FLEA}**
Flea market with collectibles & other flea market merchandise. *Est:* 1974. *Serv:* Catered, space rental starts at $20/reservations required. *Hours:* Year round Sun 9-6. *Size:* 350 spaces. *Park:* Free parking.

READING

H & T BOND BOOKSELLERS
33 Hartshorn St, 01867
(617)944-9044   **13**
Antiquarian books: United States 1870-1920, including reforms, immigration & business, poetry, first editions, modern literature, children's, music & the arts. *Serv:* Catalog, search service. *Hours:* BY APPT ONLY. *Assoc:* MARIAB. Harold/Theresa Bond

Antiques
UNLIMITED

AMERICAN & EUROPEAN FURNITURE

96 Long Pond Road
Plymouth, Mass. 02360
(508) 746-4100
Lawrence B. Bill ~ President

HOURS:
10 - 5:30 DAILY, 12 - 4:00 SUNDAY
OR BY APPOINTMENT

REHOBOTH

MADELINE'S ANTIQUES INC
164 Winthrop St Rte 44, 02769
(508)252-3965   **{GR62}**
A huge showroom on 2 floors with oak & mahogany, glassware, jewelry & linens. *Pr:* $1–5000. *Est:* 1968. *Serv:* purchase estates. *Hours:* Sep-Jun Mon-Sat 10-5, Sun 12-5; Jul-Aug CLOSED MON. *Size:* Huge. *CC:* MC/V. *Park:* On site. *Loc:* I-95 Exit 16: I-195E, take Exit 4 (Rte 44E), L off exits, 3/4 MI past Int of Rte 118, on the L.

MENDES ANTIQUES
52 Blanding Rd Rte 44, 02769
(508)336-7381   **37**
Large selection of American furniture from the 18th & early 19th C, specializing in antique, four-poster rope beds of all sizes. *Serv:* Delivery in New England, shipping anywhere. *Hours:* Daily 9-6 Sun 11-6. *Loc:* 7 MI E of Providence.

JIM NEARY ANTIQUES
11 New St, 02769
(508)252-4292   **22**
Cane & wicker supplies, replacement hardware, shipping, mail orders welcome. *Hours:* By chance/appt. *CC:* MC/V. *Loc:* Off Rte 44.

REHOBOTH VILLAGE SHOPPES
380 Winthrop St Rte 44 E, 02769
(508)252-5334   **{GR20}**
Twenty dealer group shop featuring a large selection of paintings from the 19th & early 20th C, many by local artists, antiques, furnishings & accessories, Oriental rugs, sterling silver & estate jewelry. *Est:* 1990. *Serv:* Estates liquidated, appraisals, consignments solicited. *Hours:* Mon-Sat 10-5 Sun 12-5. *Loc:* On Rte 44 off Rte 24.

RICHMOND

WYNN A SAYMAN
Old Fields, 01254
(413)698-2272   **63**
A large & comprehensive selection of fine 18th & early 19th C English ceramics - primarily for collectors - shown in a Federal period country home. *Pr:* $600–29000. *Est:* 1980. *Hours:* BY APPT ONLY. *Size:* Medium. *Assoc:* AADLA. *Park:* On site. *Loc:* Call for directions.

ROCKLAND

YE PRINTERS' ANTIQUES
267 Union St, 02370
(617)878-3440   **{GR8}**
Glass, china, linens & used furniture. *Pr:* $2–500. *Est:* 1984. *Serv:* Brochure, purchase estates. *Hours:* Mon-Sat 11-5. *Size:* Medium. *Assoc:* SSADA. Marie A Davis *Park:* In front. *Loc:* Rte 123, Union St at K-Mart Plaza, 1 MI on R.

ROCKPORT

FIVE CORNERS ANTIQUES
At Five Corners, 01966
(508)546-7063   **67**
Quilts & collectibles. *Hours:* By chance/appt. *Assoc:* NSADA.

MOUNT VERNON ANTIQUES
Box 66, 01966
(508)546-2434   **21 48 80**
Patchwork & appliqued quilts, hooked rugs, calico day dresses, embroidery, tapestry, lace & unusual textiles. *Pr:* $25–

20000. *Est:* 1973. *Serv:* Appraisal, conservation, consultation, interior design, repairs, restoration. *Hours:* By chance/appt. *CC:* V. Elizabeth Enfield *Park:* In front.

RECUERDO
20 Main St, 01966
(508)546-9471   **4 47 77**
Small shop featuring antique & period jewelry dated from Georgian period through 1940's, silver & smalls (Tiffany, Jensen, Lalique). *Pr:* $5–10000. *Serv:* Appraisal, purchase estates, consultation. *Hours:* Apr-Dec daily 11-5, Jan-Mar by chance/appt. *CC:* AX/MC/V. *Assoc:* GIA. Arlene Vincent *Park:* In front. *Loc:* End of Rte 128 N; follow signs to Rockport.

THE FRAMERY
11 School St, 01966
(508)546-2825   **66 70 71**
Restoration & reproduction of 18th & 19th C frames, a selection of antique prints & orders for design & carving of custom frames. *Est:* 1979. *Hours:* Mon-Fri 8:30-5:30 Sat 9-1 or by appt. *CC:* MC/V. Gloria Upton *Loc:* Rte 128 N to Rte 127 to Rockport.

YE OLDE LANTERN ANTIQUES
28 Railroad Ave, 01966
(508)546-6757   **36 44 63**
Fine furniture & accessories from the 18th, 19th & 20th C specializing in glass & porcelains from the early Victorian period thru the 20th C, also featuring a nice selection of estate jewelry. *Pr:* $10–5000. *Est:* 1970. *Serv:* Appraisal, consultation, purchase estates. *Hours:* Apr-Dec Mon-Sat 10-5, Jan-Mar BY APPT ONLY. *Size:* Medium. Matt Jackson *Park:* On site. *Loc:* Rte 128N to Rockport, from 5 Corners, L to Railroad Ave (Rte 127), across from RR station.

ROWLEY

FRANK D'ANGELO INC
53 Bradford St, 01969
(508)948-2137   **37 59**
17th, 18th & 19th C country & formal furniture, paintings & accessories in original as found condition & finish. *Serv:* Appraisal, purchase estates, shipping. *Hours:* Mon-Sat by chance/appt. *Assoc:* NEA NSADA SADA. *Loc:* In The Isaac Kilbourne House off Rte 133.

GINNY'S FLEA MARKET
Rtes 1A & 133, 01969
(508)948-2591   **{FLEA}**
Outdoor antiques & collectibles flea market. *Serv:* Catered, shady areas available, rental space $10 no reservation required. *Hours:* May-Oct Sun. *Loc:* On the grounds of the Rowley Antique Center.

NORTH FIELDS RESTORATIONS
PO Box 741, 01969
(508)948-2722   **5 74**
A complete line of antique building materials for 17th & 18th C house restoration, specializing in wide antique pine, oak & chestnut flooring. Also selling complete dismantled houses & barns delivered for re-construction on a new site, $5000-25000. *Serv:* Reconstruction on site, brochure, consultation, restoration. *Hours:* BY APPT ONLY. Mark Phillips *Park:* On site. *Loc:* I-95 Exit 54A: to Rte 133E, follow to Rte 1A, go into Rowley center, Todd Farm. Showroom located 1/8 MI past center on the R.

ROWLEY ANTIQUE CENTER
Rtes 1A & 133, 01969
(508)948-2591   **{GR35}**
Furniture, glass, china, quilts, jewelry &

metalwork. *Hours:* Tue-Sun 10-4:30 & Mon holidays. *Assoc:* NSADA. *Park:* On site. *Loc:* On the grounds of Ginny's Flea Market across from Mobil Station.

RYEFIELD ANTIQUES & INTERIORS
Rte 1A, 01969
(508)948-2085   **2 77 86**
Specializing in sterling, fireplace fittings, wicker, cane & reed supplies, furniture - all periods. *Hours:* Daily 10-4:30, Jan weekends only. Jeff Legro *Park:* On site. *Loc:* At the Int of 1A & 133.

SALT MARSH ANTIQUES
224 Main St Rte 1A, 01969
(508)948-7139   **{GR11}**
Two full floors in a restored 1805 barn, packed with furniture, paintings, Oriental rugs & decorative items. *Pr:* $25-3000. *Est:* 1985. *Serv:* Purchase estates, repairs, restoration. *Hours:* Year round daily 9:30-4:30PM. *Size:* Large. *CC:* AX/MC/V. *Assoc:* NADA SPNEA. Robert Cianfrocca *Park:* On site. *Loc:* Rte 95N Exit Rte 133E: to Rte 1A, L at lights Rte 1A, 1 MI on L.

TODD FARM
Rte 1A, 01969
(508)948-2217   **{GR31}**
A general line of antiques with furniture & collectibles pine, oak, mahogany, clocks, linens, paintings, prints, glass, china, pottery, toys, primitives, antique tools, books, & architectural materials. *Hours:* House Thu-Fri 10-4 Barn Mon-Fri 10-4 Both Sat-Sun 10-5. *Assoc:* NSADA. *Park:* On site. *Loc:* 38 min from Boston 1 MI N of Jct of Rtes 133 & 1A.

VILLAGE ANTIQUES
201 Main St Rte 1A, 01969
{GR30}
Specializing in glass & china on two floors. *Hours:* Wed-Sun 10:30-4:30. *CC:* MC/V. *Assoc:* NSADA. *Park:* On site.

SALEM

AMERICAN MARINE MODEL GALLERY
12 Derby Sq, 01970
(508)745-5777   **4 54 56**
Representing the finest in the art of marine models, antique models & models to order. *Serv:* Restoration, appraisal. *Hours:* Tue-Sat 10-4 or BY APPT. *CC:* AX/MC/V. *Assoc:* ICMM ISFAA SHA USNRG. R Michael Wall *Park:* In front. *Loc:* 2 blocks W of Peabody Museum.

ASIA HOUSE
18 Washington Sq W, 01970
(508)745-8257   **60 63 77**
Fine Oriental antiques from Japan, China & Southeast Asia & books on related subjects. *Pr:* $100–15000. *Est:* 1977. *Serv:* Appraisal. *Hours:* Mon-Sat 12-5, Win: CLOSED MON. *CC:* AX/MC/V. Emile Dubrule *Park:* On site. *Loc:* On Rte 1A in the Hawthorne Hotel on the Salem Common.

P A BURKE ANTIQUES INC
121 Essex St, 01970
(508)745-9478   **38 39 60**
Large shop of 18th & 19th C English & Continental furniture, Chinese export porcelain & accessories. *Pr:* $500–25000. *Serv:* Appraisal & purchase estates, mainly to the trade. *Hours:* Year round daily by chance/appt, appt suggested. Paul A Burke Jr *Park:* In front.

CANAL STREET ANTIQUES MARKET
266 Canal St, 01970
(508)744-0123   {FLEA}
Indoor weekly flea market of antiques & collectibles. Admission $.50. *Serv:* Catered, indoors, heated. *Hours:* Every Sun 8:30-4. *Size:* 200 dealers. *Assoc:* NSADA. *Park:* Nearby. *Loc:* Rte 128 Exit 25E: take Rte 114 E to Salem, R at Rte 1A onto Canal St.

R A DI FILLIPO ANTIQUES
Essex St, 01970
21 38
Featuring Continental furniture & accessories, Oriental rugs, glass, china, paintings. *Est:* 1972. *Hours:* Tue-Sat 10-5.

HAWTHORNE ANTIQUES
Essex St, 01970
(508)744-3502   **36 55 73**
Furniture, musical instruments, paintings & sculpture. *Hours:* Tue-Sat 11-6. Nancy D Denzler *Loc:* Across from the Hawthorne Hotel.

MARCHAND'S LAFAYETTE ANTIQUES
159 Lafayette St, 01970
(508)744-7077   **29 36 60**
Oriental china, paintings, decorative accessories & furniture. *Pr:* $25–500. *Serv:* Appraisal, purchase estates. *Hours:* BY APPT ONLY. *Assoc:* NSADA.

MARINE ARTS GALLERY
135 Essex St, 01970
(508)745-5000   **4 56 59**
Largest dealer in fine 18th & 19th C marine paintings in the Northeast displaying on 3 floors. *Serv:* Appraisal, framing, consultation, restoration, free color brochure. *Hours:* Mon-Sat 9-4. *Size:* Large. *Assoc:* AADLA NEAA.

Shows: ELLIS. Russell Kiernan *Park:* Nearby. *Loc:* Directly across from the Peabody Museum.

PHILLIPS CLOCK SHOP
542 Loring Ave, 01970
(508)741-1333   **23 68**
A fine clock, pocket watch & wristwatch shop; repairing all fine clocks & watches; specializing in sale & service of Chelsea clocks. *Serv:* Buy, on sight repair, restoration. *Hours:* Year round Mon-Sat 9-5. *Size:* Medium. *CC:* AX/MC/V. *Assoc:* NAWCC. *Park:* On site. *Loc:* Rte 1A to Vinnin Sq, to Loring Ave, past Fantasy Island Restaurant, next to Tony Lena's.

PICKERING WHARF ANTIQUES GALLERY
Derby & Congress Sts, 01970
(508)741-3113   **{GR30}**
Furniture, paintings, glass, china, jewelry, silver, textiles, country furniture & Oriental rugs in two huge rooms. *Est:* 1982. *Serv:* Appraisal, purchase estates, shipping. *Hours:* Win: daily 10-5 Sun 12-5, Sum: daily 10-6 Sun 12-6 Fri til 8. *Size:* Huge. *CC:* AX/MC/V. *Assoc:* NSADA. Nancy Denzler *Park:* On site. *Loc:* At the corner of Derby & Congress Sts.

UNION STREET ANTIQUES
Pickering Wharf, 01970
(508)745-4258   **23 47 63**
Porcelains, furniture, jewelry, collectibles, restored clocks & watches. *Est:* 1984. *Hours:* Year round daily. *Assoc:* NSADA.

SANDISFIELD

COUNTRY ANTIQUES & PRIMITIVES
New Hartford & Dodd Rds, 01255
(413)258-4834   **27**
Large selection of country & primitives including old cupboards, tables, chairs, benches, blanket chests, weathervanes & hundreds of smalls. *Hours:* Weekends 8-5 Weekdays by chance/appt. *Assoc:* BCADA. Elaine Ziegler *Loc:* From Great Barrington take Rte 23 to Rte 57 & look for sign.

SAUGUS

ANOTHER ERA
419 Essex St, 01906
                                      4 8
Silverware, toys, household furnishing, lamps, embroidery, needlework, ceramics, glassware, American furniture, old tins, advertising signs, paintings, prints & sculpture. *Est:* 1968. *Serv:* Appraisal, auction, accept phone bids, consultation, purchase estates. *Hours:* Mon-Sat 9:30-4:30. *CC:* MC/V. *Assoc:* MSAA NAA NEAA. Florence M Lionetti *Park:* In front. *Loc:* Rte 1 Melrose Exit: Essex St, R on Main St, 1 MI.

SCITUATE

GREENBUSH FIREHOUSE
34 Country Way, 02040
(617)545-6770   **{GR}**
A charming house full of antiques, collectibles & vintage clothing. *Hours:*

Daily 10-5 CLOSED MON. Sandy
Loring Jacobs *Loc:* Near Int of Rtes 3A
& 123.

GREENHOUSE ANTIQUES
182 First Parish Rd, 02066
(617)545-1964   **23 50**
Two rooms of antiques & collectibles,
specializing in early lighting & clocks.
Pr: $10–1000. *Est:* 1987. *Serv:* Ap-
praisal, purchase estates, clock repairs,
restoration. *Hours:* Year round Thu-Sat
11-4:30 or BY APPT. *Size:* Medium.
CC: MC/V. *Assoc:* SSADA. Irving A Ver-
soy *Park:* On site. *Loc:* Rte 3A to First
Parish Rd (Town Hall & Police Station),
1 1/2 MI (past Common) on L.

SEEKONK

ANTIQUES AT HEARTHSTONE
HOUSE
15 Fall River Ave, 02771
(50)336-6273*   **27 29 36**
15 rooms filled with country & formal
furniture in restored & "as found" condition, pewter, brass, copper & decorative
accessories. *Pr:* $2–20000. *Est:* 1974.
Serv: Purchase estates, appraisal,
delivery. *Hours:* Mon-Sat 10-5 Sun 12-5
or BY APPT.. *Size:* Huge. *CC:* MC/V.
Assoc: SNEADA. Bob Woods *Park:* On
site. *Loc:* I-95 from N or S to Re 195 at
Providence RI Rte 195E to MA Exit 1,
Rte 114A N across Rte 44, around bend
on L.

RUTH FALKINBURG'S DOLL SHOP
208 Taunton Ave, 02771
(508)336-6929   **32**
Antique dolls, toys & other small items.
Hours: Mon-Fri 11-3 Sat 12-4 Sun 2-4
best call ahead CLOSED WED. *Assoc:*
SNEADA. Nancy Fredricks

HIDDEN GARDEN ANTIQUES
370 Taunton Ave Rte 44, 02771
(508)336-6057   **45 47**
Fountains & garden ornaments & jewelry & silver. *Hours:* By chance/appt.
Assoc: SNEADA. John George

LEONARD'S ANTIQUES INC
600 Taunton Ave Rte 44, 02771
(508)336-8585   **4 36 43**
Two large floors of fine antique furniture
specializing in American four poster
beds. Classic reproduction furniture by
Eldred Wheeler, Jenkins Plaud & other
fine local craftsmen is on display in the
Tudor-style house. *Pr:* $200–10000. *Est:*
1933. *Serv:* Appraisal, catalog, consultation, custom woodwork, repairs. *Hours:*
Mon-Sat 8-5 Sun 1-5. *Size:* Huge. *CC:*
MC/V. *Assoc:* NEAA SNEADA. Jeffrey
B Jenkins *Park:* On site. *Loc:* 195 Exit 1:
N on Rte 114A, bear R at Old Gristmill
Tavern, R at next light onto Rte 44, on L
at top.

PENNY LANE ANTIQUES/NEW
ENGLAND
288 Fall River Ave, 02771
(508)336-5070   **35 46 71**
15 elegant showrooms featuring French
country & Victorian furniture - complete restoration services, specializing in
Gesso/Gold heat restoration. *Pr:* $25–
5000. *Est:* 1986. *Serv:* Appraisal, consultation, conservation, custom
woodwork, interior design. *Hours:* Daily
11-5. *Size:* Large. *Assoc:* NEAA
SNEADA. David M Murray *Park:* On
site. *Loc:* Rte 195E to RI/MA line Exit
1N: on Rte 114A, R at Fork, 1/2 MI on
R.

SHARON

ANTIQUARIAN BOOKWORM
22 Sentry Hill Rd, 02067
(617)784-9411   **13**

Antiquarian books: Americana, architecture, Civil War, Western Americana,
travel & exploration. *Serv:* Appraisal,
catalog. *Hours:* By appt. *Assoc:* ABAA
MARIAB. Billie Weetall

MICHAEL GINSBERG BOOKS INC
PO Box 402, 02067
(617)784-8181   **13 51**

Antiquarian books: Americana, bibliography, Civil War, explorations &
voyages, Indians, maps, atlases, religion,
theology, travel & Western Americana.

Serv: Appraisal, catalog, search service.
Hours: By appt. *Assoc:* ABAA MARIAB.
Loc: 25 MI S of Boston.

SHEFFIELD

CUPBOARDS & ROSES
Rte 7 PO Box 426, 01257
(413)229-3070   **41 63 69**

Specializing in 18th & 19th C paint-
decorated chests & armoires from the
European Alps in a spectacular post &
beam setting. Antiques & unique accessories. *Est:* 1988. *Serv:* Brochure, consultation, custom woodwork, interior
design, replication. *Hours:* Jul-Sep Daily
10-5, Oct-Jun Wed-Mon 10-5. *Size:*
Large. *CC:* MC/V. *Park:* On site. *Loc:*
On Rte 7 S of Sheffield.

Antiques from New England Homes

Good & Hutchinson INC
ASSOCIATES
Mail: Star Route, Box 147, Tolland, MA 01034
Route 7 (on the Green), Sheffield, MA 01257   (413) 229-8832 or (413) 258-4555
Member of the Art & Antiques Dealers League of America, Inc.

1750 HOUSE ANTIQUES
S Main St, 01257
(413)229-6635 **23 44 55**
American, French & European clocks, music boxes & phonographs, fine glass, china, furniture & decorative accessories. *Serv:* Expert clock repairs. *Hours:* Always open. *Assoc:* BCADA. Frances Leibowitz *Park:* On site. *Loc:* On Rte 7.

ANTIQUE CENTER OF SHEFFIELD
Rte 7, 01257
(413)229-3400 **{GR}**
Broad range of antiques & collectibles. *Est:* 1982. *Hours:* Thu-Sun 10-5, else by chance. K J Cooper *Park:* On site. *Loc:* Across from Sheffield Library.

ANTHONY'S ANTIQUES
South Main St, 01257
(413)229-8208 **29 39 63**
In a restored Berkshire barn, a handsome collection of Staffordshire, Chinese Export porcelain, English formal & country dining & library furniture, decorative accessories, mirrors & a large selection of botanical prints. *Est:* 1987. *Serv:* Decorative porcelains to be made into lamps. *Hours:* Daily 10:30-5:30 B. *Size:* Medium. *Assoc:* BCADA. Anthony Bonadies *Park:* In front. *Loc:* On Rte 7 in South Sheffield.

BLACKBIRD ANTIQUES
N Main St Rte 7, 01257
(413)229-8648 **36 47 67**
Jewelry, furniture, quilts, pottery, silver & American collectibles from 1850-1950. *Hours:* Fri-Mon 10:30-5:30 Tue-Wed by chance. *CC:* MC/V. *Assoc:* BCADA. Andrea Wolfand *Park:* In front. *Loc:* N of Sheffield Ctr.

BRADFORD GALLERIES LTD
N Main St Rte 7, 01257
(413)229-6667 **4 8**
Monthly estate auctions of furniture, sterling silver, oil paintings, oriental rugs, porcelain, brass, bronzes & prints. *Serv:* Catered, order bids accepted. Appraisal for insurance & estates. *Hours:* Daily 9:30-4:30. *Assoc:* BCADA. William Bradford *Park:* On site. *Loc:* 6 MI S of Great Barrington.

CARRIAGE HOUSE ANTIQUE FURNITURE RESTORATION
County Rd, 01257
(413)229-3367 **19 69 71**
Antique furniture restoration service including repairs, refinishing, veneer repair & replacement, color matching & duplication of broken & missing parts. *Est:* 1960. *Serv:* Restoration, replication, repairs, interior woodworking. *Hours:* Mon-Fri 9-5, weekends by appt. Erik Schutz Cabinetmaker *Park:* On site. *Loc:* Rte 7 to Sheffield, Maple Ave to County Rd until Custom Extrusion, bear R on to County Rd, approx 1 1/5 MI on the R.

CARRIAGE TRADE ANTIQUES
159 Undermountain Rd Rte 41, 01257
(413)229-2870 **47 53 85**
Carriage barn specializing in unusual antique jewelry, vintage clothing & accessories, boxes, mirrors, furniture & small. *Serv:* Consignment. *Hours:* CLOSED TUE. Arthur & Linda Segal

CENTURYHURST BERKSHIRE ANTIQUE GALLERY
Main St Rte 7, 01257
(413)229-3277 **{GR20}**
Quality multi-dealer gallery in a new post & beam building with American & European furniture, fine quality china, pottery, American clocks, paintings & prints, dolls, decorative accessories, textiles, brass, pewter, copper, tools & many early smalls. *Est:* 1989. *Serv:* Brochure. *Hours:* Daily 9-5. *CC:* AX/MC/V. Judith T Timm *Park:* On site. *Loc:* From NYC:

I-95 Rte I-287 to Taconic Pkwy to Rte 23, Rte 23 E to Rte 7, Great Barrington S to Sheffield.

CENTURYHURST ANTIQUES
Main St Rte 7 Box 486, 01257
(413)229-8131 **{GR}**
Two large rooms in a ca 1800 Colonial specializing in antique American clocks & a large selection of early Wedgwood, Jasperware, china & country furniture. *Est:* 1980. *Hours:* Daily 9-5. *Size:* Medium. *CC:* AX/MC/V. *Assoc:* BCADA. Judith Timm *Park:* On site. *Loc:* From NYC: I-95 Rte I-287 to Taconic Pkwy to Rte 23 Exit: R (E) on Rte 23 to Rte 7, Great Barrington, R (S) to Sheffield.

CORNER HOUSE ANTIQUES
Main St & Old Mill Pond Rd, 01257
(413)229-6627 **27 86**
Specializing in antique wicker furniture & accent pieces. Traditional wicker sets as well as rare & unusual collector's items. Full line of styles in natural, original paint or custom finish. Also a diverse selection of American country furniture. *Est:* 1977. *Serv:* Repairs, restoration, custom painting. *Hours:* Year round, most days 10-5, please call if coming a distance. *Size:* Medium. *Assoc:* BCADA. Kathleen Tetro *Park:* On site. *Loc:* 1 MI N of Sheffield Ctr, on L.

COUNTRY TOWNE ANTIQUES LTD
Main St Rte 7, 01257
(413)528-0775 **1 21 35**
18th & 19th C American & Continental formal & country furniture, Oriental rugs. *Est:* 1983. *Serv:* Purchase partial or entire estates, appraisal. *Hours:* Year round daily 10-5. *Size:* Large. *CC:* MC/V. *Park:* On site. *Loc:* On Rte 7 at the Great Barrington/Sheffield town line.

DARR ANTIQUES AND INTERIORS
S Main St, 01257
(413)229-7773 **37 39 50**
A large diversified selection of fine 18th & 19th C American, English, Continental & Oriental furniture, paintings, lamps & accessories displayed in two buildings in elegant room settings. Specializing in furniture & appointments for the dining room. *Pr:* $150–25000. *Serv:* Consultation, interior design. *Hours:* May-Oct daily 10-5, Nov-Apr Thu-Mon. *Assoc:* BCADA. Robert R Stinson *Park:* On site. *Loc:* On Route 7.

DOVETAIL ANTIQUES
N Main St Rte 7, 01257
(413)229-2628 **23 37 68**
Always a large selection of 18th & 19th

DOVETAIL ANTIQUES

Open all year

American Clocks • Country Furniture
Redware • Spongeware • Stoneware

Route 7 Sheffield, MA 01257   413~229~2628

C American wall, shelf & tall case clocks compatible with country interiors. Country furniture mostly in old paint or finish, redware, spongeware & stoneware. No glass or china. *Pr:* $20–12500. *Est:* 1976. *Hours:* Wed-Mon 11-5 Tue by chance/appt. *Size:* Medium. *CC:* MC/V. *Assoc:* BCADA NAWCC. David Steindler *Park:* On site. *Loc:* On Rte 7, 3/4 MI N of the ctr of Sheffield on E side of road.

EGH PETER AMERICAN ANTIQUES
Rte 7, 01257
(413)229-8881   **27 34 37**
18th & 19th C American painted country furniture in original or early surfaces, folk art & related decorative arts. *Est:* 1976. *Hours:* Open Fri-Mon, midweek by appt (203)824-1112. *Assoc:* ADA BCADA. Evan Hughes Peter Ermacora *Park:* On site. *Loc:* On Rte 7 between Susan Silver & the Bradford galleries.

FALCON ANTIQUES
176 Undermountain Rd, 01257
(413)229-7745   **16 36 81**
Two floors of American & English smalls, copper, brass, pewter & treen, American & English country furniture, plus a fine selection of woodworking tools for the collector, decorator or user. Custom furniture made to order on the premises. *Pr:* $10–2500. *Est:* 1973. *Serv:* Custom woodwork. *Hours:* Open most days 10-5 or by appt. *Size:* Medium. *CC:* MC/V. *Assoc:* BCADA. Peter Habicht *Park:* On site. *Loc:* Rte 41, 5 MI N of Int of Rtes 41 & 44, 7 MI from Rte 7 Sheffield Ctr, follow signs @ Berkshire School Rd.

GOOD & HUTCHINSON ASSOCIATES
Main St Rte 7, 01257
(413)229-8832   **39 60 63**
Specializing in American, English & Continental furniture, paintings, fine pottery, china & silver for museums & antiquarians. *Serv:* Appraisal. *Hours:* Mon-Sat 10-5 Sun 1-5. *Assoc:* AADLA BCADA. *Shows:* ELLIS. David Good *Park:* On site. *Loc:* On The Green, near Tanglewood & Jacob's Pillow.

FREDERICK HATFIELD ANTIQUES
S Main St Rte 7, 01257
(413)229-7986   **29 47 59**
18th & 19th C Country & formal furniture, jewelry, silver, paintings. Furniture as found & refinished. Some 20th C collectibles. *Est:* 1957. *Hours:* Daily 10-5 & BY APPT. *Assoc:* BCADA. *Park:* On site. *Loc:* 1/5 MI S of Post Office.

KUTTNER ANTIQUES
South Main St Rte 7, 01257
(413)229-2955   **29 37 39**
American & English furniture & decorative accessories of the 18th & 19th C. *Est:* 1987. *Hours:* Wed-Mon 11-5:30 CLOSED TUE. *Size:* Large. *Assoc:* BCADA. *Park:* In front. *Loc:* 1 MI S of Sheffield Village Green on Rte 7.

DAVID J LE BEAU FINE ANTIQUES
South Main St Rte 7, 01257
(413)229-3445   **36 44 77**
Featuring furniture, pottery, porcelain, silver & accessories from the late Federal & Victorian periods & Orientalia. *Serv:* Appraisal. *Hours:* Wed-Sun 9:30-6 or by appt. *CC:* MC/V. *Assoc:* ASA BCADA. *Loc:* Just S of Berkshire School Road.

HOWARD S MOTT INC
Main St Rte 7S, 01257
(413)229-2019   **9 13 33**
Antiquarian book dealers in rare books &

first editions, broadsides, 18th C British pamphlets, English & American literature (16th-20th C), juveniles, autographs, West Indies to 1860, golf & tennis before 1900. Located in a ca 1780 Federal house. *Est:* 1936. *Serv:* Appraisal, catalog, restoration. *Hours:* Appt requested. *Size:* Large. *Assoc:* ABAA BCADA MARIAB. Donald N Mott *Park:* In front. *Loc:* On Rte 7 1/2 Mii S of the Post Office.

OLE T J'S ANTIQUE BARN
S Main St Rte 7, 01257
(413)229-8382   **27 29 36**
Two floors of antiques & collectibles from around the world - Oriental, African, European & early American - including jewelry, furniture, paintings, rugs, lamps & art objects & fine collection of New Guinea art. *Est:* 1985. *Serv:* Purchase estates, consultation, interior design. *Hours:* Daily 10-dark, call Tue, Wed before coming. *Size:* Medium. *CC:* MC/V. Theodore J Fuchs *Park:* On site. *Loc:* Rte 7 1 1/2 MI S of Sheffield; 6 MI S of Gt Barrington, 3 1/2 MI from Canaan, CT.

SUSAN SILVER ANTIQUES
N Main St Rte 7, 01257
(413)229-8169   **29 39 53**
18th & 19th C American, English & Continental fine formal furniture & decorative accessories including a large selection of writing tables, desks, bookcases, linen presses, sideboards & decorative accessories. *Hours:* Daily 10-5 CLOSED TUE. *Size:* Large. *Assoc:* BCADA. *Park:* In front. *Loc:* On Rte 7.

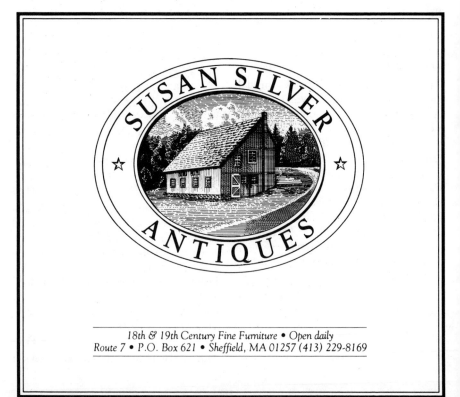

18th & 19th Century Fine Furniture • Open daily
Route 7 • P.O. Box 621 • Sheffield, MA 01257 (413) 229-8169

LOIS W SPRING
Ashley Falls Rd Rte 7A, 01257
(413)229-2542   **27 37**

18th & 19th C American furniture - country & formal - in a 10 room house & barn. Early lighting, woodenware, pottery, paintings & brass. *Hours:* Sat Sun 10-5 weekdays by chance/appt. *Assoc:* BCADA. *Park:* On site. *Loc:* Between Ashley Falls & Sheffield 2 MI S of the Village green.

THREE LITTLE INDIANS
Rte 41 Undermountain Rd, 01257
(413)229-7977   **37 47 82**

A large barn full of American southwestern antiques including trunks, cupboards, leather pouches, serapes, earthenware bowls, woven baskets, primitive paintings, enamelled coffee pots, mostly Indian jewelry. *Est:* 1990. *Hours:* Sat-Sun 10-5. Elaine Herman *Park:* On site.

DAVID M WEISS ANTIQUES
Rte 7, 01257
(413)229-2716   **1 29 37**

A small shop with quality 18th & 19th C formal & country furniture, china, paintings & select accessories. *Hours:* Open weekends or by appt. *Size:* Medium. *Assoc:* BCADA. *Park:* On site. *Loc:* From Boston: I-90 to Rte 7 in Sheffield, From NY: Taconic Pkwy to Rte 23 to Rte 7.

SHELBURNE

GOOD'NUFFS
Mohawk Trail, 01370
(413)625-2144

Paintings, collectibles, antiques with new

items coming in daily. *Hours:* Tue-Sat 10-5 and by chance/appt. Nancy Goodnow Becki Burnham *Park:* Nearby.

ORCHARD HILL ANTIQUES
Colrain Rd, 01370
(413)625-2433   **16 27 81**

Shop & barn annex containing a collection of country furniture, lamps, tools, brass & copper accessories. *Pr:* $5–3000. *Serv:* Appraisal, interior design. *Hours:* Fri 3-6 Sat,Sun 10-6 else by chance/appt. *Size:* Medium. Jeffrey C Bishop *Park:* On site. *Loc:* From Greenfield, Rte 2W, 4 MI, R at Duck Pond Inn onto Colrain Rd, 1/2 MI off Rte 2 (Mohawk Trail).

SHELBURNE FALLS

APPLE BLOSSOMS ANTIQUES
12 Main St, 01370
(413)625-6431   **27**

Country furniture & decorative accessories. *Hours:* Thu-Sat 10-4 Sun 12-4. Judy Turner *Park:* Nearby. *Loc:* In the center of town.

CALL'S SHELBURN COUNTRY SHOP
Rte 2 Mohawk Trail, 01370
(413)625-2041   **27 44 50**

A country shop with glassware, oil lamps, baskets, tools, stoneware, cupboards, & a selection of fine used furniture. *Hours:* Daily 10-4. *Loc:* I-91 Exit 6: 5 MI W on Rte 2.

CHARLEMONT HOUSE GALLERY
6 State St Rte 2A, 01370
(413)625-2800   **44 60 63**

Specializing in Staffordshire, 19th C pressed pattern glass & Orientalia. *Serv:* Appraisal. *Hours:* Tue-Sat 10-5 Sun 12-

5; win: weekends & BY APPT. Janice H Weisblat *Loc:* Next to the Bridge of Flowers in Shelburne Falls.

DIFFERENT DRUMMER
69 Bridge St, 01370
(413)625-8353
Antiques, collectibles, used furniture, a little bit of everything. *Hours:* Tue-Sat 10-5 by chance or appt. *Park:* Nearby.

LUELLA MC CLOUD ANTIQUES
Ashfield Rd Rte 112, 01370
(413)625-2215   **27 34**
A true country shop with country furniture, accessories & folk art including fireplace & hearth accessories, early lightings, Toleware, yellowware, copper, brass. *Est:* 1960. *Hours:* By chance/appt. *Loc:* 10 MI W of Greenfield.

RAINVILLE'S TRADING POST
Rte 112 Colrain Rd, 01370
(413)625-6536   **81**
A collection of antiques, tools, furniture, & collectibles. *Serv:* Buy, sell, swap or trade anything from a plate to an estate. *Hours:* Tue-Sun 9-5 CLOSED MON. *Park:* In front.

SHELBURNE COUNTRY SHOP
Rte 2, 01370
(413)625-2041
Antiques, collectibles & used furniture. *Hours:* Wed-Sun 10-4. *Park:* Nearby.

YANKEE PASTIME ANTIQUES
Rte 112 N, 01370
(413)625-2730   **40**
A large selection of refinished & as-found American oak furniture & antiques. *Hours:* Fri-Sun 9-5 weekdays by appt.

ANDREW'S AXIOMS

Clark's Commentary on Reference Books

**If you have just bought a painting
and are looking up the details of the artist in a dictionary,
you will find that the man who signed it had a different Christian name.**

If he had the same Christian name, he was dead when he painted it.

****

Clark's Commentary on Price Guides

Any piece you you have just bought will not be illustrated.

**Any illustration of a piece that might be similar will have a single feature
so different that it cannot be used for comparison.**

Reprinted with permission from *guide to the Antique Shops of Britain 1989.*
copyright The Antique Collectors Club, Great Britain

SOMERVILLE

FAUX-ARTS ASSOCIATES
40 Dartmouth St, 02145
(617)666-3965   **70**
Special finishes for floors, walls & furniture including wall glazes, murals, marbleizing, stenciling, gilding & trompe l'oeil. *Serv:* Reproduction. *Hours:* BY APPT. Diana Thayer

LONDONTOWNE GALLERIES
380 Somerville Ave, 02143
(617)625-2045   **5 42 45**
Warehouse of fine antiques, country pine, classical garden ornamentation, French country & architectural artifacts. *Est:* 1979. *Serv:* Financing available, appraisal, restoration, modification. *Hours:* Mon-Sat 10-4:30 Sun 12-4. *Size:* Large. *CC:* MC/V. *Assoc:* NEAA. William J Herbert Sr *Park:* On site. *Loc:* In Union Sq, 3/4 MI from Harvard Sq.

ROBT E SMITH
20 Vernon St, 02145
(617)625-3992   **19 43 70**
Period furniture design & reproductions. *Est:* 1973. *Serv:* Brochure ($3), furniture restoration. *Hours:* Mon-Fri 8-5 weekends. *Park:* On site. *Loc:* From McGrath Hwy, W on Broadway, L on Central, R on Vernon, 1 MI from Int of Broadway & McGrath Hwy.

SOUTH BELLINGHAM

COYLE'S AUCTION GALLERY
21 Westminster Ave, 02019
(508)883-1659   **8**
Permanent antique auction gallery. *Serv:* Accept consignments. *Hours:* Daily 9-5;

Auctions every other Tue night. *Assoc:* MFAA. Michael Coyle *Park:* On site. *Loc:* I-495 Exit 16: follow signs to Woonsocket RI, stay on King St to Rte 126S, S 300 yds to Old Colony Gas.

SOUTH BRAINTREE

ANTIQUES & THINGS
826 Washington St Rear, 02184
(617)843-4196   **36 63 66**
Furniture, china, Stueben, pottery, linens, prints, glass jewelry & paintings. *Hours:* Mon-Fri 8-4 Sat 8-12 Call first on weekends. *Loc:* Across from Town Hall.

SOUTH EGREMONT

ANTIQUES & VARIETIES
Main St, 01258
(413)528-0057   **33 34 47**
Antiques & a variety of figures, animals & toys personally picked with an eye for humor, the unusual, whimsy, folk art; precisely organized in well-lighted display cases in a most interesting store. *Hours:* May-Aug Mon-Sun 10-5:30 else Fri-Sun 10-5:30 wkdays by chnce. *CC:* AX/MC/V. *Assoc:* BCADA. Sid Schatzky *Park:* On site. *Loc:* In ctr of town at the Sign of the Juggler.

BIRD CAGE ANTIQUES
Main St Rte 23, 01258
(413)528-3556   **32 41 47**
American painted country furniture & folk accessories, jewelry & silver, glass & china, toys & dolls. No reproductions. Everything from 19th C primitives to 20th C high style. *Pr:* $10–2500. *Est:* 1958. *Serv:* Purchase single pieces or en-

tire estates, appraisal, brochure. *Hours:* Daily 9-5 & BY APPT. *Size:* Medium. *CC:* AX/MC/V. *Assoc:* BCADA. Arnold/Marilyn Baseman *Park:* In front. *Loc:* NYS Thruway Exit 21: Rte 23E past Hillsdale, on R in Post Office building; or I-90 Lee Exit: Rte 75 to Rte 23W, 3 MI to shop.

COUNTRY LOFT ANTIQUES
Rte 23 Hillsdale Rd, 01258
(413)528-5454 **36 44 47**

American country furniture, early pattern glass, lamps, mirrors, woodenware & accessories. *Hours:* Thu-Sun 10-5 by chance. *CC:* MC/V. *Assoc:* BCADA. Tom Millot *Park:* On site.

DOUGLAS ANTIQUES
Rte 23, 01258
(413)528-1810 **40 67 83**

Victorian oak furniture, custom mahogany furniture, quilts 1820-1940, rolltop & flat top desks, Hoosiers, tables & chests, chairs, servers, bookcases, file cabinets & dressers. *Hours:* Wed-Mon 10-5:30 Tue by chance. *Assoc:* BCADA. Douglas Levy *Park:* On site. *Loc:* Behind the Weathervane Inn.

BRUCE & SUSAN GVENTER BOOKS
Tyrrell Rd Rte 23, 01258
(413)528-2327 **13 66**

Antiquarian books - specializing in 19th C hand-colored prints, authentic manuscript leaves from the 13th to the 15th C, rare & unique books, fashion, costume, cookbooks, calligraphy, antique reference books & a large general stock. *Pr:* $1–2500. *Est:* 1980. *Serv:* Purchase estates. *Hours:* Wed-Sun 10:30-5 or BY APPT. *Size:* Medium. *Assoc:* MARIAB. *Park:* On site. *Loc:* 1 MI E of NY state border; 2 1/2 MI W of S Egremont post office on Tyrrell Rd just off Rte 23.

HOWARD'S ANTIQUES
Hillsdale Rd Rte 23, 01258
(413)528-1232 **46 50**

American country furniture including large extension tables, chairs, bookcases, chests of drawers & washstands. Early American electric, kerosene & gas lighting, chandeliers, sconces, floor lamps & table lamps. *Est:* 1975. *Serv:* Consultation, interior design, lighting repairs & restoration. *Hours:* Mon, Wed-Fri 10-5, Sat-Sun 10-6, CLOSED TUE. *Assoc:* BCADA. Lynda & Jeff Howard *Park:* On site. *Loc:* 2 MI W of South Egremont, 1 MI E of New York line.

LITTLE HOUSE STUDIO
Old Sheffield Rd, 01258
(413)528-9517 **27 34**

American country furniture, collectibles, decorative accessories & folk art. *Serv:* Custom painted & cut lampshades. *Hours:* Wed-Sat 10-5 Sun 1-5. *Assoc:* BCADA. Libby & Milt Fett *Park:* On site. *Loc:* Across from the Egremont Inn.

RED BARN ANTIQUES
Rte 23, 01258
(413)528-3230 **29 36 50**

Furniture, glass, accessories & large selection of early lighting - electric, gas & kerosene. *Est:* 1943. *Serv:* Appraisal, restoration, auction. *Hours:* Daily 10-5. *CC:* MC/V. *Assoc:* NAA. John Walther *Park:* On site. *Loc:* At the Int of Rtes 23 & 41.

GLADYS SCHOFIELD ANTIQUES
Rtes 23 & 41, 01258
(413)528-0387 **36 44 50**

Furniture, china, glass & lamps. *Est:* 1949. *Serv:* Appraisal. *Hours:* Fri-Mon 10-5 Sun 1-5. *Park:* On site.

ELLIOTT & GRACE SNYDER ANTIQUES
Undermountain Rd Rte 41, 01258
(413)528-3581   **45 37 80**
18th & 19th C American furniture & decorative arts, including folk art & period garden furnishings. *Hours:* Appt suggested. *Assoc:* ADA BCADA NHADA. *Park:* On site. *Loc:* Rte 41 1/2 MI S of Rte 23.

SPLENDID PEASANT
Rte 23 & Old Sheffield Rd, 01258
(413)528-5755   **27 34 65**
Two buildings of 18th & 19th C country furniture, specializing in original paint & finish, unusual folk art, early quilts & decorative accessories. *Est:* 1987. *Serv:* Interior Design. *Hours:* Daily 9:30-5:30. *Assoc:* BCADA. Martin & Pamela Jacobs *Park:* In front. *Loc:* 1 block from S Egremont center.

SOUTH NATICK

COMING OF AGE ANTIQUES
22 Elliot St Rte 16, 01760
(508)653-9789   **3 29 58**
In the John Eliot historic district: glass, china, furniture, tools, handcrafts & jewelry. *Pr:* $5–1500. *Est:* 1981. *Serv:* Consultation. *Hours:* Tue-Sat 11-4 Sun 1-4. *CC:* AX/MC/V. *Assoc:* SADA. Rosamond H Haley *Park:* In front. *Loc:* Rte 128 Wellesley Exit: Rte 16, 6 MI.

KENNETH W RENDELL INC
46 Eliot St, 01760
(617)237-1492 FAX
(617)431-1776   **9 13**
Antiquarian bookseller featuring autograph letters, manuscripts, & documents, ancient writing, medieval manuscripts & Western Americana. *Est:*

1959. *Serv:* Appraisal, cable "Autographs Boston". *Hours:* Mon-Fri 9-5 Appt preferred. *CC:* AX/MC/V. *Assoc:* ABAA. *Park:* Nearby. *Loc:* From Wellesley College, Rte 16 W about 2 MI. Across from the John Eliot Church.

KENNETH W VAN BLARCOM AUCTIONEER
63 Eliot St, 01760
(508)653-7017   **4 8 25**
Individual antiques & estates appraised, purchased & sold on consignment. Terms to consignor - 20%. Buyers premium - 10%. *Serv:* Appraisal, accept mail & phone bids, brochure, consultation. *Hours:* Mon-Fri 9-2 BY APPT or BY APPT. *Assoc:* AR. *Park:* On site.

SOUTHAMPTON

SOUTHAMPTON ANTIQUES
172 College Hwy Rte 10, 01073
(413)527-1022   **23 40 83**
Three large barns filled with a large selection of quality oak & Victorian furniture - as found & restored. *Hours:* Thu-Sat 10-5 Sun 12-5, CLOSED AUG. *Size:* Huge. *CC:* DC/MC/V. *Assoc:* PVADA. Meg Cummings *Park:* On site. *Loc:* I-90 Exit 3: L onto Rte 10, N for 7 MI or from Northampton take Rte 10S for 8 MI.

SOUTHBOROUGH

ANTIQUE MALL AT SOUTHBOROUGH
24 Turnpike Rd, 01772
(508)879-2221 FAX
(508)460-6054   **{GR90}**
A broad range of antiques & collectibles

including furniture, oil paintings, watches, postcards & baseball cards. *Hours:* Mon-Tue 10-6 Wed-Fri 10-9 Sat 10-6 Sun 12-6. *CC:* MC/V/AX. Roberta Paulas *Park:* On site. *Loc:* I-90E Exit 12: West on Rte 9 1 MI to Brickyard Square on R.

GOLDEN PARROT
22 E Main St, 01772
(508)485-5780   **25 36 44**

Baskets, tins, country furniture, glass, collectibles & consignment items. *Hours:* Mon-Fri 1-5 Sat,Sun by chance/appt. *Assoc:* SADA. Glen Urquhart *Loc:* Off of Rte 85 on Rte 30.

MAPLEDALE ANTIQUES
224 Boston Rd, 01772
(508)485-5947   **29 36**

Furniture, accessories & collectibles. *Hours:* Daily 2-5, all day Sat, CLOSED SUN. *Assoc:* SADA. Eleanor J Hamel *Loc:* Rte 30 E 1/4 MI W of Framingham line.

TEN EYCK BOOKS
PO Box 84, 01772
(508)481-3517   **13**

Antiquarian books: children's, fishing & hunting, illustrated & literature. *Serv:* Catalog. *Hours:* Call ahead advised. *Assoc:* MARIAB. Arthur Ten Eyck

SOUTHBRIDGE

SECOND FIDDLE AUCTIONS
62 Elm St, 01550
(508)765-0370   **13**

Auctioneers of antiques & books of significance. *Est:* 1964. *Serv:* Appraisal, auction, purchase estates. *Hours:* BY APPT ONLY. *Assoc:* MARIAB. Roland Boutwell *Park:* On site. *Loc:* From Sturbridge, MA take Rte 131 approx 5 MI; turn R on Rte 198 (which is also Elm St).

SUN GALLERIES
299 South St, 01550
(508)765-5540   **59**

19th & early 20th C American Impressionists, social realists & abstract art. *Hours:* BY APPT ONLY. Eric Glass

SOUTHFIELD

ANTIQUES @ BUGGY WHIP FACTORY
Main St, 01259
(413)229-2433   **{GR38}**

A group shop specializing in early & primitive American antiques. *Serv:* Lunch in Boiler Room Cafe. *Hours:* Jun-Dec daily 10-5, Jan-May Fri-Mon 10-5. Don Coffman *Loc:* 8 MI N of Int of Rtes 44 & 272 in CT. Across from the new Marlborough Fire Station.

OLDE–AN ANTIQUES MARKET
Main St Rte 272, 01259
(413)229-3140   **{GR20}**

Antique jewelry, art glass, porcelain, silver, rare books, lamps & pottery & small furniture. *Hours:* Daily 10-5. Joan & Howard Basis *Loc:* At the Buggy Whip Factory 15 min SE of Great Barrington, 10 min N of Norfolk, CT.

SOUTHWICK

BARKING FROG COLLECTIBLE CO
108 Congamond Rd Rte 68, 01077
(413)569-3291   **{GR}**

Multi-dealer shop with toys, quality oak furniture, baseball memorabilia & cards,

comics & comic collectibles. *Est:* 1990.
Hours: Tue-Sun 10-5 CLOSED MON.
John Cammisa *Loc:* Located on Rte 168.

SPRINGFIELD

ANTIQUARIA
60 Dartmouth St, 01109
(413)781-6927   **37 83**
Specializing in American Victorian antique furniture. *Serv:* Catalog $4. *Hours:*
Tue-Sat 10-5 by chance/appt. Dan
Cooper

ANTIQUES ON BOLAND WAY
1500 Main St, 01115
(413)746-4643   **{GR15}**
Featuring furniture & accessories from
all periods. *Pr:* $25–10000. *Est:* 1990.
Serv: Appraisal, purchase estates. *Hours:*
Mon-Sat 9:30-5:30. *Size:* Large. *CC:*
AX/MC/V. Paul R Tuller *Park:* On site.
Loc: Located at Bay State West.

JOHNSON'S SECONDHAND
BOOKSHOP
1379 Main St, 01103
(413)732-6222   **13**
Antiquarian books: general stock featuring fine art, local history, remainders &
children's. *Serv:* Search service. *Hours:*
Mon-Sat 9-5:30 Thu til 9. *Assoc:*
MARIAB. Jim Ward

STOCKBRIDGE

ANTIQUES AT TOM CAREY'S
PLACE
Sergeant St, 01262
(413)298-3589   **23 27 50**
An elegant shop of carefully selected
pieces displayed in room settings -

specializing in American clocks, 18th-
19th C country furniture, lamps, glass.
Hours: Daily BY APPT, CLOSED
TUE. *Assoc:* BCADA. Lucille Nickerson
Park: Nearby. *Loc:* Behind Mission
House, off Main St.

DOUGLAS ANTIQUES
Rte 7, 01262
(413)298-3104   **36**
Custom mahogany furniture. *Hours:*
Wed-Mon 10-5:30, Tue By chance.
Park: On site.

ENCORES ANTIQUES
Main St, 01262
(413)298-4765   **29 63**
A small shop with furniture, Art Deco,
framed prints, decorative accessories &
faux bamboo. *Pr:* $25–250. *Est:* 1988.
Hours: Wed-Sun 11-5. *Assoc:* BCADA.
Pauline F Nault *Park:* In front. *Loc:*
Across the street from the Red Lion Inn.

OVERLEE FARM BOOKS
PO Box 1155, 01262
(413)637-2277   **13**
Antiquarian books: explorations &
voyages, history, literature, nautical &
Herman Melville. *Serv:* Catalog. *Hours:*
BY APPT. *Assoc:* MARIAB. Martin &
Sally Torodash

REUSS ANTIQUES & ARTS CENTER
Pine & Shamrock Sts, 01262
(413)298-4074   **66**
Two floors of art & antiques, specializing
in Audubon & nature prints & antiques
in pine, cherry & walnut in a restored
1855 house. *Serv:* Appraisal, repair.
Hours: May-Jan daily 10-4. *Size:* Large.
CC: MC/V. *Assoc:* BCADA. Vern Reuss
Park: On site. *Loc:* 1 block N of Red
Lion Inn.

JOHN SANDERSON ANTIQUARIAN BOOKS
W Main St, 01262
(413)274-6093   **13**

Select stock of rare books from the 16th C onward - including literary 1st editions, science, medicine, economics, inscribed & signed books, children's literature, art reference, travel & Americana. **Pr:** $35–1500. **Est:** 1976. **Serv:** Appraisal, catalog, purchase estates, search service. **Hours:** Visitors welcomed by appt. **Size:** Medium. **CC:** MC/V. **Assoc:** ABAA MARIAB. John R Sanderson **Park:** In front. **Loc:** Call for directions.

STONEHAM

FRANK C KAMINSKI INC
193 Franklin St, 02180
(617)438-7595   **4 8**

Auctioneer dealing in early American & European antiques, paintings, furniture, rugs, silver, clocks, glass, porcelain, sculpture, photography, jewelry, militaria, Indian items, toys & automobiles. Historic real estate a specialty. **Est:** 1978. **Serv:** Appraisal, accept mail/phone bids, brochure, consultation, purchase estates. **Hours:** Office hours 9-5, appt suggested. **Assoc:** NAA. **Park:** On site. **Loc:** I-93 Exit 36: Montvale Rd to R on Main, 2 blocks, L onto Franklin, 1 MI on L, only 10 min from Boston.

STOUGHTON

WESTERN HEMISPHERE INC
144 West St, 02072
(617)344-8200   **13**

Antiquarian books: business, economics, government documents, Americana & periodicals. **Hours:** Mon-Fri 9-5 BY APPT ONLY. **Assoc:** ABAA. Eugene L Schwaab Jr

STURBRIDGE

ANTIQUE CENTER OF STURBRIDGE
Main St Rte 20, 01566
(508)347-5150   **{GR25+}**

Displaying furniture, china, glass, jewelry & metalware. **Hours:** Wed-Mon 10-5. **Park:** In front. **Loc:** In the center of town.

THE COPPERSMITH
Main St Rte 20, 01566
(508)347-7038   **16 29 50**

Handcrafted lighting specialist. One of the largest selections of handcrafted early American lighting in copper, tin & brass in New England. Sconces, chandeliers & accessories. Retail showroom - wholesale inquiries welcome. **Est:** 1982. **Serv:** Catalog ($3), reproduction. **Hours:** Wed-Fri 12-5, Sat-Sun 10:30-5, Mon-Tue by chance/appt. **CC:** MC/V. **Park:** On site. **Loc:** 1/4 MI past Sturbridge Village & entrance, opposite Sturbridge Yankee Workshop on Rte 20.

THE GREEN APPLE
On the Common Rte 131, 01566
(508)347-7921   **27 34**

Antiques, American folk art & country

furnishings. *Est:* 1975. *Hours:* Mon-Sat 10-9 Sun 10-6. *CC:* MC/V. Elaine Cook Chris Wilson *Park:* In front. *Loc:* Next door to the Publick House 1/4 MI from Rte 20.

STURBRIDGE ANTIQUE SHOPS
200 Charlton Rd Rte 20, 01566
(508)347-2744   **{GR75}**

Furniture, decorative accessories, glass, china & porcelain. *Hours:* Mon-Fri 9-5 Sat,Sun 10-5. *CC:* MC/V. Robert Hopfe *Park:* On site. *Loc:* 6 MI E of Brimfield, 2 MI E of Old Sturbridge Village & 1/2 MI E of I-84 & I-90.

YESTERDAYS ANTIQUE CENTER
Rte 20, 01566
(508)347-9339   **{GR45}**

Furniture & decorative accessories. *Hours:* Daily 10-5. Ken Boland *Park:* On site. *Loc:* Located in the heart of Sturbridge, 200 yds from Old Sturbridge Village.

SUDBURY

THE ANTIQUE EXCHANGE OF SUDBURY
236 Concord Rd, 01776
(508)443-8175   **29 44 63**

Large assortment of fine American & European furniture, fine porcelain, glass & Oriental items, as well as rugs, chandeliers, tapestries, Sedres, Royal Doulton, Dresden, steins, Wedgwood, Majolica, silver, Staffordshire, flow blue, Minton & more. *Est:* 1987. *Serv:* High-quality consignments accepted. *Hours:* Wed-Sat 10:30-6 or BY APPT, CLOSED SUN. *Size:* Large. Jeanie Quirk *Park:* On site. *Loc:* Rte 20 at

Wayland to Rte 27N to Sudbury Cen, L at lights to Concord St, look for small sign; shop in barn behind house.

BEARLY READ BOOKS INC
320 Boston Post Rd Rte 20, 01749
(508)443-4034   **13**

Antiquarian books: history, military, science fiction, detective fiction, first editions & cookery. *Serv:* Search service. *Hours:* Tue-Fri 10-6, Sat 10-5, Sun 6 weeks before Christmas 12-5. *Assoc:* MARIAB. David Van Buskirk

FARMHOUSE COLLECTIBLES
170 Hudson Rd, 01776
(508)443-6593   **1 25 27**

In a converted old barn - vintage home accessories, furniture, clothing & jewelry on consignment. *Est:* 1986. *Hours:* Wed-Sun 12-4 CLOSED JUL. *Size:* Medium. Jane Bramberg *Park:* In front. *Loc:* Rte 20 in Wayland,to Rte 27 N to Sudbury Ctr, straight to Hudson, 1 MI on R.

MAGGIE FLOOD
357 Boston Post Rd, 01776
(508)443-7324   **85**

Romantic dresses created from antique fabrics & laces & an assortment of folk art. *Pr:* $20–1000. *Est:* 1985. *Serv:* Dresses to order. *Hours:* Tue-Sat 10-5:30, Thu til 9, CLOSED SUN. *CC:* AX/MC/V. *Park:* On site. *Loc:* From the Wayside Inn, E on Rte 20 for 5 MI.

SUNDERLAND

DAN FLEMING RESTORATION MATERIAL
168 N Main St, 01375
(413)665-2421   **65**

Restoration materials & some ephemera. *Hours:* BY APPT ONLY. Dan Fleming

OINONEN BOOK AUCTIONS
PO Box 470, 01375
(413)665-3253   **8 13**

Auctions of fine & rare books. *Est:* 1980.
Serv: Appraisal, auction, catalog ($5, $8
subscription available). *Hours:* BY
APPT ONLY. *Assoc:* MARIAB NEBA
PVADA.

SWANSEA

AMERICAN ART & ANTIQUES INC
11 Maiden Ln, 02777
(508)678-9563   **59 66 71**

A diverse inventory of American paintings from early 19th to mid 20th C. *Pr:*
$500–50000. *Serv:* Conservation, res-
toration. *Hours:* BY APPT. Mel Davey
Park: On site. *Loc:* I-195, 15 min from
Fall River, or Providence, call for directions.

FERGUSON & D'ARRUDA
1 Main St, 02777
(508)674-9186   **5 36**

Diverse line of furniture, textiles, architectural elements & garden accessories. *Hours:* By chance/appt. *Assoc:*
NHADA. *Loc:* 5 min from I-95.

TAUNTON

JO-ANN E ROSS
1679 Somerset Ave Rte 138, 02780
(508)824-8255   **36 59**

Folk art paintings, country period furni-
ture & band boxes. *Hours:* BY APPT
ONLY. *Park:* On site. *Loc:* From Fall
River, MA: N on Rte 138 just over
Dighton-Taunton line, Colonial house
on W side of the road.

TAUNTON FLEA MARKET
Rte 44, 02780
(508)880-3800   **{FLEA}**

Indoor/outdoor flea market of antiques,
collectibles & other flea market mer-
chandise. Admission Adults $1.00
Children under 12 free. *Est:* 1988. *Serv:*
Catered. *Hours:* Every Sun 8-5. *Size:*
Huge. *Park:* On site.

TEMPLETON

1800 HOUSE ANTIQUES, LTD
Rte 101, 01468
(508)939-8073   **27 44 63**

Small country antiques attractively displayed in a bright new shop - part of a

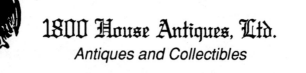

1800 House Antiques, Ltd.
Antiques and Collectibles

June and Don Poland

(508) 939-8073/939-2576   Templeton
(Route 101 - Phillipston)   Mass. 01468

large, grey restored Federal farmhouse.
Companion barn loft offers furniture in
the rough & collectibles. *Pr:* $10–2000.
Est: 1986. *Hours:* Daily 10-5, CLOSED
Thanksgiving, Christmas, New Year's
Day. June & Don Poland *Park:* On site.
Loc: Rte 2 Petersham Exit: toward Peter-
sham, L at Rte 101 toward Templeton,
approx 6 MI, grey Federal house on L.

CHETWOOD ANTIQUES
Rte 2A, 01468
(508)939-8641   **65 83**
Victorian, early primitive, custom & for-
mal antiques. *Serv:* Auction & appraisal.
Hours: Sun & Mon 9-5 & BY APPT.

PAUL C RICHARDS AUTOGRAPHS
INC
High Acres, 01468
(508)630-1228   **9 13 33**
Wide range of original autographs of
historically important personages, 15th
C to the present, including Presidents,
historical, military, literary, scientific,
music & the arts, world leaders, offered
in letters, documents & signed images.
Pr: $25–300000. *Serv:* Appraisal, catalog
$5, consultation. *Hours:* Year round
daily 10-5 Sat BY APPT. *Size:* Large.
Assoc: ABAA MARIAB. *Park:* On site.
Loc: Approx 1 MI off Rte 2 in northern
Worcester County, call for specific directions.

WRIGHT TAVERN ANTIQUES
The Common, 01468
(508)939-8879   **16 27 50**
Country furniture, primitives, brass,
iron, tin, wooden accessories & lighting
of kerosene era. *Hours:* Year round by
chance/appt. *Assoc:* PVADA. George
Pushee *Park:* In front. *Loc:* Next to the
library.

TOLLAND

MARIE WHITNEY ANTIQUES
Rte 57 Box 148, 01034
(413)258-4538   **36 60**
Three barns of furniture & decorative
accessories. *Hours:* Mon-Sat BY APPT
ONLY.

TOWNSEND

MARTHA BOYNTON ANTIQUES
1 Greeley Rd, 01469
(508)597-6794   **41**
Furniture in original paint, doorstops,
baskets, spongeware, mourning pictures,
mourning brooches & memorial
samplers. *Hours:* By chance/appt. *Assoc:*
NHADA. *Loc:* Corner Rte 119 &
Greeley Rd.

HARBORSIDE ANTIQUES
Rte 119 & Spaulding St, 01469
(508)597-8558   **{GR16}**
New stock daily from private homes in-
cluding oak furniture, clocks, quilts,
glass, ephemera, jewelry, dolls, lamps,
books & silver. *Est:* 1982. *Hours:* Wed-
Sun 10-5. *CC:* V/MC. Gloria Mc Caffrey
Loc: I-495 to Rte 119 & corner of
Spaulding St.

TOWNSEND COMMON ANTIQUES
11 Brookline St, 01469
(508)597-8044   **36**
Specializing in 17th, 18th & 19th C furniture & accessories for the serious
dealer & collector. *Serv:* Search. *Hours:*
Daily by chance/appt. *Assoc:* NHADA.
Frank Tammaro *Loc:* 4 1/2 MI S of NH
at Jct of Rte 13N & 119, at N end of town
common.

TOWNSEND HARBOR

CHERRY HILL ANTIQUES
67 Main St, 01469
(508)597-8903   **33**
Antiques, collectibles & advertising items. *Hours:* Wed-Sat 10-4:30. Ben/Joan Moran

UPTON

DAVID ROSE ANTIQUES
36 W Main St, 01568
(508)529-3838   **1 29 36**
American furniture of the 18th & 19th C, appropriate smalls & paintings. Trade inquiries invited. *Serv:* Purchase estates. *Hours:* Tue-Fri 10-5, Sat 10-4, CLOSED SUN, Mon by chance. *Size:* Medium. *CC:* MC/V. *Assoc:* NHADA SADA. *Park:* In front. *Loc:* I-495 Exit 21B: 4 MI to Rte 140, R on 140, approx 1 MI on L.

WABAN

ANTIQUE RESEARCHERS
PO Box 79, 02168
(617)969-6238   **26**
Quality research on problem issues & questions relating to art & antiques that can be investigated using library resources & related materials. No buying, selling or appraisals. *Hours:* BY APPT, call after 7:30 weekday evenings.

PRIPET HOUSE ANTIQUE PRINTS
PO Box 90, 02168
(617)235-7557   **66**
A fine collection featuring natural his-tory prints with decorative french mats & museum standard framing. *Est:* 1984. *Hours:* BY APPT. *CC:* MC/V. Elizabeth King *Loc:* Call for directions.

DIANA J RENDELL INC
177 Collins Rd, 02168
(617)969-1774   **9 13**
Antiquarian bookseller featuring autograph letters, manuscripts, antiquities & illuminated pages. *Hours:* BY APPT ONLY. *Assoc:* ABAA.

WAKEFIELD

BACK-TRACK ANTIQUES
243 North Ave, 01880
(617)246-4550   **{GR6}**
Featuring a wide selection of furniture, glassware & collectibles. *Hours:* Mon-Fri 11-6 Sat 8-4 Sun 10-3. *Loc:* Rte 128 Exit 39: 1 1/5 MI to Wakefield.

LANTERN & BREEZEWAY
935 Main St, 01880
(617)245-1713   **44 63**
Featuring fine glass & china, furniture, accessories, primitives & estate jewelry. *Hours:* Mon-Sat 10-4 Thu til 8. *CC:* MC/V. *Assoc:* NSADA. *Park:* On site. *Loc:* Rte 128 Exit 39: Follow North Ave 2 MI then R @ Dunkin Donuts on Main St. 1 MI on R.

WALTHAM

HAROLD M BURSTEIN & CO
36 Riverside Dr, 02154
(617)893-7494   **13 33 66**
Antiquarian books: Americana, American literature, books about books, children's, English literature & weaving.

Serv: Appraisal, catalog, search service. *Hours:* BY APPT. *Assoc:* ABAA MARIAB. Eunice K Burstein

THE PRINTER'S DEVIL
282 Moody St, 02021
(617)646-6762   **13 72**

Unique shop specializing in antique medical instruments, books & prints dealing with the history of medicine. *Pr:* $45–10000. *Est:* 1973. *Serv:* Appraisal, catalog, consultation, purchase estates. *Hours:* BY APPT ONLY. *Size:* Large. *CC:* AX/MC/V. *Assoc:* ABAA, ABA, MARIAB. Barry A Wiedenkeller *Park:* On street. *Loc:* Central Waltham shopping area.

RESTORATION SERVICES
621 Main St #3, 02154
(617)647-7865   **68 71**

Highest quality conservation & invisible restoration of antiques - specializing in porcelain, glass & lacquer, as well as pottery gold leaf, sculpture & ivory - the full range of objets d'art. *Serv:* Conservation, restoration. *Hours:* Mon-Fri 8-5 appt suggested. *Assoc:* AIC NECA. Neil Dale *Park:* Nearby lot. *Loc:* Directly across from Waltham City Hall on Main St (Rte 20), second floor.

SPNEA CONSERVATION CENTER
Lyman Estate 185 Lyman St, 02154
(617)891-1985   **26 37 74**

Technical expertise for conservation of early finishes: paint, wood, plaster & stone. State-of-the-art materials & expert craftsmanship for consolidation & repair on site or at Center's laboratories. Historic bldgs, furniture, upholstery & wood conserv. *Est:* 1972. *Serv:* Brochure, conservation, consultation, repairs, restoration. *Hours:* All year Mon-Fri 9-5 BY APPT. *Park:* On site. *Loc:* 1/2 MI off Rte 20.

WAYLAND

GREAT MEADOWS JOINERY
Box 392, 01778
(508)358-4370   **19 43 76**

Creating & designing Shaker & American country furniture reproductions, selecting the finest examples of the genre. Repetoire prominently features Shaker designs. *Pr:* $800–5000. *Est:* 1986. *Serv:* Catalog $2, custom woodwork, reproduction. *Hours:* Year round daily 9-5 BY APPT. *Size:* Medium. Gene Cosloy *Park:* On site. *Loc:* 5 min from Wayland Ctr, call for specific directions.

WAYLAND ANTIQUE EXCHANGE
303A Boston Post Rd, 01778
(508)358-7452   **25**

Consignment shop offering old & antique furniture, rugs, oils, china, glass, jewelry & toys. *Hours:* Tue-Sat 10-4. *Assoc:* SADA. Ruth Newell *Loc:* Wayland Village.

YANKEE CRAFTSMAN
357 Commonwealth Rd Rte 30, 01778
(508)653-0031   **36 50 71**

Antique lighting & furniture, featuring one of the country's most extensive collections of antique lighting fixtures. *Est:* 1968. *Serv:* Appraisal, consultation, restoration, repair. *Hours:* Year round 7 days/week 10-5. *Assoc:* NEAA SADA. Bill Sweeney *Loc:* Near The Villa.

WELLESLEY

D B STOCK ANTIQUE CARPETS
MAIL: PO Box 82-251, Wellesley, 02181
(617)244-5815   **3 4 21**

Specializing in selected antique & old

Oriental carpets in very good to excellent condition; Northwest Persian carpets (Serapi & Biojar) a specialty; roomsize & small collector's carpets. *Pr:* $2000-50000. *Serv:* Appraisal, Purchase estates. *Hours:* BY APPT. *Size:* Medium. *Assoc:* N. *Shows:* RI. *Park:* In front *Loc:* Please call for directions.

THE CINNABAR COMPANY
464 Washington St, 02181
(617)239-1267   **37 38 60**

Fine arts from the 19th & early 20th C & European, American & Oriental furniture & decorative accessories from the 19th & 20th C. *Est:* 1990. *Serv:* Architectural consultation to institutions & residences. *Hours:* Mon-Sat 10-5 Call for summer hours. *Size:* Medium. *CC:* AX. Sam Guiffre *Park:* In front. *Loc:* Rte 16 W from Rte 128 approx 4 MI.

EUROPEAN MANOR
566 Washington St, 02181
(617)235-8660   **38 80**

European furniture, French Provencal cottons, handpainted marbleized papers, ceramics & accessories. *Serv:* Custom fabrication. *Hours:* Mon-Sat 10-5:30.

MARCUS & MARCUS ANTIQUES
184 Worcester Rd Rte 9, 02181
(617)239-0611   **38 66**

Three floors of both European & American furniture & accessories. Large collection of botanical prints & antique mirrors. Several hundred accessories in stock at all time. *Pr:* $50–10000. *Serv:* Custom framing, furniture painting, flower arranging. *Hours:* Mon-Sat 10-5, CLOSED last 2 weeks of AUG. *Size:* Large. *CC:* MC/V. Beth Marcus *Park:* On site. *Loc:* Rte 128 Exit Rte 9W: 2nd Cedar St Exit (Needham), bear R over bridge, 1st L at light, on R next to "The Wok".

SPIVACK'S ANTIQUES
54 Washington St, 02181
(617)235-1700   **29 37 39**

One of New England oldest & largest shops, direct importers of European furniture & accessories. Also carry American furniture & accessories. *Pr:* $100–15000. *Hours:* Mon-Fri 8:30-5:30 Wed 8:30-9. *Size:* Huge. *CC:* AX/MC/V. *Park:* On site. *Loc:* I-90 to Rte 128S to Rte 16, 1/2 MI on Rte 16 to Washington St, on the L.

TERRAMEDIA BOOKS
19 Homestead Rd, 02181
(617)237-6485   **13**

Antiquarian books: travel & exploration, Africa, Asia, Americana. *Serv:* Appraisal, catalog, search service. *Hours:* BY APPT. *Assoc:* ABAA MARIAB. Elias N Saad, PhD

WELLESLEY HILLS

ERNEST KRAMER FINE ARTS & PRINTS
PO Box 37, 02181
(617)235-0112 FAX
(617)237-3635   **59 66 78**

Specializing in late 19th & 20th C American & European prints & drawings. Select works by Cadmus, Chamberlain, Clark, Crane, Hassam, Heintzelman, Kappell, Kronberg, Lewis, Lozovlick, Markham, Nason, Orr, Pennell, Pleissner, Ripley, Roth & many more. *Pr:* $150–7500. *Serv:* Appraisal, catalog ($10), consultation. *Hours:* BY APPT ONLY. *CC:* MC/V. Ernest S Kramer *Park:* On site. *Loc:* Off Rte 16 in Wellesley Hills; call for appt & specific directions.

LACES UNLIMITED
339 Washington St, 02181
(617)235-6812   **48**

Imported laces: valances, tablecloths, panels, curtains & spreads. ***Hours:*** Mon-Sat 10-5. ***Park:*** Nearby. ***Loc:*** In the Wellesley Hills train depot.

WENHAM

FIREHOUSE ANTIQUES
148 Main St Rte 1A, 01984
(508)468-9532   **36**

Fine furniture & antiques, including the largest selection of brass & iron beds in New England. ***Hours:*** Daily 10-4, Sat & Sun til 5, CLOSED WED.

HENDERSON'S
300 Main St, 01984
(508)468-4245   **29 63 77**

Furniture, accessories, silver & Oriental porcelains. ***Hours:*** Mon-Sat 9-5:30 Sun by chance.

WEST BOYLSTON

PUDDLE DUCK ANTIQUES
9 Maple St Rte 140, 01583
(508)835-3825   **{GR25}**

Quality group shop occupying two floors of a restored country barn with diversified selection of antiques & collectibles, from country primitives to Arts & Crafts. ***Est:*** 1982. ***Serv:*** Purchase estates. ***Hours:*** Year round Tue-Sun 10-5, CLOSED MON. ***Size:*** Medium. Walt & Nancy Gunderman. ***Park:*** On site. ***Loc:*** On Rte 140, 1/4 MI S of W Boylston Center on the Heritage Trail.

THE DEACON'S BENCH
18 N Main St Rte 140, 01583
(508)835-3858   **{GR16}**

Furniture, art, stoneware, tools, pottery, glass, china, prints, lamps, linens, jewelry & reference books. ***Hours:*** Tue-Sat 10:30-4:30 Sun 11-4 CLOSED MON. ***Size:*** Large. Cynthia A Secord ***Loc:*** I-190 Exit 5: S on Rte 140.

OBADIAH PINE ANTIQUES
160 W Boylston St Rte 12, 01583
(508)835-4656   **23 27 40**

Country furniture, oak, walnut, baskets, lamps, clocks, jewelry & glass. ***Hours:*** By chance/appt. Linda Toppin ***Loc:*** Rte 190 Exit 4: to Rte 12, L on W Boylston 3/4 MI.

THE ROSE COTTAGE
24 Worcester St Rtes 12 & 140, 01583
(508)835-4034   **{GR8}**

A turn of the century barn featuring primitives, toys, Black memorabilia, costume & fine jewelry, linens, large & small furniture, collectibles & some reproduction pieces. ***Pr:*** $1-1000. ***Est:*** 1970. ***Serv:*** Purchase estates, repairs, restoration. ***Hours:*** May-Dec Tue-Sat 11-5, Sun 1-5; Jan-Apr Fri-Sat 11-5, Sun 1-5. Loretta Kittredge ***Park:*** On site. ***Loc:*** I-90, 495N to Rte 290 to Rte 140N.

WEST BRIDGEWATER

RABBIT PATCH ANTIQUES
21 N Main St, 02319
(508)587-8585   **63**

Specializing in Blue Willow. ***Est:*** 1990. ***Hours:*** Fri-Sat 11-5 Sun 12:30-5. Joanne Damaris ***Loc:*** Near Jct of Rte 106 & 28.

RECOLLECTIONS
17 N Main St, 02379
(508)584-7981
An eclectic offering of antique furnishing & accessories. *Hours:* Tue-Sun 10-5. Elinor Peabody *Loc:* Rtes 106 & 28.

SHUTE AUCTION GALLERY
50 Turnpike St, 02379
(508)588-0022   **4 8**
Liquidation of estates & fine antiques. *Serv:* Auction, appraisal. *Hours:* Office hour Mon-Fri 9-5. *Assoc:* MSAA SSADA. Philip C Shute

WEST BRIDGEWATER ANTIQUES MARKET
337 West Center St Rte 106, 02379
                              {GR}
A group shop with furniture, primitives, china, glass, toys, paintings, post cards, jewelry, Victoriana & dolls. *Hours:* Daily 11-4:30 Sun 12-4. *Loc:* 12 Mi from Rte 24.

WILLOWBROOK
Rte 106 35 E Center St, 02379
(508)580-1019   **43 46**
Large, elegant showroom featuring the finest quality antique reproduction furniture & accessories, paintings & Oriental rugs. *Serv:* Interior design, appraisal, consultation, purchase estates. *Hours:* Sep-Apr Tue-Sat 10-5 Sun 12-5, May-Aug CLOSED SUN. *CC:* MC/V. Frank Silvia *Loc:* Rte 24 Exit 16 A: go through 2 sets of lights, shop on L.

WEST BROOKFIELD

BOOK BEAR
W Main St Rte 9, 01585
(508)867-8705   **13**
Antiquarian books: psychology, anthropology, military, religion & theology, technical books. *Serv:* Appraisal, catalog. *Hours:* May-Nov 7 days 10-6, Dec-Apr Wed-Sun 10-6. *Size:* 40,000 books. *Assoc:* MARIAB. Al Navitski

WEST CHESTERFIELD

TIMOTHY GORHAM CABINET MAKER
1 Ireland St, 01084
(413)296-4061   **19**
One-man shop specializing in reproductions using traditional joinery & methods. Casework, tables, chairs, turnings & carving made from air-dried native woods including tiger maple, cherry, walnut & pine. *Pr:* $300–5000. *Est:* 1980. *Serv:* Custom woodwork, repairs, reproduction, restoration. *Hours:* Most days. *Loc:* In West Chesterfield at the corner of Rte 143 & Ireland St.

SUSAN K RILEY SEAT WEAVER
1 Ireland St, 01084
(413)296-4061   **68 70 71**
Specializing in natural rush seat replacement - also splint & cane. *Hours:* By chance/appt.

TEXTILE REPRODUCTIONS
666 Worthington Rd, 01084
(413)296-4437   **14 46 74**
Goods for 18th & 19th C textile furnishings, needlework & clothing reproductions. Wide assortment of fabrics, threads, tapes, hardware & other supplies for replicating textile goods. Finished goods also available. *Est:* 1983. *Serv:* Catalog ($3/$12), minor conservation, consultation, interior design, repair. *Hours:* BY APPT ONLY. *CC:* MC/V. *Assoc:* NTHP SPNEA. Edmund Smith

WEST GRANVILLE

IVES HILL ANTIQUES
Ives Hill Main Rd Rte 57, 01034
(413)357-8703 **37 67**
Large barn showroom nestled in the
Berkshire hills featuring American
country & period furnishings & accessories. *Pr:* $25–6000. *Hours:* May-Oct
Wed-Sun 12-5, else BY APPT. *Size:*
Medium. Dee Bates *Park:* On site. *Loc:*
1 MI W of West Granville Ctr, on Rte 57
opposite the Granville State Forest Rd.
13 MI W of Westfield.

WEST NEWBURY

HELIGE ANDE ARTS
85 Church St, 01985
(508)363-2253 **26 46 71**
19th C decorative arts techniques, both
custom & restoration work, early paint
matching in restoration a specialty.
Painting techniques include: stenciling,
graining, marbleizing, wall glazing &
dragging & reverse painting on glass.
Serv: Consultation, interior design, restoration. *Hours:* BY APPT. Ingrid San-
born *Park:* On site. *Loc:* I-95N Exit Rte
113 (Newburyport): W 5 MI to ctr of
West Newbury, R on Church St.

THE JOY OF BOOKS
320 Main St Rte 113, 01985
(508)363-2343 **13**
Americana, children's books, fine bindings, military, nautical, New Englandiana, poetry. *Serv:* Appraisal. *Hours:*
Mon-Sat 10:30-4:30 other times by appt.
Size: 5,000 books. *Assoc:* MARIAB. Russ
Joy

MOODY-RIDGEWAY HOUSE
803 Main St, 01985
(508)465-8046 **13 51 66**
Books, maps & prints. *Hours:* BY APPT
ONLY. *Assoc:* NSADA.

VALYOU AUCTIONS
PO Box 132, 01985
(508)363-2946 **8 25**
Country consignment auction almost
every Wednesday. Licensed in ME, MA,
NH & VT. *Est:* 1973. *Serv:* Consult-
ation, purchase estates. *Hours:* BY
APPT. *CC:* MC/V. *Assoc:* MSAA NAA
NHAA VAA. LeRoy N Valyou *Park:* On
site. *Loc:* 495 Exit 53 (Broad St): N 1/4
MI to Horizons Function Hall in Mer-
rimac, MA.

WEST NEWTON

CONSIGNMENT GALLERIES
1276 Washington Ave, 02165
(617)965-6131 **25**
Antiques & collectibles: furniture, china,
sterling, jewelry, lamps, mirrors, chandeliers, glass, objets d'art, pottery, bronzes, copper & brass. *Serv:* Accept
consignments. *Hours:* Mon-Sat 9:30-5
Fri until 7. *Park:* In front. *Loc:* Additional parking available in lot behind
Brigham's.

WEST STOCKBRIDGE

ANDERSON & SONS SHAKER TREE
Rtes 41 & 102, 01266
(413)232-7027 **70 76**
Handcrafted Shaker reproductions
produced on commission. *Serv:*
Reproduction. *Hours:* BY APPT. Peter
Anderson

SAWYER ANTIQUES AT SHAKER MILL
Shaker Mill Depot St, 01266
(413)232-7062   **27 37 76**

Early American furniture & accessories - formal, Shaker & country. *Serv:* Appraisal. *Hours:* Fri-Sun 10-5 BY APPT. *Assoc:* ASA BCADA. Edward S Sawyer *Park:* On site. *Loc:* On the bridge at Rtes 102 & 41.

WEST TOWNSEND

ANTIQUE ASSOC AT JOSLIN TAVERN
519 Main St, 01474
(508)597-2330   **{MDS80}**

Fine antiques & Americana displayed in a colonial tavern by more than 90 carefully-selected, quality dealers. *Pr:* $25–25,000. *Est:* 1987. *Serv:* Ship worldwide, 800# = "1(800)562-SOLD", financing available. *Hours:* Daily 10-5. *Size:* Large. *CC:* MC/V. *Park:* In front. *Loc:* In a historic grey & white tavern on Rte 119 W of Antique Associates at West Townsend.

ANTIQUE ASSOC AT WEST TOWNSEND
473 Main St, 01474
(508)597-8084   **{MDS80}**

Eighty quality dealers specializing in Americana, period, country & formal furniture, decorative arts & accessories displayed in an 18th C Colonial house. *Pr:* $25–25000. *Est:* 1984. *Serv:* Ship worldwide, 800# ="1(800)562-SALE", financing available. *Hours:* Daily 10-5. *Size:* Large. *CC:* MC/V. Lynne C Hillier *Park:* On site. *Loc:* On Rte 119 in West Townsend.

DELANEY ANTIQUE CLOCKS
435 Main St, 01474
(508)597-2231   **23**

Largest selection of antique American tall clocks in the country, as well as fine examples of other clocks & period furniture. Tall clocks are guaranteed. *Pr:* $25–250000. *Est:* 1968. *Serv:* Crate & ship anywhere, will set up your clock anywhere on East. Seaboard. *Hours:* Sat-Sun 9-5 Mon-Fri by chance/appt. *Size:* Large. John & Barbara Delaney *Park:* On site. *Loc:* Rte 2 from Boston or Rte 128 to Rte 119 to West Townsend; shop is on R, 2 MI from 2nd light in Townsend.

GARY SULLIVAN ANTIQUES
435 Main St, 01474
(508)597-2680   **37**

Specializing in American furniture of the Federal period, with emphasis on formal furniture, at affordable prices for collectors & dealers. *Hours:* Sat-Sun 10-5 weekdays by chance/appt. *Assoc:* SADA. *Park:* On site. *Loc:* Next to John Delaney on Rte 119.

WEST VILLAGE ANTIQUES
434 Main St, 01474
(508)597-8475   **36 40 44**

Merchandise from area homes & estates including furniture, oak & glass. *Est:* 1978. *Serv:* Purchase estates. *Hours:* Thu-Sun 10:30-5. Dick Fiorentino *Park:* In front. *Loc:* On Rte 119.

WESTBOROUGH

1753 HOUSE ANTIQUES
22 Morse St, 01581
(508)366-4566   **37 59**
18th & 19th C American furniture & paintings. *Hours:* BY APPT ONLY. *Assoc:* SNEADA. Elizabeth Keller

HARDWICKE GARDENS
Rte 9, 01532
(508)366-5478   **45**
Garden items for country & formal gardens including Victorian fencing & gates, cast & wrought iron garden furnishings, stone bird basins, iron cauldrons & kettles, pony & goat carts, will pumps, granite posts. *Hours:* Mon-Sat 9-5:30, Sun 10-5:30.

MAYNARD HOUSE
11 Maynard St, 01581
(508)366-2073   **27 43**
Country shop featuring cupboards, tables, baskets, herb loft & exclusive line of upholstered country sofas & wing chairs representing 1750-1820. *Serv:* Catalog. *Hours:* Thu-Sun 10-5 BY APPT. *Assoc:* SADA. Betty Urquhart *Loc:* Off Rte 135.

OLDE SCHOOLHOUSE ANTIQUES
196 E Main St Rte 30, 01581
(508)366-1752   **16 27 65**
Country furniture, primitives, decorative items in brass, copper & tin. *Hours:* Wed-Fri 1-5 Sat 9:30-5:30. *Assoc:* SADA. Doris A Dall

PUSHCART PLACE
86 E Main St, 01581
(508)366-6116   **34 50 63**
Folk art, pottery, lamps, tin, iron & old tools displayed in pushcarts & stalls.

Hours: Daily 10-5:30 Thu til 8. *Assoc:* SADA. Bunnie Cummings *Loc:* Rte 30 at Water St near Rte 9.

SALT-BOX HOUSE ANTIQUES
9 Maynard St, 01581
(508)366-4951   **27 36 41**
Early, painted country furniture & accessories, along with a select line of custom upholstered sofas & wing chairs. *Serv:* Fabrics by Greeff, Waverly, Schumacher. *Hours:* Thu-Sun 10-5 or BY APPT. *Assoc:* SADA. Margaret M Gure *Park:* Ample. *Loc:* I-495 Exit 23B: W to Rte 9W to Rte 135E, R on Rte 135, 3rd R is Maynard St.

WESTFIELD

ABC ANTIQUES
658 Montgomery Rd, 01085
(413)562-4715   **42**
Featuring pine furniture & related accessories for a country look. *Hours:* Thu-Sat 10-5, Sun 12-5 or BY APPT. *Assoc:* PVADA. Eloise & Sam Adair

ANTIQUE MARKETPLACE
One Broad St, 01085
(413)562-9562   **{GR90}**
Three floors of antiques & collectibles located in a unique, restored post office, c 1912, including furniture, pottery & porcelain, glass, paintings, pewter, copper & brass, dolls & toys, folk art, jewelry, clocks & watches, primitives, prints, & more. *Est:* 1986. *Serv:* Appraisal, purchase estates. *Hours:* Daily 10-5 Sun 12-5. *Size:* Huge. *CC:* MC/V. Paul R Tuller *Park:* On site. *Loc:* I-90 Exit 3: 18 MI S of Northampton, located at Jct of Rtes 10-202 & 20.

JOYCE & DAUGHTERS
243 Elm St Rte 10, 01085
(413)562-0528   **40 83**
Oak & Victorian furniture, accessories &
Hummels. *Hours:* Daily 10-4.

WESTFORD

ANTIQUES ORCHARD
83 Boston Rd, 01886
(508)692-7161   **{GR40}**
Furniture, toys, clocks, export porcelain,
linens & accessories on 2 floors. *Pr:* $25–
2500. *Est:* 1982. *Hours:* Daily 10-5 Sun
11-5. *Assoc:* SADA. Sally Cady *Park:* On
site. *Loc:* I-495 Exit 32: Go E a short
distance on the R.

WOLF'S DEN ANTIQUES
139 Concord Rd Rte 225, 01886
(508)692-3911   **29 36**
A selection of furniture including oak,
walnut, mahogany, wicker, clocks,
Oriental rugs, sterling & china. *Hours:*
Sat & Sun or by appt. Roberta L Wolf
Loc: I-495 Exit 31 or 32:.

WESTON

JANE CHORAS, BOOKS
225 Winter St, 02193
(617)237-9828   **13 33**
Antiquarian books: children's,
ephemera, first editions, illustrated,
science fiction & fantasy. *Hours:* BY
APPT. *Assoc:* MARIAB.

HOLLYDAY HOUSE
55 Chestnut St, 02193
(617)894-4361   **29 59 74**
Consultants in 18th C period rooms,
specializing in early bed hangings & interior wood paneling. Computerized
database on early wood panelling sites.
Carrying antiques, accessories & paintings. *Est:* 1986. *Serv:* Consulting on
non-structural aspects of 18th C homes.
Hours: BY APPT. Thomas Hollyday
Loc: Call for directions.

M & S RARE BOOKS INC
45 Colpitts Rd, 02193
(617)891-5650   **9 13**
Antiquarian books: American literature,
Americana, broadsides & posters, first
editions, history of science, Judaica,
medicine, philosophy, Western
Americana & Black history. *Serv:* Appraisal, catalog. *Hours:* By chance, call
ahead advised. *Assoc:* ABAA MARIAB.
Daniel G Siegel

WESTPORT

A QUIET PLACE
1615 Drift Rd, 02790
(508)636-8390   **30 34 76**
Early baskets, decoys, folk art, Shaker,
dolls & accessories. *Hours:* BY APPT.
Assoc: SNEADA. Al & Penny Hadfield

WING CARRIAGE HOUSE
1151 Main Rd, 02790
(508)636-2585   **{GR3}**
Fine antique & estate jewelry & carefully
chosen selection of furnishings including
primitives, quilts & silver. *Est:* 1971.
Serv: Purchase estates. *Hours:* Jan-May
Wed-Sat 12-5, Jun-Dec Mon-Sat 12-5.
CC: MC/V. F Travis *Park:* In front. *Loc:*
195 to Rte 88, L at Hixbridge Rd & L
onto Main Rd.

WESTWOOD

THE APPRAISERS' REGISTRY
Box 261, 02090
(617)326-6762 FAX
(617)329-4680   **4 26**
Appraisals of fine arts, jewelry, rare books, guns, Asian art, coins & stamps for insurance & estates purposes. *Est:* 1979. *Serv:* Photographic inventories. *Hours:* Mon-Sat BY APPT. Michael F Wynne-Willson

PEG WILLS ANTIQUES
PO Box 305, 02090
(617)762-6684   **36 56 67**
American antiques for country or townhouse, furniture, Dedham & Dorchester pottery, hooked rugs, quilts, Indian & nautical items - always a good supply of items for decorators. *Serv:* Purchase estates. *Hours:* BY APPT ONLY. *Assoc:* SADA. *Loc:* Call for Appt.

WHATELY

MJ DENEHY CARPENTRY
5 Conway Rd, 01093
(413)665-4344   **19 43 70**
Raised panel walls & doors, wide pine & fine hardware. Custom 18th C building, design & restoration. *Serv:* 18th C building design & restoration, custom woodworking. *Hours:* By chance/appt. Michael J Denehy *Loc:* From 91 S Whately Exit take Rte 5 & 10 N, L on Christian Lane, R at Whately Inn, R on Conway Rd, 2nd house on L.

WILBRAHAM

MURRAY BOOKS
473 & 477 Main St, 01095
(413)596-9372   **13 33 66**
Stock of old & rare books for collectors & dealers & ephemera of all sorts. *Serv:* Appraisal, purchase estates. *Hours:* BY APPT ONLY. *Size:* Medium. *Assoc:* ABAA MARIAB. Paul M Murray *Park:* On site. *Loc:* 8 MI E of Springfield, 2 MI S of N Wilbraham on 20, phone for directions.

WILLIAMSBURG

COUNTRY FINE ANTIQUES
25 South St, 01096
(413)268-3298   **36 42 65**
Changing stock of 18th & 19th C country primitives & accessories, including some textiles, some finer quality pieces of the period, pine furniture with painted & unpainted woods. *Pr:* $25–500. *Est:* 1986. *Serv:* Appraisal, consultation, interior design. *Hours:* Sat-Sun 12-5:30 Fri by appt. Susan Netto *Park:* In front. *Loc:* In Williamsburg turn at Williamsburg General Store on to South St, 1/4 MI on L.

GEORGE THOMAS LEWIS
78 Old Goshen Rd, 01096
(413)268-7513   **4 8**
Estate appraisers & liquidators specializing in primitives, silverware, household furnishings, clocks, lamps, glassware & American furniture. *Assoc:* NEAA.

**R LOOMIS
FURNITURE/CABINETMAKER**
R219B, 01096
(413)628-3813   **19 43 70**
Fine furniture & cabinetmaking - in all styles, but specializing in Queen Anne & Chippendale periods. Each piece individually crafted. *Est:* 1974. *Serv:* Catalog ($3), cabinetmaking, custom woodwork, reproduction. *Hours:* BY APPT. Russ Loomis, Jr *Park:* On site. *Loc:* Call for appt and directions.

RUMPLESTILTSKIN
206 Main St Rte 9, 01096
(413)268-7604   **5 50 74**
Extensive inventory of architectural originals, including doors, fireplace mantels, stained glass, beveled glass, lighting fixtures, hardware, columns, handrails, spindles, wrought iron fencing, gates, church pews & cobblestone. *Serv:* Appraisal, delivery. *Hours:* Mon-Sat 9:30-6 Sun 12-6. Paul Britt *Loc:* On Northampton/Williamsburg town line.

WILLIAMSTOWN

COLLECTOR'S WAREHOUSE
105 North St, 01267
(413)458-9686   **44 48 63**
A general line of antiques & collectibles including china, glass, linens, books, prints, tools, toys, furniture, vintage clothing. *Est:* 1985. *Hours:* Wed-Sat 12-5 or by appt. *CC:* MC/V. Deborah Elder *Park:* On site. *Loc:* Off Rte 7 next to Le Country Restaurant in the Mc Clelland Press Building.

FRAME SHOP GALLERY
181 Main St, 01267
(413)458-3486   **23**
Specializing in pocket & wristwatches.

Also early military items, paintings & rugs. *Est:* 1954. *Hours:* Mon Wed Fri 10-4 & by appt. Edward A Straub *Loc:* 1/4 MI E of Howard Johnson's, next to Four Acres Motel.

WINCHENDON

TOY TOWN ANTIQUES
Rte 12, 01475
(508)297-2411   **40**
Specializing in turn-of-the-century & refinished oak furniture including tables, cabinets, chairs, dining room sets, sideboards & bedroom furniture. *Hours:* Wed-Sun. *CC:* MC/V. Ron Quesnel

WINCHESTER

KOKO BOODAKIAN & SONS
1026 Main St, 01890
(617)729-5566   **21 26 71**
Experts in Oriental rugs offering fine quality rugs for sale or trade to the discriminating collector. Complete restoration a specialty. *Est:* 1938. *Serv:* Consultation, appraisal, cleaning, complete restoration, repair. *Hours:* Tue-Sat 9:30-5 Thu til 9 CLOSED SUN, MON.

LION'S HEAD ANTIQUES
225 East Street, 01890
(617)729-7519   **36 59 66**
Paintings, prints, furniture, walking sticks, Majolica, export porcelain, paisley shawls, hooked rugs. *Est:* 1990. *Hours:* Mon-Fri 8:30-5 Sat-Sun by chance/appt. *Loc:* Next to the Indoor Tennis Center.

LUCKY LADY BOUTIQUE
41 Thompson St, 01890
(617)729-1154   **{GR}**
A collection of furniture, decorative accessories & smalls. *Est:* 1990. *Hours:* Mon-Sat 10-5. *CC:* MC/V.

WINCHESTER ANTIQUES
71 Cross St, 01980
(617)721-0550   **27 34 77**
Country furniture, folk art, quilts, china, silver, jewelry, paintings, prints, old toys, wind-ups & cast iron. *Hours:* Tue-Fri 11-5 Sat 10-5 or by appt. *CC:* MC/V. *Loc:* Between Washington St & Rte 38.

WOBURN

PATRICK J GILL & SONS
9 Fowle St, 01801
(617)933-3275   **68 71**
Complete restoration of silver, pewter, brass & copper including repairing, refinishing & plating. Over 75 years experience - specializing in plating (gold, silver & rhodium) all work performed on premises. *Est:* 1911. *Serv:* Repairs, restoration. *Hours:* Mon-Sat 9-5. *CC:* MC/V. Joe Gill *Park:* On site. *Loc:* I-93 Montvale Ave Exit: to Woburn Ctr rotary, take Rte 38S, 1st lights take L onto Fowle.

WORCESTER

ART & ANTIQUE GALLERY INC
4 Old English Rd, 01609
(508)753-7332   **59**
Featuring an inventory of over 1000 paintings of 17th thru 20th C American & European artists. *Hours:* By appt only.

J & N FORTIER INC
484 Main St, 01608
(508)757-3657   **24 79**
Worcester's largest antique coin & stamp store. *Serv:* Appraisal, purchase estates. *Hours:* Mon-Sat 10-5 Wed til 7 Sum: CLOSED SAT. *Size:* Medium. *CC:* MC/V. Naomi Fortier *Park:* Nearby lot.

HAMMERWORKS
6 Freemont St, 01603
(508)755-3434   **50**
Handmade Colonial lighting including chandeliers, sconces, hardware, andirons, candlestands in copper, brass, iron & tin. *Serv:* Lighting catalog $3, ironware catalog $1.

JEFFREY D MANCEVICE INC
PO Box 413 West Side Station, 01602
(508)755-7421   **13**
Antiquarian books: early printing, history of science, incunabula, medicine, early religion, theology, early mathematics, Renaissance & humanism. *Serv:* Catalog. *Hours:* BY APPT. *Assoc:* ABAA MARIAB.

O'REILLY/EINSTADTER LTD
36 Franklin St, 01608
(508)797-1178   **60 63 82**
Fine Asian antiques in a museum setting. Folk art, tribal art, furniture & jewelry. *Serv:* Appraisal. *Hours:* Mon-Fri 9:30-6:30 Sat 10-6 Sun 12-6. *Loc:* Across the St from City Hall.

ISAIAH THOMAS BOOKS & PRINTS
980 Main St, 01603
(508)754-0750   **13 52 66**
Paperbacks & rare books in all fields, located in a Victorian house, including Americana, first editions, local history, miniature books & prints. *Serv:* Appraisal, search service. *Hours:* Tue, Thu, Fri, 12-5 Wed 12-8 Sat 9-5 call ahead

Sun. *CC:* MC/V. *Assoc:* ABAA MARIAB. Jim Visbeck *Park:* In front. *Loc:* Near Clark University, 1 MI from Worcester's City Hall.

WORTHINGTON

COUNTRY CRICKET VILLAGE INN
Huntington Rd Rte 112, 01098
(413)238-5366   1 36 50
Furniture, lighting & collectibles displayed in a charming country restaurant. *Pr:* $10–1000. *Est:* 1980. *Serv:* Purchase estates. *Hours:* Daily 10-6 CLOSED TUE. *Size:* Medium. *CC:* AX/MC/V. *Assoc:* PVADA. Donald F Bridgeman

Park: On site. *Loc:* Northampton Rte 9W to Rte 143 to Worthington Rte 112S.

WRENTHAM

WRENTHAM ANTIQUE MARKETPLACE
513 South St Rte 1A, 02093
(508)384-2811   {GR45}
Fine antiques & collectibles. *Est:* 1987. *Serv:* Appraisal, consultation, custom woodwork, interior design, purchase estates. *Hours:* Tue-Fri 10-6 Sat 10-5 Sun 12-5. *Size:* Medium. *CC:* AX/MC/V. *Park:* On site. *Loc:* 495 Exit 15: Rte 1A to Wrentham.

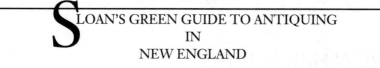
▼

New Hampshire

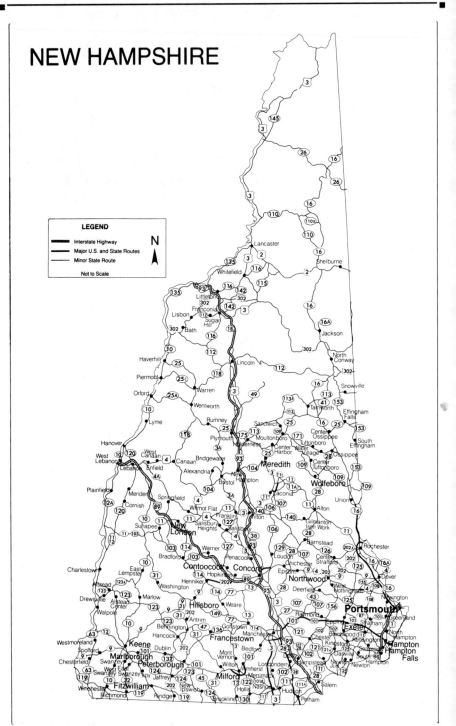

ALEXANDRIA

ALEXANDRIA WOOD JOINERY
Plumer Hill Rd, 03222
(603)744-8243   **19 68 70**
Expert antique furniture reproduction, chair seating, cane & splint. Custom designed & manufactured cabinets & furniture. *Serv:* Custom woodwork. *Hours:* Tue-Fri 10-5 Sat 10-3, please call first. *Size:* Large. George G Whittaker *Park:* In front. *Loc:* Willow St from Rte 3A in Bristol across from town offices, take L fork 1 MI up, 1st set of bldgs on R after fork.

ALSTEAD

PAPERMILL VILLAGE ANTIQUES
Rtes 12A & 123, 03602
(603)835-6418   **{GR}**
Quality 18th & 19th C American furniture, paintings, smalls, folk art & toys located in a picturesque mill on Cold River. *Serv:* Furniture restoration. *Hours:* May-Oct Daily 11-5 by chance/appt. R W Viegener *Park:* On site. *Loc:* On Cold River, 30 min from Keene, 10 min from Bellows Falls, VT.

ALTON

FLEUR-DE-LIS ANTIQUES
Rte 11, 03809
(603)875-6555   **44 63**
Early American pattern glass, cup plates, china, clocks & art glass. *Serv:* Clocks bought & sold, repair. *Hours:* Jun-Labor Day daily 10-4 CLOSED MON & TUE. *Assoc:* NHADA. Audrey S Ritchie

AMHERST

AMHERST OUTDOOR ANTIQUE MARKET
Rte 122 S, 03031
(617)641-0600   **{FLEA}**
Indoor/outdoor market with antiques, collectibles & an antique auto swap on the last Sunday of the month. Free admission. *Est:* 1960. *Serv:* Catered, spaces start at $5 for 20' X 30'. *Hours:* Apr 15-Oct Sun 6-2. *Size:* 200 spaces. *Park:* Parking available for $1. *Loc:* Rte 3N Exit 7W: 7 MI to 122 S, go L for 2 MI.

AMHERST VILLAGE ANTIQUE SHOP
101 Boston Post Rd, 03031
(603)673-5946   **37 38 83**
Diversified stock of American & Continental furniture & decorative accessories; specializing in refinished trunks. *Pr:* $25-5000. *Est:* 1974. *Hours:* By chance/appt. *Size:* Medium. Ralph Bolnick *Park:* On site. *Loc:* In the village center just off the Village Green.

THE BOOKWORM
Rte 101 Salsburg Sq, 03031
(603)673-2475   **13**
General stock of new & used books. *Hours:* Mon-Sat 10-5:30, Thu til 8, Sun 12-5. *Size:* 12,000 books. *Assoc:* NHABA. Laurie Saxon

CARRIAGE SHED ANTIQUES
35 Walnut Hill Rd, 03031
(603)673-2944   **27**
Country furniture & quality accessories. *Est:* 1955. *Serv:* Appraisal, purchase es-

tates. **Hours:** May 3-Nov 11 Thu-Sun 10-5 & by appt. **Assoc:** NHADA. Arlene Smith **Park:** On site. **Loc:** Off Rte 101, 1 MI up Walnut Hill Rd.

HOWLAND'S ANTIQUES SHOWS
Route 101 A, 03031
(603)673-2737   **{FLEA}**

A country show of antiques & collectibles. **Serv:** Catered, rental space $18. **Hours:** Apr 8-Oct 14 Sun 7-2. **Park:** On site. **Loc:** Rte 3 N Exit 7 W (101A W)..

ANTRIM

BACKWARD LOOK ANTIQUES
Rte 9, 03440
(603)588-2751   **{GR10}**

Primitives, furniture, horsedrawn vehicles, tools, folk art, Sandwich Glass & tole. **Hours:** Daily 10:30-5:30. **Assoc:** GSAAA NHADA. Bob McNeil **Loc:** On the Keene-Concord Rd at entrance to Hawthorne College.

COURT'S CUPBOARD ANTIQUES
Rtes 202 & 31, 03440
(603)588-2455   **40 42**

Refinished pine, Victorian oak furniture & accessories. **Hours:** Usually open, Win by chance. **CC:** MC/V. **Assoc:** NHADA. Dick Court **Loc:** Just S of Antrim.

BEDFORD

BEDFORD CENTER ANTIQUES
7 Meetinghouse Rd, 03102
(603)472-3557   **27 36 44**

Furniture, glass, china, silver, paintings & country antiques. **Serv:** Appraisal,

video taping. **Hours:** By chance/appt CLOSED JAN,FEB. **Assoc:** NEAA NHADA. Elaine Tefft

BELL HILL ANTIQUES
Rte 101 & Bell Hill Rd, 03102
(603)472-5580   **{GR20}**

Country furniture, primitives, folk art, quilts & textiles, rugs, hearth accessories, prints, toys, silver, glass & china displayed in room settings. **Est:** 1974. **Hours:** Year round daily 10-5. **CC:** MC/V. **Assoc:** GSAAA NHADA. Sharon S Kace **Loc:** In Houck Realty Bldg; half way between Townsend, MA & Rte 4 in NH.

CLOAK & DAGGER BOOKS
9 Eastman Ave, 03102
(603)668-1629   **13**

Out-of-print & rare books relating to nonfiction espionage, intelligence, true spy, codes & ciphers, guerrilla, terrorism & POW escapes. **Serv:** Catalog. **Hours:** BY APPT ONLY. **Size:** 10,000 books. **Assoc:** NHABA. Dan D Halpin, Jr

DRUMMER BOY ANTIQUES
278 Wallace Rd, 03102
(603)472-3172   **1 6 65**

Primitives, Americana, general antiques, Civil War & military & early photography. **Hours:** BY APPT. **Assoc:** NHADA. Hank Ford

---

BRADFORD

KALONBOOKS
Rte 114, 03221
(603)938-2380   **13**

Antiquarian books: Americana, science fiction (HC & PB), general stock. **Serv:**

Catalog. **Hours:** Sat-Sun 1-5, Jul & Aug
Wed-Sun 1-5. **Size:** 10,000 books. **Assoc:**
NHABA. Rod Jones

JEF & TERRI STEINGRIBE
Hogg Hill Rd, 03221
(603)938-2748 27
Country furniture & accessories. **Hours:**
All year BY APPT. **Assoc:** NHADA.

BROOKLINE

1786 HOUSE ANTIQUES
274 Milford Rd Rte 13, 03033
(603)673-1918 23 36 77
Formal & country furniture, clocks, silver, glass, paintings & other early American accessories. **Serv:** Clock restoration. **Hours:** Year round Sat-Mon 11-4 & BY APPT. **Loc:** 3 MI S of Milford, NH on Rte 13.

BROOKLINE VILLAGE ANTIQUES
Rte 130, 03033
(603)673-0081 40 42 48
Antique cooperative featuring oak, pine, linens, kitchen items, glass, mahogany, china & jewelry. **Hours:** Daily 10-5 CLOSED TUE. Ron Pelletier **Loc:** 1 hr from Boston.

CANAAN

AMERICAN CLASSICS
Canaan St Lake, 03741
(603)523-7139 34 37 67
American country furniture, paintings, quilts, hooked rugs & folk art. **Hours:** Jun-Labor Day BY APPT. **Assoc:** NHADA. Meryl Weiss **Loc:** Just past Cardigan Mt School.

ERNIE'S ANTIQUES
RR 1 Box 106, 03741
(603)523-4226 27 40 65
Two floors of country pine & oak furniture, cupboards & accessories located in a large barn. **Pr:** $25–3000. **Est:** 1987. **Hours:** Year round Tue-Sun 9-5. **Size:** Medium. Ernest R Eastman **Park:** On site. **Loc:** Take rd at blinking light to Canaan St, 3 MI on R.

CANTERBURY

CRABTREE'S COLLECTION
353 Baptist Rd, 03224
(603)783-9394 13
Antiquarian books: nature studies, outdoors & a general stock. **Hours:** By chance/appt. **Size:** 12,000 books. **Assoc:** NHABA. Penny Crabtree

CENTER HARBOR

ACCENTS FROM THE PAST
Rte 25, 03226
(603)253-4088 36 50 63
Specializing in refinished furniture, American art pottery & early electric lamps. Carriage house & barn open for browsing. **Hours:** Sum Tue-Sun 10-5. **Assoc:** NHADA. Anna Miller **Loc:** Across from Longwood Farms.

HOLIDAY HOUSE ANTIQUES
Bean Rd at Center Harbor, 03226
(603)253-6891 36 63 77
Antiques, furniture, china, silver & glass. **Hours:** Apr-Oct daily 9-5 CLOSED MON. **Assoc:** NHADA. Edith L Murphy **Loc:** Off Rte 25.

CENTER SANDWICH

C & D ANTIQUES
Mt Israel Rd, 03227
(603)284-7109   **50 63 65**
Barn full of primitives, furniture, china, glass, lamps & pictures. *Hours:* May-Oct daily 10-5 or by chance/appt. *Assoc:* NADA NHADA. Ciril Klarik *Park:* On site. *Loc:* Rte 93 Exit 23: Rte 3 to lights, R onto Rte 25 (Meredith), L at Bean Rd, L at Sandwich Notch Rd, 1/4 MI to Mt Israel Rd.

HILL COUNTRY BOOKS
Box 268, 03227
(603)284-7008   **13**
Literature & biography. *Hours:* May 15-Columbus Day weekend Tue-Sat 10-5 else by appt. *Size:* 15,000 books. *Assoc:* NHABA. John E Perkins *Loc:* In the village Historic District.

CENTER STRAFFORD

BERT & GAIL SAVAGE
Rte 126, 03815
(603)269-7411   **27 34**
Early 19th C country furniture, folk art & accessories, Adirondack-type items & Indian clubs. *Hours:* All year BY APPT. *Assoc:* AADA NHADA.

CENTER TUFTONBORO

GOLDEN PAST ANTIQUE MARKET
Rte 109A, 03816
(603)569-4249   **{GR9}**
Nine-dealer group shop featuring primitives, linen, sterling, furniture, china, political items, paper, post cards, books & jewelry. *Hours:* May-Oct daily 10-5. *Assoc:* NHADA. *Loc:* Between General Store & school.

CHARLESTOWN

ANTIQUES CENTER
Main St, 03603
(603)826-3639   **33 36 44**
China & glass, primitive & formal furniture & ephemera. *Est:* 1973. *Hours:* Mon-Sat 10:30-4:30 Sun 1-4:30. *Assoc:* NHADA. William Orcutt

CHESTER

BLACKBRIAR ANTIQUES
Rte 121, 03036
(603)887-4062   **83**
Specializing in furniture & accessories from the Victorian era. *Hours:* Sat & Sun 10-4. *Loc:* On the Chester-Auburn line.

HAYLOFT BARN ANTIQUES
161 Derry Rd Rte 102, 03036
(603)887-3616   **36 44**
Country & Victorian furniture & accessories including large selection of flow blue. *Hours:* Year round by chance/appt. *Assoc:* NHADA. Dottie & Dan Dwyer

OLDE CHESTER ANTIQUES
Raymond Rd Rte 102, 03036
(603)887-4778   **16 27 28**
Early country furniture with emphasis on paint, early smalls, wooden primitives, stoneware, copper & iron. *Hours:* By chance/appt. *Assoc:* NHADA. Betty Priest

WALNUT HILL ANTIQUES
Walnut Hill, 03036
(603)887-2627   **27**
18th & 19th C American country furniture & accessories - most in original surface & condition. *Hours:* By
chance/appt. *Assoc:* NHADA. Bob
Leonard *Loc:* 3 MI S of Chester Center
on Rte 121.

CHESTERFIELD

HEMLOCK HILL ANTIQUES
Cross Rd, 03466
(603)256-3281   **28 42 76**
Country pine & Shaker furniture, quilts,
crocks, decoys pewter & accessories.
Hours: Sum 9-5:30 CLOSED TUE,
Sep-May Fri-Mon 9-5:30. *Assoc:*
GSAAA NHADA. Shiela Kinnare *Loc:*
Off Rte 9.

THE STONE HOUSE ANTIQUES
Jct 9 & 63, 03443
(603)363-8097   **{GR}**
Quality antiques in room settings in an
1831 stone house. Furniture, linens,
smalls, china.. *Pr:* $25–5000. *Est:* 1990.
Serv: Appraisal, interior design, framing.
Hours: Tue-Sun 10-5. *Size:* Large. *Park:*
On site. *Loc:* Jct Rtes 9 & 63, on Spofford
Lake.

CHICHESTER

DOUGLAS H HAMEL
Staniels Rd, 03301
(603)798-5912   **1 37 76**
Shaker furniture & accessories for the
serious collector. *Est:* 1966. *Hours:* BY
APPT. *Assoc:* NHADA.

CONCORD

ART RUG
74 N Main St, 03301
(603)224-3099   **21**
Superior selection of hand knotted
Orientals with a constantly changing
stock of nearly 1000 rugs, ranging from
antiques to new. *Pr:* $100–15000. *Est:*
1968. *Serv:* Appraisal, consultation, purchase estates, repairs, restoration. *Hours:*
Tue-Sat 9-5. *Size:* Medium. *CC:* MC/V.
Assoc: NHADA. *Park:* Local garage.
Loc: 1 block S of State Capitol Building.

THE BOOK MILL
485 N State St, 03301
(603)224-2270   **13**
Specializing in modern first editions &
science fiction. *Hours:* Tue-Sat 10-5:30.
Size: 25,000 books. *Assoc:* NHABA.
Rainer Van Rossum

CARR BOOKS
51 N Spring St, 03301
(603)225-3109   **13**
General stock of antiquarian books,
manuscripts & paper. *Hours:* BY APPT
ONLY. *Size:* 1,000 books. *Assoc:*
NHABA. Roberta Carr

PIERCE & THOMPSON BOOK CO
3 Pleasant St 2nd flr, 03301
(603)225-5411   **13 33 51**
Antiquarian, out-of-print & rare books,
maps & prints primarily from the 18th &
19th C. *Pr:* $25–500. *Est:* 1975. *Serv:*
Appraisal, purchase estates, search services. *Hours:* By chance/appt. *Size:*
1,000 books. *CC:* MC/V. *Assoc:*
NHABA. Craig B Holmes *Park:* In
front. *Loc:* From N/S: I-93, any Concord
exit; From E: Rte 4 to Concord; From
W: Rtes 202 & 9 or I-89; on corner of
Main & Pleasant Sts.

CONTOOCOOK

ANTIQUES & FINDINGS
Main St, 03229
(603)746-5788 **36**

Interesting variety of antique furniture & accessories to early 20th C. *Hours:* Apr-Nov daily 10-5, a call ahead advised. *Assoc:* NHADA. Audrey Gardner

ANTIQUES ON THE HILL
Woodwell's Garrison, 03229
(603)746-3088 **44 47 77**

Ceramics, glass, handwork, jewelry, silver, woodenware. *Hours:* All year Tue, Thu, Sat, Sun by chance/appt. *Assoc:* NHADA. Marjorie Ross *Loc:* Off Rte 103.

EMERY'S BOOKS
Duston Rd Rte 2, 03229
(603)746-5787 **13 51**

Early books, travel, atlases, literature & Americana. *Hours:* By chance/appt. *Size:* 5,000 books. *Assoc:* NHABA. Ron Emery

GOLD DRAGON ANTIQUES
Rte 127, 03229
(603)746-3466 **23 44 63**

Art & pattern glass, Oriental porcelains, pottery, cloisonne & clocks. *Pr:* $5–2000. *Hours:* Daily 11-5. *Size:* Medium. *Assoc:* NHADA. Philip B Cole *Park:* On site. *Loc:* I-89 Exit 6: 1 MI to Contoocook, follow Rte 127 thru village to Park Ave Shopping Ctr, 3rd house on R.

PIATT'S COPPER COW
Briar Hill Rd, 03229
(603)746-4568 **27 80**

Country furniture, cupboards, early ac-cessories & textiles. *Hours:* By chance, call ahead suggested. *Assoc:* NHADA. Gail Piatt

SHIRLEY D QUINN ANTIQUES
Rte 3 Box 348, 03229
(603)746-5030 **27 67 80**

Country furniture & accessories, quilts, textiles & children's things. *Hours:* BY APPT. *Assoc:* NHADA VADA.

CORNISH

NATHAN SMITH HOUSE
RR 2 Rte 12A, 03745
(603)675-2951 **37 41 76**

A country shop in an historic 1791 Federal house on the Connecticut river. Specializing in unusual, high-quality American furniture & accessories, including Shaker, iron, tin, glass, items in original paint, paintings & early lighting. *Pr:* $25–2000. *Hours:* Apr 15-Oct 15 Mon-Sat 8-7, or by chance/appt. Daniel B Eastman *Park:* On site. *Loc:* I-91 Exit 8: R on Rte 131 to NH, then L on Rte 12A for 4 1/2 MI.

DERRY

ANTIQUE STOP
179 Rockingham Rd, 03038
(603)434-1212 **{GR10}**

Fine furniture, glass, primitives & much more. *Hours:* Daily 10-5. Sandy Ambiehl *Loc:* Minutes N of MA border on Rte 28.

BERT BABCOCK BOOKSELLER
9 E Derry Rd, 03038
(603)432-9142 **13**

Modern first editions, signed & association copies, poetry, broadsides & rare books. *Hours:* Daily BY APPT. *Size:* 7,000 books. *Assoc:* ABAA NHABA.

GRAND VIEW FARM FLEA MARKET
Rte 28 & Rte 28 bypass S, 03038
(603)432-2326 **{FLEA}**
Indoor/outdoor flea market with antiques, collectibles & other flea market merchandise. Admission is 50 cents for adults. *Est:* 1981. *Serv:* Catered, space rental starts at $15 for 16' X 20' space. *Hours:* Year round Sun 7:30-3:30. *Size:* 250 spaces. *Park:* On site.

DOVER

MICHAEL G BENNETT AUCTIONS
Pickering Rd, 03820
(603)335-1694 **8**
All antique, estate & collectible aution services; in-house appraisal service; licensed in ME, NH, VT & MA; terms to consignor - adjustable; buyers' premium - 10%, if necessary. *Est:* 1978. *Serv:* Auctioneer, appraisal, mail & phone bids, catalog, purchase estates. *Hours:* All year BY APPT. *Assoc:* NHADA. *Loc:* From Boston: I-95 to Portsmouth, NH (Spaulding Tnpk) through Dover toll booth to Exit 9, cross hwy, go 3 1/2 MI, then R.

DUBLIN

WILLIAM LARY ANTIQUES
Gold Mine Rd, 03444
(603)563-8603 **30 34 76**
18th & 19th C country & formal furniture, quality accessories including art, Shaker, paint, decoys & folk. *Hours:* Open all year Tue-Sat 10-5. *Assoc:*

GSAAA NHADA. *Loc:* 3 MI W of Peterborough on Rte 101, R on Gold Mine Rd, 1st house on R.

PETER PAP ORIENTAL RUGS INC
Main St Rte 1, 03444
(603)563-8717 **21 80 82**
An internationally recognized gallery featuring antique carpets, textiles & tribal weavings. Hard to find sizes in stock or will locate. *Pr:* $200–150000. *Est:* 1976. *Serv:* Appraisal, consultation, purchase estates, repairs, restoration. *Hours:* Mon-Sat 10-5. *Size:* Large. *CC:* MC/V. *Assoc:* NHADA. *Park:* On site.

ANN & DAN WALSH
Snow Hill Rd, 03444
(603)563-8542 **16 63**
Accessory items, pewter, brass, porcelains & soft paste. *Hours:* All year by chance/appt. *Assoc:* NHADA. *Loc:* Rte 101, S on Upper Jaffrey Rd, 1 MI, R on Snow Hill Rd to marked driveway.

DURHAM

WISWALL HOUSE ANTIQUES
Wiswall Rd, 03824
(603)659-5106 **29 37 40**
Specializing in restored American 19th C furniture, brass lighting, mirrors & decorative accessories & a good variety of general merchandise. *Est:* 1975. *Serv:* Appraisal, purchase estates. *Hours:* Feb-Dec Wed-Sat 10-6 Sun 12-4, Nov-Dec Wed-Sat 10-dark. *Assoc:* GSAAA NHADA. Joan Carter *Loc:* From Durham Rte 108 S toward Newmarket 1.5 MI, R on Bennett Rd, go to end, R on Packers Falls then L onto Wiswall Rd.

EAST LEMPSTER

PETER HILL INC
Maplewood Manor, 03605
(603)863-3656   **37 50 83**
Significant 19th C American furniture, fine & decorative arts for collectors & museums. *Est:* 1961. *Serv:* Appraisal, conservation, purchase estates, consultation. *Hours:* BY APPT. *Park:* On site. *Loc:* Call for directions.

EAST SWANZEY

HAYS SCULPTURE STUDIO
399 Whitcomb Rd, 03446
(603)352-0572   **71**
A small studio offering personalized attention to the restoration of wood sculptures, specializing in carousel figures. *Serv:* Custom woodwork, repairs, replication, reproduction, restoration. *Hours:* BY APPT ONLY. *Park:* On site.

ENFIELD

DANA ROBES WOOD CRAFTSMEN INC
Rte 4A Lower Shaker Village, 03748
(603)632-5385   **19 43 76**
Shaker reproduction furniture & crafts workshop & showroom in Shaker reproduction barn in the Enfield Shaker community. Custom furniture in the Shaker tradition is also created on special order basis. *Pr:* $19–3400. *Est:* 1981. *Serv:* Catalog ($3), custom woodwork, reproduction, interior design. *Hours:* Jun-Sep Mon-Sat 9-5 Sun 1-5 Oct-May

Mon-Sat 9-5. *Size:* Large. *CC:* MC/V. Ronald Boehm *Park:* On site. *Loc:* I-89 Exit 17: 5 1/2 MI E on Rte 4A. Located in Lower Shaker Village on Mascoma Lake.

EPPING

PLEASANT HILL ANTIQUES
7 Pleasant St, 03042
(603)679-5447   **27**
Early American country furniture & quality accessories. *Hours:* Jun-Oct by chance/appt. Marcha R Latwen *Loc:* Rte 127 1/2 MI W of Rte 125.

EPSOM

BOB & RITA BECKER
Rte 4, 03234
(603)736-8115   **29 34 36**
Furniture, accessories, folk art & collectibles. *Hours:* Year round. *Assoc:* NHADA. *Loc:* Brown barn 1 1/2 MI E of Epsom Circle.

THE BETTY HOUSE
North Rd, 03234
(603)736-9087   **36 81**
Four barns full of a general assortment of antiques including furniture, household items of wood, tin or iron & large collection of tools. *Hours:* By chance/appt. *Assoc:* NHADA. Charles Yeaton *Loc:* 1/2 MI off Rte 4 on North Rd.

COPPER HOUSE
Rte 4, 03234
(603)736-9798   **50 70 87**
Copper & brass lighting in traditional styles, copper weather vanes & cupolas. *Est:* 1976. *Serv:* Reproductions, catalog.

Hours: Thu-Sat 12-5 Sun 10-5 or BY APPT. **Size:** Medium. **CC:** MC/V. **Loc:** On Rte 4: 15 min E of Concord, 3/4 MI E of Epsom Traffic Circle.

EXETER

A THOUSAND WORDS
65 Water St, 03833
(603)778-1991   **13 66**

Antiquarian books: scholarly non-fiction, modern literary first editions, Western Americana & natural history prints. **Hours:** Mon-Fri 10-7 Sat 10-5 Sun 12-4. **Size:** 10,000 books. **Assoc:** NHABA. Jennifer Segal

HOLLIS & TRISHA BRODRICK
Box 40, 03833
(603)778-8842   **15 37 63**

Early New England decorative arts & accessories, English ceramics, iron, brass, lighting, Delft, combware, bottles, textiles & American furniture. **Hours:** BY APPT. **Assoc:** NHADA.

HERSCHEL B BURT
93 Linden St, 03833
(603)778-8633   **23**

American clocks & timepieces. **Est:** 1958. **Serv:** Appraisal. **Hours:** BY APPT. **Loc:** Call for directions.

COLOPHON BOOK SHOP
117 Water St, 03833
(603)772-8443   **13**

19th & 20th C literary first editions, literary bibliographies, press books, association & inscribed books, books about books & auction catalogs. **Hours:** Mon-Sat 9-5. **Size:** 2,500 books. **Assoc:** ABAA NHABA. Robert Liska

DECOR ANTIQUES
11 Jady Hill Cir, 03833
(603)772-4538   **36 63 77**

Prints & paintings, furniture, glass, china, silver & books. **Serv:** Custom framing. **Hours:** Tue-Sat 10-5 by chance. **Assoc:** NHADA. **Park:** On site. **Loc:** From 108 S (Portsmouth Ave) Exeter, take R at lights, next L.

EXETER OLD BOOK BARN
200 High St, 03833
(603)772-0618   **13**

Scholarly general stock of antiquarian books featuring Asia, Scotland, music & dancing. **Hours:** Daily 10-5. **Size:** 10,000 books. **Assoc:** NHABA. Anthony M Tufts

OCTOBER STONE ANTIQUES
56 Jady Hill Ave, 03833
(603)772-2024   **27**

Country furniture & unusual accessories. **Hours:** Year round by chance/appt. **Assoc:** NHADA. Linda J Rogers **Loc:** Next to Exeter Country Club.

FARMINGTON

THE BOOKERY
62 N Main St Rte 153, 03835
(603)755-4471   **13**

Military specialty but a good selection of maritime, art, nature, biography, business & economics. **Pr:** $5–300. **Est:** 1975. **Serv:** Appraisal, free catalog, purchase estates. **Hours:** Fri 10-6 or by chance/appt. **Size:** 6,000 books. **Assoc:** NHABA. Robert M Colpitt **Park:** On site, in front. **Loc:** From Rte 11 turn to Rte 153, go through town of Farmington, shop is two blocks up on L.

FITZWILLIAM

ANTIQUES PLUS & STRAWBERRY ACRES
Rte 12, 03447
(603)585-6517   **{GR55}**

Primitives, glass, furniture, dolls & toys. *Est:* 1979. *Serv:* Restaurant open Fri-Sun 11-3. *Hours:* Daily 10-5. *Park:* On site. *Loc:* 3 MI from MA line, 2 MI S of Jct of Rte 119.

BLOOMIN' ANTIQUES
On The Village Green, 03447
(603)585-6688   **27 37**

American country & formal furniture & related accessories, American & European art. *Serv:* Auction. *Hours:* Mon-Sat 10-5, nights by appt, Sun by chance. *Assoc:* NHADA. Gary L Taylor *Park:* Nearby.

CLOCKS ON THE COMMON
Village Common, 03447
(603)585-3321   **23**

Specializing in antique clocks. *Serv:* Buy, sell & repair antique clocks. *Hours:* Most afternoons by chance/appt, call ahead advised. *Assoc:* NHADA. John H Fitzwilliam *Park:* In front. *Loc:* Yellow house on Village Common, off Rte 119.

DAVIS HOMESTEAD ANTIQUES
Lower Troy Rd Old Rte 12, 03447
(603)585-7759   **27 29**

Formal & country furniture, china & decorative accessories. *Hours:* Year round by chance/appt, call if coming from distance. Mildred Davis *Loc:* Off Rte 12 N of the Fitzwilliam Inn.

DENNIS & DAD ANTIQUES
Rte 119, 03447
(603)585-9479   **36 44 63**

General line of glass, china, furniture & accessories. *Serv:* Wholesale only. *Hours:* By chance/appt CLOSED SUN. *Assoc:* NHADA. Dennis Bedard *Loc:* Off Rte 12 heading E, 5th house on L.

EDDY'S ANTIQUES & STAMPS
Rte 12, 03447
(603)585-6679   **44 64 79**

Specializing in stamps, postcards & art glass. *Hours:* Daily 9-5 CLOSED SUN. Henry Eddy *Loc:* 4 MI S of Int of Rte 12 & 119.

FITZWILLIAM ANTIQUE CENTER
Jct Rtes 12 & 119, 03447
(603)585-9092   **{GR43}**

18th & 19th C country furniture & accessories, folk art, antique reference books, rugs, paintings, glass & china. *Hours:* Mar-Oct Mon-Sat 10-5 Sun 12-5 Nov-Feb Close at 4:00. *Size:* Large. *Assoc:* GSAAA NHADA. Warren Legsdin *Loc:* Just S of the Int of Rtes 12 & 119.

WILLIAM LEWAN ANTIQUES
Old Troy Rd, 03447
(603)585-3365   **1 27 41**

Actively changing inventory of early & country furniture, art, folk art & appropriate accessories. *Pr:* $25-5000. *Est:* 1972. *Serv:* Appraisal, purchase estates. *Hours:* All year by chance/appt. *Size:* Medium. *Assoc:* NHADA. *Park:* On site. *Loc:* 4 1/2 MI from Fitzwilliam Village, W on Rte 119 look for sign for turn.

OLD VILLAGE SCHOOLHOUSE
Rte 119, 03447
(603)585-9208   **27 65 67**

Featuring country & primitive items, including country store items, toys, textiles, quilts & clothing. *Hours:* Daily 10-5. *Loc:* Near the Int of Rte 12 & 119.

RAINY DAY BOOKS
Rte 119, 03447
(603)585-3448   **13 33 66**

Antiquarian books: General stock specializing in travel, exploration, polar, mountaineering, European royalty, textile history, women's studies, cookbooks, children's books, science, technology, paper & prints. *Pr:* $10–300. *Est:* 1980. *Serv:* Appraisal, catalog, purchase estates. *Hours:* May-Nov 15 Thu-Mon 11-5, Nov-Apr by chance/appt. *Size:* 10,000 books. *Assoc:* ESA NHABA. Frank & Lucia Bequaert *Park:* On site. *Loc:* 15 MI S of Keene, NH on Rte 12; 1 block W on Rte 119 from Int of Rtes 12 & 119.

RED BARN ANTIQUES
Old Richmond Rd, 03447
(603)585-3134   **28 44 59**

Art, decorated stoneware, cut glass, American primitives, Victorian & country items. *Hours:* Year round 10-4, CLOSED TUE & WED. *Assoc:* NHADA. Arlene Rich *Loc:* 1/4 MI behind Fitzwilliam Inn, 5th house on R, heated red barn on the hill.

FRANCESTOWN

THE FRANCESTOWN GALLERY
Main St, 03043
(603)547-6635   **34 59**

Early 19th & late 18th C New England antiques, folk art, paintings & textiles. *Hours:* By Chance/Appt. Ann & Dave Stewart

BERT MC CLEARY AUCTIONEER
Turnpike Rd, 03043
(603)547-2796   **4 8**

Auctioneers & appraisers buying/selling single items or whole estates. *Hours:* Call for information.

MILL VILLAGE ANTIQUES
Rte 136E New Boston Rd, 03043
(603)547-2050   **23 30 65**

Duck & fish decoys, clocks, country furniture, primitives, glass, china, collector items & ice cream & chocolate molds. *Est:* 1982. *Hours:* Year round by chance/appt. *Assoc:* GSAAA. Derald Radtke *Park:* On site. *Loc:* 1/2 MI E of Francestown Town Hall.

NAN SHEA ANTIQUES
PO Box 129, 03043
(603)547-3523   **63**

Majolica & Chinese export porcelain. *Est:* 1984. *Hours:* BY APPT ONLY. *Assoc:* GSAAA. Nancy Shea *Loc:* Call for directions.

STONEWALL ANTIQUES
New Boston Rd Rte 136, 03043
(603)547-3485   **36 41 44**

Selected formal, country & painted furniture, glass, china, paintings, primitives, decorator & collector items. *Hours:* Year round by chance/appt. *Assoc:* GSAAA NHADA. Elsie E Mikula *Park:* Off street. *Loc:* 1 MI E of Village Rte 136.

THE TYPOGRAPHEUM BOOKSHOP
Bennington Rd, 03043
                    13

Specializing in 20th C British & European literature, private press books & fine bindings. *Pr:* $10–200. *Est:* 1976. *Serv:* Catalog - quarterly (free). *Hours:* By chance/appt. R T Risk *Park:* On site. *Loc:* Francestown is about 12 MI from Peterborough; shop is 1 MI N of the village on Rte 47.

WOODBURY HOMESTEAD ANTIQUES
1 Main St, 03043
(603)547-2929 **47 50**

Specializing in kerosene lamps, mirrors & jewelry of the Victorian era. *Pr:* $25–5000. *Est:* 1983. *Serv:* Appraisal, consultation, interior design, purchase estates, repairs. *Hours:* Year round by chance/appt suggested. *Assoc:* GIA GSAAA NHADA NTHP. Alan R Thulander *Park:* In front. *Loc:* On the Town Common at Jct of Rtes 136 & 47.

FRANCONIA

COLONIAL COTTAGE
Blake Rd Sugar Hill, 03580
(603)823-5614 **16 53 63**

Six rooms brimming with early New England furniture & formal decorative accessories including American glass, lamps & lanterns, brass, copper, pottery & porcelain all charmingly displayed. *Hours:* Sum & Fall 9-4:30 daily, Nov-May by chance/appt. *Size:* Medium. Lauren/Eleanor Howard *Park:* On site. *Loc:* 1 1/2 MI up Blake Rd off Rte 117.

FRANKLIN

EVELYN CLEMENT
45 Central St, 03235
(603)934-5496 **13**

Antiquarian books featuring some unusual subjects & a general stock including early technical, New Hampshire & White Mountains. *Hours:* By chance/appt. *Assoc:* NHABA.

FREEDOM

FREEDOM BOOKSHOP
Maple St Box 247, 03836
(603)539-7265 **13 33**

General stock of antiquarian books of the 19th & 20th centuries with emphasis on literature, poetry, the Arts, books on books & 20th C history. Literary magazines seen by appt. Small gallery of 19th & 20th C American paintings, watercolors & prints. *Pr:* $5–1000. *Est:* 1987. *Serv:* Catalogs issued, mail order, purchase libraries. *Hours:* Jun 15-Oct 15 Sun-Tue 11-5 else by chance. *Size:* 10,000 books. *CC:* MC/V. *Assoc:* MABA NHABA. George L Wrenn *Park:* On site. *Loc:* From Int of Rted 16 & 25, approx 5 MI E then 1/2 MI N on Rte 153; follow signs to village - 1/4 MI E of bridge in village ctr.

GILFORD

LOUISE FRAZIER BOOKS
380 Morrill St, 03246
(603)524-2427 **13**

A general stock of antiquarian books. *Hours:* By chance/appt. *Size:* 15,000 books. *Assoc:* NHABA.

VISUALLY SPEAKING
778 Gilford Ave Rte 11A, 03246
(603)524-6795 **13 66**

General stock of antiquarian books with emphasis on nonfiction, prints & paper. *Hours:* By chance/appt. *Size:* 3,000 books. *Assoc:* NHABA. Barbara French

GILMANTON IRON WORKS

STEPHEN P BEDARD
Durrell Mountain Farm, 03837
(603)528-1896   **43 46 69**
Windsor chair replications using the same procedures & locally grown woods as those utilized by 18th C chairmakers. Authentic to their period in every detail, including line, form & technique. *Est:* 1980. *Serv:* Catalog $3. *Hours:* BY APPT.

GOFFSTOWN

SACRED & PROFANE
New Boston Rd Rte 13, 03035
(603)627-4477   **13**
Antiquarian books with an emphasis on art/illustrated, leatherbound, theology & religion from 17th-20th C. *Hours:* Mon 6-8 Sat,Sun 1-4. *Size:* 4,000 books. *Assoc:* NHABA. H Donley Wray

VESSELS OF TIME
RFD #1 Rte 13, 03045
(603)774-7710   **63**
Specializing in American art pottery including Roseville, Weller, Royal Haeger & also featuring stoneware. *Hours:* By chance/appt. Jim Campbell

GORHAM

TARA
Glen Rd, 03581
(603)466-2624   **66**
19th C prints & maps of the White Mountains. *Hours:* By chance/appt. Doug Philbrook *Loc:* Call for directions.

GOSHEN

NELSON ANTIQUES & USED BOOKS
Brook Rd, 03752
(603)863-4394   **13 14 36**
Antiques from marbles to Morris chairs; plus, 40,000 used, old, rare books - fiction & non-fiction, illustrated Americana, science fiction, 1st editions, ephemera & prints. *Pr:* $1–500. *Est:* 1974. *Serv:* Brochure, purchase estates, search services. *Hours:* July-Labor Day by chance/appt; Labor Day-Jun Thu-Mon by appt. *Size:* 40,000 books. *Assoc:* NHABA. Audrey Nelson

GREENLAND

DANIEL OLMSTEAD ANTIQUES/AUCTION
1119 Portsmouth Ave, 03840
(603)431-1644   **8**
Featuring auctions of antiques fresh from New England private homes; Americana auctions, estate sales, specialty sales of tools, ephemera, advertising & toys. *Serv:* Appraisal, purchase estates, accept mail bids. *Hours:* By chance/appt. *Assoc:* NHAA.

WILLIAM THOMPSON
ANTIQUARIAN BKS
10 Tide Mill Rd, 03840
(603)431-2369   13
Antiquarian books: Specializing in
Americana, military, science, technology
& sporting. *Est:* 1986. *Serv:* Appraisal,
purchase estates. *Hours:* By chance/appt,
call ahead advised. *Size:* 5,000 books.
Assoc: NHABA. *Park:* On site. *Loc:* I-95
Exit 3: 2 1/2 MI W on Rte 101.

GUILD

PAUL & MARIE MAJOROS
Sunapee Rd Rtes 11 & 103, 03754
(603)863-3165   13
General stock of books & paper. *Hours:*
By chance/appt. *Size:* 10,000 books.
Assoc: NHABA.

HAMPTON

RONALD BOURGEAULT
ANTIQUES
694 Lafayette Rd Rte 1, 03842
(603)926-8222   1 4 39
Formal & country Americana, English &
Oriental objects from estates. *Serv:*
Consultant to museums, auction, ap-
praisal. *Hours:* BY APPT ONLY. *Assoc:*
NHADA. *Shows:* ELLIS WAS. *Park:* In
front.

GARGOYLES & GRIFFINS
Old Rte 1 On The Moors, 03842
(603)926-3744   5 36 83
Specializing in heavily carved furniture,
Victoriana, stained glass & architectural
antiques. *Est:* 1984. *Serv:* Appraisal, pur-

chase estates. *Hours:* Daily 10-5. T M
Bennett *Park:* On site. *Loc:* Just S of Rte
51.

HISTORIC HARDWARE LTD
821 Lafayette Rd, 03842
(603)926-8315   50 70
Restoration-quality period hardware,
lighting & decorative accessories - including Leforte reproduction furniture.
Serv: Catalog ($2), custom woodwork,
reproduction, restoration. *Hours:* Mon-
Sat 9-5. *CC:* MC/V. *Assoc:* NTHP
SPNEA. John R DeWaal *Park:* On site.
Loc: I-95N Exit 2 in NH: L after toll, Rte
51, 1st R (Rte 101), top of Exit turn R, L
at light, 1 MI N on R.

GUS JOHNSON ANTIQUES
21 Fern Rd, 03842
(603)964-9752   37
American country & formal furniture.
Hours: BY APPT.

NORTHEAST AUCTIONS
694 Lafayette Rd, 03842
(603)926-3545 FAX
(603)926-9200   4 8
Regular auctions of antique formal &
country American & European furniture, clocks, paintings, decorative arts &
oriental carpets. 10% buyer's premium.
Est: 1987. *Serv:* Appraisal, accept
mail/phone bids, consultation. *Hours:*
Call for appt or schedule. Ronald Bourgeault *Loc:* Many auctions held at Center
of New Hampshire Holiday Inn,
Manchester NH but always call for
directions.

H G WEBBER
49 Lafayette Rd, 03842
(603)926-3349   21 23 44
Large barn filled with variety of merchandise, featuring furniture, rugs,
clocks, china & glass. *Pr:* $25–16000.
Est: 1950. *Serv:* Appraisal, auction, pur-

chase estates, reproduction. *Hours:* Tue-Sat, Sun 1-5. *Assoc:* NAA NAWCC. Robert S Webber *Park:* On site. *Loc:* I-95 Exit 2: follow Rte 51E to Rte 1, turn L, 1 block on R.

HAMPTON FALLS

ANTIQUE TEXTILE COMPANY
Shoppers Village Rte 1, 03844
(603)929-0076 **80**
A unique shop specializing in all kinds of antique textiles & pretty Victorian decorative accessories. *Est:* 1990. *Hours:* Mon-Thu 10-3. Melanie Rahiser

ANTIQUES NEW HAMPSHIRE
Rte 1, 03844
(603)926-9603 **{GR50}**
Antiques in a large restored late Victorian house & barn including formal & country furniture & smalls. *Est:* 1987. *Hours:* Daily 10-5. *Size:* Large. *Assoc:* NHADA. Bob Hudson *Park:* On site. *Loc:* I-95 Exit 1 or 2: Between Rtes 51 & 107.

ANTIQUES ONE
80 Lafayette Rd Rte 1, 03844
(603)926-5332 **{GR50}**
A two-story house, carriage house & barn filled with a diversified selection of smalls & furniture. *Serv:* Reference books on antiques. *Hours:* Mon-Sat 10-5 Sun 12-5. Alma Libby *Park:* On site. *Loc:* I-95 Exit 1: Rte 1N, 2 MI.

ANTIQUES AT HAMPTON FALLS
Lafayette Rd Rtes 1 & 88, 03844
(603)926-1971 **{GR35}**
Antiques in a 3-story barn including fine furniture, primitives, smalls & collectibles. *Est:* 1987. *Hours:* Mon-Sat 10-5

Sun 12-5. *Size:* Large. William Low *Park:* On site. *Loc:* I-95 Exit 1: 2 MI N on Rte 1.

APPLE COUNTRY ANTIQUES
286 Exeter Rd Rte 88, 03844
(603)772-0624 **22**
Chairs: reed, rush, cane & splint. *Hours:* Tue-Sat 10-4.

THE BARN AT HAMPTON FALLS
44 Lafayette Rd Rte 1, 03844
(603)926-9003 **{GR}**
Specializing in fine American & European antique furniture & accessories including wardrobes, dining sets, bedroom furniture, upholstered furniture, office furnishings & estate jewelry. *Est:* 1977. *Serv:* Consultation, interior design, delivery service available. *Hours:* Year round daily 10-5. *Size:* Huge. Barry Welker *Park:* On site. *Loc:* I-95 Exit 1: N of Rte 107.

PAUL MC INNIS INC
356 Exeter Rd, 03844
(603)778-8989 **8**
Auctions of antiques & Americana. 10% buyers premium. *Hours:* Call for appt & schedule. *Assoc:* NAA. *Loc:* I-95 Exit 2: Rte 51 for 1 1/4 MI to exit for 101D, L to SS, R onto 101W for 1 1/4 MI, L onto Rte 88.

HANCOCK

THE BARN OF HANCOCK VILLAGE
Main St, 03449
(603)525-3529 **36 59**
Quality 19th C antiques, china, paintings, furniture, glass & decorative accessories. *Hours:* May-Oct, Nov-Apr BY APPT, CLOSED MON. *Size:* Medium.

Assoc: GSAAA NHADA. Helen M
Pierce **Loc:** Across from John Hancock
Inn.

THE GANLEY GALLERY
Orchard House Box 746, 03449
(603)525-4939   **59**
Specializing in the paintings of 19th century New England artists. **Est:** 1989.
Hours: By chance or appt. **Park:** In
front. **Loc:** Just off Rte 137 between
Dublin & Hancock.

HARDINGS OF HANCOCK
Depot St, 03449
(603)525-3518   **16 27**
Small country furniture, woodenware,
ironware, lighting, tin, brass, copper &
primitive accents. **Hours:** Year round by
chance/appt. **Assoc:** GSAAA NHADA.
Loc: 1/4 MI W from the John Hancock
Inn on Rte 123; red house on the point.

OLD BENNINGTON BOOKS
Box 142, 03449
(603)525-4035   **13**
Antiquarian books - literary first editions, poetry, detective fiction,
Americana, fine & rare books. **Pr:**
$5000–25000. **Est:** 1982. **Serv:** Appraisal, purchase estates, search service.
Hours: BY APPT ONLY. **Size:** 3,000
books. **Assoc:** GSAAA NHABA. Alan
Lambert **Park:** In front. **Loc:** 1/4 MI
from ctr of Hancock on Old Bennington
Road.

HANOVER

COUNTRY LOOK ANTIQUES
Main St, 03755
(603)643-4553   **27**
Country furniture & accessories. **Hours:**
Year round Mon-Sat 9-5 or by appt.
Assoc: NHADA. Constance Campion

G B MANASEK INC
35 S Main St Suite 22, 03755
(603)643-5634 FAX
(603)643-2227   **13 51 66**
Antiquarian books, rare maps, atlases,
manuscripts, prints & astronomy. No
general OP inventory. **Hours:** Wed-Fri
10-4 Sat 11-3. **Size:** 1,000 books. **Assoc:**
ABAA NHABA NHADA. Francis J
Manasek

MARIE-LOUISE ANTIQUES
Lyme Rd, 03755
(603)643-4276   **47 63 77**
Fine silver, china, glass & jewelry. **Serv:**
Flatware matching service. **Hours:** BY
APPT ONLY. **Assoc:** AAA NHADA.
Paul J Fredyma **Loc:** 3 MI N of Hanover
on Rte 10.

HAVERHILL

SUZANNE BRUCKNER ANTIQUES
Rte 10, 03765
(603)989-5575   **27**
Quality country furniture & accessories.
Pr: $25–5000. **Hours:** All year by
chance/appt suggested. **Assoc:** NHADA.
Park: On site. **Loc:** S of the Village
Green, across from the Victorian on
Main St.

THE VICTORIAN ON MAIN STREET
Rte 10, 03765
(603)989-3380   **48 80 85**

A Victorian house brimming with antique & vintage clothing, linens, lace, hooked & rag rugs, textiles, silverplate, antiques & curiosities from home & abroad in four large rooms. *Est:* 1981. *Hours:* Mid Jun-mid Oct Thu-Mon 10-5, Appt suggested. *Size:* Large. Ann Hayden & Susan Hellis *Park:* In front. *Loc:* S of the Village Green on Rte 10.

HENNIKER

OLD NUMBER SIX BOOK DEPOT
26 Depot Hill Rd, 03242
(603)428-3334   **13**

Antiquarian books: history, science, medicine, New England, social sciences, psychiatry, psychology & psychoanalysis. *Serv:* Appraisal, catalog. *Hours:* Daily 12:30-5:30 or BY APPT. *Size:* 90,000. *Assoc:* NHABA. Helen & Ian Morrison

RONALD J ROSENBLEETH INC
28 Western Ave, 03242
(603)428-7686   **4 8**

Auctioneer & appraiser specializing in fine estates, antiques & real estate. *Serv:* Appraisal. *Hours:* Mon-Fri 8-5 & BY APPT. *Assoc:* NAA NEAA.

HILLSBORO

APPLEYARD ANTIQUES
Rte 9, 03244
(603)478-5344   **36**

Large shop displaying a wide variety of furniture dating from late 1700s - some refinished - & some smalls & primitive

paintings. *Pr:* $25-3500. *Est:* 1983. *Serv:* Brochure, refinishing. *Hours:* Daily 10-6, call in advance if coming from a distance. *Size:* Medium. *CC:* MC/V. *Assoc:* NHADA. Wally Appleyard *Park:* On site. *Loc:* 1 MI W from Int of Rtes 202 & 9, Hillsboro, on Rte 9.

BARBARA'S ANTIQUES
74 Bridge St Rte 149, 03244
(603)464-3451   **27 44 63**

Refinished country furniture, accessories, glass, china & primitives. *Hours:* Mar 15-Dec 15 by chance/appt. *Assoc:* NHADA. Barbara Murphy

LOON POND ANTIQUES
School St, 03244
(603)464-5647   **29 36**

Country & formal furniture, early lighting & accessories. *Est:* 1980. *Hours:* Thu-Mon 10:30-5:30 Tue-Wed by chance/appt. *Assoc:* NHADA. Dean Lowry *Park:* On site. *Loc:* 4 MI N of Rtes 202 & 9.

STEPHEN SANBORN CLOCK REPAIR
Bridge St, 03244
(603)464-5382   **68 71**

Clocks. *Serv:* Repair & restoration. *Hours:* BY APPT. *Assoc:* NHADA.

CHERYL & PAUL SCOTT ANTIQUES
Bear Hill Rd, 03244
(603)464-3617   **29 36**

18th & 19th C furniture & appropriate accessories. *Hours:* BY APPT. *Assoc:* NHADA.

THE SHADOW SHOP
Preston St, 03244
(603)464-4038   **9 13 33**

Antiquarian books & ephemera, stereo views, manuscripts, business graphics & children's books. *Hours:* Tue-Sat 10-5 by

chance/appt, Win: BY APPT ONLY.
Assoc: GSAAA. Lois Meredith **Loc:** Rtes
202 & 9, turn N at Reade & Woods
Insurance Co, 3rd house on R.

TATEWELL GALLERY
Jct Rtes 9 & 31, 03244
(603)478-5756 FAX
(603)478-5711   **36 50 59**
A wide selection of quality antiques &
fine art. Frame shop offers affordable
custom framing with a selection of over
600 frame styles. **Pr:** $25–25000. **Serv:**
Appraisal, custom framing. **Hours:** May-
Oct Tue-Sun 10-5 or by chance/appt;
Nov-Apr Mon-Thu 10-5. **CC:**
AX/MC/V. **Assoc:** GSAAA NHADA.
Jack Tate Don Boxwell **Park:** On site.
Loc: Next to Pierce homestead.

**RICHARD W WITHINGTON
AUCTIONEER**
590 Center Rd, 03244
(603)464-3232   **4 8**
Forty years experience in selling antiques & fine furnishing - mostly estate
auctions & doll auctions. 10% buyer's
premium. **Est:** 1948. **Serv:** Appraisal.
Hours: Call for appts & schedule. **Assoc:**
NAA. Richard W Withington

WYNDHURST FARM ANTIQUES
Rte 2, 03244
(603)464-5377   **44**
A variety of antiques specializing in pattern glass. **Hours:** May 15-Oct 15 by
chance/appt. **Assoc:** NHADA. David &
Rosa Webb

YOUR COUNTRY AUCTIONEER
Center Road Box 339, 03244
(603)478-5723
Largest tool auctioneer in northeast with
twenty years experience in selling fine
antique & more recent tools of the trade,
including woodworking, blacksmithing
& boatbuilding. **Est:** 1970. **Serv:** Auc-

tions, appraisal, purchase single items,
shops, estates & furnishings. **Hours:** Call
for appt. **Assoc:** AAA NEAA. Richard A
Crane

HILLSBORO CENTER

BEAR TRACK FARM ANTIQUES
Hillsboro Center, 03244
(603)478-3263   **23 36 65**
Clocks, watches, country furniture,
primitives, toys & unusual smalls. **Hours:**
All year by chance/appt. **Assoc:**
NHADA. Pat & Jack Mc Laughlin **Loc:**
2 MI past Hillsboro Center toward E
Washington.

HOLDERNESS

WILLIAM F DEMBIEC ANTIQUES
Squamm Lakes Rd Rtes 3 & 25, 03245
(603)968-3178   **30**
General line of antiques & collectibles.
Hours: Jun 17-Sep 4 10-5, Sep-Jun by
chance/appt. **Assoc:** NHADA. **Loc:** I-93
Exit 24: 3 MI to Rtes 3 & 25.

SQUAM LAKE GALLERY
Rtes 3 & 25, 03245
(508)887-8996   **29 59**
Specializing in paintings of the White
Mountain School & American decora-
tive arts. **Hours:** Best to call ahead for an
appt. Jeanne A Demers **Loc:** Across from
the Inn on Golden Pond short of the
village approx 3 MI, in a barn.

HOLLIS

HOPKINTON

THE BLUE LANTERN ANTIQUES
28 Pine Hill Rd, 03049
(603)465-2624　　　　**16 44 56**
Marine antiques, country furniture, early
glass, brass & copper. **Hours:** May-Dec
Fri,Sat 10-5 or BY APPT, CLOSED
AUG. **Assoc:** NHADA. Martha Davis
Loc: Off Rte 130.

THE COOPERAGE
Rte 130 Ash St, 03049
(603)465-3322　　　　**27 29 36**
Consigned antiques in a restored 1830
setting in Hollis village. **Pr:** $20–3000.
Est: 1988. **Serv:** Consultation, purchase
estates. **Hours:** Tue-Sat 10-5, Sun 12-5,
please call ahead. **Size:** Medium. **CC:**
MC/V. **Park:** On site. **Loc:** Directly opposite post office.

HOLLIS FLEA MARKET
Silver Lake Rd Rte 122, 03049
(603)882-6134　　　　**{FLEA}**
Outdoor flea market with antiques, collectibles & other flea market merchandise. **Est:** 1965. **Serv:** Catered, space
rental is $12 for 16' X 22' space. **Hours:**
Apr-Nov 15 Sun 7 til ?. **Size:** 125 spaces.
Park: Parking is $1. **Loc:** Rte 3 Exit 7 W:
8 MI to Rte 122, turn L, go 1 1/2 MI.

GEORGE LA BARRE GALLERIES INC
Box 746, 03049
(800)842-7000　　　　**9**
Early stocks & bonds & autographs.
Hours: Daily 9-5. **Assoc:** NADA.

ANDERSON'S ANTIQUES INC
South Rd, 03229
(603)746-3364　　　　**37 59 63**
Fine New England furniture, lamps,
china, glass, Chinese export porcelain &
decorative accessories for the discriminating & knowledgeable collector.
Est: 1948. **Hours:** Appt suggested. **Size:**
Medium. **Shows:** ELLIS. Mabel A
Lomas **Park:** On site. **Loc:** Just S of Int of
Rtes 103 & 202.

ROLAND & JOYCE BARNARD ANTIQUES
Hopkinton, 03229
(603)224-6889　　　　**37 23**
Specializing in American furniture &
clocks. **Hours:** BY APPT. **Assoc:**
NHADA.

CHURCHILLBOOKS
Hopkinton, 03229
(603)746-4260 FAX
(603)746-5606　　　　**13**
Sir Winston Churchill: books by him,
about him or related to his life & times.
Serv: Mail order catalog issued periodically. **Hours:** Mon-Fri 9-5 or by
chance/appt. **Size:** 1,000 volumes. **Assoc:**
NHABA. Richard Langworth

MEADOW HEARTH
Briar Hill Rd, 03229
(603)746-3947　　　　**29 37 67**
Early American furniture, quilts &
general line of decorative accessories. **Pr:**
$5–3000. **Est:** 1938. **Hours:** Apr 15-Nov
Appt suggested, Dec-Apr 14 BY APPT
ONLY. **Size:** Medium. **Assoc:** NHADA.
John Howe **Park:** On site. **Loc:** From
Hopkinton Village, Rd opposite Cracker
Barrel, to L of church is Briar Hill Rd, 1
MI up rd, L onto dirt Rd, house on R.

THE SOULES-ANTIQUES
Blaze Hill Rd, 03229
(603)746-4527   **16 42 57**
Refinished furniture, samplers, brass, lamps & other decorative accessories. *Pr:* $10–2000. *Est:* 1970. *Hours:* Year round by chance/appt, please call ahead. *Assoc:* NHADA. Dot & Bob Soule *Park:* On site. *Loc:* Off Rte 103 between Hopkinton & Contoocook, N on Gould Hill Rd 3/4 MI. L on Blaze Hill, 2nd Driveway on R.

WOMEN'S WORDS BOOKS
RR4 Box 322 Straw Rd, 03229
(603)228-8000   **13**
Specializing in all areas of women's studies. *Est:* 1976. *Serv:* Search service, special collections development, catalog, purchase estates. *Hours:* BY APPT. *Size:* 3,000 books. *CC:* MC/V. *Assoc:* NHABA. Nancy Needham

WAYNE & PEGGY WOODARD ANTIQUES
Hopkinton Village, 03229
(603)746-3313   **16 37 57**
18th & 19th C American, French & English furniture & accessories, brass, samplers, spongeware & Gaudy Welsh. *Pr:* $50–10000. *Est:* 1972. *Serv:* Purchase estates. *Hours:* May-Nov daily 10-5, appt suggested. *Size:* Large. *CC:* AX/MC/V. *Assoc:* NHADA. *Park:* On site. *Loc:* I-89 Exit 4: approx 1 MI on Rte 103.

HUDSON

COLONIAL SHOPPE
20 Old Derry Rd, 03051
(603)882-2959   **2 22 27**
Country & primitive furniture, kitchen & hearth accessories, treenware, early iron. *Serv:* Refinishing, repairs. *Hours:* By chance/appt. *Assoc:* GSAAA NHADA. Carol Murray *Loc:* Rte 102, turn onto Old Derry Rd at Hudson Motor Inn.

JACKSON

RED SHED ANTIQUES
Rte 16, 03846
(603)383-9267   **65 81**
Primitives, tools, kitchenware, furniture & a general line. *Pr:* $25–800. *Hours:* Jun-Oct 15 Mon-Sat 10:30-5 CLOSED SUN. *CC:* MC/V. *Assoc:* NADA NHADA. *Park:* On site. *Loc:* 1/2 MI N of Covered Bridge, on rd to Mt Washington.

JAFFREY

AT THE SIGN OF THE FOX
3 Blackberry Ln, 03452
(603)532-6897   **37 66 67**
Fine early American & country furniture, accessories, paintings, prints, hooked rugs & quilts. *Hours:* BY APPT ONLY. *Assoc:* NHADA.

INDIAN SUMMER ANTIQUES
54 Main St, 03452
(603)532-4401   **30 34**
Folk art, fish decoys, woodenware, cast iron doorstops & ashwood baskets. *Est:* 1960. *Serv:* Appraisal. *Hours:* Thu-Sat 10-5. *Park:* Nearby. *Loc:* Across from the bandstand.

THE TOWNE HOUSE
30 Ellison St, 03452
(603)532-7118   **50**
Antiques, lamps, lamp parts & shades.

Hours: All year daily 10-5 CLOSED SUN. **Assoc:** NHADA. Tat Duval **Loc:** Off E Main St.

KEENE

ANDERSON GALLERY
21 Davis St, 03431
(603)352-6422   **48 77**
A sophisticated collection of 19th C silver & very fine linens. **Hours:** BY APPT. **Assoc:** AAA GSAAA NHADA. Thelma E Anderson

EAGLE BOOKS
19 West Street, 03431
(603)357-8721   **13**
Antiquarian Books: Specializing in the WPA Writer's Project. **Est:** 1990. **Hours:** Mon-Sat 10-5 else by appt. **Size:** 12,000 books. **Assoc:** NHABA. Sylvia Felix **Park:** Park at Central Square.

FAIRGROUNDS ANTIQUE CO-OP
50 Summit Rd, 03431
(603)357-0679   **{GR40}**
Furniture, glassware, primitives & country. **Hours:** Daily 10-5. **Loc:** The Cheshire Fairgrounds.

WASHINGTON STREET GALLERY
117 Washington St, 03431
(603)352-2194   **59 66 67**
Antique furniture, quilts, paintings, prints & small accessories. **Serv:** Framing of oils & prints. **Hours:** By chance/appt. **Assoc:** NHADA.

KENSINGTON

PETER SAWYER ANTIQUES
50 Moulton Ridge Rd, 03833
(603)772-5279   **23 37**
Specializing in American clocks from tall case to Connecticut shelf & wall clocks; also a collection of New England furniture. **Hours:** By chance/appt. **Assoc:** NHADA. **Loc:** 1 hr N of Boston, 10 min off I-95.

KINGSTON

COUNTRY BARN ANTIQUES
Rte 107 N off Rte 125, 03848
                        {GR}
Collectibles, quality used furniture,. **Hours:** Thu-Mon 10:30-4:30 Sun 12-5. Dave Augur

RED BELL ANTIQUES
Rte 125, 03848
(603)642-5641   **{GR30}**
China, furniture, jewelry, quilts, tools & primitives. **Hours:** Daily 10-5. **CC:** MC/V.

LACONIA

AGORA COLLECTIBLES
373 Court St, 03246
(603)524-0129   **32**
Specializing in dolls & furniture, also antiques & collectibles, doll & toy hospital & new dolls. **Hours:** All year by chance/appt. **Assoc:** NHADA. Alice & John Ortakles

BARN LOFT BOOKSHOP
96 Woodland Ave, 03246
(603)524-4839   **13**

Antiquarian books specializing in children's & New England. *Hours:* By chance/appt. *Size:* 9,000 books. *Assoc:* NHABA. Lee Burt

COTTON HILL BOOKS
RFD 6 Box 298, 03246
(603)524-4967   **13**

Antiquarian books: New England, art, gardening & general stock. *Hours:* By chance/appt. *Assoc:* NHABA. Elizabeth K Emery

BARBARA B HARRIS BOOKS
RFD 1 Box 199A, 03246
(603)524-5405   **13**

General stock featuring nature, gardening, children's, dolls, biography & New England. *Hours:* By chance/appt. *Size:* 4,000 books. *Assoc:* NHABA. *Loc:* Call for directions.

THE HOFFMANS
Union Rd, 03246
(603)528-2792   **16 27 28**

Early American country furniture & accessories, pewter, baskets, quilts & crocks. *Hours:* All year, call ahead. *Assoc:* NHADA. *Loc:* I-93 Exit 20: 5 1/3 MI N on Rte 3, R on Union Rd at Double Decker Restaurant, 2 1/2 MI on R.

LANCASTER

BRETTON HALL ANTIQUITIES
12 Cottage St, 03584
(603)788-2202   **13**

General stock of books specializing in New Hampshire & White Mountain.

Hours: May 25-Oct daily 10-4, else by chance/appt. *Assoc:* NHABA. Richard C Force

ELM STREET & STOLCRAFT BOOKS
20 Elm St, 03584
(603)788-4844   **13**

General stock of used & out-of-print books. *Hours:* Mid May-Mid Oct Mon-Sat 10-5, else BY APPT ONLY. *Size:* 100,000 books. *Assoc:* NHABA. Albert Tetreault

GRANARY ANTIQUES
North Rd, 03584
(603)788-2790   **36 63 67**

Quilts, furniture, china & miniature lamps. *Hours:* Apr 15-Jan 19 daily 8-6. *Assoc:* NHADA. Louise Martin *Loc:* 1 MI N from town.

ISRAEL RIVER BOOKS
44 Main St, 03584
(603)788-3966   **13**

15-20th C bookbinding, astronomy, gastronomy, natural history, science, literature, Greek & Roman classics, White Mountains & Americana. *Hours:* Jun-Oct Wed-Sat 10-6, Sun 12-4; Nov-May Sat 10-6, Sun 12-4. *Size:* 5,000 books. *Assoc:* NHABA. Melissa & James Robin

LANCASTER MALL & ANTIQUES MARKET
18 Middle St, 03584
(603)788-2421   **{GR9}**

Group shop & art gallery located in the White Mountains. *Pr:* $1–3500. *Est:* 1987. *Hours:* Tue-Sat 10-6. *Size:* Large. *CC:* MC/V. *Loc:* From St Johnsbury VT: Rte 2E, from ME: Rte 2W, from Concord NH: Rte 93N to Rte 3N at Franconia.

THE SHOP IN THE BARN
7 Prospect St Rte 3, 03584
(603)788-2313   **32 36 50**
Furniture, china, glass, jewelry, lamps, lampshades, toys & books. *Hours:* Jun-Oct 15 daily 9-5 Sat 9-4 CLOSED SUN. *Assoc:* NHADA. Rosalie McGraw *Park:* On site. *Loc:* Opposite Soldier's Park.

LEBANON

TIMEPIECE ANTIQUES
Powerhouse Arcade, 03748
(603)298-5223   **23 44**
Rare & unusual examples of high-quality Early American & English glass & a large collection of carriage clocks. *Hours:* By chance/appt. Christopher M English

LISBON

HOUSTON'S FURNITURE BARN
Rtes 302 & 117, 03585
(603)838-5920   **36**
Used furniture, antiques & collectibles. *Hours:* All year.

LITTLETON

ANDY'S BOOK SHOP INC
78 Main St, 03561
(603)444-7740   **13**
Eclectic selection of general used & out of print books. *Est:* 1985. *Serv:* Search services. *Hours:* Mon-Sat 10-5, Sun BY APPT. *Size:* 14,000 books. *Assoc:* NHABA. Andrew & Robin Gutterman *Park:* In front, nearby lot. *Loc:* I-93 Exit 42 (to Main St): located between Carl's Shoes & The Outlet across from Clay St.

THE BEAL HOUSE INN & ANTIQUES
247 W Main St, 03561
(603)444-2661
Furniture & smalls. *Serv:* Intimate country inn. *Hours:* Daily 10-4 or BY APPT, CLOSED WED. *CC:* AX/MC/V. *Assoc:* GSAAA. James Carver *Loc:* Jct of Rtes 302 & 18.

NILA PARKER
17 Redington St, 03561
(603)444-5628   **63**
Flow blue china. *Hours:* By chance/appt, call ahead suggested.

LONDONDERRY

RALPH KYLLOE ANTIQUES
298 High Range Rd, 03053
(603)437-2920   **37**
Specializing in Old Hickory, Adirondack, twig, antler & rustic furnishings. *Serv:* Purchase single items or sets. *Hours:* BY APPT ONLY.

THE PITKINS AUCTION
8 Rosinni Rd, 03053
(603)434-2784
Monthly auctions held on Fridays at Grandview Farm in Derry. *Hours:* Call anytime & to confirm auction. Al Pitkin

THE TATES ANTIQUES
449 Mammoth Rd Rte 128, 03053
(603)434-0272   **27 37**
Specializing in New England country furniture & accessories, old & new

finishes. *Hours:* All year by chance/appt. *Assoc:* GSAAA NHADA. *Loc:* I-93 Exit 5: 2 MI.

NHADA. Richard Malfait *Park:* On site. *Loc:* Loudon Village Exit off Rte 106 at Jct Rte 129, then 1st R, 2nd L.

LOUDON

LYME

CHIMES & TIMES CLOCK SHOP
RFD 8 Box 225C Rte 129, 03301
(603)435-7900   23

Quality antique clocks. *Pr:* $75–15000. *Est:* 1980. *Serv:* Appraisal, consultation, repairs, restoration. *Hours:* Appt suggested. *Size:* Medium. *Assoc:* NAWCC. Ralph J Dickerson *Park:* On site. *Loc:* Int Rtes 106 & 129, take Rte 129 4 MI E, located at sharp curve in the road.

COUNTRY ANTIQUES
Rte 129E, 03263
(603)435-6615   27 34 59

Country formal furniture, folk art, paintings & quality accessories. *Hours:* All year by chance/appt. Fred Cadarette *Loc:* 12 MI from Concord on Rte 129E off Rte 106N.

GODIVA ANTIQUES
RFD 13 Box 38, 03301
(603)798-5729   77 16 37

Silverware, pewter, household furnishings, ceramics & American & English furniture. *Serv:* Appraisal. *Hours:* By chance/appt, call ahead advised. *Assoc:* NEAA. Pat Smith

LOUDON VILLAGE ANTIQUE SHOP
Oak Hill Rd, 03263
(603)783-4741

A general line focusing on turn of the century, with some refinished pieces. *Hours:* All year by chance/appt. *Assoc:*

FALCON'S ROOST ANTIQUES
N River Rd, 03768
(603)353-9815   37

Fine American 18th C & early 19th C formal & country furniture & accessories located in a restored 18th C cape & barn. *Pr:* $25–7500. *Serv:* Bed & breakfast, appraisal, consultation, purchase estates. *Hours:* By chance/appt. *Assoc:* CADA NHADA VADA. Marilyn Bierylo *Park:* On site. *Loc:* I-91 Exit 14 to Lyme: 1st L after crossing CT River Bridge 2 1/2 MI on river side.

JOHN & MARJORIE RICE ANTIQUES
Rte 10, 03768
(603)795-4641   47 77

Southwestern findings, silver, jewelry & cowboy & Indian. *Hours:* May 15-Oct 15 call ahead. *Assoc:* NHADA. *Loc:* 9 MI N of Hanover.

MANCHESTER

ANITA'S ANTIQUARIAN BOOKS
1408 Elm St, 03101
(603)669-7695   13

Antiquarian books specializing in New Hampshire, paper & stamps; majority of stock is pre-1920. *Hours:* Mon-Sat 9:30-5, call ahead advised. *Size:* 50,000 books. *Assoc:* NHABA. Michael Danello

ROBERT M O'NEILL FINE BOOKS
416 Chestnut St, 03103
(603)666-5808 **13**
Fine bindings, press books & New Hampshire-related. *Hours:* Mon-Sat 10-4:30. *Size:* 4,000 books. *Assoc:* NHABA.

VICTORIAN BARN ANTIQUES
364 Bridge St, 03101
(603)622-1524 **1 37**
A fine selection of American furnishings & accessories 1800-1920. *Est:* 1982. *Serv:* Appraisal, purchase estates. *Hours:* Sat-Sun 12-5. *Size:* Medium. *CC:* MC/V. *Park:* On site. *Loc:* I-93 Exit 8: follow Bridge St.

MARLBOROUGH

1836 GRANITE HOUSE
Main St Rte 101, 03455
(603)876-4218
Antiques & collectibles. *Hours:* Open weekends May-Nov and by chance/appt. Reva Fields *Loc:* 5 MI E of Keene.

FATHER TIME ANTIQUES
208 E Main St, 03455
(603)876-4278 **40 83**
Oak & Victorian furniture, china cabinets, roll tops, chairs, Hoosier cabinets, tables & beds in three large rooms. *Hours:* Tue, Thu-Sun 10-4:40, else by chance/appt. *Loc:* On Rte 101W.

HOMESTEAD BOOKSHOP
Rte 101, 03455
(603)876-4213 **12 13**
Children's books, Americana, regional, history, cookery, military, art, crafts, antiques & fiction. *Serv:* Appraisal, bookbinding, repairs, search service. *Hours:* Mon-Fri 9-5 Sat & Sun 9-4:30. *Size:*

45,000 books. *CC:* MC/V. *Assoc:* NHABA. Robert Kenney Prudence L Ross *Park:* In front. *Loc:* On Rte 101 just E of Marlborough Village next to Wilbur Brothers Supermarket.

THOMAS R LONGACRE
726 Jaffrey Rd Rte 124, 03455
(603)876-4080 **29 37 59**
American country & formal furniture including early New England pieces & appropriate accessories. *Est:* 1971. *Hours:* All year appt advisable. *Assoc:* NEAA NHADA. *Loc:* 3 1/2 MI E on Rte 124, off Rte 101.

BETTY WILLIS ANTIQUES INC
Rte 124 Jaffrey Rd, 03455
(603)876-3983 **37 38 39**
Large selection of American, English & European furniture & appropriate accessories of the 18th & 19th C. *Pr:* $500–50000. *Serv:* Consultation, interior design, purchase estates. *Hours:* By chance/appt. *Size:* Large. *Assoc:* NHADA. Nancy Willis *Park:* On site. *Loc:* From Keene, NH E on Rte 101 to Marlborough; at Int of Rtes 10, 1 & 24, R on 124, 2 1/2 MI to shop.

WOODWARD'S ANTIQUES
166 Main St Rte 101, 03455
(603)876-3360 **27**
Country furniture refinished & in the rough. *Hours:* All year by chance/appt. Terry Woodward

MARLOW

PEACE BARN ANTIQUES
Forest Rd Rte 123N, 03456
(603)446-7161 **16 27 65**
A country home, barn & herb garden offering early furniture, decorative ac-

cessories & pewter. *Hours:* Apr-Nov by chance/appt. *Assoc:* GSAAA NHADA. Ace Ells *Loc:* Red barn & cape at edge of village.

MEREDITH

THE OLD PRINT BARN
Winona Rd, 03253
(603)279-6479   **66**
Antiques & modern prints, etchings, engravings, serigraphs, mezzotints. 18th, 19th, & 20th C prints from New Hampshire, America, Europe & Japan. *Est:* 1976. *Serv:* Framing, restoration, appraisal, brochure, consultation, purchase estates. *Hours:* Jun-Oct 15 daily 10-6, Oct 16-May BY APPT ONLY. *Size:* Large. *CC:* MC/V. *Assoc:* NHADA. Sophia Lane. *Park:* On site. *Loc:* From Hart's Restaurant on Rte 3, 1 1/2 MI on Rte 104 to blinking light, R on Winona Rd. No sign, LANE on mailbox.

ALEXANDRIA LAMP SHOP
Main St & Marketplace Ln, 03253
(603)279-4234   **50**
Antique kerosene, gas & electric lighting, lamp supplies, brass lighting, fabric shades, country-style pine & oak furniture, prints, jewelry, glassware, tools, reference books & collectibles. *Hours:* Mon-Sat 11-6 Sun 1-5 CLOSED WED (except Summer). *Assoc:* NHADA. Fran Governanti

BURLWOOD ANTIQUE CENTER
Jct Rtes 3 & 104, 03253
(603)279-6387   **{GR170}**
Two floors of smaller antiques, 1 floor of furniture, displayed in a converted 18th C barn. *Est:* 1983. *Hours:* May-Oct daily 10-5. *Size:* Huge. *CC:* MC/V. *Assoc:*

NHADA. Thomas Lindsey *Park:* On site. *Loc:* I-93 Exit 23: to Rte 104E, 9 MI to Jct of Rte 3, turn R, 100 yds up on R.

GORDONS ANTIQUES
Rte 3, 03253
(603)279-5458   **44 63 83**
Turn-of-the-century antiques including porcelains, linens, jewelry, art glass, pottery, vintage clothing, lamps, sterling silver, clocks, furniture & decorative objects. *Pr:* $2–5000. *Est:* 1981. *Serv:* Purchase estates. *Hours:* May-Oct 10-5, Sun 11-4; Nov-Dec Wed-Mon 11-4; Else, call. *Size:* Medium. *CC:* AX/MC/V. *Assoc:* NHADA. Marlene/Charlie Gordon *Park:* On site. *Loc:* Rte 93 N Exit 23: to Rte 104 E to end, R on Rte 3, 1 1/2 MI S on L after Harpers Boat yard.

MARY ROBERTSON - BOOKS
Rte 3 & Parade Rd, 03253
(603)279-8750   **13**
General stock specializing in old & new children's & needlwork craft books. *Hours:* Sum: daily 10-5, Spring/Fall most days 12-4. *Assoc:* ABAA NHABA.

MERRIMACK

JEANNINE DOBBS COUNTRY FOLK
PO Box 1076, 03054
(603)424-7617   **34 41 67**
18th & 19th C painted furnishings & accessories, baskets, samplers, quilts, hooked rugs, folk art & woodenware. *Hours:* BY APPT. *Assoc:* NHADA.

MILFORD

THE ANTIQUE WAREHOUSE
Jct 101 & 101A W Elm St, 03055
(603)673-6062   **{GR117}**

Refinished furniture, glass, paintings, jewelry, country items, china, baseball cards, trains, & ephemera. *Hours:* Daily 10-5 Thu til 8. *Size:* Huge. Matthew Bole

MILFORD ANTIQUES
14 Nashua St, 03055
(603)672-2311   **47**

Jewelry, general antiques & furniture. *Est:* 1955. *Serv:* Appraisal, evaluations. *Hours:* Daily 10-5. Mary Dugan *Park:* On site. *Loc:* Near the rotary, across from the library.

NEW HAMPSHIRE ANTIQUE CO-OP INC
Rte 101-A Elm St, 03055
(603)673-8499   **{GR288}**

A professionally run group shop featuring period furniture, pottery & porcelain, glass & collectibles, including dealer displays in 148 locked showcases. *Est:* 1983. *Serv:* Appraisal, purchase estates. *Hours:* Daily 10-5. *Size:* Huge. *CC:* MC/V. *Assoc:* GSAAA NHADA. Sam Hackler *Park:* On site. *Loc:* Rte 3 Exit 7W: Rte 101A into Milford 1 1/2 MI W of ctr of Milford.

OLD STUFF FLEA MARKET
Rte 101 A, 03055
(603)878-2510   **{FLEA}**

Flea market of antiques & collectibles. *Serv:* Dealer space $10. *Hours:* Sun & holiday Mon 8-4. *Loc:* At the Milford drive-in movie theater.

THE RENAISSANCE MAN
275 Elm St Rte 101-A, 03055
(603)673-5653   **19 70 71**

Custom woodworking, museum-quality restoration, specializing in hand-rubbed oil finished reproduction true to early American design & technique, wood carving & parts reproduced. *Serv:* Consultation, interior design, repairs, replication, reproduction. *Hours:* BY APPT ONLY. Walter Haney MFA *Park:* On site. *Loc:* Rte 3 Exit 101A: to Milford, approx 9 MI, 1 1/2 MI past Milford Town Green, located at NH Antique Co-op.

VICTORIA PLACE
88 Nashua St Rte 101A, 03055
(603)673-7101   **39**

Imported English furniture, antiques & accessories. *Hours:* Daily 10-5. *Size:* Medium. *CC:* MC/V. *Park:* In front. *Loc:* Rte 3 Exit 7W.

MONT VERNON

CANDLEWICK ANTIQUES
Main St Rte 13N, 03057
(603)673-1941   **34 63 80**

Country furniture, folk art, early china & glass, toys, textiles & Christmas ornaments. *Hours:* Sat,Sun 11-5, else by chance/appt. *Assoc:* NHADA. Jessie Anderson *Park:* On site.

THE YELLOW BARN
Blood Rd, 03057
(603)673-3612   **40 42**

Large selection of furniture including oak, pine, mahogany & walnut. *Hours:* Daily 10-5 CLOSED WED. Ed Richardson

MOULTONBORO

ANTIQUES AT MOULTONBORO
Old Rte 109S, 03254
(603)476-8863　　　　**1 36**
In a restored 1840 New England cape 3 rooms of quality country & formal furniture, folk art, glass & other accessories. Barn is stocked with Americana, collectibles & furniture - refinished or rough. *Pr:* $10–2000. *Serv:* Refinishing. *Hours:* May-Oct Sat-Sun 10-5, Mon-Fri & Nov-Apr by chance/appt. *Size:* Medium. *Assoc:* NHADA. Jack May *Park:* In front. *Loc:* Just off Rte 25, on Old Rte 109, Moultonboro Ctr.

BENCHMARK ANTIQUES
Rte 25, 03254
(603)253-6362　　　　**27**
Country furniture, accessories & collectibles. *Hours:* All year daily 10-5 by chance/appt. *Assoc:* NHADA. Gene Kincaid *Loc:* Opposite the Red Hill Motel.

CARL & BEVERLY SHELDRAKE
Stone Crop Farm, 03254
(603)544-9008　　　　**29 36**
18th C country furniture & related accessories. *Hours:* By chance/appt. *Loc:* S of Moultonboro on Severance Rd, between Rtes 109 & 171 near Lake Winnipesaukee.

MT SUNAPEE

RED SLEIGH
Rte 103, 03782
　　　　34 42 65
Country pine, primitives, folk art & smalls. *Pr:* $10–1500. *Serv:* Consult-
ation, purchase estates, repairs, restoration. *Hours:* Jun-Oct by chance/appt. Joan Pirozzoli *Loc:* Rte 103B to base of Mt Sunapee, located at E end of traffic circle.

NASHUA

ANTIQUE CLOCK REPAIR & APPRAISAL
10 Sargent Ave, 03060
(603)889-5784　　　　**4 68**
Appraisal & repairs to clocks. *Hours:* BY APPT. *Assoc:* AWI NAWCC. Lennie Brand *Loc:* Rte 3 Exit 6.

PAUL HENDERSON
50 Berkeley St, 03060
(603)883-8918　　　　**13**
Antiquarian books: genealogies & local history. *Serv:* Catalog, search services. *Hours:* By chance/appt. *Assoc:* NHABA.

HOUSE OF JAMES ANTIQUES
523 Broad St Rte 130, 03063
(603)882-4118　　　　**{GR35}**
Furniture, china, glass, collectibles, ephemera, toys & crafts. *Hours:* Wed-Mon 10-5 CLOSED TUE. Jim Prece *Loc:* Rte 3 Exit 6: Rte 130 W.

NASHUA ANTIQUES SHOWS
Saint Stans Hall, 03060
(617)329-1192　　　　**{FLEA}**
Regularly scheduled Sun antiques show in St. Stans Hall. Admission $2. *Est:* 1977. *Serv:* Catered, space rental starts at $55, reservations needed. *Hours:* Mid Oct-mid April Sun 7:30-1. *Size:* 65 dealers. Jack Donigian, Manager *Park:* Free parking. *Loc:* Rte 3 Exit 6: 2nd L onto Blue Hill Ave.

RUSTIC ACCENTS INC
69 Main St, 03060
(603)882-4112   **27 65**
Country, primitives & decorative accessories. *Hours:* All year by chance/appt. *Assoc:* NHADA. Ken Pike

NEW IPSWICH

ESTELLE M GLAVEY INC
Rte 124, 03071
(603)878-1200   **21 36 59**
Two brick Colonials with rooms of quality stock including country & formal furniture, paintings & rugs. *Est:* 1964. *Hours:* All year by chance/appt, CLOSED MON. *Assoc:* NHADA.

NEW LONDON

THE BLOCK HOUSE
Hominy Pot Rd, 03257
(603)927-4623   **30 78**
Decoys, sporting artifacts, sporting prints & paintings. *Hours:* All year by chance/appt. Doug Knight *Loc:* Call for directions.

LEE BURGESS ANTIQUES
Little Sunapee Rd, 03257
(603)526-4657   **27**
Fine country furniture, Canton & accessories. *Hours:* BY APPT. *Assoc:* NHADA.

BURPEE HILL BOOKS
Burpee Hill Rd, 03257
(603)526-6654   **13**
General Americana, early printed books, books on art & collecting & paper. *Serv:* Catalog. *Hours:* By chance/appt. *Assoc:* NHABA. Alf E Jacobson

PRISCILLA DRAKE ANTIQUES
33 Main St, 03257
(603)526-6514   **36 44 63**
Furniture, glass, china & accessories. *Hours:* Jul-Aug Tue-Sat 10-4, May Jun & Sep by chance/appt. *Assoc:* NHADA.

MAD EAGLE INC FINE ANTIQUES
Rte 11, 03257
(603)526-4880   **16 37 63**
Fine early American furniture & choice accessories - both country & formal - & Oriental rugs. *Pr:* $1–16000. *Est:* 1961. *Hours:* May 15-Oct 15 Mon-Sat 1-5, also by appt. *Size:* Large. *Park:* In front. *Loc:* I-89 Exit 11: 2 MI E.

NEWINGTON

NEWINGTON STAR CENTER
25 Fox Run Rd, 03801
(603)431-9403   **{FLEA}**
Indoor flea market with antiques, collectibles & flea market merchandise. Free admission. *Est:* 1979. *Serv:* Catered, air conditioned, rentals start at $10 for tables. *Hours:* Year round Sun 9-5. *Size:* 100 spaces. *Park:* Free parking. *Loc:* I-95: Portsmouth rotary to Spaulding Tnpk to Fox Run Rd.

NEWTON

STEVEN J ROWE
One N Main St, 03858
(603)382-4618   **27**
Country furniture & fine accessories in original condition. *Hours:* All year BY APPT. *Assoc:* NHADA. *Loc:* I-495 Exit 53: 4 MI.

NORTH BARNSTEAD

COOPER SHOP ANTIQUES
Box 43 Peacham Rd, 03225
(603)776-7191   **27 29 32**
An 1820 Cooper shop housing a collection of country antiques a wide variety of unusual & choice accessories. *Pr:* $25–1000. *Hours:* Jun-Oct 15 Thu-Sat 10-5 Sun 12-5 or by chance/appt. *Size:* Medium. *Assoc:* NHADA. Bea Nelson *Park:* On site. *Loc:* From Concord, NH, take Rte 4 E to Epsom rotary, then Rte 28 N for 13 1/2 MI; follow state signs to shop; 1 MI off Rte 28.

NORTH CONWAY

ANTIQUES & COLLECTIBLES BARN
Rtes 16 & 302, 03860
(603)356-7118   **{GR40}**
Antiques & collectibles, including jewelry, silver, rugs, ephemera, linens, quilts & period lighting. *Serv:* Consultation, search service. *Hours:* Daily 10-5. *Size:* Large. *CC:* AX/MC/V. *Assoc:* NHADA. Mardy Friary *Park:* On site. *Loc:* 1 1/2 MI N of N Conway Village.

GRALYN ANTIQUES, INC
Main St, 03860
(603)356-5546   **36 44 65**
19th C American art of the White Mountain School. *Est:* 1922. *Hours:* By chance/appt. *Size:* Large. *CC:* DC/MC/V. *Assoc:* NHADA. Robert/Dorothy Goldberg *Park:* On site. *Loc:* Across from Red Jacket Hotel, 2 MI N of Jct 16 & 302.

RICHARD M PLUSCH ANTIQUES
Main St Rtes 6 & 302, 03860
(603)356-3333   **29 59 63**
A diverse selection of fine period furnishings & accessories, glass, china, silver, Orientalia, rugs, clocks, 19th C paintings & prints, country & some formal furniture. Always an interesting collection of quality antiques. *Pr:* $5–5000. *Serv:* Appraisal, consultation, purchase estates. *Hours:* Sum: daily 10-5 & BY APPT, Win: Sat 10-5 Sun 12-5. *Size:* Medium. *Assoc:* NHADA. *Loc:* In the heart of the White Mountains 3 hrs N of Boston.

NORTH HAMPTON

NORTH HAMPTON ANTIQUE CENTER
One Lafayette Rd Rte 1, 03862
(603)964-6615   **{GR22}**
Antiques & collectibles. *Hours:* Year round Mon-Sat 10-4 Sun by chance/appt. *Assoc:* NHADA.

NORTHUMBERLAND

POTATO BARN ANTIQUES CENTER LTD
Rte 3, 03582
(603)636-2611   **{GR70}**
A group shop with a wide variety of antiques & collectibles, featuring old tools, jewelry & vintage clothing. *Est:* 1988. *Hours:* Apr-Dec 9-5 daily, Jan-Mar Fri-Sun 10-4. *CC:* MC/V. Ernie & Janice Yelle *Park:* In front. *Loc:* 4 1/2 MI N of Lancaster, NH fairgrounds on Rte 3.

NORTHWOOD

BRADBURY/NEWELL HOUSE
Rte 4, 03261
(603)942-5602   **37 1**
18th C house filled with Americana &
quality accessories. **Hours:** Sat-Tue 10-4
or by appt. **Assoc:** NHADA. Fern
Eldridge **Loc:** Adjacent to Town Hall.

BUTTERCHURN ANTIQUES
Rte 4, 03261
(603)942-5842   **27 36 65**
Traditional shop with emphasis on
quality, authenticity & diversity, featur-
ing country primitives & furniture, com-
plemented by a variety of smalls &
collectibles. **Pr:** $25–1000. **Est:** 1988.
Serv: Appraisal, purchase estates. **Hours:**
Daily 10-5 CLOSED WED. **Size:**
Medium. **CC:** MC/V. **Assoc:** NHADA.
John St Laurent **Park:** On site. **Loc:** Rte
4E, shop is 4 1/2 MI from Int of Rte 28
(Epsom traffic circle).

COUNTRY TAVERN OF NORTHWOOD
498 Rte 4, 03261
(603)942-7630   **{GR55}**
Quality American antiques in an 18th C
tavern & barn, room settings, early
country furniture, folk art, quilts & textiles, toys, rugs, baskets, distinctive
smalls & primitives. **Hours:** All year
Mon-Sat 10-5 Sun 12-5. **Size:** Large.
CC: MC/V. **Assoc:** NHADA. Bob
Schmitt **Loc:** On Rte 4 W of Rte 202.

DRAKE'S HILL ANTIQUES
Rte 202A, 03261
(603)942-5958   **63**
English china 1820-1860, country furni-
ture & accessories for the country home.
Hours: All year by chance/appt. **Assoc:**
NHADA. James & Nancy Boyd

THE EAGLE
Rte 4, 03261
(603)942-8136   **{GR10}**
Country furniture, primitives, smalls,
Victorian, collectibles. **Hours:** Daily 10-
5. Jay Miller **Loc:** W of Rte 202.

HAYLOFT ANTIQUE CENTER
Box 5A Rte 4, 03261
(603)942-5153   **{GR120}**
Clocks, tools, treen, rugs, early bottles,
silver, copper, lanterns, jewelry & furniture & the coffee pot is always on. **Pr:**
$25–1000. **Est:** 1985. **Serv:** Purchase es-
tates. **Hours:** Daily 10-5. **Size:** Huge.
CC: MC/V. **Assoc:** NHADA. **Park:** In
front. **Loc:** On Rte 4 Antique Alley near
Rte 7.

JOHNSTONE ANTIQUES
Main St Rte 107 N, 03261
(603)942-5684   **{GR}**
A full selection of 18th & 19th C
American country furniture, including
cupboards, tavern tables, candlestands,
farm tables, lift-top blanket chests, pie
safes, corner cupboards, sets of chairs,
unusual folk art, fine accessories & quilts.
Est: 1965. **Serv:** Crate on premises &
ship nationwide. **Hours:** Daily 10-5
evenings by appt, call ahead advised.
Assoc: NHADA. **Loc:** 1/4 MI off Rte 4 on
Rte 107 in the heart of Antique Alley.

JUNCTION ANTIQUE CENTER
Rtes 4 & 202, 03261
(603)942-5756   **{GR40}**
Specializing in fine quality country &
formal furnishings & accessories,
glassware, china & art. **Hours:** Mon-Sat
10-5 Sun 12-5. **CC:** MC/V. **Loc:** Near the
Jct of Rtes 202 & 4.

NORTHWOOD INN ANTIQUE CENTER
454A Route 4A, 03261
(603)942-5611   **{GR}**

Ten rooms of furniture, prints, paintings, fine glass & china. *Serv:* Purchase estates, delivery available. *Hours:* Mon-Fri 9:30-4:30, Sat-Sun 10-5. *CC:* MC/V. Stuart Frye *Park:* On site. *Loc:* On Rte 4 Near Int of Rte 202.

PARKER FRENCH ANTIQUE CENTER
Rte 4, 03261
(603)942-8852   **{GR135}**

The cornerstone at Antique Alley & oldest group shop in Northwood, featuring jewelry, silver, paintings & furniture. *Est:* 1974. *Serv:* Appraisal, purchase estates. *Hours:* Daily 10-5. *Size:* Huge. *Assoc:* NHADA. Caroline French & Gordon Millar *Park:* In front. *Loc:* Midway between Concord & Portsmouth, 12 MI W of Lee traffic circle, 6 MI E of Epsom traffic circle.

PIONEER AMERICA
Rte 4 & Upper Bow St, 03261
(603)942-8588   **63 65 66**

A two-story 19th C barn filled with country & primitives, stylish Victorian, textiles, farm collectibles, glass, china & more. *Hours:* Year round 10-5. *Size:* Medium. *CC:* MC/V. *Assoc:* NHADA. Joel Aiello *Loc:* On Antique Alley.

TOWN PUMP ANTIQUES
Rte 4 Box 288, 03261
(603)942-5515   **{GR}**

Three spacious floors of furniture, glass & collectibles. *Est:* 1975. *Serv:* Purchase estates. *Hours:* Daily 9-5 Sun 10-5. *Size:* Large. Joanie Ebberson *Loc:* On Rte 4 between Rte 202 & Rte 107.

THE WHITE HOUSE ANTIQUES
Rte 4, 03261
(603)942-8994   **{GR}**

Featuring ephemera & including furniture, decorative accessories & glassware. *Serv:* Purchase estates. *Hours:* Daily 10-5. Joe Trovato *Loc:* Just W of Rte 202.

WILLOW HOLLOW ANTIQUES
Rte 4, 03261
(603)942-5739   **{GR20}**

Two floors of small antiques, primitives, advertising, paper, Americana, postcards, glass & toys. Heated/air conditioned. *Serv:* Catalog. *Hours:* Daily 10-5. *CC:* MC/V. *Assoc:* NHADA. Nancy Winston *Loc:* Rte 4 beyond Town Hall, on L 1/2 MI from Concord.

OSSIPEE

FLAG GATE FARM ANTIQUES
Rte 28, 03864
(603)539-2231   **44 50**

Two large floors furnished with period antiques, Irish pine, antique lighting & glassware, cut glass, pattern glass, art glass, lace & miniature lamps. *Pr:* $25–6600. *Serv:* Bed & breakfast. *Hours:* All year daily 11-5 or BY APPT. *Size:* Large. *CC:* MC/V. *Assoc:* AAA. Marion M Ingemi *Park:* On site. *Loc:* On Rte 28 in Ossipee 1/4 MI S off Rte 16, N of Portsmouth.

GRANT HILL ANTIQUES
Ossipee, 03814
(603)539-2431   **71**

Antiques, collectibles & furniture restoration. *Hours:* Year round by chance/appt, CLOSED MON in winter. *Assoc:* NHADA. Marion & Bruce Rines *Loc:* Next to Town Hall in Ossipee Ctr.

GREEN MOUNTAIN ANTIQUE CENTER
Rte 16, 03864
(603)539-2236   **{GR75}**

Glass, china, primitives, tools, furniture, books, linens, vintage clothing, jewelry & coins. *Est:* 1982. *Hours:* Year round Sun-Thu 9-5, Fri-Sat 9-8. *Size:* Huge. *Assoc:* NHADA. *Loc:* 1/2 MI N of Jct of Rte 28.

THE STUFF SHOP
Box 5 Rte 171, 03864
(603)539-7715   **23 27**

Diverse selection of antiques & collectibles, primarily country with a large selection of clocks & watches. *Pr:* $10–1000. *Est:* 1960. *Serv:* Appraisal, lamp repair. *Hours:* Apr-Oct 12 daily 9-5. *Size:* Medium. *CC:* MC/V. *Assoc:* AAA. Len Wenant *Park:* In front. *Loc:* Rte 16 to Rte 28W on Rte 171, 6th house on L from Rte 28.

TERRACE ROOM ANTIQUES
Rte 16, 03864
(603)539-2253   **27 14 36**

Group shop featuring country, books, furniture, jewelry, silver & paper. *Hours:* Daily 10-5, later in summer. *CC:* AX/MC/V. *Assoc:* NHADA. *Loc:* 1/2 MI N of Rte 28 on Rte 16, in Sunny Villa shops.

PELHAM

CARTER'S BARN ANTIQUES
520 Mammoth Rd Rte 128, 03076
(603)883-3269   **40 42**

Early pine, oak, mahogany & walnut furniture. *Serv:* Stripping, refinishing. *Hours:* Wed-Sun 10-5. *Size:* Large. *CC:* MC/V. Dave Carter

PETERBOROUGH

BRENNANS ANTIQUES
130 Hunt Rd, 03458
(603)924-3445   **65 81**

Country furniture, primitives, woodenware, tin, iron, early tools & decorative accessories. *Hours:* BY APPT. *Assoc:* GSAAA. Judy Brennan

THE COBBS ANTIQUES
83 Grove St, 03458
(603)924-6361   **21 34 41**

Quality primitive, country, formal & painted furniture, paintings, rugs, fabrics, folk art, porcelains, glass & silver. *Serv:* Appraisal. *Hours:* Mon-Sat 9:30-5. *Assoc:* NHADA. Charles M Cobb *Loc:* 1 block N of Int of Rtes 202 & 101.

OLD TOWN FARM ANTIQUES
121B Old Town Farm Rd, 03458
(603)924-3523   **21 27 59**

Period & country furniture, Oriental rugs, decorative accessories, paintings & smalls. *Hours:* Daily 10-5 Sun & Holidays call ahead. *Size:* Large. *Assoc:* NHADA. Robert & Hope Taylor *Loc:* From 101W, S on Rte 202 1 MI R on Old Jaffrey Rd, R on Old Town Farm Rd, big red barn on R.

PETERBOROUGH USED BOOKS & PRINTS
76 Grove St, 03458
(603)924-3534   **13 51 66**

Rare & unusual books & prints, as well as maps, manuscripts & ephemera. *Pr:* $1–500. *Est:* 1987. *Serv:* Appraisal, consultation, purchase estates, search service. *Hours:* Mon-Sat 9:30-4:30. *Size:* Medium. *Assoc:* GSAAA. *Park:* In front or rear. *Loc:* From Int of Rtes 101 & 202, W on Grove St.

PETERBOROUGH ANTIQUES
76 Grove St, 03458
(603)924-7297 **{GR20}**
Offering a large & varied selection of 18th, 19th & 20th C furniture, art & accessories. *Pr:* $5–10000. *Est:* 1988. *Serv:* Appraisal, auction, purchase estates. *Hours:* Mon-Sat 10-5, Apr 15-Dec 24 also Sun 12-4. *Size:* Medium. *CC:* MC/V. *Assoc:* NHADA. Bruce D Cobb *Park:* On site. *Loc:* Just off Rte 101 headed N of Peterborough; follow state hwy signs.

PLAINFIELD

PLAINFIELD AUCTION GALLERY
Plainfield, 03781
(603)675-2549 **4 8**
Auctioneer specializing in fine antiques. *Serv:* Auction, appraisal, purchase single items or complete estates. *Hours:* Call for appt or schedule. William A Smith *Loc:* I-89 Exit 20: S on Rte 12-A from West Lebanon Plaza 7 MI..

PLYMOUTH

PAULINE CHARON ANTIQUES
Texas Hill Rd, 03264
(603)968-7975 **27 65**
Country furniture & primitives. *Hours:* All year by chance. *Assoc:* NHADA. *Loc:* I-93 Exit 24: N on Rte 3, after bridge turn L & look for signs (distance of 3 1/2 MI).

SUSAN B LARSEN ANTIQUES
Texas Hill Rd, 03264
(603)968-7510 **20 23 47**
Jewelry, daguerreotypes & clocks.

Hours: By chance/appt. *Assoc:* NHADA. *Loc:* Next house on R after Pauline Charon.

PORTSMOUTH

BOOK GUILD OF PORTSMOUTH
58 State St, 03801
(603)436-1758 **13**
Antiquarian books: general stock, maritime history, New England, travel & exploration, children's & illustrated. *Serv:* Catalogs, search service. *Hours:* Mon-Sat 9:30-5:30, Sun 12-5. *Size:* 35,000 books. *Assoc:* NHABA. Doug Robertson

MARGARET SCOTT CARTER INC
175 Market St, 03801
(603)436-1781 **16 27 57**
Needlework, furniture & country accessories, old woodworking tools, & folk art in a pleasant little shop near the harbor. *Hours:* Daily 10-5 CLOSED SUN. *Assoc:* NHADA. *Park:* Nearby. *Loc:* I-95 Exit 7: 2 min E.

COBBLESTONES OF MARKET SQUARE
10 Market St, 03801
(603)436-4468 **29 37 39**
English & American antiques, collectibles & accessories with an emphasis on prints. *Hours:* Memorial Day Weekend-Dec daily, Fri til 9, Win: CLOSED SUN. *CC:* MC/V. *Loc:* Up the road from the Sheraton Hotel.

THE DOLL CONNECTION
117 Market St, 03801
(603)431-5030 **32**
Dolls ranging from 1820-1950, doll accessories - including clothes, doll house furniture. *Est:* 1973. *Serv:* Doll restora-

tion service, appraisal, consultation. *Hours:* Mon-Sat 10-4. Helen Jarvis *Loc:* I-95N Exit 7: 3/4 MI.

GARAKUTA COLLECTION
65 Bow St, 03801
(603)433-1233   **60**

Japanese woodblocks, Tansu & Mingei, Asian arts, textiles & antiques, & folk art. *Est:* 1986. *Serv:* Consultation. *Hours:* Jun-Sep 6 Tue-Sat 11-6 Sun 11-5. Sylvia & Phil Chaplain *Park:* Nearby. *Loc:* On the waterfront.

LA BOMBA
102 State, 03801
(603)433-0818

Specializing in art moderne & fiestaware, cocktail shakers & other collectibles of the 1940s & 1950s. *Hours:* By chance/appt. Julie Vanasse *Park:* Nearby. *Loc:* Across from the Strawbery Banke Guild.

W MORIN FURNITURE RESTORATION
181 Hill St, 03801
(603)431-7418   **26 68 71**

Careful restoration of antique furniture paying particular attention to original construction details with an eye to making as few alterations as possible. *Serv:* Conservation, consultation, repairs, custom finishes. *Hours:* Mon-Fri 10:30-5 Appt suggested. *Assoc:* NEAA. Will Morin *Park:* On site. *Loc:* I-95 Exit 3: Rte 101, R at SS, 1/4 MI, L on to Islington, L on to bridge, 2nd L on to Hill, end of St on R.

PARTRIDGE REPLICATIONS
63 Penhallow St, 03801
(603)431-8733   **46 69 80**

18th C handcrafted replicas, documented fabrics & decorative accessories. *Est:* 1978. *Serv:* Interior design. *Hours:* Mon-Sat 10-4:30. *CC:* MC/V. Ted Partridge *Loc:* 1 block N of Market Square.

PORTSMOUTH BOOKSHOP
110 State St, 03801
(603)433-4406   **13**

Specializing in fine arts, children's illustrated, travel, literature & antiquarian. *Hours:* Tue-Sun 10-6, expanded hours in Summer. *Size:* 12,000 volumes. *Assoc:* NHABA. Brian DiMambro

THE TRUNK SHOP
23 Ceres St, 03801
(603)431-4399   **36 68 71**

On Portsmouth harbor, a long established dealer in fine old trunks. *Est:* 1978. *Serv:* Finishing & restoring of old trunks. *Hours:* Year round Mon-Thu 11-6 Fri-Sat 11-9 Sun 12-6, CLOSED TUE. *CC:* MC/V. David Edelstein *Park:* Nearby. *Loc:* 1/2 block off Bow St.

TRUNKWORKS
68 State St, 03801
(603)431-3310   **13 40 81**

Specializing in trunks, rare books, jewelry, golden oak furniture & musical instruments. *Serv:* Restoration, refinishing, appraisal. *Hours:* Mon-Sat 11-5 Sun 12-5. *Assoc:* NEAA. Cesar A Chanlatte

THE VICTORY ANTIQUES
96 State Street, 03801
(603)431-3046   **37 42 81**

Specializing in European & American country pine & formal furnishings, old woodworking tools, collectible clothing & jewelry. *Pr:* $10–2500. *Est:* 1988. *Serv:* Appraisal, purchase estates. *Hours:* Mon-Sat 10-5, Sun 12-5. Cesar A Chanlatte *Park:* In front. *Loc:* Across from the Strawbery Banke Guild.

ED WEISSMAN
110 Chapel St, 03801
(603)431-7575   **16 36**
Pre-1840 American furniture, American,
European & Oriental 15th-early 19th C
accessories, concentrating on metalware,
located in a charming 19th C ship
captain's home. *Est:* 1956. *Serv:* Appraisal, consultation, purchase estates.
Hours: Jun-Nov BY APPT. *Assoc:* ISA
NHADA. *Loc:* In town.

WISTERIA TREE
18 Ladd St, 03801
(603)431-8920   **47**
Antique & estate jewelry. *Est:* 1978.
Hours: Jan-Apr Wed-Sat 10-5, May-Dec
Mon-Sat 10-5, or eves by appt. *CC:*
MC/V. Oreen Audette *Park:* Nearby.
Loc: Across from In Town parking
garage - elevator side.

RAYMOND

BURT DIAL COMPANY
Rte 107 N, 03077
(603)895-2879   **23 31 71**
Hand painted clock dials & glass tablets
restored & refinished. Silver & silver/gilt
dial refinishing also a specialty. *Est:*
1923. *Hours:* Mon-Fri 9-5, weekends
call for appt.

RICHMOND

RANDALLANE ANTIQUES
240 Bullock Rd, 03470
(603)239-4818   **32 65**
Located in Richmond's oldest home
(1763), carefully selected antiques
specializing in country primitives &
early toys. *Pr:* $10–2000. *Est:* 1982.

Serv: Appraisal, brochure, consultation,
interior design, purchase estates. *Hours:*
Wed-Sat 10-4 by chance/appt. *Park:* On
site. *Loc:* Rte 32 to Bullock Rd.

SPINNING WHEEL ANTIQUES
135 Old Homestead Hwy Rte 32, 03470
(603)239-6208   **27**
Specializing in country furniture & accessories. *Hours:* All year by
chance/appt. *Assoc:* NHADA. Ron &
Ronna Frazier *Loc:* 7/10 MI from Int of
Rtes 32 & 119.

THE YANKEE SMUGGLER
122 Fitzwilliam Rd Rte 119, 03470
(603)239-4188   **1 27 37**
Specializing in American country &
painted furniture & unusual quality accessories. *Serv:* Antiques purchased.
Hours: Daily by chance or appt. *Assoc:*
VADA NEAA. Ted & Carole Hayward
Loc: On Rte 119 12 MI S of Keene or 7
MI W of Fitzwilliam & 1/4 MI E of Rte
32.

RINDGE

SCOTT BASSOFF/SANDY JACOBS
Box 1558 Robbins Rd, 03461
(603)899-3373   **37**
Early American furniture & accessories.
Hours: Appt advisable. *Assoc:* NHADA.
Loc: Rte 202 to Thomas Rd, 3 MI,
brown cape with red picket fence.

ROCHESTER

PETER CARSWELL ANTIQUES
293 Pond Hill Rd, 03867
(603)332-4264   **1 36 65**
Wide selection from New England

homes with emphasis on country & formal furniture & accessories in as-found condition. *Pr:* $25–10000. *Serv:* Appraisal, auction, purchase estates. *Hours:* Daily by chance/appt. *Size:* Medium. *Assoc:* NHADA. *Park:* On site. *Loc:* W of Rochester approx 3 MI watch for sign on Rte 202.

RUMNEY

JOHN F HENDSEY -BOOKSELLER
Quincy Rd, 03266
(603)786-2213   **13**

Fine & rare books in all fields, New Hampshire's oldest rare book auction firm. *Serv:* Appraisal. *Hours:* BY APPT ONLY. *Size:* 5,000 books. *Assoc:* ABAA NHABA.

VILLAGE BOOKS
Main St, 03266
(603)786-9300   **13 33**

Antiquarian books: general New England Americana, White Mountains, hunting, fishing & ephemera. *Hours:* BY APPT ONLY. *Size:* 1,500 books. *Assoc:* NHABA. Ann Kent

SALISBURY HEIGHTS

BARKER'S OF SALISBURY HEIGHTS
Rte 4, 03268
(603)648-2488   **36 44 81**

Furniture, tools & glass. *Hours:* Daily 9-5. *Loc:* Opposite the library.

SANBORNVILLE

ARTHUR'S ANTIQUES
RR1 Box 140, 03872
(603)522-9715   **7 27 76**

A wide range of items from early & country to Arts & Crafts to Art Deco. Ephemera, linens & occasional Shaker items. *Pr:* $25–1000. *Est:* 1959. *Serv:* purchase estates. *Hours:* 9-5 daily & by appt, CLOSED TUE. *Size:* Medium. *CC:* MC/V. *Assoc:* NHADA. Arthur I Mooers *Park:* On site. *Loc:* From Rochester NH, N on Rte 16 to Sanbornville traffic light, L on Rte 109, 4th bldg on R.

SANDWICH

ANTIQUES & AUCTIONS LTD
Rtes 113 & 113A, 03227
(603)284-6600   **65 67**

Primitives, quilts, tin, furniture, china, glass & baskets. *Hours:* Mid Jun-Mid Oct daily 10-5 CLOSED WED,SUN. *Assoc:* NHADA. Harold & Renee Bonnyman *Loc:* 4 MI from Ctr Sandwich.

ANTIQUES & COLLECTIBLES
Sandwich, 03227
(603)284-6474   **27 32**

Selected general line featuring country, toys, advertising & unusual accessories. *Hours:* May-Oct most days 11-7 or by chance/appt. *Assoc:* NHADA. Jeanne Smith

THE CENTER ANTIQUES
Sandwich, 03227
(603)284-6828

General stock of antiques & collectibles.

Hours: May-Jun Thu-Sat 10-5, July-Oct 15 Mon-Sat 10-5, else by appt. *Assoc:* NHADA.

SEABROOK

STONE HOUSE ANTIQUES
855 Lafayette Rd Rte 1, 03874
(603)474-3668   **21 37 59**
Early New England furniture, paintings, hooked rugs & accessories. *Hours:* All year daily 10-4 CLOSED MON. *Assoc:* NHADA. Edwin Page *Loc:* I-95 Exit 1: 1 MI N on Rte 1.

SHELBURNE

CROW MOUNTAIN FARM ANTIQUES
Star Route North Rd, 03581
(603)466-2509   **36 66 81**
Two rooms of carefully selected items from New England, including furniture, tools, prints, paintings, tinware, stoneware & accessories. *Pr:* $50–25000. *Est:* 1972. *Serv:* Appraisal, conservation, consultation, purchase estates, restoration. *Hours:* May-Oct daily 9-5, Nov-Apr please call ahead. *Size:* Medium. *Assoc:* NHADA. Ben Werner *Park:* On site. *Loc:* 1 MI E of Philbrook Farm Inn - North Rd, Shelburne 2 1/2 MI off Rte 2.

SNOWVILLE

SLEIGH MILL ANTIQUES
Snow Rd, 03832
(603)447-6791   **28 50 83**
A mill full of antiques, accessories & authentic 19th C lighting. *Est:* 1982. *Serv:* Shipping. *Hours:* By chance/appt. Edith Dashnau *Park:* On site. *Loc:* 6 MI S of Conway NH off Rte 153.

SOUTH HAMPTON

R G BETTCHER RESTORATIONS
Rte 107A, 03827
(603)394-7546   **5 16 74**
Quality 18th C architectural materials, early braced frame buildings & early ironware for restoration. *Hours:* By chance/appt. *Assoc:* NHADA. Bob Bettcher

SPRINGFIELD

THE COLONEL'S SWORD
Four Corners Rd, 03284
(603)763-2112   **39 44 63**
English & American furniture, glass, china, paintings, Oriental export porcelain & military items. *Hours:* May-Jun Sep-Oct weekends, Jul-Aug Sat-Thu 10-5, else by appt. *Assoc:* NHADA. Caye & Dick Currier

LAZY FOX ANTIQUES ET GALLERIE
Springfield, 03284
(603)763-2122   **36 63 32**
English, European, American furniture,

porcelains, attic treasures, dolls & child-related items. *Hours:* Jun-Oct 10-5 or BY APPT. *Assoc:* NHADA. Jacki Beam

SPRING HILL FARM ANTIQUES
Four Corners Rd, 03284
(603)763-2292   **44 63 77**

China, glass, silver, country things, linens & prints. *Hours:* May-Oct daily 10-4. *Assoc:* NHADA. Robert Moore Daniel Daly *Loc:* I-89 Exit 12A.

STRATHAM

COMPASS ROSE ANTIQUES
17 Winnicut Rd, 03885
(603)778-0163   **1 6 32**

Diverse selection of general antiques, with accent on country smalls & fine furniture. *Pr:* $10–5000. *Est:* 1981. *Serv:* Appraisal, consultation, purchase estates. *Hours:* Apr-Dec daily 10-4 Sun 12-4, CLOSED THU. *Size:* Medium. *Assoc:* GSAAA NHADA. Laurie Clark *Park:* In front. *Loc:* From Portsmouth: Rte 101W toward Exeter to ctr of Stratham, L on Winnicut Rd, 1 block from Rte 101.

THE COURTYARD EMPORIUM
Portsmouth Ave, 03885
(603)772-6835   **{GR}**

Furniture, glass, prints, linens, dolls, trunks, rugs, baskets, lamps & books. *Hours:* Apr-Dec 25 Mon-Fri 11:30-5 Sat 10-5 Sun 12-5. *Assoc:* NHADA. *Loc:* Next to Little Italy Restaurant.

OLDE TANNERY ANTIQUES
249 Portsmouth Ave Rte 101, 03885
(603)772-4997   **2 37 50**

Early 18th & 19th C American furniture, lighting, iron hearth equipment & acces-

sories. *Hours:* Daily 10-5 by chance/appt. *Assoc:* NHADA. *Loc:* On Rte 101.

JOHN PIPER HOUSE
Sandy Point Rd, 03885
(603)778-1347   **1 27 65**

Early American, country furniture & accessories pre-1860 in an 18th C barn. *Pr:* $25–8000. *Est:* 1980. *Hours:* By chance/appt. *Size:* Medium. *Assoc:* NHADA. Barbara/Graeme Mann *Park:* On site. *Loc:* I-95 to Rte 101W to Stratham approx 5 1/2 MI, R onto Sandy Point Rd, opposite Stratham Hill Park.

SUGAR HILL

ELEANOR LYNN/ELIZABETH MONAHAN
Rte 117, 03585
(603)823-5550   **37**

Fine American period furniture & decorative accessories. *Hours:* BY APPT ONLY. *Shows:* ELLIS. *Park:* On site. *Loc:* W of Franconia on Rte 117, near the museum.

SUNAPEE

FRANK & BARBARA POLLACK
Box 344, 03782
(603)763-2403   **1 34 37**

American primitive paintings, furniture, folk art, toleware, textiles, decorative arts of the 20th C, jewelry (Bakelite & silver), Arts & Crafts furniture. *Hours:* Jun-Aug 15 BY APPT. *Assoc:* ADA NHADA. *Loc:* Call for directions.

TAMWORTH

SANDERS & MOCK ASSOCIATES
Box 37, 03886
(603)323-8749   **8**
Auctioneers specializing in fine antiques, Americana & fine arts collections. Large, modern gallery with offices in New London & Tamworth, NH & Portland, ME. *Est:* 1972. *Serv:* Appraisal, auction, brochure, catalog, consultation, purchase estates. *Hours:* Mon-Fri 8:30-4:30 Sat,Sun BY APPT. *Assoc:* CAI. Wayne Mock, CAI

TROY

RED SHED
Central Sq, 03465
(603)242-6473   **40 42 81**
Pine & oak furniture, clocks, iron & brass beds, cast iron stoves, tools & collectibles. *Hours:* Daily 10-5 CLOSED SUN,MON. *Loc:* On Rte 12.

SMITH HOUSE ANTIQUES
60 N Main St, 03465
(603)242-3046   **27 80**
Specializing in textiles, country furniture & accessories. *Hours:* Year round by

chance/appt. *Assoc:* NHADA. Jerry Smith *Loc:* On Rte 12 across from the Citgo station.

TUFTONBORO

DOW'S CORNER SHOP
Rte 171 & Ledge Hill Rd, 03864
(603)539-4790   **7**
An old-fashioned shop in a well-stocked, large barn, specializing in Art Deco. *Est:* 1948. *Hours:* May 15-Oct 15 daily 10-5 CLOSED TUE, else by chance/appt. *Size:* Large. *Assoc:* NHADA. *Loc:* Rte 171 between Rtes 16 & 25.

THE EWINGS
Federal Corner Rd, 03816
(603)569-3861   **37 34**
18th & early 19th C American furniture & appropriate accessories, art & folk art of all periods. *Hours:* Seasonally BY APPT. *Assoc:* NHADA.

LOG CABIN ANTIQUES
Rte 109A & Ledge Hill Rd, 03816
(603)569-1909   **1 48 64**
Small shop off the beaten path with a general line of antiques & collectibles including linens & postcards. *Pr:* $5–250. *Est:* 1968. *Serv:* Purchase estates. *Hours:* Memorial Day-Labor Day Fri-

Farquhar Antiques
Prospect Hill Road
Walpole, NH 03608
603/756-4871

Yellow Grain
Painted Drysink

Sun 9-5. *Size:* Medium. *Assoc:* NHADA. Betty & Harold Holmquist *Park:* On site. *Loc:* From Wolfeboro, Rte 109A, 6 MI to Int of 109A & Ledge Hill Rd, on corner opposite Ctr Tuftonboro School.

UNION

CARSWELL'S ANTIQUES
Rte 153, 03887
(603)473-2304   **23 27 47**

Country furniture, primitives, yellow ware, clocks & folk art. *Hours:* All year by chance/appt. *Assoc:* NHADA. Kippy & Diana Carswell

WALPOLE

FARQUHAR ANTIQUES
Prospect Hill Rd, 03608
(603)756-4871   **28 36 44**

Period, Empire, Victorian & country furniture, art glass, decorated stoneware, coverlets, quilts & accessories. *Serv:* Purchase estates. *Hours:* Daily 9-5 by chance/appt. *Assoc:* NHADA VADA. Ramon & Mary E Farquhar *Park:* On site. *Loc:* Prospect Hill Rd is off S Main St.

GOLDEN PAST OF WALPOLE
Rte 12, 03608
(603)756-3974   **23 37 59**

Fine collection of oil paintings, stained glass windows, American & Victorian furniture, Oriental rugs, china, quilts & clocks. *Hours:* Apr 15-Dec 15 daily. *Assoc:* NHADA. Woody & Judy Boynton *Park:* On site.

WARNER

LINDA L DONOVAN
Melvin Mills Rd, 03278
(603)456-3718   **71**

Conservation & restoration of oil paintings. *Hours:* BY APPT. *Assoc:* AIC. *Loc:* I-89N Exit 9: W on Rte 103 for 4 1/2 MI to Melvin Mills Rd.

OLD PAPER WORLD
Rte 103, 03278
(603)456-3338   **13 33 9**

Rare books & ephemera, large stock of paper collectibles including manuscripts, photographs, maps, rare prints, newspapers, post cards, postal, automotive, science. *Est:* 1980. *Serv:* Appraisal, paper conservation, purchase estates, restoration. *Hours:* Daily 10-4 or by chance/appt. *Assoc:* NHABA ESA. Christopher Stotler *Park:* On site. *Loc:* I-89 Exit 9: 1 1/2 MI W, (20 MI W of Concord, NH), on Rte 103.

WASHINGTON

HALF-MOON ANTIQUES
Half-Moon Pond Rd, 03280
(603)495-3663   **29 36**

Furniture & accessories. *Hours:* Year round. *CC:* AX. *Assoc:* NHADA.

TINTAGEL ANTIQUES
Rte 31, 03280
(603)495-3429   **27 63 81**

Country furniture & accessories, tools, frames, quilts & hooked rugs. *Serv:* Pewter repair. *Hours:* Tue-Sat 10-5 by chance or appt. *Assoc:* NHADA. Sally Krone *Loc:* 1 MI N of village on Rte 31.

WEARE

NEW HAMPSHIRE BOOK AUCTIONS
92 Woodbury Rd, 03281
(603)529-1700   **8 13**
Auctions of books, prints, maps & ephemera held May to November. Experienced cataloguers in rare Americana, early printed books, plate books & modern first editions. *Est:* 1985. *Serv:* Catalog ($15 sub), accept consignments, appraisal, purchase estates. *Hours:* May-Nov BY APPT on non-auction days. *Size:* Medium. *Assoc:* NHABA. Richard & Mary Sykes *Park:* On site. *Loc:* 12 MI W of Concord, Rte 13 to Rte 77, 20 MI W of Manchester, Rte 114 to 77 at corner of Rte 77 & Woodbury Rd.

SYKES & FLANDERS ANTIQUARIAN BKS
92 Woodbury Rd PO Box 86, 03281
(603)529-7432   **13 51 66**
A collector's stock of general fine & rare books, maps & prints with emphasis on 19th & 20th C first editions, Americana, White Mountains, modern first editions including detective fiction, New Hampshire, illustrated books, travel & exploration. *Pr:* $25–5000. *Est:* 1975. *Serv:* Appraisal, free catalog, purchase estates. *Hours:* Apr-Dec BY APPT. *Size:* Medium. *Assoc:* ABAA NHABA NHADA. Richard & Mary Sykes *Park:* On site. *Loc:* 12 MI W of Concord via Rte 13 to Rte 77, 20 MI W of Manchester via Rte 114 to Rte 77, at Jct of Woodbury Rd & Rte 77.

FRED P WHITTIER III
Greenleaf Farm, 03281
(603)529-2936   **8**
Auctions of antique furniture & furnish-ings from area estates. No buyer's premium or reserves. *Serv:* Auctioneer. Jeffrey Wigsten

WENTWORTH

THE RE-STORE ANTIQUES
Rtes 25 & 25A, 03282
(603)764-9395   **71**
Restored turn-of-the-century furniture, specializing in rolltop desks. *Hours:* Daily 10-5.

RETOUCH THE PAST
Rte 25, 03282
(603)764-5851   **1 22 71**
Refinished trunks & lamps with assorted smalls. *Serv:* Repairs, restoration. *Hours:* By chance/appt. Robert Stover *Park:* In front. *Loc:* I-93 Exit 26: Rte 25 to Wentworth (15 MI), across from Town Common on Rte 25.

WEST LEBANON

COLONIAL PLAZA ANTIQUES
Rte 12A, 03784
(603)298-7712   **{FLEA}**
Giant flea market with antiques, collectibles, estate jewelry, furniture, old books, old clothes, dolls, old tools, post cards, stamps, paintings, bottles & more. *Est:* 1976. *Serv:* Catered, restrooms, space rentals start at $13.50. *Hours:* Daily 9-5 Sun outside May-Oct. *Size:* 90 spaces. Norman Patch *Park:* Free parking. *Loc:* I-89 Exit 20.

PARTRIDGE REPLICATIONS
The Power House Rte 12A, 03784
(603)298-6066   **46 69 80**
18th C handcrafted replicas, docu-

mented fabric & decorative accessories. *Est:* 1978. *Serv:* Interior design. *Hours:* Mon-Sat 10-4:30. *CC:* MC/V. Ted Partridge

WINDHAM ANTIQUES
PO Box 401, 03784
(802)295-6997   **36 63 76**
Fine 18th & 19th C furniture & accessories, including fireplace accessories, early soft paste & porcelain, early flint glass, exceptional woodenware, including items in good old paint, Shaker items, early brass & iron, anything unusual or of merit. *Pr:* $20–4000. *Serv:* Appraisal, consultation. *Hours:* BY APPT. *Assoc:* GSAAA. Andrew Katz *Loc:* Please call for directions.

WEST NOTTINGHAM

MERRY HILL FARM
Rte 4 & Merry Hill Rd, 03291
(603)942-5370   **{GR}**
Specializing in country furniture, folk art, oak & Victorian furniture & decorative accessories. *Hours:* Daily 10-5, Sun 12-5. *Loc:* W of the Lee Traffic circle.

WEST SWANZEY

MRS HORTON'S YARD SALE SHOPPE
Rte 10 S, 03469
(603)352-0331   **32 44 48**
General line including furniture, dolls, linen, jewelry, Art Deco & glassware. *Hours:* Mon-Fri 9-6, Sat-Sun 9-5. *CC:* AX/MC/V. Al Horton *Park:* On site. *Loc:* 6 MI S of Keene, NH on Rte 10.

KNOTTY PINE ANTIQUE MARKET
Rte 10, 03469
(603)352-5252   **{GR300}**
Antiques & collectibles featuring glass, silver, jewelry, iron, pottery, furniture, primitives, rugs, quilts, art glass, china, pewter, dishes, toys, advertising. *Serv:* Air conditioned, coffee shop, non dealer admission $2. *Hours:* Year round daily 9-5 except Thanksgiving, X-Mas, New Year's. Joan E Pappas *Park:* On site. *Loc:* 5 MI S of Keene.

FREDERICK MAC PHAIL ANTIQUES
Rte 10, 03469
(603)352-4062   **24 40 83**
Large selection of antiques featuring oak & Victorian furniture, collectibles, coins & toys. *Est:* 1982. *Serv:* Auctions, appraisal. *Hours:* Sat,Sun 10-5 or BY APPT, weekdays by chance/appt. *Assoc:* ANA NHAA NHNA. *Park:* On site. *Loc:* From Keene: 4 MI S of Ramada Inn. From S: just past Swanzey Historical Museum.

WESTMORELAND

THE ANTIQUES SHOPS
Rte 12, 03467
(603)399-7039   **{GR40}**
Decorative accessories, glass, pottery & porcelain, linens & metalware & postcards. *Est:* 1987. *Hours:* Daily 10-5. *Size:* Large. *CC:* MC/V. *Assoc:* NHADA. Larry Muchmore *Park:* On site. *Loc:* Rte 12N, 7 MI N of Keene.

HURLEY BOOKS & CELTIC CROSS BOOK
Rte 12, 03467
(603)399-4342   **13**
Specializing in Protestant religion, farm-

ing & horticulture, miniature books, printing & early imprints. *Pr:* $1–1000. *Est:* 1966. *Serv:* Catalog $1. *Hours:* By chance/appt. *Size:* 35,000 books. *Assoc:* NHABA. Henry Hurley *Park:* In front. *Loc:* Rte 12, 10 MI W of Keene.

WHITEFIELD

THE FAIRWEATHER SHOP
65 Jefferson Rd Rte 116, 03598
(603)837-9806   **44 63**

Specializing in glass & china with an emphasis on quality. *Serv:* Appraisal, consultation, purchase estates. *Hours:* Jun-Nov Mon-Sat 10:30-5, Sun 1:30-4:30. *Assoc:* NHADA. *Loc:* 1/2 MI from blinking light in Whitefield.

WILMOT FLAT

PLEASANT ACRES ANTIQUES ETC
Campground Rd, 03287
(603)526-4662   **27**

Country accessories. *Hours:* By chance/appt. *Loc:* Off Rte 11.

YE OLDE SHAVEHORSE
WORKSHOP
Kearsarge Valley Rd, 03287
(603)927-4900   **{GR11}**

A variety of antiques & collectibles located on one floor in a gambrel building, with an adjoining restoration shop. *Est:* 1986. *Serv:* Custom woodwork, repairs, restoration. *Hours:* Daily 9-5. *Size:* Medium. *CC:* MC/V. *Assoc:* GSAAA. Dick H Bacon *Park:* In front. *Loc:* I-89 Exit 11: 5 MI E on Rte 11, 1 MI from Rte 11 on R.

WILTON

NOAH'S ARK ANTIQUES CENTER
Rte 101, 03086
(603)654-2595   **{GR150}**

An interesting assortment of furniture & decorative accessories. *Est:* 1984. *Hours:* Daily 10-5 Sun 9-5. *Assoc:* GSAAA. Audrey Dolloff, Mgr *Park:* On site.

WINCHESTER

FAT CHANCE ANTIQUES
102 N Main St, 03470
(603)239-6423   **24 64 79**

Post cards, maps, prints, sheet music, wicker, coins & stamps. *Hours:* Sat, Sun, Mon 11-4 CLOSED WIN. Robert Evans *Loc:* 1/2 MI N of town on Rte 10.

GOOD OLD DAYS ANTIQUES
50 Main St, 03470
(603)239-8818   **{GR40}**

Featuring a fine selection of antique & collectable reference books, also glass & hunting & fishing memorabilia. *Est:* 1987. *Serv:* Appraisal & purchase estates. *Hours:* Year round daily 9-5. *CC:* AX/MC/V. Kenneth P Lovell *Park:* In front, nearby lot. *Loc:* Jct of Rtes 10 & 119 at the lights.

THE HALOWEEN QUEEN
4 Lawrence St & Rte 10, 03470
(603)239-8875   **32 64 66**

350,000 old post cards, posters, music, prints, paintings, toys, tin & porcelain signs, advertising, glass, china & books. *Serv:* Buy, sell, trade. Appraisals & investment consultations. *Hours:* By chance/appt. Chris Russell *Park:* Nearby. *Loc:* On Rte 10 North of Rte 119.

RICHARD WHITE ANTIQUES
98 N Main St, 03470
(603)239-4445　　　**1 21 23**

Fine 18th & early 19th C furniture & accessories including clocks & Oriental rugs. *Pr:* $100–10000. *Serv:* Appraisal, purchase estates. *Hours:* By chance/appt. *Size:* Medium. *Park:* On site. *Loc:* Rte 10.

WOLFEBORO

AUCTIONS BY BOWERS & MERENA INC
Box 1224, 03894
(603)569-5095　　　**8 24**

Specializing in numismatic auctions of collections having a minimum value of $2,000. *Est:* 1953. *Serv:* Appraisals, catalog. *Hours:* Call for appt or schedule. Q. David Bowers

RICHARD G MARDEN
Elm St, 03894
(603)569-3209　　　**34 44 63**

Staffordshire historical china, spatterware, gaudy Dutch, Leeds & other early china for the American market, small folk art items & early American glass. *Pr:* $10–10000. *Serv:* Appraisal, auction, free catalog, consultation, purchase estates. *Hours:* By chance/appt. *Park:* On site. *Loc:* 100 MI N of Boston.

MONIQUE'S ANTIQUES
4 Brummitt Ct, 03894
(603)569-4642　　　**44 77 85**

Glass, china, silver, jewelry, furniture & vintage clothing. *Hours:* By chance/appt. *Assoc:* NHADA. Jean Raditzky

NEW ENGLAND GALLERY
RR 2 Box 959, 03894
(603)569-3501　　　**14 59**

18th-early 20th C American, European & Old Master paintings, watercolors & prints. *Pr:* $200–100000. *Serv:* Purchase, consignment, appraisal, consultation, conservation, catalog on. *Hours:* Jun-Oct 15 BY APPT. Arthur Fraumeni

RALPH K REED ANTIQUES
Pleasant Valley Rd, 03894
(603)569-1897　　　**10 39 56**

Furniture - mainly English campaign chests, boxes & sea chests in camphorwood, teak, mahogany & pine. Old mercury barometers a specialty. *Pr:* $50–5000. *Est:* 1965. *Hours:* All year by chance/appt. *Assoc:* NHADA. *Park:* On site. *Loc:* 3 MI off Rte 28 on Pleasant Valley Rd, 2 MI S of Wolfeboro.

TOUCHMARK ANTIQUES
S Main St Rte 28, 03894
(603)569-1386　　　**27 42 65**

Country barn on Rust Pond specializing in country primitives, pine furniture & decorative items. *Pr:* $25–1000. *Est:* 1974. *Serv:* Appraisal, purchase estates, restoration. *Hours:* May-Oct daily 10-5 BY APPT ONLY. *Size:* Medium. *CC:* MC/V. *Assoc:* NHADA. Anne Roome & Helen Bradley *Park:* On site. *Loc:* From downtown Wolfeboro, 2 1/2 MI S on Rte 28 on L.

SLOAN'S GREEN GUIDE TO ANTIQUING IN
NEW ENGLAND

Rhode Island

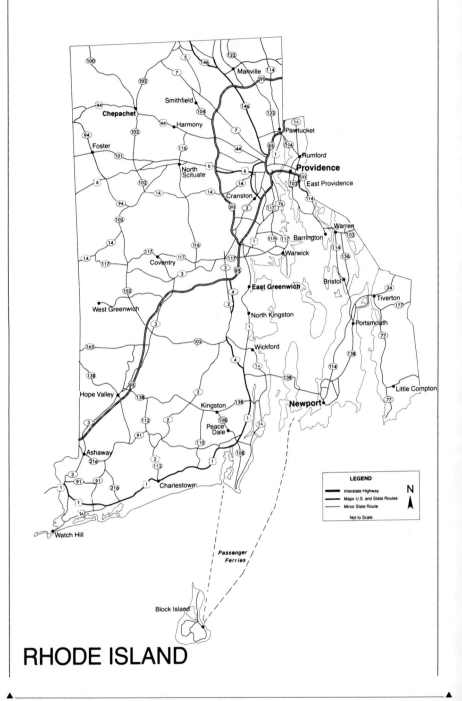

RHODE ISLAND

ASHAWAY

ASHAWAY ANTIQUES STORE
20 High St Rte 216, 02804
(401)377-8116   **16 37 67**
1850 country store with early American
furniture in old finish & paint, quilts,
coverlets, hooked rugs, needlework,
Staffordshire, coin silver, brass, copper,
tin, iron, paintings, folk art, kitchenware
& wood. *Pr:* $1–2500. *Est:* 1978. *Serv:*
Appraisal, consultation, interior design.
Hours: By chance/appt. *Size:* Medium.
Assoc: SNEADA. Sally Van Den Bossche
Park: In front. *Loc:* I-95 CT Exit 93: 1
MI E on Rte 216 to ctr of Ashaway Village, on L after crossing river.

BRIGGS HOUSE ANTIQUES
18 High St Rte 216, 02804
(401)377-4464   **44 59 63**
Rhode Island & New England artist
paintings, glass, porcelain, furniture.
Hours: Weekends 10-5 & BY APPT.
Carol Prendergast

STEPHEN P MACK
Chase Hill Farm, 02804
(401)377-8041   **5 71 74**
A selection of fine historic structures -
including houses, barns, farms & period
rooms - ready for reconstruction on the
owner's site. *Hours:* BY APPT. *Park:* On
site. *Loc:* S of I-95 at the CT-RI line.

BARRINGTON

GAIL ASHBURN HADLEY
Barrington, 02806
(401)245-2454   **36 66 47**
Period furniture & accessories, framed
prints, jewelry, smalls, country & formal;
general line fine antiques & collectibles.
Serv: Will purchase single items or estates. *Hours:* BY APPT. *Assoc:*
SNEADA.

CHAIRS OF OLD
5 Evergreen St, 02806
(401)245-8049   **36 48 44**
Chairs, linens & cut glass. *Hours:* BY
APPT. *Assoc:* SNEADA. Al & Joan
Beech

ROBBERT J DOHERTY GALLERY
10 George St, 02806
(401)431-1320   **4 21**
A small collection of antique & vintage
Oriental rugs & weavings. *Serv:* Appraisal, advice, search services. *Hours:*
BY APPT ONLY.

FIRESIDE ANTIQUES &
COLLECTIBLES
8 Knapton St, 02806
(401)245-3137
General line of antiques & collectibles.
Hours: BY APPT. *Assoc:* SNEADA.
Margaret A Wheeler

STOCK EXCHANGE
57 Maple Ave, 02806
(401)245-4170   **36 47 77**
Fine quality used home furnishings-
china, crystal, jewelry, sterling, glassware
& good quality furniture on three floors.
Serv: Consignment. *Hours:* Tue-Sat 10-
4. *Size:* Large. Jan Hess *Park:* On site.
Loc: From I-95, Rte 114S to Barrington,
R at red light at Town Hall, 5 bldgs down
on R.

BRISTOL

ALFRED'S
327-331 Hope St, 02809
(401)253-3465   **29 36 44**
Furniture, glass, china, flow blue, postcards, lamps, shades, silver, general line. *Est:* 1971. *Serv:* Appraisal. *Hours:* Daily 10-5. *CC:* AX/MC/V. *Assoc:* SNEADA. Alfred Brazil *Park:* In front. *Loc:* On Rte 114.

**ROBERT BARROW,
CABINETMAKER**
412 Thames St, 02809
(401)253-4434   **43 71**
Traditional & contemporary handmade Windsor poster beds & tables. *Est:* 1978. *Serv:* Catalog ($3), restoration. *Hours:* Tue-Sat 8-5 BY APPT. *Loc:* I-95E Exit 7: Rte 114S to Bristol, on Thames St along the water.

CENTER CHIMNEY
44 State St, 02809
(401)253-8010   **44 16 65**
Glass, brass, primitives, linens, jewelry, furniture & accessories. *Serv:* Appraisals. *Hours:* Mon-Sat 1-5. *Assoc:* SNEADA. *Shows:* RI. John & Lee White

L & T RESPESS BOOKS
557 Hope St, 02809
(407)254-0225   **13**
Antiquarian books: Americana, especially Southern, English & American literature & sporting. *Serv:* Appraisal, catalog. *Hours:* Appt suggested. *Assoc:* MARIAB. Lin & Tucker Respess

CAROLINA

JAMES E SCUDDER
Rte 112, 02812
(401)364-7228   **36 44 63**
Furniture, glass, china & decorative accessories. *Hours:* By chance/appt. *Loc:* Located on Rte 112.

CHARLESTOWN

ARTIST'S GUILD & GALLERY
5429 Post Rd Rte 1, 02813
(401)322-0506   **59**
Specializing in 19th & 20th C art. *Serv:* Conservation, frame repair & gilding. *Hours:* Thu-Sun 10-5 appt suggested. Ruth Gulliver *Loc:* Across from Ninigret Pond.

BUTTERNUT SHOP
Old Post Rd Rte 1A, 02813
(401)364-6121   **27 65**
Primitives & country accessories. *Hours:* May-Nov daily. Florence S Ide

FOX RUN COUNTRY ANTIQUES
Jct Rtes 1 & 2, 02813
(401)364-3160   **27 44 65**
Country & primitives, furniture, jewelry, glassware, china, Orientalia & lighting devices. *Hours:* Wed-Sun 10-4. Irene Larsen *Loc:* Jct of Rtes 1 & 2, across from the Charlestown Village.

GENERAL STANTON INN
Old Post Rd, 02813
(401)364-8888   **{FLEA}**
Outdoor flea market with antiques, collectibles & flea market merchandise. Free admission. Inn on grounds. Breakfast. *Est:* 1965. *Hours:* Mar 15-Nov Sat

& Sun 7-4. *Size:* 175 spaces. Angelo & Janice Falcone *Park:* Free parking. *Loc:* From CT, I-95N Exit 92, Rte 2 for 3 MI, R on 78, L on Rte 1 for 12 MI N; From Providence, call for directions.

MILL BROOK ANTIQUES
4436 Old Post Road, Cross Mills, 02813
(401)364-8064   **43**
Danish country pine furniture including wardrobes, blanket chests & nightstands. *Est:* 1989. *Hours:* Tue-Sun 10-5. Sally Fazzone *Loc:* In the heart of Charlestown at the Cross Mills Int of Old Post Rd.

SALT BOX ANTIQUES
Rte 1, 02813
(401)322-0598   **1 37 34**
Country furniture & accessories. *Pr:* $15–3500. *Est:* 1985. *Hours:* Seasonal daily 11-5. *Size:* Large. *CC:* MC/V. *Assoc:* SNEADA NEAA. Merle Giuliano *Park:* On site. *Loc:* I-95 Exit 1: S on Rte 216 to Rte 1, turn L go approx 1/4 MI.

CHEPACHET

CHEPACHET ANTIQUE CENTER
Rtes 44 & 102, 02814
(401)568-2455
Quality general line. *Est:* 1986. *Serv:* Appraisal, auction, custom woodwork, interior design, purchase estates. *Hours:* Fri-Sun 10-5. *Size:* Large. *Park:* On site. *Loc:* 150 yards N of Rte 44 on Rte 102 between Purple Cat Restaurant & Chepachet Pharmacy.

CHESTNUT HILL ANTIQUES
One Victory Hwy, 02814
(401)568-4365   **40 64**
Fiesta, azalea, refinished oak furniture, jewelry, post cards & country. *Hours:*

Wed-Sat 10-5, Sun 12-5, CLOSED Dec 15-Mar 15. *Loc:* 1 block N of Chepachet Ctr on Rte 102.

KIMBALL HOUSE 1753
Main St, 02814
(401)568-0416   **27**
Country antiques & smalls offered in natural surroundings. *Est:* 1987. *Serv:* Consignments accepted. *Hours:* Thu-Sat 11-5 Sun 12-5. *Assoc:* SNEADA. Phillip Tetreault *Park:* On street. *Loc:* I-395 Exit 97: Rte 44E or Rte 295 Greenville Exit, Rte 44W.

COVENTRY

CANDLE SNUFFER
28 Maple Root Rd, 02816
(401)397-5565   **50 71**
A complete lamp shop - specialists in restored lighting, oil & electric. Large inventory of lamp parts, over 5000 glass & fabric lampshades. *Pr:* $25–1500. *Est:* 1968. *Serv:* Repairs, restoration. *Hours:* Tue-Sat 9-5. *Size:* Medium. Phyllis Sodergren *Park:* On site. *Loc:* I-95 Exit 6: N for 1 MI, L at 1st light, L again;located in a red bldg with white picket fence.

THE LEAPING STAG ANTIQUES
Coventry, 02816
(401)821-9214   **65 14 1**
General line of fine antiques & collectibles, specializing in primitives, books & Americana. *Hours:* BY APPT. *Assoc:* SNEADA.

PAST PERFECT
Coventry, 02816
(401)821-9592

Buying & selling interesting & unusual old items. *Hours:* BY APPT. *Assoc:* SNEADA. John & Coni Mathieu

REMEMBER WHEN ANTIQUES
14 Old North Rd, 02816
(401)822-4581   **47 32**

Antique jewelry, dolls & fine china. *Hours:* By chance/appt. *Assoc:* SNEADA. Edward Viens & Samuel Orsini

THE SNOOTY FOX
Coventry, 02816
(401)397-4594   **65 48 21**

Country antiques, primitives, restored trunks, linens, prints, hooked rugs & accessories. *Serv:* Buying country antiques & trunks. *Hours:* BY APPT. *Assoc:* SNEADA. Sharon Garceau

---

CRANSTON

BERT'S BROWSE AROUND SHOP
Cranston, 02910
(401)942-7629   **36 50 23**

Furniture, lamps, clocks, Hummel, paintings & postcards. *Serv:* Purchase estates, appraisal. *Hours:* BY APPT. *Assoc:* SNEADA.

DENNIS ANTIQUES
PO Box 10251, 02910
(401)781-5694   **36 7 17**

Fine furnishings & art, bronzes, Deco, fine collectibles & 20th C design. *Serv:* Purchase single items & estates. *Hours:* By chance/appt. *Assoc:* SNEADA. Dennis Devona

GOLD 'N TIQUES
728 Pontiac Ave, 02910
(401)461-8500   **47 23 77**

Antique jewelry, vintage watches, diamonds, sterling, gold & collectibles. *Serv:* Bonded estate appraisals. *Hours:* Mon-Sat 9:30-5. *Assoc:* SNEADA. Anthony & Judy Vieira

JEFFREY HERMAN
Box 3599, 02910
(401)461-3156   **71 77**

Restoration & hand finishing of sterling, coin, pewter, brass & mixed metal holloware, flatware & dresserware. Full line of silver polishing supplies. Fully equipped & insured silversmithing studio with a central alarm system. *Est:* 1984. *Serv:* Catalog, price list, conservation, restoration, repairs. *Hours:* BY APPT ONLY. *Assoc:* SAS.

MEMORY LANE ANTIQUES
Cranston, 02910
(401)781-7222   **47 44 50**

Jewelry, china, glass, lamps, wicker, dolls, furniture & general line. *Serv:* Purchase estates, single items. *Hours:* BY APPT. *Assoc:* SNEADA. Christine Bernard

PAULINE & JOHN SAMBAIN ANTIQUES
221 Beckwith St, 02910
(401)785-1468   **36**

Furniture, unusual accessories & found objects. *Hours:* BY APPT. *Assoc:* SNEADA.

EAST GREENWICH

BOTANICA
37 Main St, 02818
(401)295-2992   **45 66**

Vases, teapots, garden accessories &

botanical prints. *Hours:* Mon-Sat 9:30-5:30. *CC:* AX/MC/V. *Loc:* Across the street from EG Armory.

HARBOUR GALLERIES
253 Main St, 02818
(401)884-6221   **47 71**

Fine antique & estate jewelry & large selection of cameos. *Serv:* Appraisal, consultation, purchase estates, repairs, restoration. *Hours:* Tue-Sat 11-5 Fri 11-8. *CC:* AX/DC/MC/V. *Assoc:* GIA NEAA SNEADA. *Park:* Nearby lot. *Loc:* I-95 E Greenwich Exit (Division St): to Main St (1 MI from I-95).

BARBARA MOSS ANTIQUES
4196 Post Road, 02818
(401)884-7843   **47 60**

Specializing in antique jewelry & Orientals. *Hours:* BY APPT. *Assoc:* SNEADA.

ROSE PETAL COTTAGE
164 Main St, 02818
(401)885-7533   **47**

General line of antique & collectible jewelry. *Hours:* Tue-Sat 11-5. *Assoc:* SNEADA. Linda Dino Pope

SERENDIPITY CORNER
247 Main St, 02818
(401)884-7990   **36 7 44**

Small furniture, collectibles, Deco, china, glass art & jewelry. *Hours:* Mon-Sat 11-4. *Assoc:* SNEADA. Bunny Jackson & Kimberly Smith

WILD GOOSE CHASE
312 Main St, 02818
(401)885-4442   **67 48 36**

Specializing in antique quilts, also linens & furniture. *Hours:* Thu-Sat 11-4 or BY APPT. *Assoc:* SNEADA.

EAST PROVIDENCE

BEATRICE BRABYN ALLEN ANTIQUES
PO Box 4123, 02914
(401)434-9376   **60 59**

Fine Oriental art specializing in Chinese embroidery & seed stitch couching, paintings, primitive wood blocks & fine natural fabrics. *Hours:* BY APPT. *Assoc:* SNEADA.

BEVERLY CHALKO ANTIQUES
337 N Broadway, 02914
(401)434-9376   **42 67**

Pine furniture, woodenware, quilts & country things. *Hours:* Tue-Sat 9:30-5. *Assoc:* SNEADA.

FOSTER

COUNTRY BARN
Rte 6 Pole 153, 02825
(401)647-7116   **27 42**

Country furniture & accessories, painted & refinished, fine oak & walnut all displayed in a 19th C barn. *Hours:* Fri-Sat 10-4, Sun 11-5. *Assoc:* SNEADA. Bill & Donna Dorsey

HOPE VALLEY

C & B HIDDEN TREASURES
41 Highview Ave Box 57, 02832
(401)539-7547

Antiques & collectibles, buying estates small & large. *Hours:* BY APPT. *Assoc:* SNEADA. Chuck Stolze & Bruce Roger

DUKSTA'S ANTIQUES
40 Arcadia Rd, 02832
(401)539-2095   **36**

Twelve rooms full, including a three-room art gallery in a silo; one of the area's largest shops with a lot of furniture & collectibles. *Pr:* $2–5000. *Est:* 1987. *Serv:* Auction, interior design, purchase estates. *Hours:* Year round daily 10-5 or by appt. *Size:* Huge. Charles B Duksta *Park:* On site. *Loc:* I-95 Exit 3B: go thru 1st traffic light, R onto Arcadia Rd, 1/2 MI, 1st farm on R.

HOPKINTON

THE ELEGANT DRAGON
Thurston-Wells House Rte 3, 02833
(401)377-9059   **31 60**

Exotic Orientalia - unusual & unique Far Eastern antique treasures from China, Japan, Korea, Malaysia, Tibet, bronzes, porcelains, root, wood, hardstone & soapstone carvings, baskets, weapons, elegant rosewood display stands & cabinets. *Pr:* $1–10,000. *Hours:* All year by chance/appt. *Size:* Medium. *CC:* MC/V. Norma H Schofield *Park:* On site. *Loc:* I-95 Exit 1 to RI: N at top of ramp (sign for Hopkinton), 3/4 MI on L.

JOHNSTON

CAROUSEL ANTIQUES
2948 Hartford Ave Rte 6, 02919
(401)934-1966   **27 36 44**

Quaint store of quality antiques & collectibles including furniture, glassware, lamps, clocks, telephones & country items. *Serv:* Purchase estates, restoration. *Hours:* Year round Thu-Sun 11-5, Mon-Tue by chance, CLOSED WED. *Park:* In front. *Loc:* Rte 95 to Rte 195W to 295 to Rte 6.

HERITAGE ANTIQUES
1932 Atwood Ave, 02919
(401)231-9393   **27 63 65**

A small but full shop specializing in primitives & quality china, primarily Limoges. *Pr:* $10–1000. *Est:* 1987. *Serv:* Sat-Sun 10-5 By chance or appt. *Assoc:* SNEADA. Gladys Crees *Park:* In Front. *Loc:* 1 1/2 MI NW from Rtes 5 & 6 on Atwood Ave.

LITTLE COMPTON

BLUE FLAG ANTIQUES
601 W Main Rd, 02837
(401)635-8707   **5 37 59**

Paintings, drawings, 19th C furniture, photographs & a broad range of curious & unusual things, from primitives to industrial design. *Pr:* $5–2500. *Est:* 1983. *Serv:* Appraisal on. *Hours:* Jun-Oct 15 daily 1-5; Oct 15-May Sat-Sun 1-5,else by appt. *Size:* Medium. *Assoc:* SNEADA. Sarah Harkness *Park:* On site. *Loc:* Rte 77 2 MI below turn off to Little Compton Ctr & 2 MI above Harbor on R.

THE GALLERY ON THE COMMONS
PO Box 932, 02837
(401)635-8935   **21**

Antique & semi-antique Oriental rugs, country & formal furniture & accessories. *Serv:* Appraisal. *Hours:* Sat,Sun 11-4 or BY APPT. *Assoc:* ASA. Nancy Walker

MIDDLETOWN

LAMP WORKS
510 E Main Rd, 02840
(401)847-0966   **50 68 75**
Restored antique lighting, restoration & repair of all types of lighting, custom lighting. **Pr:** $200–2500. **Serv:** Repairs, restoration. **Hours:** Mon-Sat 10-5 CLOSED SUN. **Size:** Medium. **CC:** AX/DC/MC/V. Allan Leach **Park:** On site. **Loc:** Located in East West crossing - at the Int of E Main Rd & Aquidneck Ave.

NEWPORT

AARDVARK ANTIQUES
475 Thames St, 02840
(401)849-7233   **5 45 50**
Architectural antiques, garden statuary, ornaments, iron fence, gates, stained glass & decorative lighting. **Est:** 1967. **Serv:** Appraisal, conservation, restoration, repairs 1-800-446-1052. **Hours:** Mon-Sat 10-5. **CC:** MC/V. **Assoc:** NADA. Arthur Grover **Park:** On site.

ALL THINGS ORIENTAL OF NEWPORT
8 Franklin St, 02840
(401)841-5267   **50 60 70**
Specializing in antique porcelain lamps with custom silk shades, antique export porcelain, Korean chests, lacquerware, paintings, mirrors & jewelry. **Est:** 1988. **Serv:** Custom silk shades. **Hours:** Daily 10-5 or by appt. **Assoc:** NADA. Joan Potter **Park:** Nearby. **Loc:** Near the corner of Franklin & Thames Sts.

ANCHOR & DOLPHIN BOOKS
30 Franklin St, 02840
(401)846-6890   **13**
Select stock of old & rare books with emphasis on works relating to the history of design, especially books on gardens, landscape architecture, early horticulture & the decorative arts. **Pr:** $5–5000. **Est:** 1979. **Serv:** Appraisal, catalog $1, purchase estates. **Hours:** Year round by chance/appt. **Assoc:** ABAA ILAB MARIAB NADA. Ann Marie Wall **Park:** On street. **Loc:** Downtown Newport between Thames & Spring Sts, 1 block N of Memorial Blvd, near post office in the ctr of Antique District.

ANTIQUES ETC
516-518 Thames St, 02840
(401)849-7330   **1 21 82**
18th & 19th C furniture, nautical, Indian baskets, beadwork, rugs, paintings, jewelry, linens, quilts, silver, china, lamps. **Serv:** Accept quality consignments. **Hours:** Daily 11-5 or by appt. **Assoc:** NADA. Janet Guy **Loc:** Between Dearborn & Holland Sts.

ARMAN'S NEWPORT
P O Box 3239, 02840
(401)683-4044 FAX
(401)683-6000   **4 8 25**
Fine antiques & art in a gallery setting. **Hours:** Call for hours.

BELLEVUE ANTIQUES
121 Bellevue Ave, 02840
(401)846-7898   **41 63 47**
Furniture, decorative accessories, porcelain & painted items. **Hours:** By chance/appt. **Assoc:** NADA.

BLACK SHEEP ANTIQUES
54 Spring St, 02840
(401)846-6810   **44 56 67**
Unusual combination of antiques & collectibles located in the center of

Newport's Historic District. Specializing in nautical antiques with ship models, boats-in-bottles, half-hulls, marine art, quilts, baskets, lace, linen, pottery, prints & more. *Pr:* $25–4000. *Est:* 1987. *Serv:* Restoration of nautical items; custom display cases. *Hours:* May-Dec Tue-Sat 11-5, Sun by chance; Jan-Apr Tue-Sat 11-5. *CC:* AX/MC/V. *Assoc:* NADA. Joyce M Botelho *Park:* In front. *Loc:* Near the Int of Touro & Spring Sts.

ARAKEL H BOZYAN STORE
140 Bellevue Ave, 02840
(401)847-0012   **21 58**

Antiques, Oriental rugs & objets d'art. *Est:* 1880. *Hours:* Afternoons. *Assoc:* NADA. *Park:* Nearby.

C & J ANTIQUES
32 Franklin St, 02840
(401)847-0555   **50 60**

Furnishings, Oriental items, lamps & lighting repair. *Est:* 1990. *Hours:* Daily 11-5. *Assoc:* NADA. Corry Ayling *Park:* Nearby.

C & T ANTIQUE DEALERS
42 Spring St, 02840
(401)461-3130   **50**

General line including antique furniture, lamps & accessories. Nationwide auctioneer & appraiser. *Serv:* Antique lamp restoration. *Hours:* Tue-Sat 12-5 (Except Brimfield weeks). *Assoc:* NADA SNEADA. John Clayton

CARRIAGE HOUSE ANTIQUES
99 Spring St, 02840
(401)849-0709   **48 56 67**

Unusual combination of antiques & collectibles featuring nautical items, lamps, candlesticks, antique linens & quilts. *Est:* 1990. *Hours:* Tue-Sat 10-5 by chance or appt. *Assoc:* NADA. *Park:* Nearby.

THE CLASSIC TOUCH
515 Thames St, 02840
(401)849-1717   **23 41**

Eclectic collections of international antiques, entertaining accessories, specializing in fine 19th C clocks. *Pr:* $10–10000. *Est:* 1984. *Serv:* Custom painted furniture, art of the painted finish. *Hours:* Daily 10-5 by chance/appt. *Size:* Medium. *Assoc:* NADA. Diane Beaver *Park:* On site. *Loc:* Bellevue Ave, L on Casino Terrace, Bellevue Plaza.

TERESA COOK ANTIQUES
38 Franklin St, 02840
(401)828-2798   **44 47 48**

Glassware, china, jewelry & linens. *Hours:* Daily 10:30-2:30.

COUNTRY PLEASURES LTD
104 Spring St, 02840
(401)849-6355   **39 42**

Antique British & Irish cut pine furniture, antique farmhouse pine, British & American collectibles & accessories. *Est:* 1985. *Hours:* Mon-Sat 11-5 Sun 12-4. *CC:* MC/V. *Assoc:* NADA. *Park:* Nearby. *Loc:* Corner Spring & Mary St.

THE DOLL MUSEUM
520 Thames St, 02840
(401)849-0405   **32 52**

A fine collection of antique & modern dolls on permanent display & collectible miniatures. *Pr:* $10–5000. *Serv:* Doll hospital, appraisals, repairs. *Hours:* Wed-Mon 10-5 Sun 12-5. *CC:* MC/V. *Assoc:* NADA. Linda Edward *Park:* In front.

THE DRAWING ROOM OF NEWPORT
221 Spring St, 02840
(401)841-5060   **37 46**

Fine antiques from Newport estates including Moser glass, Empire porcelain, icons, Russian enamels, Zsolnay, fine art glass, Black-a-moors, gas shades, military & medals. Always interested in buying unusual items. **Pr:** $100–10000. **Serv:** Appraisal, brochure, consultation, purchase estates, restoration. **Hours:** Daily 11-5 & BY APPT. **Size:** Medium. **CC:** MC/V. **Assoc:** NADA. Federico Santi **Loc:** From Boston: Rte 24 onto Island to Rte 138 or Rte 114 to Newport, from NYC: I-95N follow signs to Newport Bridge.

ETHEL'S OLD PLACE
233 Spring St, 02840
(401)841-5060   **17 50 83**

19th C high-style furniture, fabrics, gas chandeliers & lighting devices including solar, sinumbra, argand, gas sconces, newel post lamps. **Serv:** Appraisal, consultation, interior design, purchase estates, repairs. **Hours:** Thu-Sat & Mon, appt suggested. **Size:** Medium. **CC:** AX/MC/V. John Gacher **Loc:** Next to the Spa.

FAIR DE YORE
170 Spring St, 02840
(401)849-5582   **34 47 48**

Linens, folk art crafts, old & new jewelry. **Est:** 1982. **Hours:** Daily 12-5, CLOSED WED. **CC:** DC/MC/V. **Assoc:** NADA. Hazel Pharis **Park:** Nearby. **Loc:** 1 block from Thames St.

CHRISTOPHER FOSTER GLASS WORKS
10 Marlborough St, 02840
(401)847-4178   **50 70 71**

Restoration of stained glass. Will design & build windows to specification. Restoration of leaded lamp shades. Custom leaded lamp shades made to order. **Est:** 1964. **Hours:** By chance/appt. **Assoc:** NADA. **Park:** Nearby. **Loc:** 1 1/2 blocks NE of Brick Market.

FULL SWING
474 Thames St, 02840
(401)849-9494   **7 46 80**

Furnishings & accessories 1920s to 1950s. Extensive collection of vintage yardage & draperies, wicker, bamboo & rattan (seasonal), re-covered in vintage fabrics. From Art Deco bedrooms to atomic modern living rooms. **Pr:** $25–1500. **Serv:** Nationally recognized source for vintage textiles. **Hours:** Jun-Sep Mon-Sat 10-6, Oct-May Mon-Sat 11-6. **Size:** Medium. **CC:** AX/MC/V. **Assoc:** NADA. Michele Mancini **Park:** In front. **Loc:** Heart of shopping district, on 1st st parallel to Harbor.

A & A GAINES
40 Franklin St, 02840
(401)849-6844   **23 56 60**

Period furniture, clocks, China trade porcelain, nautical items & Oriental silver. **Serv:** All pieces guaranteed. **Hours:** Tue-Sat 11-5 or BY APPT. **Assoc:** NADA. **Shows:** BAS RI. Alan Gaines **Park:** Nearby. **Loc:** Just off Thames St on Antique Row.

GALLERY '76 ANTIQUES INC
83 Spring St, 02840
(401)847-4288   **36 63 77**

Period furniture, accessories, silver, porcelain, jewelry, fine 19th C export & European porcelain & clocks. **Hours:** Daily 10-5:30 CLOSED SUN. **CC:** AX/MC/V. **Assoc:** NADA. Barbara Leis **Park:** Nearby. **Loc:** Between Colony House & Trinity Church.

JOHN GIDLEY HOUSE 1744
22 Franklin St, 02840
(401)846-8303   **36 50 58**

Fine furniture, lighting fixtures & decorative arts. **Pr:** $100–20000. **Hours:** Tue-Sat 11-5. **Size:** Medium. **Assoc:** AAA

NADA. Carl Ritorno *Loc:* Across Franklin St from main post office just off America's Cup Ave.

HARRY GREW
PO Box 172, 02840
(401)846-7372   **36 59 63**

American paintings, British ceramics, Staffordshire & furniture. *Est:* 1977. *Hours:* BY APPT. *Loc:* Call for directions.

THE GRIFFON SHOP
76 Bellevue Ave, 02840
(401)847-0179   **25**

Consigned antiques & collectibles from Newport estates. *Est:* 1988. *Serv:* Consignment. *Hours:* Tue-Sat 10-4. *Assoc:* NADA. *Park:* On site. *Loc:* At the Newport Art Museum.

HYDRANGEA HOUSE GALLERY
14 Bellevue Ave, 02840
(401)846-4435   **29**

In the Hydrangea House Inn, a variety of antiques, decorative accessories & fine art. *Hours:* Tue-Sun 12-5. *Assoc:* NADA.

JB ANTIQUES
33 Franklin St, 02840
(401)849-0450   **58 59 63**

Fine antique furniture, pottery & porcelain, paintings & prints, inkstand, lamps, mirrors, Sheffield, toleware. *Serv:* Appraisal. *Hours:* Daily 10-5. *CC:* AX/MC/V. *Assoc:* NADA. Jacqueline Barratt *Park:* Nearby. *Loc:* 1/2 block E of Thames St.

JENNIFERS
29 Bull St, 02840
(401)849-8857   **36 47 50**

Eclectic second-hand shop featuring quality used furniture, art, household items, costume jewelry & lamps. *Hours:*

Mon-Sat 10-5 Sun 12-5. *CC:* AX. Frank Moquin *Park:* Nearby. *Loc:* Across from the Bellevue Shopping Center.

R KAZARIAN/ANTIQUES
35 Franklin St, 02840
(401)846-3563   **1 5 34**

American & European furniture, architectural & garden details & folk art. *Hours:* Daily 11-5. *CC:* MC/V. *Assoc:* NADA. *Park:* Nearby.

ROGER KING GALLERY OF FINE ART
21 Bowen's Wharf 2nd & 3rd fl, 02840
(401)847-4359   **4 59 71**

Specializing in important American paintings of the 19th & early 20th C. *Est:* 1973. *Serv:* Appraisal, conservation, consultation, purchase estates, restoration. *Hours:* Year round daily 12-5 (extended summer hours) appt suggested. *Size:* Medium. *CC:* AX/MC/V. *Assoc:* NADA NEAA. Roger King *Park:* Nearby lot. *Loc:* Opposite the Clarke Cooke House.

LAMP LIGHTER ANTIQUES
42 Spring St, 02840
(401)849-4179   **23 37 50**

Specializing in oil lamps, clocks, American furniture & Currier & Ives prints. *Est:* 1976. *Hours:* Mon-Sat 11-5. *Assoc:* NADA. Al Lozito

MAINLY OAK LTD
489 Thames St, 02840
(401)846-4439   **40 53 86**

Oak furniture, mirrors & wicker. *Serv:* Refinishing. *Hours:* Mon-Sat 10-5, Sun 12-4, CLOSED TUE. *CC:* MC/V. John Majewski *Park:* On street. *Loc:* Downtown.

R A NELSON, ANTIQUES & INTERIORS
59 Bellevue Ave, 02840
(401)846-8256   **38 29**
Selected European antique furnishings & accessories of finest qualtiy. *Serv:* Interior design. *Hours:* Tue-Sat 10-5 by chance or appt. *Assoc:* NADA. Richard A Nelson

NEW ENGLAND ANTIQUES
60 Spring St, 02840
(401)849-6646   **27 59 63**
American art, country, English transfer china, glass, flow blue & items in original paint. *Pr:* $20–2000. *Hours:* Mon-Sat 11-5 & BY APPT. *CC:* AX. *Assoc:* NADA. *Loc:* Int of Spring & Touro Sts in the heart of 18th C Newport, across from Touro Synagogue.

NEWELL'S CLOCK RESTORATION
79 Thames St, 02840
(401)849-6690   **71**
Restoration of fine antique clocks & timepieces. *Est:* 1972. *Serv:* Repairs, restoration. *Hours:* Mon-Sat 10-1 2:30-5:30 appt suggested. *Assoc:* AWI NADA NAWCC. A F Newell *Park:* In front. *Loc:* 1/2 block N of Marlborough St on W side of Thames St.

NEWPORT ANTIQUES
471 Lower Thames St, 02840
(401)849-2105   **{GR}**
A great variety of old things. *Hours:* Daily during the season, weekends off season. *Assoc:* NADA.

THE NEWPORT GALLERY LTD
337 Thames St Ste 4, 02840
(401)849-8218   **56 59**
Fine 19th & 20th C marine paintings & selections of coastal fine art. *Hours:* Mon-Sat 10-6 Sun 11-6 BY APPT. *CC:* AX/MC/V. *Loc:* Perry Mill Market, at st level of Bay Club Hotel.

NEWPORT SCRIMSHAW COMPANY
337 Thames St, 02840
(401)846-8666   **56 58**
Antique American scrimshaw, quality American Oriental & European antique ivory carvings. *Serv:* Appraisal, repairs. *Hours:* Daily 10-5 Sun 12-5. *CC:* MC/V. Chet Gotauco *Park:* Nearby. *Loc:* Perry Mill Market.

OLD FASHION SHOP
38 Pelham St, 02840
(401)847-2692   **1 21 63**
Americana, furniture, accessories, Oriental rugs & porcelains. *Est:* 1959. *Hours:* Mon-Sat 1-5. *Assoc:* NADA. *Park:* Nearby. *Loc:* At sign of the Hand, 3 houses down from corner of Pelham & Spring Sts.

JILL OLTZ ANTIQUES
24 Franklin St, 02840
(401)846-7010   **5 45 50**
A special collection of unusual furniture & accesssories, including garden, lighting & architecturals on Newport's Antique Row. *Est:* 1990. *Serv:* Antique show management, consultation, interior design, purchase estates. *Hours:* Year round Wed-Sat 10-6 or by chance or appt. *CC:* MC/V. *Assoc:* PSMA. *Park:* Nearby. *Loc:* Just off Thames St.

PETTERUTI ANTIQUES
105 Memorial Blvd W, 02840
(401)849-5117   **58 59 86**
Unique antique wicker, fine paintings, 19th C bronzes, quality furniture & objets d'art. *Serv:* Appraisal, consultation. *Hours:* May-Nov daily 10-5 Sun 12-5. *CC:* AX/MC/V. *Assoc:* NADA. Carmine Petteruti Jr *Park:* Off street. *Loc:* Below Int of Memorial Blvd & Spring St.

RAMSON HOUSE ANTIQUES
36 Franklin St, 02840
(401)847-0555   **43 50 63**

Antiques & fine reproductions of furniture, desks, lamps, Oriental porcelains & decorative accessories. *Est:* 1978. *Serv:* Repair lamps, interior design. *Hours:* Mon-Sat 11-5, Sun 12-4. *CC:* MC/V. *Assoc:* NADA. Joan DeDionisio *Loc:* On Antique Row.

SIMMONS & SIMMONS
223 Spring St, 02840
(401)849-7281   **13 33 66**

Books, prints, paper, curios, Arctic material, advertising, paper theatres & modern 1st editions. *Hours:* By chance/appt. *Assoc:* NADA. Eric Simmons

ALICE SIMPSON ANTIQUES
40 1/2 Franklin St, 02840
(401)849-4252   **47 77 80**

Specializing in Victorian silver plate, textiles & jewelry. *Serv:* Appraisal. *Hours:* By chance. *CC:* MC/V. *Loc:* 1/2 block from Newport post office.

SMITH MARBLE LTD
44 Franklin St, 02840
(401)846-7689   **36 44 63**

Specializing in fine antiquities, works of art, objects of vertu, silver, porcelains, glass, furniture, tapestries & rugs. *Est:* 1970. *Serv:* Appraisal, consultation, interior design. *Hours:* May-Nov Mon-Sat 10-5 Sun 12-5 BY APPT (508)838-2019. *CC:* AX/MC/V. *Assoc:* NADA. Ada V Smith *Park:* Nearby. *Loc:* Corner of Franklin & Spring.

TRITON ANTIQUES
160 Spring St, 02840
(401)847-6077   **27 29**

Specializing in American country furniture, paintings, linen, porcelain & glassware. *Hours:* Sat-Wed 11:30-4:30 CLOSED THU & FRI. *Assoc:* NADA. Herbert Motz

WILLIAM VAREIKA FINE ARTS
212 Bellevue Ave, 02840
(401)849-6149   **59 66**

Offering 18th, 19th & early 20th C American paintings, drawings & prints by important artists, i.e. Bierstadt, Church, Gifford & Kensett. Two large floors in a museum-like setting, located on Newport's historic Bellevue Avenue. *Pr:* $500–500000. *Serv:* Appraisal, brochure, catalog, conservation, consultation, restoration. *Hours:* Mon-Sat 10-6 & BY APPT. *Size:* Large. *Assoc:* NADA NEAA. *Park:* Nearby lot. *Loc:* From N: Rte 124S to Rte 114 to central Newport. From W: Rte 138 & Newport Bridge, 1 block S of Int'l Tennis Hall of Fame.

MICHAEL L WESTMAN FINE ARTS
135 Spring St, 02840
(401)847-3091   **59 66**

Esoteric & decorative arts, fine arts & folk art from all periods & cultures. *Pr:* $100–5000. *Serv:* Appraisal. *Hours:* By chance/appt. *Size:* Medium. *Assoc:* NADA. *Loc:* Next to Trinity Church.

GUSTAVES JS WHITE
37 Bellevue Ave, 02840
(401)849-3000   **8 29 36**

Auctions of antique & estate furniture, decorative accessories. 10% buyer's premium. Auctions on site or in Portsmouth, RI auction gallery. *Hours:* Daily 9-4. Michael R Corcoran

NORTH KINGSTOWN

LAFAYETTE ANTIQUES
814 Ten Rod Rd Rte 102, 02852
(401)295-2504   **37 83**
Early American & Victorian furniture.
Hours: Tue-Sun 11-5. Chet Chandron-
net *Loc:* I-95 S to Rte 4 to Rte 102,
approx 1 MI down Rd, just outside of
Wickford.

LILLIAN'S ANTIQUES
7442 Post Rd Rte 1, 02852
(401)885-2512   **44 47 86**
Antique jewelry, china, glass, paintings,
furniture, wicker & general line. *Serv:*
Purchase estates. *Hours:* Thu-Sun 1-5 or
BY APPT. *Assoc:* SNEADA. Lillian
Anderson

MENTOR ANTIQUES
7512 Post Rd Rte 1, 02852
(401)294-9412   **39 29**
Carefully selected English furnishings &
decorative accessories, specializing in armoires & wardrobes. *Hours:* Daily 10-6.
CC: MC/V. *Assoc:* SNEADA. *Shows:* RI.
Marry Gormally *Park:* On site. *Loc:* I-
95, on Rte 1 in North Kingston: at the
bright red English telephone box.

NORTH SMITHFIELD

ROCKING CHAIR ANTIQUES
1090 Eddie Dowling Hwy, 02895
(401)762-5566
Quality antiques & collectibles. *Hours:*
BY APPT. *Assoc:* SNEADA. Frank/Bar-
bara Lesowski

PAWTUCKET

CRINOLINES & OLD LACE
Pawtucket, 02862
(401)725-2285   **48 65 67**
Linens, primitives, military, costume
jewelry & quilts. *Hours:* BY APPT.
Assoc: SNEADA. Jennie Simonian

MY THREE SONS
201 Pine St, 02862
(401)722-4488   **36 44**
Furniture, glassware, china & general
line of antiques & collectibles. *Hours:*
Tue-Fri 10-6, Sat 10-4:30, CLOSED
SUN, MON. *Size:* Large. *Assoc:*
SNEADA. Pauline/Frank Lefebvre

PEACE DALE

**ANTIQUITY RESTORATIONS &
REPRO'S**
22 Kersey Rd, 02883
(401)789-2370   **68 70 71**
Antique sales, repair & refinishing, furniture reproductions, carriage & sleigh
restoration. *Est:* 1984. *Serv:* Repairs,
reproduction, restoration. *Hours:* Mon-
Fri 8-5 Sat 9-5. Jim Harmon *Park:* On
site. *Loc:* 2 MI from Univ of RI off Rte
108.

PORTSMOUTH

BENJAMIN FISH HOUSE ANTIQUES
934 E Main Rd, 02871
(401)683-0099   **37 60 63**
Dedham pottery, Dorchester, early
American furniture, accessories, Heisey
& Oriental porcelain. *Est:* 1980. *Hours:*

Year round Mon-Sat 10-5 Sun 12-4. **Assoc:** SNEADA. Charles Crouch **Park:** Plentiful, nearby. **Loc:** On Rte 138 2 doors from Portsmouth Historical Society.

PROVIDENCE

125 BENEFIT STREET ANTIQUES
125 Benefit St, 02903
(401)274-6330   **36 50 53**
In a renovated 1851 house a collection of antique furniture, porcelain, brass, mirrors, glass & lighting fixtures. **Serv:** Interior design services. **Hours:** Tue-Sat 12-5. **CC:** AX/MC/V. Nancy Taylor **Park:** At rear of shop. **Loc:** I-95E, S Main St Exit: R on Meeting St, L at top of hill, 2 blocks on R.

ANTIQUES BEAUTIFUL
69 Governor St, 02906
(401)434-0275   **{GR4}**
Five rooms featuring period furniture, custom mahogany, cherry, pine & oak, Oriental rugs, paintings, glassware, antique jewelry & country items. **Pr:** $25–2500. **Serv:** Appraisal, consultation, interior design, purchase estates, repair. **Hours:** Mon-Fri 9:30-5. Dennis Vieira **Park:** On site. **Loc:** I-95E Exit 6: R onto Warren Ave, R at light onto Broadway, 1 1/2 MI on L, I-95W Exit 6: R onto Broadway, 1 1/3 MI on L.

BERT GALLERY
Omni-Biltmore Hotel, 02903
(401)751-2628   **59**
Specializing in important Rhode Island artists who worked in Providence at the turn of the century. **Pr:** $150–10000. **Est:** 1983. **Serv:** Appraisal, conservation, restoration, purchasing. **Hours:** Sep-May Mon-Fri 11:30-5; Jun-Aug Tue-Fri

11:30-5; or by appt. **Size:** medium. **CC:** MC/V. Catherine Little Bert **Park:** Local garage. **Loc:** I-95 N/S Exit 22: downtown, R on Dyer St, Hotel directly on R.

PATSY BRAMAN ANTIQUES
122 Brook St, 02906
(401)351-1614   **{GR3}**
Specializing in American antiques & decorative arts. **Hours:** Tue-Sat 12-5 & by appt; Sum: Wed-Sat 11-5.

BRASSWORKS
379 Charles St, 02904
(401)421-5815   **68 71**
Repair, restoration & polishing of brass, copper, pewter & silver. **Serv:** Brochure available. **Hours:** Mon-Fri 9-5 Sat 9-3. **CC:** AX/MC/V. **Loc:** I-95 Exit 24.

CELLAR STORIES BOOKS
190 Mathewson St, 02903
(401)521-2665   **13 14**
Antiquarian books: First editions, literature, Rhode Island history, science fiction & fantasy, theatre. **Pr:** $1–2000. **Serv:** Appraisal, purchase estates, repair, search service. **Hours:** Mon-Sat 10-6. **Size:** Medium. **Assoc:** MARIAB. Michael K Chandley **Park:** Nearby lot.

MARTIN CONLON AMERICAN ANTIQUES
PO Box 3070, 02906
(401)831-1810   **37**
Fine American furniture & accessories of the 18th & 19th C. **Est:** 1986. **Serv:** Auction, consultation, conservation. **Hours:** BY APPT. **Loc:** 3 min from I-95, call for directions.

CORNERSTONE BOOKS
139 Brook St, 02906
(401)861-7244   **13**
Antiquarian books - Brown University, Rhode Island, architecture of Rhode Is-

land, black-American culture. *Pr:* $5–2000. *Est:* 1983. *Serv:* Appraisal, catalog, search service, repairs. *Hours:* Wed-Sat 12-6 & by appt. *Size:* Medium. *Assoc:* MARIAB. Ray Rickman *Park:* In front.

CAROL LOMBARDI ANTIQUES
PO Box 5954, 02903
(401)521-4656   1 38 47

American & European decorative art & furnishings, antique jewelry & period & custom furniture. *Serv:* Appraisal, interior design, purchase estates. *Hours:* BY APPT. *Assoc:* SNEADA NEAA. Carol Lombardi

METACOMET BOOKS
Box 2479, 02906
(401)861-7182   13

Americana, literature, science, technology, women & general. *Serv:* Appraisal, catalog, search service. *Hours:* BY APPT. *Assoc:* MARIAB. James Sanford *Loc:* 2 min from I-95, call for directions.

MY FAVORITE THINGS
Arcade Bldg, 02903
(401)831-3332   18 48 77

Specializing in antique lace & linen, sewing items, buttons & buckles, sterling silver smalls & jewelry. *Pr:* $25–500. *Hours:* Dec 27-Nov 24 Mon-Sat 10-6, Nov 25-Dec 24 daily 10-9. *Size:* Medium. *CC:* AX/MC/V. Patricia Mc Garty *Park:* Nearby lot. *Loc:* In Historic Arcade Bldg, between Westminster & Weybosset sts in downtown Providence.

QUE ANTIQUES
Box 2367A, 02906
(401)751-7991   62 66

Specializing in prints: botanicals, horticulturals, early advertising & photographs. *Hours:* By appt. Kathie Florsheim

THE REEL MAN
PO Box 752 Annex Station, 02901
(401)941-6853   78

Antique fishing tackle including complete vintage outfits - rod, reel, line & lure - creels, nets, bobbers, tackle boxes, angling paraphernalia, artwork, shadow boxes & framed displays. Mail order catalog issued 3-4 times per year. *Serv:* Consultation, appraisal, repair, refinishing, restoration, int design   n. *Hours:* By appt.

SEWARD'S FOLLY, BOOKS
139 Brook St, 02906
(401)272-4454   13

First editions, literary criticism & biography, philosophy, poetry & Rhode Island history. *Pr:* $1–2000. *Est:* 1976. *Serv:* Purchase estates, search services. *Hours:* Wed-Fri 12-6 Sat 9-6 Sun 12-6 Mon, Tue by chance/appt. *Size:* Medium. *Assoc:* MARIAB. Schuyler Seward *Park:* In front. *Loc:* 8-10 blocks S of Brown Univ, on E side of Providence.

SUNNY DAYS
287 Thayer St, 02906
(401)274-5570   47 85

Fine antique clothing & jewelry for men & women including 1920's beaded dresses, Victorian whites, Deco, bags, tuxedoes & rhinestones. *Est:* 1981. *Hours:* Mon-Sat 11-6 Sun 12-5 CLOSED SUN in summer. *CC:* MC/V. *Assoc:* SNEADA. Lois Hollingsworth *Park:* On street. *Loc:* On the E side of Providence, in the heart of the college area.

TYSON'S OLD & RARE BOOKS
334 Westminster St, 02903
(401)421-3939   13

American literature, Americana, first editions, travel, Rhode Island history, better books in all fields. *Est:* 1935. *Serv:*

Appraisal, catalog, search service. *Hours:* Mon-Fri 11-5 most Sat 11-4. *Assoc:* MARIAB. Mariette P Bedard *Park:* Behind building. *Loc:* 5 min from I-95.

BARBARA WALZER BOOKSELLER
175 Ontario St, 02907
(401)785-2277   **13**
Women's history, general antiquarian & collection development - rare & unusual books & ephemera.. *Hours:* By appt. *Assoc:* ABAA.

YESTERYEAR ANTIQUES
409 Wickenden St, 02903
(401)331-0262   **7 39 50**
Victorian furniture, Deco, lamps, prints, books & glassware. *Hours:* Wed-Fri 10-6, Sat 10-5, Sun 12-5, CLOSED MON, TUE. *Assoc:* SNEADA. Eleanor Williams

ZEXTER ANTIQUES
460 Wickendon St, 02903
(401)272-6905   **29 36**
A large selction of 18th & 19th C furniture & decorative accessories. *Hours:* Mon-Sat 9-5.

ZUZU'S PETALS
288 Thayer ST, 02906
(401)331-9846   **47 85**
Antique clothing & jewelry, 1900-1960.. *Est:* 1989. *Hours:* Mon-Sat 11-6 Sun 12-5 Sum: CLOSED SUN. *CC:* MC/V. *Park:* On street. *Loc:* On the east side of Providence in the heart of the college area near Brown University.

RIVERSIDE

SUE CHRISTIE
20 Star Ave, 02915
(401)433-2568   **23 27 81**
General line of antiques & collectibles including clocks, tools, small country accessories, glass & china. *Hours:* BY APPT. *Assoc:* SNEADA.

DONALD K SMITH
75 Boyden Blvd, 02915
(401)438-4084   **44**
Glassware, china, Disney & black collectibles. *Hours:* By chance/appt. *Assoc:* SNEADA.

JAMES TEIXEIRA
75 Boyden Blvd, 02915
(401)438-4084   **33 44 32**
Postcards, souvenirs, glass, china, toys & collectibles. *Hours:* By chance/appt. *Assoc:* SNEADA.

RUMFORD

IPO'S ATTIC
Rumford, 02916
(401)434-0466   **67 27 1**
Specializing in quilts, period & country furniture, Americana & quality accessories. *Hours:* BY APPT. *Assoc:* SNEADA. Jim & Judi Wims

PURPLE OPAL
36 Hood Ave, 02916
(401)438-5240   **36 44 93**
China, furniture, glass, inkwells, jewelry, tobies & unusuals. *Hours:* By chance/appt. *Assoc:* SNEADA. Joyce & Tony Gomes

SAUNDERSTOWN

MIMOSA TREE
10 Baneberry Trail Box 534, 02874
(401)294-9286   **36 33 60**

Small furniture, documents & Oriental accessories. *Hours:* BY APPT. *Assoc:* SNEADA. Bill Flynn & Valerie Felt

STEPHANIE ADAMS WOOD
PO Box 444, 02874
(401)294-2787   **59 73 80**

American furniture, textiles, paintings, sculptural objects & accessories. *Hours:* BY APPT. *Assoc:* NHADA.

SMITHFIELD

MARTY'S ANTIQUE AUCTION SERVICE
RFD 4 Mountaindale Rd, 02917
(401)231-8246   **8**

Auctions of antiques & estate liquidations. Licensed & bonded. Auction hall in Foster, RI. *Hours:* Auctions held Tue at 7; Call for more information. *Assoc:* SNEADA. Marty Austin

SMITHFIELD RARE BOOKS
Deer Run Trail, 02917
(401)231-8225   **13**

Antiquarian books on medicine, science, natural history, better biographies of scientists & physicians. *Serv:* Catalog, search service. *Hours:* By appt. *Assoc:* MARIAB. Michael Elmer

TIVERTON

METAL RESTORATION SERVICES
43 Wm S Canning Blvd Rte 81 S, 02878
(401)624-6486   **26 68 71**

Conservation, restoration, refinishing & spray coating of metal antiques made of gold, silver, bronze, copper, brass, pewter & tin. Lighting fixture work from lamps to chandeliers. No work done on jewelry. *Est:* 1980. *Serv:* Conservation, consultation, repair, restoration. *Hours:* Mon-Fri 8-4:30 Sat 8-12, appt suggested. *Size:* Large. Peter M Pflock *Park:* In front. *Loc:* From Rte 24 S of Fall River, MA, take Exit for Rte 81 S Adamsville RI, take 2nd driveway on R marked Canning Pl Bus Condos.

WAKEFIELD

DOVE AND DISTAFF ANTIQUES
365 Main St, 02879
(401)783-5714   **29 37**

Early American furniture & accessories. *Serv:* Restoration, refinish, upholstery & drapery workshop, lampshades. *Hours:* Mon-Fri 8-5 Sat 8-12. Caleb Davis *Loc:* Rte 1 Wakefield Exit: take Main St into Old Wakefield.

HELEN C FERRIS
135 Whitford St, 02879
(401)783-7389   **23 27**

Clocks, country furniture & smalls. *Hours:* BY APPT. *Assoc:* SNEADA.

OLDE TOWNE SHOPPE
14 Columbia St, 02879
(401)782-1230   **{GR}**

Antiques, collectibles, books, furniture

& sterling. *Hours:* Tue-Sat 10-4. *Assoc:* SNEADA. Bob & Shirley Anderson *Loc:* Across from the movie theater.

THE RATHBUN GALLERY-SHAKER
Rose Hill Farm 1101 Mooresfield, 02879
(401)789-5380   **37 76**
A complete line of Shaker antiques for the beginning or established collector. *Pr:* $35–70000. *Serv:* Appraisal, consultation. *Hours:* BY APPT. *Size:* Medium. Richard Schneider *Loc:* Please call for directions.

TREASURES OF ROYAL T
22 Browning St RR8A, 02879
(401)789-4143
Antiques & collectibles. *Hours:* BY APPT. *Assoc:* SNEADA. Royal & Hazel Thompson

---

WARREN

CHRISTIE & HADLEY ANTIQUES
160 Water St, 02885
(401)245-2711   **29 47**
Eclectic decorative accessories, smalls, jewelry & small furniture. *Est:* 1987. *Hours:* Tue-Sat 1-5. Suzanne Christie *Park:* On street. *Loc:* Just off Rte 114.

WARWICK

ANTIQUE HAVEN
30 Post Rd, 02888
(401)785-0327   **44 63**
Hand-painted china, Limoges, crystal & general line. *Hours:* Mon-Sat 11-4 or by appt anytime. *Assoc:* SNEADA. Claire Silverman

CONSTANTINE'S FINE FURNITURE
334 Knight St 4th Fl, 02887
(401)884-5441   **43 59 60**
Reproduction & antique furniture, Chinese & European marble sculpture, paintings & decorative accessories. *Serv:* Appraisal. *Hours:* Mon-Sat 9-5. *CC:* V. *Park:* Plenty. *Loc:* In the Pontiac Mills Building 1, 4th Floor.

THE EMPORIUM
1629 Warwick Ave, 02889
(401)738-8824   **47 64 77**
Fine jewelry, costume jewelry, kitchen collectibles, glassware, furniture, silver, paintings, china & post cards. *Est:* 1983. *Hours:* Daily 11-5 CLOSED WED,SUN. *CC:* MC/V. *Park:* In front. *Loc:* In back of Green Airport.

FORTUNATE FINDS BOOKSTORE
16 W Natick Rd, 02886
(401)737-8160   **13**
Antiquarian books- Rhode Island, genealogies, documents, general books, travel, children, fiction & nonfiction. *Pr:* $5–500. *Est:* 1958. *Serv:* Appraisal, catalog. *Hours:* Fri-Sat 9-5 & BY APPT. *Park:* On site. *Loc:* Across from the Warwick Mall off Rte 5.

JO-ART GLASS
288 Natick Ave, 02886
(401)737-7554   **44**
China, crystal, depression glass & collectibles. *Hours:* BY APPT. *Assoc:* SNEADA. Josephine Brown

RAY & ESTELLE NELSON
2855 Post Rd, 02886
(401)739-8644   **27**
Specializing in country furniture. *Hours:* BY APPT. *Assoc:* SNEADA.

THE SCHOOLMASTER'S WIFE
598 Warwick Neck Ave, 02889
(401)739-4366   **27**

General line specializing in country furniture. *Hours:* By chance/appt. *Assoc:*
SNEADA. Nancy & Carl Johnson

TIQUES & TIBLES
359 Greenwich Ave #132, 02886
(401)737-6882   **44 48 67**

Antiques & collectibles specializing in all
types of glass, linen, quilts & fine china.
Hours: BY APPT. *Assoc:* SNEADA.
Jackie St Germain

WATCH HILL

A TO Z ANTIQUES
185 Watch Hill Rd, 02891
(401)348-8775   **64**

Barn full of interesting items-smalls,
postcards, etc. *Hours:* All year by
chance/appt. Adelaide S Zanke *Loc:* 5 MI
outside of Westerly toward the beaches.

THE BOOK & TACKLE SHOP
7 Bay St, 02891
(401)596-0700   **13 64 66**

Antiquarian books - rare science & medical books, sea voyages, exploration,
cookery, children's, music & rare post
cards, fine bindings, early printings &
engravings. *Pr:* $5-10000. *Est:* 1955.
Serv: Appraisal, auction, purchase estates, search service. *Hours:* May-Oct
daily 9-5, Nov-Apr BY APPT. *Size:*
Large. *CC:* MC/V. *Assoc:* ABAA
MARIAB. Bernard Gordon *Park:* In
front. *Loc:* 10 MI from CT/RI border on
US Rte 1, 7 MI from Westerly RI, accessible by boat on Watch Hill RI Harbor.

THE COUNTRY STORE AT WATCH
HILL
19 Bay St, 02891
(401)596-6540   **27 42**

Specializing in country pine antiques,
wicker furniture & accessories. *Hours:*
May 15-Oct 15 Mon-Sat 10-9.

OCEAN HOUSE
ANTIQUES/CURIOSITIES
Ocean House 2 Bluff Ave, 02891
(401)348-8161   **44**

Heisey & general line. *Hours:* Late Jun-
Labor Day nights only 6:30-9:30. Carole
B Lacey

SECOND IMPRESSION ANTIQUES
84 1/2 Bay St, 02891
(401)596-1296   **86**

Specializing in antique wicker furniture -
Victorian, Bar Harbor, Art Deco, Lloyd
Loom, American pine furniture & accessories. *Serv:* Restoration of furniture &
wicker. *Hours:* Tue-Sat 10-5. *CC:*
AX/MC/V. *Loc:* On the right driving
into the village on Bay St.

WEST GREENWICH

MARTONE'S GALLERY
699 New London Tnpk, 02816
(401)885-3880   **8 44**

Auctioneer of antique furniture, rugs &
glassware 10% buyer's premium. *Serv:*
Appraisal, mailing. *Hours:* Call for appt
or schedule. *CC:* AX/MC/V. Jack Martone *Park:* On site. *Loc:* Rte 95 Exit 7.
20 min from CT border.

WEST KINGSTON

EIGHTEENTH CENTURY WOODWORKS
272 James Trail, 02892
(401)539-2558   **19 69 70**

Reproductions of Colonial beds, adapting antique beds to modern uses, featuring cannonballs, pencil posts, canopy field beds, low posts & variations, tavern tables & tea tables. *Pr:* $2000–8000. *Est:* 1969. *Serv:* Custom woodwork, catalog ($3), repairs, replication, reproduction. *Hours:* Mon-Fri 9-5 Sat 9-12, Sun BY APPT; by chance/appt after 5. Ray Clidence *Park:* On site. *Loc:* I-95 Exit 3A: follow Rte 128 approx 3 MI, L onto Hillsdale for 2 1/2 MI, R onto James Trail, go 1 MI.

PETER POTS AUTHENTIC AMERICANA
494 Glen Rock Rd, 02892
(401)783-2350   **28 29**

Stoneware, period furniture, decorative & collectible items. *Hours:* Mon-Sat 10-4 Sun 1-4, CLOSED MAJOR HOLIDAYS. *CC:* AX/MC/V. Oliver Greene *Loc:* I-95 to Rte 138 W, approx 5 or 6 MI, watch for signs.

WEST WARWICK

ROSEWOOD ANTIQUES
1630 Main St, 02893
(401)823-3196   **47 14 33**

Antiques, collectibles, jewelry, old books, comics, dolls & postcards. *Hours:* By chance/appt. *Assoc:* SNEADA. Mae & Gene Childs

WESTERLY

TOOLS & BOOKS LTD
Old Potter Hill Rd, 02891
(401)377-8270   **14 81**

18th & 19th C carpenter's tools, rare out-of-print books & furnishings for the workshop or library. *Hours:* By chance/appt. *Assoc:* SNEADA. Bruce & Allison Goodsell *Loc:* Rte 95 Exit 1: R onto Rte 3, 2 MI, R at blinking light/Maxton Hill Rd, L at end, R over bridge, 1st house on L.

WESTERLY ENTERPRISES
28 Canal St, 02891
(401)596-2298   **24 47**

Rare coins, jewelry, art, antiques & collectibles. *Hours:* Tue-Sat 10-5. *CC:* MC/V. George Champlin *Loc:* Rte 955 to Rte 3, 6 MI, across from China Village restaurant & RR station.

WICKFORD

THE BALL & CLAW
1 W Main St, 02852
(401)295-1200   **43 51 59**

Exemplary pieces of handcrafted 18th C furniture. Period oil paintings & watercolors, export porcelain, early maps, quilts, weathervanes, pewter & pottery. *Est:* 1988. *Serv:* Catalog($2), custom woodwork, replication, reproduction. *Hours:* All year daily 10-5, Sun 12-5. *CC:* AX/MC/V. Jeffrey Greene *Park:* In front, nearby lot.

WOONSOCKET

WYOMING

THE CORNER CURIOSITY SHOPPE
56 Crawford St, 02895
(401)766-7678   **36 44 65**
Furniture, glassware, linens, pottery & other fine antiques & collectibles. *Est:* 1988. *Serv:* Sell reference books. *Hours:* Wed-Sun 11-5 or BY APPT. *CC:* MC/V. *Assoc:* SNEADA. Glen & Diane Turner *Park:* On street. *Loc:* Rte 146A to Park Ave 1 MI to Crawford St.

BRAD SMITH
Jct Rtes 112 & 138, 02898
(401)539-2870   **29 36 59**

Furniture, paintings & decorative accessories.

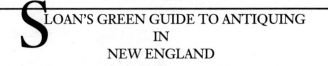

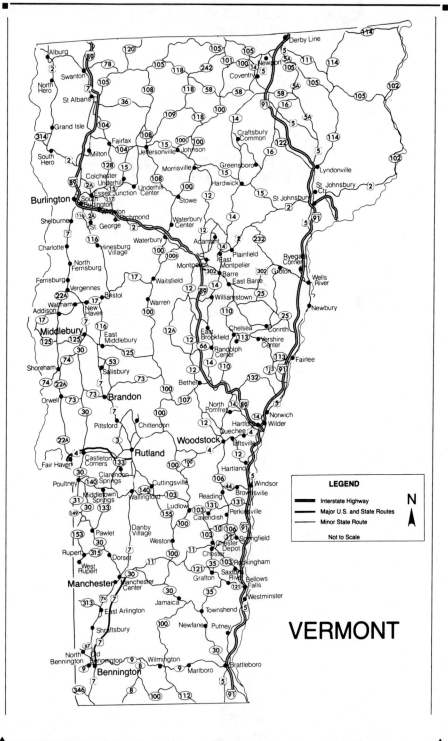

VERMONT

LEGEND

Interstate Highway
Major U.S. and State Routes
Minor State Route

Not to Scale

N

ADDISON

OLD STONE HOUSE ANTIQUES
Old Stone House Rd Rte 22A, 05491
(802)759-2134   **36 44 63**

Choice furniture, glass, china, Orientals, primitives & large selection of glazed pottery. *Hours:* All year 9-5 by chance/appt. *Assoc:* VADA. Walter Washburn *Park:* On site. *Loc:* 1 MI N of Addison 4 Corners and 12 MI W of Middlebury.

BARRE

ARNHOLM'S ANTIQUES
891 N Main St, 05641
(802)476-5921   **47**

Antique & estate jewelry. *Est:* 1940. *Hours:* BY APPT ONLY. *Assoc:* AAA VADA. Rachel Arnholm *Park:* On site. *Loc:* On Rte 302 between Barre & Montpelier.

BARTON

THE WEE SHOP
Pleasant St, 05822
(802)525-6534

An old red barn full of interesting antiques. *Hours:* Year round by chance/appt CLOSED SUN. *Assoc:* VADA. Elizabeth G Lewis

BELLOWS FALLS

ARCH BRIDGE BOOKSHOP
142 Westminster St 2nd fl, 05101
(802)463-9395   **13**

Specializing in WW II, American West, Civil War, biographies & history. *Hours:* By chance/appt. *Size:* 6,000 books. *Assoc:* VABA. Barbara Whitehead *Park:* Nearby. *Loc:* Westminster St is Rte 5, S end of Bellows Falls Village.

BENNINGTON

FOUR CORNERS EAST INC
307 North St, 05201
(802)442-2612   **37 38 59**

Constantly changing stock of fine American antiques, including furniture, paintings, rugs & accessories. *Est:* 1973. *Serv:* Appraisal, shipping. *Hours:* Daily 10-5 CLOSED TUE. *CC:* AX/MC/V. *Assoc:* AADLA VADA. Douglas L Millay *Park:* On site.

NEW ENGLANDIANA
121 Benmont Ave, 05201
(802)447-1695   **13**

Antiquarian books: Americana, biography & autobiography, genealogies, history, religion, religion, theology & social sciences. *Pr:* $1–100. *Est:* 1961. *Serv:* Catalog $2 for 4 issues. *Hours:* Mon & most weekdays 8-4:30. *Size:* 7,500 books. *Assoc:* VABA. Roger D Harris *Park:* In front. *Loc:* From US Rte 7 take River St between A&P & Mazda dealer 2 blocks to shop on corner of Benmont Ave.

NOW AND THEN BOOKS
439 Main St, 05201
(802)447-1470   **13**

General line of used & out-of-print books featuring cookbooks & children's. *Hours:* Wed-Sat 11-4, Mon-Tue by chance. *Assoc:* VABA. Frances Stockman *Loc:* Rte 9, 1 block E of US Rte 7.

BRANDON

BRANDON ANTIQUES
Country Club Rd & Rte 73E, 05733
(802)247-3026   **34 37 80**

19th C American formal & country furniture, specializing in cannonball beds, textiles, chests & cupboards. Folk art for the knowledgeable. *Est:* 1963. *Hours:* Most days 10-5, call ahead. *Assoc:* VADA. Warren Kimble *Park:* On site. *Loc:* 1 1/2 MI from ctr of town, across from 2nd hole of Neshobe Golf Course.

H GRAY GILDERSLEEVE ANTIQUES
57 Park St, 05733
(802)247-6684   **34 65**

Primitives, folk art & the unusual. *Est:* 1960. *Hours:* BY APPT. *CC:* MC/V. *Loc:* Park St-Rte 73: 1/2 block from the Brandon Inn.

KENNEDY'S ANTIQUES
2143 Towne Farm Rd, 05733
(802)247-0047   **28 44 67**

A selection of pattern glass, art glass, stoneware, furniture, quilts & Bennington ware. *Hours:* All year by chance/appt. *Loc:* 3 1/2 MI N of Brandon, 1st R after Sea Shell City, go 1/2 MI then R again, 2nd house on L - Call for better directions.

NUTTING HOUSE ANTIQUES
40 Park St Rte 73E, 05733
(802)247-3302   **27 34 80**

Country & early American furniture - refinished or original surface, folk art, textiles & decorative accessories. *Pr:* $60–3000. *Est:* 1984. *Serv:* Appraisal, restoration, shipping. *Hours:* Year round most days 10-5. *CC:* MC/V. *Assoc:* VADA. Pamela Laubscher *Park:* On site. *Loc:* Rte 7 to 73E.

BRATTLEBORO

BLACK MOUNTAIN ANTIQUE CENTER
Rte 30, 05301
(802)254-3848   **{GR50}**

Furniture, glassware, china, stoneware, milk bottles, books, ephemera, tools & jewelry. *Hours:* Daily 10-5. Charles Stokes *Park:* On site. *Loc:* 2 MI N of downtown Brattleboro on Rte 30.

BRATTLEBORO BOOKS
34 Elliot St, 05301
(802)257-0177

Antiquarian books: general stock history, literature, mythology, folklore, militaria, children's. *Hours:* Mon-Sat 9:30-6. *Size:* 20,000 books. *Assoc:* VABA. Dwayne Whitehead *Park:* Nearby. *Loc:* In the center of town.

PAUL LAWTON & SON
PO Box 551, 05301
(802)254-8969   **4 8**

Twice weekly sales in the gallery Wednesday evening & Saturday except when Saturday sale is on another site. Annual antique auction on Labor Day. No buyer's premium. *Est:* 1951. *Serv:* Appraisal, auction house, accept mail/phone bids. Terry W Lawton

BRISTOL

TERRY HARPER BOOKSELLER
117 North St Box 37, 05443
(802)453-5088   **13**
Americana, historical, rare & scarce books with emphasis on condition. *Serv:* Appraisal, purchase estates. *Hours:* BY APPT. *Size:* Medium. *CC:* MC/V. *Assoc:* VABA. *Park:* On site. *Loc:* Shop at Jct of Rtes 7 & 116, call for directions to home.

BURLINGTON

ASHLEY BOOK COMPANY
26 Summit Ridge, 05402
(802)863-3854   **13**
Press books & fine printing, illustrated books, American & English literature, books about books & skiing. *Hours:* BY APPT ONLY. *Assoc:* VABA. George & Gloria Singer

BYGONE BOOKS
31 Main St, 05401
(802)862-4397   **13 66**
General stock of used & out-of-print books & some prints. *Serv:* Appraisal, search service. *Hours:* Mon-Sat 9:30-5:30. *Size:* 11,000 books. *Assoc:* VABA. Sallie Soule *Park:* On site. *Loc:* Two doors from Battery St.

CODEX BOOKS
148 Cherry St, 05401
(802)862-6413   **13**
Specialzing in out-of-print & scarce books on philosophy, religion, the occult & literary criticism. *Serv:* Appraisal, catalog, search service. *Hours:* Mon-Sat 10:30-5:30, Sun By APPT. *Size:* 12,000

books. Don Norford *Park:* On site. *Loc:* Downtown Burlington, across from post office.

CONANT CUSTOM BRASS INC
270 Pine St, 05401
(802)658-4482   **16 50 71**
A mix of fine brass & copper antiques & unusual one-of-a-kind treasures all set in a bustling workshop. Stock three hundred restored antique light fixtures & hundreds of glass shades. *Pr:* $5–5000. *Est:* 1979. *Serv:* Custom brass, brochure, consultation, repairs, reproduction, restoration. *Hours:* Mon-Fri 9-5 Sat 12-4. *Size:* Large. *CC:* MC/V. Stephen W Conant *Park:* On site. *Loc:* Rte 89N Exit 14W: W on Rte 2 into Burlington, cross Church St, St. Paul St & turn L on Pine St, 2 blocks down.

COLIN & ELIZABETH DUCOLON
41 University Terr, 05401
(802)863-1497   **44 80**
Early textiles, flint glass & rural paint. *Hours:* BY APPT. *Assoc:* VADA.

JAMES FRASER
309 S Willard St, 05402
(802)658-0322   **13**
Antiquarian books: Stock Market & Wall Street, economics, business, political, social & cultural history. *Hours:* BY APPT ONLY. *Assoc:* ABAA. James Fraser

TAILOR'S ANTIQUES
68 Pearl St, 05401
(802)862-8156   **44 65**
Primitives, glass, china & art. *Est:* 1958. *Hours:* Mon-Fri 8-5 Sat 8-4. *Park:* In front. *Loc:* Near the post office.

WEBB & PARSONS NORTH
147 Main St 2nd Fl, 05401
(802)658-5123   **34**
Contemporary, folk & outsider art.
Hours: Mon-Sat 10-5:30. *Loc:* 2 doors
down from the Flynn Theater.

CASTLETON CORNERS

OLD HOMESTEAD ANTIQUES
Rte 4A, 05732
(802)468-2425   **21 44 65**
Lamps, Oriental rugs, glass, china,
primitives, vintage clothing, choice
linens, some furniture & early
Americana. *Est:* 1963. *Serv:* Consult-
ation. *Hours:* May-Nov by chance/appt
CLOSED SUN. *Assoc:* VADA. Alma
Gibbs Donchian

CHERLOTTE

MILES PAINTINGS & ANTIQUES
RR1 Box 1518 Churchill Rd, 05445
(802)425-3711   **30 34 59**
Paintings, American Indian items,
decoys & folk art. *Serv:* Appraisal, consultation. *Hours:* Year round by
chance/appt. Jason Miles *Loc:* 2 MI S of
Shelburne Vil 1/10 mile E off Rte 7 on
Curchill Rd.

CHESTER

1828 HOUSE
Rte 103 N of Chester, 05143
(802)875-3075   **35 36 39**
Wide selection of quality 18th & 19th C
English & French country furniture en-
hanced by elegant decorative accessories
attractively displayed in an 18th C carriage shed. *Pr:* $25–5000. *Serv:*
Brochure. *Hours:* May 15-Oct 15 daily
10-5 BY APPT ONLY. *CC:* MC/V.
Assoc: VADA. Jane W Thrailkill *Park:*
On site. *Loc:* Between Chester & Ludlow.

WILLIAM AUSTIN'S ANTIQUES
Rte 103 Maple St, 05143
(802)875-3032   **40**
Large selection of quality country oak
pieces. *Serv:* Shipping. *Hours:* Daily 9-
5. William Smith *Loc:* Int of Rtes 103N
& 11.

**THOMAS MAKON AMERICAN
ANTIQUES**
Rte 103, 05143
(802)875-4246   **1 37**
A variety of authentic early American
antiques. *Est:* 1989. *Hours:* Daily by
chance/appt. *Assoc:* VADA. *Loc:* I-91
Exit 6: 7 MI N on Rte 103 N, 1st R after
Chester General Store then 1/4 MI to
end.

CLARENDON SPRINGS

CLARENDON HOUSE ANTIQUES
Clarendon Springs Rd, 05777
(802)438-2449   **23 28 85**
Country furniture, vintage clothing,
clocks, paintings, rugs & stoneware. *Est:*
1973. *Serv:* Appraisal, purchase estates.
Hours: All year by chance/appt. Tony
Costantino *Loc:* 3 MI S of West Rutland
off Rte 133.

COLCHESTER

MATTESON GALLERY OF ARTS
Prim Rd Rte 127, 05446
(802)862-3422 **36 59 67**
Antiques & art: deco furniture, paintings, prints, quilts, glass, silver, jewelry, tools, clocks & watches, decoys, folk art & collectibles. *Pr:* $25–50000. *Est:* 1971. *Serv:* Appraisal, conservation, custom woodwork, purchase estates, restoration. *Hours:* By chance/appt. *Size:* Medium. David Matteson *Park:* Nearby lot. *Loc:* From Burlington: Rte 127N into Colchester, to Prim Rd. I-89 Exit 16: N on Rtes 2 & 7 to Rte 127 to Prim Rd.

COVENTRY

YESTERYEAR SHOP
Box 58, 05825
(802)754-2129
Antiques & collectibles. *Hours:* May 15-Oct 15 Mon-Sat 10-5 Sun 1-5 & BY APPT. *Assoc:* VADA. Marion C Conway *Park:* On site. *Loc:* Rte 5 Coventry Village.

CRAFTSBURY COMMON

CRAFTSBURY COMMON ANTIQUARIAN
Box 69, 05827
(802)586-9677 **13**
Antiquarian books: maritime, Americana, illustrated, travel & natural history. *Hours:* BY APPT. Ralph Lewis

CUTTINGSVILLE

HAUNTED MANSION BOOKSHOP
Rte 103, 05738
(802)492-3462 **13**
Two floors of an 1880s Victorian: Vermontania, Americana, art, travel, Europe, cookbooks, natural history, antiques, Civil War, New Englandiana, illustrated books & juveniles. *Pr:* $3–300. *Est:* 1968. *Serv:* Appraisal, brochure, purchase estates. *Hours:* May-Oct Mon-Sat 10-5 or by appt. *Size:* 60,000 books. *Assoc:* VABA. Clint Fiske *Park:* On site. *Loc:* Rte 103, 10 MI S of Rutland.

DANBY

DANBY ANTIQUES CENTER
Main St, 05739
(802)293-9984 **{GR25}**
Eleven rooms & barn filled with 18th & 19th C American country & formal furniture & related accessories, accent on stoneware, folk art, textiles & some architectural pieces. *Pr:* $25–10000. *Est:* 1982. *Serv:* Appraisal, brochure. *Hours:* Apr-Dec Daily 10-5, Jan-Mar Thu-Mon 10-5. *CC:* AX/MC/V. *Assoc:* VADA. Agnes Franks *Park:* On site. *Loc:* 13 MI N of Manchester, 1/4 MI off Rte 7, watch for state signs.

MAIN STREET ANTIQUES CENTER
Main St, 05739
(802)293-9919 **{GR10}**
18th, 19th & 20th C furniture, decorative accessories, antique linens & lace, & collectibles. *Est:* 1987. *Hours:* Daily 10-5. *CC:* MC/V. *Park:* In front. *Loc:* On old Rte 7 in Danby.

DERBY LINE

CARRIAGE HOUSE ANTIQUES
29 Main St, 05830
(802)873-3606   **16 36 81**

Furniture, glass, Oriental rugs, china, paintings, prints, copper, tools, primitives & treen. *Est:* 1987. *Serv:* Appraisal. *Hours:* May-Oct 15 daily 10-5; Oct 16-Apr daily 12-5. *CC:* MC/V. Sarah M Noble *Park:* On site. *Loc:* In the house.

TRANQUIL THINGS
43 Main St, 05830
(802)873-3454   **13**

General stock of used & out-of-print books & some antiques. *Hours:* Usually open afternoons or by chance/appt. *Assoc:* VABA. Richard Wright *Loc:* I-91 Derby Line Exit: L at the T (Castle Ave), which becomes Main St.

DORSET

THE ANGLOPHILE ANTIQUES
The Old Schoolhouse Rte 30, 05251
(802)362-1621   **52 63 77**

Large stock of authentic English antiques in an old schoolhouse, emphasis on 18th & 19th C china, jewelry, amber, tortoise, silver, brass & copper, tea caddies & boxes & large selection of miniature china. *Pr:* $20–2000. *Hours:* Daily 10-5; Nov-May by appt. *Size:* Medium. *Assoc:* VADA. Dorothy R Jones *Park:* On site. *Loc:* Rte 30, 4 MI N of Manchester Ctr, to Jct of Rte 7A (Main St), 2 MI S of Dorset Village Green.

MARIE MILLER
Rte 30, 05251
(802)867-5969

Specializing in in antique quilts with over 200 in stock. *Hours:* Seven days 10-5. *Assoc:* VADA. *Loc:* 4 1/2 MI N of Manchester.

VIRGINIA POPE INC
Box 537, 05251
(802)867-5945   **29 34 59**

American & European folk art, portraits & decorative arts. *Hours:* BY APPT ONLY. *Assoc:* NHADA.

EAST ARLINGTON

EAST ARLINGTON ANTIQUE CENTER
Old Mill Rd, 05252
(802)375-9607   **{GR25}**

Country & formal furniture, primitives, Oriental rugs, paintings, jewelry, china & glass. *Est:* 1987. *Serv:* Appraisal, purchase estates. *Hours:* Year round daily 9-5. *CC:* MC/V. Phil Elwell *Park:* On site. *Loc:* Located in the Post Office Building across from the Candle Mill Village between Rtes 7 & 7A.

GEBELEIN SILVERSMITHS
Box 157, 05252
(802)375-6307   **77**

Antique silver including American 18th C, Arts & Crafts & Chinese export. *Hours:* BY APPT. *Assoc:* VADA. Dave Thomas *Park:* Nearby.

EAST BARRE

FARR'S ANTIQUES
Rte 110, 05649
(802)476-4308   **27 44 65**
Country & Victorian furniture, glass, china, primitives, baskets, tools & clocks. *Est:* 1967. *Hours:* All year by chance. *CC:* MC/V. *Assoc:* VADA. Edward Farr *Loc:* 4 MI E of Barre on Rte 302, turn R, 1/4 MI on Rte 110.

EAST MIDDLEBURY

MIDDLEBURY ANTIQUE CENTER
Rtes 7 & 116, 05740
(802)388-6229   **{GR56}**
Over 50 dealers displaying a large inventory of furniture & smalls changing weekly. *Est:* 1987. *Serv:* Brochure. *Hours:* Year round daily 9-6. *Size:* Large. *CC:* MC/V. Francis/Dianne Stevens *Park:* On site. *Loc:* Halfway between Rutland & Burlington, on corner of Rtes 7 & 116.

EAST MONTPELIER

JEFFREY R CUETO ANTIQUES
Murray Rd RD 1 Box 125, 05651
(802)223-5175   **1 37**
American furniture, country & formal, clocks & country store items. *Pr:* $50–5000. *Serv:* Appraisal, purchase estates. *Hours:* By chance/appt. *Size:* Medium. *Assoc:* NAWCC VADA. *Park:* On site. *Loc:* Take R on Towne Hill Rd at top of Main St, 1/2 MI, L on Murray Rd for 1/2 MI, red farmhouse.

EAST POULTNEY

RIVERS EDGE ANTIQUES
RD 2 Box 1412, 05764
(802)287-9553   **66 59 78**
Paintings, American & European sporting & miscellaneous prints, books, china, linen, quilts, jewelry & furniture. *Hours:* May-Oct Thu-Sat 10-5 else by chance/appt. Charlotte & Wm Osbourne *Loc:* On the Gorge in E Poultney, 1/10 MI S of Rte 140.

ESSEX JUNCTION

ALL THINGS CONSIDERED
16 Lincoln St Rte 2A, 05452
(802)878-8166   **1 36 37**
Uncluttered browsing featuring oak, Victorian & primitive furniture, glassware, china, watches, clocks, prints, collectibles & a large selection of quality mid-century furniture. *Pr:* $10–1500. *Est:* 1984. *Serv:* conservation, custom woodwork, purchase estates, repairs & more. *Hours:* Mon-Fri 10-5, Sat 9-5, Sun 11-3. *Size:* Medium. *CC:* DC/MC/V. Sam & Fran Kinghorn *Park:* In front, on site. *Loc:* 400 feet N of the Five Corners in Essex Junction.

FAIR HAVEN

BRICK HOUSE
45 S Main St Rte 22A S, 05743
(802)265-3614   **21**
Ten rooms of antiques from local estates. *Hours:* Tue-Sun 10-5 or by appt. William Barsalow

FOUNDATION ANTIQUES
148 N Main St, 05743
(802)265-4544 **34 65**
Specializing in Quimper, graniteware &
art pottery in 3 separate display areas. *Pr:*
$1–10000. *Serv:* Appraisal, consultation,
purchase estates, brochure, catalog.
Hours: Apr 15-Jan 15 Daily 9-5 appt
advised. *Size:* Large. *Assoc:* VADA.
Stephen G Smith *Park:* On site. *Loc:*
Approx 300 yds N of Village Green.

FAIRFAX

THE BOOKSTORE
223 Main St, 05454
(802)849-2209 **13**
General stock of used books & paperbacks, some rare & out-of-print. *Est:*
1979. *Hours:* May 15-Oct 15 by
chance/appt. *Assoc:* VABA. Arthur &
Louise Wold *Park:* In front. *Loc:* I-89
Exit 18: 6 MI.

THE CAT'S MEOW ANTIQUES
Rte 104, 05454
(802)849-6065 **7 47 85**
Small, friendly shop specializing in Art
Deco, vintage clothing & accessories,
costume jewelry, small collectibles,
Oriental, cat collectibles & dolls. *Pr:*
$10–500. *Est:* 1984. *Hours:* Most week-
days, weekends & winter by
chance/appt. Bonnie Groves *Park:* On
site. *Loc:* I-89 Exit 18: Rte 7 to Rte 104A,
6 MI turn R toward Fairfax Village, 2 MI
at bottom of hill on R, watch for sign.

FAIRLEE

EDITH M ACKERMAN
4 Woodland Terr, 05045
(802)333-4457 **44**
Depression, Heisey, Fostoria &
Cambridge glass. *Serv:* Mail order.
Hours: By chance/appt. *Assoc:* Nat'l
Heisey. *Loc:* Off Lake Morey Rd.

FERRISBURG

TWIN MAPLES ANTIQUES
RR 1 Box 167, 05456
(802)877-3486 **63**
China, glass & prints specializing in Buf-
falo Pottery. *Est:* 1980. *Hours:* Daily by
chance/appt. Roger & Agnes Northon
Loc: 3/4 MI S of Dakin Farm on Rte 7, 3
1/2 MI N of Rte 22A, Vergennes.

GRAFTON

GABRIELS' BARN ANTIQUES
Inn @ Woodchuck Hill Farm, 05146
(802)843-2398 **34 36 65**
A carefully selected inventory of country
furniture & unusual decorative accessories: decorated stoneware, pottery,
decoys, treen, pewter & copper, paintings, gameboards, porcelain & china -
Canton, flow blue, yellowware & spongeware. *Pr:* $25–3500. *Serv:* Appraisal,
brochure, purchase estates, country inn
on premises. *Hours:* May-Oct daily 10-
5. *Size:* Medium. *CC:* MC/V/AX. *Assoc:*
VADA. Anne Gabriel *Park:* In front.
Loc: I-95 Exit 5: Rte 121 W to Grafton,
shop & inn are 2 MI W of village on
Middletown Rd.

GRAFTON GATHERING PLACE
Sylvan Rd, 05146
(802)875-2309   **27 36**
Specializing in period furniture, country pieces & the appropriate accessories. *Hours:* By chance/appt, CLOSED TUE, call ahead suggested in winter. *Assoc:* VADA. Mary Pill *Loc:* I-91 Exit 6: Rte 103 8 MI to Sylvan Rd, 2 1/2 MI to shop.

PICKLE STREET ANTIQUES
Rte 121, 05146
(802)843-2533   **27 28 67**
Country furniture, primitives & a fine selection of quilts. *Hours:* All year by chance/appt. *Assoc:* VADA. Virginia McMahon *Loc:* 1/4 MI E of the Village, ctr of Grafton.

GROTON

STEPHEN JONES ANTIQUES
N End of Lake Groton, 05046
(802)584-3858   **27 33 64**
Country furniture, paintings, accessories, paper goods & post cards. *Hours:* By chance or call ahead.

OLD BOOKS
US Rte 302, 05046
(802)584-3748   **13**
A general stock of antiquarian books. *Hours:* By chance/appt. *Assoc:* VABA. Faye Jordan

HARDWICK

WILLIAM F HILL
Box 15, 05843
(802)472-6308   **8**
Auctions of antiques & estates including on site auctions. No buyer's premium. *Est:* 1957. *Serv:* Accept mail/phone bids, brochure, consultation, purchase estates. *Hours:* Year round daily. *Assoc:* NAA.

OLD FIREHOUSE ANTIQUES
Mill St, 05843
(802)472-6166   **{GR10}**
Pine furniture & quilts in an historic old fire house. *Est:* 1985. *Hours:* Daily 9:30-5, Sat til 4, Sun 12-4. Jean Hanzl *Park:* On site. *Loc:* In town across from the Post Office.

HINESBURG

HAWK'S NEST ANTIQUES & DECOYS
Silver St, 05461
(802)482-2076   **27 30 41**
Specializing in fine American folk art including decoys by well-known carvers, period furniture, accessories, quilts & fabrics. *Hours:* BY APPT ONLY. *Assoc:* NHADA VADA. Loy & Rae Reynolds Harrell *Loc:* 1 MI S of village.

WALKER HOUSE ANTIQUES
Rte 116 Charlotte Rd, 05461
(802)482-3410   **27 65**
Country furniture & accessories, primitives & collectibles. *Hours:* Apr-Oct Sat,Sun, else by chance/appt. Daphne Walker *Loc:* In the village.

JAMAICA

ANTIQUES ANONYMOUS
Rte 30, 05343
(802)874-4207   **24 28 67**
Furniture, crocks, quilts, coins, toys, advertising, political, photos, books & Ver-

mont memorabilia. *Est:* 1979. *Serv:* Appraisal, conservation, purchase estates, repairs. *Hours:* By chance/appt. Andrew Avery *Loc:* 2 houses S of bank.

JEFFERSONVILLE

1829 HOUSE ANTIQUES
Rte 15, 05464
(802)644-2912   {GR20}
Country antiques in a turn-of-the century barn, heated in the winter. *Est:* 1976. *Serv:* Purchase estates, shipping. *Hours:* Mon-Sat 9-5. *Size:* Large. *CC:* MC/V. Richard Hover *Loc:* 2 1/2 MI E of Jeffersonville on Rte 15.

MARY'S GLASS & COLLECTIBLES
RR 1 Box 249, 05464
(802)644-8878   **16 44 48**
Small shop featuring depression & collectible glass, kitchen collectibles, linens, old books, tinware & some small furniture. *Hours:* By chance/appt. Mary Edwards *Park:* On site. *Loc:* Int Rtes 15 & 108: N on Rte 108 1/2 MI, Rte 109, 1st house on L.

JOHNSON

MEL SIEGEL & JUSTIN GALLANTER
Rte 15 W of Johnson Village, 05656
(802)635-7838   **1 40 63**
Country antiques, refinished pine & oak furniture, primitives, majolica, spongeware, Quimper, jewelry, glass, china, tools, advertising & general line. *Pr:* $10–35000. *Est:* 1959. *Serv:* Purchase estates. *Hours:* May-Oct daily 9-5:30. *Size:* Medium. *Assoc:* VADA. *Park:* On site. *Loc:* From Burlington: E on Rte 15.

LUDLOW

LUDLOW ANTIQUE & GIFT CENTER
Rte 103, 05149
(802)228-7335   {GR12}
Furniture, wood stoves, tools, tin books, china, glass silverware, period clothing & jewelry. *Est:* 1986. *Hours:* Year round daily 10-5. *CC:* MC/V. *Park:* On site. *Loc:* 2 MI S of Ludlow.

RED CLOVER ANTIQUES
119 Main St, 05149
(802)228-4333   **27 28 81**
Farmhouse furniture, glass, tools, stoneware & quilts. *Serv:* Repairs. *Hours:* Sat-Sun 9-5. *CC:* MC/V. *Park:* On site. *Loc:* 1/2 MI S of Okemo Mountain Ski Area.

LUNENBERG

ATTIC SHOP ANTIQUES
S Lun Rd, 05906
(802)892-5907   **27**
Specializing in country antiques. *Hours:* May-Nov by chance/appt. *Assoc:* NHADA. Pat Briggs *Loc:* Just off Rte 2, L at PO if headed W; R if from E. 23 MI E of St Johnsbury.

LYNDONVILLE

GREEN MOUNTAIN BOOKS & PRINTS
100 Broad St, 05851
(802)626-5051   **13 66**
Antiquarian books: Americana, history, art & antiques. *Serv:* Catalog. *Hours:*

Mon-Thu 10-4 Fri 10-6 Sat 10-1. *Assoc:* VABA. Ralph Secord *Loc:* Corner of Depot & Broad St.

MANCHESTER

ANTIQUES BY JK MEIERS
Rte 7A, 05254
(802)362-3721

An array of interesting & unusual antiques displayed in an old village home. *Hours:* Year round by chance/appt. *Assoc:* VADA. *Park:* RV parking avail.

THE CLOCK EMPORIUM
Highland Ave, 05254
(802)362-3328   **23 32 55**

A choice selection of antique clocks & music boxes on display. *Pr:* $25–4000. *Est:* 1976. *Serv:* One year guarantee, repairs, old toy trains bought & repaired. *Hours:* Tue-Sat 10-5. *CC:* MC/V. Edward H Voigt *Park:* On site. *Loc:* Highland Avenue, near Barnumville.

HOOKED RUG RESTORATION
Box 542, 05254
(802)867-2252   **21 71**

Restoration of hooked rugs, including, backing, binding, repair of tears & holes. *Serv:* Restoration, free estimates. *Hours:* BY APPT ONLY. Linda Eliason

JOHNNY APPLESEED BOOKSHOP
Main St Rte 7, 05254
(802)362-2458   **13**

Regional Americana, fine & rare bindings, first editions, American history, hunting, fishing & angling & rare books. *Hours:* All year daily 9:30-5. *Assoc:* VABA. Frederic F Taylor *Loc:* In the village.

PARAPHERNALIA ANTIQUES
Rte 7A, 05254
(802)362-2421   **17 38 77**

Continental antiques, collectibles, jewelry, furniture, bronzes, silver bibelots & perfume bottles. *Est:* 1967. *Serv:* Appraisal. *Hours:* Jun-Oct 11:30-6 by chance/appt. *Assoc:* VADA. Anne Alenick *Park:* On site. *Loc:* 1/2 MI S of Manchester Village.

STEVENSON GALLERY
Rte 7 N, 05254
(802)362-3668   **34 59**

Fine art: specializing in American artists & American folk art. *Hours:* Thu-Tue 10-5 never at lunch. *CC:* MC/V. Timothy J Stevenson *Park:* In front. *Loc:* 2 1/2 MI N of Manchester Ctr next to Carriage Trade & 1812 Antique Ctr.

MANCHESTER CENTER

1812 HOUSE ANTIQUE CENTER
Rte 7N, 05255
(802)362-1189   **{GR}**

Items from kitchen, bedroom & parlor to shop, barn & sugarhouse - rag rugs, copper molds, American antiques, pictures, oil paintings, crocks, collectibles, tools, guns & trade cards. *Est:* 1984. *Hours:* Apr-Dec daily 10-5, Jan-Mar Thu-Mon 10-5. *CC:* MC/V. Sara H Symons *Park:* On site. *Loc:* 2 1/3 MI N of Manchester Ctr on Rte 7, next to Enchanted Doll House.

BELLWETHER GALLERY
Rte 7A, 05255
(802)362-4811   **21 43 50**

18th & 19th C country furniture & accessories, quality scrubbed pine, fine reproduction furniture, decorative accessories, dhurries, kilims, rag rugs, baskets & lighting. *Hours:* Mon-Sat 10-5 Sun 11-4. Ann Spencer *Loc:* 1/2 MI S of the village light across from the Jelly Mill.

BREWSTER ANTIQUES
Corner Bonnet & School Sts, 05255
(802)362-1579   **44 47 77**
Antique & estate jewelry, sterling flatware & holloware, china, glass, paintings & small furniture. *Est:* 1945. *Hours:* May-Jan Mon-Sat 10-5 call ahead, else by chance. *Assoc:* VADA. *Park:* Nearby. *Loc:* 1 block W of Rte 7 on Rte 30.

CARRIAGE TRADE ANTIQUES CENTER
Rte 7, 05255
(802)362-1125   **{GR31}**
Decorative glass, porcelain, Victorian & country furniture. *Hours:* Apr-Dec daily 10-5, Jan-Mar Thu-Mon 10-5 & BY APPT. *CC:* MC/V. Tom Kingery *Park:* On site. *Loc:* 2 1/2 MI N of Manchester Ctr on Rte 7.

CENTER HILL PAST & PRESENT ANTIQUES
Center Hill, 05255
(802)362-3211   **{GR23}**
Two large floors of country antiques & furniture (pine, oak, painted), folk art, collectibles, quilts & quality crafts. Furniture restoration & refinishing can be arranged. *Pr:* $2–5000. *Est:* 1980. *Serv:* Custom woodwork, reproduction, restoration. *Hours:* May-Dec daily 10-5, Jan-Apr Fri-Sat 10-5, Sun 11-4 by appt. *Size:* Large. *CC:* MC/V. Jeffrey Metzger *Park:* On site. *Loc:* Located on Center Hill, just off Rtes 11/30 & Rte 7.

MANCHESTER FLEA MARKET
Jct Rte 11 & Rte 30, 05255
(802)362-1631   **{FLEA}**
Indoor/outdoor market with antiques, collectibles & other flea market merchandise. Free admission. Auction service runs Thu at 6 on same premises. *Est:* 1970. *Serv:* Catered, space rental starts at $15 for 20'. Reservation required. *Hours:* May-Oct Sat 9-5. *Size:* 35 spaces. *Park:* Free parking. *Loc:* From Manchester Ctr take Bromley Mountain Rd approx 3 MI.

BARBARA B TRASK APPRAISALS
PO Box 1752 Rte 7N, 05255
(802)362-2214   **4 34 59**
Personal property appraisals for insurance, estate settlement, property division, sale. Commission sales on selected items, personal advisory service for purchasers & for sellers. *Serv:* Appraisal, consultation. *Hours:* Apr-Dec by chance/appt. *Assoc:* ASA VADA. *Loc:* Rte 7, N of Manchester Ctr, opposite post office.

MARLBORO

THE BEAR BOOKSHOP
Butterfield Rd, 05344
(802)464-2260   **13**
General line of used & rare books, especially strong in scholarly & academic areas, music, art & literature. *Pr:* $1–500. *Est:* 1975. *Hours:* Spring-Labor Day daily 10-5 Fall by appt. *Size:* 25,000 books. *CC:* MC/V. *Assoc:* VABA. John Greenberg *Park:* On site. *Loc:* 1/2 MI S of Rte 9, 1 MI E of Hogback Mtn, turn is approx 13 MI W of Int of I-91 & Rte 9 in Brattleboro (Exit 2).

MIDDLEBURY

MIDDLETOWN SPRINGS

THE ALLEY BEAT
8 Mill St, 05753
13

General stock of used books, featuring contemporary poetry, women's interests & Buddhist studies. *Hours:* Mon-Sat 10-5, Sun 11:30-4:30 (summer & fall). Garland Martin

BROOKSIDE ANTIQUES
Historic Marbleworks, 05753
(802)388-0312
27 34

Country furnishings, accessories, folk art, pewter, china, crystal, tiin ware, depression glass. *Hours:* Daily 9-5. Joan & Murray Korda

OTTER CREEK OLD & RARE BOOKS
20 Main St, 05753
(802)388-3241
13

Antiquarian books: used books,. *Hours:* Year round Mon-Sat 10-5 CLOSED SUN. *Size:* 20,000 books. Lois B Craig *Park:* Nearby. *Loc:* Next to the post office.

C TILEY ANTIQUES
91 Court St Rte 7, 05753
(802)388-7569
32 53

Toys & looking glasses. *Hours:* Apr-Nov by chance/appt. *Assoc:* VADA. Candy Tiley

VILLAGE STORE OF MIDDLEBURY
Rte 7, 05753
(802)388-6476
16 30 80

Country furniture, primitives, decoys, baskets, wood, iron, brass, tin, linens & textiles. *Hours:* All year by chance/appt. *Assoc:* VADA. Jean Panicucci *Loc:* 4 MI S of Middlebury.

CLOCK DOCTOR INC
South St Rte 133, 05757
(802)235-2440
23

European & American mechanical clocks; mixture of tall clocks, wall clocks & shelf clocks. *Est:* 1976. *Serv:* Restoration, repairs. *Hours:* Year round by chance/appt. *Assoc:* VADA. Alan L Grace *Loc:* 1/4 MI from Int of Rtes 133 & 140.

THE LAMPLIGHTER
South St Rte 133, 05757
(802)235-2306
50

A large selection of old oil lamps & hanging lamps. *Est:* 1976. *Hours:* Jun-Oct Tue-Sun 10-5, else by chance/appt. *Assoc:* VADA. Jim & Janet Webber *Park:* On site.

NIMMO & HART ANTIQUES
South St, 05757
(802)235-2388
29 39 63

17th & 18th C furniture & decorations, pottery & porcelains, oak, walnut, fruitwoods, nice selection of drop leaf tables, chests & chairs. *Est:* 1965. *Serv:* Appraisal. *Hours:* By chance/appt. *Shows:* WAS, ELLIS, PHILA. *Loc:* 1 block from crossroads of village.

OLD SPA SHOP ANTIQUES
Rte 133 & 140 On Village Green, 05757
(802)235-2366
23 36 83

Specializing in the Victorian styles & 19th C formal furniture & diverse accessories. *Est:* 1978. *Hours:* All year 10-5 by chance/appt. *Size:* Medium. *Assoc:* NAWCC VADA. Janna Rupprecht *Park:* On site. *Loc:* From Rutland: Rte 4 to W Rutland then Rte 133W into Middletown Springs.

MILTON

BARSALOW AUCTIONS
15 Main St, 05468
(802)893-2660 **8**

Estate auctions conducted on site throughout Vermont. *Est:* 1958. *Serv:* Appraisal, brochure, consultation, purchase estates, mailing list. *Hours:* Jun-Oct. *Assoc:* NAA VAA. Charles M Barsalow *Park:* On site. *Loc:* Approx 15 MI N of Burlington.

MONTPELIER

GLAD RAGS FINE VINTAGE CLOTHING
6 State St, 05602
(802)223-1451 **47 48 85**

Very select clothing for men, women, infants & children. Fashion accessories & decorative objects 1800-1950. Victorian glass, art glass, pottery, porcelain, textiles. Outrageous & elegant costume & antique jewelry-sterling, Hobe, Haskell, Trifari & more. *Pr:* $5–1000. *Est:* 1988. *Hours:* Year round Mon-Sat 10:30-5:30. *CC:* MC/V. *Loc:* I-89 Exit 8: in downtown Montpelier.

GREAT AMERICAN SALVAGE COMPANY
3 Main St, 05602
(802)223-7711 **5 74**

Nation's largest architectural antiques dealer with 5 showrooms on East Coast. Computerized inventory of over 25,000 pieces in more than 100 categories. Showroom, warehouses & workshops in Montpelier, VT. *Serv:* Custom wood-work, newsletter. *Hours:* Year round Mon-Sat 9-5. *Size:* Huge. *CC:* AX/MC/V. *Park:* On site.

MORRISVILLE

BRICK HOUSE BOOKSHOP
RFD #3, Box 3020, 05661
(802)888-4300 **13**

A wide selection of hardcovers & paperbacks in all subjects. *Pr:* $1–200. *Est:* 1977. *Serv:* Appraisal, brochure, search service. *Hours:* Tue-Sun 10-5 Mon BY APPT. *Size:* 40,000 books. *CC:* MC/V. *Assoc:* VABA. Alexandra Heller *Park:* On site.

NEW HAVEN

COLLECTOR'S EMPORIUM ANTIQUE CTR
Rte 7, 05472
(802)877-2853 **{GR29}**

Furniture, primitives, baskets & collectibles. *Est:* 1985. *Serv:* Purchase estates. *Hours:* Daily 10-5. *Size:* Medium. *Park:* On site. *Loc:* 2 MI S of Vergennes on Rte 7.

NEWBURY

OXBOW BOOKS
Rte 5, 05051
(802)866-5940 **13 33 64**

Vermontania, literature, old post cards, books & paper antiques. *Hours:* Jun 15-Labor Day By chance/appt. *Assoc:* VABA. Peter Keyes

NEWFANE

HEDY JEFFERY ANTIQUES
Rte 30, 05345
(802)365-4507   **63 66 67**
Country & formal furniture, accessories, fine china, quilts, linen, paintings, prints & maps. *Hours:* May-Oct 10-5 most days, all year BY APPT. *Assoc:* VADA. *Loc:* 1/2 MI S of the Common.

NEWFANE ANTIQUES CENTER
Old Rte 30, 05345
(802)365-4482   **{GR20}**
Three floors of quality antiques & collectibles from the 19th & early 20th C. *Pr:* $50–2000. *Est:* 1985. *Hours:* Daily 10-5; Jan-Mar CLOSED WED. *Size:* Large. *CC:* MC/V. *Assoc:* VADA. Anne M King *Park:* On site. *Loc:* 10 MI from Brattleboro, Rte 30, 1st R past Rick's Tavern.

NEWFANE FLEA MARKET
Rte 30, 05345
(802)365-7775   **{FLEA}**
Outdoor market with antiques, collectibles & other flea market merchandise. Free admission. *Est:* 1963. *Serv:* Catered, spaces start at $15. *Hours:* Year round Sun 9-5. *Size:* 150 spaces. *Park:* Free parking. *Loc:* 1 MI N of downtown Newfane.

NU-TIQUE SHOP
Box 35, 05345
(802)365-7677   **13**
Town histories, poetry, novels, medical, Civil War, genealogy & out-of-print books. *Hours:* Sat-Wed 10:30-4:30. *Assoc:* VABA. Don Kent

SCHOMMER ANTIQUES
Rte 30 N Of Village Common, 05345
(802)365-7777   **36 44 66**
19th C furniture, china, glass, prints, table settings & paintings, displayed in a white Victorian listed in the National Register of Historic Houses. *Est:* 1967. *Hours:* Sum & Fall: daily, Win & Spring: by chance/appt. *Assoc:* VADA. William Schommer *Loc:* Next to Vermont National Bank.

SIBLEYS VILLAGE WORKSHOP
Rte 30, 05345
(802)365-4653   **27**
Fine classic & country antiques, featuring tin of the 1800s. *Pr:* $25–500. *Est:* 1982. *Serv:* Custom woodwork, purchase estates, repairs, restoration. *Hours:* Year round Mon-Sun 10:30-4:30. *Size:* Medium. *CC:* MC/V. Alta Sisley *Park:* In front. *Loc:* 2 MI S of Newfane Village on Rte 30.

NORTH BENNINGTON

J JOHNSON NATURAL HISTORY BOOKS
RD 1 PO Box 513, 05257
(802)442-6738   **13**
Antiquarian books relating to natural history, birds, botany, zoology, travels & explorations. *Hours:* BY APPT ONLY. *Assoc:* ABAA. Betty Johnson

NORTH FERRISBURG

MARTIN HOUSE ANTIQUE CENTER
Corner of Rte 7 & Hollow Rd, 05473
(802)425-2874   **{GR15}**
Eleven rooms & 3 barns country: furni-

ture, primitives, art glass, sporting collectibles, country Irish pine furniture, linens, toys, jewelry, folk art & architectural antiques. *Serv:* Full time cabinet maker, dismantle homes/barns. *Hours:* Apr-Oct Daily 10-6, Win: Tue-Sun 10-5 CLOSED JAN 1-15. *Size:* Huge. Carol Anderson *Park:* On site. *Loc:* 4 MI N of Vergennes, 12 MI S of Shelburne.

NORTH POMFRET

R H ADELSON ANTIQUARIAN BOOKS
HC69 Box 23, 05053
(802)457-2608   13
Antiquarian books: voyages, travel & exploration, Pacific region, Americana, children's, Africa & illustrated. *Serv:* Appraisal, brochure, catalog, purchase estates. *Hours:* BY APPT ONLY. *Assoc:* ABAA VABA. Richard Adelson

NORWICH

LILAC HEDGE BOOKSHOP
Main St, 05055
(802)649-2921   13
Antiquarian books: many in arts & literature. *Hours:* Thu-Sun 10-5 Mon-Wed by chance/appt. *Size:* 9,000 books. *Assoc:* VABA. Robert Ericson *Loc:* 1 MI from Dartmouth College, across from the Norwich Inn.

OLD BENNINGTON

ANTIQUE CENTER AT OLD BENNINGTON
60 West Rd Rte 9, 05201
(802)442-4801   {GR26}
From Oriental to country: furniture, china, glass, paintings, pottery, porcelain, brass, primitives & folk art. *Hours:* Daily 9:30-5:30. *CC:* AX/MC/V. Cathy Rathbun *Loc:* 1/2 MI S from Bennington Museum at Camelot Village.

ORWELL

HISTORIC BROOKSIDE FARMS ANTIQUE
Rte 22A, 05760
(802)948-2727   {GR}
Country furnishings, accessories, folk art, pewter, china, crystal, tin ware, depression glass, wooden ware, prints, quilts, farm tools, paintings, 17th, 18th & early 19th C English furniture & early lighting. *Est:* 1983. *Serv:* Appraisal, purchase estates. *Hours:* Always open. *Assoc:* VADA. Joan & Murray Korda *Park:* On site. *Loc:* 1 1/4 MI S of Rte 73.

PAWLET

EAST WEST ANTIQUES
Rte 30, 05761
(802)325-3466   36 42 60
Located in an old, charming barn, extensive collection of southeast Asian antiques & artifacts as well as Irish scrubbed pine. *Est:* 1986. *Hours:* Jun-Sep 13 daily by chance/appt; CLOSED MON. *Size:*

Huge. *CC:* MC/V. *Park:* On site. *Loc:*
Outside of Manchester (15 MI), take Rte
30 N to Pawlet.

PITTSFORD

**ART INTERIORS
ANTIQUES-PITTSFORD**
Rte 7, 05763
(802)483-6766   **59 80 81**

Featuring a wide selection of paintings,
furniture, Orientalia, tools, glass, fabric
& accessories. *Hours:* Wed-Sat 10-5 or
by chance/appt. *Loc:* Just N of Rutland
on Rte 7, across from the library.

**COUNTRY BARN ANTIQUE
CENTER**
Rte 7, 05763
(802)483-9409   **{GR35}**

Authentic 18th C post & beam barn with
glass, used furniture, china, primitives &
collectibles. *Hours:* Daily 9-6. *CC:*
MC/V. Jim Owen *Park:* On site. *Loc:*
Furnace Brook Marketplace, 7 MI N of
Rutland.

IRON HORSE ANTIQUES INC
RFD 2 Box 245 B, 05763
(802)483-2111   **8 65 81**

Specializing in antique tools & books on
tools, with 2 absentee auctions per year.
Pr: $5–3000. *Est:* 1970. *Serv:* Appraisal,
auction, publisher of The Fine Tool
Journal. *Hours:* Jun-Dec Mon-Sat 10-5
Sun 12-5, Jan-May Fri-Sun 10-5. *Size:*
Medium. *CC:* MC/V. *Assoc:* MADA.
Park: On site. *Loc:* Rte 7, 4 MI N of
Rutland at Int Rte 4 E & 7, opposite
Sawdi's Steak House.

PITTSFORD GREEN ANTIQUES
Box 428, 05763
(802)483-6221   **{GR}**

Porcelain, glass, paintings, prints, linens,
jewelry, silver, books & furniture. *Serv:*
Purchase estates. *Hours:* Mon-Sat 9:30-
5:30 Sun 12-5 CLOSED WED. *CC:*
MC/V. Lynne Cleveland *Park:* On site.
Loc: Call for directions.

PLAINFIELD

THE COUNTRY BOOKSHOP
RFD #2 Box 1260, 05667
(802)454-8439   **13**

Out-of-print & scarce books, books on
bells & folk culture. *Serv:* Appraisal,
catalogs. *Hours:* By chance/appt. *Assoc:*
VABA. Benjamin Koenig *Loc:* Turn off
Rte 2 at the blinker, located beside the
church.

POULTNEY

DEN OF ANTIQUITY
Furnace St, 05764
(802)287-9914   **40 53 63**

Oak furniture, mirrors, glass, china & oil
lamps. *Est:* 1985. *Hours:* Mar-Dec Mon-
Sun 10-6 CLOSED JAN,FEB. Ted
Bachman *Loc:* On Rte 30 in Poultney.

THINGS OF YESTERYEAR
63 Main St, 05764
(802)287-5202

A wide variety of antiques & collectibles.
Est: 1984. *Hours:* Jul-Labor Day Mon-
Sat 9-5 else Tue-Sat 9-5 CLOSED JAN-
MAR 15. *CC:* MC/V. Jo Trombley *Park:*
On site. *Loc:* Rte 30 into Poultney, R at
light, on the R.

PUTNEY

UNIQUE ANTIQUE
Main St Rte 5, 05346
(802)387-4488   **11 13 33**
Antiquarian books, maps, prints, original
art, photography, ephemera & a small
inventory of unusual antiques. *Pr:* $10–
5000. *Est:* 1977. *Serv:* Appraisal, purchase estates. *Hours:* By chance/appt.
Assoc: AHPCS ESA VABA VADA.
Jonathan Flaccus *Park:* On site. *Loc:* I-
91 Exit 4: 7 MI N of Brattleboro.

QUECHEE

ANTIQUES COL. AT WATERMAN HOUSE
Rte 4, 05059
(800)272-7489   **{GR150}**
Three floors of quality antique furniture,
art, decorative accessories & a wide
variety of choice collector's items in a
unique refurbished antique farmhouse
complex. *Pr:* $25–25000. *Est:* 1990.
Serv: Appraisal, brochure, consultation.
Hours: Daily 10-5, call ahead advised
during Mar-Apr. *Size:* Large. *CC:*
AX/MC/V. Susan G Saiderman *Park:* In
front. *Loc:* I-89 N Exit 1: W on Rte 4 to
Int of Waterman Hill Rd in Quechee, 4
MI on R.

PEDLER'S ATTIC
Rte 4, 05059
(802)296-2422   **40 42 84**
Oak & pine furniture, glass, wagon
wheels, sleighs & cupboards. *Serv:* Stripping & refinishing. *Hours:* Tue-Sun 9-6.
Loc: By Quechee Gorge.

QUECHEE BOOKS
Rte 4 at I-89 Box 597, 05059
(802)295-1681   **13**
Antiquarian books: Americana, militaria,
sciences, history, social science & New
England. *Hours:* Daily 9:30-5:30, even-
ings in summer. *Size:* 25,000 books. *CC:*
MC/V. *Assoc:* VABA. Ian Morrison &
Duane Whitehead *Park:* On site. *Loc:*
I-89N Exit 1: 1 MI, I-89S Exit 1: 100
yds.

TIMBER VILLAGE ANTIQUE CENTER
Rte 4, 05059
(802)295-1550   **{GR300}**
Antiques, collectibles, furniture, glass,
china, porcelain, primitives, paintings,
prints & quilts. *Pr:* $1–5000. *Est:* 1985.
Hours: May 26-Oct 9:30-5:30 daily,
Nov-Apr 10-5 daily. *CC:* AX/MC/V.
Park: On site. *Loc:* I-91 Exit 10: 6 MI on
Rte 4; I-89 Quechee Exit 2 MI on Rte 4.

RANDOLPH CENTER

PAGE JACKSON ANTIQUE GALLERY
Ridge Rd, 05061
(802)728-5303   **27 63 66**
Country & formal furniture & acces-
sories, original prints, Navajo rugs &
American art pottery. *Hours:* All year by
chance. *Assoc:* VADA. *Loc:* I-89 Exit 4: 2
MI N of Randolph Ctr on Ridge Road.

READING

LIBERTY HILL ANTIQUES
Rte 106, 05062
(802)484-7710   **27 81**
Country furniture refinished or as-

found, accessories & woodworking tools.
Hours: May 15-Oct. *Assoc:* VADA.
James & Susan Mulder *Loc:* S of Mill
Brook Antiques.

MILL BROOK ANTIQUES
Rte 106, 05062
(802)484-5942   **27 28 37**
Country shop & barn filled with furni-
ture, primitives, stoneware & china.
Hours: All year by chance/appt. *Assoc:*
VADA. Nancy Stahura *Loc:* 11 MI S of
Woodstock.

YELLOW HOUSE ANTIQUES
Rte 106, 05062
(802)484-7799   **1 67 76**
A small shop of fine Shaker, 18th & early
19th C American furniture, decorative &
folk art, with an emphasis on provincial
New England forms & museum-quality
community Shaker pieces. *Serv:* Consultation, purchase estates. *Hours:* By
chance/appt. *Size:* Medium. *Assoc:*
NHADA VADA. Elizabeth/James Har-
ley *Park:* On site. *Loc:* 10 MI S of the
Woodstock Green, on the E side of Rte
106.

RICHMOND

**VINCENT J FERNANDEZ
ORIENTAL RUG**
Rte 2, 05477
(802)434-3626   **21**
New, used, semi-antique & antique
Oriental rugs, including Persian,
Turkish, Caucasian, Turkoman, Pakis-
tani, Indian & Chinese. Also buying &
selling, expert cleaning & mothproofing
& a general line of antiques. *Pr:* $50–
9000. *Est:* 1976. *Serv:* Appraisal, conservation, interior design, purchase estates,
restoration. *Hours:* Appt suggested.

Size: Medium. *Assoc:* NEAA ORRA
VADA. *Park:* On site. *Loc:* On Rte 2, 2
1/2 MI E of Richmond Ctr.

ROCKINGHAM VILLAGE

STEPHEN-DOUGLAS ANTIQUES
Meetinghouse Rd, 05101
(802)463-4296   **1 37**
18th & early 19th C American furniture
& decorative accessories from country
homes for collectors who appreciate
quality. Interesting smalls. *Hours:* APPT
PREFERRED. *Assoc:* NHADA.
Stephen Corrigan *Park:* On site. *Loc:*
I-91 Exit 6: 1 MI.

RUTLAND

THE ANTIQUE CENTER
67-71 Center Street, 05701
(802)775-3215   **{GR45}**
Post cards, baseball cards, Depression,
art & cobalt glass, jewelry & prints, bottles & tins, silver plate, etc. *Est:* 1986.
Hours: Year round Mon-Fri 9:30-5:30
Sat 9:30-5 Sun 12-5. *CC:*
AX/DC/MC/V. Kayce Hinton *Park:* On
street. *Loc:* 2 blocks off Rte 7 in
downtown.

CLARENDON HOUSE ANTIQUES
Woodstock Ave Rte 4 E, 05701
(802)773-6550   **27 34 37**
Two full stories of country & formal fur-
niture, folk art, toys, paintings, Oriental
& hooked rugs, stoneware, silver & glass.
Est: 1989. *Serv:* Appraisal, purchase es-
tates. *Hours:* Mon-Sat 10-4. *CC:* MC/V.
Tony & Bonnie Constantino *Loc:* Rte 4
E, 500 ft past the Rutland Mall.

CONWAY'S ANTIQUES & DECOR
90 Center St, 05701
(802)775-5153   **21 37 63**

Pewter, primitives, silverware, toys, household furnishings, clocks, embroidery, needlework, woven textiles, ceramics, glassware, American, Continental, English & French furniture, dolls, Orientalia, paintings & sculpture & rugs. *Est:* 1956. *Serv:* Appraisal, conservation, repair, refinish upholstery. *Hours:* Mon-Fri 9:30-5 CLOSED AT NOON, Sat til 12 or BY APPT. *CC:* MC/V. *Assoc:* NEAA. Thomas D Conway *Loc:* 1 block W of Rte 7.

EAGLE'S NEST ANTIQUES
53 Prospect St, 05701
(802)773-2418   **32 52 65**

Primitives, fine china, lamps, dolls, kettles, jewelry, silver, bottles, copper & miniatures. *Est:* 1950. *Hours:* All year Sat,Sun by chance. *Assoc:* VADA. James Lemmo *Loc:* 2 short blocks from Rte 7.

FREEMAN JEWELERS
76 Merchants Ave, 05701
(802)773-2792   **4 47 68**

An extensive antique & estate jewelry department, featuring many one-of-a-kind & collectible items. Repairs & restorations done on premises. *Pr:* $25–25000. *Est:* 1890. *Serv:* Annual August estate jewelry extravaganza, appraisal, purchase estates. *Hours:* Mon-Thu, Sat 9:30-5:30 Fri til 9 CLOSED SUN. *CC:* AX/DC/MC/V. *Assoc:* AGS GIA. Ron Marcus *Park:* In front. *Loc:* Downtown Rutland.

PARK ANTIQUES
75 Woodstock Ave Rte 4E, 05701
(802)775-4184   **28 36 65**

Period furniture, primitives, jugs, crocks, glass, china, jewelry, quilts, paintings & folk art. *Est:* 1982. *Serv:* Purchase estates. *Hours:* Tue-Sun 10-5. *CC:* AX/MC/V. *Assoc:* VADA. John Smart *Park:* On site. *Loc:* 1/2 MI from Rte 7, on Rte 4E on the way to Killington.

RUTLAND ANTIQUES
Rte 7, 05701
(802)775-6573

In a 150-year-old Vermont farmhouse, an interesting variety of reasonably-priced, locally-acquired antiques. *Pr:* $5–10000. *Serv:* Appraisal, consultation, purchase estates. *Hours:* Tue-Sat 9-5 Sun 10-5. *Size:* Medium. *CC:* MC/V. *Assoc:* NEAA VADA. Joanna Seward *Park:* On site. *Loc:* Approx 3 MI N of the Jct of Rtes 4 & 7, on Rte 7, red farmhouse on the R.

TRULY UNIQUE ANTIQUES
Rte 4E, 05701
(802)773-7742   **27 84**

Country oak, pine & walnut furniture & accessories. *Serv:* Furniture refinishing. *Hours:* Year round daily 9-6. *CC:* AX/MC/V. Joanne Fratrich *Loc:* 2 1/2 MI E of Jct of Rtes 4 & 7 in Rutland.

TUTTLE ANTIQUARIAN BOOKS INC
26 S Main St, 05701
(802)773-8229   **13 51**

Antiquarian books: genealogies, general & New England Americana, maps, atlases & Orientalia. *Hours:* Mon-Fri 8-5 Sat 8-4. *Assoc:* ABAA VABA. Charles E Tuttle *Loc:* On Rte 7 S.

WALDRON & RHODES FINE JEWELERS
10 Stratton Rd, 05701
(802)747-4500   **4 47**

Fine antique jewelry, master jeweler on premises for repair & restoration of estate jewelry. *Serv:* Estate & insurance appraisals, purchase estates, repair, restoration. *Hours:* Daily 9-6 Wed. *Assoc:* GIA ISA NEAA. John A Waldron Jr CG *Loc:* Off Rte 4 on Stratton Rd.

SALISBURY

SALISBURY FLEA MARKET
Rte 7, 05769
(802)352-4424   **{FLEA}**
Indoor flea market with antiques, collectibles & ephemera. Friday night tailgate auctions Jun-Oct at 6. Free admission. *Est:* 1983. *Serv:* Catered. *Hours:* Daily 10-5. *Size:* 25 spaces. *Park:* Free parking. *Loc:* S of Middlebury.

SAXTONS RIVER

SCHOOLHOUSE ANTIQUES
Rte 121, 05154
(802)869-2332   **1 27 65**
Two floors of country furniture, some refinished & a nice selection of accessories. *Pr:* $10–2000. *Hours:* Daily 9-5 or by chance. *Size:* Medium. *Assoc:* VADA. Faith Boone Sandy Saunders *Park:* On site. *Loc:* 2 1/5 MI W of Saxtons River on Rte 121.

SIGN OF THE RAVEN
Main St Rte 121, 05154
(802)869-2500   **1 59**
Big red barn with fine early American antiques & new gallery showing early & contemporary fine oils, watercolors & prints with exceptional assortment of decorative accessories. *Pr:* $25–25000. *Est:* 1968. *Serv:* Appraisal, brochure. *Hours:* May-Nov by chance/appt. *Assoc:* VADA. Mary Ellen Warner *Park:* On site. *Loc:* 5 MI W of 91 & Bellows Falls on Rte 121.

SHAFTSBURY

THE CHOCOLATE BARN ANTIQUES
Rte 7A, 05262
(802)375-6928   **29 36**
Two floors of antiques, 200 antique chocolate molds used to form Swiss chocolate figures, furniture & decorative accessories in period room settings in 1842 sheep barn. *Est:* 1976. *Hours:* Daily 9:30-5:30. *CC:* MC/V. Lucinda D Gregory *Park:* On site. *Loc:* 8 MI N of Bennington on historic Rte 7A.

TOWN HOUSE ANTIQUES
Rte 7A, 05262
(802)442-5574   **50**

Specializing in 19th & early 20th C lighting & lamps with a general selection of antiques. *Hours:* Fri-Mon 10:30-4 in season. Charles Bollinger *Loc:* Rte 7A N of Bennington.

SHELBURNE

GADHUE'S ANTIQUES
Rte 7, 05482
(802)985-2682   **44 65 80**

Early furniture, glassware, china, textiles & primitives. *Hours:* Win: by chance/appt. *Assoc:* VADA. Rene Gadhue

HARRINGTON HOUSE 1800
Rte 7, 05482
(802)985-2313   **1**

Americana - glass, primitives & books. *Hours:* Jun-Oct by chance. *Assoc:* VADA. Henrietta Panettieri *Loc:* 1/2 MI N of the Shelburne Museum.

SHOREHAM

LAPHAM & DIBBLE GALLERY INC
Main St, 05770
(802)897-5531   **51 59 66**

19th & early 20th C American paintings, prints & maps. *Serv:* Painting conservation. *Hours:* Year round Tue-Sat 9-5. *Assoc:* VADA. Rick Lapham

SOUTH BARRE

COUNTRY LOFT ANTIQUES
Middle Rd, 05670
(802)476-8439   **27**

Country furnishings & accessories in as-found or refinished condition. *Est:* 1984. *Hours:* All year by chance. *Assoc:* VADA. Marilyn J Carbonneau *Park:* On site. *Loc:* 2 1/4 MI S on Rte 14 from Barre.

SOUTH BURLINGTON

ETHAN ALLEN ANTIQUE SHOP INC
1625 Williston Rd, 05403
(802)863-3764   **27 63 66**

American period & country furniture & accessories, china & prints. *Est:* 1939. *Hours:* Daily 10-4:30 Sun BY APPT. *Assoc:* VADA. Nathan E Merrill *Loc:* I-89 Exit 14E: E of Burlington.

SPRINGFIELD

18TH CENTURY DESIGN ASSOCIATES
397 Massey Rd, 05156
(802)885-1122   **5 70 71**

Traditional architecture, reproduction & preservation of antique architecture of America, 1670-1900. Also historic documentation & research, building & site design, antique procurement, contractor directory & supervision of projects, sub-contracting. *Est:* 1980. *Serv:* Catalog ($3), consultation, custom woodwork, interior design, repairs. *Hours:* Mon-Fri 9-6 BY APPT ONLY. Leigh Johnson *Park:* On site. *Loc:* Off

I-91 along the Connecticut River, in Old Massey homestead off Craig Hill Rd, S of the village.

ST ALBANS

PAULETTE'S ANTIQUES
Fairfield Hill, 05478
(802)524-5664   **16 40 44**
Furniture, Victorian, country & oak; cut glass, china, brass - including a variety of candlesticks - iron, clocks, art quilts & linens. *Hours:* Daily 9-5 Sun BY APPT. Marge Paulette *Loc:* I-89 Exit 19: Rte 36E.

ST GEORGE

AJ BELIVEAU BOOKS
Rte 2A Goose Creek Farms, 05495
(802)482-2540   **13**
Antiquarian books: Vermontiana, military & Americana. *Hours:* BY APPT. *Assoc:* VABA.

ST JOHNSBURY

JOHN HALE ANTIQUES
13 Mill St, 05819
(802)748-2231   **27 40 42**
A large 2-story warehouse with furniture "as found" & restored. Constantly changing inventory. Dealers always welcome. *Est:* 1987. *Serv:* Repairs, Restoration. *Hours:* Mon-Sat 9-5 or by chance/appt. *Size:* Medium. *CC:* MC/V. *Park:* On site. *Loc:* I-91 Exit 20: Rte 5 N.

SIGN OF THE DIAL CLOCK SHOP
63 Eastern Ave, 05819
(802)748-2193   **23 71**
Specializing in antique American & European clocks, pocket watches & older wristwatches. *Pr:* $1–7000. *Est:* 1967. *Serv:* Appraisal, repairs, restorations. *Hours:* Mon-Fri 8-5:00 Sat,Sun by appt. *Size:* Medium. *CC:* MC/V. *Assoc:* AWI NAWCC VADA. Richard Diefenbach *Park:* In front. *Loc:* Easter Ave is in the center of St Johnsbury & connects the upper & lower levels.

STOWE

ENGLISH COUNTRY AT STOWE
1 Pond St, 05672
(802)253-4420   **16 42 48**
Country & pine furniture, copper & brass, wooden boxes, linens, prints & toys. *Hours:* Wed-Mon 10:30-4 or by appt. *Assoc:* VADA. Louise Reed

GREEN MOUNTAIN ANTIQUES OF STOWE
Main St, 05672
(802)253-4369   **36 67 77**
Fine line of selected antiques, furniture, primitives, quilts, silver & decorative accessories. *Hours:* Jul-Oct 10-5 daily, Nov-Jun 11-5 CLOSED WED. *Assoc:* VADA. Judy Foregger

SWANTON

RAY & AL'S ANTIQUES
41 Liberty St, 05488
(802)868-4715   **32 48**
Linens, hand lamps, small primitives,

flow blue, doll stands, dolls & accessories. *Hours:* Mon-Sat 10-5 Sun by chance. Eveline Letourneau

TANSY FARM ANTIQUES
Rte 7, 05488
(802)868-2340   **40 42 67**
Pine, oak, primitives, quilts & folk art. Lorraine Raleigh *Loc:* On Rte 7, 1 MI S of Swanton.

TAFTSVILLE

FRASER'S ANTIQUES
Happy Valley Rd, 05073
(802)457-3437   **27 32 34**
Village barn filled with country antiques including baskets, country furniture, quilts, coverlets, samplers, wrought & cast iron, folk art, soft paste, stoneware, yellowware, woodenware, hooked & woven rugs. *Pr:* $25–2500. *Serv:* Show management. *Hours:* All year by chance/appt. *Size:* Medium. *Assoc:* VADA. Bob Fraser *Park:* On site. *Loc:* 3 MI E of Woodstock, just off Rte 4, turn at Taftsville Country Store.

TOWNSHEND

ANTIQUE BOUTIQUE
Rte 30, 05353
(802)365-4631   **48 67**
Quilts, linens, country furniture, & a general line. *Hours:* Year round by chance/appt. *Assoc:* VADA. Joan Russell *Loc:* In the Village.

COLT BARN ANTIQUES
Peaked Mountain Rd, 05353
(802)365-7574   **1 34 65**
A small barn, filled with country furni-

ture & accessories, cupboards, drop leaf tables, chairs, mirrors, unusual folk art & iron tools. *Hours:* Year round daily 9-5. *Size:* Medium. *Assoc:* NHADA VADA. Howard Graff *Park:* In front. *Loc:* 2 MI N of Townshend toward Grafton on Rte 35 follow state signs 2 MI.

A RICHTER GALLERY
Rte 30, 05353
(802)365-4549   **66**
Antique prints including botanicals, etchings, illustrative art. *Est:* 1989. *Serv:* Archival framing. *Hours:* By appt.

TOWNSHEND FLEA MARKET
Townshend Family Park Rte 30, 05353
(802)365-4373   **{FLEA}**
Flea market with antiques, collectibles & other flea market merchandise. Free admission. *Est:* 1984. *Serv:* Catered, picnic tables, space starts at $5 for 20' X 30'. *Hours:* May-Oct Sun 7-6. *Size:* 50 spaces. *Park:* Free parking. *Loc:* 30 MI N of Brattleboro.

VERGENNES

BRADY GALLERIES INC
RR 3, 05491
(802)388-3350   **29 37 59**
19th & 20th C paintings, 18th & 19th C American furniture & accessories. *Hours:* All year Tue-Sat 1-5 & BY APPT. Rosemary Brady

FACTORY MARKETPLACE ANTIQUES
Rte 22A at Kennedy Brothers, 05491
(802)877-2975   **{GR150}**
In a renovated Vermont creamery, silver, glass, tinware, lamps, railroad memorabilia, jewelry, bottles, linens & more. *Pr:* $10–1000. *Est:* 1987. *Hours:*

Apr-Dec daily 9-6, else 10-5. *Size:* Huge.
CC: AX/MC/V. Edwin R Grant *Park:*
On site. *Loc:* 22 MI S of Burlington, Rte
7 to Rte 22A, 1/2 MI S on Rte 22A to
Kennedy Bros on L.

FITZ-GERALDS' ANTIQUES
Rte 7, 05491
(802)877-2539   **23 36 81**
Shop with furniture, tools & clocks &
barn with furniture-as-found. *Hours:*
Mon-Sat by chance/appt CLOSED
SUN. *Assoc:* VADA. G M Fitz-Gerald

WAITSFIELD

RARE & WELL DONE BOOKS
Rte 100, 05674
(802)496-2791   **13**
19th & 20th C first editions, natural history & evolution. *Hours:* BY APPT.
Assoc: VABA. Cathleen G Miller *Loc:*
Across from Bridge St.

THE STORE INC
Rte 100, 05673
(802)496-4465   **37 39**
A wide selection of 19th C American &
British country antiques housed in a
beautiful 1834 Methodist meeting house
with exposed beams & old church windows. *Pr:* $25–7000. *Est:* 1965. *Serv:* In-
terior design. *Hours:* Daily 10-6. *Size:*
Large. *CC:* AX/MC/V. *Assoc:* VADA.
Jacqueline Rose *Park:* In front, nearby
lot. *Loc:* S on Rte 100, large, red bldg on
L.

WALLINGFORD

COUNTRY HOUSE ANTIQUES
Rte 7, 05773
(802)446-2344   **37**
American country & formal furniture &
accessories. *Hours:* All year. *Assoc:*
VADA. Wayne & Eleanor Santwire *Loc:*
1 MI S of Village.

TOM KAYE ANTIQUES LTD
Mooney Rd, 05773
(802)446-2605   **39 56 72**
Importers of fine quality 18th C English
formal & country furniture, specializing
in library & office furnishings, with
marine, medical & scientific instruments. *Hours:* BY APPT ONLY. *Assoc:*
VADA.

WALLINGFORD ANTIQUE
CENTER
Main St Rte 7, 05773
(802)446-2450   **{GR}**
Country primitives, oak, European,
paintings, dolls & collectibles. *Serv:*
Shipping. *Hours:* May-Oct daily 10-5,
Nov-Apr Thu-Sun 10-5, or by appt.
Assoc: VADA. Richard Savery *Loc:* Next
door to shops at 16 S Main.

YANKEE MAID ANTIQUES
Rte 7, 05773
(802)446-2463   **27 65 80**
Early country furniture in original con-
dition & refinished, primitives, baskets,
textiles & appropriate accessories.
Hours: BY APPT. *Assoc:* VADA. Lynne
N Gallipo

WALTHAM

C J HARRIS ANTIQUES
Maple St Extension, 05491
(802)877-3961   **36 65 76**
Furniture in old paint, primitives, baskets, Shaker & folk art. *Hours:* BY APPT. *Loc:* 2 1/5 MI S of Vergennes.

WARREN

WARREN ANTIQUES
Old Rte 100 Box 74A, 05674
(802)496-2864   **32 36 66**
Large selection of restored oak & walnut Victorian furniture, custom mahogany, iron banks & tin toys, Fiestaware, tobacco tins & advertising, framed prints, restored electric lighting & marble sinks. *Hours:* Year round daily 10-5. *Assoc:* VADA. Neal Harrington *Loc:* Off Rte 100 in the Village.

WATERBURY

EARLY VERMONT ANTIQUES
Rte 100N, 05676
(802)244-5373   **{GR20}**
American country furniture & decorative accessories. *Est:* 1985. *Hours:* Year round daily 10-5. *CC:* MC/V. *Loc:* Across from Ben & Jerry's.

SUGAR HILL ANTIQUES
Rte 100 N, 05676
(802)244-7707   **{GR}**
A group shop with furniture & decorative accessories. *Hours:* Tue-Sat 10-5 by chance.

WATERBURY CENTER

SIR RICHARD'S ANTIQUE CENTER
Stowe Rd Rte 100, 05677
(802)244-8879   **{GR}**
American & Victorian furniture, glass, post cards, pottery, quilts, books, dolls, silver, jewelry, stoneware, lighting & Oriental rugs. *Est:* 1967. *Hours:* Daily 10-5. *Size:* Large. Richard Woodard *Park:* On site. *Loc:* I-89 Exit 10: 4 MI toward Stowe.

WEST RUPERT

AUTHENTIC DESIGNS
36 The Mill Rd, 05776
(802)394-7713   **68 69 70**
Meticulously crafted reproduction lighting fixtures of Colonial & early American design in solid brass, maple, pewter & tin. Over 300 models displayed in room settings. Catalog $3. *Pr:* $100–5000. *Serv:* Appraisal, repairs, replication, reproduction, restoration. *Hours:* Daily 9-5 Sat BY APPT. *Size:* Large. *CC:* MC/V. *Assoc:* NEAA. Dan Krauss *Park:* On site. *Loc:* Follow state directional signs.

WESTMINSTER

LARSON'S CLOCK SHOP
Main St Rte 5, 05158
(802)722-4203   **23**
Hundreds of antique clocks in many styles. *Serv:* Shipping, catalog (send SASE). *Hours:* By chance/appt sug-

gested. *Assoc:* NAWCC VADA. Lindy Larson *Loc:* Across from Town Hall in village.

WESTON

FREIGHT WAGON ANTIQUES
The Millyard Main St, 05161
(802)824-6909   **27 34**

Country antiques & furniture, including harvest tables, chairs, tinware & folk art. *Hours:* Daily 10-5. Judy Grant

GAY MEADOW FARM ANTIQUES
Trout Club Rd, 05161
(802)824-6386   **27**

Country & period furniture & accessories. *Hours:* May 15-Oct. *Assoc:* VADA. Harriet Sisson *Park:* In back. *Loc:* Turn at post office on Rte 100, follow signs to the 2nd L, look for decoy in front.

WILLISTON

GREEN MOUNTAIN CLOCK SHOP
73 Essex Rd Rte 2A N, 05495
(802)879-4971   **23 55 71**

Specializing in antique, tower & grandfather clocks & cylinder & disk musical boxes. *Pr:* $100–10000. *Est:* 1974. *Serv:* Appraisal, custom woodwork, repairs, restoration, locator service. *Hours:* Jan-Dec Mon-Fri 9-5 Sat 9-1. *Size:* Medium. *CC:* AX/MC/V. *Assoc:* GMTS NAWCC VADA. Pat Boyden *Park:* On site. *Loc:* I-89 Exit 12: (Williston-Essex Jct), 2 2/3 MI N.

MERRILL'S AUCTION GALLERY
27 James Brown Dr, 05401
(802)878-2625   **8**

Specializing in estate & antique auctions at gallery & on site; under tents during summer season; No buyer's premium. *Est:* 1967. *Serv:* Appraisal, brochure, catalog, consultation, absentee bids accepted. *Hours:* All year BY APPT ONLY. *Size:* Large. *Assoc:* NAA, VAA. Duane E Merrill *Park:* On site. *Loc:* I-89 Exit 12: (Williston/Essex Jct), N on Rte 2A for 2 1/2 MI, L on to James Brown Dr, watch for auction signs.

SIMPLY COUNTRY
Rte 2 Tafts Corner, 05495
(802)879-8681   **40 53**

Refinished furniture, oak, pine & wicker, roll top desks, plant stands, mirrors, floor lamps & country decorating items. *Hours:* Year round Mon-Sat 10-5. *Size:* Medium. *CC:* MC/V. Audrey Chetti *Park:* On site. *Loc:* I-89 Exit 12: 1/5 MI N.

WILMINGTON

PINE TREE HILL ANTIQUES
123A Higley Hill Rd, 05363
(802)464-2922   **27 34**

Quality country furniture, antique accessories, old paint & folk art. *Hours:* Open daily by chance/appt. *Assoc:* VADA. Steve Gerben Bob Buckley *Loc:* 3 MI E of Rte 100.

WILMINGTON FLEA MARKET
Rtes 9 & 100, 05363
(802)464-3345   **{FLEA}**

Outdoor flea market of antiques & collectibles & other flea market merchandise on 10 acres. *Serv:* Space rental $15 Catered. *Hours:* Memorial Day

Weekend through Oct Sat-Sun. *Size:* 100 dealers. Pete & Sally Gore *Park:* Free parking.

WINDSOR

L T HALL APPRAISALS
PO Box 190, 05089
(802)674-9336 **4**
Appraisals of antique furniture, decorative arts for insurance, estate & division of property; also, professional documents prepared. *Est:* 1981. *Hours:* BY APPT ONLY. *Assoc:* ASA VADA. Louise Hall

---

WOODSTOCK

CHURCH STREET GALLERY
4 Church St Rte 4, 05091
(802)457-2628 **36 67 63**
Fine antiques, carefully chosen & arranged - period furniture, mirrors, lamps, porcelain, crystal, art work, accessories, majolica & Quimper. *Pr:* $10–10000. *Est:* 1916. *Hours:* Daily 10-5:30, Sun 12:30-5. *Size:* Medium. *CC:* AX/MC/V. *Assoc:* VADA. Lillian C Phelan *Park:* On site. *Loc:* Just W of the Woodstock Green, on Rte 4, near the churches.

COUNTRY WOODSHED
Rte 12N, 05091
(802)457-2490 **36 65**
New England country furniture, both refinished & original condition & related accessories. *Pr:* $25–1000. *Est:* 1966. *Hours:* Mon-Sat 9-5 by chance/appt. *Size:* Medium. *Assoc:* VADA. Emerson Johnstone *Park:* On site. *Loc:* 2 1/2 MI N from the ctr of town on Rte 12.

LOFTY IDEAS
Rte 4, 05091
(802)457-1922 **27**
Barn full of interesting things from the area, including furniture, tools & smalls. *Hours:* May-Oct weekends or by appt. *Assoc:* VADA. Pia Nichols

PLEASANT STREET BOOKS & EPHEMERA
48 Pleasant St, 05091
(802)457-4050 **9 13 33**
Antiquarian books, baseball cards, ephemera & Vermontiana. *Pr:* $1–1000. *Est:* 1986. *Hours:* Jun-Oct 11-5, Nov-May Thu-Sun 11-5. *Size:* Medium. *CC:* MC/V. *Assoc:* VABA. Harry Saul Jr *Park:* on site. *Loc:* Rte 91, Exit 9, 20 min from Dartmouth College on Rte 4 in Woodstock.

SLOAN'S GREEN GUIDE TO ANTIQUING IN NEW ENGLAND

Indexes

ALPHABETICAL INDEX OF BUSINESS NAMES

125 Benefit Street Antiques, *Providence, RI* 406
1736 House Antiques, *West Chatham, CC* 92
1750 House Antiques, *Sheffield, MA* 315
1753 House Antiques, *Westborough, MA* 337
1774 House Antiques, *Wells, ME* 228
1784 House Antiques, *Canton, CT* 103
1786 House Antiques, *Brookline, NH* 347
1800 House Antiques, Ltd, *Templeton, MA* 328
1812 House Antique Center, *Manchester Center, VT* 427
1828 House, *Chester, VT* 420
1829 House Antiques, *Jeffersonville, VT* 426
1830 House Antiques, *Yarmouth Port, CC* 93
1836 Granite House, *Marlborough, NH* 369
1840 House Antiques, *Norwich, CT* 145
1847 House Antiques, *Pine Meadow, CT* 148
1860 House Of Antiques, *Darien, CT* 110
1895 Shop, *Bernard, ME* 188
18Th Century Design Associates, *Springfield, VT* 438
5 Church Street Antiques, *Mystic, CT* 133
The Old Print Barn, *Meredith, NH* 370
D B Stock Antique Carpets, *Wellesley, MA* 331
A Summer Place, *Guilford, CT* 122
H B Watson Jr & Dorothy Watson, *Wellfleet, CC* 90
Madison, *Great Barrington, MA* 278
Puddle Duck Antiques, *West Boylston, MA* 333
Mac Sonny's Flea Market, *North Reading, MA* 301
John Hale Antiques, *St Johnsbury, VT* 439
Joel Einhorn American Furniture, *Woodbury, CT* 173
A Room With A Vieux, *Brookline Village, MA* 260
A Thousand Words, *Exeter, NH* 353
A To Z Antiques, *Watch Hill, RI* 411
ABC Antiques, *Westfield, MA* 337
ABCDef Bookstore, *Camden, ME* 192
ARK Antiques, *New Haven, CT* 137
Aardenburg Antiques, *Lee, MA* 286
Aardvark Antiques, *Newport, RI* 399
Don Abarbanel, *Ashley Falls, MA* 243
Abington Auction Gallery, *Abington, MA* 240
Able To Cane, *Warren, ME* 228
Acampora Art Gallery, *New Canaan, CT* 134
Accents From The Past, *Center Harbor, NH* 347
Edith M Ackerman, *Fairlee, VT* 424
Acme Antiques, *Hallowell, ME* 202
Charles & Barbara Adams, *Middleboro, MA* 293
R H Adelson Antiquarian Books, *North Pomfret, VT* 432
The Advanced Collector, *West Haven, CT* 165
Agora Collectibles, *Laconia, NH* 365
Arne E Ahlberg, *Essex, CT* 115
Arne E Ahlberg, *Guilford, CT* 122
Edwin C Ahlberg, *New Haven, CT* 137
Albert Arts & Antiques, *Hyannis, CC* 80

Albert Meadow Antiques, *Bar Harbor, ME* 186
Alberts-Langdon Inc, *Boston, MA* 245
Albion Used Books, *Amherst, MA* 240
Janice Aldridge Inc, *Nantucket, CC* 82
Alexander's Jewelry, *Northampton, MA* 301
Alexandria Lamp Shop, *Meredith, NH* 370
Alexandria Wood Joinery, *Alexandria, NH* 345
Alfred Trading Company, *Alfred, ME* 184
Alfred's, *Bristol, RI* 394
All Things Considered, *Essex Junction, VT* 423
All Things Oriental Of Newport, *Newport, RI* 399
Beatrice Brabyn Allen Antiques, *East Providence, RI* 397
The Alley Beat, *Middlebury, VT* 429
Allinson Gallery Inc, *Coventry, CT* 108
Alphabet Books & Antiques, *Andover, MA* 242
Amber Spring Antiques, *Lanesborough, MA* 285
Sheila B Amdur - Books, *Mansfield Center, CT* 130
America's Past, *Stratford, CT* 161
American Art & Antiques Inc, *Swansea, MA* 328
American Classics, *Canaan, NH* 347
American Classics, *Westport, CT* 166
American Country Collection, *Camden, ME* 192
American Decorative Arts, *Northampton, MA* 301
An American Gallery, *Kent, CT* 125
American Marine Model Gallery, *Salem, MA* 311
American Tradition Gallery, *Greenwich, CT* 120
American Worlds Books, *Hamden, CT* 123
Americana Antiques, *Essex, MA* 270
Americana Antiques, *Peabody, MA* 304
Amherst Antiquarian Maps, *Amherst, MA* 240
Amherst Outdoor Antique Market, *Amherst, NH* 345
Amherst Village Antique Shop, *Amherst, NH* 345
Amusement Arts, *Burlington, CT* 102
Anchor & Dolphin Books, *Newport, RI* 399
Anchor Farm Antiques, *Thomaston, ME* 226
Anderson & Sons Shaker Tree, *West Stockbridge, MA* 335
A Mathews Anderson Antiques, *Essex, CT* 115
Bruce W Anderson Antiques, *New Milford, CT* 140
Anderson Gallery, *Keene, NH* 365
Anderson's Antiques Inc, *Hopkinton, NH* 363
Andover Books & Prints, *Andover, MA* 242
Andrews & Andrews, *Belfast, ME* 187
Andy's Book Shop Inc, *Littleton, NH* 367
Hope R Angier, *Wiscasset, ME* 232
The Anglophile Antiques, *Dorset, VT* 422
Anita's Antiquarian Books, *Manchester, NH* 368
Ann Marie's Vintage Boutique, *New Haven, CT* 137
Annex Antiques, *Essex, MA* 270
Another Era, *Saugus, MA* 312
Antique & Folk Art Shoppe, *Somers, CT* 155

Antique Assoc At Joslin Tavern, *West Townsend, MA* 336

Antique Assoc At West Townsend, *West Townsend, MA* 336

Antiques At Sign Of The Bluebird, *Littleton, MA* 288

Antique Books, *Hamden, CT* 123

Antique Boutique, *Townshend, VT* 440

The Antique Center, *Rutland, VT* 435

Antique Center Of Northampton, *Northampton, MA* 301

Antique Center At Old Bennington, *Old Bennington, VT* 432

Antique Center Of Old Deerfield, *Deerfield, MA* 267

Antique Center Of Sheffield, *Sheffield, MA* 315

Antique Center Of Sturbridge, *Sturbridge, MA* 326

Antique Center Of Wallingford, *Wallingford, CT* 162

Antique Clock Repair & Appraisal, *Nashua, NH* 372

The Antique Company, *Brookline Village, MA* 260

Antique Corner, *New Haven, CT* 137

The Antique Exchange Of Sudbury, *Sudbury, MA* 327

Antique Furniture Restoration, *Woodbury, CT* 173

Antique Haven, *Warwick, RI* 410

Antique Ireland Inc, *Boston, MA* 245

Antique Mall At Southborough, *Southborough, MA* 323

Antique Marketplace, *Westfield, MA* 337

Antique Porcelains Ltd, *Boston, MA* 246

Antique Poster Collection Gall., *Ridgefield, CT* 151

Antique Researchers, *Waban, MA* 330

Antique Restoration At Granary, *Lenoxdale, MA* 287

The Antique Shop, *Marblehead, MA* 289

Antique Stop, *Derry, NH* 350

Antique Textile Company, *Hampton Falls, NH* 359

The Antique Warehouse, *Milford, NH* 371

Antique Wicker, *Bernard, ME* 188

Antan Antiques Ltd, *Greenwich, CT* 120

Anthony's Antiques, *Sheffield, MA* 315

Antiquaria, *Springfield, MA* 325

Antiquarian Bookworm, *Sharon, MA* 314

The Antiquarian Scientist, *Dracut, MA* 268

The Antiquarium, *Bethany, CT* 98

Antiquers III, *Brookline, MA* 259

Antiquewear, *Marblehead, MA* 289

Antiquity Restorations & Repro's, *Peace Dale, RI* 405

Antiques & Art Associates, *Somers, CT* 155

Antiques & Auctions Ltd, *Sandwich, NH* 381

Antiques & Collectibles Barn, *North Conway, NH* 374

Antiques & Collectibles, *Sandwich, NH* 381

Antiques & Findings, *Contoocook, NH* 350

Antiques & Interiors At The Mill, *Greenwich, CT* 120

Antiques & Things, *South Braintree, MA* 321

Antiques & Varieties, *South Egremont, MA* 321

Antiques 'N Things, *Litchfield, CT* 127

Antiques 608, *Dennis, CC* 75

Antiques And Herbs Of Riverton, *Riverton, CT* 152

Antiques Anonymous, *Jamaica, VT* 425

Antiques At Canton Village, *Canton, CT* 103

Antiques At Forge Pond, *East Bridgewater, MA* 269

Antiques At Hearthstone House, *Seekonk, MA* 313

Antiques At The Hillmans, *Searsport, ME* 223

Antiques At Moultonboro, *Moultonboro, NH* 372

Antiques Beautiful, *Providence, RI* 406

Antiques By JK Meiers, *Manchester, VT* 427

Antiques Center, *Charlestown, NH* 348

Antiques Depot of Saybrook Jct., *Old Saybrook, CT* 146

Antiques Etc, *Newport, RI* 399

Antiques From Powder House Hill, *Farmington, ME* 200

The Antiques Market, *New Haven, CT* 137

Antiques New Hampshire, *Hampton Falls, NH* 359

Antiques Of Tomorrow, *Milford, CT* 132

Antiques On Boland Way, *Springfield, MA* 325

Antiques On Nine, *Kennebunkport, ME* 206

Antiques On The Hill, *Contoocook, NH* 350

Antiques One, *Hampton Falls, NH* 359

Antiques Orchard, *Westford, MA* 338

Antiques Plus & Strawberry Acres, *Fitzwilliam, NH* 354

Antiques Red Lion, *Dennis, CC* 75

The Antiques Shops, *Westmoreland, NH* 387

Antiques Tools & Catalogs, *Athol, MA* 244

Antiques Unlimited, *Darien, CT* 110

Antiques Unlimited Inc, *Plymouth, MA* 307

Antiques Col. at Waterman House, *Quechee, VT* 434

Antiques at Clarks Corner, *Lincolnville, ME* 208

Antiques at Eagle's Nest, *Marshfield, MA* 292

Antiques at Hampton Falls, *Hampton Falls, NH* 359

Antiques at Madison, *Madison, CT* 128

Antiques At Tom Carey's Place, *Stockbridge, MA* 325

Antiques at Topsham Fair Mall, *Topsham, ME* 226

Apex Antiques, *Belfast, ME* 187

Apple Blossoms Antiques, *Shelburne Falls, MA* 319

Apple Country Antiques, *Hampton Falls, NH* 359

Apple Tree Hill Antiques, *New Fairfield, CT* 136

Appleton Antiques, *Brookline, MA* 259

Appleyard Antiques, *Hillsboro, NH* 361

Appraisal Associates, *Trumbull, CT* 162

The Appraisers' Registry, *Westwood, MA* 339

Apropos, *West Falmouth, CC* 92

Araby Rug, *Boston, MA* 246

Arch Bridge Bookshop, *Bellows Falls, VT* 417

Archives Historical Autographs, *Wilton, CT* 169

Arethusa Book Shop, *New Haven, CT* 137

Arman's Newport, *Newport, RI* 399

Armchair Books, *Orange, MA* 304

Arnholm's Antiques, *Barre, VT* 417

Eva Arond, *Lexington, MA* 287

Around The Corner Antiques, *Newtonville, MA* 299

The Arringtons, *Wells, ME* 228

Ars Antiqua Books, *Bloomfield, CT* 99

Ars Libri, *Boston, MA* 246

James E Arsenault Bookseller, *Bath, ME* 186

Art & Antique Gallery Inc, *Worcester, MA* 341

Art Interiors Antiques-Pittsford, *Pittsford, VT* 433

Art Rug, *Concord, NH* 349

Arthur's Antiques, *Sanbornville, NH* 381

Artist's Guild & Gallery, *Charlestown, RI* 394

Artistic Ventures Gallery, *West Haven, CT* 165

Arundel Antiques, *Arundel, ME* 184

Arvest Galleries Inc, *Boston, MA* 247

As Time Goes By Antiques, *Essex, MA* 270

Ashaway Antiques Store, *Ashaway, RI* 393

Gail Ashburn Hadley, *Barrington, RI* 393

Ashley Book Company, *Burlington, VT* 419

Ashley Falls Antiques, *Ashley Falls, MA* 243

Asia House, *Salem, MA* 311

At The Sign Of The Fox, *Jaffrey, NH* 364

Atlas Amusement, *Plainville, CT* 149

Attic Shop Antiques, *Lunenberg, VT* 426

Attic Treasures, *Ridgefield, CT* 151

Auburn Antique & Flea Market Inc, *Auburn, MA* 244

Auction Barn, *New Milford, CT* 140

Auctions By Bowers & Merena Inc, *Wolfeboro, NH* 389

Auntie Bea's Antiques, *Caribou, ME* 194

Aunties Attic Antiques, *Martha's Vineyard, CC* 81

Aurora Borealis Antiques, *Falmouth, CC* 78

William Austin's Antiques, *Chester, VT* 420
Authentic Designs, *West Rupert, VT* 442
Authentic Reproduction Lighting, *Avon, CT* 97
Autrefois Antiques, *Boston, MA* 247
Autrefois II, *Brookline, MA* 259
Autumn Pond Antiques, *Bolton, CT* 100
Avanti Antique Jewelry, *Nantucket, CC* 83
Avery & Cox Ltd, *Salisbury, CT* 153
Avery's Antiques, *Framingham, MA* 275
B & B Autographs, *Randolph, MA* 307
BC Books, *Somers, CT* 155
Bert Babcock Bookseller, *Derry, NH* 350
Back-Track Antiques, *Wakefield, MA* 330
Backward Glance Antique Mall, *Harrison, ME* 204
Backward Goose, *Bristol Mills, ME* 190
Backward Look Antiques, *Antrim, NH* 346
Bacon Antiques, *Hartford, CT* 123
Bad Corner Antiques & Decoration, *Lakeville, CT* 126
F O Bailey Antiquarians, *Portland, ME* 218
James R Bakker Antiques Inc, *Cambridge, MA* 261
Balcony Antiques, *Canton, CT* 103
The Ball & Claw, *Wickford, RI* 412
Bananas, *Gloucester, MA* 276
Bancroft Book Mews, *Newtown, CT* 144
Robert T Baranowsky, *Plainville, CT* 149
Barbara's Antiques, *Hillsboro, NH* 361
Patricia & Keith Barger, *Essex, CT* 116
Barker's of Salisbury Heights, *Salisbury Heights, NH* 381
Barking Frog Collectible Co, *Southwick, MA* 324
The Barn At Cape Neddick, *Cape Neddick, ME* 193
The Barn At Hampton Falls, *Hampton Falls, NH* 359
The Barn At Windsong, *Harwich, CC* 79
The Barn Door, *Caribou, ME* 194
Barn Loft Bookshop, *Laconia, NH* 366
The Barn On 26 Antique Center, *Gray, ME* 202
Barn Stages Bookshop, *Newcastle, ME* 213
The Barn of Hancock Village, *Hancock, NH* 359
Roland & Joyce Barnard Antiques, *Hopkinton, NH* 363
Barnstable Stove Shop, *West Barnstable, CC* 91
Barnstable Village Antiques, *Barnstable, CC* 71
Barridoff Galleries, *Portland, ME* 218
The Barrow Bookstore, *Concord, MA* 265
Robert Barrow, Cabinetmaker, *Bristol, RI* 394
Amabel Barrows Antiques, *Wilton, CT* 169
Barsalow Auctions, *Milton, VT* 430
Barter Shop, *Norwalk, CT* 145
Scott Bassoff/Sandy Jacobs, *Rindge, NH* 380
John Bauer/Sonia Sefton Antiques, *Newfield, ME* 214
Michael J Baumann, *Newburyport, MA* 296
William M Baxter Antiques, *Brewster, CC* 71
Bay Street Antiques, *Boothbay Harbor, ME* 189
The Bay Tree Antiques, *Woodbury, CT* 173
Bayberry Antiques, *North Chatham, CC* 85
Beach Plum Antiques, *Yarmouth Port, CC* 93
The Beal House Inn & Antiques, *Littleton, NH* 367
Francis Bealey American Arts, *Essex, CT* 116
The Bear Bookshop, *Marlboro, VT* 428
Bear Track Farm Antiques, *Hillsboro Center, NH* 362
Bearly Read Books Inc, *Sudbury, MA* 327
Beaufurn Inc, *South Norwalk, CT* 155
Beauport Antiques, *Gloucester, MA* 277
Beauport Inn Antiques, *Ogunquit, ME* 215
Beaux Arts, *Southbury, CT* 156
Bob & Rita Becker, *Epsom, NH* 352
Neal Beckerman Antiques, *Brookline Village, MA* 260
Stephen P Bedard, *Gilmanton Iron Works, NH* 357
Bedelle Inc, *Boston, MA* 247
Bedford Center Antiques, *Bedford, NH* 346

Belcher's Antiques, *Deer Isle, ME* 196
Belgravia Antiques Inc, *Boston, MA* 247
AJ Beliveau Books, *St George, VT* 439
Gerald W Bell Auctioneer, *Yarmouth, ME* 234
Bell Farm Antiques, *York, ME* 235
Bell Hill Antiques, *Bedford, NH* 346
Bellevue Antiques, *Newport, RI* 399
Bellwether Gallery, *Manchester Center, VT* 427
Benchmark Antiques, *Moultonboro, NH* 372
Michael G Bennett Auctions, *Dover, NH* 351
R & B Bennett, *Damariscotta, ME* 195
Deborah Benson Bookseller, *West Cornwall, CT* 164
Berdan's Antiques, *Hallowell, ME* 202
The Bergeron's Antiques, *Killingworth, CT* 126
Berkshire Antiques, *Pittsfield, MA* 305
Berkshire Hills Coins & Antiques, *Pittsfield, MA* 305
Bernardston Books, *Bernardston, MA* 244
Bernheimer's Antique Arts, *Cambridge, MA* 261
Berry Patch Antiques, *East Winthrop, ME* 198
Bert Gallery, *Providence, RI* 406
Bert's Browse Around Shop, *Cranston, RI* 396
Millicent Rudd Best, *Weston, CT* 166
R G Bettcher Restorations, *South Hampton, NH* 382
Betteridge Jewelers Inc, *Greenwich, CT* 120
The Betty House, *Epsom, NH* 352
Betty's Trading Post, *Lincolnville Beach, ME* 210
Bibliolatree, *East Hampton, CT* 114
Biddeford Antique Center, *Biddeford, ME* 188
Big Chicken Barn-Books & Antique, *Ellsworth, ME* 198
James Billings Antiques, *Boston, MA* 247
Bird Cage Antiques, *South Egremont, MA* 321
Bit Of Country, *New Milford, CT* 140
Bittersweet Antiques, *Gaylordsville, CT* 118
The Black Goose, *Marblehead, MA* 289
Black Mountain Antique Center, *Brattleboro, VT* 418
Black Sheep Antiques, *Newport, RI* 399
Black Swan Antiques, *New Preston, CT* 142
Blackbird Antiques, *Sheffield, MA* 315
Blackbriar Antiques, *Chester, NH* 348
Blackwood March, *Essex, MA* 270
David & Dale Bland Antiques, *Hebron, CT* 124
Richard Blaschke, *Bristol, CT* 101
Bldg 38 Antique Center, *Orange, MA* 304
Robin Bledsoe Bookseller, *Cambridge, MA* 261
The Block House, *New London, NH* 373
Bloomin' Antiques, *Fitzwilliam, NH* 354
Blue Cape Antiques, *Littleton, MA* 288
Blue Flag Antiques, *Little Compton, RI* 398
The Blue Lantern Antiques, *Hollis, NH* 363
Blue Unicorn, *Boothbay, ME* 189
Blue Willow Farm Antiques, *Manchester, ME* 211
Blueberry Hill Farm, *Rangeley, ME* 221
The Blueberry Patch, *Hope, ME* 204
Mr & Mrs Jerome Blum, *Lisbon, CT* 127
Bo & Co, *Woodstock, VT* 179
Bo-Mar Hall Antiques, *Wells, ME* 228
Sharon Boccelli & Co Antiques, *Cambridge, MA* 261
James Bok Antiques, *Fairfield, CT* 117
H & T Bond Booksellers, *Reading, MA* 308
Bonsal-Douglas Antiques, *Essex, CT* 116
Koko Boodakian & Sons, *Winchester, MA* 340
Book & Tackle Shop, *Chestnut Hill, MA* 265
The Book & Tackle Shop, *Watch Hill, RI* 411
Book Addict, *Sanford, ME* 223
Book Barn, *Niantic, CT* 144
The Book Barn, *Wells, ME* 229
Book Bear, *West Brookfield, MA* 334
The Book Block, *Cos Cob, CT* 107

Book Cellar, *Freeport, ME* 200
The Book Collector, *Newton, MA* 297
The Book Den East, *Martha's Vineyard, CC* 81
The Book Exchange, *Plainville, CT* 149
Book Guild Of Portsmouth, *Portsmouth, NH* 378
Book Marks, *Amherst, MA* 241
The Book Mill, *Montague, MA* 293
The Book Mill, *Concord, NH* 349
Book Pedlars, *Cundys Harbor, ME* 195
Book Store, *Canton, CT* 103
Bookcell Books, *Hamden, CT* 123
The Bookery, *Farmington, NH* 353
Booklover's Attic, *Belfast, ME* 187
Books & Autographs, *Eliot, ME* 198
Books & Birds, *Manchester, CT* 129
Books About Antiques, *Woodbury, CT* 174
Books Bought And Sold, *Madison, ME* 211
Books With A Past, *Concord, MA* 265
Books by the Falls, *Derby, CT* 113
The Bookstore, *Fairfax, VT* 424
The Bookworm, *Amherst, NH* 345
Borssen Antiques, *Belgrade, ME* 188
Thomas G Boss-Fine Books, *Boston, MA* 247
Boston Antique Cooperative II, *Boston, MA* 247
Boston Book Annex, *Boston, MA* 247
Boston Book Annex, *Jamaica Plain, MA* 285
Boston Brass Works, *Dennis, CC* 76
The Boston Hammersmith, *Boston, MA* 248
Boston Road Antiques, *Groton, MA* 280
Botanica, *East Greenwich, RI* 396
Ronald Bourgeault Antiques, *Hampton, NH* 358
Richard A Bourne Co Inc, *Hyannis, CC* 80
Martha Boynton Antiques, *Townsend, MA* 329
Pam Boynton, *Groton, MA* 280
Bert & Phyllis Boyson, *Brookfield, CT* 101
Arakel H Bozyan Store, *Newport, RI* 400
Bradbury/Newell House, *Northwood, NH* 375
Bradford Galleries Ltd, *Sheffield, MA* 315
Brady Galleries Inc, *Vergennes, VT* 440
Patsy Braman Antiques, *Providence, RI* 406
Brandon Antiques, *Brandon, VT* 418
Brass & Bounty, *Marblehead, MA* 290
Brass Buff Antiques, *Newton, MA* 297
The Brass Bugle, *Cornwall Bridge, CT* 107
Brass Ring Antiques, Inc., *Woodbury, CT* 174
Brass and Friends Antiques, *Hallowell, ME* 202
Brassworks, *Providence, RI* 406
Brassworks Antiques Center, *Haydenville, MA* 284
Braswell Galleries, *Norwalk, CT* 145
Brattle Book Shop, *Boston, MA* 248
Brattleboro Books, *Brattleboro, VT* 418
Brennans Antiques, *Peterborough, NH* 377
Breton House, *Brewster, CC* 71
Bretton Hall Antiquities, *Lancaster, NH* 366
Brewster Antiques, *Manchester Center, VT* 428
William Brewster Antiques, *Brewster, CC* 71
Brewster Farmhouse Antiques, *Brewster, CC* 71
Briar Patch Antiques, *Plainville, MA* 307
Brick House, *Fair Haven, VT* 423
Brick House Antiques, *Stockton Springs, ME* 226
Brick House Antiques, *Essex, MA* 270
Brick House Bookshop, *Morrisville, VT* 430
Bridge Antiques, *North Weymouth, MA* 301
Briggs House Antiques, *Ashaway, RI* 393
Brimfield, *Brimfield, MA* 258
Brimfield Antiques, *Brimfield, MA* 258
Britannia Bookshop, *New Preston, CT* 142
British Country Antiques, *Woodbury, CT* 174
Brodney Inc, *Boston, MA* 248

Hollis & Trisha Brodrick, *Exeter, NH* 353
Broken Shell Gallery, *Canton, CT* 103
Bromer Booksellers Inc, *Boston, MA* 248
Maury A Bromsen Associates Inc, *Boston, MA* 248
Brookline Village Bookshop, *Brookline Village, MA* 261
Brookline Village Antiques, *Brookline Village, MA* 261
Brookline Village Antiques, *Brookline, NH* 347
Brookside Antiques, *Middlebury, VT* 429
Brookside Antiques, *New Bedford, MA* 295
Brookside Antiques, *Orland, ME* 216
The Brown Jug, *Sandwich, CC* 88
Paul Brown-Books, *Old Mystic, CT* 146
Brown-Corbin Fine Art, *Lincoln, MA* 288
The Browser's Box, *New Milford, CT* 140
Suzanne Bruckner Antiques, *Haverhill, NH* 360
Brunswick Art and Antiques, *Brunswick, ME* 191
Brush Factory Antiques, *Centerbrook, CT* 104
Bryn Mawr Book Shop, *New Haven, CT* 137
Patricia Buck Emporium, *Kingfield, ME* 208
Buckley & Buckley Antiques, *Salisbury, CT* 153
Buddenbrooks, *Boston, MA* 249
Antiques @ Buggy Whip Factory, *Southfield, MA* 324
Bunker Hill Antiques, *Jefferson, ME* 205
Bunker Hill Relics, *Charlestown, MA* 264
Bunkhouse Books, *Gardiner, ME* 201
Lee Burgess Antiques, *New London, NH* 373
P A Burke Antiques Inc, *Essex, MA* 270
P A Burke Antiques Inc, *Salem, MA* 311
T J Burke Oriental Rugs, *Bangor, ME* 185
Burke's Bazaar-Poet's Antiques, *Gloucester, MA* 277
Burlwood Antique Center, *Meredith, NH* 370
Burpee Hill Books, *New London, NH* 373
J R Burrows & Company, *Jamaica Plain, MA* 285
Harold M Burstein & Co, *Waltham, MA* 330
Burt Dial Company, *Raymond, NH* 380
Herschel B Burt, *Exeter, NH* 353
Business In The Barn, *Hadlyme, CT* 122
E R Butler & Sons, *Marblehead, MA* 290
Butler Fine Art, *New Canaan, CT* 134
Butterchurn Antiques, *Northwood, NH* 375
Butternut Shop, *Charlestown, RI* 394
By Shaker Hands, *Great Barrington, MA* 278
Bygone Books, *Burlington, VT* 419
Bygone Days, *Great Barrington, MA* 278
C & B Hidden Treasures, *Hope Valley, RI* 397
C & D Antiques, *Center Sandwich, NH* 348
C & J Antiques, *Newport, RI* 400
C & T Antique Dealers, *Newport, RI* 400
CC Cancer Consignment Exchange, *Yarmouth Port, CC* 93
Cache, *Falmouth, CC* 79
Cackleberry Farms Antiques, *Canterbury, CT* 102
Joan F Caddigan, *Hanover, MA* 282
S Calcagni Fine Arts & Antiques, *Washington Depot, CT* 163
Calico Country Antiques, *Marblehead, MA* 290
Calista Sterling Antiques, *Ellsworth, ME* 198
Call's Shelburn Country Shop, *Shelburne Falls, MA* 319
Henry Thomas Callan Fine Antique, *East Sandwich, CC* 78
Camden Passage Ltd, *Boston, MA* 249
Canal Street Antiques Market, *Salem, MA* 311
Candle Snuffer, *Coventry, RI* 395
Candlelight & Cobblestones, *Camden, ME* 192
Candlewick Antiques, *Mont Vernon, NH* 371
The Cane Workshop, *Barkhamstead, CT* 98

Ives Hill Antiques, *West Granville, MA* 335
J & S Enterprises, *North Brookfield, MA* 300
JB Antiques, *Newport, RI* 402
Page Jackson Antique Gallery, *Randolph Center, VT* 434
Bernice Jackson Fine Arts, *Concord, MA* 266
Martha Jackson Quilts, *New Canaan, CT* 135
Jeff Jacobs Flea Market Inc, *Plainville, CT* 149
Jandra's Woodshed, *Fort Fairfield, ME* 200
Jane's Collectiques, *Orleans, CC* 87
Jasmine, *New Haven, CT* 139
Hedy Jeffery Antiques, *Newfane, VT* 431
Jennifers, *Newport, RI* 402
Frank C Jensen Antiques, *Woodbury, CT* 176
Jer-Rho Antiques, *Gloucester, MA* 277
Jewett City Emporium, *Jewett City, CT* 124
Jo-Art Glass, *Warwick, RI* 410
Johnny Appleseed Bookshop, *Manchester, VT* 427
Gus Johnson Antiques, *Hampton, NH* 358
J Johnson Natural History Books, *North Bennington, VT* 431
Johnson's Secondhand Bookshop, *Springfield, MA* 325
Johnson-Marsano Antiques, *Hallowell, ME* 203
Johnston Antiques, *Franklin, MA* 275
Johnstone Antiques, *Northwood, NH* 375
Emy Jane Jones Antiques, *Darien, CT* 110
Stephen Jones Antiques, *Groton, VT* 425
Joneses Antiques, *Great Barrington, MA* 279
Joppa Bay Antiques, *Newburyport, MA* 297
Jerard Paul Jordan, *Ashford, CT* 97
Jordan Delhaise Gallery Ltd, *Westport, CT* 167
Jerard Paul Jordan Gallery, *Ashford, CT* 97
R Jorgensen Antiques, *Wells, ME* 230
Albert Joseph & Co, *Naugatuck, CT* 134
Tom Joseph & David Ramsay, *Limerick, ME* 208
Josko & Sons Auctions, *Fairfield, CT* 117
The Joy Of Books, *West Newbury, MA* 335
Joyce & Daughters, *Westfield, MA* 338
Julia & Poulin Antiques, *Fairfield, ME* 199
John D Julia Antiques, *Fairfield, ME* 199
James D Julia Auctioneers, *Fairfield, ME* 199
The Jumping Frog, *Hartford, CT* 123
Junction Antique Center, *Northwood, NH* 375
Priscilla Juvelis Inc, *Boston, MA* 254
Kahn's Antique & Estate Jewelry, *Great Barrington, MA* 279
Kaja Veilleux Art & Antiques, *Newcastle, ME* 213
Kalonbooks, *Bradford, NH* 346
Frank C Kaminski Inc, *Stoneham, MA* 326
Milton H Kasowitz, *New Haven, CT* 139
Kay Bee Furniture Company, *Boston, MA* 254
Tom Kaye Antiques Ltd, *Wallingford, VT* 441
R Kazarian/Antiques, *Newport, RI* 402
JJ Keating Inc, *Kennebunk, ME* 205
Judith A Keating, *GG, Kennebunk, ME* 205
Joyce B Keeler - Books, *North Monmouth, ME* 215
Keezer's Harvard Community Exchange, *Cambridge, MA* 262
Jean Kennedy Antiques, *West Barnstable, CC* 91
Kennedy's Antiques, *Brandon, VT* 418
Kenniston's Antiques, *Pittsfield, ME* 217
Kent Antiques Center, *Kent, CT* 125
Joseph Kilbridge Antiques, *Groton, MA* 281
Kimball House 1753, *Chepachet, RI* 395
King Cane, *Stonington, CT* 159
Roger King Gallery Of Fine Art, *Newport, RI* 402
Kings Way Books & Antiques, *Brewster, CC* 72
The Kingsleigh 1840, *Lee, MA* 286
Paul Klaver, *Arlington, MA* 242

Paul & Susan Kleinwald Inc, *Great Barrington, MA* 279
Kloss Violins, *Needham, MA* 294
Knollwood Antiques, *Boston, MA* 254
Knollwood Antiques, *Lovell Village, ME* 211
Knotty Pine Antique Market, *West Swanzey, NH* 387
Jeff Koopus, *Harrison, ME* 204
Ernest Kramer Fine Arts & Prints, *Wellesley Hills, MA* 332
Alice Kugelman, *West Hartford, CT* 165
Kuttner Antiques, *Sheffield, MA* 317
Ralph Kylloe Antiques, *Londonderry, NH* 367
L & M Furniture, *Northampton, MA* 302
George La Barre Galleries Inc, *Hollis, NH* 363
La Bomba, *Portsmouth, NH* 379
La Caleche, *Darien, CT* 110
La Chaise de France, *Florence, MA* 274
Laces Unlimited, *Wellesley Hills, MA* 333
Lafayette Antiques, *North Kingstown, RI* 405
Lakeside Antiques, *East Winthrop, ME* 198
Lamb House Fine Books, *Guilford, CT* 122
Lame Duck Books, *Jamaica Plain, MA* 285
Lamp Glass, *Cambridge, MA* 263
Lamp Lighter Antiques, *Newport, RI* 402
Lamp Works, *Middletown, RI* 399
The Lamplighter, *Middletown Springs, VT* 429
Lancaster Mall & Antiques Market, *Lancaster, NH* 366
Landmark Antiques, *New Bedford, MA* 295
L A Landry Antiques, *Essex, MA* 271
Langenbach Fine Arts & Antiques, *Kingston, MA* 285
Lantern & Breezeway, *Wakefield, MA* 330
Lapham & Dibble Gallery Inc, *Shoreham, VT* 438
Susan B Larsen Antiques, *Plymouth, NH* 378
Larson's Clock Shop, *Westminster, VT* 442
William Lary Antiques, *Dublin, NH* 351
Leif Laudamus, *Rare Books, Amherst, MA* 241
Laurel City, *Winsted, CT* 172
Paul Lawton & Son, *Brattleboro, VT* 418
The Layne Galleries, *East Longmeadow, MA* 269
Lazy Fox Antiques et Gallerie, *Springfield, NH* 382
David J Le Beau Fine Antiques, *Sheffield, MA* 317
James Le Furgy Antiques & Books, *Hallowell, ME* 203
Le Manoir Country French Antique, *Southbury, CT* 157
Le Perigord, *Longmeadow, MA* 289
The Leaping Stag Antiques, *Coventry, RI* 395
Jesse Caldwell Leatherwood, *East Sandwich, CC* 78
J Leeke Preservation Consultant, *Sanford, ME* 223
Jenny Lees Antiques, *Milford, CT* 132
Edward J Lefkowicz Inc, *Fairhaven, MA* 274
Willem & Inger Lemmens Antiques, *Halifax, MA* 282
Leonard's Antiques Inc, *Seekonk, MA* 313
Leone's Appraisers & Auctioneers, *Lebanon, CT* 127
Lepore Fine Arts, *Newburyport, MA* 297
les classiques, *Woodbury, CT* 179
Les Trois Provinces, *Colchester, CT* 106
Leslie's & Mayfair Antiques, *Boston, MA* 254
Levett's Antiques, *Camden, ME* 192
William Lewan Antiques, *Fitzwilliam, NH* 354
Lewis & Wilson, *Ashley Falls, MA* 243
George Thomas Lewis, *Williamsburg, MA* 339
Liberty Hill Antiques, *Reading, VT* 434
Liberty Way Antiques, *Greenwich, CT* 121
Lighthouse Antiques & Promotions, *Fall River, MA* 274
Lil-Bud Antiques, *Yarmouth Port, CC* 93
Lilac Cottage, *Wiscasset, ME* 232
Lilac Hedge Bookshop, *Norwich, VT* 432
The Lilac Shed Antiques, *Washington, ME* 228

Miriam Lillian, *Woodbridge, CT* 172
Lillian's Antiques, *North Kingstown, RI* 405
Lime Rock Farm Antiques, *New Milford, CT* 141
Limerock Farms Antiques, *Marble Dale, CT* 130
D W Linsley Inc, *Litchfield, CT* 127
Lion's Head Antiques, *Winchester, MA* 340
Lion's Head Books, *Salisbury, CT* 153
Lippincott Books, *Bangor, ME* 185
Liros Gallery, *Blue Hill, ME* 189
Lissard House, *New Canaan, CT* 135
Litchfield Antiques Center, *Litchfield, CT* 127
Litchfield Auction Gallery, *Litchfield, CT* 127
Little House Of Glass, *Old Saybrook, CT* 147
Little House Studio, *South Egremont, MA* 322
Nathan Liverant & Son, *Colchester, CT* 106
Lloyd Antiques, *Hanover, MA* 283
The Loft Antiques, *Richmond, ME* 221
Lofty Ideas, *Woodstock, VT* 444
Log Cabin Antiques, *Tuftonboro, NH* 384
Lombard Antiquarian Map & Prints, *Cape Elizabeth, ME* 193
Carol Lombardi Antiques, *Providence, RI* 407
London Lace, *Boston, MA* 254
Londontowne Galleries, *Somerville, MA* 321
Thomas R Longacre, *Marlborough, NH* 369
Longview Antiques, *Gorham, ME* 202
R Loomis Furniture/Cabinetmaker, *Williamsburg, MA* 340
Loon Pond Antiques, *Hillsboro, NH* 361
Loon's Landing Antiques, *Damariscotta, ME* 195
Ken Lopez Bookseller, *Hadley, MA* 281
Thomas Lord Cabinetmaker, *Canterbury, CT* 102
Lord Randall Bookshop, *Marshfield, MA* 292
Lord Seagrave's, *Northport, ME* 215
Lordship Antique Auto Inc, *Stratford, CT* 161
Loudon Village Antique Shop, *Loudon Village, NH* 368
Samuel L Lowe Jr Antiques Inc, *Boston, MA* 255
J & J Lubrano, *Great Barrington, MA* 279
A Lucas Books, *Fairfield, CT* 117
Robert F Lucas, *Blandford, MA* 245
Lucky Lady Boutique, *Winchester, MA* 341
Ludlow Antique & Gift Center, *Ludlow, VT* 426
Ludwig's Antiques, *West Barnstable, CC* 91
Eleanor Lynn/Elizabeth Monahan, *Sugar Hill, NH* 383
Russell Lyons, *Ashley Falls, MA* 243
Lyons' Den Antiques, *Hanover, ME* 204
M & S Rare Books Inc, *Weston, MA* 338
MAH Antiques, *North Edgecomb, ME* 214
Mac Donald's Military, *Eustis, ME* 199
Michael S Mac Lean Antiques, *Washington Depot, CT* 164
Frederick Mac Phail Antiques, *West Swanzey, NH* 387
MacDougall-Gionet Antiques/Assoc, *Wells, ME* 230
Stephen P Mack, *Ashaway, RI* 393
Mad Eagle Inc Fine Antiques, *New London, NH* 373
Paul Madden Antiques, *Sandwich, CC* 88
Madeline's Antiques Inc, *Rehoboth, MA* 308
Maggie's Antiques, *Harwichport, CC* 79
Magic Horn Ltd, *East Haddam, CT* 113
The Magnolia Shoppe, *Cheshire, CT* 104
Mary Mahler Antiques, *Stonington, CT* 159
Main Street Antiques, *Essex, MA* 272
Main Street Antiques Center, *Danby, VT* 421
Main Street Arts & Antiques, *Gloucester, MA* 277
Main Street Cellar Antiques, *New Canaan, CT* 135
Main(E)ly Books, *Skowhegan, ME* 224

Maine Antique Merchants Ltd, *Lincolnville Beach, ME* 210
Mainely Antiques, *Hallowell, ME* 203
Mainly Oak Ltd, *Newport, RI* 402
Maison Auction Company Inc, *Wallingford, CT* 163
K Maisonrouge Antiques Ltd, *Washington Depot, CT* 164
Val Maitino Antiques, *Nantucket, CC* 83
Paul & Marie Majoros, *Guild, NH* 358
Thomas Makon American Antiques, *Chester, VT* 420
G B Manasek Inc, *Hanover, NH* 360
Jeffrey D Mancevice Inc, *Worcester, MA* 341
Manchester Flea Market, *Manchester Center, VT* 428
Elizabeth S Mankin Antiques, *Kent, CT* 125
Kenneth & Ida Manko, *Moody, ME* 212
Manor Antiques, *New Canaan, CT* 135
Dorvan Manus Restoration/Gilding, *Westport, CT* 167
Maple Avenue Antiques, *Farmington, ME* 200
Mapledale Antiques, *Southborough, MA* 324
The Maples, *Damariscotta, ME* 195
Marblehead Antiques, *Marblehead, MA* 290
Marchand's Lafayette Antiques, *Salem, MA* 311
Marcia & Bea Antiques, *Newton Highlands, MA* 299
Marcoz Antiques Inc, *Boston, MA* 255
Marcoz Antiques & Jewelry, *Boston, MA* 255
Marcus & Marcus Antiques, *Wellesley, MA* 332
Richard G Marden, *Wolfeboro, NH* 389
Marie-Louise Antiques, *Hanover, NH* 360
Marika's Antique Shop Inc, *Boston, MA* 255
Marine Antiques, *Wiscasset, ME* 232
Marine Arts Gallery, *Salem, MA* 311
Maritime Auctions, *York, ME* 235
Maritime Museum Shop, *Kennebunkport, ME* 206
Market Place, *Buzzards Bay, CC* 73
Marlboro Cottage Art & Interiors, *New Marlborough, MA* 296
Marston House American Antiques, *Wiscasset, ME* 232
Martin House Antique Center, *North Ferrisburg, VT* 431
Martingale Farm Antiques, *Morris, CT* 133
Martone's Gallery, *West Greenwich, RI* 411
Marty's Antique Auction Service, *Smithfield, RI* 409
Mary's Glass & Collectibles, *Jeffersonville, VT* 426
Peter L Masi Books, *Montague, MA* 293
Mathom Bookshop & Bindery, *Dresden, ME* 197
Mattaquason Arts & Antiques, *Chatham, CC* 74
Matteson Gallery Of Arts, *Colchester, VT* 421
Mattozzi & Burke Antiques, *Groton, MA* 281
Matz & Pribell, *Cambridge, MA* 263
Maurer & Shepherd, *Joyners, Glastonbury, CT* 119
Mavis, *Kent, CT* 126
Timothy Mawson Books & Prints, *New Preston, CT* 143
Maynard House, *Westborough, MA* 337
Mayo Auctioneers & Appraisers, *Trenton, ME* 227
Maypop Lane, *Sandwich, CC* 88
Mc Blain Books, *Hamden, CT* 123
Thomas Mc Bride Antiques, *Litchfield, CT* 128
Mc Caffrey Booth Antiques, *Brookfield, CT* 101
Bert Mc Cleary Auctioneer, *Francestown, NH* 355
Kevin B Mc Clellan Appraiser/Auc, *Rowayton, CT* 153
Luella Mc Cloud Antiques, *Shelburne Falls, MA* 320
Paula T Mc Colgan Inc, *Harvard, MA* 283
Paul Mc Innis Inc, *Hampton Falls, NH* 359
Phill A Mc Intyre & Daughters, *Anson, ME* 184
Jean S Mc Kenna Book Shop, *Beverly, MA* 345
H P Mc Lane Antiques Inc, *Darien, CT* 110
Dan Mc Laughlin Antiques, *Hallowell, ME* 203

McKay's Antiques, *Gardiner, ME* 201
McLeod Military Collectibles, *Brewer, ME* 190
McMorrow Auction Company, *Mechanic Falls, ME* 212
The Meadow Gallery, *Groton, MA* 281
Meadow Hearth, *Hopkinton, NH* 363
Mechanical Music Center Inc, *South Norwalk, CT* 155
Meeting House Antiques, *Oxford, ME* 216
Mellin's Antiques, *Redding, CT* 150
J Thomas Melvin, *Bethel, CT* 99
Memories, *Great Barrington, MA* 279
Memories, *Hallowell, ME* 203
Memory Lane Antique Center, *Coventry, CT* 108
Memory Lane Antiques, *Cranston, RI* 396
H Mendelsohn Fine European Books, *Cambridge, MA* 263
Mendes Antiques, *Rehoboth, MA* 308
Mentor Antiques, *North Kingstown, RI* 405
Merlyn Auctions, *North Harwich, CC* 86
Robert L Merriam, *Conway, MA* 266
Merrill's Auction Gallery, *Williston, VT* 443
Merrimac's Antiques, *Orrington, ME* 216
Merry Hill Farm, *West Nottingham, NH* 387
Merrymeeting Antiques, *Topsham, ME* 226
Merrythought, *Ashford, CT* 97
Metacomet Books, *Providence, RI* 407
Metal Restoration Services, *Tiverton, RI* 409
Meurs Renehan, *Clinton, CT* 105
Michael Black Designs, *Old Lyme, CT* 146
Micklestreet Rare Books/Mod 1sts, *East Lebanon, ME* 197
Middle Haddam Antiques, *Middle Haddam, CT* 131
Middlebury Antique Center, *East Middlebury, VT* 423
Miles Paintings & Antiques, *Charlotte, VT* 420
Milford Antiques, *Milford, NH* 371
Milford Emporium, *Milford, CT* 132
Milford Green Antiques Gallery, *Milford, CT* 132
Milk Street Antiques, *Portland, ME* 219
George E Milkey Books, *Springvale, ME* 225
Mill Brook Antiques, *Reading, VT* 435
Mill Brook Antiques, *Charlestown, RI* 395
Mill House Antiques, *Woodbury, CT* 176
Mill Village Antiques, *Francestown, NH* 355
Jim Miller Antiques, *East Haddam, CT* 113
Marie Miller, *Dorset, VT* 422
Ken Miller's Flea Market, *Northfield, MA* 303
Milling Around, *Newcastle, ME* 213
Mimosa Tree, *Saunderstown, RI* 409
George R Minkoff Inc, *Great Barrington, MA* 279
Lee Mohn Antiques & Art, *Wallingford, CT* 163
Monique's Antiques, *Wolfeboro, NH* 389
Monroe Antique Center, *Monroe, CT* 132
Moody-Ridgeway House, *West Newbury, MA* 335
Constance Morelle Books, *Haverhill, MA* 283
C W Morgan Marine Antiques, *Martha's Vineyard, CC* 82
W Morin Furniture Restoration, *Portsmouth, NH* 379
Morin's Antiques, *Auburn, ME* 184
Morrell's Antiques, *Gardiner, ME* 201
Edward Morrill & Son, *Newton Centre, MA* 298
The Morris House, *New Canaan, CT* 135
Mortar & Pestle Antiques, *Wellfleet, CC* 90
Woody Mosch Cabinetmakers, *Bethlehem, CT* 99
Thomas Moser Cabinetmakers, *Portland, ME* 219
Barbara Moss Antiques, *East Greenwich, RI* 397
Mother Goose Antiques, *Hallowell, ME* 203
Howard S Mott Inc, *Sheffield, MA* 317
Mountain Crest Antiques, *Hadley, MA* 282
Mount Vernon Antiques, *Rockport, MA* 309

Much Ado, *Marblehead, MA* 290
J Muennich Associates, *Inc, Cheshire, CT* 104
Mullin-Jones Antiquities, *Great Barrington, MA* 280
Gerald Murphy Antiques Ltd, *Woodbury, CT* 177
Murray Books, *Wilbraham, MA* 339
Robinson Murray III Bookseller, *Melrose, MA* 293
Claire Murray Inc, *Nantucket, CC* 83
Museum Gallery Book Shop, *Fairfield, CT* 117
The Music Emporium, *Cambridge, MA* 263
Musical Wonder House, *Wiscasset, ME* 233
My Favorite Things, *Newport, RI* 407
My Three Sons, *Pawtucket, RI* 405
Mystic Fine Arts, *Mystic, CT* 133
Mystic River Antiques Market, *Mystic, CT* 133
Joseph Louis Nacca, *West Haven, CT* 165
Nadeau's Auction Gallery, *Colchester, CT* 106
Nantucket House Antiques, *Nantucket, CC* 83
Nantucket Lightship Baskets, *Nantucket, CC* 84
Nashua Antiques Shows, *Nashua, NH* 372
Nautical Antiques, *Kennebunkport, ME* 206
Nancy Neale Typecraft, *Bernard, ME* 188
Jim Neary Antiques, *Rehoboth, MA* 308
Cheryl Needle Books, *Chelmsford, MA* 264
Ellen Neily Antiques, *Essex, MA* 272
Nelson Antiques & Used Books, *Goshen, NH* 357
Nelson Rarities, *Inc, Portland, ME* 219
Ray & Estelle Nelson, *Warwick, RI* 410
R A Nelson, *Antiques & Interiors, Newport, RI* 403
Nelson-Monroe Antiques, *Boston, MA* 255
Seth Nemeroff Bookseller, *Northampton, MA* 302
Never Say Goodbye, *Higganum, CT* 124
Neville Antiques, *Cushing, ME* 195
New Bedford Antiques Company, *New Bedford, MA* 295
New Canaan Antiques, *New Canaan, CT* 135
New Creation Antiques, *Old Saybrook, CT* 147
The New England Antique Toy Mall, *Hudson, MA* 285
New England Antiques, *Newport, RI* 403
New England Gallery, *Wolfeboro, NH* 389
New England Gallery Inc, *Andover, MA* 242
The New England Shop, *Bethlehem, CT* 99
New England Shop, *Old Greenwich, CT* 145
New Englandiana, *Bennington, VT* 417
New Hampshire Antique Co-op Inc, *Milford, NH* 371
New Hampshire Book Auctions, *Weare, NH* 386
New Preston Antiques Center, *New Preston, CT* 143
New To You Ltd, *Southbury, CT* 157
The Newbury Galleries Antiques, *Boston, MA* 255
Newbury Street Jewelry & Antique, *Boston, MA* 255
Newcastle Antiques, *Newcastle, ME* 214
Newell's Clock Restoration, *Newport, RI* 403
Newfane Antiques Center, *Newfane, VT* 431
Newfane Flea Market, *Newfane, VT* 431
Newington Star Center, *Newington, NH* 373
Steve Newman Fine Arts, *Stamford, CT* 158
Newport Antiques, *Newport, RI* 403
The Newport Gallery Ltd, *Newport, RI* 403
Newport Scrimshaw Company, *Newport, RI* 403
Nice Stuff, *West Rockport, ME* 231
Nickerson's Antiques, *Yarmouth Port, CC* 93
Nimmo & Hart Antiques, *Middletown Springs, VT* 429
Nininger & Company Ltd, *Woodbury, CT* 177
No 5 Kennebec Row Antiques, *Hallowell, ME* 203
Noah's Ark Antiques Center, *Wilton, NH* 388
Nobody Eats Parsley, *Norfolk, CT* 144
Ronald Noe Antiques, *Stonington, CT* 159
Hilary & Paulette Nolan, *Falmouth, CC* 79
Nonesuch House, *Wiscasset, ME* 233

PAGE NUMBERS FOR QUICKCODE™ INDEX

INDEX BY QUICKCODE™
CATEGORY

Essex Junction, *All Things Considered* 423
Johnson, *Mel Siegel & Justin Gallanter* 426
Reading, *Yellow House Antiques* 435
Rockingham Village, *Stephen-Douglas Antiques* 435
Saxtons River, *Schoolhouse Antiques* 437
Saxtons River, *Sign Of The Raven* 437
Shelburne, *Harrington House 1800* 438
Townshend, *Colt Barn Antiques* 440

2 Andirons/Fenders

Cape Cod
Brewster, *The Pflock's-Antiques* 72
Sandwich, *Shawme Pond Antiques* 89
Connecticut
Cheshire, *Fine Arts Associates Of Cheshire* 104
Essex, *The Essex Forge* 116
New Canaan, *Sallea Antiques Inc* 135
Woodbury, *Kenneth Hammitt Antiques* 175
Woodbury, *Woodbury Blacksmith & Forge Co* 178
Massachusetts
Amherst, *R & R French Antiques* 241
Boston, *Howard Chadwick Antiques* 249
Brimfield, *Brimfield Antiques* 258
Marblehead, *S & S Galleries* 291
Rowley, *Ryefield Antiques & Interiors* 310
New Hampshire
Hudson, *Colonial Shoppe* 364
Stratham, *Olde Tannery Antiques* 383

3 Antiquities

Cape Cod
Sandwich, *Faulconer House Antiques* 88
Connecticut
Greenwich, *Vintage Ladies* 122
Ridgefield, *Island House Antiques* 151
Maine
Boothbay Harbor, *Bay Street Antiques* 189
Newcastle, *Newcastle Antiques* 214
Massachusetts
Arlington, *Paul Klaver* 242
Boston, *Camden Passage Ltd* 249
Cambridge, *Bernheimer's Antique Arts* 261
Cambridge, *Hurst Gallery* 262
South Natick, *Coming Of Age Antiques* 323
Wellesley, *D B Stock Antique Carpets* 331

4 Appraisal

Cape Cod
East Dennis, *Robert C Eldred Co Inc* 77
Hyannis, *Richard A Bourne Co Inc* 80
Hyannis, *Hyannis Auction* 80
Martha's Vineyard, *Island Auctioneers* 81
Orleans, *Frank H Hogan Fine Arts Inc* 87
Connecticut
Avon, *Lawrence C Goodhue Inc* 97
Cheshire, *J Muennich Associates, Inc* 104
Chester, *Sage Auction Galleries* 105
Clinton, *Hey-Day Antiques* 105
Clinton, *Van Carter Hale Fine Art* 106
Coventry, *Allinson Gallery Inc* 108
Danbury, *Deer Park Books* 109
Deep River, *Jas E Elliott Antiques* 112

East Haddam, *Connecticut River Bookshop* 113
Essex, *Essex Auction & Appraisal* 116
Greenwich, *Betteridge Jewelers Inc* 120
Greenwich, *Chelsea Antiques of Greenwich* 120
Greenwich, *Schutz & Company* 122
Litchfield, *Litchfield Auction Gallery* 127
Madison, *Schafer Auction Gallery* 129
Ridgefield, *Gerald Grunsell & Associates* 151
Rowayton, *Kevin B Mc Clellan Appraiser/Auc* 153
South Glastonbury, *Riba Auctions* 155
South Windsor, *John A Woods, Appraisers* 156
Southbury, *The Honey Pot* 157
Southport, *Hansen & Co* 157
Southport, *Pomeroy Anderson* 157
Stamford, *Fendelman & Schwartz* 158
Stratford, *Lordship Antique Auto Inc* 161
Trumbull, *Appraisal Associates* 162
Wallingford, *Maison Auction Company Inc* 163
Washington Depot, *Des Jardins Oriental Rugs* 163
West Hartford, *Samuel S T Chen* 164
West Hartford, *Alice Kugelman* 165
Weston, *Millicent Rudd Best* 166
Weston, *Sandi Oliver Fine Art* 166
Westport, *Connecticut Fine Arts, Inc* 167
Wethersfield, *Clearing House Auction Galleries* 169
Wilton, *Amabel Barrows Antiques* 169
Woodbury, *Woodbury House* 178
Maine
Belfast, *Andrews & Andrews* 187
Kennebunk, *Judith A Keating, GG* 205
Portland, *F O Bailey Antiquarians* 218
Trenton, *Mayo Auctioneers & Appraisers* 227
Massachusetts
Arlington, *Paul Klaver* 242
Bolton, *Skinner Inc* 245
Boston, *Brattle Book Shop* 248
Boston, *Bromer Booksellers Inc* 248
Boston, *Maury A Bromsen Associates Inc* 248
Boston, *Roy K Eyges Inc* 251
Boston, *Fusco & Four Associates* 252
Boston, *Grogan & Company* 253
Boston, *Harper & Faye Inc* 253
Brockton, *Ben Gerber & Son Inc* 258
Brookline, *Nancy A Smith Appraisal Assoc* 260
Cambridge, *Christie, Manson & Wood* 261
Cambridge, *F B Hubley & Co* 262
Cambridge, *Hurst Gallery* 262
Canton, *Gabriel's Auction Co Inc* 264
Chestnut Hill, *Dale Pollock Appraisal Services* 265
Dedham, *Century Shop* 267
Deerfield (South), *Douglas Auctioneers* 268
Essex, *L A Landry Antiques* 271
Gloucester, *Gloucester Fine Arts* 277
Gloucester, *Jer-Rho Antiques* 277
Gloucester, *Ten Pound Island Book Co* 277
Halifax, *Willem & Inger Lemmens Antiques* 282
Hingham, *Pierce Galleries Inc* 284
Lee, *Caropreso Gallery* 286
Lee, *Henry B Holt Inc* 286
Marshfield, *Willis Henry Auctions* 292
Needham, *Kloss Violins* 294
Newburyport, *Christopher L Snow Associates* 297
North Attleboro, *Ryan's Antiques & Auctions* 300
North Dartmouth, *S Hankin Textile Conservation* 301
Rockport, *Recuerdo* 309
Salem, *American Marine Model Gallery* 311
Salem, *Marine Arts Gallery* 311
Saugus, *Another Era* 312

10 Barometers

11 Baseball Cards

12 Bookbinding/Restoration

13 Books/Antiquarian

14 Books

15 Bottles

16 Brass/Pewter/Metalware

Kensington, *Peter Sawyer Antiques* 365
Lebanon, *Timepiece Antiques* 367
Loudon, *Chimes & Times Clock Shop* 368
Ossipee, *The Stuff Shop* 377
Plymouth, *Susan B Larsen Antiques* 378
Raymond, *Burt Dial Company* 380
Union, *Carswell's Antiques* 385
Walpole, *Golden Past Of Walpole* 385
Winchester, *Richard White Antiques* 389

Rhode Island
Cranston, *Bert's Browse Around Shop* 396
Cranston, *Gold 'N Tiques* 396
Newport, *The Classic Touch* 400
Newport, *A & A Gaines* 401
Newport, *Lamp Lighter Antiques* 402
Riverside, *Sue Christie* 408
Wakefield, *Helen C Ferris* 409

Vermont
Clarendon Springs, *Clarendon House Antiques* 420
Manchester, *The Clock Emporium* 427
Middletown Springs, *Clock Doctor Inc* 429
Middletown Springs, *Old Spa Shop Antiques* 429
St Johnsbury, *Sign Of The Dial Clock Shop* 439
Vergennes, *Fitz-Geralds' Antiques* 441
Westminster, *Larson's Clock Shop* 442
Williston, *Green Mountain Clock Shop* 443

24 Coins/Medals

Cape Cod
Brewster, *Kings Way Books & Antiques* 72
Connecticut
Avon, *Eagle's Nest* 97
Greenwich, *Chelsea Antiques of Greenwich* 120
Madison, *Ordnance Chest* 129
Westport, *Sam Sloat Coins, Inc* 168
Winsted, *Laurel City* 172
Maine
Lincolnville Beach, *Betty's Trading Post* 210
Roxbury, *Yankee Gem Corp* 222
Massachusetts
Franklin, *Johnston Antiques* 275
Pittsfield, *Berkshire Hills Coins & Antiques* 305
Worcester, *J & N Fortier Inc* 341
New Hampshire
West Swanzey, *Frederick Mac Phail Antiques* 387
Winchester, *Fat Chance Antiques* 388
Wolfeboro, *Auctions By Bowers & Merena Inc* 389
Rhode Island
Westerly, *Westerly Enterprises* 412
Vermont
Jamaica, *Antiques Anonymous* 425

25 Consignment

Cape Cod
Brewster, *William Brewster Antiques* 71
Hyannis, *Hyannis Auction* 80
Martha's Vineyard, *Island Auctioneers* 81
Martha's Vineyard, *Island Treasure of Nantucket* 81
North Harwich, *Merlyn Auctions* 86
Yarmouth Port, *CC Cancer Consignment Exchange* 93
Connecticut
Darien, *Rose D'Or* 111

Enfield, *Encore Consignment* 115
Essex, *Essex Auction & Appraisal* 116
Greenwich, *Consignments Etc* 120
Greenwich, *Estate Treasures of Greenwich* 120
Guilford, *Cornucopia Antique Consignments* 122
Madison, *On Consignment Of Madison* 129
Milford, *Stock Transfer* 132
Mystic, *5 Church Street Antiques* 133
New Canaan, *The Silk Purse* 136
New Milford, *Cricket Hill Consignment* 140
New Preston, *Village Barn & Gallery* 143
Old Lyme, *The Elephant Trunk* 146
Ridgefield, *Hunter's Consignments Inc* 151
Rowayton, *Williams Port Antiques* 153
Southbury, *New To You Ltd* 157
Stonington, *Peaceable Kingdom* 160
Torrington, *Country Auction Service* 161
Westport, *Consignmart* 167
Woodbury, *The Polished Sneaker* 177
Maine
Trenton, *Mayo Auctioneers & Appraisers* 227
Massachusetts
Boston, *Collector's Shop* 249
Cambridge, *Christie, Manson & Wood* 261
Cambridge, *F B Hubley & Co* 262
Essex, *The White Elephant Shop* 273
Needham, *On Consignment Galleries* 294
Newton, *Give & Take Consignment Shop* 298
South Natick, *Kenneth W Van Blarcom Auctioneer* 323
Southborough, *Golden Parrot* 324
Sudbury, *Farmhouse Collectibles* 327
Wayland, *Wayland Antique Exchange* 331
West Newbury, *Valyou Auctions* 335
West Newton, *Consignment Galleries* 335
Rhode Island
Newport, *Arman's Newport* 399
Newport, *The Griffon Shop* 402

26 Consultation/Research

Cape Cod
Nantucket, *Professional Art Conservation* 84
Connecticut
Cheshire, *Fine Arts Associates Of Cheshire* 104
Clinton, *Van Carter Hale Fine Art* 106
Madison, *P Hastings Falk Sound View Press* 129
Old Saybrook, *New Creation Antiques* 147
South Windsor, *John A Woods, Appraisers* 156
Southport, *Pomeroy Anderson* 157
Westport, *Professional Art Conservation* 168
Maine
Sanford, *J Leeke Preservation Consultant* 223
Massachusetts
Boston, *The Fortress Corporation* 252
Boston, *Heritage Art* 253
Brookline, *Nancy A Smith Appraisal Assoc* 260
Lincoln, *Brown-Corbin Fine Art* 288
North Attleboro, *Ryan's Antiques & Auctions* 300
North Dartmouth, *S Hankin Textile Conservation* 301
Waban, *Antique Researchers* 330
Waltham, *SPNEA Conservation Center* 331
West Newbury, *Helige Ande Arts* 335
Westwood, *The Appraisers' Registry* 339
Winchester, *Koko Boodakian & Sons* 340

28 Crocks/Stoneware

29 Decorative Accessories

30 Decoys

31 Display Stands/Glass

32 Dolls/Toys

37 Furniture/American

Cape Cod

40 Furniture/Oak

41 Furniture/Painted

42 Furniture/Pine

45 Garden Accessories

51 Maps

Boston, *Goodspeed's Book Shop Inc* 252
Essex, *The Scrapbook* 272
Fairhaven, *Edward J Lefkowicz Inc* 274
Franklin, *Johnston Antiques* 275
Gloucester, *William N Greenbaum* 277
Sharon, *Michael Ginsberg Books Inc* 314
West Newbury, *Moody-Ridgeway House* 335
New Hampshire
Concord, *Pierce & Thompson Book Co* 349
Contoocook, *Emery's Books* 350
Hanover, *G B Manasek Inc* 360
Peterborough, *Peterborough Used Books & Prints* 377
Weare, *Sykes & Flanders Antiquarian Bks* 386
Rhode Island
Wickford, *The Ball & Claw* 412
Vermont
Rutland, *Tuttle Antiquarian Books Inc* 436
Shoreham, *Lapham & Dibble Gallery Inc* 438

52 Miniatures
Maine
Searsport, *Gold Coast Antiques* 223
Massachusetts
East Arlington, *Henry Deeks* 269
Northampton, *Lilian C Stone Antiques* 303
Worcester, *Isaiah Thomas Books & Prints* 341
Rhode Island
Newport, *The Doll Museum* 400
Vermont
Dorset, *The Anglophile Antiques* 422
Rutland, *Eagle's Nest Antiques* 436

53 Mirrors
Cape Cod
West Barnstable, *Wisteria Antiques* 91
Connecticut
Riverton, *Uncovering The Past* 152
Somers, *Antique & Folk Art Shoppe* 155
Woodbury, *Crossways Antiques* 175
Woodbury, *Kenneth Hammitt Antiques* 175
Maine
Damariscotta, *Thru The Looking Glass* 196
Wells, *The Farm* 229
Massachusetts
Boston, *Autrefois Antiques* 247
Boston, *Marcoz Antiques & Jewelry* 255
Boston, *The Newbury Galleries Antiques* 255
Boston, *Reruns Antiques* 256
Brookline Village, *A Room With A Vieux* 260
Brookline Village, *Brookline Village Antiques* 261
Brookline, *Jerry Freeman Ltd* 259
Essex, *P A Burke Antiques Inc* 270
Great Barrington, *Paul & Susan Kleinwald Inc* 279
Lee, *The Kingsleigh 1840 Antiques* 286
New Marlborough, *Marlboro Cottage Art & Interiors* 296
Norwell, *Stonehouse Antiques* 303
Sheffield, *Carriage Trade Antiques* 315
Sheffield, *Susan Silver Antiques* 318
New Hampshire
Franconia, *Colonial Cottage* 356

Rhode Island
Newport, *Mainly Oak Ltd* 402
Providence, *125 Benefit Street Antiques* 406
Vermont
Middlebury, *C Tiley Antiques* 429
Poultney, *Den Of Antiquity* 433
Williston, *Simply Country* 443

54 Models
Cape Cod
Martha's Vineyard, *Shipwright Gallery* 82
Nantucket, *Four Winds Craft Guild* 83
Connecticut
Stonington, *Quester Gallery* 160
Maine
Freeport, *Port 'N Starboard* 201
Wiscasset, *Marine Antiques* 232
Massachusetts
Hudson, *The New England Antique Toy Mall* 285
Salem, *American Marine Model Gallery* 311

55 Music/Musical Instruments
Cape Cod
Provincetown, *Remembrances Of Things Past* 88
Connecticut
Bloomfield, *Ars Antiqua Books* 99
Danbury, *Orpheus Books* 109
East Hampton, *Martin Roenigk* 114
Norwalk, *Barter Shop* 145
South Norwalk, *Mechanical Music Center Inc* 155
Yalesville, *Unique Antiques & Collectibles* 180
Maine
Ellsworth, *Eastern Antiques* 199
Wiscasset, *Musical Wonder House* 233
Massachusetts
Boston, *The Collector* 249
Boston, *Skinner Inc* 257
Cambridge, *The Music Emporium* 263
Georgetown, *Thomas A Edison Collection* 276
Great Barrington, *Madison* 278
Needham, *Kloss Violins* 294
Orange, *Orange Trading Company* 304
Salem, *Hawthorne Antiques* 311
Sheffield, *1750 House Antiques* 315
Vermont
Manchester, *The Clock Emporium* 427
Williston, *Green Mountain Clock Shop* 443

56 Nautical/Marine Items
Cape Cod
Brewster, *The Homestead Antiques* 72
Buzzards Bay, *Heritage Antiques & Jewelry* 73
Chatham, *Olde Village Country Barn* 74
Chatham, *The Spyglass* 74
Dennis, *Hyland Granby Antiques* 76
East Sandwich, *Jesse Caldwell Leatherwood* 78
Martha's Vineyard, *C W Morgan Marine Antiques* 82
Nantucket, *Four Winds Craft Guild* 83
Nantucket, *Nina Hellman* 83
Nantucket, *Val Maitino Antiques* 83
Nantucket, *Puffin Antiques* 84

57 Needlework/Samplers

58 Objets d'Art

59 Oil Paintings

64 Post Cards

65 Primitives

66 Prints/Drawings

67 Quilts/Patchwork

71 Restoration/Conservation

Vermont
Burlington, *Conant Custom Brass Inc* 419
Manchester, *Hooked Rug Restoration* 427
Springfield, *18Th Century Design Associates* 438
St Johnsbury, *Sign Of The Dial Clock Shop* 439
Williston, *Green Mountain Clock Shop* 443

72 Scientific/Medical
Cape Cod
Falmouth, *Aurora Borealis Antiques* 78
Nantucket, *Tonkin Of Nantucket* 85
Wellfleet, *Mortar & Pestle Antiques* 90
Connecticut
Greenwich, *Hallowell & Co* 121
New Haven, *The Antiques Market* 137
Weston, *Sandi Oliver Fine Art* 166
Maine
Portland, *George L Collord III* 218
Wiscasset, *Marine Antiques* 232
Massachusetts
Marblehead, *Historical Technology Inc* 290
Newburyport, *Paul & Linda De Coste* 296
Newton, *Brass Buff Antiques* 297
Waltham, *The Printer's Devil* 331
Vermont
Wallingford, *Tom Kaye Antiques Ltd* 441

73 Sculpture
Connecticut
Burlington, *Amusement Arts* 102
Litchfield, *Peter H Tillou - Fine Arts* 128
Stamford, *Steve Newman Fine Arts* 158
Massachusetts
Boston, *Arvest Galleries Inc* 247
Boston, *Childs Gallery* 249
Boston, *Comenos Fine Arts* 250
Brookline Village, *Neal Beckerman Antiques* 260
Essex, *Comenos Fine Arts & Antiques* 271
Salem, *Hawthorne Antiques* 311
Rhode Island
Saunderstown, *Stephanie Adams Wood* 409

74 Services to Period Homes
Cape Cod
West Barnstable, *Barnstable Stove Shop* 91
West Barnstable, *Salt & Chestnut Weathervanes* 91
Connecticut
Ashford, *Jerard Paul Jordan Gallery* 97
Bethlehem, *Woody Mosch Cabinetmakers* 99
Bristol, *Richard Blaschke* 101
Chester, *Period Lighting Fixtures* 105
Glastonbury, *Maurer & Shepherd, Joyners* 119
Wilton, *The Pine Chest, Inc.* 170
Woodbury, *Ramase* 177
Maine
Sanford, *J Leeke Preservation Consultant* 223
Massachusetts
Boston, *New England Center/Antique Conservation* 249
Brookline, *Renovators Supply* 260
Groton, *Old Fashioned Milk Paint Company* 281

Jamaica Plain, *J R Burrows & Company* 285
Marblehead, *Evie's Corner* 290
Rowley, *North Fields Restorations* 310
Waltham, *SPNEA Conservation Center* 331
West Chesterfield, *Textile Reproductions* 334
Weston, *Hollyday House* 338
Williamsburg, *Rumplestiltskin* 340
New Hampshire
South Hampton, *R G Bettcher Restorations* 382
Rhode Island
Ashaway, *Stephen P Mack* 393
Vermont
Montpelier, *Great American Salvage Company* 430

75 Shipping/Packing/Storage
Cape Cod
Chatham, *Mildred Georges Antiques* 74
Dennis, *Clipper Shipping & Packaging* 76
Massachusetts
Boston, *The Fortress Corporation* 252
Marblehead, *E R Butler & Sons* 290
Newburyport, *Somewhere in Time* 297
Rhode Island
Middletown, *Lamp Works* 399

76 Shaker
Connecticut
Bethlehem, *Woody Mosch Cabinetmakers* 99
Maine
Belfast, *Avis Howells Antiques* 187
Cape Elizabeth, *Hanson's Carriage House* 193
Saco, *F P Woods, Books* 222
Searsport, *Primrose Farm Antiques* 224
Massachusetts
Great Barrington, *By Shaker Hands* 278
Harvard, *The Harvard Antique Shop* 283
Lee, *Ferrell's Antiques & Woodworking* 286
Lee, *Pembroke Antiques* 287
Lenox, *Charles L Flint Antiques Inc* 287
Lenox, *October Mountain Antiques* 287
Marshfield, *Willis Henry Auctions* 292
Wayland, *Great Meadows Joinery* 331
West Stockbridge, *Anderson & Sons Shaker Tree* 335
West Stockbridge, *Sawyer Antiques At Shaker Mill* 336
Westport, *A Quiet Place* 338
New Hampshire
Chesterfield, *Hemlock Hill Antiques* 349
Chichester, *Douglas H Hamel* 349
Cornish, *Nathan Smith House* 350
Dublin, *William Lary Antiques* 351
Enfield, *Dana Robes Wood Craftsmen Inc* 352
Sanbornville, *Arthur's Antiques* 381
West Lebanon, *Windham Antiques* 387
Rhode Island
Wakefield, *The Rathbun Gallery-Shaker* 410
Vermont
Reading, *Yellow House Antiques* 435
Waltham, *C J Harris Antiques* 442

INDEX TO
MULTIPLE DEALER SHOPS,
GROUPSHOPS
AND FLEA MARKETS

MULTIPLE DEALER SHOPS

GROUP SHOPS

FLEA MARKETS

Antiques Dealers
Auction Houses
Period Restoration Specialists
Antiquarian Booksellers

WE WOULD LIKE to consider you for listing in "Sloan's Green Guide to Antiquing in New England". Please attach your card to this sheet of paper and mail it to:

The Antique Press
105 Charles Street - 140
Boston, MA 02114

AFFIX YOUR BUSINESS CARD HERE

or call 1-800-552-5632